THE WALKERTON INQUIRY

The Honourable Dennis R. O'Connor, Commissioner

180 Dundas St. W., 22nd Floor
Toronto, ON M5G 1Z8

Tel: Toronto Area   (416) 326-4498
        Outside Toronto Area   1-877-543-8598
Fax: (416) 327-8782

Ontario

LA COMMISSION
D'ENQUÊTE WALKERTON

L'honorable Dennis R. O'Connor, Commissaire

180, rue Dundas Ouest, 22 étage
Toronto, ON M5G 1Z8

Tél: Région de Toronto   (416) 326-4498
        À l'extérieur de Toronto 1-877-543-8598
Télée: (416) 327-8782

May 23, 2002

The Honourable David Young
Ministry of the Attorney General
720 Bay Street, 11th Floor
Toronto, Ontario
M5G 2K1

Dear Mr. Attorney,

With this letter I transmit my Part 2 report of the Walkerton Inquiry.

Yours very truly,

Dennis R. O'Connor
Commissioner

Encl.

Walkerton
220 Trillium Court, P.O. Box 789, Bldg. 3, Unit 4, Walkerton, ON N0G 2V0   (519) 881-3936 (tel.)   (519) 881-4706 (fax)
220 Cour Trillium, C.P. 789, édifice 3, pièce 4, Walkerton, ON N0G 2V0   (519) 881-3936 (tél.)   (519) 881-4706 (fac.)

Part Two

Report of the Walkerton Inquiry:

A Strategy for Safe Drinking Water

The Honourable Dennis R. O'Connor

Published by
Ontario Ministry of the Attorney General

© Queen's Printer for Ontario 2002

Cover Design: Tania Craan Design

ISBN: 0-7794-2560-X

Copies of this and other Ontario Government publications are available from
Publications Ontario at 880 Bay St., Toronto. Out-of-town customers may
write to Publications Ontario, 50 Grosvenor St., Toronto M7A 1N8.
Telephone (416) 326-5300 or toll-free in Ontario 1-800-668-9938.
Fax (416) 326-5317. Internet: www.publications.gov.on.ca. The hearing
impaired may call toll-free in Ontario 1-800-268-7095. MasterCard and Visa
are accepted. Cheques and money orders should be made payable to the
Minister of Finance. Prepayment is required.

Contents

Chapter 1   An Overview

Chapter 2   Government Oversight of the Delivery of Drinking Water: Introduction

Chapter 3   A Multi-Barrier Approach to Drinking Water Safety

Chapter 6   Drinking Water Treatment Technologies

Chapter 7   Drinking Water Distribution Systems

Chapter 8   Monitoring and Measurement

Chapter 9   The Role of Laboratories

Chapter 10   The Role of Municipal Governments

Chapter 11   The Management of Municipal Water Systems

Chapter 12 The Certification and Training of Operators

Chapter 13   The Provincial Government Role in Overseeing Drinking Water Systems

Chapter 16   The Process of Part 2 of the Inquiry

Appendix A   An Interjurisdictional Comparison of Water Quality Standards

Chapter 1 An Overview

Contents

Chapter 1   An Overview

1.1   Introduction

In the aftermath of the water-borne outbreak in Walkerton, the Government of Ontario established this public Inquiry.[1] The first part of the Inquiry's mandate directed me to report on the events in Walkerton and the causes of the tragedy. The report for Part 1 was released in January 2002. The second part of the mandate directed me to make recommendations to ensure the safety of drinking water across the province. This volume is the Part 2 report.

This report results from a very thorough public process that involved the active participation of a wide array of individuals and groups with interest and expertise in the many issues relating to the safety of drinking water. In the process, the Inquiry reviewed the most current literature in the area, the best practices in water management and regulation employed in jurisdictions around the world, and the latest in science and technology. I am satisfied that I have had the benefit of the best available experience, expertise, and advice to assist in developing a set of reasonable and practical recommendations.

In this report, I make recommendations for improvements to each of the main components of Ontario's water delivery system.[2] However, readers should not conclude that Ontario's existing system needs radical reform. It does not. We can be proud of the high level of expertise and competence that our leading water providers exhibit. The challenge is to ensure that the best practices are implemented across the province. A review of outbreaks in jurisdictions around the world shows that many of the failures that played a role in the Walkerton tragedy have also been contributing factors on other occasions.[3] We must take seriously the lessons learned from these experiences so as to avoid similar failures in the future.

For the convenience of readers, I first set out a brief executive summary of my recommendations. That is followed by a discussion of some of the principles and themes that underlie the approach I have adopted throughout the report

[1] Throughout this report, the terms "the Inquiry" and "the Commission" are used interchangeably.
[2] These recommendations should be read together with the recommendations made in the Part 1 report of this Inquiry.
[3] S. Hrudey et. al., 2002, "A fatal waterborne disease outbreak in Walkerton, Ontario: Comparison with other waterborne outbreaks in the developed world," proceedings at the International Water Association World Water Congress Health-Related Water Microbiology Symposium, Melbourne, Australia, April 7–12.

and then by a more complete overview of the recommendations that are contained in the body of the Part 2 report. The chapter concludes with a complete listing of the Part 2 recommendations. The remaining chapters contain the full text of my report.

1.2   Executive Summary

The recommendations in this report are divided into five areas.

1.2.1   Source Protection

The first barrier to the contamination of drinking water involves protecting the sources of drinking water. I recommend that the Province adopt a watershed-based planning process, led by the Ministry of the Environment (MOE) and by the conservation authorities[4] (where appropriate), and involving local actors. The purpose is to develop a source protection plan for each watershed in the province. The plans would be approved by the MOE and would be binding on provincial and municipal government decisions that directly affect drinking water safety. Large farms, and small farms in sensitive areas, would be required to develop water protection plans that are consistent with the watershed-based source protection plans.

1.2.2   Standards and Technology

The next set of barriers to the contamination of drinking water relies on having in place effective standards and technology for treating water and for monitoring its quality as it makes its way to the consumer. I recommend that Ontario's standards and technology be continually updated according to the most recent knowledge and experience. The processes for doing so should be open and transparent.

---

[4] Conservation authorities were established in Ontario in 1946. There are currently 36 conservation authorities in the province. Their functions include controlling potential flood damage, and in many cases they also perform watershed management, including planning, education, prevention, and monitoring. In managing particular watersheds, they also protect lands and wetlands for recreation and wildlife and have the power to acquire lands and build structures such as reservoirs and dams.

1.2.3   Municipal Water Providers

Over 80% of Ontarians get their drinking water from municipal sources. I therefore recommend that all municipal water providers be required to adopt a quality management approach for their water systems. As a condition of provincial approval, municipalities would be required to have an accredited operating agency (either internal or external) and to have an approved operational plan for their water system. There would be mandatory training for all water system operators, and grandparented operators would be required to pass certification examinations within two years.

1.2.4   Provincial Oversight

The provincial government is responsible for regulating and overseeing the safety of Ontario's drinking water. I recommend that the government strengthen the way in which it fulfills this responsibility. In particular, I recommend that the Province adopt a government-wide drinking water policy and a *Safe Drinking Water Act* for Ontario, and that it establish two specialized branches within the MOE. These branches would be responsible, respectively, for watershed planning and for overseeing water systems. It is essential for the Province to strictly enforce drinking water regulations and to commit sufficient resources, financial and otherwise, to enable the MOE to play this role effectively.

1.2.5   Special Cases

Special approaches are needed in two areas: small water systems and First Nations water supplies. For those small systems that are currently captured by regulatory standards, I recommend that the Province allow variances from regulatory standards only where the owner demonstrates that safety will not be compromised, and never for cost reasons alone. For those small systems that serve the public but that do not currently fall under regulatory standards – such as those at rural restaurants and campgrounds – I recommend that they be given the option either to comply with regulatory standards or to post a notice at every tap that the water is not potable. For First Nations water supplies, I recommend that the Province make available on request the services of the Ontario Clean Water Agency (OCWA), along with other technical assistance, as well as training.

Readers involved with the water industry will find most of the recommendations familiar. The recommendations are based on the best practices found in other jurisdictions and on the most current thinking of those with experience and expertise in the industry. For example, watershed-based management planning has been adopted in Europe and Australia and is already being used in a few Ontario watersheds. Also, the concept of quality management for water providers is becoming broadly accepted by the water industry throughout North America, Europe, and Australia. Quality management systems, which have been used in other industries for years, are currently used by some Ontario water providers. Given the importance of water industry practices to public health, the time has come to make quality management mandatory for municipal water providers. Finally, few informed observers, if any, would argue against the need for the Province to ensure that drinking water systems are overseen in a consistently strong and effective manner.

1.3   General Principles

This section outlines a number of general principles and themes that underlie the approach I have adopted throughout the report.

While it is not possible to utterly remove all risk from a water system, the recommendations' overall goal is to ensure that Ontario's drinking water systems deliver water with a level of risk so negligible that a reasonable and informed person would feel safe drinking the water.[5]

The risks of unsafe drinking water can be reduced to a negligible level by simultaneously introducing a number of measures: by placing multiple barriers aimed at preventing contaminants from reaching consumers, by adopting a cautious approach to making decisions that affect drinking water safety, by ensuring that water providers apply sound quality management and operating systems, and by providing for effective provincial government regulation and oversight.

I discussed the multiple-barrier concept in section 4.2 of the Part 1 report, and it is a recurring theme throughout this Part 2 report. The multiple-barrier approach is well-entrenched in the water industry, for good reasons. Putting in place a series of measures, each independently acting as a barrier to passing

---

[5] I address standards setting with regard to vulnerable subpopulations in Chapter 5 of this report.

water-borne contaminants through the system to consumers, achieves a greater overall level of protection than does relying exclusively on a single barrier (e.g., treatment alone or source protection alone). A failure in any given barrier will not cause a failure of the entire system. The challenge is to ensure that each of the barriers is functioning properly, so that together they constitute the highest level of protection that is reasonably and practically available.

My recommendations are intended to improve both transparency and accountability in the water supply system. Public confidence will be fostered by ensuring that members of the public have access to current information about the different components of the system, about the quality of the water, and about decisions that affect water safety. Public confidence will also be raised by ensuring that those who make decisions about drinking water safety are accountable for the consequences of those decisions.

Taken together, the recommendations constitute an overall approach to reducing to negligible levels the risks that can affect drinking water. It is important to invest resources so as to achieve the greatest combined reduction of risk for a reasonable cost. In my view, the risk reduction that could result from implementing the recommendations in both of my reports makes the costs of their implementation well worth bearing. I asked Strategic Alternatives, a respected consulting firm, to estimate the costs of implementing all the recommendations, as well as the cost increases that have resulted from the steps that the provincial government has already introduced since the Walkerton tragedy.[6]

In summary, Strategic Alternatives estimates the following:

• One-time cost of implementing this Inquiry's recommendations: $99 million to $280 million.

• Ongoing annual cost of implementing the Inquiry's recommendations: $17 million to $49 million per year.

---

[6] Strategic Alternatives et al., 2002, "The costs of clean water: Estimates of costs arising from the recommendations of the Walkerton Inquiry," Walkerton Inquiry Commissioned Paper 25. I want to emphasize that the Strategic Alternatives report contains estimates based on the assumptions set out in that report. Strategic Alternatives made those assumptions based on its expertise and on available information. While I have no reason to disagree with those assumptions, they should not be considered to constitute the details of the recommendations made in this report. In implementing the recommendations, the Province and municipal governments may find it necessary to adopt different assumptions in some cases.

- One-time cost of steps taken by the provincial government since the Walkerton tragedy: $100 million to $520 million.[7]

- Ongoing annual cost of steps taken by the provincial government since the Walkerton tragedy: $41 million to $200 million per year.

These costs may be allocated among the provincial government, municipalities, and individuals in a variety of ways. No matter how they are allocated, given that this province has over 11 million people (and assuming that the Strategic Alternatives estimates are reasonably accurate), the overall cost of safe water for Ontario would still compare favourably with that in other jurisdictions, as well as with expenditures typically made by Ontario households for other services. According to Strategic Alternatives, the total costs of my recommendations, including the one-time costs amortized over 10 years at 7% interest, would amount to an average of between $7 and $19 per household per year.[8] Comparing the average water rates with those for less essential services such as cable television, telephones, or Internet access makes this point powerfully.

The cost of the Walkerton tragedy itself also makes for a compelling comparison. A study commissioned by the Inquiry estimates the economic impact of the Walkerton events to be more than $64.5 million.[9] Of course, this figure does not include the tragedy's great impact in terms of human suffering and loss of life. Still, it does show that from an economic standpoint alone, the costs of a system failure can be enormous.

I have approached the recommendations with a view toward using existing structures and institutions wherever those structures are able to carry out my recommendations. For example, I recommend that the provincial government's responsibility for protecting water sources be implemented on a watershed basis through the already existing conservation authorities, rather than by establishing new local bodies to fulfill this role. If a conservation authority is unable to carry out the new responsibility, the MOE itself should do so. I expect that the use of existing institutions will facilitate the adoption of these recommendations and reduce the costs of implementing them.

---

[7] These estimated costs relate only to implementing Ontario Regulation 459/00 and Ontario Regulation 505/01.

[8] The actual costs for a given household may vary considerably.

[9] J. Livernois, 2002, "The economic costs of the Walkerton water crisis," Walkerton Inquiry Commissioned Paper 14.

Since Dr. John Snow's 1854 discovery in London, England, that drinking water could kill people by transmitting disease, the developed world has come a long way toward eliminating the transmission of water-borne disease. The Walkerton experience warns us that we may have become victims of our own success, taking for granted our drinking water's safety. The keynote in the future should be vigilance. We should never be complacent about drinking water safety. Circumstances change. Ontario's population will likely continue increasing, as will the intensity and the types of human activities that can threaten drinking water sources. New pathogens and chemical contaminants will continue to emerge. We will be able to minimize risk to a negligible level in the future only if we constantly monitor the design and management of our water delivery systems to ensure that we are always employing the safest practices available. The recommendations in this report are aimed at achieving this important objective.

1.4   Specific Recommendations

Here I discuss more fully the recommendations summarized in section 1.2.

1.4.1   Source Protection (Chapter 4)

In a multiple-barrier system for providing safe drinking water, the first barrier involves selecting and protecting reliable, high-quality drinking water sources.

A strong source protection program offers a wide variety of benefits. It lowers risk cost-effectively: keeping contaminants out of drinking water sources is an efficient way of keeping them out of drinking water. This is particularly so because standard treatments cannot effectively remove certain contaminants. And protecting drinking water sources can in some instances be less expensive than treating contaminated water so that it meets required safety standards.

The public strongly favours source protection as a key component of our water system. No other aspect of the task of ensuring drinking water safety received as much attention during the town hall meetings that this Inquiry held across

Ontario. Source protection was also one of the main issues identified by the parties with standing in the Inquiry.[10]

I recommend a source protection system that includes a strong planning component on an ecologically meaningful scale – that is, at the watershed level.

Drinking water source protection, as one aspect of watershed management, makes the most sense in the context of an overall watershed management plan. In this report, I restrict my recommendations to those aspects of watershed management that I think are necessary to protect drinking water sources, but I want to emphasize that a comprehensive approach for managing all aspects of watersheds is needed and should be adopted by the province. Source protection plans should be a subset of the broader watershed management plans.

The following are some of the main elements of the source protection system I envision:

> **Leadership from the Ministry of the Environment (MOE):** I recommend that the MOE be the lead provincial agency with regard to all aspects of providing safe drinking water, including source protection. The MOE would establish the framework for developing the watershed-based source water protection plans, would help to fund and participate in their development, and would approve the completed plans.

> **A local planning process:** To ensure that local considerations are fully taken into account, and to develop goodwill within and acceptance by local communities, source protection planning should be done as much as possible at a local (watershed) level, by those who will be most directly affected (municipalities and other affected local groups). Where possible, conservation authorities should coordinate the plans' local development. Otherwise, the MOE itself should undertake the coordination role. I envision the process as being completely open to public scrutiny.

---

[10] I granted standing on being satisfied that a party had an interest in the Inquiry's subject matter and could bring a useful perspective to the issues being considered. In the Part 2 process, I granted standing to 36 parties. The parties who were granted standing are listed in Chapter 16 of this report.

Approval by the MOE: Once draft plans are developed at the watershed level, I envision that they would then be subject to MOE approval. Requiring approval will provide consistency of approach across watersheds and should help prevent undue influence by local interests.

Effective plans: If source protection plans are to be meaningful, they must be respected by the various actors in a watershed. Once the MOE has approved a plan, therefore, provincial Permits to Take Water and Certificates of Approval for sewage treatment plants and any other activities that pose a threat to water quality will have to be consistent with the approved plan. In cases involving a significant direct threat to drinking water sources, municipal official plans and zoning decisions will also need to be consistent with the local source protection plans. In all other situations, municipal official plans and zoning decisions should at least take the relevant source protection plans into account.

The chapter on source protection also includes a number of recommendations relating to specific potential sources of contamination, including sewage treatment plants, septage and biosolids, septic tanks, agriculture, and industrial activity. The thrust of all of these recommendations is that no discharges into drinking water sources should be permitted unless they are consistent with watershed-based source protection plans. In particular, I envision requiring large farms in all locations and smaller farms in sensitive areas to develop water protection plans for MOE approval. In addition, I recommend that there be minimum regulatory requirements for agricultural activities that create impacts on drinking water sources. The objective of these recommendations is to ensure that the cumulative effect of discharges from farms in a given watershed remains within acceptable limits. For smaller farms in areas that are not considered sensitive, I recommend continuing and improving the current voluntary programs for environmental protection.

1.4.2   Standards and Technology (Chapters 5 to 9)

I make a number of recommendations directed at improving the process by which standards are set. I propose making the federal–provincial process for establishing water quality guidelines more transparent and more accessible to public participation. I also propose that Ontario establish an Advisory Council on Standards to provide a broader range of expertise in the provincial standard-setting process. Both suggestions are aimed at obtaining more assistance, at little cost, in this critical area.

In addition, I make specific recommendations for improving a number of current practices in setting standards. These recommendations relate to such matters as turbidity levels, disinfection by-products, heavy metals and priority organics, selecting appropriate treatment processes, continuous monitoring of operational measurements, and collecting and testing samples.

These recommendations should not be viewed as a criticism of Ontario's current water quality standards. Indeed, I have no doubt that the current standards were established with great concern for the safety of the province's drinking water. Rather, the specific proposals are intended to bring Ontario's regulatory standards and practices into line with the most current developments in technology and the best practices adopted elsewhere. These proposals may be viewed as part of the continuing process of ensuring that our standards are consistent with the most up-to-date information and practices.

1.4.3   Municipal Water Providers (Chapters 10 to 12)

Over 80% of Ontarians are served by municipally owned water systems. Although municipalities are permitted to sell their systems, there was no suggestion during the Inquiry that any municipalities are even considering doing so. Moreover, nothing I heard during the Inquiry led me to conclude that I should make recommendations about the ownership of municipal systems in order to address water safety issues. The recommendations in this area are therefore premised on continued municipal ownership.

There are, however, a number of different ways in which a municipality may choose to manage and operate the water system it owns. Possible approaches include a variety of internal management structures, regionalization or consolidation with other municipalities, and contracting with external operating agencies such as the Ontario Clean Water Agency, various private operators, or other municipalities. There are advantages – and, in some cases, drawbacks – to each choice. What is best for a particular municipality will depend on its circumstances. The first consideration, however, in choosing any management or operational structure should always be safety. It will be through the process of mandatory accreditation and operational planning that we will gain assurance about the competence of operating agencies, whether public or private.

I recommend that each municipality review the available options, with provincial guidance where required, to determine the management structure that will best promote the safety of its drinking water. This review should be done in the light of a number of my recommendations, including those involving mandatory accreditation and operational planning. But whatever management structure is chosen, the arrangement must be such that the municipality, as the system's owner, remains accountable for the provision of safe drinking water.

To promote accountability, I recommend that the persons designated by a municipality to oversee the management and operation of its water system be held to a statutory standard of care for the safety of the water, similar to the duty of a director of a corporation.

Perhaps the most significant recommendations in this report address the need for quality management through mandatory accreditation and operational planning. Sound management and operating systems help prevent, not simply react to, the contamination of drinking water. In this vein, I recommend requiring all operating agencies to become accredited in accordance with a quality management standard – a standard that will be developed by the industry and others knowledgeable in the area and mandated by the MOE. Accreditation is designed to ensure that operating agencies have systems in place at the organizational level that will enable them to deliver safe water. Also, as part of the quality management approach, I recommend that each municipality be required to have an operational plan for its water system. I anticipate that the accreditation standard and the requirement for operational plans can be tailored to accommodate systems of different sizes and complexity.

In addition, I recommend that mandatory certification for individual operators continue and that those operators who have received their certification by way of grandparenting be required to meet current standards regarding experience and knowledge, demonstrated by passing an examination at the appropriate level, within two years. I also propose that the MOE develop a curriculum for operator training and that mandatory training requirements specifically emphasize water quality and safety issues.

Finally, I recommend that municipalities be formally required to raise adequate resources to pay for their water systems. Water safety is promoted by sound fiscal management. I propose requiring each municipality to have a financial plan that provides for full cost recovery and for proper asset management in accordance with provincially established standards. Provincial subsidies should be available only in exceptional cases – specifically, when safety is at risk and when no other alternatives, either technological or managerial, are available.

Before leaving this topic, I want to comment on the additional burden these recommendations will place on municipalities. For many, the added burden will not be great. The well-run water systems, while not currently accredited, already practise quality management and already have financial plans that should be easily adaptable to the newly mandated standards. However, for some systems, particularly smaller ones, these proposals will involve a significant amount of work. But that is not an adequate reason for not implementing them. The Walkerton tragedy and other outbreaks have taught us the vital importance of sound management. Any adjustments made for small communities should be based on their water systems' relative lack of complexity and lower risk, and should never compromise safety. Some of my recommendations, especially those involving mandatory accreditation and operational planning, may lead certain municipalities to conclude that they should no longer manage their water system internally, and to move to an alternative model, either by joining their system with that of a neighbouring municipality or by engaging the services of an external operating agency.

1.4.4   Provincial Oversight (Chapter 13)

The intent of the recommendations in this area is to strengthen provincial oversight of water delivery systems. In the Part 1 report, I found several failures in the way the provincial government exercised its oversight role in relation to the Walkerton tragedy, and I made specific recommendations aimed at addressing those failures. Taken together, the recommendations in the two reports will, in my view, improve the quality of provincial policy and provide for effective oversight across the province.

With regard to policy, I recommend that the Province develop a comprehensive, source-to-tap, government-wide drinking water policy and enact a *Safe Drinking Water Act* embodying the important elements of that policy. I also propose that the Ministry of the Environment (MOE) take the lead in developing and implementing the policy.

I recommend that two new branches be created within the MOE. The Watershed Management Branch would be responsible for overseeing the watershed-based planning process described in section 1.4.1. It is important that the provincial government's responsibilities for watershed management be coordinated in one place – a place where there is sufficient expertise to manage the process. This new branch would be responsible for developing the framework for watershed planning, participating in the locally based process of developing the plans, and approving the draft plans. In the event that draft plans are not developed as required at the local level, this branch of the MOE would step in and take charge of the process. Having a centralized MOE branch dedicated to watershed management should promote consistency in planning across the province and provide the expertise and support necessary for ensuring that good plans are developed.

I also propose establishing a specialized Drinking Water Branch within the MOE. This branch would be responsible for overseeing drinking water treatment and distribution systems. The skills and knowledge needed for the tasks of regulating and overseeing drinking water providers and systems differ significantly from those required for performing most of the ministry's other responsibilities. Within this branch, I recommend creating a new position: the Chief Inspector – Drinking Water Systems. This person would be responsible for the inspections program. I suggest that individual inspectors should have the same qualifications as, or higher qualifications than, the operators of the systems they inspect. The Drinking Water Branch would oversee and be responsible for the quality management accreditation program proposed in section 1.4.3. The Drinking Water Branch would also be responsible for granting most of the approvals necessary for operating a drinking water system. I recommend a new form of approval – the owner's licence – that will collect in one set of documents all the approvals and conditions necessary for operating a waterworks.

To date, the MOE's Investigations and Enforcement Branch (IEB) has investigated – and, where appropriate, prosecuted – those suspected of non-compliance with regulatory requirements. I am satisfied that the IEB should remain, as currently constituted, a separate branch within the ministry. For the most part, this arrangement has worked well. In my view, the necessary independence from inspections and abatement can be maintained without establishing a new agency outside the ministry. However, I do recommend that the new provincial policy on drinking water provide for strict enforcement of drinking water regulations and that it apply equally to all operating agencies, including the municipalities and OCWA.

Finally, I urge the government to proceed with the proposed Integrated Divisional System and to either include in that system, in one database, or otherwise provide central access to, information related to source protection, information about each drinking water system in Ontario, and all other data that might reasonably be required by the Drinking Water Branch and by the local boards of health.

Chapter 11 of the Part 1 report discusses in some detail the budget reductions within the MOE. Implementing a number of the recommendations I make in this Part 2 report will involve expenditures aimed at ensuring that the MOE is able to carry out its oversight role fully and effectively. It will be essential for the Province to provide the MOE with sufficient resources, financial and otherwise, to enable it to act on these recommendations.

1.4.5   Special Cases (Chapters 14 and 15)

In Chapters 14 and 15 of this report, I discuss two kinds of systems that warrant special consideration: small water systems and First Nations reserves, respectively.

1.4.5.1   *Small Water Systems*

There are two categories of small water systems. The first category comprises systems covered by Ontario Regulation 459/00, which sets out water quality, treatment, monitoring, and other requirements for systems that serve more than five households or that have more than a specified capacity. During the Inquiry, I heard at length that Ontario Regulation 459/00's current requirements are financially onerous for many small communal systems.

For some municipal systems, following the recommendations in this report regarding accreditation, operational plans, and financial plans may indeed increase expenses, at least temporarily. To address concerns about the costs of regulatory requirements, I recommend allowing water systems, whether municipally or privately owned, to apply for a variance from provincially imposed standards, including those currently found in Ontario Regulation 459/00. Any such variance should be granted solely on the basis of a satisfactory risk assessment. In some cases, the nature of the water source or the use of specialized technology may ensure water safety without the need of meeting the full regulatory requirements.

I also recommend that in future, the Province refuse to approve water systems that will not be economically viable under the regulatory regime necessary for ensuring water safety in that system. Problems regarding the costs of regulatory compliance should be addressed before approval is granted.

Existing systems that are not economically viable under the current regulatory regime should be required to explore all available management and technological options in order to find the most cost-effective way of providing safe water. If, in the end, no alternatives can be found and currently authorized systems are not affordable beyond a predetermined point, I recommend provincial assistance. I expect that few such cases will occur, and they should be phased out, if possible, over time.

The second category of small systems that present a troubling concern comprises privately owned systems that do not come within Ontario Regulation 459/00 but that serve drinking water to the public: that is, establishments with their own wells, such as rural restaurants, gas stations, summer camps, resorts, schools, hospitals, and businesses. In December 2001, the provincial government passed Ontario Regulation 505/01, which sets out certain requirements for some of these types of water providers. But that regulation applies only to water providers whose systems serve designated facilities, such as schools, nursing homes, and hospitals. I agree with this initiative. I recommend, however, that Ontario Regulation 505/01 be extended to *all* those who own a water system that is not covered by Ontario Regulation 459/00 but that serves the public. For those whose systems are not covered by Ontario Regulation 505/01 as now written, I propose giving them a choice: either comply with the regulation or post a sign at every tap saying that the water is not potable.

Finally, I address privately owned wells that serve fewer than six residences and that do not serve the public. I propose that the owner of any such system remain responsible for the safety of his or her own water. I recommend that the province improve education programs aimed at informing the owners of private wells about the potential dangers to drinking water and about the technology available for treating water within private systems. The province should encourage regular testing by private well owners and should continue to make free microbiological tests available through local health units.

1.4.5.2   *First Nations Water Systems*

Constitutionally, First Nations reserves fall within the jurisdiction of the First Nations themselves and of the federal government. Because this is a provincial inquiry, my recommendations in this regard must be circumscribed.

The water provided on many First Nations reserves is some of the poorest-quality water in the province. Residents of Ontario's First Nations reserves are also Ontario residents. I therefore suggest to the First Nations and to the federal government that the water quality standards for reserves should be no lower than those that apply elsewhere in the province and that those standards should be made legally enforceable. To assist with this objective, I recommend that when asked, Ontario make its resources and expertise available, on a cost-recovery basis, to help improve the water quality on reserves. In particular, I suggest that the Ontario Clean Water Agency be available to operate water systems on reserves and that the MOE make its inspections, abatement, and training programs available to reserves as well. I also suggest that the First Nations, where appropriate, be involved in the watershed-based source protection planning process I recommend (see section 1.4.1).

1.5   The Balance of This Report

In addition to the recommendations described above, this report includes an overview of the current regulatory scheme (Chapter 2) and a discussion of the multiple-barrier approach (Chapter 3). Chapter 16 describes the process followed during Part 2 of this Inquiry. When read together, Chapter 14 in the Part 1 report and Chapter 16 in this Part 2 report provide a complete description of this Inquiry's process.

In the course of its work, the Inquiry accumulated a substantial library of materials. Papers were commissioned from distinguished experts in the areas most relevant to the work of Part 2 of the Inquiry, and the parties with standing contributed another large set. All of these papers, as well as a selection of the many submissions received from the general public, will be available on the Inquiry's Web site, www.walkertoninquiry.com, until December 31, 2002, and all are included on a compact disc that also contains the Part 1 and Part 2 reports. The Inquiry's general records – including the originals of these materials, as well as transcripts of hearings and documents introduced in evidence – are deposited in the Provincial Archives.

1.6   Summary

The people of Ontario are entitled to safe, high-quality drinking water. For the most part, they have enjoyed just that. But improvement is clearly necessary in a number of areas. This report examines the statutory, regulatory, technological, management, and operational systems and processes currently in place for supplying Ontario's drinking water. My aim throughout is to identify any weaknesses in those areas and to propose ways to correct those weaknesses. My recommendations touch on all dimensions of Ontario's water system and on all the actors within it. If the recommendations in this Part 2 report and those contained in the Part 1 report are implemented, I am confident that Ontarians will enjoy safe drinking water well into the future.

1.7   List of Part 2 Recommendations

The following is a list of all recommendations in Part 2.[11]

Source Protection (Chapter 4)

Recommendation 1
Drinking water sources should be protected by developing watershed-based source protection plans. Source protection plans should be required for all watersheds in Ontario.

Recommendation 2
The Ministry of the Environment should ensure that draft source protection plans are prepared through an inclusive process of local consultation. Where appropriate, this process should be managed by conservation authorities.

Recommendation 3
Draft source protection plans should be reviewed by the Ministry of the Environment and subject to ministry approval.

Recommendation 4
Provincial government decisions that affect the quality of drinking water sources must be consistent with approved source protection plans.

---

[11] As a result of the broader perspective afforded to me by Part 2, some of my Part 2 recommendations do not exactly reflect those in Part 1. Where this occurs, my Part 2 recommendations should take precedence.

Recommendation 5
Where the potential exists for a significant direct threat to drinking water sources, municipal official plans and decisions must be consistent with the applicable source protection plan. Otherwise, municipal official plans and decisions should have regard to the source protection plan. The plans should designate areas where consistency is required.

Recommendation 6
The provincial government should provide for limited rights of appeal to challenge source protection plans, and provincial and municipal decisions that are inconsistent with the plans.

Recommendation 7
The provincial government should ensure that sufficient funds are available to complete the planning and adoption of source protection plans.

Recommendation 8
Conservation authorities (or, in their absence, the Ministry of the Environment) should be responsible for implementing local initiatives to educate landowners, industry, and the public about the requirements and importance of drinking water source protection.

Recommendation 9
Septic systems should be inspected as a condition for the transfer of a deed.

Recommendation 10
The Ministry of the Environment should not issue Certificates of Approval for the spreading of waste materials unless they are compatible with the applicable source protection plan.

Recommendation 11
The Ministry of the Environment should take the lead role in regulating the potential impacts of farm activities on drinking water sources. The Ministry of Agriculture, Food and Rural Affairs should provide technical support to the Ministry of the Environment and should continue to advise farmers about the protection of drinking water sources.

Recommendation 12
Where necessary, the Ministry of the Environment should establish minimum regulatory requirements for agricultural activities that generate impacts on drinking water sources.

Recommendation 13
All large or intensive farms, and all farms in areas designated as sensitive or high-risk by the applicable source protection plan, should be required to develop binding individual water protection plans consistent with the source protection plan.

Recommendation 14
Once a farm has in place an individual water protection plan that is consistent with the applicable source protection plan, municipalities should not have the authority to require that farm to meet a higher standard of protection of drinking water sources than that which is laid out in the farm's water protection plan.

Recommendation 15
The Ministry of the Environment should work with the Ministry of Agriculture, Food and Rural Affairs, agricultural groups, conservation authorities, municipalities, and other interested groups to create a provincial framework for developing individual farm water protection plans.

Recommendation 16
The provincial government, through the Ministry of Agriculture, Food and Rural Affairs in collaboration with the Ministry of the Environment, should establish a system of cost-share incentives for water protection projects on farms.

Recommendation 17
The regulation of other industries by the provincial government and by municipalities must be consistent with provincially approved source protection plans.

Standards (Chapter 5)

Recommendation 18
In setting drinking water quality standards, the objective should be such that, if the standards are met, a reasonable and informed person would feel safe drinking the water.

Recommendation 19
Standards setting should be based on a precautionary approach, particularly with respect to contaminants whose effects on human health are unknown.

Recommendation 20
Regarding drinking water quality research, I encourage Health Canada and other agencies to adopt as a priority the development of sufficiently detailed definitions of the susceptibility of vulnerable population groups to drinking water contaminant exposures to allow appropriate adjustments in drinking water quality guidelines.

Recommendation 21
I suggest that the federal–provincial process for proposing drinking water quality guidelines be refined to provide for greater transparency and public participation.

Recommendation 22
I suggest that the Federal–Provincial Subcommittee on Drinking Water focus on drinking water quality guidelines. I encourage Health Canada to commit the required scientific support to the federal-provincial process for proposing drinking water quality guidelines.

Recommendation 23
I encourage the federal government to adopt standards that are as stringent as, or more stringent than, Ontario Regulation 459/00 for all federal facilities, Indian reserves, national parks, military installations, and other lands under federal jurisdiction in Ontario.

Recommendation 24
The provincial government should continue to be the government responsible for setting legally binding drinking water quality standards.

Recommendation 25
In setting drinking water quality standards for Ontario, the Minister of the Environment should be advised by an Advisory Council on Standards.

Recommendation 26
The Advisory Council on Standards should have the authority to recommend that the provincial government adopt standards for contaminants that are not on the current federal–provincial agenda.

Recommendation 27
The Advisory Council on Standards should consider whether to replace the total coliform test with an *E. coli* test.

Recommendation 28
No formal maximum contaminant level for protozoa should be established until real-time tests are available. The objective, as with bacterial and viral pathogens, should be zero, and the regulations should so state; but the standard should be a treatment standard, specified in terms of log removal dependent on source water quality.

Recommendation 29
The provincial government should seek the advice of the Advisory Council on Standards regarding the desirability of a turbidity limit that is lower than the limit specified in the federal–provincial *Guidelines*.

Treatment (Chapter 6)

Recommendation 30
All raw water intended for drinking water should be subject to a characterization of each parameter that could indicate a public health risk. The results, regardless of the type of source, should be taken into account in designing and approving any treatment system.

Recommendation 31
The Advisory Council on Standards should review Ontario's standards for disinfection by-products to take account of the risks that may be posed by the by-products of all chemical and radiation-based disinfectants.

Recommendation 32
The provincial government should support major wastewater plant operators in collaborative studies aimed at identifying practical methods of reducing or removing heavy metals and priority organics (such as endocrine disruptors) that are not removed by conventional treatment.

Recommendation 33
The Ministry of the Environment should be adequately resourced to support a water sciences and standards function in relation to drinking water.

Distribution (Chapter 7)

Recommendation 34
The provincial government should encourage the federal government, working with the Standards Council of Canada and with advice from municipalities, the water industry, and other stakeholders, to develop standards for materials, including piping, valves, storage tanks, and bulk chemicals, that come into contact with drinking water.

Recommendation 35
As part of an asset management program, lead service lines should be located and replaced over time with safer materials.

Monitoring (Chapter 8)

Recommendation 36
All municipal water providers in Ontario should have, as a minimum, continuous inline monitoring of turbidity, disinfectant residual, and pressure at the treatment plant, together with alarms that signal immediately when any regulatory parameters are exceeded. The disinfectant residual should be continuously or frequently measured in the distribution system. Where needed, alarms should be accompanied by automatic shut-off mechanisms.

Recommendation 37
Every municipal water provider should be responsible for developing an adequate sampling and continuous measurement plan as part of its operational plan, as recommended in Chapter 11 of this report.

Recommendation 38
Sampling plans should provide for sampling under the conditions most challenging to the system, such as after heavy rainfalls or spring floods.

Recommendation 39
Ontario Regulation 459/00 should be modified to require standard protocols for the collection, transport, custody, labelling, testing, and reporting of drinking water samples, and for testing all scheduled contaminants, that meet or better the protocols in *Standard Methods.*

Recommendation 40
Where remoteness dictates that samples for bacteriological analysis cannot be delivered to a lab either within regulated times or under guaranteed conditions, the Ministry of the Environment should determine the feasibility of alternative means of providing microbiological testing that meet the requirements of *Standard Methods.*

Laboratories (Chapter 9)

Recommendation 41
The provincial government should phase in the mandatory accreditation of laboratories for all testing parameters, and all drinking water testing should be performed only by accredited facilities.

Recommendation 42
The Ministry of the Environment should licence and periodically inspect, as required, environmental laboratories that offer drinking water testing; as with water treatment operations, continuing accreditation should be a condition of licence.

Recommendation 43
The results of laboratory accreditation audits should be provided to the Ministry of the Environment and should be publicly available.

The Role of Municipal Government (Chapter 10)

Recommendation 44
Municipalities should review the management and operating structure for their water system to ensure that it is capable of providing safe drinking water on a reliable basis.

Recommendation 45
Given that the safety of drinking water is essential for public health, those who discharge the oversight responsibilities of the municipality should be held to a statutory standard of care.

Recommendation 46
The provincial government should provide guidance and technical advice to support municipal reviews of water systems.

Recommendation 47
The provincial government should require municipalities to submit a financial plan for their water system, in accordance with provincial standards, as a condition of licence for their water systems.

Recommendation 48
As a general principle, municipalities should plan to raise adequate resources for their water systems from local revenue sources, barring exceptional circumstances.

Recommendation 49
Municipal contracts with external operating agencies should be made public.

Recommendation 50
The role of the Ontario Clean Water Agency in offering operational services to municipalities should be maintained. The provincial government should clarify the Ontario Clean Water Agency's status and mandate. In particular, OCWA should be:

- an arm's-length agency with an independent, qualified board responsible for choosing the chief executive; and

- available to provide standby emergency capabilities.

Quality Management (Chapter 11)

Recommendation 51
The provincial government should require all owners of municipal water systems, as condition of their licence (see Recommendation 71), to have an accredited operating agency, whether internal or external to the municipality.

Recommendation 52
Accreditation should be based on an independent audit and a periodic review by a certified accrediting body.

Recommendation 53
The Ministry of the Environment should initiate the development of a drinking water quality management standard for Ontario. Municipalities, the water industry, and other relevant stakeholders should be actively recruited to take part in the development of the standard. The water industry is recognized as an essential participant in this initiative.

Recommendation 54
The Ministry of the Environment's Drinking Water Branch (see Recommendation 69) should have the responsibility for recognizing the drinking water quality management standard that will apply in Ontario and for ensuring that accreditation is properly implemented.

Recommendation 55
The drinking water quality management standard should come into force by a date to be fixed by the provincial government. All municipalities should be required under the *Safe Drinking Water Act* (see Recommendation 67) to have an operating agency for their water system accredited within a specified time.

Recommendation 56
The provincial government should require municipalities to have operational plans for their water systems by a date to be fixed by the provincial government.

Recommendation 57
Operational plans should be approved and reviewed as part of the Ministry of the Environment approvals and inspections programs.

Recommendation 58

The Ministry of the Environment should work with Emergency Measures Ontario and water industry associations to develop a generic emergency response plan for municipal water providers. A viable and current emergency response plan, and procedures for training and periodic testing of the plan, should be an essential element of mandatory accreditation and operational planning.

Training of Individual Operators (Chapter 12)

Recommendation 59

The Ministry of the Environment should continue to require the mandatory certification of persons who perform operational work in water treatment and distribution facilities. Education, examination, and experience are essential components of ensuring competence.

Recommendation 60

The Ministry of the Environment should require water system operators who currently hold certificates obtained through the grandparenting process to become certified through examination within two years, and it should require operators to be recertified periodically.

Recommendation 61

The Ministry of the Environment should require all applicants for an operator's licence at the entry level to complete a training course that has a specific curriculum to ensure a basic minimum knowledge of principles in relevant subject areas.

Recommendation 62

The Ministry of the Environment should develop a comprehensive training curriculum for operators and should consolidate the current annual training requirement in Ontario Regulation 435/93 and the proposed requirement of ministry-approved training into a single, integrated program approved by the Ministry of the Environment.

Recommendation 63

The Ministry of the Environment should take measures to ensure that training courses are accessible to operators in small and remote communities and that the courses are tailored to meet the needs of the operators of these water systems.

Recommendation 64

The Ministry of the Environment should meet with stakeholders to evaluate existing training courses and to determine the long-term training requirements of the waterworks industry. The ministry should play an active role in ensuring the availability of an array of courses on the subjects required to train operators.

Provincial Government (Chapter 13)

Recommendation 65

The provincial government should develop a comprehensive "source to tap" drinking water policy covering all elements of the provision of drinking water, from source protection to standards development, treatment, distribution, and emergency response.

Recommendation 66

The Ministry of the Environment should be the lead ministry responsible for developing and implementing the "source to tap" Drinking Water Policy.

Recommendation 67

The provincial government should enact a *Safe Drinking Water Act* to deal with matters related to the treatment and distribution of drinking water.

Recommendation 68

The provincial government should amend the *Environmental Protection Act* to implement the recommendations regarding source protection.

Recommendation 69

The provincial government should create a Drinking Water Branch within the Ministry of the Environment to be responsible for overseeing the drinking water treatment and distribution system.

Recommendation 70

The provincial government should create a Watershed Management Branch within the Ministry of the Environment to be responsible for oversight of watershed-based source protection plans and, if implemented, watershed management plans.

Recommendation 71
The Ministry of the Environment should require the owners of municipal water systems to obtain an owner's licence for the operation of their waterworks. In order to obtain a licence, an owner should have:

- a Certificate of Approval for the facility;

- a Permit to Take Water;

- approved operational plans;

- an approved financial plan; and

- an accredited operating agency.

Recommendation 72
The provincial government should create an office of Chief Inspector – Drinking Water Systems.

Recommendation 73
Inspectors should be required to have the same or higher qualifications as the operators of the systems they inspect and should receive special training in inspections.

Recommendation 74
The Ministry of the Environment should increase its commitment to the use of mandatory abatement.

Recommendation 75
The Ministry of the Environment should increase its commitment to strict enforcement of all regulations and provisions related to the safety of drinking water.

Recommendation 76
The Ministry of the Environment should initiate a process whereby the public can require the Investigations and Enforcement Branch to investigate alleged violations of drinking water provisions.

Recommendation 77

A steering group should be established within each public health unit area in the province, comprised of representatives of affected local hospitals, municipalities, local Ministry of the Environment offices and local boards of health, for the purpose of developing in a coordinated fashion emergency response plans for the control of, or the response to, infectious diseases and public health hazard outbreaks.

Recommendation 78

The provincial government should ensure that programs relating to the safety of drinking water are adequately funded.

Recommendation 79

The Ministry of the Environment should create an Integrated Divisional System which provides central electronic access to information:

- relevant to source protection;

- relevant to each drinking water system in Ontario (including a description of the system, trend analyses, water quality, and systems data);

- required by the Drinking Water Branch (including for approvals and inspections); and

- required by local Boards of Health.

Recommendation 80

The Drinking Water Branch should prepare an annual "State of Ontario's Drinking Water Report," which should be tabled in the Legislature.

Small Systems (Chapter 14)

Recommendation 81

Ontario Regulation 459/00 should apply to any system that provides drinking water to more than a prescribed number of private residences.

Recommendation 82

The Ministry of the Environment should establish a procedure under which owners of communal water systems may apply for a variance from provincial regulations only if a risk analysis and management plan demonstrate that safe drinking water can be provided by means other than those laid down in regulations.

Recommendation 83

The provincial government should not approve water systems that would not be economically viable under the regulatory regime existing at the time of the application.

Recommendation 84

Approved systems that are not economically viable under the improved regulatory scheme should be required to explore all managerial, operational, and technological options to find the most economical way of providing safe drinking water. If the system is still too expensive, the provincial government should make assistance available to lower the cost per household to a predetermined level.

Recommendation 85

The application of Ontario Regulation 505/01 should be broadened to include all owners of water systems that serve the public for a commercial or institutional purpose and that do not come within the requirements of Ontario Regulation 459/00.

Recommendation 86

With regard to private drinking water systems that are not covered by either Ontario Regulation 459/00 or Ontario Regulation 505/01, the provincial government should provide the public with information about how to supply water safely and should ensure that this information is well distributed. It should also maintain the system of licensing well drillers and ensure the easy availability of microbiological testing, including testing for E. coli.

Recommendation 87

The provincial government should review the current practices for the delivery of drinking water in bulk and the need for a regulatory framework in this area.

First Nations (Chapter 15)

Recommendation 88
Ontario First Nations should be invited to join in the watershed planning process outlined in Chapter 4 of this report.

Recommendation 89
I encourage First Nations and the federal government to formally adopt drinking water standards, applicable to reserves, that are as stringent as, or more stringent than, the standards adopted by the provincial government.

Recommendation 90
I encourage First Nations and the federal government to consider moving to a quality management standard over time, even if the consequence is that several communities, perhaps both reserve and non-reserve, might collaborate on a regional basis, or that First Nation communities might choose to contract with others to manage their water supply systems.

Recommendation 91
The provincial government should require the Ontario Clean Water Agency (OCWA) to offer its services to First Nations band councils for operating on-reserve water systems on a normal commercial basis.

Recommendation 92
The provincial government should actively offer, on a cost-recovery basis, its training facilities and curriculum to First Nations water system operators.

Recommendation 93
As a matter of principle, the provincial government should make technical assistance, drinking water testing, inspection, and enforcement available to First Nations communities on a cost-recovery basis, if requested.

Chapter 2   Government Oversight of the Delivery of Drinking Water: Introduction

Contents

Chapter 2 Government Oversight of the Delivery of Drinking Water: Introduction

2.1 Overview

This chapter is an introduction to the provincial government's responsibility in relation to the delivery of safe drinking water in Ontario. It is descriptive only and does not contain any recommendations. It has three components: (1) an examination of the constitutional responsibility for drinking water; (2) a brief review of the province's current approach to the oversight function; and (3) a review of the recommendations for change made in the Gibbons Report.[1] Substantial portions of the full report focus on the various elements involved in delivering safe drinking water, from source protection through treatment and distribution to the management and financing of drinking water systems. I return to the topic of provincial oversight in Chapter 13. In that chapter, I examine in detail the government's role and make recommendations for areas in which I think improvements are necessary. I note that the majority of drinking water systems are owned by municipalities. I deal with the role of municipal governments in Chapter 10.

2.2 The Constitutional Responsibility for Drinking Water

A useful starting point for examining the government oversight role is a brief discussion of how the responsibility for drinking water fits into the allocation of powers between the federal and provincial governments set out in the *Constitution Act, 1867*. Traditionally, provincial governments have taken the lead in regulating most aspects of the safety of drinking water, and the majority of my recommendations, both here and in the Part 1 report, are aimed at the provincial and municipal levels of government. Although this lead responsibility of the province is consistent with the allocation of powers set out in the Constitution, there is constitutional authority for significant federal participation in the area. Specifically, a number of federal powers, including those over navigation, fisheries, and agriculture, as well as the broad peace, order, and good government and federal spending powers, authorize a significant federal involvement in the subject matter. In addition, the federal responsibility for Indians and lands reserved for Indians results in a substantial federal role for drinking water safety on First Nations reserves.

---

[1] Executive Resource Group, 2001, *Managing the Environment: A Review of Best Practices* (Toronto) [hereafter Gibbons Report].

2.2.1   Drinking Water as a Constitutional Subject Matter

The power to legislate with respect to drinking water has not been expressly assigned in the Constitution. It is necessary, therefore, to assess the subject matter and determine which of the assigned heads of power set out in sections 91 or 92 or elsewhere in the Constitution relate to it. The regulation of the safety of drinking water has two general components: the regulation of drinking water sources and the regulation of treatment and distribution. There is some overlap between the two functions, but the first is generally concerned with environmental regulation and the second deals with public health, safety, and convenience. Although the environment and public health are not referred to as specific heads of power in the Constitution, there is a history of interpretation by the courts addressing issues of constitutional responsibility for these matters.[2]

It is now well established that neither the environment nor public health are within the exclusive jurisdiction of any level of government. Whether a particular level of government has the power to legislate depends on what aspect of the environment or public health the legislation relates to. The Supreme Court of Canada has referred to a shared responsibility. Justice La Forest, in *Friends of Oldman River v. Canada*,[3] stated that in relation to the environment,

> the *Constitution Act, 1867* has not assigned the matter of "environment" *sui generis* to either the provinces or Parliament. The environment, as understood in its generic sense, encompasses the physical, economic and social environment touching several of the heads of power assigned to the respective levels of government . . .

> It must be recognized that the environment is not an independent matter of legislation under the *Constitution Act, 1867* and that it is a constitutionally abstruse matter which does not comfortably fit within the existing division of powers without considerable overlap and uncertainty.[4]

---

[2] See R. Foerster, 2002, "Constitutional jurisdiction over the safety of drinking water," Walkerton Inquiry Commissioned Paper 2, pp. 3–14.

[3] [1992] 1 S.C.R. 3.

[4] Ibid. at 42, per La Forest J. See also *R. v. Crown Zellerbach Canada Ltd.* (1998), 49 D.L.R. (4th) 161 at 200–201 (S.C.C.), per La Forest J.:

> To allocate the broad subject-matter of environmental control to the federal government under its general power would effectively gut provincial legislative jurisdiction... In Canada, both federal and provincial levels of government have extensive powers to deal with these

A similar shared jurisdiction has also been recognized in respect of public health.[5]

2.2.2 Provincial Jurisdiction

Four powers set out in section 92 of the Constitution provide the provinces with a broad jurisdiction over drinking water safety: local works and undertakings (s. 92(10)); property and civil rights in the province (s. 92(13)); matters of a local or private nature (s. 92(16)); and municipal institutions in the province (s. 92(8)). In addition, section 109 gives the provinces jurisdiction over natural resources. This is reinforced by section 92A, which provides the provinces with exclusive jurisdiction over the development, conservation, and management of non-renewable resources. The provinces also have jurisdiction, held concurrently with the federal government, to regulate with respect to agriculture in each province.[6]

These powers have enabled provincial governments to legislate with respect to both the environment and public health.[7] Pursuant to these powers, the Ontario government has passed a broad variety of legislation relating both directly and

---

matters. Both have enacted comprehensive and specific schemes for the control of pollution and the protection of the environment. Some environmental pollution problems are of more direct concern to the federal government, some to the provincial government. But a vast number are interrelated, and all levels of government actively cooperate to deal with problems of mutual concern...

  To allocate environmental pollution exclusively to the federal Parliament would, it seems to me, involve sacrificing the problems of federalism enshrined in the Constitution. As Professor William R. Lederman has indicated in his article, "Unity and Diversity in Canadian Federalism: Ideals and Methods of Moderation"... environmental pollution "is not a limited subject or theme, [it] is a sweeping subject or theme virtually all-pervasive in its legislative implications." If, he adds, it "were to be enfranchised as a new subject of federal power by virtue of the federal general power, then provincial power and autonomy would be on the way out over the whole range of local business, industry and commerce as established to date under the existing heads of provincial powers." And I would add to the legislative subjects that would be substantially eviscerated the control of the public domain and municipal government.

La Forest J. wrote for the dissent, but this aspect of his decision was not contested by the majority; see also *Friends of the Oldman River*, supra note 3 at 41.

[5] See P.W. Hogg, 1992 (looseleaf) *Constitutional Law of Canada*, vol. 1 (Toronto: Carswell) at 18-11–18-12; *Schneider v. The Queen*, [1982] 2 S.C.R. 112. Note also that shared jurisdiction in these areas is emphasized by s. 36 of the *Constitution Act, 1982*, which commits both levels of government to provide essential public services of measurable quality to all Canadians.

[6] *Constitution Act, 1967,* s. 95.

[7] See, for example, *Schneider v. The Queen*, supra note 5; and *Canadian National Railroad Co. v. Ontario* (1991), 3 O.R. (3d) 609 (Div. Ct.); aff'd (1992) 7 O.R. (3d) 97.

indirectly to the safety of drinking water, including the *Ontario Water Resources Act*,[8] the *Environmental Protection Act*,[9] the *Environmental Assessment Act*,[10] the *Health Protection and Promotion Act*,[11] and the *Farming and Food Production Protection Act*.[12] None of these enactments has been challenged as being beyond the jurisdiction of the province.[13]

In general, provincial jurisdiction is sufficiently broad to enable the province to regulate virtually all matters relating to the safety of drinking water. There are, however, two exceptions to this statement: regulation that conflicts with valid federal legislation, and regulation relating to Indians and lands reserved for Indians.

2.2.3   Potentially Conflicting Federal Jurisdiction

There are a number of federal powers pursuant to which legislation aimed at the safety of drinking water could be enacted by Parliament. These powers include navigation and shipping (s. 91(10)); seacoasts and inland fisheries (s. 91(12)); federal works and undertakings (s. 91(29) and s. 92(10)); canals, harbours, rivers, and lake improvement (s. 108); and a concurrent jurisdiction over agriculture in all or any of the provinces (s. 95). In addition, a number of conceptual powers exist, including trade and commerce (s. 91(2)); the spending power (s. 91(1A)); criminal law (s. 91(27)); and peace, order, and good government (s. 91), any of which could also be used to authorize federal action. Many of these powers have been used to justify federal legislation in the area, especially in relation to environmental matters.[14] The power over seacoasts and fisheries is the jurisdictional basis for the *Fisheries Act*, which contains a

---

[8] R.S.O. 1990, c. O.40 [hereafter OWRA].

[9] R.S.O. 1990, c. E.19, s. 1(1) [hereafter EPA].

[10] R.S.O. 1990, c. E.18, as amended, s. 1(1).

[11] R.S.O. 1990, c. H.7.

[12] S.O. 1988, c. 1.

[13] See, however, the discussion below about challenges to the provincial regulation of federal undertakings such as railways.

[14] See, for example, the *Canada Water Act*, R.S.C. 1985, c. C-11, which sets out a comprehensive water resource management scheme. See also *Friends of Oldman River v. Canada*, supra note 3, in which federal legislation requiring an environmental assessment on new undertakings was found to apply to the construction of a dam on a river located wholly within the province of Alberta; and *Northwest Falling Contractors v. The Queen* (1980), 113 D.L.R. (3d) 1(S.C.C.), in which the Supreme Court of Canada found no constitutional difficulty with s. 33(2) of the *Fisheries Act*, R.S.C. 1985, c. F-14, which prohibited the deposit of substances "deleterious to fish" in waters frequented by fish. However, this result should be contrasted with *Fowler v. The Queen* (1980), 113 D.L.R. (3d) 513 (S.C.C.), where similar legislation that was not as clearly related to "fisheries" was struck.

number of environmental prohibitions aimed at the protection of fish habitats but which have a broad effect on source protection.

The federal spending power has also been used by Parliament as authority to enact legislation directed to health care and infrastructure spending, including national standards for hospital insurance, medical care, and student housing programs – all as conditions of federal financial contributions to these regimes.[15] The federal government also participates in establishing drinking water guidelines through a federal–provincial subcommittee. This important activity is discussed in detail in Chapter 5 of this report.

The special responsibility of the federal government with respect to Indians and Indian lands is discussed below.

Although broad federal powers exist, the courts have not interpreted them so as to place undue limitations on the provinces' ability to legislate with respect to matters concerning drinking water. The doctrine of paramountcy does apply, but it has not been used to limit provincial authority to any great extent. The doctrine provides that in areas where both the federal and the provincial governments have jurisdiction, any conflicts are resolved in favour of the federal legislation. However, the doctrine has developed from its original form, in which jurisdictional conflict was found to exist whenever the provincial legislation encroached upon the federal power, to the present form, in which an actual conflict between federal and provincial legislation must be found before provincial legislation will be struck down.[16] For example, provincial legislation requiring a report to be made by a business that discharges waste into the Thunder Bay harbour has been upheld despite the fact that the "harbour" is under federal jurisdiction.[17] Similarly, a provision in Ontario's *Environmental Protection Act*[18] making it an offence to discharge a contaminant into the environment that "causes or is likely to cause impairment of the quality

---

[15] Such initiatives have been upheld by the courts in *Re Canada Assistance Plan*, [1991] 2 S.C.R. 525; *Eldridge v. British Columbia*, [1997] 3 S.C.R. 624 (upholding the *Canada Health Act*); and *Central Mortgage and Housing Corporation v. Co-op College Residences* (1975), 13 O.R. (2d) 394 (C.A.) (upholding federal loans for student housing).

[16] As then Chief Justice Dickson stated in *Multiple Access Ltd. v. McCutcheon*, [1982] 2 S.C.R. 161, at 191: "In principle there would seem to be no good reason to speak of paramountcy and preclusion except where there is actual conflict in operation as where one enactment says 'yes' and the other says 'no': 'the same citizens are being told to do inconsistent things'; compliance with one is defiance of the other." See also *Bank of Montreal v. Hall*, [1990] 1 S.C.R. 121; and *Ontario v. Canadian Pacific Ltd.* (1993), 13 O.R. (3d) (C.A.); aff'd, [1995] 2 S.C.R. 1028.

[17] *Canadian National Railroad Co. v. Ontario*, supra note 7.

[18] EPA, s. 13 (1)(a).

of the natural environment or any use that can be made of it" was found to apply to a controlled burn of dead grass on a CP Railway right-of-way conducted pursuant to CP's obligations under the *Railway Act*.[19]

Generally, the division of powers in the Constitution allows a reasonable degree of flexibility in regard to the allocations of responsibility relating to the matters that are necessary to achieve safe drinking water. The combination of the powers conferred on the provinces in the Constitution and, no doubt, the practical advantages of provincial regulation have resulted in the provinces assuming primary responsibility for most issues relating to the safety of drinking water. However, there are also substantial benefits to be had from a federal role in certain aspects of the subject matter. I will return in other chapters to the practical advantages of cooperation between the two levels of government, especially in areas such as source protection and standards development. Here, I only wish to point out that such cooperation is constitutionally permissible.

2.2.4   Indians and Lands Reserved for Indians

One exception to what I have set out above relates to Indians and lands reserved for Indians – a jurisdiction that has been reserved for Parliament in section 91(24) of the Constitution. The federal government has traditionally taken the view that this section permits Parliament to legislate with respect to First Nations on matters that ordinarily fall under provincial jurisdiction.[20] Indeed, in relation to drinking water, the *Indian Act* explicitly authorizes First Nations to make bylaws relating to the construction of water courses, "public wells, cisterns, reservoirs and other water supplies."

Despite this express allocation, arguments exist to support a provincial power with respect to Indians and Indian lands. Specifically, there are cases that have held that provincial laws "of general application" also apply to Indians and on Indian lands.[21] Much has been written about who among federal, provincial, and First Nations governments should be responsible or empowered to regulate the various aspects of Indian life. Not surprisingly, the matter is controversial. However, I do not believe it would serve any purpose for me to enter this

---

[19] *Ontario v. Canadian Pacific Ltd.*, supra note 16.

[20] See, for example, the *Indian Act*, R.S.C. c. I-6, s. 1, which covers a broad range of activities relating to Indians, including the purposes for which reserve lands may be used for property and civil rights, and education.

[21] See Foerster, pp. 36–41, particularly note 55.

debate. As I discuss in Chapter 15, the safety of drinking water on First Nations lands in Ontario faces serious problems, which will not be resolved by jurisdictional squabbles among the federal, provincial, and First Nations governments.

The province of Ontario has much to offer First Nations communities in terms of technical assistance and know-how. Although it would be inappropriate for the provincial government to impose such assistance, it would clearly be helpful for the provincial, federal, and local First Nations levels of government in each aboriginal community to sit down and work out an approach for ensuring drinking water safety. Similarly, in regard to the recommendations on source protection that I make in Chapter 4, it would be beneficial for aboriginal communities in each watershed to be given the opportunity for involvement in the watershed-based source protection planning process that I am recommending.

2.3   Overview of the Current Provincial Approach

2.3.1   Ministries with Responsibilities Relevant to the Safety of Drinking Water and Relevant Legislation

2.3.1.1   *The Ministry of the Environment*

The Ministry of the Environment (MOE) is currently the key player in the management of the drinking water system.[22] It administers both the *Environmental Protection Act* (EPA) and the *Ontario Water Resources Act* (OWRA) – the two statutes most directly related to the safety of drinking water.[23] The MOE sets standards for water quality and applies those standards through a system of approvals, permits, certification, monitoring, inspection, and enforcement. It can take action to ensure compliance or it can initiate prosecutions or applications for court orders to prevent damage. The legislation

---

[22] The Ministry of the Environment was created in 1972. It absorbed the Ontario Water Resources Commission, which constructed and operated water and sewage works from 1956 to 1971.

In describing current provincial government oversight of drinking water, I rely heavily on the following papers: N. d'Ombrain, 2002, "Machinery of government for safe drinking water" Walkerton Inquiry Commissioned Paper 4; and J. Merritt and C. Gore, 2002, "Drinking water services: A functional review of the Ontario Ministry of the Environment," Walkerton Inquiry Commissioned Paper 5.

[23] As noted above, however, they are by no means the only pieces of legislation affecting the subject matter.

also authorizes the MOE to approve the taking of water, the construction of water and sewage treatment facilities, and the licensing of well contractors and technicians.

Key Legislation: The EPA is Ontario's principal environmental statute; several of its sections deal with protecting water sources. Section 6 of the Act prohibits the discharge into the natural environment of any contaminant in excess of the limits prescribed in regulations. However, animal wastes disposed of in accordance with normal farm practices are exempt from section 6.

Section 6 must be read together with section 14, which prohibits discharges that cause or are likely to cause an adverse effect. From my reading, section 14, which applies "despite any other provision of the Act," has the overall effect of narrowing the animal waste exemption if such wastes cause or are likely to cause certain types of adverse effect. The problem is that section 14 is unclear. While it creates a prohibition against the discharge of contaminants into the environment that cause an adverse effect, there is then an attempt, in section 14(2), to exempt certain agricultural discharges so long as they are "disposed of in accordance with normal farm practices." The exemption relates to some but not all of the definition of "adverse effect" contained in the Act. The result, which I discuss in detail in Chapter 4, is needlessly confusing.

"Normal farm practices" are not defined in the EPA. Instead, they are determined by the Normal Farm Practices and Procedures Board under the *Farming and Food Production and Protection Act, 1998* which is discussed in some detail later in this chapter.

Further confusion results from the overlap of these provisions with the OWRA, section 30 of which makes it an offence to discharge or permit the discharge of "any material of any kind into or in any waters … that may impair the quality of the water." The term "may impair the quality" is not defined. There is no exemption for normal farm practices for this section. The scope of the prohibition in the OWRA is expressed in different terms than is the prohibition in section 14 of the EPA (i.e., discharges that have an adverse effect). Absent the exemption for some farming activities, the EPA section 14 prohibition seems to be very similar to the OWRA section 30 prohibition.

The EPA has been used interchangeably with the OWRA to control water pollution. Like the OWRA, the EPA contains provisions for control orders (s. 7), stop orders (s. 8), and prevention orders (s. 18). In addition, the EPA provides for remedial orders (s. 17) that can require the clean-up of damage that has already occurred. Farm operations are exempt from requirements for certificates of approval for discharges by virtue of section 9(3) of the EPA.

Other relevant environmental legislation administered by the MOE includes the *Environmental Assessment Act*,[24] the *Environmental Review Tribunal Act 2000*,[25] the *Drainage Act*,[26] and the *Pesticides Act*.[27] In addition, Ontario also has an *Environmental Bill of Rights, 1993*[28] which gives the public a right to be consulted prior to certain governmental decisions affecting them. For example, the EBR allows members of the public to review approvals issued under the OWRA before they are issued. It also provides a mechanism for the public to request investigations of environmental compliance. A member of the public may request that the MOE investigate any suspected violation of a prescribed Act, regulation, or approval (Part V). If the complainant does not receive a response or receives a response that he or she considers unreasonable, a legal proceeding in respect of harm to public resources, including water, can be commenced (Part VI).

The government has introduced but not yet passed a new *Nutrient Management Act* (Bill 81), which, among other things, provides for the passage of regulations respecting the management of materials containing nutrients. It is possible that the MOE may be designated as the ministry responsible for the administration of this Act.

The OWRA serves a dual purpose in dealing with both environmental protection and the treatment and distribution of drinking water. It is the main statute for the management and protection of surface water and groundwater in the province and makes the Minister of the Environment responsible for "the supervision of all surface waters and ground waters in Ontario" for the purposes of the Act.[29] The OWRA also empowers the MOE to "control and regulate the collection, production, treatment, storage, transmission, distribution and use of water for public purposes and to make orders with respect thereto."[30] The Act:

---

[24] R.S.O. 1990, c. E.18.
[25] S.O. 2000, c. 26, Sched. F.
[26] R.S.O. 1990, c. D.17.
[27] R.S.O. 1990 c. P.11.
[28] S.O. 1993, c. 28.
[29] OWRA, s. 29.
[30] Ibid., s. 10 (3).

- prohibits the discharge into water of polluting materials that may impair the quality of water;

- enables the MOE to take remedial and enforcement action to protect water quality;

- provides a regime for overseeing water taking, water wells, water supply and treatment facilities, and sewage works; and

- enables the Ontario Clean Water Agency (OCWA) to operate municipal and sewage works.

Policy Guidelines: Prior to August 2000, the province applied two main policy guidelines to decisions about drinking water protection and management: the Ontario Drinking Water Objectives (ODWO)[31] and the Chlorination Bulletin.[32]

The ODWO were first introduced in 1964. They were last revised in 1994 and superseded by Ontario Regulation 459/00 in August 2000. The ODWO included:

- maximum acceptable concentrations in drinking water of substances that are harmful to human health or that may interfere with the taste, odour, or appearance of drinking water;

- minimum sampling requirements;

- circumstances in which notification of the MOE was required;

- a definition of unsafe drinking water and instructions about who was to be notified in the event it was detected;

- a requirement that all public water supply systems using groundwater be sampled for the following physical parameters: turbidity, disinfectant residuals, volatile organics, inorganics, nitrates/nitrites, and pesticides and PCBs; and

---

[31] Ontario, Ministry of the Environment, Water Policy Branch, "Ontario Drinking Water Objectives" (1994 revision).
[32] Ontario, Ministry of the Environment, Water Policy Branch, "Chlorination of Potable Water Supplies," Technical Bulletin 65-W-4 (updated March 1987).

- monitoring requirements, including continuous disinfectant residual monitoring for systems serving more than 3,300 people from surface water or groundwater under the influence of surface water.

The ODWO were a guideline and were thus not legally binding. However, the MOE sometimes made compliance with the ODWO a condition of a Certificate of Approval, and the ODWO or portions of them were also sometimes made conditions of Field Orders.

The Chlorination Bulletin was first introduced in the 1970s. It provided detailed information about a number of areas, including determinations of when disinfection was required, minimum chlorine residuals, chlorination equipment, and monitoring.

Regulation 459/00: In August 2000, following the Walkerton outbreak, the policy approach described above was altered with the passage of a new Drinking Water Protection Regulation, Ontario Regulation 459/00. The revised ODWO and the Chlorination Bulletin are now contained in a document entitled "Ontario Drinking Water Standards" (ODWS) and referred to in the new regulation.

Key requirements under the regulation include:

- the increased testing and treatment of water (minimum levels of treatment, sampling, and analysis);

- mandatory regular water sampling by all waterworks and testing by accredited labs;

- stricter procedures for reporting contamination;

- more frequent inspections (a report of each facility is to be submitted to the municipality and the MOE every three years);

- the upgrading of existing water treatment systems and facilities;

- the issuance of quarterly reports by large waterworks;

- the notification of both the Medical Officer of Health and the MOE of adverse water quality; and

- public access to all sample results, approvals, and orders.[33]

The regulation places the onus for ensuring water treatment, testing, reporting, and the publicizing of results, as well as corrective action, on the owners of facilities. It does not, however, regulate or provide any guidelines for the activities of the regulator.

Regulation 505/01: In 2001, the provincial government passed Ontario Regulation 505/01, which requires designated types of small water systems, to which Ontario Regulation 459/00 does not apply, to meet certain treatment requirements. The designated systems include those that provide water to at-risk groups, such as the young, the elderly, and the infirm.[34]

Organizational Structure: The MOE is organized into divisions, branches, regions, and regional district and area offices that carry out its functions (see Figure 2.1). It has four divisions:

- Integrated Environmental Planning (policy and planning);

- Environmental Sciences and Standards (science and standards);

- Operations (delivery); and

- Corporate Management (human resources and *Environmental Bill of Rights*).

The Integrated Environmental Planning Division: The Integrated Environmental Planning Division provides policy planning, program development, and long-term thinking for the MOE. The division is organized by media (land use, air, and water). The Water Policy Branch is responsible for developing programs and policies related to the quality and quantity of Ontario's drinking water. Representatives from the Water Policy Branch lead the Drinking Water Coordination Committee (DWCC), an interministerial committee with a mandate to coordinate the implementation of the MOE's drinking water program.

The Environmental Sciences and Standards Division: The Environmental Sciences and Standards Division supplies the MOE with the science base used

---

[33] O. Reg. 459/00, ss. 5–11.

[34] O. Reg. 505/01 is discussed in greater detail in section 14.4 of this report.

Figure 2.1 Organization of the Ministry of the Environment, 2002

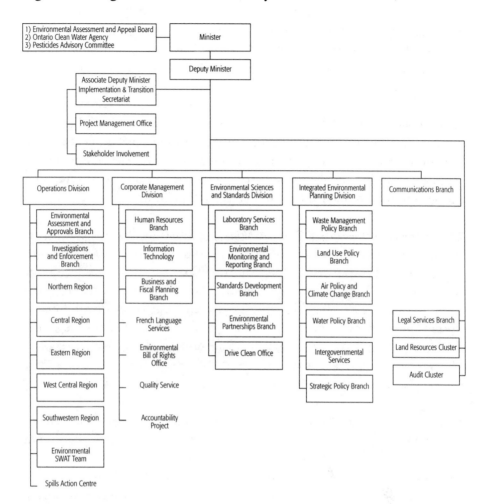

to develop standards and monitor programs. The division consists of four branches. The Laboratory Services Branch provides analytical support for monitoring and regulatory programs. It oversees the MOE laboratory in Toronto, which provides all testing services.[35] The Environmental Monitoring and Reporting Branch maintains air and water monitoring activities, such as the Drinking Water Surveillance Program (DWSP) and the Great Lakes Sampling Program. The Standards Development Branch develops drinking water standards (ODWS) and has representation on the DWCC and the Federal–Provincial–Territorial Subcommittee on Drinking Water. The Environmental Partnerships Branch supports (non-regulatory) pollution prevention partnerships between government and industry. Such programs include grants to municipalities for waste and wastewater management.

The Operations Division: The Operations Division is divided into five regions: Northern, Central, Eastern, Southwestern, and West Central. These regional offices in turn oversee 15 district and 16 area offices that are responsible for the delivery of MOE programs at a local level, including those directed at the quality of drinking water and drinking water source protection. Environmental officers, investigations officers, and administrative staff work out of regional/district/area offices; technical support staff are primarily located in the regional offices. Communal water is one of the 15 programs for which the regional offices have responsibility.

Environmental officers (also referred to as abatement officers or field staff) in the regions perform inspections of sewage and water treatment plants and respond to complaints of environmental violations.

The work of the branches of the Operations Division is intended to ensure compliance with environmental laws. The Environmental Assessment and Approvals Branch issues permits, licences, and Certificates of Approval for new or modified water and sewage facilities under the OWRA, the EPA, the *Environmental Assessment Act*, and the *Pesticides Act*. The Investigations and Enforcement Branch (IEB) investigates suspected violations of environmental legislation and is responsible for all aspects of environmental enforcement. Investigation officers in the IEB collect the evidence and lay the charges for environmental prosecutions.

---

[35] Before 1996, three regional laboratories, in London, Kingston, and Thunder Bay, handled routine testing for municipalities. Only the Toronto laboratory currently exists.

The Operations Division also runs the Spills Action Centre (SAC) and the Environmental SWAT Team. The SAC is a province-wide system staffed by environmental officers on a 24-hour basis. Its role is to record reports of spills and other urgent environmental matters and to coordinate a response. Spills must be reported when they impair or are likely to impair the quality of the natural environment (e.g., water) or pose adverse health risks.[36]

The Environmental SWAT Team is a recent addition to the Operations Division. Environmental officers and investigation officers conduct inspection sweeps of sectors that have high non-compliance rates and/or present a high risk to public health. None of the sectors currently being inspected by the Environmental SWAT Team is directly related to drinking water.

The Corporate Management Division: The Corporate Management Division includes administrative support functions such as the Human Resources Branch, Information Management and Technology Branch, Business and Fiscal Planning Branch, and French Services. The Environmental Bill of Rights staff is also included in this division.

2.3.1.2   *The Ministry of Natural Resources*

The Ministry of Natural Resources (MNR) does not play a major role in the provision of safe drinking water. It is the lead ministry for programs primarily related to water quantity, including drought and low water levels; flood forecasting, warning, and emergency response; watershed management; dams; water diversions, transfers, and withdrawals; and water conservation. The MNR works closely with local conservation authorities, and is currently developing a groundwater-monitoring network with the MOE.

The MNR administers the *Conservation Authorities Act*,[37] which provides for the creation of conservation authorities,[38] which are charged with furthering the conservation, restoration, development, and management of natural resources (other than gas, oil, coal, and minerals) in their areas.[39] An authority can regulate the use of water from surface waters in its area; regulate or prohibit

---

[36] The SAC received initial calls from Walkerton residents at the onset of the *E. coli* outbreak in Walkerton and initiated the first response.

[37] R.S.O. 1990, c. C.27.

[38] Ibid., s. 3.

[39] Ibid., s. 20.

any alterations to a watercourse; and prohibit the construction of structures in areas susceptible to flooding or erosion.[40]

2.3.1.3   *The Ministry of Health and Long-Term Care*

The Ministry of Health and Long-Term Care (Ministry of Health) oversees public health administration at the local level under the *Health Protection and Promotion Act*. Currently there are 37 health units in the province, each of which is supervised by a board of health and directed by a local Medical Officer of Health. The health units act independently of the municipalities and the province (who both provide resources), but the province sets the regulatory framework for the boards' operation and maintains an advisory role.

Interaction between the Ministry of Health and the MOE is critical to the provision of safe drinking water. The Ministry of Health is involved in the development of drinking water standards. Further, under Ontario Regulation 459/00, the local health unit is to be notified (by the waterworks owner and by the testing laboratory) of adverse water quality results.[41] The Medical Officer of Health may then take action under the *Health Protection and Promotion Act* and Ontario Regulation 459/00, including issuing a boil water order or advisory.[42]

Also related to the safety of drinking water, when a complaint is made that a health hazard related to environmental (or occupational) health exists in the area covered by the local health unit, the local Medical Officer of Health is to notify the responsible ministry, and, in consultation with the ministry, investigate and determine whether the health hazard exists.[43] Medical Officers of Health can issue orders to remedy conditions they consider health hazards.[44]

Further, Ministry of Health laboratories can test water quality if requested to do so by the Medical Officer of Health or by waterworks operators and owners, including the owners of private wells. Although the ministry does not monitor water quality, it provides water quality advice to the MOE through a technical committee on water microbiology.

---

[40] Ibid., s. 28.
[41] O. Reg. 459/00, ss. 8(2), 8(3)(a).
[42] O. Reg. 459/00, s. 9; *Health Protection and Promotion Act*, s. 13.
[43] *Health Protection and Promotion Act*, s. 11.
[44] Ibid., s. 13.

2.3.1.4 *The Ministry of Agriculture, Food and Rural Affairs*

The Ministry of Agriculture, Food and Rural Affairs (OMAFRA) also has an important role in relation to the safety of drinking water in Ontario. It has the mandate to regulate aspects of agricultural activity, including the management of animal waste – a major cause of water contamination.

To date, the province has not passed specific legislation restricting or regulating farm activities. Instead, it has provided certain exemptions to farm activities from some environmental statutes. In addition, it has put in place several voluntary programs that encourage environmentally sound practices. As to the exemptions granted to farmers in legislation, I received several submissions arguing that the exemptions were too broad and should be narrowed. It struck me that there was some misunderstanding about the extent of these exemptions. Let me summarize.

Prohibitions Against Pollution

As noted above:

- Section 30 of the OWRA prohibits the discharge into water of contaminants that have a deleterious effect and contains no exemption for farm activities;

- Section 6 of the EPA prohibits the discharge of contaminants into the natural environment in excess of the limits prescribed in regulations but normal farm practices are exempt; and

- Section 14 of the EPA prohibits discharges of contamination into the natural environment that cause adverse effects. Some exemptions exist for normal farm practices but not for discharges that injure or damage property, cause a material discomfort to any person, or have an adverse effect on human health or impair safety.

The continued effect of the EPA and the OWRA is that farm practices that have deleterious effects or cause specified adverse effects are prohibited.

Immunity Against Civil Action

Section 6(1) of the *Farming and Food Production Protection Act*, which provides that a farmer is not liable in nuisance for a disturbance resulting from normal farm practices, does not apply to the contamination of waters. Disturbances are defined as coming from odour, dust, flies, light, smoke, noise, and vibration. Consequently, there is no immunity from civil action for farmers who engage in farming practices that contaminate water.

Municipal Bylaws

Section 6 of the *Farming and Food Production Protection Act* exempts normal farm practices from municipal bylaws.

It is not clear which ministry will ultimately be responsible for the proposed *Nutrient Management Act, 2001* (Bill 81).[45] Although I am recommending that the MOE be the responsible ministry, it is possible that OMAFRA will have an important role to play. Under the Act, provincial regulations can be passed that establish standards respecting the management of material containing nutrients, including the management of farm practices that use this material. The Act will require farmers and other generators of nutrients to comply with those standards. It also provides for the enforcement of the standards by provincial officers.[46] I deal with the regulation of farmers in detail in Chapter 4.

2.3.1.5   *The Ministry of Municipal Affairs and Housing*

The Ministry of Municipal Affairs and Housing (MMAH) has a role in the oversight of the drinking water process through its administration of the *Planning Act*.[47] Land use planning can play an important role in the protection

---

[45] The Act does not identify a lead ministry. At the September 7, 2001, Walkerton Inquiry Public Hearing #5, Peter Wallace (on behalf of the government) acknowledged that the Ministry of the Environment generally has a lead on enforcement (Transcript, p. 79) and is the lead ministry with respect to water (Transcript, p. 76).

[46] The bill contains amendments to the *Environmental Protection Act*, the *Highway Traffic Act*, the *Ontario Water Resources Act*, the *Pesticides Act*, and consequential amendments to the *Farming and Food Production Protection Act, 1998* [hereafter FFPPA]: *Compendium* <www.gov.on.ca/OMAFRA>.

[47] R.S.O. 1990, c. P.13.

of surface water and groundwater. Although the *Planning Act* does not deal expressly with drinking water quality in Ontario, it requires most municipalities to develop official plans. An official plan sets out future land use plans for a municipality and may address matters relating to water use and water quality, including expected water use, discharge and runoff into water courses relating to the patterns of land use (e.g., industrial withdrawal and consumption of water and discharge into water, agricultural withdrawal and discharge, and residential consumption and withdrawal). The *Planning Act* provides the Minister of Municipal Affairs and Housing with the power to amend official plans if a matter of "provincial interest" such as "the supply, efficient use and conservation of water" is, or is likely to be, affected by a plan.[48]

The *Planning Act* dictates that when exercising authority that affects a planning matter, a planning authority (such as MMAH, a council of a municipality, or the Ontario Municipal Board) "shall have regard to" policy statements issued by the provincial government. Some parts of the Provincial Policy Statement relate to land use and groundwater protection.[49]

The province has recently introduced two proposed Acts that are relevant to safe drinking water. First, it has introduced a revised *Municipal Act*, which comes into effect on January 1, 2003.[50] The Act gives municipalities broad authority and flexibility over ten "spheres of jurisdiction," including public utilities, waste management, and drainage and flood control.[51] These "spheres of jurisdiction" are intended not to be subject to specific prescriptive provisions but to be left open to the discretion of the municipality. Four additional powers are provided that will be subject to the more traditional prescriptive approach. These powers relate to the natural environment; to facilitating economic development; to the health, safety, protection, and well-being of people and protection of property; and to nuisance, noise, odour, vibration, illumination, and dust.

---

[48] *Planning Act*, ss. 2, 23(1).
[49] PPS 1.1.1(e): "A coordinated approach should be achieved when dealing with issues which cross municipal boundaries, including infrastructure and ecosystem and watershed related issues."
PPS 1.1.1(f): "Development and land use patterns which may cause environmental or public health and safety concerns will be avoided."
PPS 2.4.1: "The quality and quantity of groundwater and surface water and the function of sensitive groundwater recharge/discharge areas, aquifers and headwaters will be protected or enhanced."
PPS 2.1.5: "In prime agricultural areas, agricultural uses and normal farm practices will be promoted and protected."
[50] *Municipal Act, 2001*, S.O. 2001, c. 25.
[51] Ibid., s. 11.

The second significant legislative proposal is the *Sustainable Water and Sewage Systems Act, 2001* (Bill 155),[52] which would require all owners of water or wastewater systems to submit to the MMAH a written report on the full cost of providing water and wastewater services to the public (the "full-cost report"). The report would have to contain "such information as is required by regulation concerning the infrastructure needed to provide the water services, the full cost of providing the services and the revenue obtained to provide them and concerning such other matters as may be specified in the regulation."[53] In addition, the proposed Act would require a municipality to submit to the ministry, within six months of the approval of its full-cost report, a "cost-recovery plan" outlining how it "intends to pay the full cost" of water and wastewater services to the public.[54]

The Minister of Municipal Affairs and Housing would have the authority to approve, reject, or change both the full-cost report and the cost-recovery plan submitted by a municipality. Further, the minister could order a municipality to, in effect, pay the full cost of providing water or wastewater services, if the minister concluded that the municipality was "not implementing its approved cost recovery plan" or "not taking all necessary steps to pay the full cost of providing water services or wastewater services, as the case may be, to the public."[55] Such an order could require the municipality "to generate revenue in a specified manner or from a specified source to pay all or part of the cost of providing the services and to make specified or necessary amendments to existing contracts, resolutions or by-laws."[56] The proposed Act would require municipalities to establish and maintain "a dedicated reserve account that segregates from its general revenues the revenue allocated in its approved cost-recovery plan to pay the full cost (including operating and capital costs) of providing water services or wastewater services."[57]

---

[52] Bill 155 received first reading on December 12, 2001.

[53] Bill 155, s. 3.

[54] Ibid., s. 9. In some sections of Bill 155, the term "regulated entity" is used. For the purposes of this report, I use the term "municipality" instead, because municipalities own the overwhelming majority of communal systems.

[55] Ibid., s. 21(1).

[56] Ibid., s. 21(3).

[57] Ibid., s. 22.

2.3.2 Agencies with Responsibilities Relevant to the Safety of Drinking Water

A number of agencies and tribunals also play an important role in the regulation of drinking water.

2.3.2.1 *The Ontario Clean Water Agency*

Ontario municipalities own their water and sewage facilities. Most municipalities operate the facilities themselves (or through public utilities commissions), but about 25% of them contract out water and sewage operations – primarily to the Ontario Clean Water Agency (OCWA).[58]

Until 1993, the MOE operated many of the province's sewage and water works. OCWA was created in 1993 to remedy the apparent conflict posed by the MOE regulating its own operations.[59] OCWA initially owned some facilities, but under the *Water and Sewage Services Improvement Act, 1997*, legal title was transferred to the municipalities.

When a municipality enters into an agreement with OCWA for the provision of water and sewage services, OCWA can exercise any statutory power given to municipalities in respect of the "establishment, construction, maintenance or operation of water works or sewage works."[60] OCWA supplies the labour and management, pays for operations and maintenance, and guarantees performance and regulatory compliance.

2.3.2.2 *The Ontario SuperBuild Corporation*

The establishment of the Ontario SuperBuild Corporation was announced in the 1999 provincial budget. The purpose of SuperBuild is to consolidate the

---

[58] It has 95% of the market for municipalities that choose to outsource the operation of such facilities; the remaining 5% is operated by the private sector. At the end of 2000, the agency operated 161 water treatment and 233 sewage facilities for more than 200 municipalities; 222 of its 383 contracts were with small municipalities and were worth less than $100,000 annually.

[59] The Ontario Clean Water Agency (OCWA) was established by the *Capital Investment Plan Act*, S.O. 1993, c. 23. The Ontario Water Resources Commission (OWRC) also regulated and operated water and sewage works from 1956 until the creation of the Ministry of the Environment (MOE) in 1972.

[60] OWRA, ss. 10, 12.

province's infrastructure spending. The corporation advises the Cabinet Committee on Privatization and SuperBuild (chaired by the Minister of Finance) on infrastructure spending and spending by ministries, agencies, and provincially funded municipal infrastructure.

The Ontario Small Towns and Rural Initiative (OSTAR) is a "subsidiary initiative" administered by the MMAH that is intended to fund infrastructure capital expenditures (i.e., water and sewage works) in smaller municipalities.

2.3.2.3   *The Ontario Municipal Board*

The Ontario Municipal Board occasionally arbitrates planning disputes that affect the quality of drinking water.[61]

2.3.2.4   *The Normal Farm Practices Protection Board*

The Normal Farm Practices Protection Board referees the provisions of the *Farming and Food Production Protection Act.* It is empowered to inquire into and resolve disputes respecting agricultural operations, to determine what constitutes normal farm practice, and to make the necessary inquiries and orders to ensure compliance with its decisions.[62] The Board has its own statutory mandate and is also subject to ministerial directives, guidelines, or policy statements in relation to agricultural operations or normal farm practices.[63]

2.3.2.5   *The Environmental Commissioner*

The Environmental Commissioner assists the public in preparing complaints, reviews compliance by ministries with environmental responsibilities, and

---

[61] For example, in Perth County, where the West Perth township council passed a zoning bylaw limiting the size of livestock operations to 600 animal units and stipulating the intensity and location of manure-spreading activities, the bylaw was challenged before the Ontario Municipal Board by several farm operators and by the Ministry of Municipal Affairs and Housing. Protection of drinking water was the principal argument advanced by the council in defence of the bylaw, and the council bolstered its case by demonstrating that existing regulations are not adequately enforced. The board upheld the validity of the bylaw. The appeal to the Divisional Court was dismissed. See *Ben Gardiner Farms Inc. v. West Perth (Township)*, ([2001] O.J. No. 4394 (S.C.J. (Div. Ct.)).

[62] FFPPA, s. 4.

[63] Ibid., s. 9.

reports to the legislature on issues of environmental concern. The commissioner often reports on issues related to water quality in the province. The Environmental Commissioner's office was established under the *Environmental Bill of Rights 1993* (EBR). The EBR applies to 13 government ministries and agencies, requiring them to register plans that could have environmental impacts so that the public has an opportunity to present concerns at an independent environmental assessment.

2.3.2.6   *The Environmental Review Tribunal*

The Environmental Review Tribunal hears appeals from some MOE decisions made under the EPA, the OWRA, and the *Pesticides Act*. Under the Ontario *Environmental Assessment Act*, it also conducts hearings to assess the environmental impact of major projects such as water and sewage treatment facilities.

2.3.2.7   *Conservation Authorities*

Another important entity in the current structure is the conservation authority. There are 36 conservation authorities in Ontario. Their functions include the control of potential flood damage, and in many cases watershed management including planning, education, prevention, treatment, and monitoring. In managing particular watersheds they also protect lands and wetlands for recreation and wildlife and have the power to acquire lands and build structures such as reservoirs and dams.[64] The province establishes conservation authorities, and the relevant municipality (or municipalities, if the watershed extends into other municipalities) appoints the members. They are financed through user fees, municipal levies, and provincial grants.

2.3.3   Authorization Processes for Safe Drinking Water

The OWRA governs the procedure for approving new water facilities, including the alteration, extension, and replacement of existing facilities.

---

[64] *Conservation Authorities Act*, R.S.O. 1990, c. C.27, s. 21(1).

2.3.3.1   *Permits to Take Water*

Under the OWRA, no person shall take more than a total of 50,000 L of water in a day without a permit issued by a Director.[65] Permits are issued by the MOE's regional offices. An application must be made to the MOE for a permit to draw surface water or groundwater. The Certificate of Approval addresses the drinking water quality aspects of the water withdrawn for communal waterworks through a Permit to Take Water (PTTW).

2.3.3.2   *Certificates of Approval*

The legal owner of waterworks or sewage works (including distribution systems) that are larger than a prescribed size must obtain approval for the construction and operation of the waterworks.[66] Certificates of Approval, originally similar to building permits, were originally approvals to build a facility with specific machinery. More recent Certificates of Approval include conditions for operating, which vary because every certificate is facility-specific. Older certificates for Ontario waterworks do not refer to any operating conditions (e.g., water quality requirements). This deficiency has been corrected by Ontario Regulation 459/00, which gave the ODWO (now the ODWS) the force of law. The conditions of approval for new facilities are based on six broad criteria that are addressed as standards under the ODWS. The six standards, performance, monitoring and recording, operations and maintenance, notification and reporting, conditions as compliance/enforcement tools, and other conditions provide the basis for inspection and enforcement of compliance. Certificates of Approval issued more recently are similar to operating licences.

Licensing requirements for waterworks and sewage works are set out in Regulation 435/93 (under the OWRA). Facilities are divided into four classes, depending on the complexity of the facility. Owners must ensure that operators are properly licensed for the particular class of facility and must provide 40 hours of training per year to each operator.[67] Operators are responsible for maintaining records of monitoring and sampling and must "take all steps reasonably necessary to operate the processes within his or her responsibility in

---

[65] OWRA, s. 34(3).

[66] Ontario, Ministry of the Environment, August 2000, "Guide to applying for approval of municipal and private water and sewage works. Sections 52 and 53 Ontario Water Resources Act R.S.O. 1990," p. 1.

[67] O. Reg. 435/93, ss. 14, 17.

a safe and efficient manner in accordance with the relevant operations manuals."[68] They are also to ensure the maintenance of operating equipment and to ensure that "the processes within his or her responsibility are measured, monitored, sampled and tested in a manner that permits them to be adjusted when necessary."[69] An operator's licences may be suspended or cancelled if a contravention of the regulation results in the discharge of a pollutant into the natural environment or has an adverse effect on the health or safety of an individual.[70]

2.3.4   Compliance and Enforcement Processes

2.3.4.1   *Monitoring*

The owner of a waterworks that is capable of supplying more than 250,000 L per day and actually supplies at least 50,000 L per day on at least 88 days in a 90-day period, or that serves more than five private residences, must meet the water sampling and analysis requirements in Ontario Regulation 459/00.[71] The regulation also sets out the procedure for the notification of an adverse test result. The testing laboratory must immediately notify the owner of the waterworks, and both must immediately notify the local Medical Officer of Health and the MOE (through the Spills Action Centre).[72]

2.3.4.2   *Voluntary Monitoring*

The voluntary Drinking Water Surveillance Program (DWSP) provides the MOE with data to determine long-term trends in drinking water quality in Ontario. Waterworks operators collect raw and treated water samples on a regular basis; the samples are analyzed at the MOE laboratory to determine the presence or absence of hundreds of substances. As of the end of 1999, the DWSP monitored 162 municipal waterworks, accounting for about 88% of the population served by municipal water supplies.

---

[68] Ibid., ss. 18, 19.
[69] Ibid., s. 19.
[70] Ibid., s. 11.
[71] O. Reg. 459/00, s. 7.
[72] Ibid., s. 5.8(1)–(3).

2.3.4.3   *Inspection, Investigation, and Enforcement*

Environmental officers in the MOE's district and area offices carry out inspections of waterworks. Inspection is considered an "abatement" function (i.e., a method of achieving compliance short of investigation and enforcement). The Sewage and Water Inspection Program (SWIP) was set up by the MOE in 1990 to be responsible for inspections of sewage and water facilities.

The Investigations and Enforcement Branch (IEB) is a separate branch of the MOE. It is usually made aware of information about a violation of any relevant MOE statute or regulation through an occurrence report. If necessary, an IEB officer will start an investigation to determine whether there are reasonable and probable grounds to lay charges.

The officer may issue an order if there has been a contravention of a provision of the OWRA or EPA, or the regulations; of a provision of an order, notice, direction, requirement, or report made under the OWRA; or of a term or condition of a licence, permit, or approval made under the OWRA.[73] Orders are issued to require operators to take corrective action. The issuance of orders is usually followed by assistance with compliance, in which environmental officers work with waterworks owners and operators to correct problems brought to the MOE's attention. Operators who do not comply with the issued order or take corrective action can be prosecuted for violating the statute, regulation, certificate of approval, permit, or order.[74]

MOE "compliance activities" are actions taken and/or procedures followed by staff to ensure that legislation is complied with and regulatory requirements are followed. Non-compliance is identified through routine inspections and abatement activities, responses to spills, the addressing of complaints, or the handling of *Environmental Bill of Rights* requests for investigation.[75] The MOE decides whether abatement measures for non-compliance should be voluntary or mandatory.

---

[73] OWRA, s. 16(1). An officer might also issue orders under the EPA, such as: a stop order (s. 8), a control order (s. 7), or a remedial order (s. 17).

[74] OWRA, s. 107.

[75] Ontario, Ministry of the Environment, 1995, "Compliance guidelines," June 16, s. 2.2.0.

2.4   The Gibbons Report

After the Walkerton tragedy, the Government of Ontario retained Valerie A. Gibbons and Executive Resource Group to prepare a report and make recommendations on how the province could improve its approach to environmental regulation and oversight. The report, entitled *Managing the Environment: A Review of Best Practices,* was released in January 2001. In Gibbons's own words, the focus of the report was on "identifying best practices in other jurisdictions that could be implemented in Ontario as part of establishing this Province as a leading environmental jurisdiction and a model for others."[76]

Although the report does not focus specifically on the safety of drinking water, its focus – government regulation of the environment – is clearly relevant to my mandate. Moreover, I find the report helpful as a third-party review of the MOE's current approach. In the following sections, I set out a brief overview of what I perceive to be some of the report's more significant conclusions and recommendations, as well as my impressions of these findings and recommendations.

2.4.1   Overview of the Gibbons Report

2.4.1.1   *Review of Current Practice*

The Gibbons Report refers to a number of shortcomings of the MOE, at least in comparison with what are characterized as "best management practices" from other jurisdictions. According to the Gibbons Report, the MOE:

- is under considerable management and operational pressure;[77]

- has no coherent strategy for how to approach environmental issues.[78] (The current approach is described as "piecemeal."[79] In a similar vein,

---

[76] V.A. Gibbons, letter to A. Karakatsanis (secretary of Cabinet and clerk of the Executive Committee, January 31, 2001, included at the outset of the Executive Summary of the Gibbons Report).
[77] Gibbons Report, Executive Summary, p. 7.
[78] Ibid., p. 8.
[79] Ibid., p. 7.

the report also criticizes the absence of a strategic approach to policy development on environmental matters.);[80]

- focuses too much on a "command and control approach to achieving compliance and too little emphasis on more innovative compliance mechanisms";[81]

- is too centralized and does not delegate enough functions to other operating organizations, leaving fewer resources to focus on strategic capacity;[82]

- experiences "significant gaps in the knowledge and information required to support ... policy development."[83] (The report also identifies shortcomings in the MOE's ability to acquire and manage information.[84] In particular, the MOE needs to work on the integration of the numerous existing government databases.);[85]

- suffers from shortcomings relating to its ability to address emerging issues;[86]

- devotes insufficient resources to research and development and has no research and development strategy;[87] and

- needs to move from its current focus on risk assessment alone, to more emphasis on risk management and risk communication.[88]

As will be seen in greater detail elsewhere in my report, some of these observations are supported by the evidence and information disclosed to me in Parts 1 and 2 of this Inquiry. In particular, the absence of a top-down strategic approach, the need for more resources and for a better allocation of such resources, the need to rebuild or obtain access to sufficient expertise, and the

---

[80] Ibid., p. 20.
[81] Ibid., pp. 10–11.
[82] Ibid., p. 12.
[83] Ibid., p. 13.
[84] Ibid., pp. 14–15.
[85] Ibid., p. 16.
[86] Ibid., pp. 14–15.
[87] Ibid., pp. 17–18.
[88] Ibid., pp. 18–19.

need to better integrate the information that the MOE does have, were regular themes in the submissions made to me in both Parts 1 and 2 of this Inquiry.

2.4.1.2 *Recommendations Made in the Gibbons Report*

Two types of recommendations are made in the Gibbons Report: "strategic shifts" and more particular recommendations. At the core of the recommendations is a system-wide shift from a traditional model of environmental regulation (referred to in the report as a "command and control" model) to a "strategic approach," which

> steps beyond minimum standards to emphasize continuous improvement for all sources of pollution, cross-media and cumulative impacts, and broader public participation and access to information. It typically includes less emphasis on the role of government as "doer", i.e. protecting human health and the environment by traditional regulation and enforcement, and a greater emphasis on the role of government to provide overall *system management*, through a range of partnerships, processes, structures, and tools...[89]

According to Gibbons, this overarching shift is accomplished through five general strategic shifts:

- a "high-level, government-wide vision and goals with implementation shared across different departments";[90]

- a "new and broader emphasis on strategies to promote continuous improvement in environmental outcomes and accountability across all sources of pollution";[91]

---

[89] Gibbons Report, p. 91. I find some of the language used in the report to be somewhat vague and unclear. For this reason and to ensure that I do not misrepresent the recommendations made, I have quoted liberally from the Gibbons Report.

[90] Gibbons Report, Executive Summary, p. 3. According to Robert Breeze, the current Associate Deputy Minister of the Environment and a key member of Ms. Gibbons's team, this does not preclude lead or coordinating responsibility on the part of the MOE. See the letter from Timothy Hadwen to me dated September 17, 2001, reporting on a meeting with Mr. Paul Muldoon, Ms. Ramani Nadarajah from CELA, Commission Counsel, Robert Breeze, and others from the Government of Ontario.

[91] Gibbons Report, Executive Summary, p. 3. My interpretation of this recommendation is that it calls for less emphasis on ensuring compliance with minimum standards and for more emphasis on a goal of continuous improvement of environmental conditions.

- a "place-based approach with boundaries that make environmental sense and facilitate a cross-media, cumulative approach (such as watershed management)";[92]

- a "comprehensive, more flexible set of regulatory and non-regulatory tools and incentives";[93] and

- an approach based on "shared responsibility with the regulated community, NGOs, the public, and the scientific/technical community."[94]

In support of these "strategic shifts," the Gibbons Report makes a number of specific recommendations regarding the way in which the "new vision" will be achieved. Two overarching recommendations are made in support of these specific recommendations: the allocation of sufficient resources to carry out the role effectively,[95] and "a formal commitment to a Change Management approach and process."[96]

The specific recommendations include the following:

---

[92] Gibbons Report, Executive Summary, p. 5.

[93] Ibid. The report recognizes, however, that "a clear understanding that strong, effective, tough inspection, investigation, and enforcement are the essential backbone" (p. 6). The recommendation is that a broader range of procedures be used in addition to tough enforcement.

[94] Gibbons Report, Executive Summary, p. 6.

[95] See ibid., p. 21. In the words of the Executive Summary to the report: "Our view is that implementation and transition management cannot be accomplished within existing structures or within existing resources. Effective implementation and transition planning and oversight will require:
- Dedicated, experienced, senior leadership at the political level;
- A significant core of human and financial resources for a period of at least three to five years that will draw on additional dedicated resources from across government;
- Resources to support the development and implementation of an integrated approach to environmental compliance assurance;
- Resources to support new monitoring systems;
- New capacities to create, share and use knowledge internally and externally;
- Significant investment in information and information technology; and
- Creating new formal and informal mechanisms and approaches to broader outreach and participation of stakeholders and the public."

[96] See Gibbons Report, Executive Summary, p. 22. This recommendation appears to contemplate putting mechanisms in place to ensure that change not only occurs but is accepted by the MOE employees and the public. In the words of the report: "This approach should acknowledge and address the changes required both inside and outside the government and be infused in the process from the very beginning: identifying the need for change, creating buy-in, developing specific strategies, and implementing specific strategies."

1. *Creating an environmental management vision for Ontario:* The Gibbons Report recommends that a high-level government-wide vision of environmental management be developed in Ontario that incorporates all affected ministries. The vision should provide guidance and direction to those ministries and include an articulation of what each ministry's role in the overall strategy should be.

2. *Improving governance for environmental management:* The Gibbons Report suggests that "at some point in the future" the government should consider creating an arm's-length operating agency for the "operational/program delivery of environmental management," while retaining responsibility for "policy, program design, and monitoring, and accountability for performance."[97] The creation of an arm's-length operating agency is explicitly not recommended for the present time, because of the extensive changes that would be required over the next three to five years as a result of the other recommendations made in the Gibbons Report.[98] Although an arm's-length operating agency is not recommended for the present time, the Gibbons team clearly see advantages to such a structure. The overall impression left by the report is that such an agency should be created as soon as the other recommendations have been implemented.

3. *Implementing an integrated approach to environmental compliance assurance:* The Gibbons Report favours a move away from a primary reliance on traditional enforcement techniques to achieve compliance.[99] A "tool kit" of a variety of approaches is favoured, including enforcement, abatement, cooperative agreement, compliance assistance, and economic instruments. The four main policy ends identified in the report are controlling point-pollution sources, reducing priority-pollutant emissions, controlling non–point-pollution sources, and encouraging continuous improvement.

4. *Implementing a comprehensive environmental knowledge management strategy:* The Gibbons Report includes a number of recommendations to improve information gathering and organization mechanisms. These recommendations include ensuring that the government's overall environmental management vision include an explicit commitment to knowledge management as an important means of achieving the vision;

---

[97] See Gibbons Report, Executive Summary, p. 24.
[98] See Gibbons Report, p. 213.
[99] See Gibbons Report, Executive Summary, pp. 24–25.

that the vision be based on the framework proposed in Research Paper No. 5 and that the strategies developed be consistent with the principles outlined in that paper;[100] that there be strong senior leadership and sponsorship of initiatives; that investment be made in the technology required for an environmental knowledge management strategy; and that the strategy build on the new reporting requirements for water.

5. *Identifying and addressing emerging issues:* The Gibbons Report identifies a need for developing a process to assist in identifying emerging issues. Research Paper No. 6 commissioned by the Gibbons team reviews the processes used in some other jurisdictions and makes some broad recommendations on the basis of these processes.[101]

6. *Improving access to scientific and technical expertise:* The Gibbons Report recognizes that the MOE is slipping in regard to the scientific and technical expertise available to assist it in performing its functions. A number of recommendations are made to improve this situation.[102]

7. *Improving environmental monitoring and reporting:* As part of the overall environmental knowledge management strategy, the Gibbons Report also recommends an improved monitoring and reporting strategy for the province. The report recommends that this strategy include:

- developing a new monitoring program with early investment in improving the water quality components, including the Great Lakes, and developing indicators and biomonitoring approaches;

- integrating existing databases;

---

[100] These strategies include linking knowledge and business strategies; articulating and demonstrating the commitment to knowledge management; defining, classifying, organizing and disseminating types and sources of information and knowledge; institutionalizing and resourcing the function within the ministry; rewarding the creation, sharing, and using of information; and building networks and outreach strategies within communities of interest. See IBM Canada, "Creating leading knowledge and information management practices," Research Paper No. 5 to Gibbons Report.

[101] See P. Victor, E. Hanna, J. Pagel et al., "Emerging issues and the Ministry of the Environment" Research Paper No. 6 to Gibbons Report.

[102] These recommendations include the establishment of a research agenda, including a dedicated environmental research fund; the creation of an external research advisory committee to assist in shaping research priorities and to oversee the quality of the research acquired; the provision of ongoing staff training; and a clear link with the above-mentioned knowledge management strategy. See Gibbons Report, Executive Summary, pp. 26–27.

- making information available to the public; and

- creating an "Access Ontario Website" that provides public access to data and analytical tools.[103]

8. *Developing a policy framework for risk analysis:* The Gibbons Report recommends the development of a policy framework for environmental risk analysis that includes the creation of standardized analytical tools and expectations for use in the process; a clear articulation of the expected role and mandate of risk analysis in the decision-making process; and building on the work of the II&E Working Group led by the Ontario Ministry of Labour.

9. *Strengthening policy development:* The Gibbons Report recommends that MOE senior management commit to strengthening policy development capacity. This commitment should include the development of a separate strategic policy unit within the ministry to "focus on policy issues that require a strategic response" and to provide economic advice and analysis. The MOE should also strengthen the "program evaluation component" of the current policy development process.

2.4.1.3   *Comments*

During the public hearings in Part 2 of the Inquiry, a number of parties informed me that in their view the Gibbons Report contained many good points. I generally agree with this assessment. In particular, I agree with the observation and recommendation that the province needs to develop a government-wide strategy with respect to the environment; that within this strategy, clear roles and responsibilities must be assigned; and that the entire enterprise needs to be adequately resourced. I also agree with the recommended "area-based" approach (a watershed-based approach) and with the comments made about the need to improve what the report terms "Information Management." Moreover, as I point out in Chapter 13 of this report, I think there is merit to the suggestions that the MOE needs more resources to fulfill its mandate, more scientific and technical expertise, better environmental monitoring, and an improved information management system.

---

[103] See Gibbons Report, Executive Summary, p. 27.

I would also make these comments of an overview nature about why my report must go beyond the Gibbons Report and address the specific issues relating to the safety of drinking water:

1. The recommendations and observations made in the Gibbons Report are quite general and broad. It is easier to achieve consensus on broad or general points. However, as the range of submissions made to me in this Inquiry establishes, there is much room for controversy and disagreement in the details. For example, like the Gibbons Report, virtually everyone who made submissions to me relating to the oversight role of government agreed that the province needs an overarching water policy (or "vision," as it is referred to in the Gibbons Report). What the elements of that policy should be is an issue on which it is far more difficult to reach consensus. Details such as this were sometimes not dealt with in the Gibbons Report or, when discussed, were not put in a "safety of drinking water" context. I raise this not as a criticism of that report, but only to note that I view my mandate in relation to safe drinking water as requiring me to go further.

2. Although the general recommendation of movement away from a command and control model to a more integrated, cooperative approach that would encourage potential polluters to change their ways may be useful for some aspects of the MOE's mandate, including the abatement of pollution, it is not in my view appropriate for the regulation of drinking water safety. Drinking water safety is different from general pollution abatement in a number of important respects. First, the public health and safety concerns arising from unsafe drinking water are acute and immediate. On the treatment and distribution side, there is little or no room for simply encouraging good performance because there is no time for gradual change. If water is contaminated, people get sick or die. As a result, the system must focus on avoiding problems in the first place and on taking swift corrective action when deficiencies are identified. Second, water providers are more susceptible to government regulation than are potential polluters. There are far fewer of them, they are easily identified, and, in general, they have the same objective as the government – safe drinking water. These factors lend themselves to a command and control system. The same is also true for the entire treatment and distribution regime. Not only is it susceptible to, but I would add that it requires, rules that are clear, easily ascertained, and strictly enforced. There is no room for variations based on factors such as the impact on the local

economy or the interests of local stakeholders. As developed in detail in Chapter 13, a strict approach to oversight is a crucial feature of the government oversight function in regard to treatment and distribution. These comments are not meant as a criticism of the Gibbons Report, but as an observation that the recommendation is not appropriate for drinking water safety.

3. As part of the recommendations on alternative service delivery, the Gibbons Report suggests the possible devolution of the regulation function to the industry. When it comes to the safety of drinking water, I have concerns about such a devolution. As I develop in more detail in Chapter 13, given the public importance of a safe drinking water system, safety can best be ensured when the government is directly involved in regulation and oversight. Allowing the industry to regulate itself could involve conflicts that might have a negative impact on safety. Obviously, if it can be shown that devolution of the function enhances safety, I would not oppose such a move. However, given my concerns, I believe that the onus should be placed on those who propose a form of alternative service delivery to establish that it will enhance safety (and not merely promote efficiency), before such a change is accepted.

Where it is useful to do so, I will discuss the consistency and inconsistency of my recommendations with those of the Gibbons Report in more detail in the relevant chapters that follow.

Chapter 3   A Multi-Barrier Approach to Drinking Water Safety

Contents

Chapter 3   A Multi-Barrier Approach to Drinking Water Safety

3.1   Multiple Barriers in Drinking Water Supply

The best way to achieve a healthy public water supply is to put in place multiple barriers that keep water contaminants from reaching people.[1] The voluminous technical literature and all of the submissions made to the Inquiry on this point emphasized the importance of the multiple-barrier approach in ensuring the safety of drinking water.

Much reform in government in recent years has focused on overlap and duplication, which are considered to be sources of waste and inefficiency. In the area of public health, however, this approach has limits, because single barriers are never entirely effective. Thus, a degree of redundancy guards against the failure of any one barrier. A low tolerance for system failures requires placing a number of processes in series, each of which has a low failure rate and each of whose modes of failure is independent of the others. Every step in the chain, from water supply through treatment to distribution, needs careful selection, design, and implementation, so that the combination of steps provides the best defence against calamity if things go wrong.

---

[1] See P. Huck, testimony, Walkerton Inquiry (Part 1 Hearing, October 16, 2001), transcript p. 111: [T]he multi-barrier approach or defence in depth ... has been an approach which has long been used by the water industry ... to provide safe and secure supplies of drinking water ... [W]e don't rely only on one barrier in the system, we rely on a series of barriers"; Ontario Water Works Association/Ontario Municipal Water Association, 2001, "Final submissions relating to the provision of safe drinking water in Ontario," Walkerton Inquiry Submission, p. 73: "Watershed protection and source evaluation should be emphasized as an integral part of the multi-barrier concept of drinking water protection"; and R.G. Luthy, 2001, *Water Supplies Need Better Protection* <www4.nationalacademies.org/onpi/oped.nsf/(Op-EdByDocID)/97AF7365F3DOC7D 385256B1000777B81> [accessed May 6, 2002]: "The best approach to ensuring water quality is through application of multiple barriers to contaminants in supply, treatment, and distribution." See also D. Krewski et al., 2002, "Managing health risks from drinking water," Walkerton Inquiry Commissioned Paper 7, p. 91; L. Gammie, 2001, for Ontario Water Works Association/Ontario Municipal Water Association, "Review of Issue #5 – Drinking Water Standards – in the Krewski et al. report 'Managing health risks from drinking water,'" Walkerton Inquiry Submission, p. 4; M. Murray and K. Seiling, for the Regional Municipality of Waterloo, Walkerton Inquiry (Kitchener-Waterloo Town Hall Meeting, March 22, 2001) transcript p. 16.

Five types of barriers are commonly used in the provision of drinking water.[2] I discussed them at some length in the Part 1 report of this Inquiry and briefly summarize them here.[3]

- **Source protection** keeps the raw water as clean as possible to lower the risk that contaminants will get through or overwhelm the treatment system.

- **Treatment** often uses more than one approach to removing or inactivating contaminants (e.g., filtration may be followed by chlorination, ozonation, or ultraviolet radiation).

- Securing the **distribution system** against the intrusion of contaminants and ensuring an appropriate free chlorine residual throughout is highly likely to deliver safe water, even when some earlier part of the system breaks down.

- **Monitoring programs,** including equipment fitted with warning or automatic control devices, are critical in detecting contaminants that exist in concentrations beyond acceptable limits and returning systems to normal operation.

- Well-thought-out, thorough, and practised **responses to adverse conditions**, including specific responses for emergencies, are required when other processes fail or there are indicators of deteriorating water quality.

Although each barrier offers protection, no single barrier is perfect. Thus, an over-reliance on only one barrier at the expense of another may increase the risk of contamination. Leaving out key steps at one stage can negate the effect of other stages; for example, the uncovered storage of post-treatment water may undermine the earlier steps taken to ensure water safety.

Independent failure modes should be established; that is, barriers should be selected so that a failure of one barrier does not result in the failure of all. The disinfection part of the treatment sequence should guarantee that if the source water is polluted, bacteria do not pass through to the distribution system. It

---

[2] Different sources give different numbers of stages, usually depending on whether they include a variety of management or training activities, or stick to more technical matters. All, however, would include this basic five in one form or another. I treat quality management and effective regulation of water facilities as the means by which the five barriers are achieved.

can do this by, for example, requiring the installation of alarm-equipped chlorine monitors and possibly automatic shut-off valves. The existence of one barrier does not, therefore, mean that others can be ignored. The concept of multiple barriers entails the balanced presence of all five types of barriers, to the greatest extent possible.

Table 3.1 provides a general indication of how the multi-barrier approach might be put into effect.

Table 3.1   An Example of the Multi-barrier Approach

Hazard	Barrier	Typical Risk Management Approach
Pathogens Chemical contaminants Radionuclides	Source protection	Watershed protection plan Upgraded sewage treatment Choice of water source
Pathogens Disinfection by-products Chemical contaminants	Treatment	Water quality standards Chemically assisted filtration Disinfection
Infiltration Pathogen regrowth	Distribution system	Chlorine residual System pressure Capital maintenance plan
Undetected system failures	Monitoring	Automatic monitors Alarms and shut-offs Logbooks, trend analyses
Failure to act promptly on system failure Failure to communicate promptly with health authorities and the public	Response	Emergency response plans Boil water advisories (orders)

3.2   The Goal: Safe Drinking Water

The goal of any drinking water system should be to deliver water with a level of risk that is so negligible that a reasonable and informed person would feel safe drinking it. This goal must inform all the decisions that affect the safety of drinking water and should provide the objective against which risk assessment and management decisions are to be made. The goal as I have set it out above implies that there will always be some risk. The point made repeatedly in the literature and by those knowledgeable in the area is that removing all risk is not possible. That said, I base my approach to this issue on the premise that in regard to the safety of drinking water, the reasonable and informed public will not feel safe with anything other than the most imperceptible level of risk, a level that is simply not practical to remove.

Tying the risk assessment and management processes to the safety of drinking water and to public acceptance requires that those who make decisions affecting drinking water – the setting of standards, the selection of water sources, the choice of treatment – must involve those who bear the risks (the public) in the decision-making process. The type of confidence in the safety of drinking water that is necessary to achieve the goal I have set out will result only when members of the public are fully informed of the relevant factors leading to such decisions and are able to hold those who make the decisions accountable for the consequences of those decisions. The recommendations made throughout this Part 2 report reflect the need for transparency and accountability in the risk assessment and risk management process.

3.3   Risk Management

The multi-barrier approach is put into effect by assessing and managing the risks to drinking water safety that can be addressed by each barrier. It is important to assess the degree of each risk and to determine how to reduce it effectively in order to select the most appropriate actions for each of the barriers. Often these actions are obvious; for example, surface water should be treated by filtration before being treated by disinfection. In other situations, such as determining the acceptable concentration of a contaminant – a step relevant to the selection of a water source (barrier 1) and to the treatment of the source water (barrier 2) – the decision-making process can be far more complicated. However simple or complex a particular decision may be, it is necessary to address risk and to settle on the approach that most effectively reduces risk.

The key features of a good approach to managing risk include being preventive rather than reactive; distinguishing greater risks from lesser ones, and dealing first with the former; taking time to learn from experience; and investing resources in risk management that are proportional to the danger posed.[4]

Risk management is not a formulaic exercise best left only to the experts. Each stage in the process is informed by human values. In relation to drinking water safety, risk management means choosing among alternative strategies to reduce risk, usually on the basis of the greatest lowering of risk for available resources,

[3] Ontario, Ministry of the Attorney General, 2002, *Report of the Walkerton Inquiry, Part 1: The Events of May 2000 and Related Issues* (Toronto: Queen's Printer), pp. 108–112.

[4] Adapted from S.E. Hrudey, 2001, "Drinking water quality: A risk management approach," *Water,* vol. 26, no. 1, pp. 29–32.

or on the minimum resources needed to attain a pre-set standard. Because public perceptions and values are so fundamental to these choices, there must be effective opportunities for public debate and advice before important decisions are taken.

Risk assessment and management have become increasingly common features of public policy in recent decades.[5] Some resist this trend, in part because the activity as it is typically practised is seen as remote, bureaucratic, and insufficiently open to public involvement. For some, risk management has acquired a stereotypical image: unaccountable experts telling those who are potentially affected not to worry, that everything is under control, and that in any case those who are affected would not understand the deeply scientific arguments.[6] That approach would of course be ineffective, because risk management inevitably involves the influencing of human behaviour; alienating those who are to be protected is not helpful. The management of risks to public health is a value-driven exercise that must be informed by and must respond to the views of the public, just as it must call on the best that science can offer.[7]

3.4   The Precautionary Principle

One way to overcome the difficulties of purely rationalist risk management is to err systematically on the side of safety. A refinement of this approach is the precautionary principle, a guide to environmental action that has now been

---

[5] The federal government published its current risk management policy in 1994 and expanded on it in 2001. It devotes a Web page to listing its own publications and policies in the area. The policy is meant to guide the whole federal government. See Canada, Treasury Board Secretariat, 1994, *Risk Management Policy*; and Canada, Treasury Board Secretariat, 2001, *Integrated Risk Management Framework* <www.tbs-sct.gc.ca/pubs_pol/dcgpubs/RiskManagement/siglist_e.html> [accessed December 23, 2001]. See also Canada, Privy Council Office, 2000, *Risk Management for Canada and Canadians: Report of the ADM Working Group on Risk Management* (Ottawa: Privy Council Office); and S. Hill and G. Dinsdale, 2001, *A Foundation for Developing Risk Management Learning Strategies in the Public Service* <www.ccmd-ccg.gc.ca/pdfs/risk_mgnt_rt_e.pdf> [accessed April 17, 2002]. The basic concepts have been widely applied in fields as diverse as public health, insurance, aeronautics and aircraft design, and banking.

[6] For example, in the expert meetings, the Canadian Environmental Law Association (CELA) was skeptical about whether adequate allowances are made for vulnerable populations and whether the development of standards lags because of pressures to require unattainable proofs of harm. CELA argued for a more explicit and transparent process.

[7] See, for example, W. Leiss, 2001, *In the Chamber of Risks: Understanding Risk Controversies* (Montreal and Kingston: McGill-Queen's University Press).

recognized in international law [8] and cited with approval in a Supreme Court of Canada decision.[9] This principle, which has been formulated in many ways,[10] says that the absence of scientific certainty about a risk should not bar the taking of precautionary measures in the face of possible irreversible harm. It addresses situations in which risk cannot be estimated with any reliability and in which uncertainty prevails regarding the relationship, if any, between cause and supposed effect. Under such circumstances, precautionary measures such as investments in risk mitigation, alternative technologies, and research are called for. At worst, such an approach means that resources that might have been devoted to more productive use elsewhere may be consumed to reduce certain risks. Although this prudent approach must still take account of costs, when the potential consequences of the hazard in question are large, the precautionary principle has a role to play in practical risk management and should be an integral part of decisions affecting the safety of drinking water.

Sometimes the precautionary principle is described as an alternative to the risk management approach. It strikes me that these two approaches should be complementary. Properly applied, what they are designed to achieve is not perfect safety, but a level of risk that a broad spectrum of citizens finds tolerable. This is a pragmatic notion of safety.[11] The precautionary approach is inherent in risk management, and the need for precaution rises where uncertainties about specific hazards are expected to persist and where the suspected adverse effects may be serious or irreversible.

---

[8] "The precautionary principle/approach appears in a large number of international instruments, and Canada's obligations in that regard are governed by its expression in those instruments. Due to an absence of clear evidence of uniform State practice and opinio juris, Canada does not yet consider the precautionary principle to be a rule of customary international law": Canada, Privy Council Office, 2001, *A Canadian Perspective on the Precautionary Approach/Principle: Discussion Document* <www.pco-bcp.gc.ca/raoics-srdc/docs/precaution/Discussion/discussion-e.html> [accessed April 17, 2002]. On the other hand, the Supreme Court of Canada has said that "there may be a 'currently sufficient state practice to allow a good argument that the precautionary principle is a principle of customary international law'": *114957 Canada Ltée (Spraytech, Société d'arrosage) v. Hudson (Town)*, [2001], S.C.J. No. 42 at para. 32.

[9] *114957 Canada Ltée (Spraytech, Société d'arrosage) v. Hudson (Town)*.

[10] See, for example, K. Ogilvie, 2001, *Applying the Precautionary Principle to Standard Setting for Toxic Substances in Canada* (Toronto: Pollution Probe); J. Abouchar, 2001, "Implementation of the precautionary principle in Canada," pp. 235–267 in T. O'Riordan et al., eds., *Reinterpreting the Precautionary Principle* (London: Cameron May); and Canada, Privy Council Office, 2001.

[11] S.E. Hrudey and D. Krewski, 1995, "Is there a safe level of exposure to a carcinogen?" *Environmental Science and Technology*, vol. 29, no. 8, pp. 370A–375A.

In an ideal world, resources would be allocated so as to reduce risks to the greatest extent possible.[12] Where drinking water is involved, the costs associated with any particular barrier tend to rise the more we rely on that barrier. It therefore makes sense to invest in a balanced way in all five types of barriers.

3.5   Outbreaks of Water-borne Disease

Was the Walkerton tragedy an isolated incident brought about by an unlikely combination of events, or was it a warning of a more general problem? Unfortunately, tragedies of the sort experienced in Walkerton are not as uncommon as many may think. They typically involve the simultaneous failure of two or more barriers in systems operated with more complacency than rigour. An April 2002 paper summarizing the causes of 19 outbreaks in six countries[13] concluded that nine of the outbreaks in question resulted from source waters that were polluted during heavy precipitation, two from poorly located intakes, and three from local geographical problems – all source water problems. Three had filtration failures, and five had no or inadequate disinfection – treatment failures; six had distribution system failures; two had monitoring failures; and five had inappropriate responses to adverse conditions. It usually takes the failure of more than one barrier to cause an outbreak. Outbreaks would be more frequent if multiple barriers were not the norm.

Too often, either such outbreaks are inadequately analyzed or the results of the analyses that are done are not drawn to the attention of people who are in a position to respond to them. In England, for instance, a 1980 outbreak affected up to 3,000 residents served by the Bramham water supply. The outbreak was caused by a sewer blockage that resulted in sewage seeping through fractured limestone to contaminate one of four wells. Consumers had earlier complained about the taste of chlorine in the water, so the chlorine dose was kept below 0.01 mg/L total chlorine. When coliforms were observed in treated water, staff had no equipment with which to check chlorine levels downstream of the

---

[12] R. Dobell, 2002, "Social risk, political rationality, and official responsibility: Risk management in context," Walkerton Inquiry Commissioned Paper 13. Compare with C.G. Jardine et al., in press, "Review of risk management frameworks for environmental, human health, and occupational health risks," *Journal of Toxicology and Environmental Health:* "Seek actions that will achieve the greatest overall reduction of risk."

[13] S.E. Hrudey et al., 2002, "A fatal waterborne disease outbreak in Walkerton, Ontario: Comparison with other waterborne outbreaks in the developed world," proceedings at the International Water Association World Water Congress Health Related Water Microbiology Symposium, Melbourne, Australia, April 7–12.

dosing pump. Later it was discovered that the pump was not adding chlorine at all but was passing it straight to the drain. It was also discovered that a number of similar outbreaks with similar causes had previously occurred in Britain. An article discussing the Bramham outbreak noted that

> [e]vidently, the lessons of earlier incidents were not learnt and applied in such a way as to prevent the Bramham outbreak. However, little detailed information is available in the water supply literature about circumstances of [such] incidents. More publicity and detailed analyses are required.
>
> At borehole sites it is required to have automatic shutdown of the pumps if the residual falls below an absolute minimum level.
>
> At sources with an excellent bacteriological record...the role of the chlorine residual would be principally to act as an indicator of chlorine demand. Thus, if the source became polluted the chlorine residual would quickly drop below the acceptable minimum and would thus trigger an alarm and possibly an automatic shut-down. In-house training schemes for operators have been developed, covering the purpose of disinfection as well as the operation of chlorination and chlorine monitoring equipment.[14]

The critically important themes of vigilance and quality management arise throughout this report. In protecting public health, the first step is to ensure that adequate technology is in place. This technology in turn should be operated by trained and conscientious people as part of a well-managed organization. Together with effective oversight and regulation, these are the elements necessary to ensure a very high level of drinking water safety. A tragedy like the one in Walkerton need never happen again.

---

[14] C.S. Short, 1988, "The Bramham incident, 1980: An outbreak of water-borne infection," *Journal of the Institute of Water and Environmental Management*, vol. 2, pp. 383–390.

Chapter 4   The Protection of Drinking Water Sources

Contents

Chapter 4   The Protection of Drinking Water Sources

4.1   Overview

In this chapter, I discuss recommendations for protecting sources of drinking water in Ontario. The existing legislative framework for source protection was discussed in Chapter 2.

This chapter is divided into three areas. First I provide a brief overview of the hydrological cycle (i.e., the water cycle) in Ontario and discuss issues relating to water quantity. I then set out a recommended system for protecting drinking water sources on a watershed basis. Finally, I discuss issues relating to several specific potential sources of drinking water contaminants.

4.2   The Hydrological Cycle in Ontario

4.2.1   Introduction

Of necessity, this chapter begins with a brief and elementary review of the water cycle.[1] Water enters the atmosphere when it evaporates from the oceans and other surface waters or transpires through the leaves of plants and the breath of animals (jointly, evapotranspiration). As air rises, it cools; the water vapour in the air condenses into clouds and then falls as precipitation. Once it hits the ground, water can flow over land as runoff, entering streams, rivers, and lakes to become surface water and ultimately flowing back to the sea, or it can infiltrate or percolate through the soil to become groundwater (a process sometimes referred to as recharge), which will also flow, at a slower rate, downhill toward water bodies or the sea.

Groundwater is contained in porous, water-bearing layers of rock or unconsolidated material called aquifers. Impermeable layers of rock or clay known as aquitards may separate aquifers. An aquifer with an aquitard on top of it is said to be confined, and it may be under pressure. Generally, confined

---

[1] More detailed information on the hydrological cycle is widely available in geography, ecology, hydrogeology, and engineering texts, and on the Internet. For an Internet primer on the water cycle, see Canada, Environment Canada, 2002, *Water Is the Lifeblood of the Earth* <www.ec.gc.ca/water> [accessed April 29, 2002].

aquifers are the preferred sources of drinking water, because slow filtration through the aquitard helps to purge the groundwater of potential pathogens.[2]

Limestone underlies most of Southern Ontario. Where the cracks and fault planes in the limestone have been enlarged by the dissolution of the limestone, the resulting geology is called karst. The channels thus created allow a rapid underground flow of water, so that rather than seeping slowly through aquifers, water may move considerable distances in a short time. It is difficult to predict the pathways that may be taken by groundwater in such systems, although scientists are getting better at modelling them.[3] While the rate of groundwater flow generally measures centimetres or even millimetres per day in non-karst systems, water can travel very rapidly through karstic limestone, with ranges of up to hundreds of metres per day.

Groundwater and surface water are interconnected. Water may flow from surface sources into aquifers in one area, and then re-emerge into surface water in another. In some cases, the direction of water flow between surface water and groundwater depends on the time of year. Groundwater contributes to surface water bodies during periods of low water, while the flow is in the opposite direction during periods of high water.

4.2.2   Water Availability and Use in Ontario

The issue of water quantity in Ontario merits some discussion. Concerns about water quantity and the potential impacts of climate change were expressed by several parties and members of the public during this Inquiry. It was pointed out that although it is often said that Canada has more fresh water per capita than just about any other country, such statements usually refer to the gross stocks of water rather than the annual net runoff. A pattern of water use that exceeds annual net runoff is often compared to dipping into capital instead of living on interest. There is no question that when it comes to water resources, sustainability must be a cornerstone of public health.

---

[2] K. Howard, testimony, Walkerton Inquiry (Part 1 Hearing, October 16, 2000), transcript pp. 24–28.

[3] E.O. Frind, D.L. Rudolph, and J.W. Molson, 2001, "The case for groundwater protection in Ontario: Results of the workshop held at the University of Waterloo, May 1, 2001 – A contribution to the Walkerton Inquiry, Phase II," Waterloo, Ontario, pp. 16–19.

Ontario is certainly one of the world's favoured places with respect to the quantity of water available. Its stock of old water includes groundwater sources created millions of years ago. The annual precipitation in Ontario ranges from a low of approximately 650 mm in the Hudson Bay watershed to a high of 850 mm in the Lake Superior and Lake Huron watersheds. Some of this water cycles directly back into the air through evapotranspiration, but this leaves a staggering average runoff of approximately 12,000 cubic metres per second (m^3/s). Moreover, this amount of runoff is relatively reliable: in only 1 year in 20 is it statistically expected to be less than 7,910 cubic metres per second.

A small portion of net precipitation seeps into the ground to replace water that is extracted and consumed. Even though most of Southern Ontario is underlain by carbonate rock with a great capacity for holding water, groundwater movement is generally slow and the aquifers may not be in hydraulic connection with each other. There is therefore a danger of overtaxing local groundwater resources.

4.2.2.1   Consumptive Use Compared with Non-consumptive Use

A small proportion of water is used consumptively – that is, without returning it to the local ecosystem following use. Water lost to evapotranspiration during use, or water that is sequestered in products or exported, is said to have been consumed. In contrast, water is returned to the ecosystem following non-consumptive use. Non-consumptive uses include most of the water that is used for drinking, in industry, or for hydroelectric generation.

In fact, most activities result in some combination of consumptive and non-consumptive use. Irrigation is an example of a highly consumptive use of water – over 70% of the water is lost to evapotranspiration. On the other hand, activities like hydroelectric generation are over 99% non-consumptive.[4]

Comparing consumptive use in Ontario to total runoff shows that, in total, Ontarians consume very little of what is reliably and sustainably available. They are far from dipping into capital, according to the data in one of the

---

[4] International Joint Commission, 2000, *Protection of the Waters of the Great Lakes: Final Report to the Governments of Canada and the United States* <www.ijc.org/boards/cde/finalreport/finalreport.html> [accessed March 26, 2001].

papers commissioned for the Inquiry.[5] Much less than 1% of the average annual runoff is consumed in most of Ontario, and just under 1% (or 1.25% of reliable runoff) is consumed in the Great Lakes basin. The paper's forecasts indicate that these figures might increase to around 1.3% of the average (or 1.7% of the reliable) annual runoff in the Great Lakes basin by 2021. On the other hand, the total intake of water (which may include some double counting, because water is reused as it moves through a watershed) in 1996 was approximately 38% of the reliable annual runoff, and may rise to over 50% by 2021. These data are summarized in Table 4.1.

4.2.3   Water and Climate Change

A number of parties at the Inquiry suggested that climate change may become a significant factor in the provision of safe drinking water in the future. The report of a workshop organized in 2000 by the Soil and Water Conservation Society, the International Institute for Sustainable Development, and the Canadian Water Resources Association indicates that this may be the case.[6] The report synthesizes much of the work that has been done on the regional impacts of climate change in Canada. It suggests that Ontario may expect to see increased overall annual precipitation, with reduced snow and increased rainfall, more dramatic weather events, a greater degree of surface runoff and flooding, and less infiltration. At the same time, increased temperatures are expected to create increased evaporation, more than offsetting the increase in precipitation and resulting in a lowering of water levels in the lakes. Lower surface water levels, greater runoff, and greater evaporation could also substantially reduce the rate of recharge of groundwater.

Such changes, if they occur, will have long-term impacts on the quality and quantity of drinking water sources in Ontario.

My mandate is to make recommendations regarding the safety of drinking water and does not extend to long-term conservation or ecological management issues. However, a number of the recommendations I make below also provide

---

[5] D.M. Tate, 2002, "Water quantity and related issues: A brief overview," Walkerton Inquiry Commissioned Paper 22.
[6] Global Change Strategies International Inc. and Meteorological Service of Canada, 2000, *Water Sector: Vulnerability and Adaptation to Climate Change, Final Report* <www.c-ciarn.ca/Waterresources_jimbrucereport.pdf> [accessed April 4, 2002].

Table 4.1 Water flow and use in Ontario[7]

1996 Actual	Average Runoff (m³/sec)	Reliable Runoff (m³/sec)	Intake (m³/sec)	Consumed (m³/sec)	Consumed (% average)	Consumed (% reliable)	Intake (% average)	Intake (% reliable)
Hudson-James Bay	6000	3730						
Winnipeg	760	380						
Great Lakes	3070	2400	940	30	0.98	1.25	30.62	39.17
Ottawa	1990	1390						
Total	**11810**	**7910**	**1030**	**40**	**0.34**	**0.51**	**8.72**	**13.02**

2001 Trend Line Projection	Average Runoff (m³/sec)	Reliable Runoff (m³/sec)	Intake (m³/sec)	Consumed (m³/sec)	Consumed (% average)	Consumed (% reliable)	Intake (% average)	Intake (% reliable)
Hudson-James Bay	6000	3730						
Winnipeg	760	380						
Great Lakes	3070	2400	1000	30	0.98	1.25	32.57	41.67
Ottawa	1990	1390						
Total	**11810**	**7910**	**1100**	**40**	**0.34**	**0.51**	**9.31**	**13.91**

2021 Trend Line Projection	Average Runoff (m³/sec)	Reliable Runoff (m³/sec)	Intake (m³/sec)	Consumed (m³/sec)	Consumed (% average)	Consumed (% reliable)	Intake (% average)	Intake (% reliable)
Hudson-James Bay	6000	3730						
Winnipeg	760	380						
Great Lakes	3070	2400	1360	40	1.30	1.67	44.30	56.67
Ottawa	1990	1390						
Total	**11810**	**7910**	**1500**	**40**	**0.34**	**0.51**	**12.70**	**18.96**

[7] Modified from Tate.

tools for adaptive management on a wider basis. In particular, the "approaches to adaptation" of the climate change report that will be well supported in the recommendations of this Inquiry are as follows:

- "[p]reparing water budgets for watersheds to identify the connections between surface and groundwater, areas of vulnerability to water takings and to determine limits for water extraction";

- "[i]mproving contingency plans for extreme events";

- "[e]ncouraging best management practices in rural areas to reduce sources of pollution"; and

- "[e]ncouraging community-based environmental stewardship."[8]

4.2.4   Conclusion

For the purposes of providing drinking water to its population, Ontario has little reason for immediate concern about the gross quantity of water available. On the other hand, a large portion of that water (a volume equal to approximately 39% of the available runoff in the Great Lakes basin)[9] is at some point appropriated for human use. This amount is already large, given the amount of water in the province, and it is likely to increase substantially, to over 50% of the reliable annual runoff by 2021.

Although the vast majority of the water used by humans is returned to the ecosystem, its condition may be considerably worse than when it was withdrawn, depending on what it was used for and what sort of treatment was applied before it was returned. With such a large amount of water being returned to watersheds, which are sources of drinking water for users downstream, it is critical to ensure that all sources are protected from undue contamination.

---

[8] Ibid., pp. 67–68.
[9] See Table 4.1.

4.3   Drinking Water Source Protection

4.3.1   Overview

In a multiple-barrier system for providing safe drinking water, the selection and protection of reliable, high-quality drinking water sources is the first barrier.

A strong source protection program offers a wide variety of benefits. It lowers risk cost-effectively, because keeping contaminants out of drinking water sources is an efficient way of keeping them out of drinking water. This is particularly so because some contaminants are not effectively removed by using standard treatment methods. As a result, protecting drinking water sources can in some instances be less expensive than treating contaminated water. Moreover, protecting sources is the only type of protection available to some consumers – at present, many rural residents drink untreated groundwater from wells. The protection of those groundwater sources is the only barrier in their drinking water systems.

It is clear that the public strongly favours source protection as a key component of our water system. No other aspect of the task of ensuring drinking water safety received as much attention during the town hall meetings this Inquiry held across Ontario. Source protection was also one of the main issues identified by the Part 2 parties in the Inquiry. The parties addressed the issue in their submissions, at the expert meetings, and in the public hearings that were held from May through September of 2001.[10]

In this chapter, I recommend a source protection system that begins with a strong planning component. I also recommend that source protection planning must be carried out on an ecologically meaningful scale – that is, at the watershed level.

Because drinking water source protection is one aspect of the broader subject of watershed management, it makes the most sense in the context of an overall watershed management plan. In this report, I restrict my recommendations to those aspects of watershed management that I think are necessary to protect drinking water sources. However, I want to emphasize that a comprehensive

---

[10] As I mentioned above, these submissions can be found on the Commission's Web site.

approach is needed and should be adopted by the Province. Source protection plans should be a subset of broader watershed management plans.

Some of the main elements of the source protection system I envision are as follows:

Leadership from the Ministry of the Environment (MOE): I recommend that the MOE be the lead provincial agency with regard to all aspects of providing safe drinking water, including source protection. The MOE would establish the framework for developing watershed-based source water protection plans, would help to fund and participate in their development, and would approve the completed plans.

A watershed basis: The watershed is the most meaningful unit for drinking water source protection planning. Impacts on water resources are integrated within watersheds, not municipalities. Residents of a watershed have a common interest in water quality, regardless of political boundaries.

A local planning process: To ensure that local considerations are fully taken into account, and to develop goodwill within and acceptance by the local communities, source protection planning should be done as much as possible at a local (watershed) level, by those who will be most directly affected (municipalities and other affected local groups). Where possible, conservation authorities should coordinate the plans' local development. Otherwise, the MOE itself should undertake the coordination role. I envision the process as being completely open to public scrutiny.

Approval by the MOE: Once draft plans are developed at the watershed level, I envision that they would then be subject to MOE approval. Requiring approval will provide consistency of approach across watersheds and should help prevent undue influence by local interests.

Effective plans: If source protection plans are to be meaningful, they must be respected by the various actors in the watershed. Once the MOE has approved a plan, therefore, provincial Permits to Take Water and Certificates of Approval for sewage treatment plants and any other activities that pose a threat to water quality will have to be consistent with the approved plan. In cases involving a significant direct threat to drinking water sources, municipal official plans and zoning decisions will also need to be consistent with the local source protection plans. In all other situations, municipal official plans and zoning decisions should at least take the relevant source protection plans into account.

Those who have experience in watershed planning will find these recommendations familiar. They quite closely reflect the watershed planning process developed in 1993 by the MOE, the Ministry of Natural Resources, the conservation authorities, and other groups[11] and are consistent with the regimes for source protection and watershed management that exist in many other jurisdictions.

The legislation discussed in Chapter 2 of this report and other provincial policies provide many of the tools needed to ensure the safety of Ontario's drinking water sources. However, the system as currently structured is a patchwork that lacks a clear mandate, leadership, consistency, and coordination for the protection of drinking water sources.

The need for a coordinated, integrated approach to managing water resources is acknowledged in some of the documents the Inquiry obtained from the provincial government.[12] Importantly, even before the Walkerton tragedy, the government was beginning to move in the direction of establishing a

---

[11] Ontario, Ministry of the Environment and Energy and Ministry of Natural Resources (MOEE/MNR), 1993a, *Watershed Management on a Watershed Basis: Implementing an Ecosystem Approach* (Toronto: Queen's Printer); Ontario, Ministry of the Environment and Energy and Ministry of Natural Resources (MOEE/MNR), 1993b, *Subwatershed Management* (Toronto: Queen's Printer); Ontario, Ministry of the Environment and Energy and Ministry of Natural Resources (MOEE/MNR), 1993c, *Integrating Water Management Objectives into Municipal Planning Documents* (Toronto: Queen's Printer).

[12] The annual reports published by the Environmental Commissioner of Ontario from 1994 to 2001 discuss a recommendation that the Ministries of Environment and Energy, Natural Resources, Consumer and Business Services (formerly Consumer and Commercial Relations), Agriculture, Food and Rural Affairs, and Transportation work together to upgrade Ontario's groundwater management framework. See also Ontario Water Directors' Committee, 1999, "Policy water management: Strategic policy direction & 5-year business plan," September, submitted to Assistant Deputy Ministers; Ontario, Ministry of the Environment and Ministry of Natural Resources, 2000, "Provincial water management framework," February, submitted to the Management Board.

comprehensive water management framework for Ontario. A report prepared for the MOE by Valerie Gibbons in 2001 also supports calls for more integrated management.[13] The background paper on watershed management prepared for the Gibbons Report[14] identified best practices in watershed management that closely reflect many of the recommendations contained in this chapter.

A more integrated approach, as proposed below, is necessary to protect the quality of Ontario's drinking water sources. Protecting water resources for the purpose of maintaining or improving the quality of drinking water sources must be a primary focus of strategic planning for water at the provincial level.

4.3.2   Source Protection Plans

Recommendation 1: Drinking water sources should be protected by developing watershed-based source protection plans. Source protection plans should be required for all watersheds in Ontario.

In Chapter 13 of this report I recommend a comprehensive provincial policy for drinking water that will include a multiple-barrier system for the protection of drinking water safety. Source protection is the first barrier in that system.

Drinking water organizations around the world are increasingly recognizing the need to manage the drinking water system as a whole, including protecting sources. The American Water Works Association (AWWA), for instance, has provided a series of "white papers" on the importance of source water protection as part of a multiple-barrier system.[15] In Australia, where an extensive process of development and consultation has resulted in the production of a new set of guidelines, the need for water quality planning to extend all the way from the catchment to the consumer has been emphasized.[16]

---

[13] Executive Resource Group, 2001, *Managing the Environment: A Review of Best Practices* (Brampton, ON), vol. 1, pp. 23–27. Available at <www.ene.gov.on.ca/envision/ergreport> [accessed April 29, 2002] [hereafter Gibbons Report].

[14] Beak International Incorporated, 2001, "A review of watershed management experience," in *Ibid* vol. 2.

[15] See appendices in B. Pett, for OWWA/OMWA, 2001, "The management of manure and non-point source contamination of water quality in Ontario: Review of the Walkerton Inquiry Issue #6 reports by Goss and Johns," Walkerton Inquiry Submission.

[16] L. Gammie, for OWWA/OMWA, 2001, "Review of Issue #5 – Drinking water standards – in the Krewski et al. report 'Managing health risks from drinking water,'" Walkerton Inquiry Submission, pp. 23–25.

Most of the Part 2 parties emphasized the need for strong source protection measures. None disagreed. Many emphasized not only the importance of source protection in reducing health risks, but also the cost-effectiveness of protection as a means of keeping pathogens out of drinking water.

As part of this Inquiry, town hall meetings were held at locations around Ontario. In each city or town that we visited, I met with municipal water services staff and managers. In every case, the importance of having secure drinking water sources was brought home to me. At the town hall meetings, Ontarians from many communities voiced their concern about the protection of drinking water sources. The commissioner of engineering and public works for the Region of Waterloo said that "[s]ource water protection is ... the first and probably most cost-effective barrier in a multiple barrier or integrated approach."[17] The president of the Lake Kasshabog Residents' Association said that "[t]he future safety of drinking water in the Province is inextricably tied to the care that we take in managing the integrity of these sources."[18] The general manager of the City of Toronto Water and Waste-Water Facilities said that "[t]he protection of our drinking water sources ... is the most critical issue facing us today."[19] Ontario's Environmental Commissioner has also emphasized the need for source protection: "The true protection for all our drinking water ... lies upstream of the treatment plant."[20]

Protecting our drinking water sources must be a key part of the system for ensuring the safety of Ontario's drinking water.

The key to source protection is managing the human activities that affect drinking water sources. At present in Ontario, the main approach to managing these activities is the permit-based regulation of water takings and effluents from human activities, combined with voluntary programs for the control of non–point source pollution.[21] This approach is largely "end-of-pipe" and has

---

[17] M. Murray, Walkerton Inquiry (Kitchener-Waterloo Town Hall Meeting, March 22, 2001), transcript p. 17.

[18] T. Rees, Walkerton Inquiry (Peterborough Town Hall Meeting, April 10, 2001), transcript p. 124.

[19] M. Price, Walkerton Inquiry (Toronto Town Hall Meeting, October 29, 2001), transcript p. 11.

[20] G. Miller, Environmental Commissioner of Ontario, 2001, speech given at the Safe and Clean Drinking Water Strategies Conference, Toronto, Ontario, July 10.

[21] Sources of contaminants can generally be grouped into two classes. *Point sources* are identifiable fixed single points where contaminants are released, such as a municipal sewage outflow pipe. *Non-point sources* involve contaminants that are released from multiple or dispersed locations, such as the spreading of road salt or runoff from agricultural land.

been criticized for being applied on a serial, project-by-project basis, resulting in a failure to regulate the cumulative impacts of water use in a watershed.

A systematic land use planning approach that protects drinking water sources, including strategies like wellhead protection legislation, the mapping of groundwater aquifers, and other land use controls, is used in many other jurisdictions, including New Brunswick, Nova Scotia, and most of Europe. In Ontario, some municipalities have created bylaws to control land use for the purpose of protecting drinking water sources on an ad hoc basis, with some assistance and encouragement from the provincial government. It has been suggested, however, that the tools available to municipalities are not sufficient to allow the development of a consistent and systematic source protection plan. Moreover, as I discuss in section 4.4.5.5, municipal authority is restricted in regulating agricultural activities (which are often a source of pathogenic contamination) if the activity constitutes a normal farm practice.[22]

A watershed consists of all of the lands that drain into a particular body of water. This may be a large body of water (e.g., the Lake Ontario watershed, the Great Lakes watershed, the Ottawa River watershed) or a small one (the Lake George watershed, the Tay River watershed). Watersheds may be nested: for example, the Grand River watershed is within the Lake Erie watershed. In fact, nearly every watershed is contained within some other watershed. For practical purposes, it is often useful to define a certain major watershed and then refer to subwatersheds within it.

Watersheds are an ecologically practical unit for managing water. This is the level at which impacts to water resources are integrated, and individual impacts that might not be significant in and of themselves combine to create cumulative stresses that may become evident on a watershed level.[23]

Managing water on a watershed basis requires decision makers to recognize the impacts that upstream activities have on downstream water sources and helps ensure that decision makers take all impacts into account. Management units like municipalities or individual sites are too small to encourage decision makers to take a whole-system view when managing water and allow them to ignore the costs that are incurred outside their jurisdictions. Such externalization results

---

[22] *Farming and Food Production Protection Act, 1998*, S.O. 1998, c. 1, s. 6.
[23] Ontario, MOEE/MNR, 1993a, p. 5; Conservation Ontario, 2001, "The importance of watershed management in protecting Ontario's drinking water supplies," Walkerton Inquiry Submission, p. 14; Beak International, p. 1.

in a skewing of what planners may regard as the most cost-effective choices and hinders the sensible management of the resource.[24]

Using the watershed as the appropriate level for planning also helps to balance two competing needs: the need for local decision making and the need for a reasonable consistency of approach between localities. I think this balance can be reached by ensuring that affected groups in the watershed develop drinking water source protection plans on a watershed basis in accordance with provincially established guidelines.

The Government of Ontario, conservation authorities, and various other groups have developed a watershed planning framework that is already applied in some watersheds.[25] This may be an excellent framework for environmental management on a watershed basis, but it is optional and, importantly for this report, drinking water and the safety of drinking water sources have not received sufficient attention within this framework.

For this recommendation, I suggest that the provincial government accept the watersheds as they are currently defined for the purposes of establishing the jurisdiction of the conservation authorities. These jurisdictions have the advantage of already being in place, and they have worked well in the past. There has been no serious suggestion that watersheds should be reidentified for the purpose of the planning process I am recommending. Below, I recommend that where possible, the conservation authorities coordinate the development of watershed-based source protection plans. It therefore makes sense to adopt the jurisdictional areas within which the conservation authorities now operate for the purposes of source protection planning. Where there is no conservation authority, the MOE should define the geographic extent of the watersheds for planning purposes.

In recommending that the provincial government adopt watersheds for planning purposes, I recognize that groundwater aquifers may be located in more than one watershed. In such instances, there will be a need to coordinate the planning process among the watersheds.

The various aspects of water management cannot be separated, because the water involved is used and reused as it passes through watersheds. Several of

---

[24] Ontario, MOEE/MNR, 1993a, pp. 3–4.
[25] Ibid.

the Part 2 parties suggested that the MOE should be responsible for developing a comprehensive water management strategy that would address all aspects of water management on a watershed basis. As I have already said, it would be very difficult to develop a meaningful and useful drinking water source protection regime without a broader strategy. The recommendations I make in this chapter assume that a broader system will be in place.

It is apparent from many of the documents made available to the Inquiry that the provincial government, led by the Ministry of Natural Resources and the MOE, has been taking steps toward developing an integrated provincial water strategy.[26] The impetus for this work appears to have been successive years of low precipitation in the late 1990s and a recognition of the need to plan for low-water conditions.

However, the Province has focused on protecting water resources on the basis of the resources' ecological and recreational values, not on the basis of the critical public health goal of maintaining secure water supplies for public consumption. This focus may be due to the relatively low priority given to drinking water within the MOE in the past and the view that municipal drinking water was not a core program of the ministry.[27] The safety of Ontario's drinking water will be greatly enhanced if maintaining safe and secure drinking water supplies is a core goal of the MOE. If the ministry chooses to approach drinking water source protection as part of a larger system of watershed management, the requirements of safe drinking water should be the central focus. I do not suggest that the protection of drinking water sources will in all cases take precedence over other uses; many factors will have to be considered and balanced. However, the protection of drinking water sources should be the primary concern for achieving the balance in a particular watershed.

4.3.3   The Role of the Ministry of the Environment

There are a number of reasons why the province must take the leadership role in developing the source protection planning process and ensuring that the process is adequately funded.

---

[26] Ontario Water Directors' Committee; Ontario, MOE/MNR, 2000.

[27] I discussed this issue in the Part 1 report. See Ontario, Ministry of the Attorney General, 2002, *Report of the Walkerton Inquiry, Part 1: The Events of May 2000 and Related Issues* (Toronto: Queen's Printer), p. 272.

The process for developing watershed-based source protection plans that will be elaborated below will be locally driven. However, the product of the process (i.e., the plan), once approved by the MOE, will be binding on provincial decisions to issue Permits to Take Water and Certificates of Approval for the discharge of contaminants. The Province is the more senior level of government and cannot fairly be bound by a process in which it has not played the lead role.

Furthermore, there is a need to ensure a level of consistency among source protection plans from different watersheds, along with a need to ensure that source protection planning is carried out thoroughly and fairly. The provincial government is in the best position to achieve these goals.

Finally, ensuring that source protection is done well is a key part of the whole system of overseeing drinking water management. The Province has the ultimate responsibility for the safety of drinking water. It only makes sense that the provincial government would therefore assume the ultimate responsibility for the first critical step in the process.

Within the provincial government, the lead agency for source protection planning should be the MOE. Water source protection is closely related to other environmental objectives. This ministry already has the responsibility for overseeing both environmental regulation and the management of drinking water in Ontario. It also has a mandate to use a watershed approach to environmental management.[28] That mandate has been reinforced by the Gibbons Report.[29] Moreover, the MOE has more expertise relating to matters involved in protecting drinking water sources than do other provincial government ministries.

Taking the lead role will mean that the MOE should be responsible for the development of the watershed-based source protection framework, should participate in the development of the plans (either by working with a conservation authority or by taking on the initiative itself), and should be the final approving body for the draft plans. In Chapter 13, I recommend that the MOE establish a new Branch, the Watershed Management Branch, to carry out these functions.

---

[28] Watershed Planning Implementation Project Management Committee (WPIPMC), 1997, *An Evaluation of Watershed Management in Ontario* <www.ene.gov.on.ca/envision/techdocs/3513e.pdf> [accessed May 1, 2002], p. 18.
[29] Executive Resource Group.

4.3.4 Conservation Authorities

Recommendation 2: The Ministry of the Environment should ensure that draft source protection plans are prepared through an inclusive process of local consultation. Where appropriate, this process should be managed by conservation authorities.

The development of plans intended to protect drinking water sources is, among other things, a land use planning activity. Most land use planning is currently done at the municipal level (under provincial guidance), and the provision of drinking water is a primarily municipal function. However, as noted in section 4.3.2, source protection must be undertaken on a watershed basis – the level at which cumulative impacts on the drinking water sources become apparent. This implies the need for a planning body to operate at the watershed level, but with the full participation of the municipalities in the watershed. Such entities already exist for the watersheds that contain over 90% of Ontario's population: they are the conservation authorities (see Figure 4.1).

The role of conservation authorities in Ontario is to act as planning, coordination, and management agencies on behalf of the municipalities within a watershed. From their inception, conservation authorities have had the legislative mandate to control water levels for domestic and municipal purposes.

The first organization identifiable as a conservation authority in Ontario was established following a series of flooding events on the Grand River. The 1932 Finlayson Report, commissioned after the worst of those floods in 1929, identified the health consequences of low flow in the river and recommended the construction of a series of reservoirs. Responding to the report, the provincial government passed legislation enabling the affected municipalities to establish the Grand River Conservation Commission (GRCC) to undertake the work. The GRCC was to control the water levels of the Grand River "to ensure [a] sufficient supply of water for municipal, domestic, and manufacturing purposes."[30]

The current *Conservation Authorities Act* states the purpose of conservation authorities very broadly:

---

[30] Conservation Ontario, p. 8.

Figure 4.1 Ontario's Conservation Authorities

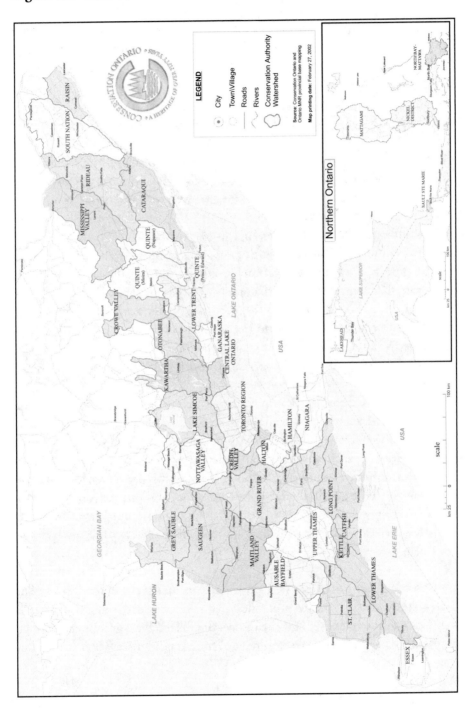

Map courtesy of Conservation Ontario

> The objects of an authority are to establish and undertake, in the area over which it has jurisdiction, a program designed to further the conservation, restoration, development and management of natural resources other than gas, oil, coal and minerals.[31]

Section 21 of the Act gives conservation authorities broad powers to carry out that mandate. Those powers include the authority necessary to develop watershed management plans and source protection plans.

The board of directors of a conservation authority consists of representatives of the authority's constituent municipalities. I have considered the possibility of recommending broadening the representation on conservation authority boards to include representatives of the MOE, Ministry of Natural Resources, or other affected groups. However, in my view, the boards of the conservation authorities should remain as currently constituted. Source protection planning will be only part of a conservation authority's responsibilities, and I am concerned that changing the representation on the board of directors without a thorough canvassing of everything conservation authorities do could compromise a conservation authority's other roles. As discussed below, those who have a specific interest in source protection planning can be adequately involved in ways other than serving on the board of directors of a conservation authority.

Many of the Part 2 parties recommended that conservation authorities have a central role in developing watershed-based source protection plans. However, a few parties were concerned that this approach could lead to inconsistency in the application of source protection in different watersheds. I am satisfied that this concern can be adequately addressed by extensive provincial government involvement in the development of the framework and process for watershed-based source protection planning, as well as in the development of the draft plans themselves, together with the requirement for final MOE approval of draft plans.

Conservation authorities are well positioned to manage the development of draft watershed-based source protection plans. They have the mandate and, in many cases, the experience and the respect of affected local groups that will be required to coordinate the development of the plans. Conservation authorities

---

[31] *Conservation Authorities Act*, R.S.O. 1990, c. C.27, s. 20(1).

will also be the appropriate bodies to integrate a broader program of watershed planning if and when such a program is implemented.[32]

I received one submission suggesting that rather than relying on the conservation authorities for source protection, river basin (or catchment) management authorities should be established to manage and regulate source protection and other regulatory aspects of drinking water provision on a watershed basis.[33] It was suggested that these bodies would also have authority for land use planning and for granting permits and licences. The number of drinking water providers in the province would be reduced to match the number and geographic extent of the catchment management authorities. This proposal was based on experiences in Europe and Great Britain. One of the principal advantages of the new authorities, it was argued, would be a greater independence from municipalities. Without such independence, it is feared, improper political influence could adversely affect the process of promoting drinking water safety.

I am not convinced that such a radical change in the governance of water and water systems is necessary. Many conservation authorities are tested, publicly respected, and accepted organizations that can build on a significant amount of goodwill in their communities and among affected local groups to facilitate source protection planning. I am reluctant to recommend the creation of new bodies when existing institutions are able to fulfill the role. If the source protection planning process receives appropriate guidance, participation, and approval from the MOE, I do not believe that there is a significant risk that municipalities will exert undue influence on the process. Moreover, I am recommending that the planning process not only include affected parties, but also be completely transparent to the public. I believe that public scrutiny affords significant protection against unreasonable behaviour. Given that the province will ultimately have to approve all source protection plans, I think there will be sufficient safeguards to address the concern that the local political actors would be able to impose unreasonable requirements on the planning process.

I recognize that the river basin model used in Europe provides a high level of coherence between source protection planning, environmental regulation, and the operation of water systems. However, I am satisfied that by involving water

---

[32] The 1993 MOEE/MNR papers on watershed management also recommended that conservation authorities take charge of the broader program of watershed planning (see Ontario, MOEE/MNR, 1993a, p. 28).

[33] M. Price, Walkerton Inquiry (Toronto Town Hall Meeting, October 29, 2001), transcript p. 15.

providers in source protection planning and by requiring the approval of watershed plans by the MOE, which is also the regulator of water systems and other environmental issues, the system I propose can also achieve this coherence.

Finally, there is a real benefit that flows from the fact that the conservation authorities are primarily representative of the municipalities. It is the municipalities that have the responsibility for land use planning. Watershed-based source protection planning will have a direct impact on land use planning. It is therefore essential that the municipalities be significantly involved in the source protection planning process so that their concerns may be considered and addressed and so that the resulting plans will enjoy greater acceptance. I am satisfied that where conservation authorities exist and have the necessary capacity, they are the organizations best positioned to bring about effective source protection planning.

I recognize that conservation authorities around the province are currently involved in a wide range of different functions and have reached varying degrees of sophistication. Some simply provide flood control in river basins, whereas others are leaders in detailed watershed management planning. It would be very difficult for some conservation authorities to take on the additional responsibilities proposed by this recommendation without a major increase in capacity and some time for development. It is up to the MOE to evaluate the ability of each conservation authority to undertake the watershed-based source protection plan development. I support capacity-building among conservation authorities, and the MOE should provide assistance in this area. However, as a practical matter, the MOE itself may need to take on the task of developing the draft watershed-based source protection plans for some watersheds.

The MOE will also have to take on the task of managing the development of draft plans in areas where there is no conservation authority. A substantial portion of the province (containing about 10% of the population) is not covered by a conservation authority. It is possible that planning will not be as complex in areas that are more remote and less densely populated than those served by conservation authorities, but nonetheless there are significant land uses, such as forestry or mining, that may have an impact on drinking water sources in those areas. It is also important to note that due to the more rural nature of these areas, many people will be using untreated individual domestic water supplies, thus increasing the importance of protecting those sources.

If a conservation authority does not produce a plan acceptable to the MOE within a prescribed time limit, the MOE should take over development of the plan. Indeed, the prospect of having the MOE step in to develop the plan when the local participants are unable to do so should serve as a significant incentive to those involved in the local planning process to reach consensus. The important point, however, is that there must be an alternative process if the local process fails to develop an acceptable plan. The MOE must provide that alternative process.

The process that applies to source protection planning should be the same whether plans are developed by a conservation authority or the MOE: there should be consultation with affected local groups, plans developed by the MOE should have the same effect as plans developed under the leadership of conservation authorities, and plans should be periodically reviewed and revised if necessary.

4.3.5 Watershed-based Source Protection Plans

4.3.5.1 *The Framework*

The provincial government should consult with conservation authorities, municipalities, environmental groups, and other affected groups to develop a provincial framework for source protection planning, including guidelines for the form, content, and the development process.

In section 4.3.5.2, I list what I consider to be many of the important elements of a watershed-based source protection plan. The Province should cooperate with the organizations that will be affected, and with those that have experience in watershed planning, to develop this framework. The Grand River Conservation Authority has received global recognition for its efforts in watershed planning, and I suggest that its model, combined with the model provided in the 1993 watershed planning framework, may be a good starting point. It will be important, however, to leave sufficient flexibility to ensure that processes and plans can be adapted to local circumstances.

The framework should include both an "ingredients list" for source protection plans and guidance on the appropriate process for plan development. This second item is very important, because the binding nature of the plans will require that all of those who are affected feel that they have been fairly involved in developing the plans.

The development of this framework should not be used as a reason to delay the implementation of watershed-based source protection planning. Excellent watershed planning models already exist in Ontario, and in my opinion adapting them to suit this purpose would not be an overly onerous task. I encourage the MOE to try to establish the framework within six to eight months after the release of this report. Further modifications or adaptations can be made as the process is implemented and as the participants learn from their experiences.

4.3.5.2   *Components of Plans*

At a minimum, watershed-based source protection plans should include the following:

- a water budget for the watershed, or a plan for developing a water budget where sufficient data are not yet available;

- the identification of all significant water withdrawals, including municipal intakes;

- land use maps for the watershed;

- the identification of wellhead areas;

- maps of areas of groundwater vulnerability that include characteristics such as depth to bedrock, depth to water table, the extent of aquifers, and recharge rates;

- the identification of all major point and non–point sources of contaminants in the watershed;

- a model that describes the fate of pollutants in the watershed;

- a program for identifying and properly decommissioning abandoned wells, excavations, quarries, and other shortcuts that can introduce contaminants into aquifers;

- the identification of areas where a significant direct threat exists to the safety of drinking water (in such cases, municipal official plans and zoning decisions must be consistent with the plan); and

- the identification of significant knowledge gaps and or research needs to help target monitoring efforts.

The objective of all this data collection and modelling should be the development of an adaptive model of risks to water sources. Such a model would indicate those areas where specific measures should be taken to protect drinking water sources. Importantly, different levels or types of required protection could be designated for different areas.

A number of Part 2 parties identified the need to undertake research on various topics, including the value of protecting wetlands and near-shore (riparian) areas in maintaining the quality of drinking water sources and the economic benefits of source protection. Such research should be integrated into the watershed-based source protection planning process and should be supported by all interested parties. Where data are not available to complete components of the plan listed above, research should make filling such gaps a priority.

Based on the vulnerability mapping, source protection plans should designate land use zones in which particular source protection measures are (or are not) needed and determine acceptable ranges of water allocations among competing uses. They should also provide operational limits concerning acceptable levels of water withdrawals and total contaminant loadings that will be considered and not exceeded by the MOE when considering applications for Permits to Take Water or Certificates of Approval for water-related contaminant releases.

Water use allocation as part of the watershed-based source protection plan deserves some further explanation, because in some areas local shortages may make this a significant issue. In section 4.3.9, I recommend that Permits to Take Water (PTTW) and Certificates of Approval for pollutant releases granted by the MOE should be consistent with source protection plans. Where it is shown through the planning process that the demand for PTTW or Certificates of Approval may exceed available supply or the system's assimilative capacity (i.e., its ability to absorb pollutants), all those desiring or holding PTTW or Certificates of Approval should participate in a corollary process that should attempt to negotiate a mutually acceptable agreement concerning water use or contaminant release allocation. If such an agreement can be produced and is acceptable to the MOE, then PTTW and Certificates of Approval granted by the MOE should follow the agreement. If the participants cannot agree on allocations, the MOE should itself determine the distribution of rights. Under neither of these circumstances should the total amount of water allocated or the total loading of pollutants under the combined PTTW or Certificates of Approval exceed the amount of water sustainably available or the system's assimilative capacity according to the watershed-based source protection plan.

I envision that the planning process would identify areas where the protected measures for drinking water sources are critical to public health and safety, and that in such cases, the plan would govern municipal land use and zoning decisions. However, other measures in the plan need not require such rigidity in the municipal decision-making process. In such instances, municipalities will be required only to have regard for the plan but will make the ultimate decision regarding how to balance the competing factors. Given that municipalities themselves will be centrally involved in the source protection planning process, I think this approach strikes a reasonable balance.

4.3.5.3   *Groundwater Management*

It is essential that watershed-based source protection planning address the management and protection of groundwater sources. Most of Ontario's population lives in large cities served by drinking water from surface water sources (in particular, the Great Lakes). However, almost 50% of smaller municipal systems use groundwater as their source. Once groundwater becomes contaminated, clean-up can be expensive and technically challenging, if it is possible at all.

Research needed to produce the information required for groundwater management has ebbed and flowed over the years. In the latter part of the 1960s and the early 1970s, Canada and Ontario were recognized as world leaders in groundwater-related research through the work of the Geological Survey of Canada and the Ontario Geological Survey. By 1987, the federal Pearce Commission report suggested that only modest attention was being paid to groundwater.[34] According to experts today, there is not enough information about groundwater resources in Ontario to manage them

---

[34] Canada, Environment Canada, 1985, *Currents of Change, Final Report: Inquiry on Federal Water Policy* (Ottawa: Environment Canada), p. 122.

properly.[35] Furthermore, the Environmental Commissioner of Ontario has found that the Ministry of the Environment often grants PTTW without making an adequate assessment of the capacity of the resource and without basing decisions on an ecosystem approach. In a 2001 report, he concluded that Ontario lacks a comprehensive framework for groundwater management.[36]

Models do exist that can (when sufficient data are available) predict groundwater movement and allow for the development of good groundwater protection strategies.[37] Indeed, in some areas where groundwater has been the traditional source of municipal drinking water, most of the needed data are available.[38]

The MOE has taken some action on this issue. In 2000, the Minister of the Environment announced a cooperative program for groundwater monitoring with Conservation Ontario, and this program has begun.[39] In January 2002, the minister announced a $10 million program to map Ontario's aquifers as a means of providing much-needed information for the protection of drinking water resources.[40] It will be critical for such efforts to contribute to a broader system of source protection planning that takes a watershed approach and acknowledges the interconnection among various water sources.

4.3.6 Participation of Affected Groups and the Public

The involvement of a broad range of affected groups in the watershed-based source protection planning process will be key to its success. The process must be seen to be broadly and fairly inclusive of the interests that will be affected. The province should involve affected groups not only to ensure the fairness of

---

[35] K. Howard, testimony, Walkerton Inquiry (Part 1 Hearing, October 16, 2001), transcript pp. 103–104; Frind, Rudolph, and Molson, pp. 10–13.

[36] Environmental Commissioner of Ontario, *Ontario's Permit to Take Water Program and the Protection of Ontario's Water Resources: Brief to the Walkerton Inquiry* <www.eco.on.ca/english/publicat/walker01.pdf> [accessed April 29, 2002] pp. i–ii.

[37] Frind, Rudolph, and Molson, pp. 16–19. However, there is room for advancement, and our understanding of groundwater transport in karstic systems like those underlying much of Ontario is improving. Policies for groundwater protection must therefore be sufficiently flexible to accommodate future improvements in our models.

[38] For example, in the Region of Waterloo extensive groundwater modelling has been undertaken and used to create groundwater protection strategies.

[39] Ontario, Minister of the Environment, 2000, *Ontario Launches Groundwater Monitoring Network* <www.ene.gov.on.ca/envision/news/0075.htm> [accessed April 30, 2002].

[40] Ontario, Minister of the Environment, 2001, *Ontario Flows $10 Million to Communities for Groundwater Studies* <www.ene.gov.on.ca/envision/news/11401.htm> [accessed April 30, 2002].

the process, but more importantly to improve it. Involving a broad cross-section of water users in the planning process will both help to ensure that all issues are considered in the planning process and bring new perspectives into the process. Affected groups and the interested public have played an essential role in this Inquiry. They have provided insights and have greatly assisted in my understanding of the issues. I am certain that watershed-based source protection planning can benefit from the same type of experience and expertise that was available to me.

The conservation authority or the MOE – whichever body is coordinating the draft plans' development – should ensure that a committee consisting of affected local groups is convened. That committee should be responsible for developing the draft watershed-based source protection plan.

A key group of participants in developing the plans will be the municipalities. Although they are represented on the conservation authorities' boards of directors, they should also take an active role in the committees that develop the plans. This role could be undertaken by water system managers or elected officials. Involving both managers and officials would ensure that the municipality is represented in both of the two main capacities in which it may be affected by source protection planning: as the water provider, and as the level of government responsible for land use zoning and setting municipal bylaws in accordance with the *Planning Act* and the *Municipal Act*. In both of these capacities, municipalities have a significant interest in source protection planning.

Some Ontario municipalities draw water from watersheds other than the ones in which they are located. These municipalities should participate in watershed-based source protection planning committees in both watersheds.

The development of watershed plans should also take place in consultation with the MOE, other ministries (Agriculture, Food and Rural Affairs; Municipal Affairs and Housing; Natural Resources; Consumer and Business Services), non-governmental organizations, and other affected groups, including local public health officials. I also encourage the federal government to participate where appropriate; particularly relevant will be representatives of Fisheries and Oceans Canada, Environment Canada, Indian and Northern Affairs Canada, and Agriculture and Agri-Food Canada. The participation of federal agencies will help ensure intergovernmental coordination in an area where constitutional jurisdiction is not always clear.

It is also highly desirable to include First Nations in watershed planning working groups where appropriate. Water does not recognize the boundaries of First Nations reserves.

Although the form of consultation may vary to accommodate local circumstances, the need for it is clear. As a general rule, consultation should err on the side of inclusion, both regarding which parties are consulted and regarding the level of involvement in the process. Consultation should never be pro forma; it should be meaningful and substantial. Interested parties must be given adequate time and information to ensure that their views are fully canvassed and considered.

Without extensive consultation, watershed plans are likely to suffer from a lack of commitment from affected groups and are less likely to be successful. Conservation authorities that have undertaken this type of planning exercise have found that when all of the affected parties gather to determine a management model, a sense of fairness tends to take hold, and solutions are created that are acceptable to all participants.

To ensure that the benefits of a variety of perspectives are brought to bear on the planning process, the Province, where appropriate, should make funding available to help public interest groups participate.

To ensure that the process is and is seen to be fair, complete, and reasonable, and as a means of discouraging any undue influence, the source protection planning process should be fully transparent to the public. Draft plans and proposals should be widely published. Meetings of the planning committee, including affected groups, should be open to public attendance – although not necessarily full public participation, which might make meetings unwieldy. Planning committees should at least invite public comment in writing at some point in the process. The MOE's decisions concerning the approval of draft watershed-based source protection plans should be subject to the requirements of the *Environmental Bill of Rights, 1993*.[41]

---

[41] *Environmental Bill of Rights*, 1993, S.O. 1993, c. 28.

4.3.7   The Ministry of the Environment's Provision of Information and Technical Assistance to Conservation Authorities

The development of watershed-based source protection plans will involve the collection and assimilation of large quantities of data. Unfortunately, watershed managers find it difficult at times to obtain from the MOE baseline information that would be helpful in their activities.[42]

The MOE is a repository of much of the key information required for watershed-based source protection planning (e.g., well drilling records). It should ensure that the information it maintains is freely available to those engaged in the planning process. The planning will be an MOE initiative that will be developed through local committees, and those committees will require access to MOE data. This collaboration should go both ways, because often the local source protection planners will be the ones collecting new data on behalf of the MOE.

I am aware that the MOE, in collaboration with related ministries, is developing information management systems and capabilities (through the Land Information Ontario initiative) in ways that will allow the collection of large volumes of standardized information for dissemination through the Internet. This is a very helpful initiative.

The MOE should also maintain a capacity for technical support for watershed-based source protection planning. This would include capabilities in geographic information systems, ecological monitoring and modelling, and other decision support tools. This technical capacity should also be available to the agencies undertaking source protection planning. Assistance will be particularly important for smaller and less well-developed conservation authorities.

4.3.8   The Approval of Watershed-based Source Protection Plans

Recommendation 3: Draft source protection plans should be reviewed by the Ministry of the Environment and subject to ministry approval.

The development of draft source protection plans will be a province-wide initiative that will often be carried out by local entities. There will be a need to ensure a degree of consistency across Ontario. Therefore, each draft plan, once

---

[42] WPIPMC, p. 14.

completed, should be submitted to the MOE for review. The MOE should review the draft plan for conformity with the framework and should also review the process that was used in developing the plan to ensure that all affected groups were fairly consulted. The MOE may return the plan with a request for revisions. When the plan is satisfactory, it should be approved.

The MOE's approvals process must be transparent and flexible. If the MOE chooses to reject a watershed-based source protection plan or a portion of a plan, it must do so for clearly and publicly stated reasons.

Some Part 2 parties expressed a concern about requiring MOE approval. It was argued that the watershed planning process has been so successful in some watersheds because it is essentially driven by the affected groups, and acceptance of the process occurs because it is a local initiative. There is some worry that too much MOE involvement or oversight might compromise some of the goodwill in the process. While I understand this concern, I do not think that requiring MOE approval will interfere with the goodwill that arises from developing plans locally. The plan, if approved, will still have local origins. In addition, the need to obtain MOE approval should be an incentive to reach reasonable compromise at the local level, and the prospect of having the MOE develop a plan if the affected local groups fail to reach consensus should inspire reasonable approaches.

Another concern about requiring MOE approval relates to the time involved. These plans are intended to evolve through a process of ongoing review and adaptation. This process is already slowed by the need to consult various affected groups during the planning process. Adding the additional step of a potentially lengthy provincial government approval could result in greater delay and considerable time spent using out-of-date plans. However, these plans will be reviewed and approved by the proposed Watershed Management Branch of the MOE. With proper staff and resources, I see no reason why the MOE, which will have participated in the plan's development, could not complete its review within no more than three months of receiving the plan. I do not think that delays of this order outweigh the substantial benefits of requiring provincial government approval of the plans.

4.3.9   The Implementation of the Plans

Recommendation 4: Provincial government decisions that affect the quality of drinking water sources must be consistent with approved source protection plans.

Watershed-based source protection plans will have implications for many different kinds of land users. The provincial government must also be bound by the plans if those plans are to be effective, because some of its decisions, such as the issuance of PTTW and Certificates of Approval for discharges, may have significant effects on drinking water sources. No Permits to Take Water or Certificates of Approval should therefore be granted for activities that would exceed the limits set by or otherwise violate the provisions of the relevant watershed-based source protection plan. The source protection plans should designate any other types of provincial decisions where consistency is required.

This approach will force a consideration of the cumulative ecological impacts of all actions in the watershed before a PTTW or Certificate of Approval is granted, rather than allowing such permits or certificates to be granted strictly on the basis of the individual application.

It will also answer the concerns of the many Part 2 parties who stated that a new approach to the granting of PPTW is needed. Their criticism was that the current approach does not sufficiently involve affected local groups in the decision and does not embrace an ecosystem approach. I agree that these are valid concerns and think that the best approach will be to make the granting of provincial PTTW and Certificates of Approval subject to the wider source protection plan, which includes a watershed approach to managing water sources.

The Energy Probe Research Foundation took this approach one step further by asking me to make the following recommendation:

> No one should have the right to contaminate a source of water. Farmers, industrial polluters, and sewage treatment plant owners should be responsible for ensuring that their wastes do not impair the quality of water. Criminal and tort liability should apply.[43]

---

[43] Energy Probe Research Foundation, 2001a, "Energy Probe Research Foundation's recommendations for Public Hearing No. 1: Guiding principles and the role of government," Walkerton Inquiry Submission, p. 1.

In my view, this recommendation is too broad and would affect matters that go beyond my mandate. It would represent a significant shift in the way water resources on the whole are managed in Ontario. I am satisfied that requiring that PTTW and Certificates of Approval conform with drinking water source protection plans is the way to protect drinking water sources while at the same time recognizing the need for certain land use activities that could have a negative effect on water. I do not think it advisable that the courts be the first recourse for determining what land use activities could constitute a threat to the safety of drinking water and should therefore not be permitted. Others with special expertise and familiarity with the local circumstances are more suited to make decisions of this nature.

Recommendation 5: Where the potential exists for a significant direct threat to drinking water sources, municipal official plans and decisions must be consistent with the applicable source protection plan. Otherwise, municipal official plans and decisions should have regard to the source protection plan. The plans should designate areas where consistency is required.

One of the key aspects of watershed-based source protection plans is that they must influence land use patterns if they are to be successful. It might therefore seem desirable to recommend categorically that municipal official plans and decisions should be consistent with all aspects of watershed-based source protection plans. This type of approach was supported by several Part 2 parties. Making such a change would confer enormous authority on the watershed-based source protection planning process to constrain municipal decision making. In a way this would be a self-imposed constraint, since conservation authorities are essentially composed of municipalities and since municipalities will be involved in the source protection planning process. However, conservation authorities are not the bodies with the ultimate authority for land use decisions; municipalities are. In my view, the planning process that I envision should intrude on the municipal authority over land use decisions only to the extent that is necessary to ensure the safety of drinking water and therefore the protection of public health.

There is a history of debate over whether municipal land use plans should be required either to "have regard to" or to "be consistent with" provincial policy statements. This same issue also arises when it comes to the question of how watershed-based source protection plans should affect municipal plans. Some elements of source protection may be more important than others, and there are legitimate planning considerations other than the quality of water. It is important that municipal policy-makers be allowed to make municipal policy, but the protection of drinking water sources should be an important priority. In my view, an acceptable approach is that municipal plans and actions must have regard to the watershed-based source protection plan unless the plan itself stipulates that municipal plans or actions must be consistent with it. The requirement for consistency would be triggered in areas where it is determined that there is a potential for a significant direct threat to drinking water sources. Thus, watershed-based source protection plans may indicate portions of the plan for which municipal plans and bylaws must either "be consistent with" or "have regard to" the watershed-based source protection plan. Allowing the watershed-based source protection planning committee members these options promotes greater flexibility and will, I believe, encourage a more proactive approach to planning. I am concerned that requiring all municipal plans and bylaws to be consistent with watershed-based source protection plans might be a disincentive to incorporating certain protective features in the plan. In the end, I take comfort from the fact that the provincial government approval of plans is required.

In section 4.3.15, I discuss the need for a provincial review of all the Acts, regulations, and policies relating to the issue of source protection. That review should provide recommendations regarding the statutory changes required to create the recommended relationship between watershed-based source protection planning and municipal planning. However, in the meantime, municipalities themselves should strive to ensure that their municipal plans are consistent with source protection plans where indicated.

Municipal sewage, storm-sewer, and combined-sewer effluents must also be consistent with the watershed plan. This will eventually be controlled through MOE Certificates of Approval, but in the meantime municipalities should monitor contaminant levels in their effluents, especially where those effluents might have an impact on downstream drinking water sources.

Under certain circumstances, it may be desirable for a municipality to grant a variance from a municipal plan that is contrary to a "be consistent with" portion of a watershed-based source protection plan. For such a variance to be granted, approval from the municipality and the MOE should be required. It would obviously make sense for the conservation authorities to be consulted about the advisability of a variance. Precedent for this type of arrangement can be found in the procedure for granting a variance from flood-plain zoning controls.

Such variances should be time limited and should be terminated if the land use is changed.

4.3.10 The Review of the Plans

Some aspects of the watershed-based source protection plans will require constant updating to reflect changing circumstances. One component of those plans should therefore be the identification of significant knowledge gaps and a plan for developing knowledge in those areas. The monitoring component of watershed-based source protection should ensure that new data are collected and used to continuously refine watershed models. These improvements must be integrated into the plan through a full and fair process. Original affected groups and new participants should be convened periodically to review and revise the plan as necessary, using a process that is defined by the MOE in cooperation with the affected groups and is similar to the one used to develop the plan.

The MOE should review and approve the revised plan, at which point it should replace the original plan.

4.3.11 Appeals

Recommendation 6: The provincial government should provide for limited rights of appeal to challenge source protection plans, and provincial and municipal decisions that are inconsistent with the plans.

There should be a narrow right of appeal for watershed-based source protection plans. I am concerned that appeals should not become commonplace and, in effect, emerge as the main forum for resolving planning issues. The right to appeal should be restricted to parties who are directly affected and should be limited to failure of a plan to conform to provincial guidelines or failure to follow the proper process in developing a plan.

There should also be provisions for appealing provincial decisions, such as the issuance of PTTWs and Certificates of Approval, or municipal decisions that are related to the source protection plans, on the basis that such decisions do not conform to the relevant plan. In the case of all such appeals, I think that the principle of administrative deference should apply and there should be provision for summary dismissal.

4.3.12 Funding Watershed Management

Recommendation 7: The provincial government should ensure that sufficient funds are available to complete the planning and adoption of source protection plans.

In considering the funding of source protection planning, three main options offer themselves. The Province or the municipalities could provide public funds, water consumers could pay through user fees, or those who discharge pollutants could pay fees when issued a Certificate of Approval. No option appears to be perfect, and I favour a combination of funding mechanisms to pay for the source protection planning process.

There is a strong argument in favour of provincial funding, on the basis of fairness. A successful watershed-based source protection planning system will provide side benefits to water users generally, including the enhancement of recreational opportunities (e.g., fishing, swimming, canoeing); stable access for rural, domestic, and industrial users; and environmental and other benefits.

The assignment (for the purposes of calculating fees) of economic benefits for a resource that lends itself to many simultaneous non-consumptive beneficial uses, as well as other uses that are only partly consumptive, is difficult. It would therefore be hard to establish a system for assigning fair portions of the cost to all users, let alone collecting those fair portions. Furthermore, if one limits the fees to PTTW or Certificates of Approval, a user-fee approach will not reach all users. Those not captured under the *Ontario Water Resources Act* or under some other environmental approvals system (for Certificates of Approval for pollution sources) will not have to bear the cost, nor will other water users (e.g., swimmers, fishers, naturalists), although they may be significant beneficiaries.

On the other hand, the proposition that source protection planning should be paid for exclusively out of provincial coffers runs contrary to the user-pay concept. It therefore seems reasonable that at least some component of the funding for source water protection should come from municipal water rates.[44]

What is clear is that watershed-based source protection planning need not be terribly expensive. The Province's review of watershed planning (which I have already observed is an analogous and highly overlapping process) notes that the cost of watershed planning pilot projects appeared to be between $160,000 and $420,000.[45] It is clear that watershed-based source protection plans cannot be developed and maintained without stable funding. As a result, I recommend that some portion of the necessary funding come from user fees. In addition, some portion of the cost should be raised by those to whom Certificates of Approval are issued for discharging pollutants. Finally, the province should contribute from general revenues a portion of the necessary cost and ensure that its portion of the funding is available on a continuous and sustainable basis. However funding is allocated among the three sources, the province should ensure that the necessary funding is in fact made available for this vitally important exercise.

4.3.13 Public Reporting

During the Inquiry, several suggestions were made regarding which organizations should be responsible for providing public reporting about source protection. One recommendation was that there should be annual or biannual provincial reports on source water protection, with a response from the various agencies involved. Another was that drinking water providers should be obliged to "assess and periodically review the vulnerability of their sources of drinking water to current or future contamination or degradation, and publicly report upon the results of such assessments."[46] Another possibility would be to ensure that

---

[44] A joint statement by Conservation Ontario, Ontario Water Works Association/Ontario Municipal Water Association, Ontario Sewage and Watermain Construction Association, and Strategic Alternatives at the Walkerton Inquiry Expert Meeting on Financing Drinking Water Systems included these principles: "Some of the costs of source protection must be recovered from water users, including private and large commercial users as well as municipalities, and from effluent discharges thus capturing the 'polluter pays' concept. The Province needs to establish policy and tools for this to happen ... Standards or guidelines from the Province are needed to guide what relevant source protection costs can be linked to drinking water supply and sewage management. A structure is needed to determine where revenues should come from and what programs to support."

[45] WPIPMC, p. 11.

[46] Concerned Walkerton Citizens and Canadian Environmental Law Association, 2001, "Tragedy on tap: Why Ontario needs a *Safe Drinking Water Act*," executive summary, Walkerton Inquiry Submission, p. 7.

the conservation authority or the MOE (whichever body is organizing the watershed-based source protection plan in a given area) should be obliged to produce annual reports.

It seems to me that there should be a role for reporting at each of these levels. However, the overarching responsibility for source protection belongs to the provincial government. The Province should provide an annual summary indicating the status of drinking water source protection plans in each watershed.

The planning itself may be coordinated on a local basis by a conservation authority or the MOE. That local authority should ensure that local source protection plans are widely available. Since these plans will be evolving, the local authority should also provide regular progress reports.

4.3.14 Education

Recommendation 8: Conservation authorities (or, in their absence, the Ministry of the Environment) should be responsible for implementing local initiatives to educate landowners, industry, and the public about the requirements and importance of drinking water source protection.

Education is a key component of a good source protection strategy. People need to understand the value of the resource and the reasons for restrictions on various types of activities. The conservation authorities (or the MOE, in their absence), as the centre of the watershed-based source protection planning effort in the watershed, will have the best access to the information resources needed for this effort. Furthermore, most conservation authorities have already taken on extensive public education roles, to which this component can be added if it is not already being delivered.

4.3.15 Legislative Review

Implementing a province-wide watershed-based source protection planning strategy may require changes to provincial legislation. Conservation Ontario, the Association of Municipalities of Ontario, and the Ontario Public Service Employees Union have all emphasized the need for changes to the *Planning Act* to enable municipalities to undertake source protection. I do note, however, that the *Planning Act* provides broad powers to the Province to affect planning through the Provincial Policy Statement. I also note that section 34 of the Act allows municipalities to control land uses in any area "that is a sensitive ground water recharge area or head-water area or on land that contains a sensitive aquifer," and section 23 provides the Minister of Municipal Affairs and Housing with the ability to require changes to municipal plans if they affect a "provincial interest" such as the one identified in section 2(e): "the supply, efficient use and conservation of ... water." It may be possible to develop a comprehensive watershed-based source protection planning system under current legislation.

In Chapter 13 of this report, I suggest that the province should review current legislation to ensure that the tools needed for implementing the watershed-based source protection regime recommended in this chapter are available.

4.3.16 The Value of Water

It has been suggested that the provincial government should charge water users for the resource – that is, assign a value to water. The principal justification for doing this would be to "reflect its scarcity"[47] and to encourage conservation – appropriate economic behaviour in the face of a scarce resource. However, I am not convinced that this is a necessary step for ensuring the safety of Ontario's drinking water. Water "used" for drinking is mostly returned to the ecosystem, and as such is not "consumed." It must be treated to acceptable standards before it is returned, and that cost is paid through sewage rates. To the extent that the water is being "used," the user is paying for treatment. Only a small proportion is lost to evapotranspiration or export.

On the other hand, it is clear that price signals can have a significant impact on water consumption. Some studies have shown up to a 40% reduction in household water use when meters and volumetric pricing (i.e., pricing based on the amount of water used, rather than a flat fee) are introduced in communities. Reducing consumption may be a key strategy in managing a municipal water system, and using price may be the best approach for doing so. It is open now for water providers to price water to include a conservation charge. I therefore see no need to make any specific recommendation in this regard.

---

[47] Energy Probe Research Foundation, 2001b, "Energy Probe Research Foundation's recommendations for Public Hearing No. 4: Source protection," Walkerton Inquiry Submission, p. 3.

4.3.17 The Enforcement of Environmental Laws and Regulations

Environmental regulations and conditions on provincial approvals must be consistently and strictly enforced.[48] During the Inquiry, I heard that the MOE's approach to enforcing conditions on Certificates of Approval, Permits to Take Water, and other environmental regulations has been subject to substantial changes from time to time, depending in part on the policies of the government of the day. In the 1990s, the MOE's tendency was to employ "voluntary compliance" techniques rather than to prosecute environmental violators.

The MOE should issue a clear statement, internally and externally, that water pollution must be tightly controlled. This means enforcing the provisions of the *Environmental Protection Act*, the *Ontario Water Resources Act* (or the *Safe Drinking Water Act* when it is ready), and the *Fisheries Act* (in collaboration with the Ministry of Natural Resources and the federal Department of Fisheries and Oceans), as well as enforcing the conditions of Certificates of Approval and Permits to Take Water. There should also be a strong statement that offending municipalities will be prosecuted, just as any other violator would be. I do not propose a "zero tolerance" policy of immediately moving to prosecute after any exceedance, but I do recommend that the enforcement tools available to the MOE be used much more readily than they have been used in the past.

Such a policy, supported by appropriate funds, should immediately help to protect the sources of drinking water. Moreover, the source water protection regime I have proposed cannot work in the absence of enforced rules concerning land uses, effluent qualities, Certificates of Approval, and Permits to Take Water.

This recommendation runs slightly counter to the Gibbons Report, which recommends an increased focus on cooperative approaches to environmental compliance.[49] As I discussed in Chapter 2 of this report, I do not mean to impugn that recommendation. I express no opinion on whether it may be appropriate for some environmental issues. However, when the environmental issue is the protection of drinking water sources, the concern is not about environmental impacts but about public health. There is little room for

---

[48] I provide greater detail on the notion of strict enforcement as it applies to drinking water in general in Chapter 13 of this report.
[49] Executive Resource Group, pp. 28–32.

negotiating voluntary compliance arrangements when public health is threatened.

Several of the Part 2 parties made extensive recommendations concerning the need for citizen enforcement of environmental regulations. I address the issue of public enforcement in Chapter 13 of this report.

4.4   Specific Threats

4.4.1   Introduction

What I have described so far in this chapter is a broad approach for developing watershed-based source protection plans. During the Inquiry, many issues regarding the regulation of particular contaminant sources were identified by commissioned paper authors, Part 2 parties, and participants in town hall meetings. This section provides recommendations concerning those issues. In general, I make recommendations on the assumption that the broader source protection plans are already in place. These recommendations can be seen as fitting into the nested approach to source protection at the site level.[50]

This section devotes more attention to regulating contaminants from agricultural sources than to regulating those from any other source. This emphasis is not intended to suggest that agricultural sources are more dangerous than any other sources. It simply reflects the difficulty of dealing with non–point source pollutants in general and with agricultural sources in particular. Agriculture represents one of the most intimate relationships that exists between humans and the rest of the natural world, and it is impossible to expect that it can be carried out without creating changes in the environment. But agriculture is also a source of contaminants that sometimes appear in drinking water, and those must be controlled.

4.4.2   Human Waste

Municipal sewage treatment plants may be significant point sources of a wide range of water contaminants. The amounts and types of contaminants released by such sources depend on the type of treatment, as is described in Chapter 6

---

[50] Ontario, MOEE/MNR, 1993a.

in this report. As the major outlets for human waste into the environment, sewage treatment plants may contribute substantial loadings of human pathogens.

An application for a Certificate of Approval for a sewage works must provide information about the concentration and volume of the effluent and about the volume and flow rate of the receiving waters.

The adequacy of Certificates of Approval for protecting drinking water sources from contaminants arising from point sources depends on the conditions attached to the certificates. Certificates should include conditions that ensure that effluents must be consistent with source protection plans. The enforcement of those provisions should be strict. One matter that concerns me is that in more than 60% of the cases in Ontario,[51] the Inquiry's examination of sewage treatment was unable to determine whether sewage treatment plants were in compliance with regulations. Of the remaining 40%, approximately 15% were out of compliance. This information should be publicly available.

Municipalities may use bylaws to determine the types of chemicals that may be deposited by sewer users. Toronto has recently amended its sewage use bylaw to provide more stringent environmental controls. The bylaw is applied to ensure that substances deposited into the city's sewers meet certain requirements. For instance, the bylaw prohibits depositing fuels, dyes, PCBs, combustible liquids, hazardous wastes, waste disposal site leachate, and many other substances into sewers. It also limits the levels of other substances that may be present in materials released into the sewers and prohibits using dilution to remain within those limits. (It is possible for the city to accept prohibited wastes by agreement.) The bylaw also requires pollution prevention planning by industrial sewer users. It is intended to ensure that chemicals that are not treated by the treatment system or those that might impair the system's functioning are not deposited into the city's sewers. [52]

Perhaps less easily controlled is what goes into storm sewers. Urban runoff, through sewers or directly into streams and rivers, may contain a wide variety of substances. These complex mixtures, which may include various chemicals, pesticides, fuels and oils, salt, pathogens, and nutrients, can be very damaging

---

[51] E. Doyle, 2002, "Wastewater collection and treatment," Walkerton Commissioned Paper 9, p. 10.
[52] City of Toronto, By-law No. 457-2000, *To regulate the discharge of sewage and land drainage* (July 6, 2000).

to the environment. Urban runoff can contribute to environmental loadings of contaminants that might cause problems in drinking water. It should therefore be taken into account in watershed-based source protection planning. Municipalities may wish to evaluate the possibility of using such technologies as constructed wetlands and stormwater retention tanks or ponds as means of containing or treating this kind of effluent. The province should support the efforts of municipalities and conservation authorities to educate people about the need to use sewers appropriately.

4.4.3 Septic Systems

Recommendation 9: Septic systems should be inspected as a condition for the transfer of a deed.

Throughout this Inquiry, I often heard about the problems related to groundwater contamination from inadequate or old and decrepit septic systems. The issue came up in expert meetings, public hearings, and town hall meetings. An alarming statistic that was often quoted is that approximately a third of septic systems are in compliance with the building code, a third are simply out of compliance, and a third could be characterized as a public health nuisance.[53]

Given these statistics, and considering that septic systems are generally located in rural areas, where groundwater is the principal source of drinking water, inadequate septic systems may present a substantial threat to some Ontario drinking water sources.

The Sewell Commission considered this problem at some length[54] and recommended that the MOE should ensure that regular inspections be carried out at the expense of septic tank owners. This conclusion was echoed in the paper prepared for this Inquiry by the Pembina Institute.[55] I support these

---

[53] See, for instance, Commission on Planning and Development Reform in Ontario, 1993, *New Planning for Ontario: Final Report* (Toronto, Queen's Printer), p. 124 [hereafter Sewell Commission]. In 1998, the *Building Code Act, 1992*, S.O. 1992, c. 23, was amended to include the regulation of septic systems, and responsibility for septic systems was transferred from the Ministry of the Environment to the Ministry of Municipal Affairs and Housing. The authority for enforcing these new provisions was delegated to municipalities, with local health units and conservation authorities maintaining responsibility in certain Northern Ontario areas.

[54] Commission on Planning and Development Reform in Ontario, pp. 124–126.

[55] M.S. Winfield and H.J. Benevides, 2001, *Drinking Water Protection in Ontario: A Comparison of Direct and Alternative Delivery Models* (Ottawa: Pembina Institute for Appropriate Development).

conclusions, and recommend that as a minimum there should be mandatory inspection of septic tanks as a condition of the transfer of a deed. The owner of the septic system should pay for these inspections. Municipalities might also wish to consider requiring septic reinspection as a condition for the issuance of building permits.

Rather than making periodic inspections mandatory for all septic systems (an enormously expensive undertaking), I suggest that the watershed-based source protection planning process address areas of particular concern. In areas with a high density of septic systems, it may be desirable to include a proactive septic reinspection program as part of the implementation of the source protection plan. A program for the inspection of septic systems should prioritize those that are located in areas of high drinking water source vulnerability as identified in the source protection plan.

Many of the Part 2 parties expressed strong support for a program of mandatory septic system inspection and septic system owner education. The Ministry of Municipal Affairs and Housing does provide guidance for communities that wish to establish a septic system reinspection program.[56] The ministry points out that reinspection may lead to the need for enforcement but does not discuss enforcement strategies.

4.4.4   Biosolids and Septage

Recommendation 10: The Ministry of the Environment should not issue Certificates of Approval for the spreading of waste materials unless they are compatible with the applicable source protection plan.

Considerable attention was also given by the Part 2 parties at the Inquiry to the issue of the spreading of biosolids (treated solid municipal waste) and septage (untreated hauled waste – e.g., materials that have been pumped out of septic tanks) on rural land as fertilizer or in land-farming operations. There was some concern about the potential impacts on water resources, although much attention was also given to the impact on neighbours' property values and

---

[56] See Ontario, Ministry of Municipal Affairs and Housing, Housing Development and Buildings Branch, 2001, *Septic Systems Re-Inspections: Information for Enforcement Agencies and Others Interested in Local Septic System Re-Inspection Initiatives* <http://obc.mah.gov.on.ca/septic.html/Septic_English_.pdf> [accessed May 7, 2002].

quality of life due to odours from the operations. These latter problems are well beyond the scope of my mandate.

In Ontario, a Certificate of Approval is required before biosolids or septage may be applied to agricultural land. In general, the application of waste must be likely to improve the quality of the soil and must not endanger the environment if it is to be approved. The document *Guidelines for the Utilization of Biosolids and Other Wastes on Agricultural Land* outlines the rules for applying wastes to agricultural lands.[57] It states that septage must not generate odours that are worse than those generated by normal farm practices and must not contain pathogens in amounts higher than would be found in digested biosolids.[58] Certificates of Approval detail the maximum levels of various potential contaminants that may be contained in the applied waste.

Some of the Part 2 parties called for a ban on the application of untreated septage or asked for stricter standards regarding biosolids that are to be applied. The Environmental Commissioner of Ontario identified a number of serious problems with the management of biosolids and septage in his 2001 report.[59] Several of these shortcomings relate directly to the protection of potential drinking water sources:

- Nutrient management plans are not required before a Certificate of Approval is granted, with the result that septage or biosolids may be applied without anyone knowing the current nutrient load being applied to the area.

- There is no requirement to consider whether the land may be a water recharge area.

- There are no restrictions on spreading on tiled land,[60] which may drain rapidly to surface waters.

---

[57] Ontario, Ministry of the Environment and Ministry of Agriculture, Food and Rural Affairs, 1996, *Guidelines for the Utilization of Biosolids and Other Wastes on Agricultural Land*, <www.ene.gov.on.ca/envision/gp/3425e.pdf> [accessed April 29, 2002].

[58] Digestion is a biological process that can be used to reduce the concentrations of pathogens in biosolids.

[59] Environmental Commissioner of Ontario, 2001, *Having Regard: 2000/2001 Annual Report* <www.eco.ca/english/publicat/ar2000.pdf> [accessed April 29, 2002], p. 54.

[60] Tiling is a technique used to improve drainage on some farmlands.

- There is no prohibition against applying septage or biosolids to frozen soil, a practice that greatly increases the chances of runoff.

The Environmental Commissioner recommended that the "MOE and OMAFRA [the Ontario Ministry of Agriculture, Food and Rural Affairs] ensure that the new legislation and policies for sewage sludge and septage address the need for overall ecosystem protection, as well as protection of groundwater recharge areas."[61]

Those parties calling for an improved management regime may be encouraged to hear of a recent U.S. initiative to bring environmental management principles and continuous improvement into the handling and spreading of biosolids. The National Biosolids Partnership program is intended to ensure that biosolids are handled not only in accordance with U.S. Environmental Protection Agency (U.S. EPA) and state standards, but also in a "community-friendly" fashion.[62] The program includes public disclosure. OMAFRA and the MOE are undertaking a study aimed at determining whether to bring such a program to Ontario.

Some Part 2 parties suggested that information about the spreading of biosolids and other waste is not made available to affected persons in a timely fashion. In his 2001 report, the Environmental Commissioner of Ontario agreed, finding that the MOE provides "no opportunity for public consultation on approvals for land spreading of sewage sludge."[63] I think this situation is unfortunate.

I am satisfied that concerns about the impact on drinking water from the spreading of biosolids and septage can be adequately addressed by the source protection planning process that I am recommending. Spreading occurs only pursuant to a Certificate of Approval, and a certificate should be issued only if the proposed spreading is consistent with the area's watershed-based source protection plan. That plan, as I point out above, will assess and limit the cumulative impact of all loadings within the watershed. As I pointed out in section 4.3.17, enforcement of the conditions of Certificates of Approval must be strict.

---

[61] Ibid., p. 56.
[62] U.S. Environmental Protection Agency, Office of Wastewater Management, 2002, *Biosolids* <www.epa.gov/owm/bio.htm> [accessed April 29, 2002].
[63] Environmental Commissioner of Ontario, 2001b, p. 53.

4.4.5   Agriculture

4.4.5.1   *Introduction*

Agriculture can be a significant source of the contaminants in drinking water. The U.S. EPA has found that the largest contributor of non–point source water pollution by volume in the United States is sediment runoff from agricultural sources.[64] Studies of rural wells in Ontario found that 34% contained elevated levels of coliform bacteria and 14% contained elevated levels of nitrates; both are indicators of agricultural contamination.[65] Moreover, at present in Ontario there is very little in the way of regulation directed to the protection of drinking water sources from the potential impacts of agriculture. For instance, there is no legally binding requirement concerning manure storage or management, nor is there an inspection program concerning manure management. There is considerably less environmental and water protection regulation of agriculture in Ontario than there is in many other Western jurisdictions.[66]

---

[64] U.S. Environmental Protection Agency, 1995, *Progress Report* (Washington, DC: EPA), as cited in C.M. Johns, 2002, "Policy instruments to manage non–point source water pollution: Comparing the United States and Ontario," Walkerton Commissioned Paper 11, p. 11.

[65] M.J. Goss, D.A.J. Barry, and D.L. Rudolph, 1998, "Groundwater contamination in Ontario farm wells and its association with agriculture. 1. Results from drinking water wells," *Journal of Contaminant Hydrology*, vol. 32, p. 267, cited in M.J. Goss et al., 2002, "The management of manure in Ontario with respect to water quality," Walkerton Inquiry Commissioned Paper 6, p. 275.

[66] Ontario does not currently have the legally binding standards and regulations that address the environmental impacts of agricultural practices that exist in many other jurisdictions. Instead, the province has a series of position statements.

In the United States, the federal regulatory framework that governs water quality specifically addresses contamination from agricultural facilities. Agricultural nutrient regulation is achieved by federally set guidelines with a concurrent federal–state enforcement authority. In general, all states must adhere to U.S. EPA standards unless they develop more stringent water quality and manure management standards. State regulations typically apply to non–point sources of pollution, such as smaller agricultural operations.

In the European Union (EU), livestock waste disposal concerns have led to regulations that require producers either to use costly waste management techniques or to scale back production. The EU Nitrate Directive, enacted as a central regulatory act in 1991, sets a nitrate concentration limit for water and a limit on residual nitrogen after land applications of manure. Regions that do not meet this directive (which applies to all member countries) are subject to more stringent policies to bring about compliance, such as limits on livestock production and expansions for export markets. Some EU members, namely the Netherlands and Denmark, have regulatory instruments that tightly control various agricultural activities by way of nutrient management plans and fines or taxes on excess nutrients.

Other Canadian jurisdictions have also enacted regulatory mechanisms targeted at protecting water quality from agricultural impacts. In New Brunswick, municipalities can designate watersheds as protected areas; such a designation prevents new agricultural activity and restricts existing

A great deal of attention in Part 2 of the Inquiry focused on regulating the potential impacts of agriculture on Ontario's drinking water sources. My main recommendation is that every large or intensive farm, and every smaller farm located in an area designated as sensitive or high-risk, be required to develop a water protection plan that is consistent with the local watershed-based source protection plan (once the latter becomes available) and is binding on the farm's activities.[67]

The purpose of the plans will be to identify the ways in which the farming operation may affect drinking water sources, including those sources used by the farmers and their families, and to determine ways of preventing or reducing those impacts. Such water protection plans might logically be part of a broader nutrient management plan or environmental farm plan.

Farm water protection plans for all farms larger than a certain size and for all farms in areas designated as sensitive or high-risk by the watershed-based source protection planning system will require MOE approval. Compliance with these plans will be mandatory. Small farms that are not in sensitive or high-risk areas should nonetheless be encouraged to undertake water protection planning, possibly as part of an environmental farm plan.

In making recommendations concerning agriculture, I am seeking a balance between two needs that were repeatedly emphasized by the Part 2 parties during the Inquiry. Many of these parties emphasized the need to ensure that the regulation of the potential impacts of farming activities on drinking water sources is approached on a watershed or ecosystem basis. A simple regulation of individual farms that does not account for the cumulative effects of all the activities in a watershed is not sufficient. Making individual farm water protection plans consistent with watershed-based source protection plans will address this issue.

---

agricultural practices. A Quebec regulation, specifically aimed at reducing pollution from agricultural sources, requires farmers to maintain an agro-environmental fertilization plan and document all manure spreading. The regulation also imposes restrictions on the time of manure application and the type of equipment used.

   (See Goss et al.; 2002, Johns; and Environmental Commissioner of Ontario, 2002, *The Protection of Ontario's Groundwater and Intensive Farming: Special Report to the Legislative Assembly of Ontario* <www.eco.on.ca/english/newsrel/00jul27b.pdf> [accessed February 18, 2002].)

[67] When I refer to a "farm" in this report, I mean an agricultural operation as defined in the *Farming and Food Production Protection Act, 1998*, S.O. 1998, c. 1, s.1(1): "'agricultural operation' means an agricultural, aquacultural, horticultural or silvicultural operation that is carried on in the expectation of gain or reward." The Act further elaborates on the definition of a farm in s. 1(2).

On the other hand, various farm groups made the point that every farm is different and that even within a given farm, circumstances often change – different fields are left fallow or planted in different crops; herd sizes grow or are reduced – according to the farm's day-to-day management needs. A system is therefore needed that is able to recognize and accommodate each farm's individual circumstances. Thus, individual farm water protection plans must be consistent with protection of the watershed while at the same time recognizing the circumstances and practicalities of the particular farm involved.

4.4.5.2   *Farmers' Commitment to the Environment*

Ontario's farmers have generally demonstrated a strong commitment to the environment. Many have been certified under the environmental farm plan program (EFP) offered by the Province, Agriculture and Agri-Food Canada, and the Ontario Soil and Crop Improvement Association. The EFP appears to me to be an excellent program that helps educate farmers about the potential environmental impacts of all facets of their operations and encourages them to take appropriate actions. The plans are not compulsory, but a large number of farms have developed them with financial assistance from the Province.[68] The Ontario Federation of Agriculture (OFA) and other farmers' organizations suggested that the EFP may be threatened by funding cuts at the provincial level. I think such cuts would be most unfortunate. The farm groups also suggested that the EFP should be developed into a certifiable quality management program for farms. Although this may be a good idea, recommending such a program would address a broad array of environmental issues and would therefore be beyond the scope of this Inquiry. However, I do envision environmental farm plans as being the means by which water protection can be achieved for those small farms that are not in areas of the watershed that are designated as sensitive or high-risk. This may, in fact, be a large majority of the farms in some watersheds.

The Ontario Farm Environment Coalition (OFEC) also advocated using a "Contract with Consumers" to encourage good environmental performance among farmers in Ontario.[69] In such a "Contract," a farmer would promise to engage in a program of continuous environmental improvement in exchange

---

[68] A $1,500 grant has been available to assist the farmer in undertaking the environmental farm plan and subsequent improvements.

[69] Ontario Farm Environmental Coalition, "Ontario farmers' commitment to the natural environment," Walkerton Inquiry Submission, p. 17.

for funding from the Province. Although I find that there is much to recommend such an approach, possibly building on the environmental farm planning process, I do not think this solution goes far enough to protect drinking water sources in all cases.

4.4.5.3   *Ministry of the Environment Lead*

Recommendation 11: The Ministry of the Environment should take the lead role in regulating the potential impacts of farm activities on drinking water sources. The Ministry of Agriculture, Food and Rural Affairs should provide technical support to the Ministry of the Environment and should continue to advise farmers about the protection of drinking water sources.

I am recommending that a regulatory regime be established for agricultural operations. It is essential that a single ministry in the provincial government be responsible for developing and enforcing regulations. Of the two obvious candidates for regulating potential agricultural impacts on drinking water sources, I prefer the Ministry of the Environment (MOE).

Placing the MOE in charge of regulating potential agricultural impacts will centralize the protection of drinking water sources within one expert ministry. The recommendations in this report will result in the MOE's having the regulatory lead for all other aspects of drinking water management. The ministry already has the lead for other environmental regulation, including the regulation of pesticide use on farms.[70] I am concerned that allowing the continuing fragmentation of responsibilities for source protection – with most activities being carried out by the MOE, and those related to agriculture being carried out by OMAFRA – could lead to a lack of clarity about roles and accountabilities and could reduce the effectiveness of source protection enforcement. The farm groups expressed concern that the MOE does not have the expertise necessary to regulate agricultural activities, but the MOE should be able to call on OMAFRA to provide technical support when necessary.

The argument in favour of centralizing the regulation of agriculture in OMAFRA is that agriculture is significantly different from other types of industries and requires specialized knowledge on the part of the regulator.

---

[70] *Pesticides Act*, R.S.O. 1990, c. P.11, s. 1.

Furthermore, OMAFRA has an established relationship with farmers and is likely to be seen as a supporter rather than as an aggressor in the agricultural community. Both these statements may be true. However, I am wary of the perception of a conflict of interest within OMAFRA, which could be seen to be simultaneously promoting the needs of the agriculture community and regulating that community. The possibility of such a perception has increased in the past few years, during which time OMAFRA has focused strongly on rural economic development and provided less attention to environmental protection. This development is reflected in the removal in 1998 of the statements concerning environmental protection from the ministry's statement of environmental values under the *Environmental Bill of Rights, 1993*, as noted by the Environmental Commissioner of Ontario.[71] Finally, while OMAFRA could be said to be expert in agricultural affairs, the MOE is expert in environmental regulation: it will be expert in the protection of drinking water generally and should have the most expertise in this area.

The MOE as the lead agency should work with OMAFRA, conservation authorities, and the agricultural community to develop an integrated approach to managing the potential impacts of agriculture on drinking water sources. This approach should include four separate elements: planning, education, financial incentives, and regulatory enforcement. Two papers prepared for the Inquiry suggest that a good policy would consist of a well-integrated combination of these four elements and would be sufficiently flexible to accommodate the different circumstances that may prevail on a number of scales (e.g., on the farm, in the watershed, in the municipality, or in the province).[72]

I agree with these authors and with the many submissions suggesting that the quality of drinking water sources should be protected from potential agricultural impacts through an integrated approach that uses all available tools. It is important that the actions of the different levels of government in this area be coordinated into a single coherent framework so as to avoid duplication and uncertainty.

Underpinning the integrated system for managing potential agricultural impacts on drinking water sources must be a strong regulatory system that will provide a minimum ("floor") level of performance that all operators must meet and

---

[71] Environmental Commissioner of Ontario, 1999, *Annual Report 1998: Open Doors* <www.eco.on.ca/english/publicat/ar1998.pdf> [accessed April 29, 2002], p. 33.

[72] Goss et al.; Johns.

that will set out the requirements of the participants. I lay this framework out in greater detail below.

4.4.5.4   *Regulatory Floor*

Recommendation 12: Where necessary, the Ministry of the Environment should establish minimum regulatory requirements for agricultural activities that generate impacts on drinking water sources.

Ontario's farmers have generally received direction from the provincial government in the form of guidelines rather than through regulation. For instance, there is currently no binding requirement for farmers to develop or follow nutrient management plans (although this situation may change under the proposed *Nutrient Management Act*). The Province has focused on a series of position statements and other Best Management Practices regarding nutrient management planning, manure storage and handling, and minimum distance separation that are intended to provide direction that is based on the best available technologies.

Some types of agricultural activities may constitute a threat to drinking water sources regardless of where they take place in a watershed. For example, manure storage and handling practices that do not follow guidelines for minimum distance separation from wellheads, or improper storage of large amounts of manure, may threaten drinking water anywhere. Such activities should be subject to province-wide regulation, not guidelines. This principle applies equally to those drinking water sources that serve those on the farms and those off. In particular, a minimum regulatory baseline or "floor" for manure storage and handling that will apply to all farms should be developed by the MOE, in consultation with OMAFRA, agricultural groups, and other affected groups.

Many jurisdictions that are in the forefront of addressing environmental issues have developed such minimum standards. In addition, I envision the possibility that watershed-based source protection plans may set out minimum standards for individual farm water protection plans in certain areas within the watershed. The point is that while flexibility and the customizing of individual farm water protection plans are important, there may be certain minimum standards that must apply to all farmers.

4.4.5.5   *Regulatory Review*

As a first step in ensuring a regulatory framework that is adequate to protect drinking water sources from potential impacts from agriculture, the MOE should review the existing regulatory framework in the light of this report.

In Part 2 of the Inquiry, much attention was focused on the exemptions granted to farms under the *Environmental Protection Act,* the immunity from nuisance actions afforded to farmers under the *Farming and Food Production Protection Act, 1998,* and the proposed *Nutrient Management Act.* In some cases, there appeared to be considerable misunderstanding about the scope of these Acts. I think it is useful to comment briefly on each of these statutes.

4.4.5.5.1   The *Environmental Protection Act*

I doubt that the exemptions granted under the *Environmental Protection Act* (EPA) protect farmers from prosecution for the pollution of water sources that causes or is likely to cause the adverse environmental effects referred to in definitions (b) to (h) of the definition of "adverse effect" in the EPA.[73] The protections provided to farmers appear to me to be much narrower than many of those who argue against them seem to understand.

Section 6 of the EPA states the following:

> (1) No person shall discharge into the natural environment any contaminant, and no person responsible for a source of contaminant shall permit the discharge into the natural environment of any contaminant from the source of contaminant, in an amount, concentration or level in excess of that prescribed by the regulations.
>
> Exception
>
> (2) Subsection (1) does not apply to animal wastes disposed of in accordance with normal farming practices.

This is a general prohibition that prevents exceedances of regulatory limits on contaminants. The exemption applies to animal wastes that are disposed of in accordance with normal farm practices, and it is very broad.

---

[73] *Environmental Protection Act*, R.S.O. 1990, c. E-19, s. 1.

However, section 14 of the EPA creates a much narrower exemption for farming activities when they cause or are likely to cause any adverse effects:

(1) Despite any other provision of this Act or the regulations, no person shall discharge a contaminant or cause or permit the discharge of a contaminant into the natural environment *that causes or is likely to cause an adverse effect.* [emphasis added]

Exception

(2) Subsection (1) does not apply, in respect of an adverse effect referred to in clause (a) of the definition of "adverse effect" in subsection 1(1), to animal wastes disposed of in accordance with normal farming practices.

Section 14(1) is a special case provision of the EPA that prevents the discharge of contaminants if there is or is likely to be an adverse effect.

The exemption provided for the disposal of animal wastes here applies only to those adverse effects contained in paragraph (a) of the definition of adverse effects. The complete definition is as follows:

1. (1) In this Act,

"adverse effect" means one or more of,

(a) impairment of the quality of the natural environment for any use that can be made of it,

(b) injury or damage to property or to plant or animal life,

(c) harm or material discomfort to any person,

(d) an adverse effect on the health of any person,

(e) impairment of the safety of any person,

(f) rendering any property or plant or animal life unfit for human use,

(g) loss of enjoyment of normal use of property, and

(h) interference with the normal conduct of business.

Although it is possible to fit any of definitions in paragraphs (b) through (h) into the definition in paragraph (a), there is a good argument that those adverse effects specifically set out in paragraphs (b) through (h) that are not referred to in the exemption in section 14(2) are caught by the prohibition in section 14(1). If this argument is correct, the MOE would be in a position to prosecute, when appropriate, for discharges causing or likely to cause the specific harms set out in paragraphs (b) through (h).

Since the EPA will form the backbone of the source protection regulatory system that I propose, the MOE should review this issue and, if necessary, seek to amend the Act to permit prosecution in appropriate cases where adverse effects occur. The MOE should also review its policies regarding the prosecution of agricultural operations under the EPA to ensure that the ministry is interpreting the legislation correctly and using it to its full extent to protect drinking water sources.

Moreover, there is no exemption provided to farmers from section 32 of the *Ontario Water Resources Act* (OWRA), the anti–water pollution statute. If, as I recommend in Chapter 13 of this report, the OWRA provision is to be removed, the MOE should make clear that farmers are not exempt from prosecution under section 14 of the EPA when adverse effects of the types described in paragraphs (b) through (h) of the EPA definition of adverse effect occur or are likely to occur. I emphasize that removing the OWRA provisions and leaving source protection issues to the EPA should not result in less protection for water sources.

4.4.5.5.2   The *Farming and Food Production Protection Act, 1998*

The *Farming and Food Production Protection Act, 1998* (FFPPA) does not create immunity for farmers from civil action relating to the contamination of drinking water. The question of civil liability for farmers is a difficult one. The preamble to the FFPPA provides as follows:

> It is in the provincial interest that in agricultural areas, agricultural uses and normal farm practices be promoted and protected in a way

that balances the needs of the agricultural community with provincial health, safety and environmental concerns.[74]

This is a laudable objective. The Act then goes on to provide the following exemption for farmers:

> 2(1) A farmer is not liable in nuisance to any person for *a disturbance* resulting from an agricultural operation carried on as a normal farm practice.[75] [emphasis added]

A disturbance is defined as follows:

> "[D]isturbance" means odour, dust, flies, light, smoke, noise and vibration.[76]

This definition does not include the release of contaminants such as nutrients or pathogens. The exemption in section 2(1) therefore does not apply to the contamination of drinking water sources. Thus, a farmer could be civilly liable for a nuisance related to the contamination of drinking water, subject to the usual defences, including statutory approval.

There are no other immunities from civil action for farmers set out in the FFPPA.

4.4.5.5.3   The *Nutrient Management Act*

Many Part 2 parties commented on the proposed *Nutrient Management Act* (Bill 81). A number of possible deficiencies were identified that could be of consequence if the Act is intended to address the issue of protecting drinking water sources:

- Nutrient management planning does not necessarily entail a consideration of the presence of microbes such as bacteria, protozoa, and viruses, or of other non-nutrient constituents of manure (although the Act does not restrict the minister from considering these things when making regulations concerning the management and handling of nutrient-containing materials such as manure).

---

[74] *Farming and Food Production Protection Act, 1998*, S.O. 1998, c. 1.
[75] Ibid., s. 2(1).
[76] Ibid., s. 1(1).

- Nutrient management plans do not necessarily take into consideration watershed-specific information.

- In the past, nutrient management planning has focused more on maximizing crop yield than on protecting water resources.

- The *Nutrient Management Act* does not provide for enforcement by members of the public.

These points suggest that the *Nutrient Management Act* as it is proposed may not be sufficient in itself to protect the sources of Ontario's drinking water from potential agricultural contaminants. The Act's effectiveness will depend on the development of appropriate regulations.

That said, the Act as it is proposed grants broad powers to the Lieutenant-Governor-in-Council to create regulations to control the use of "nutrient containing materials." These powers include the authority to make regulations concerning standards for the management of nutrient-containing materials and making those standards compulsory and enforceable. Without restricting the generality of these powers, the Act specifically mentions a number of potential regulations:[77]

- specifying the size and types of containment to be used, as well as construction standards;

- specifying the amounts of nutrient-containing materials that can be applied to lands;

- setting standards for equipment and the transportation of nutrient-containing materials;

- prescribing conditions of use;

- requiring licensing or certification;

---

[77] Draft *Nutrient Management Act,* s. 5(1); see Ontario, Ministry of Agriculture, Food and Rural Affairs, 2001, *Nutrient Management Act, 2001: Explanatory Note* <www.gov.on.ca/OMAFRA/english/agops/nutrient_management_act_2001.pdf> [accessed April 29, 2002].

- setting out the requirements of a nutrient management plan, including the requirement for the renewal of the plan;

- prohibiting the application of nutrient-containing materials, except in accordance with a nutrient management plan;

- requiring that nutrient management plans be created by qualified individuals;

- providing for the issuance of approvals and their termination;

- requiring that nutrient management plans be filed;

- enabling the minister or the minister's appointees to make changes to a nutrient management plan;

- governing the requirements for sampling and chemical analysis;

- respecting minimum distance separation guidelines; and

- requiring documentation of management.

With respect to nutrient-containing materials, the Act, if passed in its present form, would certainly provide the Province with the authority to create the tools it would need to develop the farm water protection planning system that I am recommending. There is a substantial overlap between the farm water protection planning I recommend and nutrient management planning for other purposes, and I think it may make sense to deal with both of these issues at once. In other words, it may be best to have a single Act affecting farmers that regulates both nutrient management and source water protection. However, the *Nutrient Management Act* as it is currently drafted does not provide the power to make regulations concerning other aspects of agriculture that could have impacts on drinking water sources, such as the handling of pesticides or fuels. That problem could be addressed either by broadening the scope of the regulatory power under the *Nutrient Management Act* or by integrating the drinking water source protection aspects of regulations under the Act into a broader policy that also includes regulations under the *Pesticides Act* and the *Environmental Protection Act*.

If the Province intends to use the *Nutrient Management Act* as the principal means of regulating the potential impacts of agriculture on drinking water sources, it would be better to say so clearly in a preamble to the Act. Furthermore, if the Act is used to create regulations for the protection of drinking water sources, then separate regulations specifically addressing the matter should be used. The Province should consult with farm groups, conservation authorities, and other affected groups in developing any such regulations.

As I said above, the backbone of regulating farming activity as it relates to the protection of drinking water is the development of individual farm plans. These plans, once developed, should collect in one place all of the requirements of an individual farm for protecting water sources.

4.4.5.6   *Farm Water Protection Plans*

Recommendation 13: All large or intensive farms, and all farms in areas designated as sensitive or high-risk by the applicable source protection plan, should be required to develop binding individual water protection plans consistent with the source protection plan.

Recommendation 14: Once a farm has in place an individual water protection plan that is consistent with the applicable source protection plan, municipalities should not have the authority to require that farm to meet a higher standard of protection of drinking water sources than that which is laid out in the farm's water protection plan.

I discuss the issue of what should be considered large or intensive farms for purposes of this recommendation in section 4.4.5.7.1.

These recommendations are intended to balance two competing interests. On the one hand, municipalities wish to protect the health of their communities from potential problems arising from the contamination of drinking water sources. On the other hand, the agricultural community may feel that it is being regulated from all sides. The approach I propose is that municipalities should deal with all of their drinking water source protection requirements through the watershed-based source protection planning process, in which farmers also participate. Once those plans are in place, farmers whose activities pose a risk to drinking water because of their farm's size, intensity, or location must make their binding individual water protection plans consistent with those watershed-based plans, in effect implementing the source protection measures that have been developed by the municipalities, the agricultural community, and other affected groups and that have been approved by the Province in the watershed-based process. Municipalities should not then be allowed to unilaterally impose on farmers more stringent measures for the protection of drinking water sources.[78]

This recommendation is not meant to constrain the ability of municipalities to make bylaws for any other purposes.

4.4.5.7   Planning

The first facet of the integrated approach to managing the potential impacts of agriculture should be the development of individual farm water protection plans. These plans will serve both an educational and a regulatory function.

Farmers' organizations repeatedly stressed the need to ensure that the regulation of farming activities takes into account the individual circumstances of each farm operation. It is through farm water protection planning that this would occur. The development of such plans need not be overly onerous for farmers. In short, all that will be required of a farm operation is an assessment of the ways in which the farm may create impacts on potential drinking water sources, and a plan for reducing those impacts to an acceptable level.

The level of detail and effort required in preparing such plans will vary from farm to farm, depending on the farm's size and location and the vulnerability of local drinking water sources.

---

[78] There are some legal precedents in this area. The recent Supreme Court of Canada decision in *114957 Canada Ltée (Spraytech, Société d'arrosage) v. Hudson (Town)*, [2001] S.C.J. No 42 held that the municipal power to create bylaws under a "general welfare" provision should not be constrained by the presence of Provincial regulations on the same matter, as long as the bylaws and the regulations are not in conflict and "dual compliance" is possible. On the other hand, in Ontario, s. 6 of the FFPPA specifically constrains the ability of municipalities to make bylaws restricting normal farm practices. The recent decision in *Ben Gardiner Farms Inc. v. West Perth (Township)*, [2001] O.J. No. 4394 (Ont. Civ. Ct.) held that a municipal bylaw restricting farm size did not restrict a normal farm pratice (although s. 6 of the FFPPA was not specifically referenced in the decision). I do not provide an extensive discussion of this issue here, but I appeal to the efforts of those involved in the planning process to respect the intent to have a single process of drinking water–related regulation for farmers.

Recommendation 15: The Ministry of the Environment should work with the Ministry of Agriculture, Food and Rural Affairs, agricultural groups, conservation authorities, municipalities, and other interested groups to create a provincial framework for developing individual farm water protection plans.

As I discuss above, small farms that are not in areas designated as sensitive or high-risk and that are therefore not required to develop a binding water protection plan should nevertheless be encouraged to consider the protection of drinking water sources as part of environmental farm planning.

Environmental farm plans should encourage farmers to catalogue, consider, understand, and commit to minimizing the potential impacts on drinking water sources of their practices, including the following:

- their manure management practices, including the land spreading of manure;

- the spreading of biosolids or septage;

- the use of chemical fertilizers;

- ways of dealing with stormwater runoff, including tile drainage;

- pesticide use; and

- fuel management.

This assessment could be completed by the farmer using a guidance document prepared by the MOE and OMAFRA.

A second category of farms includes large or intensive farms and small farms that are in areas specially designated as sensitive or high-risk by the watershed-based source protection plan. Each such farm will require a detailed farm water protection plan, which should include a hydrogeological assessment of the farm's operation. This two-tiered system embraces a risk-based approach to regulating agricultural impacts.[79] It has been recognized that larger farms may

---

[79] I discuss risk-based approaches in detail in Chapter 3 of this report.

require more detailed nutrient management planning,[80] and the same reasoning supports a stronger regime for planning for drinking water source protection. Small farms in sensitive or high-risk areas also pose a greater risk to drinking water sources, so they should also be subject to the more stringent regime.

The completed plans of farms in this second category should be submitted to the MOE for approval. Once approved, these plans should achieve the force of regulation, and their minimum requirements should be enforceable by the MOE.

Once again, these plans should embrace the concept of continuous improvement. If, in the process of creating a farm water protection plan, the farmer or a consultant identifies areas in which the farm is not in compliance with regulations, the farmer should take immediate action to achieve compliance.

Plans for larger farms or for farms that are in areas designated as sensitive or high-risk must be approved and held on file by the MOE. Preparing such plans may require the assistance of a third-party professional. The third party could be an expert from any of a number of fields, including agrology, agronomy, and environmental science. The key issue is that the experts' backgrounds must allow them to examine all the relevant impacts of farm activities.

4.4.5.7.1   Small Farms versus Large or Intensive Farms

The distinction between small and large farms is contentious and is necessarily arbitrary. That, however, is not a reason not to draw such a line.

There are several possible cut-offs being proposed or in use elsewhere. In its proposed nutrient management strategy, the Ontario Farm Environment Coalition (OFEC) uses a cut-off number of 150 livestock units, or 50 livestock units with a density of higher than 5 units per hectare, to distinguish between operations that it suggests should be required to produce a nutrient management plan before being issued a building permit and those that should not.[81] The ALERT/Sierra Club coalition recommended a similar number as the cut-off

---

[80] D. Armitage, Ontario Farm Environmental Coalition, Walkerton Inquiry Submission (Public Hearing, September 6, 2001), transcript p. 111.
[81] See Ontario Farm Environmental Coalition, *Nutrient Management Planning Strategy* <www.ofa.on.ca/aglibrary/Research/Nutrient%20Management%20Planning%20Strategy/ default.htm> [accessed April 30, 2002].

between a large farm and a small one.[82] The U.S. Environmental Protection Agency uses a higher number (defining fewer than 300 animal units as a small animal feeding operation),[83] but permits states to make more stringent regulations. The current draft of the *Nutrient Management Act* discusses a "large livestock operation" category that includes operations that have more than 450 livestock units.

My intention in proposing a two-tiered system is to avoid imposing undue restrictions or requirements on those who operate farms that truly pose a very small threat to drinking water sources. Based on the assumption that larger volumes of manure are more difficult to handle, larger farms present greater risks. Certainly, a larger hazard exists in the event of a catastrophic failure if a larger volume of manure is present. Still, I have heard some arguments that support and others that deny the assertion that larger operations are riskier.

Simply put, large farms create more manure, and for that reason alone they create a greater risk. If that manure is transported elsewhere, the potential risk may be smaller, and the farm water protection plans will be correspondingly adjusted. However, the sheer size of the large operation, in my view, calls for the increased protection of developing a plan that requires MOE approval.

The provincial government, in consultation with affected groups, should develop distinct definitions of "large farms" and "small farms" in view of the regime I am recommending.

4.4.5.8   *Education*

The Ministry of Agriculture, Food and Rural Affairs should work in cooperation with the Ministry of the Environment and conservation authorities to review

---

[82] D. Mills, ALERT/Sierra Club coalition, Walkerton Inquiry Submission (Public Hearing, September 6, 2001), transcript p. 39.

[83] See U.S. Environmental Protection Agency, 2000, *AFO or CAFO* <www.epa.gov/r5water/npdestek/npdcafoafovscafo.htm> [accessed January 4, 2002]. Note that the definition of "animal unit" varies from jurisdiction to jurisdiction, depending on species (e.g., cows vs. sheep), type (e.g., beef cows vs. dairy cows), and life stage. The U.S. EPA and the OFEC agree that one beef cow is 1 animal unit, but the OFEC would count two feeder cattle as 1 animal unit, whereas the U.S. EPA would count two feeder cattle as 2 animal units. Moreover, the U.S. EPA definitions are generally more conservative. Thus, it is possible that the 300 animal units discussed by the U.S. EPA and the 150 animal units discussed by the OFEC could refer to the same number of animals, depending on the individual operation.

education programs for farmers and, if necessary, develop new ones. These programs should have as their primary goal assisting farmers with the development of water protection plans.

Many would argue that this should indeed be the first element in the system for protecting drinking water sources from the potential impacts of agriculture. Two of the papers commissioned for the Inquiry found that an effective program for the control of non–point source pollution, such as that which comes from agriculture, must be supported by an effective education program if it is to work.[84] This suggestion was also supported by most parties at the public hearings. Without an effective education program that creates a desire to comply on the part of the regulated, enforcement becomes more difficult.

4.4.5.9   *Economic Incentives*

Recommendation 16: The provincial government, through the Ministry of Agriculture, Food and Rural Affairs in collaboration with the Ministry of the Environment, should establish a system of cost-share incentives for water protection projects on farms.

According to one of the papers commissioned for the Inquiry, voluntary programs that emphasize education and the adoption of suites of "best management practices" tend to be effective only insofar as they do not affect farm profitability.[85] When such programs would create significant reductions in profitability, economic incentives are generally provided. Such incentives may seem unfair to people in other industries that may not be eligible for such cost-sharing. However, farmers argue that society as a whole benefits both from environmental protection and from inexpensive food, and that farmers who do not qualify for the incentives are less likely to adopt the practices.[86] Economic incentives are a well-accepted part of managing impacts from agricultural non–point source pollutants in other jurisdictions.[87] I think they should be used, where appropriate and with due care, in Ontario.

The Inquiry's commissioned papers cited in the previous paragraph, my consultations with farm groups during the public hearings and with individual

---

[84] Goss et al., p. 24; Johns, p, 9.

[85] Goss et al., p. 22.

[86] This argument has less force in a system in which compliance is mandatory.

[87] Goss et al., p. 23; Johns, pp. 11–23.

farmers during the town hall meetings, and the written submissions I received from the farm associations amply demonstrated that the financial support of provincial programs such as the environmental farm plan program results in a high level of participation from farmers. In addition, many of the Part 2 parties that were not farm organizations were supportive of financial incentives for farmers.

However, I also understand the need to limit provincial spending. I encourage the Province to continue to provide support for environmental initiatives in general and for water protection projects on farms in particular. The selection of projects should be based on the level of environmental protection per dollar – that is, it should include a consideration of the level of support required and the sensitivity of the area to be protected.

Abandoned wells deserve special mention. There are thousands of abandoned or improperly decommissioned wells in Ontario. They create direct threats to drinking water sources because they provide a direct connection between surface water and groundwater. The vast majority of these wells are located on agricultural properties.

Such wells are a hindrance and a threat to farmers as well as to groundwater. Farmers are keen to see the wells properly decommissioned, but there can be a substantial expense associated with decommissioning. The MOE should develop a program for encouraging farmers to identify improperly decommissioned wells and should provide cost-sharing for their decommissioning.

4.4.6 Other Industries

Recommendation 17: The regulation of other industries by the provincial government and by municipalities must be consistent with provincially approved source protection plans.

A large number of other industries and activities may have an impact on sources of drinking water. Those mentioned during this Inquiry include the following:

- the spreading of road salt;

- forestry;

- mining;

- urban development; and

- industrial plants.

These industries and activities can pose just as serious threats to the safety of drinking water as those resulting from farming operations.

I envision that the potential for these activities to contaminate drinking water sources should be limited by the appropriate regulatory agencies in accordance with the watershed-based source protection plans.

In the end, I recommend that no activities, whatever the source, be permitted to contaminate drinking water sources in contravention of source protection plans.

Chapter 5   Drinking Water Quality Standards

Contents

Chapter 5   Drinking Water Quality Standards

5.1   Introduction

This chapter is about standards, specifically the drinking water quality standards that are now part of Ontario Regulation 459/00. In discussing these standards, I do not intend to offer recommendations about maximum acceptable concentrations of contaminants but to examine the process by which they are set. There was no information presented at the Inquiry to warrant alarm with respect to existing standards. This Inquiry did not examine individual standards in detail; the purpose of my recommendations regarding the process of setting standards is to provide a vehicle for public review of existing standards, where necessary, and of emerging threats to drinking water safety.

There are many other kinds of standards. Some deal with mechanical, electrical, or plumbing matters, which have a bearing – but not a central one – on matters of drinking water quality. I deal with these standards only incidentally. More important are standards for treatment, monitoring, and laboratory testing, which are dealt with in Chapters 6, 8, and 9. Finally, there are essential standards for attaining consistent high quality in management and operations, which require drinking water quality standards as a base.[1] Quality management is dealt with in Chapter 11.

The failures at Walkerton were not failures of the drinking water quality objectives as such but of the systems that were supposed to ensure they were met. Reviews of outbreaks – see Chapter 3 – suggest that this pattern holds on a larger scale. As was the case in Walkerton, operational, managerial, and regulatory failures can lead to a major breakdown.

In this chapter, I make only a few recommendations. Some are directed toward the cautious approach that should be adopted in setting drinking water quality standards. The remainder are directed toward making the system for setting standards, both at the federal and provincial levels, more transparent. There is reason to have confidence that Ontario's drinking water quality standards are

---

[1] Contrasting the two, the executive director of the American Water Works Association said: "[A] table of numbers – whether they are guidelines or strict standards – does not protect public health in and of itself. Meeting the numbers is just part of an effective program. More important to me is whether utilities have continuous quality improvement systems to verify that the entire process of delivering safe drinking water is working as it should": J.W. Hoffbuhr, 2001, "The regulatory paradox," *Journal of the American Water Works Association*, vol. 93, no. 5, p. 8.

essentially based on sound principles of risk assessment and management and that they make due allowance for precaution. Conservative and enforceable water quality standards are an important basis for a multi-barrier approach to water safety, and it is likely true that improvements in management and regulation will yield greater safety benefits than will any general tightening of Ontario's present drinking water quality standards. Nevertheless, new threats will continue to be identified and old ones will be periodically re-evaluated.

I also recommend the establishment of an expert advisory council to advise the Minister of the Environment on setting standards. There are, in particular, two areas where current standards may be obsolete: the use of total coliform as an indicator, and the apparently lax standard for turbidity. These I assign to this expert advisory council to examine, in public, along with the rest of a lengthy agenda. Finally, I have included a description of the contaminants that pose the more serious threats to drinking water and the processes by which drinking water quality standards are set in Canada and elsewhere.

5.2   Setting Drinking Water Quality Standards in Canada

Drinking water quality standards are expressed as maximum acceptable concentration (MAC) limits for certain microbes, chemicals, and physical properties. Where data are insufficient but a hazard is suspected, an interim maximum acceptable concentration (IMAC) limit may be specified. Canada's drinking water quality standards are set in two steps. First, a committee of officials from the federal, provincial, and territorial governments, working without a great deal of public involvement or political oversight, examines toxicological and epidemiological evidence as well as other information and publishes a set of recommended *Guidelines*.[2] Second, provinces and territories decide which of the contaminants and MACs ought to be adopted in their jurisdictions.

Sometimes, as was the case for many years in Ontario, the federal–provincial *Guidelines* were carried over simply as guidelines or objectives by the implementing jurisdictions. In a few provinces, they were given the force of

---

[2] Federal–Provincial–Territorial Committee on Environmental and Occupational Health, Federal–Provincial Subcommittee on Drinking Water, 1996, *Guidelines for Canadian Drinking Water Quality*, 6th ed. (Ottawa: Health Canada) [hereafter *Guidelines*]. A more updated version of the *Guidelines* can be found at <http://www.hc-sc.gc.ca/ehp/ehd/catalogue/bch_pubs/summary.pdf> [accessed April 30, 2002].

law by being made regulations under appropriate provincial legislation. In Ontario, a version of the *Guidelines* was incorporated as an objective into the Ontario Drinking Water Objectives (ODWO),[3] until shortly after Walkerton, when they were extended and incorporated into law as Ontario Regulation 459/00 under the *Ontario Water Resources Act*.[4]

Recommendation 18: In setting drinking water quality standards, the objective should be such that, if the standards are met, a reasonable and informed person would feel safe drinking the water.

I discussed this goal in more detail in Chapter 3.

Recommendation 19: Standards setting should be based on a precautionary approach, particularly with respect to contaminants whose effects on human health are unknown.

In setting up systems that affect human health, decision makers usually err on the side of safety, regardless of the costs. As discussed in Chapter 3, a refinement to this approach is the precautionary principle, a guide to environmental action that has been recognized in international law and cited approvingly by the Supreme Court of Canada.[5] Precautionary measures include setting standards to account for uncertainties, investments in risk mitigation or alternative technologies, and investments in research.[6] This prudent approach must still consider costs, but as prevention usually costs much less than remediation, the precautionary principle has a role to play in risk management and should be an integral part of decisions affecting the safety of drinking water.

Recommendation 20: Regarding drinking water quality research, I encourage Health Canada and other agencies to adopt as a priority the development of sufficiently detailed definitions of the susceptibility of vulnerable population groups to drinking water contaminant exposures to allow appropriate adjustments in drinking water quality guidelines.

------

[3] Ontario, Ministry of the Environment, Water Policy Branch (1994 revision).

[4] R.S.O. 1990, c. O.40.

[5] See *114957 Canada Ltée (Spraytech, Société d'arrosage)* v. *Hudson (Town)*, [2001] 2 S.C.R. 241.

[6] Some of the parties in Part 2 made the point explicitly: Sierra Legal Defence Fund, 2001, "A paper on the regulatory approaches to drinking water used in Canada and, selectively, abroad," and "Public submission to the Walkerton Inquiry," vol. 2, Walkerton Inquiry Submission, p. 39; and Canadian Environmental Law Association and Concerned Walkerton Citizens, 2001, "Tragedy on tap: Why Ontario needs a *Safe Drinking Water Act*," vol. 2, Walkerton Inquiry Submission, pp. 120–121.

Where identifiable groups are susceptible to certain contaminants, quality standards may be made more stringent and/or susceptible people must take measures to protect themselves. Immunocompromised people (e.g., people with AIDS, transplants, or cancer, whose drug regimes suppress immune responses) may need to take special precautions if there is a chance of *Cryptosporidium* in the water.[7] Sometimes it is practical to require general standards to take these problems into account, but at other times, medical advice and individual precautions are necessary.

5.2.1   The Federal–Provincial Subcommittee on Drinking Water

The Federal–Provincial Subcommittee on Drinking Water develops water quality guidelines as recommendations to its parent committee, the Federal–Provincial–Territorial Committee on Environmental and Occupational Health (CEOH),[8] which is composed of senior officials from the health, environment, and labour departments. The subcommittee consists of 14 mid-level managers appointed by the ten provinces, the three territories, and Health Canada. Its members are public servants who typically have regulatory experience in water or public health, but operational experience or professional qualifications in the subject are not prerequisites to appointment. The judgments they make are based on scientific evidence about risks to human health, costs, availability of suitable technologies, and the expressed views of the governments they represent. None of these categories is free of important value judgments.

Although the Walkerton Inquiry is a provincial inquiry, the standards in Ontario principally originate in the work of the federal–provincial subcommittee. Therefore, I consider it appropriate to make recommendations about that process.

Recommendation 21: I suggest that the federal–provincial process for proposing drinking water quality guidelines be refined to provide for greater transparency and public participation.

---

[7] In 2001, people drinking Vancouver's unfiltered water were warned to boil it, as a precaution, if they were immunocompromised: see British Columbia, Ministry of Health, Health File #56, February 2000, "Weakened immune systems and water-borne infections" <http://www.hlth.gov.bc.ca/hlthfile/hfile56.html> [accessed April 22, 2002].

[8] Federal–Provincial Subcommittee on Drinking Water, 1999, *Canadian Drinking Water Guidelines Development Process* (Ottawa: Health Canada).

In recent years, the work of the subcommittee has become more visible. A Web site posts summaries of its proceedings. It also posts proposed recommendations and the supporting technical evidence for public comment before they are forwarded to the parent committee.[9] Few comments are received, however. Perhaps interested parties do not understand the process or they may not know where to look for the documentation. Possibly they are unsure where, in this multi-stage federal–provincial process, they may intervene most effectively. The subcommittee may need to become more involved in active outreach.

Transparency and public participation can be advanced in several ways. I suggest that all meeting and future research agendas should be published on the Health Canada Web site, as should the full minutes (not summaries) of the subcommittee's meetings. All the risk assessment research done or commissioned by Health Canada for the subcommittee, including copies of toxicological or epidemiological papers prepared as part of the characterization of specific risks, should be freely available through the Web site. Most important, the subcommittee should document and publish the reasons for its recommendations. It should allow for dissenting or minority opinions.

The Web site should include an up-to-date schedule of scientific and regulation-making work, the subcommittee's members' names with their contact information, and requests for comments about substance or process. All the information needed to facilitate efficient and informed participation by the interested public should be freely available.

In that context, when a matter of broad public interest is being considered for regulatory change, interested parties should be encouraged to attend, write, or make submissions. Specifically, academics, consumer and environmental groups, and water industry experts should be invited to attend on an agenda basis. For more controversial issues, the subcommittee should consider asking Health Canada to undertake research on relevant public values and attitudes. Since the standards-setting process is inherently subjective, the subcommittee should consider the values of Canadians in making its decisions and not limit its considerations to science alone.

At present, a 1996 edition of the resulting *Guidelines* is sold to the public in a

---

[9] See <www.hc-sc.gc.ca/ehp/ehd/bch/water_quality.htm> and <www.hc-sc.gc.ca/ehp/ehd/bch/water_quality/consult/intro.htm> [accessed April 30, 2002].

print version. The current *Guidelines* should be made available on the Internet, free of charge.[10]

The CEOH receives recommendations from the subcommittee and in due course either passes them or sends them back for reconsideration. It also approves the subcommittee's plans for the technical and scientific work that underlies new guidelines. It is difficult to assess what value this committee brings to the process, since its proceedings are not public and there is no mechanism for public input. The CEOH does not even have a link on the Health Canada Web page. In my view, it should adopt the same procedures urged on its subcommittee in relation to transparency and public participation with respect to its own work on drinking water guidelines. The CEOH's guidance on the agenda, its reasons for accepting proposed guidelines or sending them back for further consideration, and its plans for drinking-water–related work at all levels, including the international level, should be published on the Health Canada Web site.

The first reason for opening the debate, at all levels, is that many of the decisions are inherently value-laden. Even experts do not always agree on what standards should apply.[11] It is important that the full debate on values should be as public as possible and open to comment from those who have an interest.[12] Some people may object that, if the real decisions lie with the provinces, then that is where the public debate should take place. I agree that more openness is needed at the provincial level, but the federal–provincial guidelines to a large extent set the agenda for provincial decisions, and the process establishing those guidelines should therefore be fully open to the public. In this respect, I urge the CEOH to mirror the improved process suggested for the subcommittee.

A second reason for calling for more transparency at the CEOH level is that there is always the chance that the federal government might decide to use the

---

[10] A summary table can be found on <www.hc-sc.gc.ca/ehp/ehd/bch/water_quality.htm> [accessed April 30, 2002].

[11] A pioneering work in this regard is M.F. O'Connor, 1973, "The application of multiattribute scaling procedures to the development of indices of water quality," Report 7339 (Chicago: Center for Mathematical Studies in Business and Economics, University of Chicago); cited in R.L. Keeney and H. Raiffa, 1975, *Decisions with Multiple Objectives: Preferences and Value Tradeoffs* (New York: John Wiley & Sons), pp. 431–432. This work, completed the year before the discovery of disinfection by-products, surveys water professionals and identifies 13 attractive attributes of public water supplies, which cannot all be produced at once. There was no consensus on priorities.

[12] Observers have praised the process for developing air standards in Ontario for its transparency and opportunities for public input; this may serve as a useful precedent.

Guidelines as the basis for enforceable regulations within its own domain. Ontarians whose water may be regulated federally should have the opportunity to make their views known regarding the standards to be applied.

Finally, there is a danger that decisions arrived at without public scrutiny tend toward the lowest common denominator. Standards arrived at after public debate are likely to be more demanding and less skewed by any particular interests and more acceptable to the public because of the process.

Recommendation 22: I suggest that the Federal–Provincial Subcommittee on Drinking Water focus on drinking water quality guidelines. I encourage Health Canada to commit the required scientific support to the federal–provincial process for proposing drinking water quality guidelines.

The Federal–Provincial Subcommittee on Drinking Water already has a full agenda in developing water quality guidelines. The structure, and many of the resources, for carrying out the research and analysis for setting water quality guidelines are now in place. There is a substantial benefit in having the subcommittee focus on the primary task for which it was established and for which it is equipped and qualified.

Health Canada provides the secretariat and all the subcommittee expenses, including travel and research, except for the salaries of the provincial and territorial members. The expenses can be significant. In particular, Health Canada provides the toxicological and epidemiological research that is the primary basis for characterizing public health risks. The speed at which the subcommittee can operate is effectively set by the budget that Health Canada is able to provide for this research. Goff Jenkins, the member from Ontario for many years and the chair for a period of five years, told the Inquiry that there is a considerable amount of research requested by the subcommittee that must be continually deferred for budgetary reasons.[13]

The subcommittee reportedly goes to some length to achieve consensus. This means that any of its 14 members can veto, or at least substantially delay, the passage of a particular recommendation for a guideline. Not all provinces and territories share the same pattern of past investments in treatment facilities, and because new recommendations may entail large expenditures, individual

---

[13] G. Jenkins, Walkerton Inquiry (Public Hearing, September 11, 2001), transcript pp. 20–21.

provinces and territories have, from time to time, a financial concern that may cause their members not to approve an otherwise desirable guideline. The danger is that the recommendations to the parent committee, the CEOH, may reflect only the views of the jurisdiction that seeks the least protective standards. I have been informed, for instance, that the turbidity standard would be lower but for the fact that several provinces would have to spend a great deal of money on filtration.[14]

Since the content of the *Guidelines* is non-binding and advisory, it is not necessary that unanimity exist for the recommendations to go forward. A simple, or two-thirds, majority should suffice. It is likely that the removal of the effective consensus rule would lessen the ability of a small number of jurisdictions to hold up progress toward a standard otherwise widely anticipated and accepted.

5.3   Where the Canadian *Guidelines* Apply

Recommendation 23: I encourage the federal government to adopt standards that are as stringent as, or more stringent than, Ontario Regulation 459/00 for all federal facilities, Indian reserves, national parks, military installations, and other lands under federal jurisdiction in Ontario.

The final output of the federal–provincial process is called the *Guidelines for Canadian Drinking Water Quality*, published by Health Canada and now in its sixth edition. The *Guidelines* serve as advice to the provinces and territories, and as the objective in some areas of federal jurisdiction. Alberta, Ontario, and Quebec have adopted versions of the *Guidelines* as provincial regulations. In general, the federal government policy is to apply whichever standard is stricter – the *Guidelines* or the provincial regulation or objective – to installations for which it is responsible. These include First Nations, military installations, and national parks.[15] The *Guidelines* are not regulations, however, and thus do not have the force of law: there are no penalties for a failure to comply with them.

Federal officials are obviously aware of the unenforceability of the *Guidelines* in the federal domain. One step in the right direction has been the incorporation by reference of the *Guidelines* MACs in Part IV of the *Canada Labour Code*.

---

[14] G. Jenkins, 2002, personal communication.
[15] J. Weiner, Health Canada, and J. Mills, Environment Canada, 2001, letter to H. Swain, Chair, Research Advisory Panel, Walkerton Inquiry, July 5 [Walkerton Inquiry files]. The federal government's policy and its actions sometimes diverge: see letter to H. Swain in Chapter 15.

This does not, however, require the sampling, testing, or reporting of the results, nor does it allow the prosecution of water suppliers who do not meet the quality standards.

It is important that sound and legally enforceable standards exist regardless of which of the two senior levels of government enacts them. Ontario residents drawing drinking water from areas under federal jurisdiction should not have lower standards than do other residents of the province. In this respect, it is important that this new obligation should carry requirements for sampling, testing, and enforcement that are as stringent as, or more stringent than, those standards established from time to time by Ontario regulations.

5.4   The Province's Responsibility to Implement Standards

Recommendation 24: The provincial government should continue to be the government responsible for setting legally binding drinking water quality standards.

Drinking water quality standards should, as they do now, have the force of law. I commented on this matter in the Part 1 report of this Inquiry.[16] Water quality standards should be set, on the initiative of the Minister of the Environment, by the Lieutenant-Governor-in-Council. The guidelines established from time to time by the federal–provincial subcommittee should be used as a starting point for establishing provincial standards.

For many years, as noted, the federal–provincial recommendations became "guidelines" or "objectives" in Ontario and other jurisdictions. Increased administrative flexibility resulted in weak enforcement. An offender could not be prosecuted for a breach of a guideline. In the 1980s, the MOE began to insert the Ontario Drinking Water Objectives (ODWO), as they then were, into Certificates of Approval. In the wake of Walkerton, the provincial government strengthened the process by incorporating the ODWO in Ontario Regulation 459/00. Now, recommendations from the federal–provincial process are scrutinized by the provincial government and, if found fitting, are added by Order-in-Council to the schedule in the regulation.

---

[16] Ontario, Ministry of the Attorney General, 2002, *Report of the Walkerton Inquiry, Part 1: The Events of May 2000 and Related Issues* (Toronto: Queen's Printer), pp. 355–358.

A bill before the Senate, S-18,[17] would require the federal government to regulate drinking water quality standards for the whole of Canada. This is not necessary for the protection of drinking water quality in Ontario, where the Ontario government has already established a standard more stringent than exists in the federal *Guidelines*. A federal enactment of this nature would also imply a willingness to establish a federal inspection and enforcement regime or to negotiate the delegation of those functions to the provinces.

Recommendation 25: In setting drinking water quality standards for Ontario, the Minister of the Environment should be advised by an Advisory Council on Standards.

There are two principal reasons for creating this new body.[18] First, it is reasonable for the provincial government to seek expertise from the general public. The general public provides a broad base from which to draw people highly qualified in the many relevant disciplines. Second, there are benefits in terms of transparency and public access through the use of an advisory council.

Members should be Canadians distinguished in the fields of public health, engineering, microbiology, utility operations, and other related areas, and should be appointed by Order-in-Council for overlapping terms. Relevant professional organizations, notably the Ontario Water Works Association, the Ontario Municipal Water Association, the Aboriginal Water Works Association of Ontario, the Ontario Medical Association, and the Association of Local Public Health Agencies, as well as leading non-governmental organizations with a record of interest and accomplishment in areas related to drinking water, should be solicited for nominations.

A predecessor committee, the Advisory Committee on Environmental Standards, was discontinued in 1996. Such bodies, however, are an excellent mechanism for drawing upon expert members of the community at a relatively low cost in terms of the quality of advice that is available.

The advisory council should establish its own process, solicit public views on proposed regulations, be provided with staff support by the MOE, and make appropriate recommendations to the minister. Recommendations should be

---

[17] Bill S-18, *An Act to Amend the Food and Drugs Act (Clean Drinking Water)*, 1st Sess., 37th Parl., 2001 (1st reading February 20, 2001).

[18] In subsequent chapters, I recommend that the Advisory Council on Standards also advise the minister with respect to management, treatment, testing, materials, and reporting standards.

made public and should be supported by the council's reasons. The advisory council should also provide advice to the MOE and Health Canada on drinking water research requirements; since this advice should be public, the universities and granting councils may also take note, with a consequent effect on the direction of the national research effort. The advisory council should make full use of the *Environmental Bill of Rights, 1993*,[19] and may decide to hold public hearings on matters of broad public concern. Under the *Environmental Bill of Rights*, the MOE operates a Web site where Ontario government agencies can post proposals with significant environmental impacts for public comment.[20]

5.4.1   Ontario Can Initiate as Well as React

Recommendation 26: The Advisory Council on Standards should have the authority to recommend that the provincial government adopt standards for contaminants that are not on the current federal–provincial agenda.

Although the federal–provincial subcommittee's work is important, it need not be the sole source of suggestions. Relevant work by the World Health Organization, the United States Environmental Protection Agency, and other leading authorities may be helpful, as may the work of public interest groups in Ontario. Recently, for instance, the Sierra Legal Defence Fund drew public attention to a less restrictive guideline for TCE (trichloroethylene) in Canada than exists in the United States.[21] This is the type of issue that the advisory council may wish to address.

5.5   Contaminants and Current Standards

The standards in Ontario Regulation 459/00 and the hazards posed by the contaminants they limit are worth examining in some detail. In order of decreasing risk to public health, the hazards fall into four groups. Those that can cause acute, serious, and immediate threats to public health are for the most part pathogens, such as viruses, bacteria, and protozoa. There is then a large class of chemicals that adversely affect public health in the case of long-

---

[19] S.O. 1993, c. 28, as amended.

[20] See Environmental Registry Postings for Policies, Acts, Regulations, and Instruments at <www.ene.gov.on.ca/envision/env_reg/er/registry.htm> [accessed April 30, 2002].

[21] M. Mittelstaedt, 2002, "Ottawa urged to curb solvent in tap water," *Globe and Mail*, January 16, p. A9.

term exposure: these are called chronic risks. Third are some standards that relate to the efficient operation of water treatment systems themselves, and finally, there are aesthetic standards for otherwise harmless agents affecting taste, odour, and colour.

5.5.1   Standards for Acute (Microbial) Risk

Standards for microbial risk are the most important and the most difficult to establish. Of the uncounted millions of microbes, only a tiny proportion is harmful to humans and other animals. Many, in fact, are conducive to, or compatible with, good health. Science has identified some, but by no means all, of the harmful ones, and evolutionary processes continue to create new ones. These difficulties are compounded by the serious problems of finding and characterizing microbes (see Chapter 8), so a regulatory dilemma appears.

Globally, the contamination of water by pathogenic organisms poses the most significant threat to the health of humans.[22] Several types of organisms may be implicated in the spread of water-borne illness. Viruses, bacteria, and parasites may all cause disease. A common element among many of them is that mammals (including humans) and sometimes birds are the usual source of the contaminants that may cause disease in humans.[23]

5.5.1.1   *Endemic versus Epidemic Levels of Exposure*

Illnesses that result from pathogenic organisms occur at low levels in the population almost continually. The background level of infection of a given pathogen in a population is referred to as the *endemic* rate of infection. The Inquiry heard evidence that endemic levels of exposure to some important pathogens, such as *Giardia* and *Cryptosporidium*, may be due to low-level exposure through drinking water or through other potential pathways, such as contact with pets, contaminated fruits or vegetables, or undercooked meats.

---

[22] L. Ritter et al., 2002, "Sources, pathways, and relative risks of contaminants in water," Walkerton Inquiry Commissioned Paper 10.

[23] D. Krewski et al., 2002, "Managing health risks from drinking water," Walkerton Inquiry Commissioned Paper 7, p. 77.

As much as one-third of the endemic level of exposure to enteric bacteria may be due to the low-level contamination of drinking water.[24]

Endemic exposure is with us all the time, but sometimes large populations are exposed to high concentrations of a pathogen all at once. Such exposure results in an *epidemic* – a large number of cases of the same disease occurring in a population at the same time. Walkerton was an epidemic. The recommendations in this report are cast with a view to reducing both endemic and epidemic exposure to pathogens.

5.5.1.2   *Viruses*

Viruses are tiny (typically 0.02–0.3 μm)[25] organisms consisting of little more than a strand of genetic material and a protein shell.[26] They cannot multiply outside a host, but some may survive long periods in the environment if they are provided with appropriate conditions. Any one of more than 140 enteric viruses may infect people through the digestive system. Some of these viruses cause well-known diseases, including hepatitis and meningitis; they also cause generic symptoms such as diarrhea, fever, and heart disease.[27]

There are no standards for viruses.[28] Historically, this has been justified by the small fraction of the uncountable viruses in nature that are harmful, the poorly known pathways and mechanisms by which most have their effect, and the fact that most are even more easily susceptible to chlorine than are bacteria. Among those tested, most, but not all, are easily inactivated with chlorine.

---

[24] P. Payment et al., 1991, "A randomized trial to evaluate the risk of gastrointestinal disease due to the consumption of drinking water meeting current microbiological standards," *American Journal of Public Health*, vol. 81, pp. 703–708.

[25] Krewski et al., p. 53.

[26] American Water Works Association, 1999, *Waterborne Pathogens: Manual of Water Supply Practice, M48* (Denver: American Water Works Association).

[27] Ibid.; Krewski et al., p. 54.

[28] O. Reg. 459/00 does not mention viruses. The companion O. Reg. 505/01, for "smaller water works serving designated facilities," requires the use of filtration and disinfection equipment capable of 4-log removal or inactivation of viruses. It would be better to specify one or more of the relatively resistant pathogenic viruses because "viruses" as a class have varying susceptibility to treatment.

5.5.1.3   *Bacteria*

Bacteria are small (typically 0.5–1.0 µm) single-celled organisms that are nearly ubiquitous on Earth.[29] Natural water systems contain massive communities of bacteria, most of which are free-living environmental bacteria that have no health consequences for humans. A small subset of the bacteria found in source waters may be of mammalian origin, and an even smaller subset of those is potentially pathogenic in humans.[30] Bacteria are responsible for two of the biggest historical threats to public safety through drinking water: typhoid and cholera. Although these diseases have been largely eradicated in the developed world through the disinfection of public water supplies, they are still threats in many parts of the world. However, as occurred in Walkerton, the potential exists for the bacterial contamination of drinking water to cause serious health problems in North America.

The main reservoirs for pathogenic water-borne bacteria are mammals, including humans and farm animals. Pathogenic bacteria are excreted in large numbers in the feces of mammals and work their way into source waters through surface runoff or infiltration. The ecology and health impacts of pathogenic bacteria are well described elsewhere.[31]

The regulatory requirement is that water should receive a minimum level of treatment: disinfection in the case of groundwater, chemically assisted filtration and disinfection in the case of surface water. "Disinfection" is not defined in the regulation. The Ontario Regulation 459/00 standard for pathogenic bacteria is expressed in terms of a treatment requirement if coliform bacteria, especially *E. coli*, are found in samples.[32] In essence, the operator is to increase the chlorine dose until two successive samples show no bacteria.[33]

---

[29] Krewski et al., p. 54.

[30] HDR Engineering Inc., 2001, *Handbook of Public Water Systems* (New York: John Wiley & Sons), p. 87.

[31] American Water Works Association, 1999; the Part 1 report of this Inquiry has information on the two species implicated at Walkerton – *E. coli* O157:H7 and *Campylobacter jejuni*: Ontario, Ministry of the Attorney General, 2002, *Report of the Walkerton Inquiry, Part 1: The Events of May 2000 and Related Issues* (Toronto: Queen's Printer), pp. 49–51.

[32] O. Reg. 459/00, as amended, "Drinking water protection: Larger water works."

[33] The following is included in a list of indicators of adverse water quality: "*Escherichia coli (E. coli)* or fecal coliform is detected in any required sample other than a raw water sample. (Corrective action: Increase the chlorine dose and flush the mains to ensure that a total chlorine residual of at least 1.0 mg/L or a free chlorine residual of 0.2 mg/L is achieved at all points in the affected part(s) of the distribution system. Resample and analyze. Corrective action should begin immediately and

The regulation does not oblige the water provider, even as an objective that will guide the treatment requirements, to supply water that is free of pathogenic bacteria. The regulation for small systems is likewise treatment-based but allows for new technologies by saying they must be demonstrably as good as, or better than, chlorine. Operationally, this is specified as 2-log removal or inactivation of viruses if the source is groundwater, or 4-log removal or inactivation of viruses and 3-log removal or inactivation of *Giardia* if the source is surface water.[34] No inactivation limit is set for pathogenic or other bacteria.

Recommendation 27: The Advisory Council on Standards should consider whether to replace the total coliform test with an *E. coli* test.

For a century and a half, the focus of drinking water treatment has been on bacteria. For most of that time, the approach has been to erect defences against bacteria that are known to cause gastrointestinal disease and to assume that viruses and protozoa would be equally well challenged.[35] Bacteria that spent part of their life cycle in mammalian, especially human, gut were the focus.[36] These bacteria were hard to identify, but one, *E. coli*, was a sure indicator of fecal contamination because of its enormous numbers in feces and because it has no non-fecal source.[37] However, for the better part of a century, it was hard to separate *E. coli* from other bacteria, called coliforms, which shared one specific metabolic process. Thus most standards around the world refer to coliform counts, even though there are many coliform bacteria that never pass near, or through, a mammal's intestine. Recently, better tests specific for *E. coli* have become available. It is now cheaper and quicker to measure directly the species

---

continue until *E. coli* and fecal coliforms are no longer detected in two consecutive sets of samples or as instructed by the local Medical Officer of Health.)": O. Reg. 459/00, Schedule 6.

[34] O. Reg. 505/01, "Drinking water protection – Smaller water works serving designated facilities," para. 4(3)(b); <http://www.ene.gov.on.ca/envision/WaterReg/Kit/reg505a.pdf> [accessed April 30, 2002].

[35] Authorities have long considered viruses and protozoa, but only recently have the assumptions about kill rates for *Giardia* and *Cryptosporidia* overturned longstanding practices.

[36] Virtually all the organisms that can cause water-borne gastroenteritis in humans – *Salmonella, Shigella, Campylobacter, E. coli,* and so on, as well as parasites such as *Entamoeba, Giardia, Cryptosporidia* and such viruses as hepatitis A – enter water supplies through fecal contamination.

[37] "By the late 1970s, it was established that *E. coli* was specific and abundant in human and animal feces at an average of approximately 10^9 g^{-1}": S.C. Edberg et al., 2000, "*Escherichia coli*: The best biological drinking water indicator for public health protection," *Journal of Applied Microbiology,* vol. 88, p. 109S.

of interest than the broad family of look-alike bacteria, and it is probably appropriate that regulatory standards should follow.[38]

In testing drinking water, the use of indicator organisms of some sort must remain a reality for the foreseeable future. However, the total coliform test is not efficient because of the number of non-fecal sources that can provide total coliform results.[39] This test may nevertheless have some limited value as a means for monitoring the general condition of a distribution system.

5.5.1.4   *Parasites*

Parasites are the largest of the water-borne pathogens and the leading causes of water-borne illness.[40] Most of them are larger than 3 μm in size. To put the sizes of the three types of pathogen in perspective, if viruses were the size of a marble, bacteria would be about the size of a grapefruit, and most parasites would be as big as beach balls. As with viruses and bacteria, mammals are the principal source of parasites of concern. The main parasites in drinking water are the protozoa *Giardia lamblia* (infection that leads to "beaver fever") and *Cryptosporidium parvum*;[41] several other protozoan parasites and some helminth worm eggs may be conveyed through drinking water. Protozoan parasites cause the usual array of gastrointestinal complaints. As with bacteria and viruses, infection in susceptible population groups can have much more serious health consequences.[42]

Parasites can exist outside their host for extended periods of time. Most, like *Giardia* and *Cryptosporidium*, are excreted from their hosts as cysts – dormant organisms with tough walls, which make them resistant to heat, light, and even disinfection by chlorination.

---

[38] Edberg et al.; M. Stevens, N. Ashbolt, and D. Cunliffe, 2001, "Microbial indicators of water quality – An NHMRC discussion paper," National Health and Medical Research Council, Canberra <http://www.health.gov.au/nhmrc/advice/microb.pdf> [accessed April 30, 2002]; J.B. Rose and D.J. Grimes, 2001, *Re-evaluation of Microbial Water Quality: Powerful New Tools for Detection and Risk Management* (Washington: American Academy of Microbiology).

[39] Stevens et al.

[40] American Water Works Association, 1999.

[41] HDR Engineering, p. 87.

[42] Krewski et al., pp. 57–59.

Recommendation 28: No formal maximum contaminant level for protozoa should be established until real-time tests are available. The objective, as with bacterial and viral pathogens, should be zero, and the regulations should so state; but the standard should be a treatment standard, specified in terms of log removal dependent on source water quality.

Only the provincial regulation dealing with smaller water systems, Ontario Regulation 505/01, currently says anything about protozoa, and it refers only to *Giardia*. Yet the incidence of gastrointestinal disease from *Cryptosporidium* and *Giardia* is considerable[43] because there is no practical way of detecting these organisms, or of determining their infectivity if detected, in a reasonable period of time. Small numbers – even as few as ten organisms – can give rise to disease, and a given sample from infected water may or may not contain the microbe. False positives and false negatives are prevalent in current testing methods. Even large and sophisticated operations can make serious errors: Milwaukee experienced an estimated 370,000 cases of cryptosporidiosis in 1993 (initial false negative).[44] Sydney, Australia, spent $50 million battling an epidemic that many experts now believe was merely a monitoring mistake – a series of false positives[45] – and Thunder Bay issued a boil water advisory on the basis of one report of one *Giardia* cyst in treated water.[46]

The United Kingdom has experienced a number of localized outbreaks of cryptosporidiosis, most recently in 1995 and 1997. In the aftermath of privatization, drought, and a failed legal proceeding, the United Kingdom enacted new legislation. Utilities, and their managements and directors, now face the possibility of criminal sanctions if they permit *Cryptosporidium* to contaminate the water system. The U.K. Drinking Water Inspectorate claims that its continuous and risk-based sampling techniques are workable and that storing the sampled water until the lab tests are done can obviate the risk of people drinking contaminated water while testing goes on. Many on this side

---

[43] P. Payment, 1999, "Poor efficacy of residual chlorine disinfectant in drinking water to inactivate waterborne pathogens in distribution systems," *Canadian Journal of Microbiology*, vol. 45, pp. 709–715; Payment et al., 1991.

[44] N.J. Hoxie et al., 1997, "Cryptosporidiosis-associated mortality following a massive waterborne outbreak in Milwaukee, Wisconsin," *American Journal of Public Health*, vol. 87, no. 12, pp. 2032–2035; various authors, 1993, "Fatal neglect," *Milwaukee Journal* (special reprint), September 19–26.

[45] J.L. Clancy, 2000, "Sydney's 1998 water quality crisis," *Journal of the American Water Works Association*, vol. 92, no. 3, pp. 55–66.

[46] D.W. Scott, 2002, letter to the Walkerton Inquiry, January 30.

of the Atlantic are skeptical, and a debate continues.[47] In North America, the weight of professional opinion is that the best safeguard against *Cryptosporidium* is provided by filtration rather than direct measurement. This relatively large (>4 μm, for the most part) parasite can be removed through chemically assisted filtration or through the use of membrane filters. More recently, its susceptibility to ultraviolet radiation has led to new treatment possibilities. For the present at least, the preferable approach is that the standard for *Cryptosporidium* should be based upon validated performance criteria for an effective treatment method, rather than specifying the unmeasurable absence of this particular microbe.

5.5.2 Standards for Chronic Risks

An enormous array of chemicals may be present in drinking water sources. Metals such as lead, cadmium, or chromium; organics including benzene, toluene, vinyl chloride, pesticides, herbicides, and some pharmaceuticals; radiological contaminants like radon or uranium; and even the by-products of drinking water disinfection may all be present to one degree or another. Possible sources include industry, landfills, urban runoff, sewage disposal, agriculture, atmospheric transport, and nature itself: cyanotoxin, for example, is produced by blue-green algae. Ontario Regulation 459/00 specifies maximum acceptable concentration (MAC) levels for 54 chemicals, 14 natural radionuclides, and 64 artificial radionuclides. In addition, there are interim maximum acceptable concentrations (IMACs) for another 22 chemicals. Appendix A to this report compares the limits specified in Ontario Regulation 459/00 with those in the federal-provincial *Guidelines* and the standards set by the U.S. Environmental Protection Agency, Australia, and the World Health Organization.

This Inquiry commissioned a team from the Canadian Network of Centres of Excellence in Toxicology to report on the relative risks of various types of potentially toxic contaminants in Ontario drinking water generally.[48] The brief was to quantify, as best as available data allow, the relative risks associated with

---

[47] At the AWWA annual meeting in June 2001, Michael Rouse, the head of the Drinking Water Inspectorate, defended his position stoutly. He claimed that continuous filter sampling of risky sources, strict chain of control, interim storage, and regulation-induced diligence on the part of privatized utilities had effectively eliminated *Cryptosporidium* from U.K. drinking water, and it was therefore sensible to have a regulation banning the microbe. British water providers also rely on filtration.

[48] L. Ritter et al. There are, of course, specific local contamination concerns, such as the NDMA problem at Elmira, Ontario, which was discussed at the town hall meeting in Kitchener-Waterloo on March 22, 2001.

toxic contaminants that have had demonstrated or potential effects on human health through exposure from drinking water. Some chemicals ranked low on the risk scale simply because scientific information was lacking. Those most likely to repay investment in further research were nitrates and the pesticide atrazine in rural drinking water wells, and lead and disinfection by-products in municipal systems. An expert meeting in April 2001 added fluoride, water treatment chemicals, endocrine-disrupting substances, and pharmaceuticals to the list as chemicals that should receive closer scrutiny.

The current levels are set on the basis of tests of elevated levels of the contaminant in question on laboratory animals – usually rats or mice that have been selected to be especially susceptible to possible effects. A level at which there is no observable adverse effect is determined. At this point, safety factors are entered: an order of magnitude (factor of ten) for interspecies differences in susceptibility, a correction for body mass, perhaps another order of magnitude to ensure that especially susceptible humans are not affected, and so forth. For carcinogenic chemicals, the aim is to strike a standard that would assure less than one statistically expected additional case in a population of 100,000 over a lifetime, a level below the capacity of epidemiological analysis to measure. The final recommendation for a MAC is thus usually explicitly precautionary. Nevertheless, new research sometimes results in a need to rethink a standard, and there will be substances for which, because of scientific uncertainty, further precaution is required.

5.5.2.1   *Chemical Hazards*

Arsenic: A case in point is the current controversy in the United States over arsenic.[49] The old standard, 50 parts per billion (ppb), was a rough rule of thumb struck in 1942 by the U.S. Public Health Service. In recent years, concerns have arisen that the standard is too lax. Congress asked the U.S. Environmental Protection Agency to take action, and the National Academy of Sciences was asked to provide advice. Its view was that a lower level was justified. The controversy was over how low: 20, 10, 5, and 3 ppb were all suggested. The outgoing administration made 10 ppb the limit in January 2001 – a decision that was suspended by the new administration. After an extensive review, the U.S. Environmental Protection Agency reiterated the 10

---

[49] "Senate supports tougher arsenic standard" <www.safedrinkingwater.com/alerts/alert080201.htm> [accessed August 2, 2001]. The U.S. Environmental Protection Agency's Web site has exhaustive coverage: see <www.epa.gov/safewater/arsenic.html>.

ppb limit, and the administration confirmed it. An issue arises because the expense of achieving arsenic removal at the lower end of the range is large, and some argue that the expected gain in public health is small.[50] We can expect the Federal–Provincial Subcommittee on Drinking Water to take careful note of the U.S. debate and the scientific evidence underlying it and to propose any necessary change to the Canadian *Guidelines* IMAC level of 25 ppb (0.025 mg/L). Ontario is not known to have arsenic problems, even though arsenic is often a by-product of gold mining and occurs elsewhere in groundwater in Canada. Recent news articles have reported elevated levels of arsenic in groundwater in Saskatchewan and Newfoundland. If the proceedings of the subcommittee and the Advisory Council on Standards are open and accessible, as I recommend, the public will be able to participate in the debate as it sees fit.

Arsenic has dominated the debate on inorganic chemicals in recent years. The debate has been driven by the enormous tragedy of water-borne disease arising from groundwater contaminated with arsenic in Bangladesh[51] and by the U.S. political and regulatory agenda.[52] However, a number of other chemicals are being evaluated on a preventive basis, notably hexavalent chromium, boron, vanadium, radium, cyanide, bromate, and perchlorate. These chemicals are usually present, if at all, only in very small concentrations, which poses difficult engineering questions. Ion exchange methods and enhanced membrane treatment are the focal points of much current work. The U.S. Environmental Protection Agency has a formal process in which larger water systems screen for the presence of a long list of suspect chemicals.[53]

Lead: Lead in drinking water sources can occur naturally at low levels (up to 0.04mg/L) as a result of geological deposits. This level can be increased as a

---

[50] As an example, at the June 2001 American Water Works Association annual meeting in Washington, there was a lively debate between U.S. EPA officials and local utility operators, encapsulated by one small-town water provider from the U.S. Southwest who noted that the agency's then-proposed standard of 5 ppb would require the expenditure of several thousand dollars per household per year to prevent less than one statistically predicted but empirically unmeasurable cancer in 250 years. He said he did not expect his mayor to agree to make the investment. See also F.J. Frost et al., 2002, "Evaluation of costs and benefits of a lower arsenic MCL," *Journal of the American Water Works Association*, vol. 94, no. 3, pp. 71–80.

[51] The Bangladesh–West Bengal case of naturally occurring arsenic in groundwater is extensively covered on the Internet. See, for example, <www.angelfire.com/ak/medinet.arsenic.html>, <www.unicef.org/arsenic>, and <phys4.Harvard.edu/~wilson/arsenic_project_main.html>.

[52] National Research Council, Subcommittee on Arsenic in Drinking Water, 1999, *Arsenic in Drinking Water* (Washington, DC: National Academy Press), c. 4.

[53] United States Environmental Protection Agency, 2001, "Reference guide for the unregulated contaminant monitoring regulation," EPA 815-R-01-023 (Washington, DC).

result of activities such as mining.[54] However, the principal source of lead in drinking water is lead in the distribution system. Lead piping used to be a common component of drinking water systems, and in many older systems today there remain some lead components. Lead is also much more soluble in soft water than in hard. It is therefore not surprising that there are some instances of elevated lead concentrations in distributed drinking water in Ontario.

Acute effects from lead exposure are rare. Its toxicity almost always occurs as a result of chronic exposure. The effects include a wide variety of physiological complications, including cognitive difficulties, kidney dysfunction, anemia, reproductive problems, and delayed neurological and physiological development. The U.S. Environmental Protection Agency classifies lead as a probable human carcinogen,[55] although a 1982 study by the U.S. National Academy of Sciences[56] concluded there was little evidence of carcinogenicity, mutagenicity, or teratogenicity. The effects of lead are particularly serious in children, where exposure can lead to mental retardation or death. Most exposure to lead, however, occurs through ambient air and food.[57]

Nitrates: Nitrates are found in concentrations exceeding the levels specified in Ontario Regulation 459/00 in many wells in rural Ontario. One study indicated that 14% of Ontario's rural wells contain nitrates in concentrations exceeding the MAC set out in the regulation.[58] Nitrates are also found in treated municipal water, but they rarely exceed provincial standards.[59]

The principal sources of nitrates in water are runoff from fertilized agricultural lands, feedlots, municipal and industrial waste discharges, landfill leachate, and decaying vegetation.[60] Nitrates normally occur in concentrations of less than 2 mg/L in surface water and of up to 20 mg/L in groundwater. They may be found in much higher concentrations in shallow aquifers polluted by sewage

---

[54] United States Environmental Protection Agency, 2001.

[55] J. DeZuane, 1997, *Handbook of Drinking Water Quality*, 2nd ed. (New York: John Wiley & Sons), p. 80.

[56] DeZuane, p. 83.

[57] Ibid.

[58] M.J. Goss, D.A.J. Barry, and D.L. Rudolph, 1998, "Contamination in Ontario farmstead domestic wells and its association with agriculture: 1. Results from drinking water wells," *Journal of Contaminant Hydrology*, vol. 32, pp. 267–293; cited in Ritter et al., p. 85.

[59] Ritter et al., p. 69.

[60] HDR Engineering, p. 47.

or the intensive use of fertilizers.[61] Nitrates are highly soluble in water and, as such, are not filtered out as water percolates through the ground.

Nitrate contamination above the regulation's limit of 10 mg/L is most common in agricultural areas,[62] and the presence of nitrates in groundwater is an important indicator of potential contamination from agricultural sources.

Although nitrates do not directly affect human health, they are rapidly reduced to nitrites in the gastrointestinal tract. Nitrites then bind with hemoglobin, the oxygen-carrying molecule of the blood, converting it to methemoglobin, which is not capable of carrying oxygen. In adults this does not appear to have any significant effect, but methemoglobinemia can cause serious problems in young children and lead to "blue baby syndrome," a potentially fatal condition. The difference in susceptibility may be due either to the small amount of nitrate consumed relative to body weight in adults[63] or to the fact that children under three years of age convert all ingested nitrates to nitrites in the gastrointestinal tract, whereas older people convert only about 10%.[64] There is also some indication that nitrates in high concentrations may react with other substances to create potentially carcinogenic compounds (notably nitrosamines), although the U.S. Environmental Protection Agency, one of the leading agencies examining issues of this nature, has yet to make any determination in this matter.

Fluorides: Fluorides are found in fertilizers, chemicals, and aluminum smelting, coal burning, and nuclear power plants.[65] The Federal–Provincial Subcommittee on Drinking Water revisited its guideline in 1996. Two health conditions are associated with excess fluoride. Fluorosis mottles young teeth and, in severe cases, results in enamel erosion and tooth pain, which can impair chewing. Long-term exposure to fluorides may result in skeletal fluorosis, a progressive disease in which bone density increases. Bones become more brittle and joints may stiffen, leading to reduced mobility and skeletal deformation in extreme cases.[66]

---

[61] DeZuane, p. 89.
[62] M.J. Goss et al., 2002, "The management of manure in Ontario with respect to water quality," Walkerton Inquiry Commissioned Paper 6, p. 9.
[63] HDR Engineering, pp. 47–48.
[64] DeZuane, p. 89.
[65] Health Canada, "It's your health: Fluorides and human health" <http://www.hc-sc.gc.ca/english/iyh/fluorides.html> [accessed April 30, 2002]; G. Glasser, "Fluorine pollution" <http://home.att.net/~gtigerclaw/fluorine_pollution.html> [accessed April 30, 2002].
[66] Health Canada.

There is a long-standing debate over the fluoration of water.[67] Most water providers in Ontario add fluoride, where necessary, to maintain the regulation's recommended level of 1.0 ± 0.2 mg/L, "the optimum level for control of tooth decay."[68]

Chemicals Used in Water Treatment: The chemicals used in water treatment (see Chapter 6) can, in large enough quantities, cause health problems of their own. Regulations, and standards such as those set by the U.S. National Sanitation Foundation, provide for the maintenance of chemical doses below adverse health levels. However, accidents happen: in 1998 in Camelford, Cornwall, United Kingdom, 20 tonnes of aluminium sulphate were accidentally dumped into the wrong tank at a treatment works. The consumption of contaminated water affected 20,000 households; the effects ranged from mouth ulcers to vomiting and rashes.[69]

5.5.2.2   *Disinfection By-products*

The chemicals added to water for disinfection can form disinfection by-products (DBPs). Chlorine may react with dissolved organic material in water to form trihalomethanes (THMs) and haloacetic acids.[70] At high-dose levels, some of these chemicals, when fed to mice that are bred to develop cancers easily, are carcinogenic. Clearly, DBPs should be minimized in finished water; equally clearly, doing without disinfection to prevent the occurrence of DBPs is substituting an acute risk for a relatively remote, chronic risk. The Peruvian tragedy of 1991, when officials reduced disinfection in a manner that may have contributed to infecting 320,000 people with cholera, which resulted in 3,000 deaths, shows the importance of keeping risks in proper perspective.[71] The balance of evidence is that Ontario standards for THMs have been set at

---

[67] Two examples of the opposing views of fluoridation are at <http://www.fluoridation.com> and <http://www.all-natural.com/fleffect.html>.

[68] O. Reg. 459/00, Schedule 4, note b.

[69] A draft report from the committee investigating the incident is due in 2002: <http://news.bbc.co.uk/hi/english/uk/newsid_1490000/1490142.stm> [accessed April 30, 2002].

[70] Canada, Department of National Health and Welfare, Environmental Health Directorate, Health Protection Branch, 1995, *A National Survey of Chlorinated Disinfection By-Products in Canadian Drinking Water* (Ottawa, Supply and Services Canada), p. 7. See <http://www.hc-sc.gc.ca/ehp/ehd/catalogue/bch_pubs/95ehd197.htm> [accessed April 30, 2002].

[71] C. Anderson, 1991, "Cholera epidemic traced to risk miscalculation," *Nature*, vol. 354, November 28; Pan American Health Organization, 2002, *Cholera: Number of Cases and Deaths in the Americas (1991–2001)* (Washington, DC).

quite safe levels,[72] but the human health effects of other DBPs have yet to be assessed.

In addition to a review of old standards on the basis of new evidence, there is a need to provide a first round of examination for many chemicals, particularly when a standard has been struck on the basis of the precautionary principle, in advance of experimental evidence. Cases in point include bromate, aluminum, and uranium. Ontario should contribute to the national effort, and the Ministry of the Environment (MOE) laboratory, in particular, should have as one of its missions the ability to provide authoritative advice to the provincial government on the scientific basis for standards setting.

A greater level of research effort should be devoted to DBPs of all sorts, not just those arising from chlorination. The economies of scale are considerable, however, and the effort would make the most sense if it were mounted cooperatively by many nations. Human susceptibility to toxic substances is similar everywhere. Canadians need both to contribute to the worldwide effort and to keep fully abreast of the work of others. Given the magnitude of the issue, I am of the view that Canada's contribution is best coordinated by Health Canada, working together with international bodies, leading institutions in other countries, the granting councils, the National Research Council, and the provinces. Not all provinces have the resources to be much more than consumers of this research, but this is certainly not the case with Ontario.

5.5.2.3 *Radiological Hazards*

Most countries specify maximum acceptable concentrations of contaminants or their equivalent in terms of an aggregate radiation exposure. Ontario, following the model of the federal-provincial *Guidelines*, specifies individual limits for a large number of natural and manufactured radionuclides as well as an aggregate limit. See Appendix A to this report.

---

[72] S.E. Hrudey, 1999, *Assessment of Human Health Risks in Relation to Exposure to THMs in Drinking Water* (Toronto: Pollution Probe).

5.5.3   Operational Standards

A third group of standards is related to treatment and distribution techniques. For obvious engineering reasons, water should not corrode the materials through which it flows. It should be neither too acidic nor too alkaline. It should not be so efficient an electrolyte that it promotes unwanted galvanic reactions among the metals used in water treatment and distribution systems.

Recommendation 29: The provincial government should seek the advice of the Advisory Council on Standards regarding the desirability of a turbidity limit that is lower than the limit specified in the federal–provincial *Guidelines*.

Turbidity is important because microbes can shelter themselves on, within, or behind (in the case of ultraviolet radiation disinfection) suspended particles. Moreover, to the degree that the particles have an organic origin, their downstream reaction with chlorine will not only reduce the chlorine residual but may also produce unacceptable levels of DBPs. The current standard of 1 NTU[73] is an example of the Federal–Provincial Subcommittee on Drinking Water lagging behind good practice among the better water providers, most of whom now routinely produce water at 0.3 NTU or better. Turbidity by itself has little meaning for public health. Rather, it is the consequences of turbidity that are worrisome: the lower the level, the better.

5.5.4   Aesthetic Standards

Finally, there are purely aesthetic standards. People prefer to avoid the smells associated with summer algal blooms or the tea colour of tannic northern waters. Thus, standards are set for taste, odour, and colour. These standards are not without importance from a public health standpoint: if their tap water is unappealing, people may turn to other, less secure, sources, with consequent increases in public health risk. Furthermore, aesthetic problems can indicate other water quality problems. Foul water is never acceptable.

---

[73] "Nephelometric turbidity unit: A unit for expressing the cloudiness (turbidity) of a sample," in J.M. Symons, L.C. Bradley, Jr., and T.C. Cleveland, 2000, *The Drinking Water Dictionary* (Denver: American Water Works Association), p. 495.

5.5.5   Problems in Setting Standards

In the case of drinking water safety, the pure model for setting standards implies that relationships between the amount of exposure to a drinking water contaminant (the dose) and the illness caused (the response) are known. In practice, a number of problems arise; the following are two examples.[74] First, the necessary experiments must usually be performed with animal models, but the differences between these laboratory species and humans can, and have been shown to, lead to wrong conclusions about whether a given contaminant can actually cause a given disease. For instance, chloroform in drinking water is no longer regarded by experts to be a serious cancer risk, after almost 25 years of suspicion.[75] There are also contaminants that distress humans but not the animal models.[76] Second, the laboratory animals must be exposed to high doses of contaminants to ensure that some measurable response (to be used to estimate risk) will occur with a reasonable number of experimental animals. An experimental population of 100 animals at each exposure level, for instance, can only reveal a risk of 1 in 100 or more. Attaining a high degree of statistical certainty may require unrealistically large sample populations when the contaminant is rare or the effect small. Thus the laboratory budget decision itself is an expression of relative values.

These features of dose-response determination inevitably introduce major uncertainties. Obvious ethical considerations preclude deliberate human testing,[77] although epidemiological evidence and accident case histories are sometimes able to provide key inferences about human health risk. An even more serious problem arises when the existence of a causal relationship between exposure and health is unknown – when uncertainty about causation itself

---

[74] D. Hattis and D. Kennedy, 1986, "Assessing risks from health hazards: An imperfect science," *Technology Review*, May/June, pp. 60–71.

[75] F. Pontius, 2000, "Chloroform: Science, policy and politics," *Journal of the American Water Works Association*, vol. 92, no. 5, p. 12.

[76] Odours and other sensory irritants can be severe sources of human distress, for example, but cannot be assessed by any animal models.

[77] The U.S. Environmental Protection Agency was recently criticized for proposing the use of human experiments in setting pesticide limits. Manufacturers who felt that these more accurate tests would allow higher pesticide doses favoured the move. The agency sent the matter to the National Academy of Science for a report on the ethical and scientific issues involved (*New York Times*, December 15, 2001). Human experimentation is not allowed for these purposes in Canada; drinking water standards will continue to be set by using animal models.

makes uncertainty about the form of the dose-response function pale in comparison.[78]

5.6   Emerging Issues

Ontario has no established system for examining candidates for regulation and does not mention the standard-setting process on its Web site. However, both the Federal–Provincial Subcommittee on Drinking Water and the U.S. Environmental Protection Agency publish priority lists of contaminants that are candidates for regulation.[79] Ontario does, however, have a monitoring program that can help to identify emerging issues. The Drinking Water Surveillance Program (DWSP), undertaken by the MOE Environmental Monitoring and Reporting Branch, Environmental Science and Standards Division, monitors trends and contaminant levels for a wide variety of parameters, improving our knowledge of new contaminants and supporting standards and policy development. The program is not mandatory, but as of 1997, it consisted of 145 municipal waterworks, serving 88% of the population.[80]

5.6.1   New Pathogens

New pathogens arise from time to time. Sometimes a microbe is discovered that has been quietly making people ill for a long time; at other times, a mutant form of an organism emerges. Microbes are continually evolving, just as humans and other animals are continually developing antibodies and other defences against them.[81] Some scientists view the O157:H7 strain of *E. coli* as biologically novel. Cyanobacterial and algal toxins are beginning to receive attention. There is little to be said about this as a matter of public policy, except to emphasize the necessity for a robust, long-term research effort.

---

[78] S.E. Hrudey, 1998, "Quantitative cancer risk assessment: Pitfalls and progress," *Issues in Environmental Science and Technology,* vol. 9, pp. 57–90.

[79] See <www.hc-sc.gc.ca/ehp/ehd/bch/water_quality/priority_lst.htm>; <www.epa.gov/safewater/ccl/cclfs.html> [accessed April 30, 2002].

[80] Krewski et al., p. 8.

[81] J. Diamond, 1997, *Guns, Germs and Steel* (New York: Norton); T. McMichael, 2001, *Human Frontiers, Environments and Disease: Past Patterns, Uncertain Futures* (Cambridge: Cambridge University Press). The latter is reviewed in D. Morens, 2001, "Certain diseases, uncertain explanations," *Science,* vol. 294, p. 1658.

Treatment for protozoan pathogens has been a major topic of professional debate in the past few years. This will likely continue. There will be more discussion of water-borne viruses, which as a group are poorly understood. More research is needed, not only to understand the risks they pose to people, but also to gain basic information about their sources and persistence in raw and finished waters.

5.6.2   Chemicals

The case of arsenic has been discussed above. Other chemicals that bear a closer degree of scrutiny for possible regulatory action as drinking water constituents are water-soluble pesticides and herbicides, certain industrial chemicals, nitrates (especially in agricultural areas), and the large family of chemicals, including human and veterinary antibiotics and other pharmaceuticals, that may disrupt endocrine systems in humans and other animals, in addition to other public health concerns.

5.6.2.1   *Pesticides and Herbicides*

Pesticides and herbicides are regulated by Health Canada's Pest Management Regulatory Agency, which follows the classic process of testing the substances on laboratory animals and establishing a human threshold at least an order of magnitude lower than the level at which no effects are observed in the test animals. Some pesticides and herbicides are long-lived and accumulate in the body – a substantial reason for great care. On the other hand, the worst culprits, the bioaccumulative ones, appear to be dangerous precisely because they are soluble in fats and nerve tissue and only sparingly or not at all soluble in water. The likelihood is that Canadians are more exposed to these chemicals directly and through food than through water supplies.

The only pesticide identified by one study as being a potential problem in Ontario drinking water was atrazine, detected "in 6.6 and 10.5% of approximately 1,300 domestic wells sampled in the winter and summer respectively" of Ontario farm wells surveyed in 1998.[82] This is a small number, but it indicates that atrazine may be a health risk in some parts of Ontario.

---

[82] Goss et al., 1998, cited in Ritter et al., 2002, p. 74.

Atrazine is a herbicide commonly used on corn and soybeans. The effects of chronic exposure to atrazine are not well documented.[83] However, the U.S. Environmental Protection Agency

> has found atrazine to potentially cause the following health effects when people are exposed to it at levels above the MCL [3 ppb] for relatively short periods of time: congestion of heart, lungs and kidneys; low blood pressure; muscle spasms; weight loss; damage to adrenal glands ... Atrazine has the potential to cause the following effects from a lifetime exposure at levels above the MCL: weight loss, cardiovascular damage, retinal and some muscle degeneration; cancer.[84]

The interim maximum acceptable concentration for atrazine in Ontario is 0.005 mg/L (5 ppb).

5.6.2.2   *Industrial Chemicals*

There is a wide range of industrial chemicals about which relatively little is known, at least insofar as these chemicals may be delivered in water. Lipid-soluble chemicals are not the first concern for water systems for the reasons mentioned above, but chemicals such as NDMA (nitrosodimethylamine),[85] TCE (tetrachloroethylene, used for drycleaning and industrial degreasing), MTBE (methyl-*tert*-butyl-ether, an octane enhancer), and perchlorate (an oxidant for rocket fuels) have all been matters of at least local interest in parts of the United States.[86] The Sierra Legal Defence Fund, as mentioned, has drawn

---

[83] DeZuane, pp. 268–269; <http://www.horizononline.com/MSDS_Sheets/968.txt> [accessed April 30, 2002].

[84] United States Environmental Protection Agency, Office of Water, 2002, *Technical Factsheet on Atrazine*, National Primary Drinking Water Regulation, Washington, DC <www.epa.gov/safewater/dwh/t-soc/atrazine.html> [accessed April 30, 2002].

[85] For NDMA, Ontario sets an IMAC of 0.000009 mg/L. NDMA is not mentioned in the federal–provincial *Guidelines,* which illustrates why Ontario needs its own expertise in risk assessment: NDMA is a serious, although localized, matter.

[86] The U.S. EPA's Unregulated Contaminant Monitoring Regulation requires large utilities to assist in identifying candidates for future regulation by screening three lists of possible contaminants. The difference among the lists is the degree to which analytic methods have been developed. United States Environmental Protection Agency, 2001, *Reference Guide for the Unregulated Contaminants Monitoring Regulation,* 815-R-01-023 (Washington, DC: Environmental Protection Agency), s. 1.2.

attention to TCE in the Ottawa River and to the existence of a less restrictive guideline for TCE in Canada than in the United States. The *Guidelines* do not currently have a maximum acceptable concentration for NDMA, MTBE, or perchlorate, but Ontario has an interim maximum acceptable concentration of 0.000009 mg/L for NDMA, and MTBE is on the current priority list for development of a federal–provincial guideline. TCE is subject to a maximum acceptable concentration of 0.05 mg/L in Ontario, but the World Health Organization and the United States have not yet developed a standard. Although rocket fuel intrusions into groundwater are unlikely to become a Canadian concern, the other chemicals may occur in specific locations in Ontario. Elmira, Ontario, is the unfortunate locus of serious groundwater pollution by industrial NDMA, which is water-soluble, able to penetrate skin, and known to be carcinogenic at extremely low doses.[87]

5.6.2.3   *Endocrine-Disrupting Substances*

A large and ill-defined class of pharmaceutical and other chemicals are suspected of disrupting animal endocrine systems.[88] The endocrine system consists of glands and organs that release chemical messages in the form of hormones to other parts of the body. These glands and hormones are fundamental to growth, reproduction, and behaviour. Endocrine-disrupting substances (EDS) either prevent the hormone from being released, block the hormone receptor in a cell, or mimic the hormone. These "could lead to irreversible effects in the organism or its offspring."[89] Some of these chemicals (e.g., the artificial estrogens in birth control pills) pass untransformed through the human body and are not destroyed or sequestered in sewage treatment systems. They thus pass into rivers, lakes, and ultimately oceans. There is some suspicion among fisheries

---

[87] S. Bryant, Walkerton Inquiry (Kitchener-Waterloo Town Hall Meeting, March 22, 2001), transcript pp. 197–199; see also E.O. Frind, D.L Rudolph, and J.W. Molson, 2001, "The case for groundwater protection in Ontario: Results of the workshop held at the University of Waterloo, May 1, 2001 – A contribution to the Walkerton Inquiry, Phase II," Walkerton Inquiry Submission.
[88] United States National Academy of Sciences, *Hormonally Active Agents in the Environment* (Washington, DC). See also <www.emcom.ca>, a service of the Institute for Population Health at the University of Ottawa. A recent workshop surveyed the state of research in the United States: P. Weyer, G. Parkin, and D. Riley, 2001, *Endocrine Disruptors and Pharmaceuticals in Drinking Water,* Project 2598 (Denver: American Water Works Association Research Foundation).
[89] M. Servos, G.J. Van Der Kraak, and M. Wade, 2001, "Introductory remarks: Scientific assessment of endocrine disrupting substances in the Canadian environment," *Water Quality Research Journal of Canada*, vol. 36, no. 2, p. 171 (a special issue of the journal dedicated to EDS in Canada).

and aquatic ecosystem scientists that these chemicals, even in minuscule doses, may cause reproductive anomalies in fish.

There are probably tens of thousands of EDS, or hormonally active agents, as the U.S. National Research Council calls them.[90] Some of these are well-known persistent organic chemicals. Although maximum contaminant levels have been established in the United States for several suspected EDS,[91] problems exist on several levels. Some EDS are difficult to detect at the levels required to produce adverse results. Also, their effects in the human body are slow and might not be manifested in the affected individual but in that individual's offspring, and perhaps not until the offspring mature. This slow emergence of symptoms makes the collection of scientific evidence about EDS difficult.

To date, research has mainly focused on estrogen look-alikes. Current research is concentrating on how individual substances might affect various hormonal relationships. This research is being undertaken globally. In Canada, a federal working group has been established whose terms of reference instruct it to "identify knowledge gaps from a Canadian perspective, and anticipate international developments that may influence Canadian policy."[92]

Endocrine-disrupting substances and links with human health will continue to be an area of research, both with regard to the environment as a whole and in the water industry in particular.[93] Water providers must keep up with scientific research and disseminate this information among their employees. Potential risks and treatment should be evaluated on an individual plant basis, as techniques to monitor and remove the substances are developed. Furthermore, treatment plants must communicate with the public regarding both the potential risks and the measures being implemented to mitigate them.[94]

---

[90] United States National Research Council, Committee on Hormonally Active Agents in the Environment, 2000, *Hormonally Active Agents in the Environment* (Washington, DC: National Academy Press), c. 2.

[91] American Water Works Association, 2000, *Endocrine Disruptors* <http://www.awwa.org/endocrine> [accessed April 29, 2001].

[92] M. Servos et al., 2001, "A Canadian perspective on endocrine disrupting substances in the environment," *Water Quality Research Journal of Canada*, vol. 36, no. 2, p. 331.

[93] Foundation for Water Research, 1999, *Exposure to Endocrine Disruptors Via Materials in Contact with Drinking Water*, Report No. DWI0809 <http://www.fwr.org/> [accessed May 3, 2002].

[94] R. Rhodes Trussell, 2001, "Endocrine disruptors and the water industry," *Journal of the American Water Works Association*, vol. 93, no. 2, pp. 58–65.

5.7   Standards Setting in Some Other Countries

The Australian Productivity Commission has most helpfully published a detailed comparison of standards-setting processes in Australia, the United States, Canada, New Zealand, England and Wales, France, and the European Union.[95] Following is a summary of some features that may be relevant to the discussion in Ontario.

5.7.1   United States

Drinking water standards are established as part of the *Safe Drinking Water Act*.[96] The standards apply to public water systems that have a minimum of 15 service connections or that supply more than 25 people. The U.S. Environmental Protection Agency is responsible for establishing and implementing these standards, although implementation is usually devolved to the tribal or state level, often with the agency's financial assistance.

Standards can be primary or secondary: primary standards are legally enforceable, whereas secondary standards are a guideline for aesthetic effects that can be made legally enforceable at the state level, if required. Primary standards are applied to contaminants with known or suspected adverse health effects. They may be based on a maximum concentration limit (MCL) approach or a treatment technique approach. They come into effect three to five years after being established. The United States has almost completed a new codification of its primary surface water standard, the Long-Term Stage 2 Enhanced Surface Water Treatment Rule, which will come into effect over the next several years.[97]

Before a standard is set, water problems are identified and prioritized. Substances are identified in a National Drinking Water Contaminant Candidate List (CCL), last published in 1998. On a five-year cycle, substances are prioritized, and five substances are examined in detail to see whether they warrant a primary standard; if so, a standard is drafted. The standard is based on scientific evidence

---

[95] Australia, Productivity Commission, 2000 <www.pc.gov.au/research/benchmrk/drink> [accessed April 30, 2002]. For the World Health Organization, the United States, and the state of New York, see DeZuane.

[96] See <www.epa.gov/OGWDW/sdwa/sdwa.html> [accessed April 30, 2002].

[97] M.A. Scharfenaker, 2002, "Draft LT2ESWTR out of the box," *Journal of the American Water Works Association*, vol. 94, no. 2, pp. 24–37.

as well as a broad technological assessment that includes the presence of the contaminant in the environment, risk assessment, detection technology, and removal feasibility, as well as the impacts of the standard and variations of it on health, utilities, and the economy. Within each five-year cycle, 30 unregulated contaminants are identified for monitoring by systems that serve more than 100,000 people. At the end of the cycle, the CCL is updated. Meanwhile, on a six-year cycle, existing standards are revisited and updated as necessary.

A maximum contaminant level goal (MCLG) is established by the U.S. Environmental Protection Agency (U.S. EPA) as an unenforceable guideline. This is the level at which health effects do not, or are not expected to, occur. Since the MCLG is based purely on health, it does not always coincide with technical feasibility. In these cases, the MCL is established as close to the MCLG as possible. If the MCLG is unattainable, a treatment technique standard may be established.

Once a standard has been drafted, an economic analysis is undertaken to ensure that the benefits justify the costs. A standard can be adjusted for certain system types so that the costs are justified by the risk reduction benefits. For all standards except microbial, variances can be granted to systems serving fewer than 3,300 people at a state level, if they cannot afford to comply with a rule and if they install U.S. EPA-approved technology to minimize risks. A state can grant variances to systems serving up to 10,000 people with U.S. EPA approval. Exemption periods from standards can also be granted to find alternative funding sources, but at the end of the period, the system is expected to be in full compliance. There is an obligation for the U.S. EPA, particularly in the case of small systems, to identify point-of-use or point-of-entry and low-cost options, such as modular systems, to attain standards. The U.S. EPA has a duty to identify affordable technologies that reduce contaminant levels and protect public health.

Public input is solicited throughout the standards-setting process. A key platform for this is the National Drinking Water Advisory Council.[98] Public participation is solicited at public meetings and through comments on postings on the Federal

---

[98] A 15-member committee consisting of five members of the general public, five representatives from private organizations concerned with water hygiene and supply, and five representatives from state and local agencies. Two of the representatives for private organizations have to represent rural systems. The council was formed under the *Safe Drinking Water Act* and advises the U.S. EPA on all matters relating to drinking water: National Drinking Water Advisory Council <http://www.epa.gov/safewater/ndwac/charter.html> [accessed April 30, 2002].

Register. Special meetings are held to obtain input from specific target groups, such as small businesses, minority groups, and low-income communities.

The U.S. system of full public disclosure and wide-open debate, mandated under law, can be studied by Ontarians who are interested in continuously improving standards and performance.

5.7.2 England and Wales

The European Union (EU) has incorporated World Health Organization guidelines into its *Drinking Water Directive 98/83/EC*. Enforcement is through national legislation, which must be established by a certain compliance date. In the United Kingdom, standards beyond those dictated by the EU are developed under the *Water Industry Act* (1991). A regulatory impact statement is required for standards other than those directed by the EU, as in the case for *Cryptosporidium*.

Britain's unique *Cryptosporidium* legislation arose at least in part from a failed legal proceeding (see section 5.5.1.4 of this report). In 1995, about 600 people in a town in South Devon were infected with water-borne *Cryptosporidium*. The Drinking Water Inspectorate prosecuted the water company for the event but was unsuccessful: epidemiological evidence was deemed hearsay. The *Cryptosporidium* legislation came into force in 1999 as the Water Supply (Water Quality) (Amendment) Regulations.[99] Operating agencies must perform a *Cryptosporidium* risk analysis, and if they are found to be at risk, the companies must implement a stringent monitoring program that demands continuous sampling via inline filters. Treated water cannot contain more than 1 oöcyst in 10 L of water. Failing to meet this standard is considered a criminal offence.

This is an interesting approach, but not one I would recommend for Ontario. The standards required for criminal prosecution imply extremely low levels of measurement error and a large investment in documentation, chain of custody, and the like that could better be spent on quality upgrades by water providers and on inspection and enforcement on a civil basis by the MOE.

---

[99] See <http://www.dwi.gov.uk/regs/si1524/index.htm> [accessed April 30, 2002].

5.7.3   Australia

In Australia, guidelines are developed at the Commonwealth level. A joint committee of the National Health and Medical Research Council (NHMRC) and the Agriculture and Resource Management Council of Australia and New Zealand established the current version of the guidelines in 1996. Specialist panels under this committee presented reports on micro-organisms, organic and inorganic chemicals, and radiological and physical parameters. The panels included members from universities, the NHMRC, utilities, and private industry. Territories and states are responsible for implementing these guidelines and can adopt them as standards. Various regions adopt different versions of the guidelines.

The guidelines are based on the World Health Organization's 1993 guidelines and "provide a framework for identifying acceptable drinking water quality, emphasising flexibility and community consultation."[100] They are meant to be used as part of the management framework approach to water quality. Multiple barriers are intended to constitute a comprehensive treatment system. From an Ontario perspective, the Australian "rolling revision" process is notable for, among other things, its inclusion of non-governmental people in the process and the provision of a reasoned response to commentary from the public.[101]

---

[100] Australia, Productivity Commission, p. 170.
[101] See <www.waterquality.crc.org.au/guideRR.htm> [accessed April 30, 2002].

Chapter 6   Drinking Water Treatment Technologies

Contents

Chapter 6   Drinking Water Treatment Technologies

6.1   Introduction

Part 2 of this Inquiry focuses on safe water for Ontario's future, which largely involves managing water supply systems and the policy and regulatory apparatus that governs them. The safety of the water supply also raises issues about the science and technology of water treatment and delivery. A basic understanding of the main techniques and controversies in water treatment will help the reader to understand the reasons for many of the following recommendations.

The next several chapters provide an overview of issues that are often considered straightforwardly scientific and engineering in content but that also involve issues of values and public choice. They draw heavily on a voluminous technical literature,[1] including the Inquiry's own commissioned background papers. These chapters attempt also to reflect some of the current developments in technology because current and future developments are likely to have an impact on new regulatory initiatives in the coming years.

Water can become contaminated as part of natural processes. Many contaminants are benign. The less-benign contaminants fall into two general categories, solutes and particles, which require different approaches to treatment. Solutes are chemicals that dissolve completely. Particles may be inorganic, like clay fines (colloids), or organic. Among the organic particles are micro-organisms, which themselves come in several forms – algae, protozoa, bacteria, and viruses. Again, most of these are benign with respect to human health. Only specific organisms, referred to as human pathogens, cause human disease.

The principal purpose of water treatment is to reduce the risk from pathogens and solutes to acceptable levels. Its secondary purposes include ensuring that the water is of high aesthetic quality – that is, its taste, odour, clarity, or colour do not so offend consumers that they are tempted to turn to less safe sources –

---

[1] In the chapters on treatment and distribution especially, I have relied extensively on the reference works of the American Water Works Association (AWWA), of which the Ontario Water Works Association (OWWA) is a chapter. The AWWA's *Journal* provides an excellent overview of current and emerging issues, and I also rely on its most recent volumes. The American Water Works Association bibliographic service is excellent on all technical and regulatory matters related to water supply: American Water Works Association, 2001, *Waternet,* CD-ROM (Denver: AWWA) (published by subscription every six months).

and ensuring that the water's chemical constituents do not result in operational problems in distribution systems.

This chapter provides an overview of the main treatment technologies in use and available in Ontario today.[2] It is principally descriptive and is intended as a background for the more policy-oriented chapters that follow, but I do make some recommendations here that deal more with the management of technology than with science or engineering as such.

A main point is that there are always trade-offs among objectives and that attaining all objectives is rarely possible. The problem for design engineers is optimization: how to safely meet or exceed all the regulatory standards at the lowest possible cost.

6.2   The Importance of Source

Recommendation 30: All raw water intended for drinking water should be subject to a characterization of each parameter that could indicate a public health risk. The results, regardless of the type of source, should be taken into account in designing and approving any treatment system.[3]

The choice of water treatment technologies is strongly affected by the qualities of the source water. The most basic distinction for treatment purposes is between surface and ground sources, a point that has generated a great deal of controversy over the years. Surface waters vary in quality and are always subject to some microbial contamination, therefore requiring more treatment. Groundwater not under influence from the surface may have a relatively high mineral content but generally is much less affected by contamination that is pathogenic or of

---

[2] There is a large literature on water treatment. This chapter relies on the Inquiry's own summary background paper (E. Doyle, 2002, "Production and distribution of drinking water," Walkerton Inquiry Commissioned Paper 8), as well as several of the standard works in the field, notably Canada, Department of National Health and Welfare, Health Protection Branch, 1993, *Water Treatment Principles and Applications: A Manual for the Production of Drinking Water* (Ottawa: Canadian Water Works Association); R.L. Droste, 1997, *Theory and Practice of Water and Wastewater Treatment* (New York: John Wiley & Sons); HDR Engineering Inc., 2001, *Handbook of Public Water Systems*, 2nd ed. (New York: John Wiley & Sons); American Water Works Association, 1999, *Design and Construction of Small Water Systems*, 2nd ed. (Denver: AWWA); Great Lakes–Upper Mississippi River Board of State and Provincial Public Health and Environmental Managers, 1997, "Recommended Standards for Water Works," Bulletin 42.

[3] I include in the term "treatment system" those systems that are necessary to monitor the effectiveness of the treatment in real time, such as continuous chlorine residual and turbidity monitors.

human origin. In particular, groundwater not under the direct influence of surface events will, by definition, be free of pathogens.

Most Ontarians draw their drinking water from high-quality sources: "Almost three quarters (73%) of Ontario residents served by municipal water systems drink Great Lakes water. This water is typically low in turbidity, low in microbiological contamination and low in concentration of chemicals."[4] The variations in its quality tend to be slow and predictable. The smaller the water system, however, the more likely it is to use groundwater as a source. Thus, the water may have either high mineral content or high variability, depending on whether or not it is much affected by surface events.

Some may argue that modern engineering can overcome all the problems that source water might present. This may be so, but at a price: the worse the raw water quality, the more demanding is each step in the purification process and errors or accidents tend to have more severe consequences. Research in Canada and Australia has demonstrated that where the source water quality is impaired, even treated water that meets current standards may cause 20–30% of all gastrointestinal disease. By comparison, where source water is already of high quality, treated drinking water may be responsible for up to 15% of gastrointestinal disease.[5]

6.2.1   Groundwater under the Direct Influence of Surface Water

I have come to conclude that "groundwater under the direct influence of surface water" is not a useful concept for regulatory purposes and should be dropped in favour of Recommendation 30. In the Part 1 report of this Inquiry, I

---

[4] Doyle, p. 2.

[5] P. Payment et al., 1991, "A randomized trial to evaluate the risk of gastrointestinal disease due to consumption of drinking water meeting current microbiological standards," *American Journal of Public Health*, vol. 81, pp. 703–708; P. Payment et al., 1995, "A prospective epidemiological study of gastrointestinal health effects due to the consumption of drinking water," *International Journal of Health Research*, vol. 7, pp. 5–31; M.E. Hellard et al., 2001, "A randomized, blinded, controlled trial investigating the gastrointestinal health effects of drinking water quality," *Environmental Health Perspectives*, vol. 109, pp. 773–778; P. Payment, 2001, "Tap water and public health: The risk factor," *Water*, vol. 21, p. 9.

The importance of good treatment standards, even when the watershed is well protected and the water chlorinated, is suggested by a recent epidemiological study of gastrointestinal illness in Vancouver, which does not filter its water: J. Aramini et al., 2000, *Drinking Water Quality and Health Care Utilization for Gastrointestinal Illness in Greater Vancouver* <http://www.hc-sc.gc.ca/ehp/ehd/catalogue/bch_pubs/vancouver_dwq.htm> [accessed December 1, 2001].

recommended that the Ministry of the Environment (MOE) should develop criteria for identifying groundwater under the direct influence of surface water as a means for determining treatment and treatment-monitoring requirements and as a guide to inspections.[6] On reflection, I have concluded that the distinction is difficult to make, both in theory and in practice, and in any case the design of barriers between contaminants and consumers should take into account the specific set of challenges posed by a specific water source. I would thus broaden my recommendation in the Part 1 report to read as Recommendation 30 does.

Much more effort than in the end is useful has gone into defining groundwater under the direct influence of surface water.[7] This groundwater must be treated as if it were surface water, a generally more expensive proposition and thus one that some local authorities have attempted to circumvent over the years. An example of how complex the definition may become is the following, from the United States Environmental Protection Agency:

> Groundwater under the direct influence of surface water means any water beneath the surface of the ground with significant occurrence of insects or other macro organisms, algae, or large-diameter pathogens such as *Giardia lamblia* or [for ... systems serving at least 10,000 people only] *Cryptosporidium*, or significant and relatively rapid shifts in water characteristics such as turbidity, temperature, conductivity, or pH which closely correlate to climatological or surface water conditions. Direct influence must be determined for individual sources in accordance with criteria established by the State. The State determination of direct influence may be based on site-specific measurements of water quality and/or documentation of well construction characteristics and geology with field evaluation.[8]

---

[6] Ontario, Ministry of the Attorney General, 2002, *Report of the Walkerton Inquiry, Part 1: The Events of May 2000 and Related Issues* (Toronto: Queen's Printer), p. 298.

[7] The American Water Works Association Research Foundation (AWWARF), for instance, found that none of the water quality parameters tested in a large-scale Florida study "appeared to be a good predictor of direct surface water influence on groundwater." Temperature was fairly good; colour, conductivity, turbidity successively were much poorer; and turbidity, pH, heterotrophic plate count, as well as total and fecal bacteriological data, showed no relationship between ground and surface water: J.C. Jacangelo et al., 2001, *Investigation of Criteria for GWUDI Determination* (Denver: AWWARF) <http://www.awwarf.com/exsums/2538.htm> [accessed April 16, 2002].

[8] United States Environmental Protection Agency, National Primary Drinking Water Regulations, 40 C.F.R., c. 1, § 141.2 (July 2000), p. 338. See <http://www.epa.gov/safewater/regs/cfr141.pdf> [accessed April 16, 2002].

This is a generous definition. It fails to mention any bacteria or viruses and leaves some room for individual states to exercise discretion. Interestingly, the protection against *Cryptosporidium* is less for communities under 10,000 people. The definition properly mentions rapid change in certain easily measured physical parameters but does not define "significant" or "relatively rapid."

Ontario does not formally define groundwater under the direct influence of surface water, although the concept is referred to in Schedule 2 of Ontario Regulation 459/00. I remarked in the Part 1 report of this Inquiry that the MOE's failure to apply a 1994 policy requiring continuous monitors for groundwater sources under the direct influence of surface water to Walkerton was a contributing factor in that tragedy.[9] Although the terms of reference for a current survey of potential groundwater under the direct influence of surface water contains a highly detailed statement of what such groundwater constitutes,[10] the MOE's thrust is generally to require a detailed characterization of the source water, regardless of whether it comes from a well, a lake, or a river, and to design the treatment accordingly. To be useful for specifying treatment, a definition for such groundwater would have to be quite strict, including at least the following concepts:

- no known hydrogeological connection to the surface that would allow percolation into the aquifer in less than a specified number of years;

- the complete absence, over many tests, of any positive results from a broad-spectrum bacterial test such as heterotrophic plate counts, as well as absence in tests for specific protozoa and viruses; or satisfactory results from microbial particulate analyses;

- the absence of solutes, such as nitrates, known to derive from fertilizers, sewage, or manure; and

- the absence of rapid shifts in turbidity, temperature, pH, or conductivity, as the U.S. Environmental Protection Agency suggests.

Under the circumstances, dropping this intermediate definition in favour of a focus on the more direct parameters makes sense.

---

[9] Ontario, Ministry of the Attorney General, p. 293.

[10] Ontario, Ministry of the Environment, 2001, *Terms of Reference: Hydrogeological Study to Examine Groundwater Sources Potentially under Direct Influence of Surface Water* <www.ene.gov.on.ca/envision/techdocs/4167e.pdf>.

6.3 Water Treatment Processes

A water treatment plant must be able to treat source water to meet the maximum volume demand at the poorest raw water quality levels without compromising the quality of the final product. A wide variety of processes are available, depending on the problems posed by the source water (see Table 6.1). Usually the plant selects a combination of several processes that work together to meet the required quality standard. In Ontario, a typical process is chemically assisted filtration followed by disinfection. I summarize the standard set of methods below.

Table 6.1 Water Treatment Processes

Parameter Group	Conventional Processes	Advanced Processes
Microorganisms	Chlorination Chloramination Chlorine dioxide	Membrane filtration Ultraviolet Ozone
Turbidity	Chemically assisted filtration	Flotation Granular activated carbon (GAC) Biological processes Oxidation Membrane filtration Ion exchange (humics)
Total organic carbon	Coagulation, flocculation, sedimentation	Powdered activated carbon (PAC) Flotation
Trihalomethanes	Reduced chlorine dose Elimination of pre-chlorination Improved coagulation (precursor removal) Change in disinfectant	PAC GAC Air stripping Biological precursor removal
Specific organics (other than THMs)	Air stripping GAC Oxidation	PAC Membrane filtration Biological processes
Ammonia	Breakpoint chlorination	Ion exchange Biological processes Air stripping Ferrate
Gasoline		GAC Air stripping
Nitriloacetic acid	None	Biological processes Ozonation
Pesticides	PAC	GAC Biological processes
Inorganics (heavy metals)	Chemically assisted filtration	Ion exchange Precipitation Sequestering

Table 6.1   Water Treatment Processes (continued)

Parameter Group	Conventional Processes	Advanced Processes
Mercury	None	Ferric sulphate Coagulation (inorganic Hg) Ion exchange (organic Hg)
Asbestos	Chemically assisted filtration	
Fluoride	None	Alum coagulation Lime softening Activated alumina Reverse osmosis Electrodialysis
Cyanide	Oxidation	
Iron and Manganese	Oxidation Sand filtration Greensand	Biological processes (Mn)
Hydrogen sulphide	Aeration	
Nitrite	Chlorination	Biological processes
Nitrate	Ion exchange	Biological processes
Total dissolved solids		Ion exchange Membrane filtration Electrodialysis
Hardness (Ca and Mg)	Lime-soda softening	Ion exchange
Algae	Chemically assisted filtration Application of algicides to raw water Oxidation	Coagulation Flotation
Colour	Coagulation Oxidation	Flotation
Taste and odour	Aeration Oxidation (O_3) PAC Change of oxidant/disinfectant	GAC Biological processes Membrane filtration
pH	Acid or base addition	
Radioactivity		Greensand Ion exchange (Ra, U) Air stripping (Ra)

Source: Adapted from Canada, Department of National Health and Welfare, Health Protection Branch, 1993, pp. 168–169.

6.3.1   Conventional Processes

Screening: An inexpensive process, screening puts relatively coarse screens at the intake point of the raw water and places finer screens at the water treatment plant.[11] The finer screens usually require frequent cleaning.

---

[11] Finer screens may recommend themselves in some instances. In Tasmania, migrating eels expiring in the water system recently caused foul water: D. Rose, 2001, "Dead eels in water supply," *Mercury* (Tasmania), November 2. Here, as elsewhere, the Inquiry is indebted to pioneering Australian work.

Coagulation: The next several steps "clarify water, reduce the organic load, and greatly decrease the microbial count so that subsequent disinfection will be more effective."[12] Coagulation has the further benefit of reducing the chemical disinfectant dose and thus lowering the levels of disinfection by-products.

Micro-organisms and clay colloids in water are negatively charged, a feature that stabilizes their dispersion in water. Adding positively charged (cationic) metals, such as soluble aluminum or iron salts, or cationic organic polyelectrolytes, neutralizes their charges. This destabilizes the colloidal suspensions and results in agglomeration into small flakes, or microflocs. Aluminum and iron salts hydrolyze to form a gelatinous polymer that further entraps and adsorbs clay particles and micro-organisms. Chemical reactions between the salts and free organic acids or proteins can also result in precipitation.[13] The processes are temperature and pH dependent and are less efficient in cold water, thus requiring careful attention to mixing times and pH.[14] Design mistakes may lead to this process's poor performance in winter.

Aluminum and iron salts have been used to remove colour and enhance particle removal. Their use is preferred because of their efficiency, cost, and ability to control aluminum and iron residuals for a given water quality. Synthetic coagulants (polymers or polyelectrolytes) or activated silica can also be used. They are usually more expensive, but smaller doses may be required. Polymers form gelatinous masses that entrap smaller flocs and particles more efficiently than do the metal hydroxides formed by the hydrolysis of metallic salts.

Flocculation: The process of slowly agitating the coagulated mix is known as flocculation. It allows microflocs to agglomerate, which increases the size of the floc and thereby enhances the gravity sedimentation of the larger flocs while allowing the capture of floc-adhering particles that are otherwise too tiny to be trapped in the relatively coarse filters that follow. Flocculators can be mechanical, pneumatic, or hydraulic, but the mixing action is relatively slow. Baffled channels can be effective flocculators if the velocities are maintained between 0.1 and 0.4 metres per second and the detention time is about 15–20 minutes. In a tapered flocculation process, water flows through a series of cells at decreasing speed. This allows for rapid floc formation in the early stages

---

[12] S.S. Block, 1991, *Disinfection, Sterilization and Preservation*, 4th ed. (Philadelphia: Lee and Febiger), p. 719.

[13] Ibid., pp. 719–720.

[14] HDR Engineering Inc., c. 10.

while preventing floc break-up and encouraging sedimentation in the later stages.

Sedimentation: Sedimentation is the separation of suspended material by gravity. Sedimentation basin design depends on the settling velocity of the lightest particles to be removed from suspension. This provides a nice example of the need to optimize the trade-offs among processes considered together: if flocculation is highly efficient (particles are large and heavy), sedimentation may be rapid and the tank small – but at the cost of higher dosage or the selection of a more expensive chemical coagulant.

Flotation: An alternative to sedimentation is flotation, in which solids are transported to the surface through their attachment to bubbles and are then skimmed off. This method can remove smaller particles than can sedimentation, at some cost in capital and power requirements, and is particularly suitable for waters that have a high algal content, low natural turbidity, or high colouration. Flotation is not as efficient as sedimentation for the removal of particles and turbidity and is sensitive to temperature; it performs poorly in very cold water.

Flotation is provided electrolytically or through dissolved or dispersed air.[15] In the first case, the electrolysis of water generates bubbles of hydrogen and oxygen. Dispersed air is a froth in which bubble formation and dispersion is achieved through violent agitation, or a foam in which tiny bubbles are formed when air passes through a porous medium or sparger. Dissolved air flotation is the most popular method. Small-diameter air bubbles are generated by reducing a high-pressure (345–552 kPa) saturated stream to atmospheric pressure in the bottom of the tank.[16] In all cases, bubbles attach themselves to floc or are trapped inside it, and the floc rises to the top, where it is skimmed off.

The choice of separation technique – sedimentation or flotation – depends on factors such as source water quality (presence of algae and lime or silt), objectives in turbidity and particulate removal, rapid start-up, sludge removal and disposal constraints, cost, and the skill level of the operating personnel. The design trade-off at the level of coagulation/flocculation/clarification is the choice between a high level of particle removal versus optimal conditions for the reduction of the natural organic matter, which leads to the formation of disinfection by-products. The former approach removes more micro-organisms;

---

[15] Ibid, p. 337.
[16] Canada, Department of National Health and Welfare, p. 53.

the latter limits the secondary impact of disinfecting the remaining micro-organisms with chlorine.

Sand Filtration: Clarified water then passes through a filter, conventionally a thick layer of sand and anthracite, which is occasionally overlain by granular activated carbon. Since the pore spaces in these filters are much larger than the few microns of a typical protozoan or bacterium, the coagulation and flocculation steps are critical to effective filtration.[17] The particles remaining in the clarified water fed to the filter are small, but they are still much larger than the pathogens they may contain.

Filter beds must be taken out of service periodically for backwashing when the accumulation of solids causes excessive pressure drop or particle breakthrough. The accumulated solids are evacuated by a combination of up-flow wash, with or without air scouring, and surface wash. The need for backwashing usually requires water treatment plants to have several filters arranged in parallel, so that one or two filters can be offline without reducing the rated capacity of the plant.

The effective backwashing of filters is critical to their proper performance. Air scouring, in particular, is critical to the adequate cleansing of the media of mud balls, filter cracks, and the accumulation of large macro-organisms (worms). But backwashing is also the most frequent source of filter failure.[18]

After the backwash period, commonly 5 to 60 minutes, filtered water often does not meet turbidity and particle removal goals. The efficiency of particle removal decreases following a backwash, when the filter is clean and the pores are at their maximum size.

Good practice (and regulation in the United States) now dictates that water produced during that period of "filter ripening" is sent to drain. Since the

---

[17] Following optimal coagulation, conventional filtration can result in as much as a 4- to 5-log removal of *Cryptosporidium*, but performance apparently depends on close process control: N.R. Dugan, K.R. Fox, and R.J. Miltner, 2001, "Controlling *Cryptosporidium* oöcysts using conventional treatment," *Journal of the American Water Works Association*, vol. 93, no. 12, pp. 64–76. Filter performance data from normal operations show much lower removals and a great sensitivity to chemical conditioning.

[18] R.D. Letterman, ed., 1999, *Water Quality and Treatment: A Handbook of Community Water Supplies*, 5th ed. (New York: McGraw-Hill/American Water Works Association), c. 8.

amount of water wasted during filter ripening may be 5% of overall production, it is often recycled to the head of the plant, but this may simply increase the load of micro-organisms to the plant, risking microbial breakthrough. Thus, recycling is no longer recognized as a good practice. Providing filter-to-waste facilities is an important step in lessening the overall risk of pathogen passage into finished water. Many plants in Ontario, especially the smaller ones, are not equipped with filter-to-waste piping.

The trade-off in filtration is the efficiency of particle removal versus filter productivity. It would be possible to construct particle filters with a much finer pore structure: diatomaceous earth is a good example of such a filter.[19] But the filtration rate would be unacceptably slow under gravity alone, making pressurization (an added expense) necessary. The most common trade-off facing designers is between the area and the depth of the media, that is, between the length of the filtration cycle and the initial period of particle breakthrough.

The combination of steps described so far is referred to in engineering shorthand as "chemically assisted filtration."

Disinfection: Because it removes or inactivates pathogens, disinfection is the vital step in preventing the transmission of water-borne disease. By far the most common disinfectant is chlorine, which has been in wide use for more than a century. Chlorine is effective against bacteria and viruses but not against encysted protozoa.

The effectiveness of disinfection is generally calculated for different types of disinfectants, using a complex equation based on the concentration of the disinfectant (C) and the contact time (T), which is often referred to as the CT.

The usual shorthand in the water business is to say that a particular treatment provides, for example, "3-log inactivation or removal for *E. coli*," which means that 99.9% of the *E. coli* bacteria in the raw water have been killed (or in the case of filtration, removed). Thus, 4-log means that 99.99% of the *E. coli* have been inactivated, and so on. Different standards apply for different organisms. For example, *Giardia* inactivation should have 3-log efficiency, while the usual minimum for viruses is 4-log. To quote again from the Inquiry's commissioned paper:

---

[19] Diatomaceous earth under lab conditions yields approximately 6.3-log *Cryptosporidium* removal: J.E. Ongerth and P.E. Hutton, 2001, "Testing of diatomaceous earth filtration for removal of *Cryptosporidium* oöcysts," *Journal of the American Water Works Association,* vol. 93, no. 12, pp. 54–63.

Depending on the treatment process, a substantial portion of these requirements could be achieved through filtration, often leaving a remaining disinfection requirement of 0.5-log *Giardia* inactivation and 2-log virus inactivation. Systems would then determine the *CT* required to achieve these inactivation targets, using tables provided in the regulatory literature that correlate *CT* values to different levels of *Giardia* and virus inactivation. The new Ontario standard uses this approach …

An extremely important consideration with the *CT* approach is the determination of *C* and *T*. When a disinfectant is applied to the water, it reacts with the various impurities and decays. Thus, *C* is continuously changing. Furthermore, not every element of water passes through the treatment system in the same amount of time. Some elements pass quickly while others move through eddies or stagnant regions and take longer. Thus there is no single contact time *T* that can be used to describe the entire flow of water.[20]

The most commonly used oxidants in drinking water disinfection are chlorine, ozone, and chlorine dioxide. Of these, by far the most common are chlorine gas and hypochlorite, which have been in widespread use for a century. However, concerns about the formation of potentially harmful halogenated by-products have led many water systems to adopt alternative oxidants for disinfection.

Chlorine is the oldest and most widely used disinfectant. It is effective against bacteria and viruses, though not against encysted protozoa. *Giardia* is very resistant to chlorine, whereas *Cryptosporidium* cannot be inactivated by chlorine doses that are compatible with drinking water treatment.

The most commonly used and lowest-cost form of chlorine is chlorine gas, a highly toxic chemical that must be transported (unless it is produced on-site), handled, and accounted for with great care and only by trained and certified people. Chlorine in storage or transport may pose unacceptable security risks. It can, however, be produced on-site from the electrolysis of a brine solution, avoiding the hazards associated with the transport and handling of gaseous chlorine. This is now almost the only form of chlorine used in urban European plants, and it is gaining ground rapidly in the United States.

---

[20] E. Doyle, 2002.

Sodium hypochlorite is another form of chlorine that is safer to use than chlorine gas. This option is typically provided in a water solution ranging from 5–15% available chlorine.[21] High-strength solutions degrade fairly rapidly, so low-strength solutions are preferred if the storage period is likely to last weeks or months. Calcium hypochlorite is provided as a dry solid; in commercial products it may contain between 65% and 70% available chlorine. The reaction with water occurs in a similar manner to that of sodium hypochlorite.

Whatever the source, chlorine in solution takes the form of hypochlorous acid, which partly dissociates into hypochlorite ions. Both of these forms are referred to as free chlorine. Hypochlorous acid is the most effective form of chlorine-based disinfectant. At higher pH (>7.5), the less effective hypochlorite ion will dominate, so pH control during disinfection is important. Free chlorine reacts with organic and inorganic material that is dissolved or suspended in water, as well as specifically with micro-organisms. Simply adding more chlorine to satisfy the demand caused by this non-toxic material results in higher concentrations of harmful disinfection by-products (DBPs), which in turn means that it is important to minimize total organics before the chlorination step.

Production of Chloramines: The reaction of aqueous chlorine with ammonia produces chloramines. This may be done purposely by adding ammonia to chlorinated water to convert the free chlorine residual into chloramines.[22] Monochloramine is a form of combined chlorine that, although it is less effective than free chlorine, is much more stable, which makes it particularly useful for maintaining a chlorine residual in the distribution system.

Use of Chlorine Dioxide: A strong oxidant used mainly for taste and odour control, chlorine dioxide is also used to oxidize iron and manganese. Since it is highly unstable, it cannot be transported or stored and must be produced on-site on a continuous basis. It is effective against *Giardia* and *Cryptosporidium*, and its application is mainly restricted by the limitations on its undesirable inorganic by-products, chlorate and chlorite.

Maintaining a Residual: The topic of maintaining a chlorine residual received a good deal of attention in Part 1 of the Inquiry. It is normal practice to have a chlorine residual (either free chlorine or chloramines) in the water as it leaves the treatment plant. This residual is meant to prevent the regrowth of microbes

---

[21] American Water Works Association, 1973, *Manual of Water Supply Practices: Water Chlorination Principles and Practices*, M20 (Denver: AWWA), p. 10.
[22] Letterman, pp. 12–14.

in the water until it reaches the consumer's tap. The current Ontario requirement is a free chlorine residual throughout the distribution system in concentrations of between 0.2 and 4.0 mg/L.[23]

In the 1990s, concern about the formation of chlorine disinfection by-products during distribution caused a major shift toward using chloramines in distribution systems. Chloramines are less potent but more persistent disinfectants,[24] with applied dosages ranging between 1.0 and 3.0 mg/L. Chloramines have been shown to be more efficient in controlling biofilm and in reducing the coliform-positive events in corroded distribution systems. However, they have also been linked to increased heterotrophic plate counts, at least during the transition from chlorine to chloramines.[25]

Ozonation: The main chemical alternative to chlorine, ozone is used in several of the larger treatment plants in Ontario, notably in those of Windsor and Kitchener-Waterloo. Widely used in Europe, the United States (more than 400 plants), and Quebec (more than 20 plants), ozone is used to oxidize organic matter (including trihalomethane precursors); to reduce objectionable taste, odour, and colour; and to inactivate pathogens. Ozone is effective against bacteria, viruses, and protozoa. It is one of the few disinfectants capable of inactivating *Cryptosporidium*.

Ozone's limitations include its sensitivity to temperature (all chemical disinfectants work less well at low temperatures) and the fact that ozonation increases the amount of biodegradable organic matter reaching the distribution system, which may, under favourable conditions, increase bacterial regrowth.[26] However, it is the only chemical disinfectant that will work at low water

---

[23] The requirement is not in the regulation, which simply requires disinfection, but is mentioned in the new chlorination bulletin, Procedure B13-3, which is appended to the new Ontario Drinking Water Standards (ODWS).

[24] Letterman, pp. 12–45.

[25] A shift has occurred in European practice regarding the maintenance of chlorine residuals in distribution systems. Until the events of September 11, 2001, European practice was to lower or avoid altogether the presence of chlorine in distribution systems, mainly in response to the high sensitivity of customers to taste and odour generated by chlorine. This practice has now ceased: M. Prévost, 2002, personal communication, February 4.

[26] I.C. Escobar and A.A. Randall, 2001, "Case study: Ozonation and distribution system biostability," *Journal of the American Water Works Association,* vol. 93, no. 10, pp. 77–89. Regrowth in this study of Orlando, Florida, occurred under a combination of conditions including the presence of food (biodegradable organic matter produced by ozone); temperature (>15°C); oxidant depletion (absence of residual); and material (proper housing for bacteria). Vancouver, however, chose ozonation, together with proper residual maintenance, and experienced a decline in regrowth.

temperatures (albeit with higher doses) without causing unacceptable levels of disinfection by-products. It is good at controlling taste and odour problems and is unexcelled for the control of algal toxins.

6.3.2   Disinfection By-products

Recommendation 31: The Advisory Council on Standards should review Ontario's standards for disinfection by-products to take account of the risks that may be posed by the by-products of all chemical and radiation-based disinfectants.

Disinfection by-products (DBPs) are the unintended result of drinking water disinfection and oxidation. The compounds of most concern contain chlorine and bromine atoms and may be either organic or inorganic. Precursors of DBPs include natural organic matter such as humic and fulvic acids, total organic carbon, and bromides.

Chlorine is not alone in forming DBPs, but chlorine-derived DBPs were the first to be recognized and have been the source of some controversy.[27] Chemical disinfectants in general produce DBPs by oxidation and halogen substitution in some precursor in the raw or semi-processed water. Halogenated organic DBPs include chloroform and other trihalomethanes (THMs), haloacetic acids, and haloacetonitriles. Total THM concentrations in drinking water are limited to 0.1 mg/L in Ontario. Typically, waters with high natural organic matter concentrations are at greater risk of exceeding chlorine-related DBP limits. The tea-coloured lakes and streams of northern Ontario get their characteristic colour from high concentrations of natural organic matter.

---

[27] These matters are reviewed in P.C. Singer, ed., 1999, *Formation and Control of Disinfection By-products in Drinking Water* (Denver: American Water Works Association); see also the references in note 1. Chloroform was first recognized as a by-product of water treatment in Holland: J.J. Rook, 1971, "Headspace analysis in water," (translated) *H2O*, vol. 4, no. 17, pp. 385–387; and 1974, "Formation of halogens during the chlorination of natural water," *Water Treatment and Examination*, vol. 23, pp. 234–243, cited in J.M. Symons, "Disinfection by-products: A historical perspective," c. 1, in Singer, ibid. Health Canada has a Chlorinated Disinfection By-products Task Group, whose publications are available through the Health Canada Web site. For an up-to-date summary, see S.E. Hrudey, 2001, "Drinking water disinfection by-products: When, what and why?" proceedings at the Disinfection Byproducts and Health Effects Seminar, Cooperative Research Center for Water Quality and Treatment, Melbourne, Australia, October 29.

Chlorine dioxide undergoes a wide variety of oxidation reactions with organic matter to form oxidized organics and chlorite. All three forms of oxidized chlorine species – chlorine dioxide, chlorate, and chlorite – are considered to have adverse health effects. There is no current regulation of chlorine dioxide and its by-products, chlorite and chlorate, in Ontario. The ozonation by-product of major concern is bromate, formed by the oxidation of bromide. Bromate is not regulated in Ontario but the European Union, the United States Environmental Protection Agency, the World Health Organization, Australia, and Quebec do set maximum contaminant levels for bromate.

The use of chemical disinfectants requires a balance between ensuring proper disinfection and minimizing unintended and undesirable by-product formation. In all cases and for all chemical disinfectants used, the uncertain long-term risk from DBPs must be weighed against the acute and more certain risk of inadequate disinfection. The failure to put disinfection first can have immediate and catastrophic effects, as occurred in Peru in 1991[28] and in Nigeria in 2001.[29]

Three general approaches are available to control DBPs:

- **Minimizing Natural Organic Matter before Disinfection:** Natural organic matter can be reduced through coagulation, adsorption, oxidation, or nano-filtration. This is common practice in Ontario. Chlorination DBPs can also be minimized by moving chlorine application downstream, to a later point in treatment, after some of the natural organic matter has been removed by coagulation.

- **Changing Oxidants:** The most common modifications are to use chlorine dioxide or ozone for primary disinfection, or chloramine for the residual.[30]

---

[28] A misunderstanding about relative risk led to the cessation of chlorination, with the result that at least 3,000 people died and 320,000 were made ill with cholera: C. Anderson, 1991, "Cholera epidemic traced to risk miscalculation," *Nature*, vol. 354, November 28, and Pan American Health Organization, 2002, "Cholera: Number of Cases and Deaths in the Americas (1991–2001) <www.paho.org/English/HCP/HCT/EER/cholera-cases-deaths-91-01.htm> [accessed May 1, 2002]. It is fundamental that "management actions to reduce the potential risk posed by DBPs must not compromise the microbiological quality of the drinking water": Singer, p. 113.

[29] A. Aboubakar, 2001, "Hellish scenes in Nigeria's cholera city," *Agence France Presse* (Kano), November 26; see also <http://www.theage.com.au/breaking/2001/11/27/FFXE97A4HUC.html>, [accessed May 1, 2002].

[30] "After the THM rule became effective in 1979, some water utilities had to make changes in their practices to come into compliance. [Enactment resulted, on average] in a 40 to 50 percent lessening in TTHM [total trihalomethane] concentrations for the larger utilities surveyed. ... Although the median concentration [38 µ/L] was not influenced much, utilities with high TTHM levels were

- **Optimizing Disinfection:** This can be achieved by using just enough oxidant to achieve the necessary disinfection and applying it under conditions that minimize DBP formation. One example is pH adjustment for bromate control. Lowering the pH before ozonation can almost entirely prevent bromate formation. Both overdosing and underdosing pose threats; thus, a careful assessment of *CT* based on the particular design of a facility, combined with an equally careful approach to overall risk management and a routine audit of the number of surviving micro-organisms, must be employed.[31]

All chemical disinfectants produce undesirable by-products that can and must be minimized to lower long-term risk while providing immediate disinfection and other water quality benefits. However, the current regulations in Ontario limit only the levels of chlorination DBPs, which creates a regulatory void that may cause inappropriate shifts from one oxidant to another. A balanced view is required. The proposed Advisory Committee on Standards should examine this issue.

6.3.3   Innovative Disinfection Technologies

The recent focus on chlorine-resistant micro-organisms such as *Cryptosporidium* results directly from recent outbreaks such as those in Milwaukee, the United Kingdom, and North Battleford, Saskatchewan, as well as a suspected outbreak that may never have occurred in Sydney, Australia. These outbreaks have shown the inability of conventional separation processes coupled with chlorination to ensure the reliable removal of these pathogens. In each of these cases, the treatment processes in place were theoretically capable of preventing the passage of these micro-organisms. Since *Cryptosporidium* is highly resistant to chlorine, chemically assisted filtration done in an optimal mode is the main barrier available in a conventional plant. However, an inadequate operation of treatment processes may result in the massive contamination of drinking water, with

---

able to lessen their TTHM concentrations substantially. ... Of those systems that implemented THM control measures, the majority did one or more of the following: (1) modified their point(s) of chlorine application [to follow filtration], (2) changed their chlorine dosages, and (3) adopted the use of chloramines": Symons in Singer, pp. 16–17.

[31] The U.S. Environmental Protection Agency proposed in 1978 a THM limit that would apply only to utilities serving more than 10,000 people because of a concern that "if the smaller utilities tried to alter their disinfection practice to lessen TTHM concentrations, because of a lack of technical expertise, an increased risk of microbial contamination in the finished water might result": Symons in Singer, p. 12.

dramatic consequences for the local consumers. As a result, it is now accepted practice to recommend the provision of an additional barrier to ensure the removal or inactivation of these pathogens. This provision is not yet required by regulation in Canada or the United States, although it will become a requirement in the United States with the promulgation of the Stage II Microbial/Disinfection By-product Rule in 2003. This is a clear case of practice preceding regulation to provide safer drinking water.

It is in this context that alternative technologies such as ultraviolet radiation (UV) disinfection and membrane filtration have recently been recognized as efficient technologies to remove or inactivate these chlorine-resistant pathogens in drinking water. The great interest in these technologies lies in the fact that there is no known production of DBPs as a result of using these technologies.[32] However, neither technology is a complete barrier to bacteria and viruses, and neither carries a disinfectant residual. Because of these limitations, they must be applied together with a chlorine or chloramine residual.

The need to remove or inactivate chlorine-resistant pathogens has resulted in major changes in regulations around the world and has spurred tremendous interest in the development of alternative technologies to reach that goal. As a first response to this threat, other oxidants, such as ozone and chlorine dioxide, appeared to be viable alternatives that could be used with success. However, their application may be limited by their production of undesirable DBPs.

Ultraviolet Radiation: UV technology is not new, and its application for disinfection is well established. It has been applied with success for decades to disinfect wastewater effluents. Today, the UV disinfection of drinking water is widely used in Europe, where more than 2,000 UV installations exist, and it is also common in the United States, where there are more than 1,000 installations, the majority of which are in small systems, with about 40% applied to surface water.[33]

UV is most effective when the water is already clear – when there are no particles in or behind which micro-organisms may shelter from the killing light. Hence, it is usually placed toward the end of the treatment processes.

---

[32] In the case of UV, however, this may be due in part to a lack of relevant research.

[33] United States Environmental Protection Agency, 2001, *Draft UV Guidelines*, CD-ROM (Washington, DC).

Disinfection by UV light is fundamentally different from disinfection by chemical disinfectants such as chlorine, chlorine dioxide, and ozone. UV inactivates micro-organisms by damaging their nucleic acids and preventing the micro-organisms from replicating. A micro-organism that cannot replicate may not be dead, but it cannot infect. The UV adsorption for DNA peaks at 265 nm, well within the UV range.

UV radiation is extremely effective against chlorine-resistant pathogens such as *Cryptosporidium* and *Giardia* and requires small dosages for bacterial inactivation, whereas the inactivation of certain viruses requires significantly higher dosages.

The U.S. Environmental Protection Agency's Federal Advisory Committee of 21 stakeholders has been studying the efficacy, current use, performance, reliability, and cost of UV since 1999.[34] Its economic analyses show that using UV to treat water for *Cryptosporidium* costs significantly less than using other technologies, such as membrane filtration.[35]

Concurrent with its publication of the proposed rules (LT2ESWTR and Stage II Microbial/Disinfection By-product Rule), the United States Environmental Protection Agency intends to publish the following in the summer of 2002:

- tables specifying UV doses (product of irradiance (I) and exposure time (T)) needed to achieve up to 3-log inactivation of *Giardia lamblia*, up to 3-log inactivation of *Cryptosporidium*, and up to 4-log inactivation of viruses;[36]

- minimum standards to determine whether UV systems are acceptable for compliance with drinking water disinfection requirements; and

---

[34] D.C. Schmelling, 2001, "Disinfection goals: Crypto? Viruses? Both?" proceedings at the American Water Works Association Annual Conference, Washington, DC, June 17–21.

[35] C.A. Cotton et al., 2001, "The development, application and cost implications of the UV dose tables for LT2ESWTR compliance," presentation at the Water Quality Technology Conference, Nashville, Tennessee, November; C.A. Cotton et al., 2001 "UV disinfection costs for inactivating *Cryptosporidium*," *Journal of the American Water Works Association*, vol. 93, no. 6, pp. 82–94.

[36] C.A. Cotton et al., 2001, "The development of the UV dose tables for LT2ESWTR implementation," presentation at the First International Congress on UV Technologies, International UV Association, Washington, DC, June.

- a final *UV Guidance Manual*, the purpose of which is to facilitate the design and planning of UV installations by familiarizing regulators and utilities with important design and operational issues, including redundancy, reliability and hydraulic constraints in UV system design, and design considerations with respect to plant and pipe size, water quality (e.g., UV absorbance, turbidity), lamp fouling and aging, appropriate operations, and maintenance protocols to ensure the performance of UV lamps (e.g., sleeve cleaning systems).[37]

Germany has already developed a standard[38] and has accredited eight manufacturers. The National Water Research Institute (NWRI) and the American Water Works Association Research Foundation (AWWARF) have similar guidelines, but the expected U.S. Environmental Protection Agency guidelines will set the accreditation framework in the United States. The UV guidance manual is likely to require full-scale validation testing based on German DVGW guidelines.

UV disinfection has many advantages. First, it is much less demanding on the operator than are any of the chemical disinfectants. Although the minimum dose must be met, modest overdosing is not known to create hazards. Continuous optimization is not required. A second advantage is the apparent lack of DBPs, although it must be understood that little research has been done to date, especially on the question of whether any problematic non-halogenated DBPs may be produced. The area of current concern is the production of nitrite, which can be formed from nitrate, but keeping the lamp output above 240 nm can avoid this reaction. A third advantage of UV is its excellent capacity, much better than all available oxidants, to inactivate protozoan pathogens, most notably *Cryptosporidium*. Lastly, the technology is easily scalable: it can work economically all the way from the point-of-use or point-of-entry level to that of a full-scale water plant. Perhaps the most obvious attraction of UV is its low cost. It is increasingly thought of as inexpensive insurance, and several utilities are installing UV without being compelled to do so by regulatory obligation.

---

[37] See also National Water Research Institute and American Water Works Association Research Foundation, 2000, "Ultraviolet Disinfection Guidelines for Drinking Water and Water Reuse," NWRI-00-03.

[38] Deutsche Vereinigung des Gas-und Wasserfaches eV., 1997, Arbeitsblatt W-294.

A good deal of work is being done in the United States to fine-tune and standardize the use of UV in large systems.[39] As mentioned above, the U.S. Environmental Protection Agency's Federal Advisory Committee has been studying the issue since 1999.[40] At the time of writing, the agency was circulating a draft of its forthcoming *UV Guidance Manual*. In Canada, UV has been gaining ground. The Edmonton utility Epcor ordered a UV system in December 2001. Also in 2001, Quebec reviewed its drinking water regulations, and a minimum 2-log *Cryptosporidium* removal requirement was introduced. As a result, more than 100 projects are now under review for approval by Quebec's ministry of the environment.

Membrane Filtration: If micro-organisms are not killed with chemical disinfectants or radiation, they can simply be excluded physically from the finished water. Membrane processes currently in use for drinking water production include reverse osmosis, nano-filtration, ultra-filtration (UF), and micro-filtration (MF). Nano-filtration, the most recently developed membrane process, is used to soften water, to remove DBP precursors, and more recently (in Europe) to trace contaminants such as pesticides. Ultra-filtration and micro-filtration are used to remove turbidity, pathogens, and particles from surface waters. Coagulants or powdered activated carbon (PAC) must be used in MF or UF to remove significant amounts of dissolved components such as natural organic matter, DBP precursors, taste and odour compounds, and trace contaminants such as pesticides, herbicides, and arsenic. Depending on water quality, MF and UF can be used as stand-alone separation processes in which coagulant and PAC is added, or in combination with other separation technologies such as high-rate clarification or filtration.

Membranes can be classified by such properties as geometry, molecular weight cut-off, operating pressures, and membrane chemistry, but the most common classification is by their pore size, as shown in Table 6.2. Size is critical. Protozoa are typically larger than 4 μm and bacteria larger than 0.5 μm. *E. coli* is a rod-shaped bacterium 0.5 to 2.0 μm long; *Campylobacter* is a spiral-shaped or curved bacterium from 0.2 to 0.5 μm wide and from 0.5 to 5.0 μm long.[41] Viruses

---

[39] See two papers from the June 2001 AWWA meetings in Washington, DC: R.H. Sakaji, R. Haberman, and R. Hultquist, "UV disinfection: A state perspective"; and V.J. Roquebert et al., "Design of UV disinfection systems for drinking water treatment: Issues and alternatives," proceedings at the American Water Works Association Annual Conference, Washington, DC, June 17–21.

[40] Schmelling.

[41] American Water Works Association, 1999, *Manual of Water Supply Practices: Waterborne Pathogens,* M48 (Denver: AWWA).

and viral particles can be much smaller – as small as 0.02 μm. Only recently have filters been developed that are both fine enough to exclude micro-organisms and capable of providing a high enough throughput capacity to be practical. Membrane filters are now commercially available at all suitable scales.

Table 6.2 Membrane Filter Terminology

Term	Pore size lower limit	Pressure
Micro-filtration	0.1 μm	4–10 psi
Ultra-filtration	0.01 μm	10–30 psi
Nano-filtration	0.001 μm	80–120 psi
Reverse osmosis	0.0001 μm	125–200 psi

A membrane filter looks like a large number of thin drinking straws suspended in a frame. These hollow fibres have holes in them of the desired size, so that applying positive pressure to the feed water or negative pressure to the header – sucking on the straw – pushes or draws water through the filter, leaving the impurities on the outside.

Membrane filtration is used in a number of medium-sized communities in Ontario, notably Owen Sound and Thunder Bay; Walkerton now has such a system, operated under contract by the Ontario Clean Water Agency.

One commentator observed that, from a safety point of view, membrane filtration and UV have interesting characteristics: "They have virtually eliminated the risk of chemical by-products and all of their health concerns, which mean the operator skill level and the attendants needed to adjust the processes are significantly reduced."[42] Their costs have been coming down rapidly. UV systems are already available at the scale of individual households, and a household-scale membrane system is just becoming available in Ontario at the time of writing. Maintaining home UV systems is not difficult, especially when the unit has a monitor showing that the lamp has not burned out. Membrane systems need periodic maintenance, but this may be done under contract by the same utility that rents the system to the homeowner. Household-scale UV systems now cost $400 to $1,500. Membrane systems are entering the market at about $4,000 but deal with a wider range of contaminants. The

---

[42] K. Mains, Walkerton Inquiry Submission (Public Hearing, September 12, 2001), transcript pp. 94–95.

importance of economical point-of-entry technologies for disinfection is substantial if Ontario is to reach the goal of having safe water for all its citizens. The prices may be seen as putting a notional cap on the amount that rural groundwater users need to spend.

Heat: The principle behind pasteurization, heat, is also a good killer of micro-organisms. It is applied in desalination schemes in the Middle East and other dry areas of the world. The typical flash distillation process heats the water sufficiently and for a long enough time to inactivate micro-organisms. Such expensive schemes are irrelevant in Canada.

Comparison of New Disinfection Techniques: A recently reported Wisconsin study evaluated ozone, membranes, and four kinds of UV treatment.[43] The latter's performance strongly depended on the clarity of the water. Lamps aged in predictable fashion and were readily cleaned; indeed, they performed better than the flux measurement devices did. Low-pressure, high-output (LPHO) lamps at 40 mJ/cm^2 used 43% of the power used by medium-pressure lamps (12.5 kWh/ML[44] versus 28.75 kWh/ML), but they did little for taste, odour, and colour problems, which were better dealt with by the broader energy spectrum. Ozone (O_3) required 167 to 325 kWh/ML, and performance depended on temperature and pH. UV worked superbly on *Cryptosporidium*. The first demonstration run of LPHO lamps at 45 mJ/cm^2 gave >4.7-log inactivation, the limit of measurement.

The huge Metropolitan Water District of Southern California has likewise been evaluating UV and O_3.[45] It found that a mere 3 mJ/cm^2 produced 1-log reduction, though with high variance. It saw both techniques as having a place in a multi-barrier system, noting that beyond treating bacteria, UV was a *Cryptosporidium* specialist and O_3 was good at pre-oxidation for particulate control, micro-pollutant oxidation, taste, odour, and colour reduction. Bromate, a probable carcinogen that occurs when there is substantial bromide in the raw

---

[43] E.D. Mackey, R.S. Cushing, and G.F. Crozes, 2001, "Evaluation of advanced UV disinfection systems for the inactivation of *Cryptosporidium*," proceedings at the American Water Works Association Annual Conference, Washington, DC, June 17–21.

[44] ML: megaliter, or 1,000,000 L.

[45] B.M. Coffey et al., 2001, "Comparing UV and ozone disinfection of *Cryptosporidium parvum*: Implications for multi-barrier treatment," proceedings at the American Water Works Association Annual Conference, Washington, DC, June 17–21. An interesting side point was that *Bacillus subtilis* may be a useful surrogate for *C. parvum* (r^2 = 0.93 for UV and r^2 = 0.96 for O_3).

water and that may be an ozone disinfection by-product,[46] was judged to be a treatable concern.

This work by the U.S. Environmental Protection Agency showed that, for typical installations, the ratio of cost was around 10 for micro- or ultra-filtration to 2 or 3 for ozone to 1 for UV, though the ratios are said to be narrowing even as the absolute cost numbers decline. One senior Canadian engineer thinks that ozone will eventually be replaced by high-performance membranes and UV disinfection, especially in cold climates, unless there are specific geosmin[47] and related summer taste problems, with which ozone deals well; even so, ozone can in some circumstances impart a phenolic-like taste.[48] A comparison of costs by another practising engineer showed that none of these advanced treatment costs was large, in the context of the delivered cost of potable water.[49]

6.3.4 Meeting Other Treatment Objectives

Total Organic Carbon Removal: Total organic carbon (TOC), which consists of dissolved and particulate matter, can be removed from water through coagulation or by magnetic ion exchange. It has generally not been possible to remove TOC economically, so raw waters that are high in TOC tend to be avoided if possible. As an indicator of organic DBP precursors, TOC serves as the basis for coagulation requirements in the U.S. EPA regulations.

pH Correction: The pH level may have to be corrected during the treatment process for a variety of reasons. Some chemicals are more effective at certain pH levels, so pH adjustments may be necessary to optimize disinfection. Further, some treatment processes alter pH.

Corrosion Control: In the plant and distribution system, corrosion control must include the control of environmental parameters, the addition of chemical inhibitors, electrochemical measures, and system design considerations. Corrosion control and inhibitor chemicals include polyphosphates, zinc

---

[46] Federal–Provincial Subcommittee on Drinking Water, 1999, "Bromate," establishes an IMAC of 0.01 mg/L. See <http://www.hc-sc.gc.ca/ehp/ehd/catalogue/bch_pubs/summary.pdf>.

[47] Geosmin is "the common name for *trans*-1,10-dimethyl-*trans*-9-decalol, an earthy-smelling chemical produced by certain blue-green algae and *Actinomycetes*. This odorous compound can be perceived at low nanogram-per-litre concentrations": Symons in Singer, p. 183.

[48] K. Mains, 2001, personal communication, June 18.

[49] W.B. Dowbiggin, 2001, "Advanced water treatment without advanced cost," proceedings at the American Water Works Association Annual Conference, Washington, DC, June 17–21.

orthophosphates, and silicates.[50] Electrochemical methods convert the infrastructure to a cathode (a receiver of electrons) to prevent chemical reactions from occurring or, more precisely, to confine them to the sacrificial anode.

Taste and Odour Control: Offensive taste and odour, often seasonal problems, arise most commonly as a result of generally very small amounts (ng/L) of secretions from blue-green algae and *Actinomycetes*. There are also a wide number of sources that have a human origin. No single treatment can be specified without an exhaustive characterization of the water, but in general, oxidation followed by filtration reduces the problem to manageable levels.[51]

6.3.5   Choosing an Optimal Treatment Strategy

The choice of an efficient strategy must reflect the fundamental objective of disinfection, which is to ensure the reliable removal or inactivation of pathogenic micro-organisms, thus dealing with the largest and most acute health risk. But the benefits and appropriateness of available technologies must also be evaluated in the context of the whole water system, from source water to tap. The strength and reliability of the technical barriers must reflect the risks associated with the level of contaminants in the source water. As for treatment, disinfection is the first but not the sole objective: the removal of hardness, particles, DBP precursors, natural organic matter, colour, iron, manganese, taste and odour, trace contaminants, and so on must also be taken into account when selecting the best treatment solutions.

The order in which individual treatment steps are arranged can affect both their effectiveness and the overall efficiency of the treatment processes. Some steps are affected by other processes or by water properties or constituents. Some result in by-products that must be removed. For example, the effectiveness of disinfection in general and UV irradiation in particular are maximized when turbidity is low, so these processes are usually performed after chemically assisted filtration. Treatment for iron and manganese must be followed by filtration to remove the resulting sludge. Some disinfectants form nuisance residuals that need to be removed. Moving the point of chlorine addition to the point of minimum dissolved organic carbon can reduce DBP formation. However, since disinfection is improved by maximizing contact time, a strategy favouring the reduction of DBPs may make disinfection less efficient.

[50] Canada, National Health and Welfare, p. 188.
[51] HDR Engineering Inc., pp. 538–554.

Beyond simply performing the steps in the right order, the quantities of chemical additives may have to be continuously adjusted as a result of slight changes in such raw water parameters as temperature and turbidity. Chemical disinfection is particularly delicate because the desired dose range is typically narrow to inactivate microbial pathogens and minimize DBP formation.

6.4   Water Recycling

All water is recycled through nature's hydrological cycle. The term "direct recycling" means treating wastewater so that it can be reused immediately for drinking purposes. This extreme of treatment is clearly required in some places, such as in space or in deserts, where a grave shortage of water exists alongside a relatively unconstrained demand. However, Ontario does not require such extreme measures and should not permit the increased risks that come from direct recycling. That said, it is inevitable, even in Ontario, that wastewater after treatment will be discharged into the environment to enter the source water of drinking water systems. Both California and Florida indirectly recycle water to some degree, through groundwater recharge, irrigation projects, and the like, but not without controversy.[52] However, it will not be long before an amount equal to half of Ontario's reliably available annual water supply is used, in some form, at least once. In inland areas of intense use, such as in the Grand River basin, water is now being used much more intensively than is the Ontario average. Under these circumstances, and with the example of such non-arid but industrialized regions as Europe's Rhine River valley, Ontario should at least keep up-to-date with recycling research in developed countries.

Water recycling can reduce the amount of water needing to be treated through the use of a dual water supply system. This relatively expensive technique is particularly suited to regions where raw water is costly or scarce, as in parts of the United States, the Middle East, and even northern Canada. These systems separate grey water (bath, dish, and wash water) from black water (household sewage). Black water is sent to a sewage treatment plant, as it is in traditional systems. Grey water is recycled and brought back into residences via a second local distribution system. This water is then used for non-potable purposes, such as toilet flushing and garden irrigation. Grey-water recycling systems can

---

[52] For example, see M. Zapler, 2001, "Recycled water draws scrutiny," *Mercury News* (San Jose), October 21, p. B1.

be adopted at the individual or communal level; in Australia it is used in communities ranging from 1,200 to 12,000 households.[53]

Grey water is a lesser source of pathogenic micro-organisms and parasites than sewage is, and its organic content decomposes much faster. It is not, however, an acceptable source of drinking water at present. Laundry and kitchen wastes can be heavily loaded with pathogens as well as more generalized biochemical oxygen demand.

Rainwater reclamation is similar in principle to grey-water recycling, but the reclaimed rainwater is potentially much cleaner, depending on how it is collected and stored. The water is used, untreated, for purposes not requiring water of a quality as high as that of drinking water. Although not as reliable, rainwater reclamation is a cheaper and healthier alternative to grey-water recycling. In regions where the wells produce hard water, rain barrels are common because rainwater is much softer. Its attractiveness for bathing and hair washing can lead, as in Walkerton, to breaches in system integrity through mismanaged cross-connections. There seems to be no compelling reason to prohibit rainwater use by individual households so long as there is no potential for contaminating a communal supply. The information provided to the public about individual household supplies should include advice about good practice.

There is no need for the direct recycling of grey or black water for potable uses to be permitted under Ontario Regulation 459/00.

6.5   Wastewater Treatment

Because sewage treatment plant standards and operations go beyond the mandate of this Inquiry, I make only the following recommendation, recognizing that it should be seen in the context of a larger program of reform and upgrading:

Recommendation 32: The provincial government should support major wastewater plant operators in collaborative studies aimed at identifying practical methods of reducing or removing heavy metals and priority

---

[53] N. Booker, 2000, "Economic Scale of Greywater Reuse Systems" in *Built Environmental Innovation & Construction Technology*, Number 16 (Canberra: CSIRO); see <http://www.dbce.csiro.au/inno-web/1200/economic-scale.htm> [accessed May 2, 2002].

organics (such as endocrine disruptors) that are not removed by conventional treatment.

Sewage treatment plant discharges should be brought within the cumulative loadings established under the watershed management plans recommended in Chapter 4.

A brief discussion of wastewater treatment technology is appropriate here. Technically, wastewater treatment shares many features with drinking water treatment. An impure influent must be cleaned, but not to the same standards as those required for drinking. Rather, the standards are constructed (somewhat loosely) around the notion of no harm being done to receiving waters or their fauna. It is not just technical similarity that makes the topic worthy of concern, however. Protecting source waters by introducing sewage treatment is one of the most important public health measures ever devised.[54] Treatment techniques are grouped into imperfectly defined baskets labelled as primary, secondary, and tertiary (see Table 6.3).[55]

Primary treatment involves little more than screening raw sewage, separating the grit particularly associated with infiltration and with combined storm and sanitary sewers, and sedimentation. "It is unlikely that a certificate of approval would be issued by MOE today for a new primary plant. Although several primary plants exist throughout the province, most of them face regulatory pressure to … move toward secondary treatment."[56]

Secondary treatment adds a biological reactor – active or passive, aerobic or anaerobic – in which bacteria absorb dissolved and colloidal organic matter so that they can be separated from the aqueous phase. The biological sludge that is typically separated by sedimentation can be further stabilized by digestion, in which the microorganisms metabolize the available organic matter until it is all consumed, effectively starving to death. Anaerobic digestion, the normal process in a septic tank, produces methane gas and a relatively inert sludge.

---

[54] J. Benidickson, 2002, "Water supply and sewage infrastructure in Ontario, 1880–1990s: Legal and institutional aspects of public health and environmental history," Walkerton Inquiry Commissioned Paper 1. S. Gwyn (1984) has given a wonderful account of miasmic Ottawa in the 1870s in her history of the city: *The Private Capital* (Toronto: McClelland and Stewart).

[55] E. Doyle et al., 2002, "Wastewater collection and treatment," Walkerton Inquiry Commissioned Paper 9, contains a fuller description, covering not only technology and standards, but also the current state of the art in Ontario and comparisons with a number of other jurisdictions.

[56] Doyle et al., 2002, Paper 9, p. 100.

Table 6.3   Typical Effluent Quality for Different Levels of Treatment (mg/L)

Parameter	Level of Treatment				
	Influent	Primary	Secondary	Tertiary	Objective[57]
Total suspended solids (TSS)	200	110	15	5	25
5-day biochemical oxygen demand[58] (BOD$_5$)	170	70	~15	~6	25
Total Kjeldahl nitrogen (TKN)	30	25	20	5	–
Total phosphorus (TP)	7	5	3.5	0.3	0.3

Note: In addition, typical influent carries 10⁴–10⁵ fecal coliforms and 10–100 enteric viruses per mL. Feces may contain 10⁹ bacteria per gram.
Source: E. Doyle et al., 2002, "Wastewater collection and treatment," Walkerton Inquiry Commissioned Paper 9, Tables 4.1 and 4.2, pp. 98–99.

The most common form of secondary treatment in Ontario, the century-old activated sludge process, adds air to a mechanically stirred mix, which allows aerobic micro-organisms (the active component of the activated sludge) to flourish. These organisms then consume dissolved and colloidal carbonaceous matter so that, upon separation, the clarified effluent has a much-reduced biochemical oxygen demand. Effective exploitation of activated sludge occurred only after treatment specialists realized that the settled concentrated sludge should be recycled and mixed with incoming sewage to build up a high concentration of micro-organisms that would remove the organic matter on contact. Secondary treatment may also include phosphorus removal.

Tertiary treatment is generally required when the volume of receiving water is low or zero. "A dry or perennial stream is defined by the 7Q20 rule (referring to the minimum flow recorded or predicted over a 7-day period in the past 20 years)."[59] Tertiary treatment is usually required when streams run dry or when less than 10:1 dilution is available under the "7Q20 rule." The requirement is specified in terms of more stringent limits on effluent biochemical oxygen demand, total suspended solids, total phosphorus, and ammonia nitrogen than

---

[57] This is a basic set of effluent quality standards; more stringent standards are required for more sensitive receiving waters.

[58] BOD is a generic measure of the biodegradable organic matter present in water, as exhibited by the dissolved oxygen consumed by bacteria as they decompose organic compounds. When receiving waters are overloaded with BOD, the limited supply of dissolved oxygen can be totally consumed, creating anaerobic conditions and killing all higher forms of life.

[59] Doyle et al., 2002, Paper 9, p. 111.

can be achieved through secondary treatment. Filtration, often chemically assisted, through beds of ground anthracite and fine sand, is the norm. The chemicals used for coagulation, the familiar alum or ferric chloride from drinking water treatment, assist in capturing phosphorus.

Disinfection can be added to any of these processes, although the standards required are quite different than they are for drinking water. (Ontario tolerates 100 *E. coli* colonies per 100 mL in water used for recreation.) Chlorine is the most common disinfectant, but it has all the disadvantages that were noted earlier for drinking water – handling problems, need for precise dosage, DBPs – as well as one other: the final effluent must be dechlorinated before release because even the small quantities associated with a chlorine residual in drinking water distribution systems can be harmful to aquatic fauna. Fish, crustaceans, and other aquatic organisms breathe dissolved oxygen, with the result that they will be exposed to dissolved chlorine through their respiratory apparatus as well as through their gastrointestinal tract. Across all species, the gastrointestinal tract is far less susceptible to chemical insult than are the respiratory organs, which likely explains why fish and other aquatic organisms are so much less tolerant of dissolved chlorine than are humans.

UV radiation has gained widespread acceptance for sewage disinfection in the past decade in Ontario and has been the technique of choice for treating drinking water for a longer period in Europe. According to Doyle,

> UV systems consume much more power than chlorination, but they have many advantages, including
>
> • very short retention times of one minute or less, compared to 30 minutes for chlorine (hence compact size),
>
> • non-toxic effluent,
>
> • no residual by-products such as trihalomethanes,
>
> • no need to transport, store and handle hazardous chemicals,
>
> • no need for emergency ventilation and scrubbing systems as necessary for chlorine,

- simple and accurate process control, and

- low and simple maintenance.[60]

Membrane technology is emerging as a strong competitor to UV disinfection; indeed, its first large-scale use was for the purification of wastewater in Europe. Their considerable advantages can overcome an initial cost disadvantage (which is declining). Again, Doyle states:

- They eliminate secondary clarifiers, which invariably are the limiting process in terms of plant rating and performance.

- They eliminate tertiary filtration.

- Aeration tanks can operate at a mixed-liquor suspended solids (MLSS) concentration of approximately 15,000 mg/L, compared to 2,000–5,000 mg/L for conventional plants. Simplistically, this reduces the aeration tank footprint and volume by a factor of 3 or 4, which is a dramatic difference made even more so when the elimination of clarifiers and filters is taken into account.

- Rather than reduce the size of the aeration tank, the high MLSS concentration can be used to increase solids retention time, promote nitrification, and reduce the volume of solids or sludge …

- Membrane pore sizes are small enough to strain out bacteria physically, effectively eliminating the need for disinfection.

- Effluent suspended solids are consistently maintained at <5 mg/L to non-detectable, regardless of the quality of the flocculated mixed-liquor solids, a factor crucial to the operation of conventional secondary clarifiers.[61]

For all water treatment processes, there remains the problem of getting rid of the (semi-)solid sludge left at the end of these processes. The biosolids can be

---

[60] Ibid., p. 117.
[61] Ibid., pp. 120–121.

incinerated, thus contributing to Ontario's air pollution, or they can be partially dewatered and applied to agricultural land, as discussed in Chapter 4. When biosolids are completely dried and pelletized, they may be used as an organic fertilizer. In all the recycling methods, however, the control of contamination by heavy metals and key endocrine-disrupting substances is perhaps the most intractable problem. The wide variety of endocrine-disrupting substances, the fact that many are not sequestered or degraded by conventional treatment and are apparently ubiquitous in rivers downstream from cities or intensive livestock agricultural areas,[62] is a matter for concern and will require research in many jurisdictions, both in Canada and abroad.

6.6   Emerging Water Treatment Technologies

The treatment for protozoan pathogens has been a major topic of professional debate in the past few years. The debate will likely continue, although recent developments in membranes and UV radiation technology mean that attention is shifting to application rather than technological development as such. Although most water-borne viruses seem susceptible to known disinfection and filtration techniques (occasionally at higher dose or CT rates), more discussion is needed about these viruses. As a group they are poorly understood. Research is required to determine not only the risks they pose to people, but also to gather basic information about their sources and persistence in raw and finished waters.

The report on contaminants commissioned for the Inquiry,[63] as well as the expert meeting on contaminants, proposed that the main chemical contaminants of concern for drinking water in Ontario were lead, DBPs, nitrate/nitrite, fluorides and water treatment chemicals, and, potentially, pharmaceuticals and other endocrine disruptors. Better monitoring was recommended for pesticides and herbicides. Of these substances, the knowledge base concerning soluble antibiotics, other pharmaceuticals, and endocrine disruptors appears weakest.

---

[62] K.K. Barnes et al., 2002, *Water Quality Data for Pharmaceuticals, Hormones, and Other Organic Wastewater Contaminants in U.S. Streams, 1999–2000,* Open File Report 02-94 (Iowa City, IA: United States Geological Survey).

[63] L. Ritter et al., 2002, "Sources, pathways, and relative risks of contaminants in water," Walkerton Inquiry Commissioned Paper 10. Environment Canada has published a broad review of 15 classes of hazard, summarizing current knowledge and suggesting areas for further research: Environment Canada, 2001, "Threats to sources of drinking water and aquatic ecosystem health in Canada," *NWRI Scientific Assessment Report Series 1* (Burlington, ON: National Water Research Institute) <http://www.cciw.ca/nwri/threats/threats-e.pdf>.

Because their concentrations in source waters are so low, the detection of these contaminants is difficult and expensive, and epidemiological studies are exceptionally difficult.

All of these chemicals are usually present, if at all, in very small concentrations, a situation that poses difficult engineering questions for treatment design. Ion exchange methods and enhanced membrane treatment are the focal points of much current work. The United States Environmental Protection Agency, as noted in Chapter 5, has a formal process in which larger water systems screen for the presence of any of a long list of suspect chemicals.[64] Whenever possible, the best option is to choose source waters already low in the contaminants that are difficult or expensive to sequester through conventional water treatment.

New technologies may be particularly helpful for very small systems, ranging from one to several dozen households. Sometimes, point-of-use devices may be more efficient for certain contaminants than large central facilities.[65]

Continuous improvement in water quality in response to emerging threats will require new and refined treatment techniques. A delicate balance must be achieved between innovation and reliability. A promising new treatment, if implemented without careful testing and evaluation, may have unhappy side effects or may be temperamental and require constant attention from highly skilled people to make it work as intended.

Society is properly risk-averse when it comes to public health. But an approach that unnecessarily slows the adoption of proven new techniques may have high social costs, too. The assessment, evaluation, and improvement of novel water treatment technologies prior to licensing their routine use should be done by the MOE's Drinking Water Branch.

---

[64] United States Environmental Protection Agency, 2001, "Reference Guide for the Unregulated Contaminant Monitoring Regulation," EPA 815-R-01-023 (Washington, DC) <http://www.epa.gov/safewater/standard/ucmr/ref_guide.pdf>.

[65] P.L. Gurian and M.J. Small, 2002, "Point-of-use treatment and the revised arsenic MCL," *Journal of the American Water Works Association*, vol. 94, no. 3, pp. 101–108.

6.6.1 The Role of the Ministry of the Environment in Technology Development and Evaluation

Recommendation 33: The Ministry of the Environment should be adequately resourced to support a water sciences and standards function in relation to drinking water.

At present, the MOE's Environmental Sciences and Standards Division provides scientific support in relation to drinking water, as well as other aspects of the environment. In this division, there are four relevant branches: the Standards Development Branch, the Monitoring and Reporting Branch, the Laboratory Services Branch, and the Environmental Partnerships Branch. As it relates to drinking water, the science and standards function carried out by the Standards Development Branch and the Monitoring and Reporting Branch should be transferred to the new Drinking Water Branch that I recommend in Chapter 13. I discuss the future role of the Laboratory Services Branch in Chapter 9.

In this section, I discuss the important sciences and standards function to be carried out in the new Drinking Water Branch. As I indicate in Chapter 13, this function must be adequately resourced in terms of staffing, equipment, and other resources. At a minimum, the MOE's role in this regard includes

- evaluating research that has been done elsewhere to determine whether it is applicable in Ontario;

- supporting standards-setting processes;

- ensuring that research specifically relevant to Ontario is done;

- providing specialist expertise on a regular basis to support the new Drinking Water and Watershed Management branches of the ministry in the approvals and inspection activities (Chapter 12);

- coordinating, and partly funding, collaborative research involving universities and the water industry; and

- coordinating with Environment Canada and other agencies.

Ontario once had a world-leading reputation in research on water and wastewater treatment. The Ontario Water Resources Commission (OWRC), in its research activities, had the reputation for leading all organizations in Canada and was consulted by governments around the world. In 1972, the OWRC became part of the broader MOE. The change of focus, accompanied by budgetary pressures, meant a gradual reduction in the provincial government's capacity to stay abreast of technological developments in the water field. Although the capacity for building and managing waterworks remained, the capacity for innovation waned. The best practices manuals that the OWRC and its successor once published regularly became less frequent.[66] The last of these manuals were published in 1982 and 1984.

The private sector and, somewhat later, university researchers continued the work begun by the OWRC. Through the 1970s and 1980s, large engineering firms provided the new infrastructure demanded by a growing and increasingly environmentally conscious population. Since about 1990, Ontario universities have begun to pay new attention to water treatment. The University of Waterloo, through its pioneering engineering faculty, has been a consistent leader. In recent years, the federal government has supported this regrowth with a number of endowed chairs and a new Network of Centres of Excellence, which is centred at that university. The many other university research centres include the University of Guelph Centre for Land and Water Stewardship, the Trent University Water Quality Centre, and the University of Waterloo Centre for Groundwater Research and chair in groundwater remediation.

The rise of university research contrasts strongly with the increasing financial pressure that has curtailed the MOE's research capacity. The question is whether this imbalance should continue. I start with the premise that, one way or another, the MOE will be the ministry that is required to license the application of water treatment technology in Ontario. To what degree can it rely on work done elsewhere in coming to its regulatory decisions?

A number of resources are available to the MOE. The Canadian Construction Materials Centre, part of National Research Council (NRC) Institute for Research in Construction, was established as a solution to this problem in the construction industry. It evaluates innovative materials, products, systems, and services with respect to their intended uses and applicable standards.[67] The Canadian Commission on Construction Materials Evaluation, which includes

---

[66] Ontario, Ministry of the Environment, 1982, "Guidelines for the Design of Water Treatment Works," and 1984, "Guidelines for the Design of Sewage Treatment Plants."

[67] See the Canadian Construction Materials Centre Web site <http://www.nrc.ca/ccmc/home_e.shtml> [accessed May 5, 2002].

members of the general public as well as representatives from industry and government bodies, provides policy and technical advice.

The NRC's Canadian Infrastructure Technology Assessment Centre (CITAC) offers similar services for infrastructure products. Its main focus is wastewater management technologies for residential purposes. On a fee-for-service basis, CITAC establishes testing methodologies and performance criteria. Testing is outsourced to an accredited facility for product assessment. Subsequently, CITAC evaluates the results of the assessment and provides a technical opinion on the product's suitability for use.[68]

The Environment Technology Verification (ETV) program is similar in that it "provides validation and independent verification of environmental technology performance claims."[69] ETV was once a federal concern, but it is now a private company owned by the Ontario Centre for Environmental Technology Advancement (OCETA) and operating under a licence agreement with Environment Canada. Products can be assessed within the ETV program if they are an environmental technology, provide environmental benefits, address environmental problems, or are an equipment-based environmental service.[70] These include water and wastewater treatment technologies. A recent success of the program is a novel process to remove arsenic from drinking water.

The American Water Works Association Research Foundation (AWWARF) is a principal source of research on new technology, methods, and evaluation. A strength of its large and active research program is the manner in which it uses its spending power to bring operators, university researchers, and the engineering profession together. A number of Ontario utilities are members of the AWWARF and participate in its projects, which benefit water consumers everywhere, and this cooperation should be encouraged.

The aim of the MOE should be to develop sufficient expertise for Ontario's circumstances without duplicating research and development carried out by other organizations. The MOE should have widely experienced people on staff who keep up-to-date with developments here and abroad and who evaluate those developments for the MOE's standards-setting and approvals processes. The ministry's staff should provide expert advice on whether material,

---

[68] Harry Baker, NRC, CITAC, 2002, personal communication, January.
[69] See the ETV program Web site <http://www.etvcanada.com/English/e_home.htm> [accessed May 5, 2002].
[70] Ibid.

machinery, or water quality standards that have been developed in other leading jurisdictions can and should be adopted in Ontario. They will need funds to attend conferences, to travel, and occasionally to host expert workshops on matters of Ontario interest: cold-water chemistry and the boreal source waters of much of Ontario will not attract as much attention outside our borders as we might hope. Some funding should also be made available to sponsor Ontario utilities, university scientists, and engineers in collaborative research projects of the sort that the AWWARF organizes, and resources should be available for archiving and disseminating the results of the work to interested parties in Ontario.

One implication of this approach is that the MOE staff should be allowed and encouraged by, among other things, their salary structure to develop a high level of technical proficiency, rather than relying on advancement to management as the only route to career progression.

A benefit of this approach is that it will allow the creation of an environment in which innovative Ontario companies will not have to go abroad for trials and first orders. The MOE currently applies a cautious approach in recognizing new technology, an approach that is perhaps too cautious in failing to recognize pilot plants operated in other jurisdictions. Current policy is as follows:

> Since new technologies pose a higher risk of failure, the Ministry's role is to protect public and environmental safety by ensuring that the risk of failure is reduced to an acceptably low level. This is achieved through the approvals process where the site specific application of new technology is reviewed by an engineer. Pilot plant installations are approved provided that acceptable safeguards are designed into the system to eliminate any degradation of treated water quality. Technology is considered by the Ministry to be proven usually when at least three separate installations can operate at near design capacity for three years without major failures of the process, unit or equipment to perform as designed.[71]

Given the infrequency with which wholly new installations are undertaken in Ontario, this process can take far too long. In some cases, it may be appropriate simply to adopt approvals given in other provinces or U.S. states that apply rigorous standards.

---

[71] Ontario, Ministry of the Attorney General, 2001, memorandum, Fran Carnerie to Jim Ayres, December 14.

6.7   Ontario Regulation 459/00

Treatment technologies are driven by regulatory requirements. I conclude this chapter with observations on Ontario Regulation 459/00, the current regulation addressing large waterworks, and suggestions for its improvement. I discuss Ontario Regulation 505/01, which regulates smaller systems, in Chapter 14 of this report.

Ontario Regulation 459/00, the basic regulation for larger waterworks, was created shortly after the tragic events in Walkerton. Its commendable results were that it made enforceable in law the standards for quality and sampling that hitherto had been guidelines or objectives, and it improved information management, including public access to information. The main changes introduced by the regulation are summarized here:

• Groundwater must be disinfected – in practice, with chlorine (s. 5).

• Surface water must be subjected to chemically assisted filtration and disinfection or, in the view of the MOE Director, be given equivalent or better treatment (s. 5).

• An exemption from disinfection may be made only if the equipment and chemicals for disinfection are installed and available for instant use if needed (s. 6).

• A more onerous sampling regime is enacted (s. 7) that requires, among other things, that testing be done either in a laboratory accredited for the particular test by the Canadian Association for Environmental Analytical Laboratories, operating under the aegis of the Standards Council of Canada (s. 2), or by staff certified for the procedure in question (s. 7).

• Notification requirements are formalized (addressing the non-notification problem that contributed to the severity of the Walkerton outbreak), and requirements to take any necessary corrective action and to inform the public are introduced (ss. 8–11).

• An exhaustive quarterly public reporting of test results and the actions taken are to be made available to the public (s. 12).

- Consulting engineers are to be retained every three years to make a detailed examination of the works and to prepare reports according to an MOE outline.

I pause to introduce certain documents and their customary abbreviations. The old "Ontario Drinking Water Objectives" (ODWO)[72] and the technical bulletin "Chlorination of Potable Water Supplies" (the Chlorination Bulletin)[73] are now contained in a document entitled "Ontario Drinking Water Standards" (ODWS) and referred to in Ontario Regulation 459/00, now called "Drinking Water Protection – Larger Water Works."

In considering an application for an approval, the director must now have regard to the ODWS (s. 4(2)). Although portions of the ODWS relating to sampling and analysis, standards, and indicators of adverse water quality are schedules to the new regulation, the ODWS as a whole is not part of Ontario Regulation 459/00. In the discussion that follows, I summarize the provisions of the regulation and the ODWS and make a few relatively minor suggestions for improvements.

6.7.1   The Application of Ontario Regulation 459/00

The regulation applies to all water treatment and distribution systems requiring approval under section 52(1) of the *Ontario Water Resources Act* (OWRA), which states that no person shall establish, alter, extend or replace new or existing waterworks without a Certificate of Approval granted by a director (s. 3(1)).[74]

---

[72] Ontario, Ministry of the Environment, Water Policy Branch, 1994, "Ontario Drinking Water Objectives" (1994 revision).

[73] Ontario, Ministry of the Environment, Water Policy Branch, 1987, "Chlorination of Potable Water Supplies," Technical Bulletin 65-W-4 (updated March 1987); the old Chlorination Bulletin has been replaced by "Procedure B13-3: Chlorination of Potable Water Supplies in Ontario," at p. 59 of the ODWS.

[74] Ontario Regulation 459/00, s. 3(1).

The following systems are exempt from approval under the OWRA:

- waterworks used only for supplying water that is required for agricultural, commercial, or industrial purposes and that is not required under any Act or regulation made under any Act to be fit for human consumption (s. 52(8)(a));

- waterworks not capable of supplying water at a rate greater than 50,000 L per day (s. 52(8)(b));

- privately owned waterworks that supply five or fewer private residences (s. 52(8)(c)); and

- waterworks that may be exempt by regulations made under the OWRA (s. 52(8)(d)).

In addition, Ontario Regulation 459/00 exempts the following water treatment and distribution systems from regulation:

- systems that obtain their water from another water treatment or distribution system. This exemption does not apply if the system obtaining the water is owned or operated by a municipality or the Ontario Clean Water Agency (OCWA), nor does it apply if the system obtaining the water supplies water to a municipality or the OCWA. In addition, systems that rechlorinate or otherwise treat their water do not qualify for this exemption (s. 3(2));

- systems that supply 50,000 L of water or less during 88 days or more in a 90-day period, unless the system serves more than five residences (s. 3(3)); and

- systems that do not have a capacity of supplying more than 250,000 L per day, unless the system serves more than five residences (s. 3(4)).

If any of the exemptions under section 52 of the OWRA or Ontario Regulation 459/00 are met, the system is exempt[75] from the requirements in the regulation.

---

[75] Some water treatment systems or distribution systems not covered by O. Reg. 459/00 fall under O. Reg. 505/01, Drinking Water Protection: Smaller Water Works Serving Designated Facilities.

6.7.2   Minimum Level of Treatment and Chlorination Requirements

Section 5 of Ontario Regulation 459/00 sets out the minimum requirements for water treatment. Disinfection by chlorination or an equally effective treatment is now mandatory for all water works captured by the regulation, unless a variance is granted (ss. 5(3) and 6). Groundwater sources must be treated by disinfection (s. 5(1)), whereas surface water sources must be treated by chemically assisted filtration and disinfection or other treatment capable, in the Director's opinion, of producing water of equal or better quality (s. 5(2)).

The minimum treatment requirements once found in MOE policy documents[76] are now law. However, Ontario Regulation 459/00 contains an exemption for water obtained exclusively from groundwater sources (s. 6(2)). Water obtained exclusively from groundwater sources may not require disinfection or chlorination if, among other things, the Medical Officer of Health consents, standby disinfection equipment and chemicals are readily available, and a public meeting has been held on the issue (s. 6(2)(ii),(v),(vii)).

According to Procedure B-13-3, groundwater supplies must maintain a minimum chlorine residual of 0.2 mg/L after 15 minutes of contact time prior to reaching the first customer. This minimum residual is lower than the minimum level of 0.5 mg/L identified in the Chlorination Bulletin, which allowed a 0.2 mg/L residual only in circumstances of uniformly low turbidities and in supplies that were proven free of hazardous bacterial contamination.[77]

Procedure B-13-3 sets the same minimum requirement of 0.2 mg/L after 15 minutes of contact time for surface waters. This minimum residual level is in addition to a level of treatment determined on the *CT* basis. A minimum 3-log inactivation is required for *Giardia* cysts, and a minimum 4-log inactivation is required for viruses.

The inactivation requirements for surface water also apply to groundwater under the direct influence of surface water, but under certain circumstances, inactivation may be achieved by disinfection only. However, a definition for

---

[76] Ontario, Ministry of the Environment, Water Policy Branch, 1994, pp. 8–9.
[77] Ontario, Ministry of the Environment, Water Policy Branch, 1987, p. 9.

groundwater sources under the direct influence of surface water is not included in Procedure B-13-3, the ODWS, or the regulation. The government has used a fairly complex definition in a policy document.[78]

6.7.3   Sampling and Analysis Requirements

Ontario Regulation 459/00 makes mandatory the old sampling recommendations of the ODWO (s. 7 and Schedule 2). Generally, the sampling and analysis requirements for chemical and physical parameters under the regulation are either the same as, or more stringent than, those of the ODWO. Where the ODWO only recommended continuous chlorine monitoring for surface water sources serving a population over 3,300, continuous monitoring is now mandatory for service water sources serving populations of 3,000 or more. In addition, more pesticides and volatile organics must be monitored under the regulation than under the ODWO.[79] The regulation also allows for additional sampling requirements, if necessary (s. 7(1)(b)).[80]

The regulation states that "ground water under the direct influence of surface water is considered to be surface water" for the purpose of sampling and analysis,[81] but the absence of a legal definition for such a source may make the enforceability of this provision difficult. I prefer that treatment requirements be determined on a case-by-case basis, as I laid out in section 6.2.

Under Ontario Regulation 459/00, waterworks must now use an accredited laboratory (s. 7(3)) unless they are using continuous monitoring equipment to measure operational parameters.[82] An accredited laboratory is one that has either been accredited by the Standards Council of Canada (SCC) or has obtained accreditation for analysis that, in the director's opinion, "is equivalent to accreditation" by the SCC (s. 2(1)).

---

[78] Ontario, Ministry of the Environment, 2001, "Terms of Reference for Hydrogeological Study to Examine Groundwater Sources Potentially under Direct Influence of Surface Water" <http://www.ene.gov.on.ca/envision/techdocs/4167e.pdf> [accessed April 30, 2002].

[79] Epoxide is no longer included on the list of monitored pesticides in Table D of Schedule 2 of O. Reg. 459/00.

[80] This section could theoretically be used to monitor new chemical or physical parameters that pose a health-related threat to water quality.

[81] This designation makes a continuous chlorine residual monitoring system mandatory; see Schedule 2 of O. Reg. 459/00.

[82] Operational parameters such as turbidity, pH, and chlorine residual do not have to be measured by an accredited laboratory.

An operator must ensure that the MOE has been notified of a laboratory's name (s. 7 (5)), and the laboratory cannot subcontract the analysis unless specific requirements have been met (s. 7(7)). Copies of water analysis reports submitted by a laboratory to the owner of a water treatment or distribution system must also be sent to the MOE (s. 7(10)).

Section 7(4)(c)(i) of the regulation allows holders of class 1, 2, 3, or 4 water treatment or water distribution licences to test for the operational parameters listed in Schedule 3. These operational parameters include pH, turbidity, chloramine, alkalinity, and residual chlorine. Section 7(4)(c)(ii) allows people with one year of laboratory experience or those who have passed a water quality analysis course to test for Schedule 3 operational parameters. In practice, this water quality analysis course requirement has been interpreted as a water quality analyst licence.[83] The director has a discretionary power to deem someone a water quality analyst if, in the director's opinion, the person has the necessary experience, education, and training (s. 7(4)(c)(ii)).

6.7.3.1   *Maximum Acceptable Concentrations*

The maximum acceptable concentration (MAC) and interim maximum acceptable concentration (IMAC) standards for chemical and physical parameters in Ontario Regulation 459/00 remain virtually unchanged from the standards outlined in the ODWO. One improvement is that more pesticides and volatile organics are now monitored under the regulation. Also, the list of radiological MACs has expanded from five to 78. However, radiological parameters are not measured as part of the mandatory sampling program outlined in Schedule 2 of Ontario Regulation 459/00. Radiological sampling is mentioned in section 4.4 of the ODWS, but a specific program is not identified.[84]

---

[83] See <http://www.oetc.on.ca/wqaqa.html> [accessed May 5, 2002].
[84] Section 4.4.1 of the ODWS states:

   The frequency of sampling for radionuclides is dependent on the concentration present in the supply. The higher the concentration of a radionuclide the more frequent the sampling. Where water sources are subject to discharges of radioactive waste, the sampling frequency for specific radionuclides should be increased.

   Most radionuclides can either be measured directly or expressed in terms of surrogate measurements such as gross alpha emission (e.g., radium-226) and gross beta emission (e.g., strontium-90, iodine-131, cesium-137). The gross alpha and gross beta determinations are only suitable for preliminary screening procedures. Compliance with the standards may

Consequently, sampling requirements for radiological parameters must be included in a Certificate of Approval for their MAC or IMAC standards to be legally enforced. Once their measurement is required, corrective action becomes legally enforceable by way of section 9(a) of the regulation.

6.7.3.2   *Indicators of Adverse Water Quality*

The indicators of adverse water quality under the ODWS include the ODWO indicators of unsafe and deteriorating water quality and additional indicators regarding sodium (for persons on a sodium-restricted diet) and pesticides without a MAC.

An additional indicator of adverse water quality under the ODWS occurs when "unchlorinated" water is directed into the system where chlorination is used or required.[85] Water with a chlorine residual below 0.05 mg/L is considered unchlorinated – a level that becomes the absolute minimum residual for any system covered under Ontario Regulation 459/00.

6.7.3.3   *Notification Requirements*

The regulation clarifies the confusion about the notification of adverse results. It is now mandatory for a waterworks owner to ensure that notice is given both to the local Medical Officer of Health and the MOE's Spills Action Centre when analysis shows that a MAC or IMAC has been exceeded or indicates adverse water quality (s. 8(1), (2), (3), (4)). The notice must be confirmed in writing within 24 hours (s. 8(4)). In addition to notifying the owner, private laboratories are now legally bound to the same notification requirements as the owner (s. 8(2)).

---

be inferred if these are less than the most stringent MACs … When these limits are exceeded, the specific radionuclides must be measured directly. Tritium, a gross beta emitter, must be measured separately because the screening process is not sufficiently sensitive to detect low levels of tritium.

[85] O. Reg. 459/00, Schedule 6, para. 3.

6.7.4   Corrective Action

Instead of simply recommending corrective action, the regulation makes corrective action (including resampling) mandatory and outlines the appropriate corrective action to take when an indicator of adverse quality is identified (s. 9). If a MAC or IMAC is exceeded, a second sample must be taken (s. 9(a)). The corrective action required for an indicator of adverse quality depends on the type of indicator. The detection of *E. coli* requires flushing the mains to ensure that a free chlorine residual of 0.2 mg/L is achieved in all parts of the distribution system; the flushing must continue until two consecutive samples test negative for *E. coli*.[86] In general, the corrective actions outlined in section 9 and Schedule 2 of the regulation are consistent with those previously included in the ODWO.[87]

Unfortunately, the issue of resampling is now somewhat unclear when comparing the regulation and ODWS. Section 9(a) of Ontario Regulation 459/00 specifies that "another sample" must be taken if a MAC or IMAC is exceeded. The ODWS state that "immediate resampling is required" in this instance and defines "resampling" as follows:

> Resampling should consist of a minimum of three samples to be collected for each positive sampling site: one sample should be collected at the affected site; one at an adjacent location on the same distribution line; and a third sample should be collected some distance upstream on a feeder line toward the water source ... The collection of three samples is considered the minimum number for each positive sampling site.[88]

As a result of its inclusion in the ODWS, the three-sample minimum is not a legal requirement unless it is included in a Certificate of Approval or a Director's Order. It would be preferable for the regulation to be amended to use the ODWS definition.

---

[86] O. Reg. 459/00, Schedule 6, para. 1.

[87] The language has also been improved, and confusion has been removed. The two ODWO provisions previously causing confusion (two consecutive samples detecting coliforms in the same site or multiple locations from a single submission, and more than 10% of monthly samples detecting coliforms) have been removed.

[88] See the ODWS, s. 4.2.1.1. This resampling definition is consistent with the older "special sampling" requirements in the ODWO, s. 4.1.3.

Further confusion is found in Schedule 6 of the regulation, which outlines the corrective action when "Indicators of Adverse Water Quality" are detected. The schedule uses the term "resample," but no definition is provided in either the schedule or the regulation. Some of the schedule's provisions simply state "Resample and analyze,"[89] whereas others state "Resample, take a corresponding raw water sample and analyze."[90] The preceding statement from Schedule 6 and the wording in section 9(a) imply that the term "resample" requires only one sample, not three as defined in the ODWS. The resulting inconsistency should be cleared up.

6.7.4.1   *New Requirements under Ontario Regulation 459/00*

The regulation also introduces a number of new requirements, many of which deal with information management:

- The owner of a waterworks is now required to post a warning when it does not comply with the sampling and analysis requirements for microbiological parameters or when corrective actions as outlined in the regulations have not been taken (s. 10).

- An owner must also make all information regarding the waterworks and the analytical results of all required samples available for the public to inspect (s. 11).

- Quarterly written reports must be prepared by the owner and submitted to the MOE that summarize analytical results and describe the measures taken to comply with the regulation and the ODWS (s. 12).

- Copies of these reports must be made available, free of charge, to any member of the public who requests a copy.

- Owners must submit an independent engineer's report according to the schedule contained in the regulation and submit triennial reports thereafter (s. 13).

---

[89] O. Reg. 459/00, Schedule 6, paras. 1, 4, 5, and 6.
[90] Ibid., para. 8.

- Owners must ensure that analytical results from labs and all engineers' reports are kept for at least five years (s. 14).

Changes were also introduced with respect to sampling requirements. Sections 4.1.1 and 4.2.1 of the ODWO previously addressed the frequency and location of sampling and analysis for microbiological testing. They stated:

> Frequency of analysis and location of sampling points shall be established by the operating authority under the direction of the MOEE after investigation of the source, including source protection protocol and method of treatment ...

> The minimum frequency and location of sampling is normally specified by the MOEE on the Certificate of Approval.

These references to the MOE are not directly included in either Ontario Regulation 459/00 or the ODWS. The regulation now states: "The owner of a water treatment or distribution system shall ensure that water sampling and analysis is carried out in accordance with" the regulation "or any additional requirements of an approval or an order or direction under the Act" (s. 7(1)). The ODWS says: "The site specific requirements for monitoring and analysis are reflected in the terms and conditions of the Certificate of Approval for the particular water supply system" (s. 4.1).

6.7.5   Issues Raised in the Part 1 Report of This Inquiry

The Part 1 report of this Inquiry mentions a number of confusing provisions in the ODWO and the Chlorination Bulletin.[91] These deficiencies were identified as follows:

1.   lack of clarity in section 4.1.2 of the ODWO about whether the samples referred to include treated water samples;

2.   uncertainty about the inspection required under section 4.1.4 of the ODWO when conditions of deteriorating water were detected;

---

[91] These references are found at the bottom of p. 357 of the Part 1 report of this Inquiry: Ontario, Ministry of the Attorney General, 2002, *Report of the Walkerton Inquiry, Part 1: The Events of May 2000 and Related Issues* (Toronto, Queen's Printer).

3.   the difference between the corrective actions required by section 4.1.3 of the ODWO and section 5 of the Chlorination Bulletin; and

4.   the difference in the language used in the two guidelines to set out the requirements for continuous chlorine residual monitoring.

Issue 1 concerns the section of the ODWO that listed the "Indicators of Unsafe Drinking Water" criteria. There was no definition of "distribution system." A question was raised about whether treated water samples taken from a well house were considered to be "from the distribution system." Schedule 2 of Ontario Regulation 459/00 now identifies "distribution system samples" as samples "taken in the distribution system from a point significantly beyond the point at which treated water enters the distribution system." This definition does not exactly address the question previously mentioned, but the provisions of Schedule 6 of the regulation, "Indicators of Adverse Water Quality," provide some further clarity. When identifying water samples, the Schedule 6 provisions dealing with bacteriological contamination use the following language: "any required sample other than a raw water sample." This language, in my opinion, removes any uncertainty about the location of sampling and whether a positive sample qualifies as an Indicator of Adverse Water Quality.

Issue 2 has been addressed by removing all language from the regulation and the ODWS that requires MOE inspections. I discuss the importance of inspection in Chapter 13.

Issue 3 has been dealt with by placing consistent corrective action requirements in either the regulation[92] or the ODWS.[93] However, as previously mentioned, uncertainty persists concerning the number of samples to be taken when resampling.

Issue 4 has been dealt with by including identical continuous chlorine monitoring provisions in Schedule 2 of the regulation and Table 2 of the ODWS.

I conclude this discussion of the regulation and the ODWS by observing that Ontario Regulation 459/00 represents a significant improvement in how the government addresses the treatment, monitoring, and reporting requirements. There are, however, advantages to be gained from some relatively minor changes.

---

[92] O. Reg. 459/00, s. 9 and Schedule 6.
[93] ODWS, ss. 4.2, 4.3, and 4.4.

Chapter 7   Drinking Water Distribution Systems

Contents

Chapter 7   Drinking Water Distribution Systems

7.1   Introduction

The distribution system is the final barrier before delivery to the consumer's tap. Even when the water leaving the treatment plant is of the highest quality, if precautions are not taken its quality can seriously deteriorate. In extreme cases, dangerous contamination can occur.

Distribution systems are composed of watermains, valves, hydrants, service lines, and storage facilities. This infrastructure is expensive but long-lived. Because it is largely out of sight, distribution infrastructure tends not to be a top priority in the management and financing of water systems. But as populations shift and pipes corrode, substantial ongoing investments are necessary.

This chapter is essentially descriptive and includes only two formal recommendations. It describes the various threats to the integrity of distribution systems and discusses practices relating to their construction, repair, and maintenance. In this discussion, I have tried to summarize the best current thinking on both topics, in the hope that this will assist water system owners, operators, and regulators.

7.2   The High-Quality Distribution System

A high-quality distribution system is reliable, providing a continuous supply of potable water at adequate pressure. Reservoirs within the system balance pressure and cope with peak demands, fire protection, and other emergencies without causing undue water retention, while looped watermains prevent stagnation and minimize customer inconvenience during repairs. Since water quality declines with the length of time the water remains in the system, and the rate of decline depends partly on the attributes of the distribution system, a high-quality system has as few dead ends as possible and maintains adequate flow and turnover.

A well-maintained distribution system is a critical component of a safe drinking water system. It is essential that water providers have adequate financing mechanisms in place so that their distribution systems can be properly maintained and renewed. In Chapter 10 of this report, I recommend that every municipal water provider should produce a sustainable asset management plan as part of its comprehensive financial plan. The sustainable asset management plan should include, at a minimum, an accurate characterization of all parts of the system by age, size, location, materials, maintenance history, scheduled repairs, planned capital maintenance, refurbishment, and replacement. The design of system extensions should take advantage of opportunities to optimize hydraulic characteristics and eliminate dead water.

In a well-managed system, routine maintenance and system extensions are adequately financed to minimize costs and reduce risks to public health over the asset's lifetime. Routine maintenance includes flushing, cleaning, valve exercising, and inspection.[1] Less frequent maintenance might include mechanical scraping, pigging, swabbing, chemical cleaning, or flow jetting.[2] Capital maintenance might include relining pipes, replacing valves, and repairing pumps. All maintenance is programmed through a computerized asset management system for best efficiency.

The continuous monitoring of water quality, hydraulics, and system condition is undertaken with up-to-date Supervisory Control and Data Acquisition (SCADA) systems. Data are centrally archived and used for infrastructure management. Computer models of the distribution system allow informed decisions to be made about priorities for replacement or rehabilitation. Emergency procedures are documented, and standby power is provided.

Backflow preventers stop the inflow of contaminants from cross-connections, dead ends,[3] and pipe breaks, and all customers are metered. Although meters must be replaced periodically,[4] their mere presence has been shown to reduce water demand by as much as 15% to 20%,[5] thus reducing the size and cost of distribution systems.

---

[1] E. Doyle, 2002, "Production and distribution of drinking water," Walkerton Inquiry Commissioned Paper 8, p. 76.

[2] G.J. Kirmeyer et al., 2001, "Practical guidelines for maintaining distribution system water quality," *Journal of the American Water Works Association*, vol. 93, no. 7, pp. 62–73.

[3] A special case is fire sprinkler systems, whose stagnant waters may accumulate heavy metals: S.J. Duranceau et al., 1999, "Wet-pipe fire sprinklers and water quality," *Journal of the American Water Works Association,* vol. 91, no. 7, pp. 78–90.

[4] Perhaps every 30 years for brass meters and every 15 years for plastic: M.D. Yee, 1999, "Economic analysis for replacing residential meters," *Journal of the American Water Works Association*, vol. 91, no. 7, pp. 72–77.

[5] D.M. Tate, 1990, *Water Demand Management in Canada: A State of the Art Review*, Social Science Series 23 (Ottawa: Environment Canada, Inland Waters Directorate).

7.3   Threats to System Integrity

Physical, biological, and chemical changes gradually occur as water is transported through the distribution system.[6] The causes for such changes vary; some can be prevented through changes in treatment or operating procedures, whereas changes that result from the age and quality of the infrastructure may require large capital investments.

7.3.1   Pipe Age

As pipes age, they become prone to leaks and breaks as a result of bedding failure, corrosion, the development of capacity-limiting scale or biofilm, and subtle changes in the pipe's chemical or physical properties. Coatings and cathodic protection can assist in coping with corrosive water, stray ground currents, or acidic ground conditions, but entropy always wins in the end.

Frost, traffic vibrations, the erosion of supporting ground materials, and even Ontario's mild earth tremors can cause pipes that have become weakened by age to fail. Unattended leaks may allow incursions of contaminants and result in the loss of treated water. Moreover, leaks undermine supporting ground materials, thus creating a potential for further failure of the pipes.[7]

In addition, as part of their comprehensive distribution system program, water providers should have active programs, working together with building inspectors and public health agencies, to detect and deter cross-contamination. The primary program responsibility should lie with the provider, which should develop a risk-based schedule of visits to sites that are known to pose threats. Such sites include industrial operations, car washes, interconnecting cisterns, hospitals, clinics, funeral homes, and meat and food packing plants.

---

[6] M.-C. Besner et al., 2001, "Understanding distribution system water quality," *Journal of the American Water Works Association*, vol. 93, no. 7, pp. 101–114.

[7] Finding leaks is not as difficult as it might seem. A variety of non-intrusive methods are available for doing so, including "listening" to and triangulating on the sound of leaking water. See A.N. Tafuri, 2000, "Locating leaks with acoustic technology," *Journal of the American Water Works Association*, vol. 92, no. 7, pp. 57–66; J. Makar and N. Chagnon, 1999, "Inspecting systems for leaks, pits and corrosion," *Journal of the American Water Works Association*, vol. 91, no. 7, pp. 36–46; and O. Hunaidi et al., 2000, "Detecting leaks in plastic pipes," *Journal of the American Water Works Association*, vol. 92, no. 2, pp. 82–94.

Distribution systems should have regularly tested backflow prevention valves that can prevent or at least isolate incursions. Pressure should always be higher than ambient, and distribution systems should have pressure-monitoring equipment that can detect fluctuations or drops in pressure and alert the operator when they occur.

Infrastructure is also vulnerable to amateur cross-connections and their attendant risks of contamination. It is common in areas of Ontario that depend on hard groundwater for households to use roof-fed cisterns. Such water can contain bird and rodent fecal matter as well as air-deposited contaminants. If, as frequently happens, the householder connects this supply to the household service without installing functional check valves or other backflow-preventing devices, the communal distribution system can become contaminated.[8]

As I point out in Chapter 13 of this report, the *Safe Drinking Water Act* should expressly allow for the inspection of private premises by the water provider, for emergency disconnection in the event of a public health threat, and for the refusal of service if a customer or property owner does not address the problem.

The expensive replacement of aging infrastructure can be deferred, often for many years, if repairs and rehabilitation are performed before systems deteriorate too far. Asset management planning to monitor infrastructure age and condition allows the scheduling of rehabilitation projects in advance. Sustainable asset management in relation to municipal water systems is discussed in more detail in Chapter 10 of this report.

7.3.2   Materials

Recommendation 34: The provincial government should encourage the federal government, working with the Standards Council of Canada and with advice from municipalities, the water industry, and other stakeholders, to develop standards for materials, including piping, valves, storage tanks, and bulk chemicals, that come into contact with drinking water.

---

[8] This risk is critical to system integrity: seven of the 12 largest water-borne disease outbreaks caused by distribution system contamination in the United States between 1971 and 1998 were caused by cross-connections. See G.F. Craun and R.L. Calderon, 2001, "Waterborne disease outbreaks caused by distribution system deficiencies," *Journal of the American Water Works Association*, vol. 93, no. 9, Table 5, p. 69.

Standards for materials used in water systems are necessary to guard against untested materials that provide a pathway for, or a source of, contaminants. There is no need to await a comprehensive federal law regarding materials that come into contact with all products ingested by humans. Matters specific to drinking water can be dealt with through existing mechanisms. Several major industry associations are already active in this regard. Only where existing standards fall short should effort be devoted to creating a "made in Ontario" standard.

These standards should be incorporated into building and plumbing codes as appropriate and into Certificates of Approval for new or upgraded facilities. Because the federal government has a considerable research establishment working on these topics, it makes little sense to duplicate their efforts at the provincial level, though this of course should not preclude a cooperative approach, with specific laboratories undertaking work for the benefit of all where they have established capability. Work done by Health Canada and the National Research Council (NRC) for the abandoned Bill C-76/C-14[9] should be brought forward and made part of the NRC's advisory work on building and plumbing codes, which provide an efficient and well-understood method for putting the results into practice.

Typical considerations when selecting piping material include corrosion resistance, internal surface roughness, compatibility with existing materials, susceptibility to chemical leaching or biofilm growth, cost, and use. Materials suitable for transmission may be weakened if tapped for service delivery. Mains tend to be made of cast iron or ductile iron. Occasionally they are made of wrapped steel or, in recent years, plastic. Service lines into homes are often zinc-coated iron (which may react galvanically with brass, bronze, or copper fittings), copper tubing, or in some older systems, lead pipe.

Recommendation 35: As part of an asset management program, lead service lines should be located and replaced over time with safer materials.

Human exposure to lead, especially where children are involved, has been a public health concern for several decades. The most important sources of lead used to be lead-based paint and leaded gasoline. However, lead was also frequently used in the service lines that connect homes with water mains and

---

[9] *Drinking Water Materials Safety Act*, introduced as Bill C-76 in House of Commons on December 11, 1996. Reintroduced as Bill C-14 on October 30, 1997.

in the solder used in copper plumbing. As a result, in Canada, municipalities have been phasing lead materials out of drinking water systems for a decade, and tin solder is now generally used in plumbing. Ontario's building code requires a lead content of less than 0.2% for plumbing solder used in water systems. Ontario Regulation 459/00 establishes an upper limit for lead in drinking water of 0.01 mg/L at the point of consumption. If higher levels remain after pipes have been flushed, the municipality is required to replace any lead service lines into a house. The risks are posed by a combination of lead piping and the corrosiveness of water: soft water poses a higher risk than does scale-forming hard water.

The presence of lead in drinking water is a significant health risk because even minute quantities are believed to cause neurological problems in infants and children. The U.S. Environmental Protection Agency estimates that, on average, lead in drinking water accounts for approximately 20% of all human exposure to lead.[10] In the United States, lead-free solder and piping have been required since 1986, and the 1991 Lead and Copper Rule (LCR), revised in 2000, requires the phased replacement of existing lead pipes.[11] The LCR establishes action levels (i.e., maximum limits that, if exceeded, require corrective action to be taken) of 0.015 mg/L for lead and 1.3 mg/L for copper. Maximum Contaminant Level Goals (the standard that will eventually apply in the United States when old lead pipes have all been replaced) are 0 mg/L for lead and 1.3 mg/L for copper. Techniques for addressing concerns about lead and copper include minimizing corrosion in pipes, treating source water where appropriate, investing in public education, and replacing lead service lines if levels in water exceed the action level.[12] People should be informed if the buildings they live or work in are suspected of being serviced by lead pipes so that they can check their end of the line for lead pipe as well.

7.3.3 System Design

The design of the water distribution system, including the size of the pipes, also affects integrity. The larger the diameter of the pipe, the greater the ratio

---

[10] U.S. Environmental Protection Agency, Office of Water, 2001, *Lead and Copper* <www.epa.gov/safewater/leadcop.html> [accessed May 2, 2002].

[11] G.R. Boyd et al., 2001, "Selecting lead pipe rehabilitation and replacement technologies," *Journal of the American Water Works Association*, vol. 93, no. 7, p. 75.

[12] U.S. Environmental Protection Agency, Office of Water, 1999, *Lead and Copper Rule Minor Revisions: Fact Sheet* <www.epa.gov/safewater/standard/leadfs.html> [accessed May 2, 2002].

between volume and surface area and thus the less contact between pipe material and water. But having larger-diameter pipes also slows water flow, thus increasing the risk of stagnation. The system's three-dimensional layout (e.g., the number and length of branches, slopes, curves, and so on) also affects the flow and thus influences hydraulic properties.[13] Designers must clearly balance many factors to obtain optimal performance. This task is complicated by the ever-changing size of the system and the demands placed on it.

Some elements of design are constant, however. The water distribution system should always be under a minimum of 20 psi (138 kPa) pressure[14] to prevent incursions at cracks or joints. Good pressure is facilitated by maintaining relatively constant flow rates, which also reduces pipe scouring. Curves should be minimized, with thrust restraint (usually a mass of concrete) provided where abrupt changes of direction are unavoidable. Pipes should be below the frost line, now and decades from now. High points should be equipped with air relief valves. Dead ends should be minimized, but where they are unavoidable, they should be equipped with blow-off valves for line flushing. Capacity (and hydrant spacing) should be sufficient for fire suppression, but should not lower water turnover to an extent that imperils the water's quality for drinking.

Valves are critically important components of the water delivery system and therefore need proper maintenance to avoid expensive and dangerous situations.[15] When they are working correctly, valves allow the measurement and management of water flows and the locating of leaks. Backflow preventers keep contaminants isolated. But valves can and do malfunction, often as a result of underuse. Scale, biofilm, and corrosion products occlude them. Valves that are stuck shut, broken, or not operating properly – a common problem where they are not exercised frequently – may force water to travel much farther than necessary, reducing pressure and increasing retention times.

Low pressure is particularly problematic during the peak demands caused by firefighting. Even under ordinary demand conditions, extra power may be necessary for pumping. Sometimes the hydraulic conditions in the system can lead to transient zones where pressure is lower than that in the atmosphere, with the result that pollutants are actively sucked in. In extreme cases, such

---

[13] Besner et al., pp. 101–113.

[14] Kirmeyer et al., p. 66.

[15] B. Gauley, 2000, "Valve maintenance an important 'best management practice,'" *Ontario Pipeline*, April, p. 8.

conditions can cause pipes to buckle or collapse.[16] Three-dimensional hydraulic models of a particular system can aid in identifying problems and help to maintain proper hydraulic conditions within the system.

7.3.4   Storage

Treated water is often stored in reservoirs or standpipes (water towers) before delivery. This approach may have both public health and economic advantages in allowing for treatment system optimization independent of short-term fluctuations in demand. It may also improve contact times for chemical disinfection. Although distribution system pressure is readily maintained through the use of elevated or pressurized reservoirs, the reservoir materials must not give rise to or allow contamination, reservoirs must be covered and inaccessible to the public, and retention times must not be overly long.

7.3.5   Corrosion

Most mains in Ontario are made of cast or ductile iron or, less frequently, steel. Consequently, corrosion is the most common problem in distribution systems. In addition to weakening pipe walls, corrosion can lead to the development of large tubercles (collections of material that may include scale, algae, and bacteria) inside the pipes, reducing water capacity and water pressure, which in turn increases residence times (the amount of time the water stays in the pipes) and reinforces corrosion. Meanwhile, the aesthetic quality of the water can be reduced through the release of soluble or particulate corrosion by-products. In systems using hard water, this is especially the case with new pipes, before a protective layer of scale builds up on the interior surfaces. Corrosion does not necessarily affect the safety of drinking water directly, but it will reduce the life of the pipes and, in older pipes, increase the probability of leaks, breaks, and contamination.

---

[16] A.T.K. Fok, for Environmental Hydraulics Group Inc., 2002, Walkerton Inquiry Submission.

7.3.6   Scale

Scale is usually composed of carbonate precipitates that form on pipe walls. Over time, scale will reduce flow volumes and increase headloss. Its presence, and the inclusions within it, can affect corrosion rates.

7.3.7   Sedimentation

When water is moving slowly through a pipe, particles suspended in the water may settle out into the pipe. The accumulated sediment reduces the pipe's capacity. This problem is most common in source water pipes that are situated upstream of a treatment plant, because proper treatment eliminates suspended particles. But if the water has not been treated properly, allowing excess turbidity in product water, sedimentation may also occur in the distribution system. However, even slight overtreatment of water can result in post-treatment precipitation. Thus, overdosing the water with flocculant chemicals can have the same effect as underdosing it.[17]

7.3.8   Biological Growth

Information on water retention time in every part of the storage and distribution system needs to be developed and used to schedule additional flushing in slow-flow areas in order to slow biofilm development.

Biofilm results from the growth of bacteria that can thrive in water distribution systems. Decaying algae from algal growth in insufficiently filtered surface waters is one of many possible sources of dissolved organic matter that may provide a good food source for bacterial growth. Anaerobic groundwater containing soluble iron and sulphur is a food source for two bacterial species that cause a number of aesthetic problems involving odour.[18]

---

[17] American Water Works Association, 2001, *Rehabilitation of Water Mains: Manual of Water Supply Practices, Manual M28*, 2nd ed. (Denver: AWWA), p. 1.

[18] G.C. White, 1999, *Handbook of Chlorination and Alternative Disinfectants*, 4th ed. (New York: Wiley), pp. 447–451.

Bacteria adhere to pipe walls, and their metabolic products both increase adhesion and protect the bacteria from the residual disinfectant.[19] Their biological activity can increase corrosion.[20] Further, bacteria that are adapted to low-nutrient conditions, such as can occur in distribution systems, are less susceptible to disinfectants. Once they are established, they are all but impossible to eradicate through the use of chlorine or chloramines.[21]

The regrowth of bacteria may be affected by time, temperature, sediments, and the materials used in the system. There is a direct threat to people from pathogens, and indirect threats from likely interference with coliform detection and even from the transfer of antibiotic resistance factors to pathogenic bacteria.[22]

Coliform biofilms can grow or regrow in distribution systems.[23] Age, low disinfectant residuals, warm temperatures, relatively high levels of total organic carbon, old iron pipe, and the insufficient flushing of dead ends all contribute to the growth of biofilms, sometimes to the point where bacteria, including coliforms, are released into the water. Biofilm may support the regrowth of virulent bacteria if treatment failure has occurred at the plant.[24] There are a number of methods for preventing, slowing the growth of, and removing biofilms. Control requires an ongoing, multi-faceted effort that includes monitoring, maintenance, water treatment, and management,[25] and it is not guaranteed by the use of a disinfectant residual alone.[26]

There appear to be limits to the efficacy of chlorine as a guarantor of system integrity.[27] In some ways, it may be regarded as little more than an indirect indicator; rapid changes in its measured value are a signal that something is wrong and that an investigation is required.

---

[19] American Water Works Association, 1999, *Waterborne Pathogens Manual, Manual M48* (Denver: AWWA).

[20] White, pp. 451–452.

[21] American Water Works Association, 1999.

[22] L. Evison and N. Sunna, 2001, "Microbial regrowth in household water storage tanks," *Journal of the American Water Works Association*, vol. 93, no. 9, pp. 85–94.

[23] White, pp. 461–462.

[24] P. Payment, 1999, "Poor efficacy of residual chlorine disinfectant in drinking water to inactivate waterborne pathogens in distribution systems," *Canadian Journal of Microbiology*, vol. 45, pp. 709–715.

[25] Kirmeyer et al., p. 68.

[26] R.R. Trussell, 1999, "Safeguarding distribution system integrity," *Journal of the American Water Works Association*, vol. 91, no. 1, pp. 46–54.

[27] Payment, pp. 712–715.

7.3.9   Bulk Water Reactions

Chemical reactions can occur in water as it travels through a distribution system. The longer its residence time in the system, the greater the probability that a variety of reactions will occur. Some reactions – such as the inactivation of micro-organisms by the disinfectant residual – are desirable. Others are not so helpful and can make the water aesthetically displeasing or detrimental to health. The key to avoiding risk is high-quality treatment that ensures the release of chemically stable water into the distribution system. A group of chemical reactions currently at the forefront of research are those that produce disinfection by-products (DBPs: see Chapter 6 of this report). These chemicals, chiefly trihalomethanes and haloacetic acids, may be carcinogenic if consumed over a long period of time. In the concentrations found in drinking water, the risk of becoming ill as a result of consuming DBPs is relatively small – much smaller than the risk from pathogens – but not zero. Minimizing their occurrence in a way that remains consistent with adequate disinfection should be an objective of treatment and distribution system management. DBPs are produced principally through reactions between organic matter and disinfectants, including chlorine, chlorine dioxide, and ozone. Reducing total organic carbon (TOC) in treatment through filtration – biological, granular activated carbon, ultra-, or nano-filtration – is key, as is removing TOC-containing sediment from distribution systems.

As with other aspects of distribution system management, water quality changes with age – both the system's age and the water's age (i.e., its residence time). In New Jersey, research showed that "[d]ifferent by-products responded differently to increasing time in the system."[28] The reactions proceeded more rapidly in warmer months. A study of the Laval, Québec, system demonstrated that the fate of both chlorine and dissolved organic halogens was related to the presence of corrosion by-products, the residence time of the water, and the presence of microbial biomass.[29]

Continuous disinfection should be attained by using only as much chlorine as is necessary.[30] Changing the primary disinfectant from free chlorine to ozone

---

[28] W.J. Chen and C.P. Weisel, 1998, "Halogenated DBP concentrations in a distribution system," *Journal of the American Water Works Association*, vol. 90, no. 4, p. 151.

[29] H. Baribeau et al., 2001, "Changes in chlorine and DOX concentrations in distribution systems," *Journal of the American Water Works Association*, vol. 93, no. 12, pp. 102–114.

[30] For some systems based on groundwater of known purity, a chlorine residual may be dispensed with altogether in certain jurisdictions (e.g., the Netherlands and Germany). See B. Hambsch,

or chlorine dioxide can help, as can converting the secondary disinfectant from chlorine to chloramines. Removing TOC during treatment is the optimal approach: it minimizes the consumption of disinfectant in the distribution system by contaminants other than microbes, thus allowing lower initial dosage and possibly avoiding the need for disinfectant top-up later.[31]

7.4   Good Practices in System Operation

A large and rich literature deals with good practices in system operation and maintenance.[32] Drawing together much of what has been said above, good practices in system design, operation, and maintenance include the following:

- Design the system so that it is not so large that slow turnover and high retention times degrade water quality.[33] Distribution systems can be problematic at either end of the size continuum – they can be too small to accommodate fire emergencies or too large to guarantee safe water. Overbuilding a distribution system (i.e., making it too large) can have consequences for both water quality and cost.[34]

- Make regular systematic flushing, with particular attention to dead ends and static zones, part of every maintenance program.

1999, "Distributing groundwater without a disinfectant residual," *Journal of the American Water Works Association*, vol. 91, no. 1, pp. 81–85; D. van der Kooij et al., 1999, "Maintaining quality without a disinfectant residual," *Journal of the American Water Works Association*, vol. 91, no. 1, pp. 55–64; and O. Hydes, 1999, "European regulations on residual disinfection," *Journal of the American Water Works Association*, vol. 91, no. 1, pp. 70–74.

[31] Kirmeyer et al., pp. 66–68.

[32] See, for example, HDR Engineering, pp. 680–741; and the special issue of the *Journal of the American Water Works Association* (vol. 93, no. 7) on distribution systems. Infrastructure Canada, the Federation of Canadian Municipalities, and the National Research Council are collaborating on a guide that will be a "compendium of technical best practices for decision making and investment planning as well as for the construction, maintenance and repair of municipal infrastructure," which is intended to be published in groups of 20 best practices a year for the next five years: see Canada, Treasury Board Secretariat, 2000, *Government of Canada Funds the National Guide to Sustainable Municipal Infrastructures: Innovations and Best Practices* <www.tbs-sct.gc.ca/news2000/1208_e.html> [accessed May 2, 2002].

[33] G. Burlingame, 2001, "A balancing act: Distribution water quality and operations," *Opflow*, vol. 27, no. 7, pp. 14–15.

[34] Strategic Alternatives et al., 2002, "Financing water infrastructure," Walkerton Inquiry Commissioned Paper 16, s. 5.1.

- Operate the system at a steady rate (except during emergencies) that allows for treatment optimization and the minimization of DBPs while maintaining the flexibility to cope with unexpected demand.

- Monitor water flow and basic measures of quality (disinfectant residual, turbidity, and pH, at a minimum) throughout the distribution system on a real-time basis, and adjust flows and treatment to match the changing conditions of demand or system integrity in real time.

- Monitor the condition of the distribution system itself, so that the threats to integrity mentioned above can be managed without threats to public health or excessive loss of water[35] and so that capital repairs and replacement can be scheduled on a rational basis. Timely repair or rehabilitation can often extend the lifetime of infrastructure at modest cost. "Sustainable asset management," which was recommended by a number of the parties in Part 2 of this Inquiry, is discussed in Chapter 10 of this report. One consequence of this approach is a capacity to work with other utilities to minimize multiple trenching and traffic detours.

- Maintain the network by continually improving techniques for refitting and replacement. New techniques for horizontal drilling, reaming, and pipe lining are available to extend the life of existing pipes.[36]

- Ensure that repair and maintenance crews follow industry-accepted sanitary practices when performing any maintenance activities.

- Maintain computerized models of the system that assist with everything from operational control to optimal capital investment.

---

[35] L.M. Buie, 2000, "Accounting for lost water," *Journal of the American Water Works Association*, vol. 92, no. 7, pp. 67–71.

[36] S.T. Ariaratnam, J.S. Lueke, and E.N. Allouche, 1999, "Utilization of trenchless construction methods by Canadian municipalities," *Journal of Construction Engineering and Management*, vol. 125, no. 2, pp. 76–86; American Water Works Association, 2001.

Chapter 8   Monitoring and Measurement

Contents

Chapter 8   Monitoring and Measurement

8.1   Introduction

In the Part 1 report of this Inquiry, I concluded that proper instrumentation and monitoring could have prevented the Walkerton tragedy. In this chapter, I examine the roles of monitoring and measurement in a properly functioning water supply system. Source water quality, treatment process control, distribution system integrity, laboratory services, inspection and enforcement, public confidence, and emergency responses all depend on accurate and timely information.

8.2   Timeliness

There is a fundamental divide in the ways things can be measured. Many parameters – such as temperature, turbidity, pressure, and flow rates – can be measured instantaneously (in "real time"). The results can be flashed from the points of measurement to central control points, where operators can adjust processes to maintain high quality. However, measuring other critically important parameters (notably those dealing with the presence of pathogens, but also including many chemical pollutants) require that samples be sent to laboratories for analysis. All laboratory tests take time – time during which people will consume the potentially contaminated water unless a substantial amount of stored, treated water is available. But storage may degrade water quality in other ways. This distinction between real-time and lagging (or trailing) measurements leads to two observations:

- Since it is currently impossible to measure microbial contamination in real time, the engineers who design systems and the operators who run them must rely on the treatment process to safeguard the water. Measuring the presence or absence of microbes can be used only as an after-the-fact method of auditing the integrity of treatment.

- As long as direct, real-time measurements are not possible, there are significant advantages to the development of indirect or surrogate real-time measures for microbial contaminants.

8.2.1   Real-time Measurement

Many critical measurements can be carried out in real time in the field. These continuous measures (known as inline measures) can be sent to remote locations, used for process control, archived for regulatory compliance and troubleshooting purposes, and summarized for regulatory and public use. Among the parameters that can be measured accurately and economically inline are the following:

- **Turbidity** is a measure of the total suspended solids in the water. This measure is important because pathogens are fine particles. They may be shielded by other suspended particles, a matter of particular importance in ultraviolet radiation (UV) disinfection.[1] Increases in turbidity in treated water often result from failures that have allowed the passage of pathogens through treatment, so it is particularly important to be able to make quick adjustments to disinfection doses.

- **Conductivity** is another measure of the water's ability to conduct an electrical current. The conductivity level indicates the amount of dissolved solids in the water: the higher the conductivity, the more dissolved solids the water contains.

- **pH** measures hydrogen ion activity in water, a characteristic that is related to the water's alkalinity or acidity. Monitoring pH levels is important for process optimization, structural maintenance (including corrosion control), and aesthetic objectives.

- **Temperature** is particularly relevant to raw water; the efficiency of the treatment process may vary with water temperature. Changes in water temperature may require adjustments in the treatment sequence. Many of the parameters that influence corrosion rates in the distribution system are temperature-sensitive. Maintenance of chlorine residuals in the distribution system is also affected by temperature, since certain chemicals work better at certain temperatures.

- **Pressure** is a basic measure of service quality for the treatment plant and the distribution system. It is especially important for the latter system,

---

[1] Thus, water is usually clarified before UV disinfection. One manufacturer has linked a turbidity sensor to its UV dose monitor so that the dose can be linked automatically to changes in turbidity. The efficiency of chlorination can also be reduced when pathogens are coated with particulate matter.

since rapid changes in pressure may indicate burst mains, whereas slower changes may be evidence of leaks.

- **Flow rates** help operators ensure that each part of a treatment sequence is working as designed.[2] They help localize leaks, and they allow accurate customer billing.

- **Chlorine residual** is the amount of chlorine in the water that remains available to achieve disinfection after a given contact time.[3] Free chlorine is converted in the oxidation of organic material, a process that includes the killing of pathogens. Thus the chlorine residual is a check on the adequacy of the disinfection dose. The oxidizing reaction will slow down and eventually cease with the decreasing availability of organic material to oxidize. If a chlorine residual is measurable after an appropriate contact time, it is highly likely that disinfection is complete.

Recommendation 36: All municipal water providers in Ontario should have, as a minimum, continuous inline monitoring of turbidity, disinfectant residual, and pressure at the treatment plant, together with alarms that signal immediately when any regulatory parameters are exceeded. The disinfectant residual should be continuously or frequently measured in the distribution system. Where needed, alarms should be accompanied by automatic shut-off mechanisms.

This recommendation includes and goes slightly beyond my Recommendation 11 in the Part 1 report (p. 298), requiring "continuous chlorine and turbidity monitors for all groundwater sources that are under the direct influence of surface water or that serve municipal populations greater than a size prescribed by the MOE," to include all sources, pressure monitoring, alarms, and, where required for safety, automatic shut-off valves. I understand that the government has accepted my earlier recommendation and has moved to require some 205 wells to have chlorine and turbidity monitors in place by December 31, 2002. Given the exceptional importance of this particular barrier, the compliance date should be brought forward, if possible, and the requirement should be

---

[2] In treatment processes like disinfection, coagulation, and filtration, flow rates affect process efficiency, because they affect how much time is available for chemical reactions to take place. If the flow rate is too slow, the process will not be efficient; if the flow rate is too fast, the process will not be effective. Rapid changes in flow or rates outside design parameters are undesirable; flow must therefore be monitored to track such changes.

[3] The process of disinfection using chlorine is described in more detail in Chapter 6 of this report.

extended to all drinking water systems that come within Ontario Regulation 459/00. I would, however, recommend case-by-case extensions to this compliance deadline where, in the MOE's judgment, the risk is low and local circumstances make early compliance difficult.

8.2.2 Lagging or Trailing Measures

As noted above, it is technologically impossible at present to measure some contaminant parameters in real time. This is especially true for various pathogens but also for most chemical, physical, and radiological parameters. These delays occur for various reasons, including the time it takes to transport and prepare samples, the time it takes to grow cultures, and the need for sophisticated equipment that makes inline monitoring impractical.

8.2.2.1 *Microbial Parameters*

The most significant problems associated with pathogen measurement are the lag time involved in testing and, especially for protozoa, the large number of false results. Few direct detection techniques have been developed. Those that have been developed tend to be difficult, expensive, and still not fast enough to assist in process control. Most rely on the growth of cultures in the laboratory before identification tests can be carried out. Furthermore, identification is often a tedious process of elimination based on the known characteristics of each species. DNA analysis offers promise for the future as techniques are refined, but the methods available at present are too expensive and time-consuming for routine monitoring. Many of the tests require highly qualified analysts, and small variations in method can produce significant differences in results.

In some instances, interpretation can be more complicated than the test itself. Many tests return a high percentage of false positive and false negative results. Moreover, simply knowing that a pathogen is present does not give any information regarding its likelihood of infecting people served by that system or information on other pathogens that may be present.

One solution to this problem is to identify a surrogate measure, but this is not an easy task either. Any surrogate must be easy to measure, present when the pathogen is present, and present in large enough quantities to lend itself to inexpensive detection and identification. One surrogate currently used for pathogens of fecal origin is a group of organisms termed total coliforms (TC, measured in colony forming units, or cfu, per 100 mL of water counted after a specific culturing protocol). However, coliform bacteria are a large class of bacteria that share certain metabolic traits. They are ubiquitous in soil and the vast majority are entirely harmless. Total coliforms, like the even broader class captured by a heterotrophic plate count (HPC), is primarily a measure of biological activity and does not necessarily indicate fecal contamination of any kind. Nevertheless, TC became the standard surrogate measure early in the twentieth century because inexpensive tests that measured *E. coli* alone were unavailable. Today, specific tests for *E. coli* (including both the common, non-pathogenic and the less common pathogenic strains) are quicker, less expensive, and far more reliable and meaningful than the TC test. A positive *E. coli* reading is diagnostic of fecal pollution in a way that TC cannot be, because *E. coli* thrives only in the intestinal tracts of warm-blooded animals, and it exists in huge numbers in feces.

There is an important asymmetry regarding *E. coli* as an indicator for fecal pathogens. The presence of *E. coli* is a reliable indicator of the likelihood of fecal contamination, meaning that fecal pathogens may be present. Likewise, because *E. coli* is very sensitive to chlorine disinfection, the presence of *E. coli* is a clear indication of inadequate disinfection. On the other hand, some pathogens, particularly protozoan parasites like *Giardia* and *Cryptosporidium*, may be much more resistant than *E. coli* is to chlorine disinfection. The absence of *E. coli* therefore does not assure the absence of these more resistant fecal pathogens. Viruses are generally more susceptible to disinfection than are protozoa, but some may be more resistant than *E. coli*.[5]

---

[4] D. Krewski et al., 2002, "Managing health risks from drinking water," Walkerton Inquiry Commissioned Paper 7.

[5] Enteropathogenic *E. coli* has been implicated in relatively few outbreaks of water-borne disease. The main enteric pathogens implicated in water-borne disease outbreaks in the developed world have been *Campylobacter*, *Giardia*, *Cryptosporidium*, Norwalk-like viruses, *Salmonella*, and enteropathogenic *E. coli*. In the developing world, cholera, typhoid, and hepatitis remain the primary threats. The relevant American Water Works Association manual, however, has 17 chapters on bacteria, 18 on parasites, and 8 on viruses: AWWA, 1999, *Waterborne Pathogens, Manual M48* (Denver: AWWA).

Problems with laboratory tests are exacerbated by sampling problems associated with pathogens. Micro-organisms are not uniformly distributed through a water column: when present, they are generally present intermittently and in low numbers. Samples taken from one location may or may not indicate the presence of micro-organisms in other locations. These sampling problems limit the confidence one can have in any statistical interpretation of the tests.

8.2.2.2   *Chronic Threats*

Chemical, physical, and radiological contaminants are almost always measured in a laboratory. Gas chromatography and mass spectrometry are the most frequently used methods for measuring organic contaminants. Atomic absorption spectrophotometry and inductively coupled plasma mass spectrometry are the methods of choice for measuring metals. These demanding techniques use expensive machines that must be operated by well-trained specialists. Great care is needed to separate signals, which are often exceedingly weak for trace concentrations, from background noise. This is also true with respect to measuring the radioactivity emanating from dissolved or suspended isotopes. Properly done, however, these tests can offer great quantitative precision.

8.3   Sampling

A test can only be as good as the sample on which it is performed. The location of and procedures under which the sample is taken, and the conditions under which it is transported to the lab, affect the quality and usefulness of the result. The MOE may wish to consider developing a guidance manual on the design of sampling protocols for analyses of regulated parameters that will produce more accurate and statistically representative results and allow inferences about the status and functioning of water supply systems. Those who collect the samples must have proper skills and training.

In this context, producing representative results requires going beyond taking a few samples at source, in the treatment plant, and in the distribution system. It must also entail taking measurements under conditions that challenge the system (e.g., after heavy rainfall, and at the farthest or most sluggish ends of the distribution system). It means gathering enough data to have confidence about water quality for each regulated parameter throughout the distribution system. Finally, it should include the data necessary for sustainable asset management.

In an ideal system, sampling and measurement locations would be identified using the Hazard Analysis and Critical Control Point (HACCP) framework discussed in Chapter 11 of this report. This procedure, originally developed for the food industry, focuses on key points where failure will produce the most serious impacts.[6] If implemented from source to tap, this approach would concentrate measurement effort at points that are most likely to be compromised or that reveal the most about system behaviour. The timing of measurement and the location of measurement points would aim to allow an accurate representation of the system to be monitored at any moment, to allow testing and diagnosis when things go wrong, to plan for sustainable asset management, and to respond to emergencies.[7]

Sampling design is critical to knowing with confidence both the quality of the water and the efficacy of the barriers. An overly mechanical approach could add unnecessary expense, but protocols based on HACCP and on microbial sampling under the most challenging conditions, as well as ordinary conditions, can substitute for some of the procedures that are now in place. This is one area in which MOE circuit riders, as discussed in Chapter 13 of this report, may be able to provide assistance.

At a minimum, weekly sampling of water systems should be required, as is currently the case under Ontario Regulation 459/00. This standard should include the requirement to sample certain parameters more frequently than others on the basis of a risk assessment of source water quality, which includes assessing potential sources of contamination within the watershed and the likelihood of the occurrence of contamination.

Recommendation 37: Every municipal water provider should be responsible for developing an adequate sampling and continuous measurement plan as part of its operational plan, as recommended in Chapter 11 of this report.

---

[6] For a practical example, see Canada, Canadian Food Inspection Agency, 2001, *The Food Safety Enhancement Program Manual* <www.inspection.gc.ca/english/ppc/psps/haccp/manu/manue.shtml> [accessed April 24, 2002].

[7] E. Hargesheimer, for Ontario Water Works Association/Ontario Municipal Water Association, 2001, "Measurement of source and finished water quality: Review of issue 7," Walkerton Inquiry Submission.

With MOE guidance, water providers should capitalize on the nature of their raw water and historical records, where such records are available and reliable, to produce a sampling strategy that is economical and effective for their specific location. A customized sampling plan must be designed for each individual water system. In general, such plans will result in samples being taken at different times and places in order to build a complete and reliable picture of the substances in question. An individual sample must be small enough to manage but large enough to be representative. It must be handled in a manner that maintains its characteristics between the time it is taken and the time it is analyzed. Samples must also be identified clearly and recorded in a coherent manner that indicates where and when the sample was taken. As regulatory enforcement improves, questions regarding the documentation of the chain of custody (chiefly its clarity and completeness) will assume more importance, because enforcers will need the information that a carefully documented chain of custody provides. In general, the sooner a sample is analyzed after collection, the better the results of the test.

The weather is a key influence on water quality, as well as quantity. The timing, amount, and type of precipitation all affect water quality and quantity, as do snow melts, freezing and break-up, temperature, and wind regimes. Strong correlations exist between high-rainfall events and outbreaks of water-borne disease.[8] Sampling should always take place when risk analysis shows that the system is most likely to be under abnormal stress.

> The importance of the timing of sample collection is frequently overlooked and misunderstood. If the timing of sample collection misses the target event, information gained from the program will be deceptive and the best sampling techniques and laboratory quality-control practices will not improve the final results. The only way to avoid this problem is to thoroughly understand the system being sampled.[9]

Recommendation 38: Sampling plans should provide for sampling under the conditions most challenging to the system, such as after heavy rainfalls or spring floods.

---

[8] F.C. Curriero et al., 2001, "The association between extreme precipitation and waterborne disease outbreaks in the United States, 1948–1994," *American Journal of Public Health*, vol. 91, no. 8, pp. 1194–1199.

[9] J. Bloemker and K.R. Gertig, 1999, "Water quality monitoring, sampling, and testing," ch. 3 in American Water Works Association, 1999, p. 29.

Complacency about what may be seen as a matter of routine is always a danger. The Inquiry asked two distinguished U.S. experts to visit a selection of smaller municipal water suppliers in the summer of 2001.[10] In the words of Ed Geldreich,

> Continued strings of negative coliform results over several years [have] given some utilities a false sense of security. In reality, it is normal for a water supply[,] treatment[,] and distribution system to occasionally detect coliform occurrences in a few samples each year. Several systems in this survey reported no coliform occurrences over the past 3 to 5 years. This unusual record may be due to two factors: always collecting samples from the distribution system on a specific day of the week, and maintaining a fixed pattern of sampling sites selected from the distribution system. Water utilities, particularly surface water systems and those plants that are processing groundwater [that is] under the influence of surface water, need to be more active in their dedicated vigilance for irregular contamination breakthroughs in treatment and at intermittent cross-connections in the distribution system.[11]

Recommendation 39: Ontario Regulation 459/00 should be modified to require standard protocols for the collection, transport, custody, labelling, testing, and reporting of drinking water samples, and for testing all scheduled contaminants, that meet or better the protocols in *Standard Methods*.

The volume known as *Standard Methods*[12] is the bible of sampling. It is worth noting some of the difficulties and considerations that must be taken into account in designing a sampling plan, if only because some of these considerations give rise to – or at least *should* give rise to – regulatory requirements for standardized testing. Ontario's requirements are not wholly satisfactory with regard to sampling.

---

[10] E.E. Geldreich and J.E. Singley, 2002, "Ontario water suppliers: Two experts' assessments," Walkerton Inquiry Commissioned Issue Paper 24, s. 3.

[11] Ibid., p. 17.

[12] L.S. Clesceri, A.E. Greenberg, and A.D. Eaton, 1998, *Standard Methods for the Examination of Water and Wastewater,* 20th ed. (Washington, DC: American Public Health Association, American Water Works Association, and Water Environment Federation).

Samples can be obtained manually or continuously. Either method can affect quality, the former typically through human error and the latter through contamination.

The number of samples required will depend on the desired confidence level. The more samples taken, the more representative the results.

Different substances require different sampling protocols. Samples for metal concentrations should be taken in tandem – one filtered and one not – in order to differentiate between the dissolved fraction and total amounts. Problems with adsorption onto the filter must be allowed for. Samples for most metals should be acidified for preservation (pH <2). Samples for volatile substance testing should not be taken at turbulent locations because the mixing will increase loss of these components to the atmosphere.

The conditions of surface water sources vary with area, depth, time, and discharge rates. These variations must be accounted for so that representative samples are collected.

Samples from distribution systems should be taken after the system has been flushed in order to obtain a representative sample. There may be exceptions for lead and other tests that are taken under reduced or restricted flow conditions.

To avoid contamination, bacteriological sample locations must be considered with respect to sanitary conditions in the vicinity of the sample point. Moreover, a single sample is rarely adequate for any precise evaluation. Good evaluations usually require an established baseline that has been built up over a significant length of time.

Samples should be collected in sterilized, non-reactive containers. After collection, they should be refrigerated until they are analyzed. Treated water samples must be dechlorinated to prevent biodegradation. One study proposes using larger sample volumes for greater sensitivity and measuring multiple fecal indicators to improve the reliability of assay results.[13]

---

[13] R.S. Fujioka and B.S. Yoneyama, 1999, "A microbial monitoring strategy to assess the vulnerability of groundwater sources to fecal contamination," proceedings at the 1999 American Water Works Association Conference on Water Quality Technology, Tampa, Florida, October 31–November 3.

Raw water sources should be sampled as close to the point of withdrawal as possible, without being too close to the bank or bed. For surface waters, baseline samples should be collected upstream of the intake.

In distribution systems, samples should be taken at a tap that is directly connected to the main line and yet not affected by any storage units (since otherwise stagnation could interfere). The tap should be flushed before the sample is taken. Also, the tap should always be disinfected before the sample is taken, because bacteria may have been left on the tap by a previous user, a matter that cannot be judged by visual inspection. Hand-pump wells must be flushed until the water temperature stabilizes before a sample is taken. Sample locations should include dead ends and be established in cooperation with the local health authority.

Some water providers, such as those in Toronto and Waterloo, sample much more frequently than is required by regulation so as to improve their understanding of system behaviour beyond the bare minimum. This is a desirable practice.

Sampling for comparison purposes or trend analysis requires, above all, adherence to rigid sampling and analysis protocols. The U.S. Environmental Protection Agency, for example, established an Information Collection Rule (1997–1998) to collect data on protozoa. However, the techniques used were questioned, resulting in the Information Collection Rule Supplemental Surveys, which used different techniques, a rigid experimental design for the collection of more reliable data, and quality control through a chain-of-custody approach.[14] The superiority of the data gathered in the supplemental surveys demonstrates the importance of establishing a rigid sampling and testing framework as well as central control.

Ontario Regulation 459/00 mandates sampling requirements that define in detail minimum protocols for various system sizes. These requirements are more stringent than are those recommended by the federal–provincial *Guidelines* (discussed in Chapter 5 of this report) and include weekly sampling.[15] Plant owners must also comply with any additional, site-specific requirements contained either in a Certificate of Approval or in an order issued by an MOE director. Even so, Ontario's sampling protocol can be improved in several areas:

[14] K. Connell et al., 2000, "Building a better protozoa data set," *Journal of the American Water Works Association*, vol. 92, no. 10, pp. 30–43.
[15] Hargesheimer.

- HPC counts are currently required on only 25% of distribution system samples,[16] even though high HPC can interfere with some techniques for TC detection;[17]

- there appears to be an overemphasis on TC testing, when more specific *E. coli* tests are available;[18]

- standardized methods are not prescribed for *E. coli* and TC testing;[19] and

- sample storage times are inconsistent with those in *Standard Methods*.[20]

Departures from industry-standard best practices should occur only for good and well-documented reasons. In Northern Ontario, it has become accepted practice to allow bacteriological samples to age for longer than, and to exceed the temperatures that, good practice would allow.

Recommendation 40: Where remoteness dictates that samples for bacteriological analysis cannot be delivered to a lab either within regulated times or under guaranteed conditions, the Ministry of the Environment should determine the feasibility of alternative means of providing microbiological testing that meet the requirements of *Standard Methods*.

8.4   SCADA Systems

The MOE, municipalities, and water industry associations may wish to encourage greater use of automation to promote the safe and efficient operation of water systems, both large and small.

Automation offers great potential both for public health and for efficient operations: "[T]he development of reliable analytical and supervisory control equipment … can make remote operation of a treatment facility low risk." [21]

---

[16] Ontario Regulation 459/00, Schedule 2.

[17] Hargesheimer, p. 21.

[18] M. Allen, cited in Hargesheimer.

[19] Ibid.

[20] An Ontario MOE technical brief states that microbiological analysis should be undertaken within 48 hours if the sample has been refrigerated and 4 hours if it has not; and *Standard Methods* requires analysis within 30 hours for coliform bacteria and 8 hours for HPC if refrigerated and within 1 hour if not: Hargesheimer, pp. 22–23.

[21] K. Mains, Walkerton Inquiry Submission (Public Hearing, September 12, 2001), transcript p. 97.

Good automation can allow human operators to concentrate on non-routine activities requiring judgment and experience while freeing them from boring and repetitive work that can lead to inattention.

Automation begins with real-time data collection. What the industry calls SCADA (Supervisory Control And Data Acquisition) systems combine telemetry (automated data transfer) with automated data collection technology and automated control systems. [22] Data from pumps, valves, motors, level gauges, flow gauges, pressure gauges, temperature and water quality sensors, alarms, and electrical contacts are collected at remote sites and sent to a central control point, where they can be monitored and evaluated before changes to operations are ordered. Measurements that fall outside norms can trigger alarms, automatic control sequences, and even regulatory compliance reports. Process adjustments can be undertaken manually or, in whole or in part, automatically. [23]

In more sophisticated systems, trend data and time series analyses can help to pre-empt potential problems and can also make a tamper-proof record of system operations. The highest level of SCADA system employs advanced decision models that make and execute decisions based on mathematical probabilities and data history. [24] Some systems can even test and diagnose their own components, alerting human operators to the need for new parts. Fewer people need to visit sites simply to monitor performance or adjust machinery, and the systems can be easily integrated with longer-term models that are used for scheduling preventive maintenance and capital replacement.

Automation offers two large advantages. It increases reliability by reducing the likelihood of human error. In addition, computers can respond quickly to water quality changes in order to optimize treatment processes – a matter of particular importance for assuring important performance characteristics like maximum turbidity removal.

There are many opportunities for implementing better SCADA systems in the water industry. They offer a route to high quality at reasonable cost. Reliability, the rapid detection and correction of adverse events, and scale economies that can bring these advantages to small systems are all important from a public

---

[22] A basic reference relevant to Ontario's smaller systems is A.J. Pollack et al., 1999, *Options for Remote Monitoring and Control of Small Drinking Water Facilities* (Columbus: Battelle).
[23] Applied Technology Group, Inc., 2002, *What Is SCADA?* <www.scadaproducts.com/sp_scada.html> [accessed April 20, 2002].
[24] Ibid.

health perspective. Of course, technology is no panacea. It is especially not a substitute for trained and skilled operators. But together, skilled people and good technology are more effective than either alone.

8.5 An Improved Data Collection and Management System

8.5.1 Operational and Regulatory Data Management

At the level of the individual water supplier, a good monitoring system would integrate real-time and lagging measures to produce a picture that faithfully represents the whole system, both spatially and temporally. Instruments, testing protocols, and data handling procedures would accord with established performance standards, facilitating trend analysis and intersystem comparisons. Documenting the chain of custody and improving data-archiving procedures would allow for public accountability, supplier evaluation, and system planning. Performance summaries would be made available online or in periodically published reports to customers. The MOE's current approach is commendable in this regard, but it could benefit still further by being considered in comparison to certain U.S. utilities' practices.[25] I discuss the issue of information management in some depth in Chapter 13 of this report.

8.5.2 Consumer Reporting

In regard to customer reports, water providers should report perhaps twice a year in bill-stuffer form. More detailed information should be available to any member of the public on the supplier's Web site or at its premises. The summary bill-stuffer should, at the least, report the minimum, maximum, and average values of tests for *E. coli*, *Cryptosporidium*, and *Giardia* in delivered water, together with any exceedances of the regulatory values specified in Ontario Regulation 459/00 for the reporting period. It should tell the customer how and where to get further information.

The utility may, of course, also wish to report on rates, plans, and service matters that are not so directly related to public health. Although the current Ontario Regulation 459/00 does not require summary reporting directly to

---

[25] For instance, the Internet can be used to increase public awareness and participation. See, for example, the approach described in Delaware River Basin Commission, 2000, "Utility's Web site doubles as education tool," *Journal of the American Water Works Association*, vol. 92, no. 10, p. 14.

the consumer, such reporting has become accepted practice in the United States. Many U.S. water providers devote more time and attention than is required by regulation to assuring their customers that their water does not just barely meet the quality standards but exceeds them by increasing margins.[26]

It should be understood that the purpose of such reports is to provide consumers with comprehensible summary information, not to limit their access, or that of interested non-governmental organizations, to the raw data and reports that are on file at the MOE.

8.6   Reporting to the Ministry of the Environment

What the regulator and the public need, by way of first-order reporting, is condensed information on the water system's overall performance. With regard to drinking water quality, I suggest that this information include, at a minimum, measures of water quality as delivered to the customer.

Good SCADA systems can turn data into information. After all, the amount of data needed for minute-by-minute plant operation is vastly greater than that required for accountability, whether to the water provider's governing body, to the MOE, or directly to the public. At the least, the monitoring system should be equipped with alarms, so that regulatory exceedances can be immediately detected, corrected, and reported. Better monitoring systems will sound a warning as some critical parameter moves toward a regulatory or operational limit, and they might automatically initiate actions that will deal with the problem long before the limit is reached.

---

[26] See California, Department of Health Services, Division of Drinking Water and Environmental Management, 2002, *Preparing Your California Drinking Water Consumer Confidence Report (CCR): Guidance for Water Suppliers* <www.dhs.cahwnet.gov/ps/ddwem/publications/CCR/ccrguidance1-28-02.pdf> [accessed April 22, 2002]. U.S. practice is now quite advanced in this respect. For an example of one small city's report, see City of Rapid City, 2001, *Rapid City Water Division Annual Drinking Water Quality Report: January 1, 2000–December 31, 2000* <www.rcgov.org/pubworks/water/rcccr2000.pdf> [accessed April 24, 2002].

Chapter 9   The Role of Laboratories

Contents

Chapter 9   The Role of Laboratories

9.1   Overview

Environmental laboratories conduct a wide variety of tests for water providers, including chemical, physical, and microbiological tests of raw, treated, and distributed water. Depending on the size and complexity of its system, a water provider might have anywhere from dozens to thousands of water tests conducted on a weekly basis. The laboratories' test results provide data to support informed planning and decision making regarding the multi-barrier approach, including strategies for source protection, water treatment, and the protection of the distribution system.

Laboratory testing also plays a critical role in determining whether contaminants are present in the system.[1] In this regard, water providers adopt monitoring strategies that are oriented both to assessing the performance of the multi-barrier system (and thereby preventing contamination) and to identifying and reacting to contaminants after they have entered the system. The prompt and reliable reporting of test results by laboratories is especially important in relation to the latter type of monitoring, when other barriers have failed and dangerous contaminants have entered the distribution system.

This chapter focuses on microbiological testing, because the issues that require attention are primarily in this area.

9.2   Water Testing Laboratories in Ontario

The majority of microbiological testing of municipal water systems is provided by private or municipally owned laboratories. Provincial government laboratories currently provide few testing services for municipalities; the laboratories of the Ministry of the Environment (MOE) and the Ministry of Health and Long-Term Care (Ministry of Health) were either closed or stopped providing such

---

[1] As discussed in Chapter 8, the most effective type of monitoring is real-time monitoring, such as in the case of real-time chlorine residual monitoring. Real-time monitoring is not currently available for microbiological testing, but it may be in the future. Because of the advantages to water systems, the development and implementation of such real-time testing should be encouraged.

testing in 1996.[2] The latter ministry's public health laboratories still play a significant role in testing water samples from non-municipal water systems and private wells.

Approximately 79 environmental analytical laboratories in Ontario carry out microbiological drinking water analyses.[3] The number of private laboratories that provide environmental testing increased during the 1990s; currently, approximately 55 are privately owned.[4] Their role grew dramatically after the wholesale withdrawal of provincial government laboratories from routine testing services and the consequent privatization[5] of microbiological testing services in 1996. Since then, the great majority of municipalities – those that do not own and operate their own testing laboratory – rely on private laboratories for microbiological testing. Larger water providers, such as the municipal water departments of Ottawa, Toronto, and Waterloo, commonly have in-house laboratories for water sampling and analysis, although they will contract out testing for some uncommon or hard-to-detect contaminants.[6]

9.2.1   The Current Regulation of Laboratories

In the Part 1 report of this Inquiry, I described the historical role of the MOE and Ministry of Health laboratories in testing drinking water. When water testing was privatized in 1996, private sector laboratories were not regulated by the provincial government. There were no established criteria governing quality of testing, no requirements regarding the qualifications or experience

---

[2] Before this, provincial government laboratories at both the MOE and the Ministry of Health provided a number of testing services to municipalities, including microbiological analyses of drinking water. Ontario, Ministry of the Attorney General, 2002, *Report of the Walkerton Inquiry, Part 1: The Events of May 2000 and Related Issues* (Toronto: Queen's Printer), pp. 370–371.

[3] There is little current quantitative published information on the capacity and capability of Ontario's analytical laboratories. These figures are based on interviews with senior private and public sector laboratory experts by J.E. Pagel. See J.E. Pagel, 2002, "An overview of drinking water testing laboratories in Ontario," Walkerton Inquiry Commissioned Paper 21, p. 4.

[4] Of the 79 water testing laboratories in Ontario, besides the 55 that are private, 11 laboratories are municipal, 1 is a hospital lab, and 12 belong to the Ministry of Health. Ibid., pp. 4–5.

[5] "Privitization," as I said in the Part 1 report of this Inquiry, refers to the government's 1996 discontinuation of all routine microbiological testing for municipal water systems – a move that resulted in the large majority of municipal systems turning to private sector laboratories for routine water testing. Ontario, Ministry of the Attorney General, p. 368.

[6] Pagel, p. 20.

of laboratory personnel, and no provisions for the licensing, inspection, or auditing of such laboratories by the government.[7]

In August 2000, the government passed Ontario Regulation 459/00, which requires the mandatory accreditation of environmental laboratories conducting specified tests of drinking water. The regulation also established a certification process for accredited laboratory analysts, who are now the only people allowed to test drinking water in Ontario.

The provincial government's approach to the licensing of clinical laboratories, which test specimens taken from humans (such as blood or stool specimens), provides a useful contrast. Since the early 1970s, clinical laboratories have been regulated under the *Laboratory and Specimen Collection Centre Licensing Act*.[8] Under section 9(1) and 9(11) of the Act, all laboratories that test human specimens are licensed by the provincial government through renewable 12-month licences. The government can revoke or refuse to renew a licence on a number of grounds, including the laboratory's failure to meet the standards set out in a provincial laboratory proficiency testing program. Under this program, the provincial government sets the standards to be met, and the Ontario Medical Association has been designated to carry out proficiency testing for clinical laboratories.[9] Further, the regulations under the Act prescribe the educational and experience qualifications required for laboratory personnel, the establishment of a quality control program, and the maintenance of records and submission of reports to the Province.[10]

9.3   Accreditation

The Ontario accreditation program for environmental laboratories is based on ISO/IEC[11] 17025, "General Requirements for the Competence of Testing and Calibration Laboratories." Accreditation requires a detailed on-site inspection and a continuing demonstration of the laboratory's competence to perform certain types of tests. Site audits and proficiency testing are currently carried

---

[7] Ontario, Ministry of the Attorney General, p. 367.

[8] *Laboratory and Specimen Collection Centre Licensing Act*, R.S.O. 1990, c. L.1.

[9] It is a condition of the licence that laboratories submit to proficiency testing; ibid., s. 9(14). Laboratory inspections are performed by the Ministry of Health Laboratory Services Branch staff.

[10] R.R.O. 1990, Reg. 682, "Laboratories"; and R.R.O. 1990, Reg. 683, "Specimen Collection Centres"; under the *Laboratory and Specimen Collection Centre Licensing Act*, R.S.O. 1990, c. L.1.

[11] International Organization for Standardization and International Electrotechnical Commission, respectively.

out by the Canadian Association for Environmental Analytical Laboratories (CAEAL).[12] The Standards Council of Canada (SCC) grants accreditation based on CAEAL's recommendation and conducts an annual audit of the program.[13]

A separate laboratory accreditation program exists for clinical laboratories in Ontario: the Quality Management Program for Laboratory Services, established under an agreement between the Ministry of Health and the Ontario Medical Association (OMA).[14] Accreditation under this program, as in the case of CAEAL, is based on an ISO standard.[15]

In relation to environmental laboratories, the SCC and CAEAL define accreditation as "the formal recognition of the competence of a laboratory to carry out specific tests."[16] To be accredited, laboratories are required to undergo proficiency testing, based on interlaboratory comparisons, twice a year for the relevant type(s) of testing, and to undergo site audits every 2 years.[17] Further, laboratories are required to comply with ISO/IEC standard 17025, with required corrective actions, and with CAEAL's code of ethics and publicity guidelines.[18]

---

[12] CAEAL, formed in 1989, is a non-profit organization whose members include approximately 450 environmental analytical laboratories, from both the public and private sectors, and private individuals. SCC and CAEAL, 2001, "Accreditation of laboratories in Canada with a focus on drinking water testing laboratories," p. 6; and CAEAL, n.d., "Canada's accredited environmental laboratories: A user's guide from the Canadian Association for Environmental Analytical Laboratories (CAEAL)."

CAEAL assessments of a laboratory's technical proficiency are typically carried out by teams of two to four assessors over a period of 3 to 4 days. There are 86 trained assessors in the CAEAL/SCC program, 47 of whom are employed by federal, provincial, and municipal regulatory authorities. Most assessors are from larger laboratories or from government. SCC and CAEAL, p. 3.

[13] The SCC is a federal Crown corporation created by an Act of Parliament in 1970. Its mandate is "to promote efficient and effective voluntary standardisation in Canada, where standardisation is not expressly provided for by law." The SCC represents Canada at international standards organizations such as the ISO and the International Laboratory Accreditation Cooperation (ILAC). *Standards Council of Canada Act*, R.S. 1985, c. S-16, s. 4(1). See also SCC and CAEAL, pp. 3, 5; and CAEAL, n.d.

[14] This program is one year into a five-year program that will result in external quality assessment of test performances in clinical laboratories.

[15] International Organization for Standardization, 2002, Technical Programme, ISO/DIS 15189.2, *Medical Laboratories: Particular Requirements for Quality and Competence* (Geneva: ISO).

[16] A laboratory becomes accredited by "providing evidence that they have: the personnel with the skills and knowledge; the environment with the facilities and equipment; the quality control; and the procedures, in order to produce competent test results." SCC and CAEAL, p. 1.

[17] Ibid., pp. 1, 3, 4.

[18] Ibid., p. 1.

In Part 1 of the Inquiry, I heard evidence about the organization of the accreditation program and the types of review that CAEAL auditors carry out. I was impressed by the thoroughness of the verification process and the capacity to identify areas for improvement at individual laboratories. Although a quality assurance program adds time, effort, and cost to laboratory operations, the improvements in reliability, validity, and record keeping more than offset the increased expenditure.[19] As such, drinking water testing should be performed only by accredited laboratories, as currently required under Ontario Regulation 459/00.

Recommendation 41: The provincial government should phase in the mandatory accreditation of laboratories for all testing parameters, and all drinking water testing should be performed only by accredited facilities.

The current requirement for accreditation relates only to specified tests on drinking water. A laboratory is not required to be accredited in order to test for certain chemical and radionuclide parameters. These tests are, however, directed at ensuring the safety of drinking water, and in my view the requirement for accreditation should be expanded to all testing parameters for drinking water. The Province should phase in this expansion according to a reasonable timetable, and with reference to the breadth of accreditation requirements in other provinces.[20] Overall, the MOE, as part of its oversight role, should ensure that adequate verification of laboratory testing takes place, whether through the requirements of MOE licensing (discussed below) or CAEAL accreditation.[21]

9.4   The Role of the Regulator

Recommendation 42: The Ministry of the Environment should license and periodically inspect, as required, environmental laboratories that offer drinking water testing; as with water treatment operations, continuing accreditation should be a condition of licence.

---

[19] Pagel, pp. 6–11; and CH2M HILL Canada Limited and Diamond Management Institute, 2002, "A total quality water management system for Ontario: The model water utility," Walkerton Inquiry Commissioned Paper 19, p. 100.

[20] Pagel, pp. 22–25.

[21] For example, the MOE should ensure that proper quality assurance occurs through proficiency testing, testing comparisons between laboratories, and the use of blind samples. The MOE should also require the use of standardized methods as appropriate, as I recommend in Chapter 8.

Although accreditation is a necessary step in ensuring the proficiency of testing laboratories, it is not by itself sufficient. The purpose of accreditation is to provide a means of assessing the competence of a laboratory in a given field of testing. It is not to review and verify the individual laboratory's knowledge of, and compliance with, regulatory standards. The Province therefore cannot rely on accreditation alone as a means of overseeing water testing laboratories.

The provincial government should therefore regulate water testing laboratories in the following manner. The MOE Laboratory Services Branch, using provincial standards, should license and if necessary inspect laboratories to ensure that they comply with provincial standards under Ontario Regulation 459/00, the Drinking Water Standards, and other applicable regulatory instruments. Inspections should be done only as often as required and should include unannounced inspections. The MOE's Investigations and Enforcement Branch should also be available to address any breaches of provincial standards. As recommended in Chapter 13, enforcement should be strict in this area.

I do not think the Province needs to adopt an oversight program for environmental laboratories that is nearly as extensive as the one that exists for water systems. The issues that arise in the testing of water samples are much less complex than the management and operation of even the least complex water system. The chain of custody for a water sample has fewer links, or critical control points, than does the comprehensive series of multi-barriers through which drinking water must flow before it can be considered safe for human consumption. The most important issues for a laboratory are ensuring that proper procedures are followed in tracking water samples, conducting tests, and reporting results to the water providers and provincial authorities.

This is not to say that environmental testing does not play an important role in monitoring drinking water quality.[22] Rather, the requirements in terms of oversight for laboratories are simply less than for water systems. For these reasons, I do not see the need for an extensive inspections program for environmental laboratories, so long as the accreditation program is functioning effectively.[23]

---

[22] Although testing results must be considered in relation to such issues as an operating agency's strategies for source protection, treatment, and distribution, the accuracy and timeliness of laboratory results can be characterized as vital to drinking water safety in the case of the barrier of monitoring.

[23] Inspections should be prioritized, in my opinion, according to the areas in which the MOE most expects difficulties to arise based on the history of the laboratory, the results of accreditation audits, the types of tests performed, the types of water systems served, and other relevant factors.

To the extent that it is necessary to assert its regulatory presence, the MOE should not duplicate the types of verification provided as part of accreditation.

9.4.1   Laboratory Reporting Requirements

In the Part 1 report of this Inquiry, I discussed the importance of ensuring the proper reporting of adverse water quality results to the MOE, the Medical Officer of Health, the operator, and the public. The Province addressed the need for a legally enforceable regulation in Ontario Regulation 459/00, which requires laboratories to notify the MOE, the Medical Officer of Health, and the operating agency of adverse results. In addition, the regulation includes requirements for public reporting. These requirements should remain in place.

From the perspective of the laboratory, a clearly defined method of reporting adverse results within the organization, and to external entities, should exist. This requires familiarity with the regulatory system and its requirements and open lines of communication among the treatment facility, the laboratory, the MOE, and the Ministry of Health. Guidelines that establish a time frame for reporting testing results will aid in this dialogue, as will the clear labelling of samples subject to testing under Ontario Regulation 459/00.

9.5   Improvements to the Accreditation Program

As I indicated above, the accreditation program in Ontario strikes me as an effective, well-run program.[24] That said, I think it is important that the program be fully transparent.

Recommendation 43: The results of laboratory accreditation audits should be provided to the Ministry of the Environment and should be publicly available.

For reasons of transparency, and to support the regulatory role I described above, the results of audits of laboratories for accreditation purposes should be

---

[24] The Ontario Medical Association, which is responsible for implementing an accreditation program for clinical laboratories, indicated at the Inquiry that the CAEAL program is "excellent" and that it complies with ISO standards, although the program could use some improvement in certain areas. Dr. A. Schumacher, for the Ontario Medical Association, Walkerton Inquiry Submission (Public Hearing, September 20, 2001), transcript pp. 83–85.

provided to the MOE and should be publicly available.[25] Laboratories should not be subject to privacy regulations or constrained by commercial confidentiality when dealing with samples under Ontario Regulation 459/00. Instead, they should be accountable to and act in the public interest at all times.[26]

In addition, to the extent possible, accreditation should verify the competence of a laboratory with respect not only to drinking water testing, but also to the pre- and post-testing phases of laboratory services, including the collection and transport of samples, sample handling and preparation, and the analysis and interpretation of results.[27] A chain of custody should exist for all samples, so that any sample is traceable throughout the process.[28] Efforts to adapt and expand accreditation to pre- and post-analytical phases are reportedly occurring under ISO auspices.[29]

9.6   The Role of Provincial Laboratories

9.6.1   Ministry of the Environment Laboratory Services Branch

The role of the MOE Laboratory Services Branch in relation to safe drinking water is primarily twofold. First, the branch provides routine testing services to the MOE in support of its regulatory functions including support for the inspections and enforcement functions. In my view it is important that the MOE continue to provide this function. While there may be an argument for contracting out routine testing services, such capability is useful for the government in effectively discharging its role as the regulator of private laboratories, including, as discussed above, the periodic inspection of private

---

[25] I was informed by CAEAL during the Part 2 public hearings that this requirement exists in British Columbia. R. Wilson, for the SCC/CAEAL, Walkerton Inquiry Submission (Public Hearing, September 20, 2001), transcript pp. 144–145.

[26] In this regard, CAEAL should ensure that its code of ethics permits CAEAL auditors to release information received as part of an audit to meet this requirement and to otherwise release information where it is in the public interest.

[27] I recognize that many aspects of pre- and post-testing phases – such as sampling practices, recording information, and interpreting samples in the context of a water system – are the primary responsibility of the operating agency of a water system. However, the laboratory should be expected to demonstrate that it has been informed of these aspects by the operating agency and to maintain appropriate documentation.

[28] Likewise, standardized formats should exist for tabulating results and presenting information.

[29] Dr. H. Richardson, for the Ontario Medical Association, Walkerton Inquiry Submission (Public Hearing, September 20, 2001), transcript pp. 84, 107.

laboratories. In my view an effective inspector must have a solid understanding of what is being inspected. Such an understanding is fostered by a continuing government presence in the area.

The second role of the Laboratory Services Branch is to develop and regularly re-evaluate testing protocols. At the risk of over-simplifying, this includes developing the tests necessary for water-treatment system operators to meet their monitoring obligations. A related role, which stems from the expertise in testing protocol, is the provision of expert advice to routine testing laboratories when peculiar results are obtained. The chemistry behind such tests is often complex and the expert advice available from the Laboratory Service Branch serves a valuable function.

I was told by a number of parties in Part 2 of the Inquiry that the expertise within the Laboratory Services Branch as well as the equipment available has been allowed to deteriorate over the last 10 to 15 years and that if this trend continues the branch's valuable role in the evaluation and development of testing protocols will become impaired.

The implicit question is the degree to which the function should be continued within the MOE and whether it is reasonable to rely on expertise that exists elsewhere. Although I have noted above that expertise in testing protocol serves a valuable function in relation to drinking water, a detailed review of this function – which extends well beyond drinking water into the full range of tests related to MOE activities – is beyond my mandate. It would seem to me to be appropriate for the government to conduct an evaluation of the benefits of keeping this function within the MOE and if it concludes that it is worthwhile to ensure that it is provided with adequate resources.

I also envision the Laboratory Services Branch playing a role in relation to the licensing and inspection of environmental laboratories and the oversight of the SCC/CAEAL accreditation program, as discussed above.

9.6.2   Ministry of Health and Long-Term Care Laboratories

The Ministry of Health's public health laboratories have an integral role to play in the provincial public health system by providing screening programs and specialized testing for outbreak identification, by supporting case management and outbreak investigations, and by participating in outbreak management teams for major outbreaks.

In terms of drinking water testing, one of the functions of public health laboratories is to carry out, free of charge, tests of samples submitted by private citizens who deliver water samples to local public health agencies for microbiological testing. Public health agencies should assist private citizens in understanding both the test results and the limitations of the testing.

Public health laboratories employ certified medical laboratory technicians and are not required to be accredited under the SCC/CAEAL accreditation program for tests carried out by members of the College of Medical Laboratory Technologists of Ontario.[30] Those laboratories should be required to be accredited for water testing in the same way as other laboratories are; that is, according to consistent test protocols and requirements for proficiency testing. Whether this is implemented through the SCC/CAEAL program or another accreditation program, I leave for the Province to determine.

9.7   Miscellaneous Submissions

During Part 2 of the Inquiry, I received a number of submissions regarding the role of private and public sector (especially provincial government) laboratories in relation to the microbiological testing of water samples. These included submissions by some that the Province should reverse its decision to privatize laboratory testing and, by others, that private laboratories are more competent than their public counterparts. I do not see a need, for reasons related to drinking water safety, to rely exclusively on either private or public laboratories to perform the microbiological testing of drinking water samples. Therefore, I do not consider it necessary, for reasons of safety, for the government to reverse its 1996 privatization decision. That said, all laboratories must be subject to effective supervision, both through an accreditation program and through regulatory oversight.

It was submitted to the Inquiry by one private laboratory that it is preferable for municipalities not to conduct water tests in-house because of a possible conflict of interest. I do not see this as a problem. Ensuring drinking water safety is a shared objective of the managers of both municipal water systems

---

[30] O. Reg. 459/00, s. 2(2).

and municipal laboratories. If laboratory staff are professional and well-trained and if their management systems are verified by accreditation and provincial oversight, then this will permit consistent, high-quality testing. Further, having its own laboratory gives a municipality greater control over the nature and timing of its testing and allows for better communication and cooperation among water system managers, public health officials, and laboratory staff.

Another submission made at the Inquiry was that small or remote municipalities do not have access to affordable testing services. In this regard, the Ontario Municipal Water Association (OMWA) and the Ontario Water Works Association (OWWA) recommended that municipalities be permitted to do their own presence/absence coliform testing in-house, with the condition that it be done by a water quality analyst and that a proportion of samples be analyzed by a certified lab. According to the OWWA/OMWA, such testing costs less than using accredited laboratories and the results are available more quickly. Municipalities should be encouraged to carry out in-house testing to complement or check tests done by outside laboratories. However, to maintain consistent safety standards province-wide, municipalities should not be permitted to substitute such tests for tests done by accredited laboratories according to the minimum regulatory requirements.

The OWWA/OMWA also argued that to reduce overall costs and equalize costs between urban and rural areas, laboratory services for small and remote municipalities should either be provided by or paid for by the Province. I disagree. The cost of laboratory services is part of the full cost of water services. If a small or remote municipality is unable to afford those services, it is also unlikely to be able to afford other elements of the cost of safe water, not to mention municipal programs and services generally. In those exceptional cases, I recommend in Chapter 14 that the Province make subsidies available only according to defined affordability criteria.

Chapter 10   The Role of Municipal Governments

Contents

Chapter 10   The Role of Municipal Governments

10.1   Introduction

In this chapter, I discuss issues relating to the owners of municipal water systems: municipal governments.[1] I begin by examining the role of municipal government in providing drinking water, including the options available to municipalities in relation to their water systems in light of the recommendations in this report. I then discuss financial issues relating to municipal water systems. Finally, I discuss the involvement of the private sector in the provision of drinking water and the role of the Ontario Clean Water Agency (OCWA).

In making the recommendations in this chapter, I have considered the following general objectives:

- public accountability for decisions relating to the water system,

- effective exercise of the owner's oversight responsibilities,

- competence and effectiveness in the management and operation of the system,

- full transparency in decision making.

10.2   The Role of Municipal Governments

10.2.1   Overview

A number of the recommendations I make in this report will put new burdens on municipalities with respect to their water systems. The purpose of this section is to outline some of the issues that may arise for municipalities and to suggest available options regarding the management and operating structures they adopt

---

[1] The vast majority of consumers supplied by communal water systems in Ontario are supplied by municipally owned systems; therefore, I refer throughout this chapter to "municipal" water systems. However, I intend to include within this term all owners of water works that serve municipalities. My use of the term "water system" is intended to refer to all of the physical components of a water supply system, including water supply facilities, treatment facilities, storage reservoirs, the distribution network, pumping stations, etc., serving a defined population.

for their water systems.[2] I specifically recommend that municipal decision makers review the available options with reference to the recommendations in this report. I also recommend that the provincial government support the municipal review process by offering guidance and technical assistance. Finally, I recommend that those responsible for exercising the oversight responsibilities of the municipality, as owner, be held to an explicit standard of care under the *Safe Drinking Water Act* that I propose in Chapter 13 of this report.[3]

10.2.2 Municipal Responsibility for Water Systems

Water systems in Ontario have been owned and operated by municipalities or other local institutions for well over a century. Local decision makers have governed the delivery of water services from the early days of the industry.[4] About 8.9 million Ontarians – 82% of the population – receive their drinking water from municipal water systems.[5] The systems range from single groundwater supplies to large networks of treatment plants and distribution systems.

---

[2] I use the term "management and operating structure" throughout this chapter to refer to the overall structure that municipalities adopt to ensure the sound management of the water system; however, the use of this term should not be viewed narrowly. Municipalities may wish to consider broader issues of accountability and governance in relation to the water system, especially regarding how the municipality carries out its oversight responsibility.

[3] Some of the recommendations in this chapter may also be appropriate for municipal sewage systems, given the connection between water and sewage services in many municipalities. In light of the mandate of this Inquiry, however, I generally do not make reference to sewage systems.

[4] The first communal water and sewage systems in Ontario were built in the mid-1800s. Municipal ownership and operation of these systems came about after the passage of the *Baldwin Act* in 1849. See Ontario Sewer and Watermain Construction Association, 2001, "Drinking water management in Ontario: A brief history," Walkerton Inquiry Submission.

Today, municipal authority to provide water services arises from various provincial statutes, including the *Municipal Act*, the *Public Utilities Act*, the *Local Improvement Act*, and the *Planning Act*. For a more detailed description of relevant legislation, see Strategic Alternatives, 2002a, "Governance and methods of service delivery for water and sewage systems," Walkerton Inquiry Commissioned Paper 17, pp. 13–22.

[5] The remaining 18% are served by private water systems, such as household or communal wells or direct surface water connections. See Association of Municipalities of Ontario, 2001, "Financing of municipal waterworks," Walkerton Inquiry Submission, p. 22, citing Ontario, Ministry of the Environment, 2000, *Drinking Water in Ontario: A Summary Report 1993–1997* (Toronto: Queen's Printer), p. 3. I note that the statistics in this section, and elsewhere in this report, attempt to offer the best possible approximation of current owners, operating agencies, and population served by municipal water systems in Ontario. There are certain limitations regarding the available data, drawn primarily from the MOE's Sewage and Water Inspection Program (SWIP) databases of 2001 and 1999, including the data's reference to water "plants" as opposed to "systems" as I use the term. The statistics presented here should therefore be viewed with caution.

Municipalities have historically played a central role in this area for good reason. Water is unique as a local service. It is, of course, essential to human life and to the functioning of communities; in an urban environment, it is simply not possible to go without a communal water system. Water systems are also normally built around local water sources. As the Walkerton tragedy so clearly showed, the consequences of a failure in the water system tend to be most seriously felt by those who depend on it locally. Finally, the provision of drinking water is characterized by a high degree of natural monopoly. In other words, the service – in terms of both water treatment and distribution – can realistically only be provided by a single entity. The need to ensure the accountability of that entity is acute and, as such, it is understandable why municipalities have played a central role in the provision of drinking water.[6]

Municipal ownership, and the ensuing responsibilities, should provide a high degree of public accountability in relation to the local water system. In the event of mismanagement, municipal residents are in a position to hold those responsible accountable through the electoral process. I see this as a significant advantage to municipal ownership. Although it is open to municipalities to sell their systems, there was no suggestion during the Inquiry that any municipalities are even considering doing so. Moreover, I heard nothing during the Inquiry that led me to conclude that I should make recommendations about the ownership of municipal systems in order to address water safety issues. The recommendations in this report are therefore premised on continued municipal ownership.

The decision of a municipality whether to operate its water system directly, or to engage an external operating agency, is distinct from the issue of municipal ownership. Today, roughly 70% of municipal water systems are operated directly by the municipality. About 23% are operated under contract with the Ontario Clean Water Agency (OCWA), a provincial Crown agency; roughly 6% are contracted to private companies and fewer than 1% to another municipality.[7]

---

[6] For further discussion, see A. Sancton and T. Janik, 2002, "Provincial-local relations and the drinking water in Ontario," Walkerton Inquiry Commissioned Paper 3, pp. 1–2; and Strategic Alternatives, 2002b, "Financing water infrastructure," Walkerton Inquiry Commissioned Paper 16, p. 3.

[7] In 2001, of approximately 672 communal water systems in Ontario that serve municipalities, 661 were owned by municipalities; of which 464 were operated by the municipality directly, 151 by OCWA, 42 by a private operating agency, and 4 by another municipality. In many cases, external operating agencies are contracted to operate the treatment plant only, while other components of the system – such as the distribution system – are operated by the municipal owner. Of the 11 communal systems that serve municipalities but that are not owned by municipalities, 5 in Northern

There are a number of intermunicipal agreements governing the consolidated delivery of water services among municipalities.

The provincial government plays a significant role in regulating municipal water systems.[8] As I discuss in Chapter 13, the Ministry of the Environment (MOE) enforces legislation, regulations, and policies that apply to the construction and operation of communal water systems. The dual roles of the provincial and municipal governments in relation to drinking water might be perceived as unnecessary duplication. The provincial government is primarily responsible for setting standards, approving municipal decisions in some cases, monitoring performance, and enforcing compliance with provincial standards and regulations. As the owners of water systems, municipalities are responsible for the delivery of water services in accordance with provincial standards, and for satisfying their due diligence obligations. I am satisfied that to the extent any overlap of responsibilities exists, it is a good thing; it confers a more stringent system of oversight in an area that is critical to the protection of public health.[9]

10.2.2.1   *Provincial Approval of Municipal Water Systems*

One of the regulatory functions of the MOE is to issue Certificates of Approval for water systems. In this report, I recommend certain modifications to the

---

Ontario were owned by local private water companies, 5 by industrial (mining and paper) companies, and 1 by the Province. All of these were owner-operated, except for 1 privately owned system operated by the municipality and 1 industrial system operated by OCWA.

[8] The Province has historically delivered water services directly, especially following the creation of the Ontario Water Resources Commission in 1956. However, municipalities have played by far the most significant role on the ground.

The recent trend has been for the delivery of water services to shift further back to municipalities. The MOE used to own and operate about 25% of all water and sewage treatment plants in Ontario. In 1993, the MOE's water treatment division was made into OCWA, which assumed ownership of those plants. In 1997, the *Water and Sewage Services Improvement Act* transferred ownership to municipalities. In total, 230 plants were transferred. See Association of Municipalities of Ontario, 2001, p. 23. The Province continues to provide operational services for water systems through OCWA.

[9] Sancton and Janik express this point in their issue paper to the Inquiry, arguing that the joint provincial-municipal responsibility for drinking water

is a form of double protection that should be applauded and supported.... Rather than establishing a situation in which officials at each level hope those at the other will be doing the work, they should be given the opportunity to compete with each other to be more conscientious, more alert, and more technically competent. Indeed, such a form of competition might well produce better results than exhortations of individuals within a single large organization to try harder.

Sancton and Janik, p. 50.

approvals structure for municipal water systems. As they relate to municipalities, as owners, and operating agencies, these recommendations are dealt with either in this chapter (see the list in the next paragraph) or in Chapter 11. As they relate to the provincial approvals regime in general, the recommendations are addressed in Chapter 13.

For ease of reference, I will summarize the modifications to the current approvals regime that will be necessary as a result of my recommendations. First, the owners of municipal water systems should be required to have, and to periodically renew, an MOE licence for their water system(s). Second, in addition to the current approvals requirements, an owner's licence should have the following conditions:

- a requirement to have an accredited operating agency in accordance with a provincially recognized quality management standard (discussed in Chapter 11);

- a requirement to have an operational plan for the water system – focusing on operating and performance requirements (Chapter 11); and

- a requirement to have a financial plan for the water system in accordance with provincial standards for full-cost recovery and asset management (Chapter 10).

10.2.3 Municipal Reviews of Water Systems

Recommendation 44: Municipalities should review the management and operating structure for their water system to ensure that it is capable of providing safe drinking water on a reliable basis.

It is fundamental for municipalities to have a management and operating structure for their water system that enables them to provide safe water. I am making two important recommendations to assist in this regard. First, I recommend that municipalities be required to have an agency, whether internal or external, to operate their systems. The agency should be accredited in the manner described in Chapter 11. The municipality must also submit an operational plan to the MOE for their water system(s). Second, I recommend that those responsible for exercising the municipality's oversight responsibilities be held to a statutory standard duty of care. I note that, for municipalities, the first recommendation will be a significant step in satisfying the second.

For some municipalities, these recommendations will necessitate a new approach to how they manage their water system. A review of their water system in advance of mandatory accreditation and operational planning to accommodate the new requirements is required. The review should be undertaken in light of recent changes in the industry and regulatory standards, as well as the recommendations in this report.[10] There is no one-size-fits-all solution. Municipalities can decide for themselves how best to structure the delivery of water services within the provincial regulatory framework. I do not see a need for the provincial government to prescribe specific changes to the municipal governance structure except in the most extreme circumstances of non-compliance.

As part of their review, municipalities, especially smaller ones, will need to consider whether there are opportunities to regionalize or consolidate their water system with neighbouring municipalities. I refer below to the recent experience of Chatham-Kent in this regard. Of course, this option may not be feasible for some municipalities. Other options to consider are whether to operate the water system through a municipally controlled operating agency, such as an internal department, or to engage an external operating agency, such as OCWA, another municipality, or a private company to run the system. Whatever the case, I note that municipalities will be required to have an accredited operating agency and to submit an operational plan for the water system to the MOE (see Chapter 11).

Many municipal decision makers are no doubt already well down this road. The intent of the discussion here is to assist them in the process, not to undermine or criticize the important work now underway. Further, I do not suggest that all municipalities need to undergo an all-encompassing review of every legal, financial, and managerial aspect of their water system. The review need not involve extensive time and resources. In most cases, I expect that municipalities will have sufficient internal expertise to address these issues

---

[10] The most significant recommendations in this regard are those dealing with mandatory accreditation and operational planning, discussed in Chapter 11, and the standard of care, discussed in Chapter 10. However, other recommendations will also be relevant, especially those dealing with watershed planning (Chapter 4), financial planning (Chapter 10), public-private issues (Chapter 10), and small systems (Chapter 14).

without having to obtain a great deal of outside help, especially if provincial guidance is available as I recommend below. Some municipalities may have recently undergone many aspects of the review I envision and it makes no sense for them to repeat the process unnecessarily.

Finally, I recognize that municipalities in Ontario have undergone significant restructuring in recent years.[11] As the Association of Municipalities of Ontario (AMO) pointed out at the Inquiry, this has included:[12]

- the elimination of provincial grants and the introduction of a Community Reinvestment Fund;[13]

- the expansion of the number and range of functions that municipalities are required to deliver and finance;

- the restructuring of the electricity sector;

- the overhauling of the valuation system for the property tax assessment base;

- changes to municipal discretion over property tax rates according to provincial legislation that caps rate increases for certain classes of properties; and

- a reduction in the number of municipalities and municipal politicians by 45% and 40%, respectively, through amalgamations.

As a result of these reforms, I was informed that there is a significant degree of "re-structuring fatigue" in the municipal sector.[14] I do not intend through my

---

[11] During 1989–2001, municipal governments have faced, in the words of AMO, "some of the most dramatic, all encompassing changes since the introduction of the *Baldwin Act* of 1849." Association of Municipalities of Ontario, 2001, p. 3.

[12] Ibid.

[13] According to the Ministry of Municipal Affairs and Housing, the Community Reinvestment Fund "is provided by the Province to municipalities to balance new costs with new revenues" following the introduction of Local Services Realignment in 1998. See <www.mah.gov.on.ca/inthnews/backgrnd/20010819-2.asp>.

[14] According to AMO, the degree and speed of change, especially during the last six years, has been "extremely challenging for municipal governments," and has taken place in the context of fairly restrictive financial circumstances, inability to use deficit financing, pressure to freeze or reduce property taxes, and a large share of expenditures that is non-discretionary. See Association of Municipalities of Ontario, 2001, p. 3.

recommendations to initiate a whole new wave of municipal restructuring. However, considering the restructuring that has occurred, the ongoing changes to the water industry, the recommendations of this Inquiry, and the lessons of Walkerton, I am satisfied that now is an appropriate time for municipalities to review the operating and management structure for their water system.

10.2.4 Survey of Options

In this section, I discuss a variety of options that municipalities should consider when reviewing their water system. The options presented below do not address all the issues that municipalities may wish to consider in light of their oversight responsibilities or the recommendations coming out of this report. Rather, they focus on a central issue: the operating and management structure of the water system. A summary of the available options is provided in the following table.

Table 10.1 Summary of Options for Municipal Water Systems

Operating Agency	Options
1. Municipal operating agency	a. Municipal department b. Public utilities commission c. Municipally owned corporation
2. Regional water provider	a. Regional governments b. Intermunicipal agreements
3. External operating agency	a. Ontario Clean Water Agency b. Another municipality c. Private operating agency

10.2.4.1   *Municipal Operating Agency*

A municipality may decide to operate its own water system, either directly through the municipal administrative structure, or through an operating agency that the municipality owns and controls. Historically, many municipal water systems were run by public utilities commissions, creatures of municipalities that were governed by elected commissioners on behalf of the municipality. Following recent reforms in the electricity sector, the majority of municipalities have disbanded their public utilities commissions and most now run the water system through a municipal department or a separate municipal corporation.[15]

Municipal Department

Most communal water systems in Ontario are operated by a department of the municipality. The strength of this model, according to the AMO, lies in the integration of decisions about the water system with other municipal functions, such as public health, land use planning, and economic development. A municipal water department may also be able to achieve greater economies of scale, according to AMO, by sharing administrative services with other municipal departments.[16]

This model is criticized by some for two main reasons. First, it leads to the diversion of water-related revenues from the water system to other municipal programs and services. This cross-subsidization can occur directly, where water-related revenues or reserve funds are simply redirected elsewhere. It can also occur indirectly, such as where a municipality overcharges the water department for general municipal services, or where the municipality does not remit interest earned from water-related reserve funds to the water system. Cross-subsidization becomes a safety issue when it interferes with the adequate funding of the water system. The basic purpose of the water rate, after all, is to provide a sustainable and identifiable source of revenues for water services. In light of this, I recommend in section 10.3 of this chapter that municipalities be required to have a financial plan for the water system according to provincial standards for full-cost recovery and asset management.

---

[15] See N. d'Ombrain, 2002, "Machinery of government for safe drinking water," Walkerton Inquiry Commissioned Paper 4, p. 63. Until the late 1990s, public utilities commissions commonly provided both water and electricity to local ratepayers. This situation changed with the passage of the *Energy Competition Act*, which received Royal Assent on November 7, 1998. The Act required municipal councils to establish new companies under the *Ontario Business Corporations Act* to own and operate local electrical assets. Municipalities had to decide (1) whether or not to continue to own and operate their electric utility (and as such become the shareholder of the new company) and (2) whether the utility would be a commercial or a not-for-profit company. See Sancton and Janik, p. 45; Strategic Alternatives, 2002a, p. 23. One impact of this policy change, according to Sancton and Janik, was that public utilities commissions no longer dealt with electricity, "causing many municipal councils (and various participants in the municipal restructuring process) to question whether they are needed at all." Sancton and Janik, p. 45.

[16] Association of Municipalities of Ontario, Walkerton Inquiry Submission (Expert Meeting, June 20–21, 2001).

Second, the model is criticized on the basis that municipal councillors may not have sufficient knowledge or interest in the water system to adequately fulfill their oversight responsibilities. The response to this concern is straightforward. Since the municipality owns the water system, it is incumbent on the municipal council to ensure that its system is competently managed and operated. To make this responsibility as clear as possible, I recommend in section 10.2.5 the adoption of a statutory standard of care for owners of municipal water systems, and in Chapter 11 the adoption of mandatory quality management for municipal water providers.

Public Utilities Commission

Public utilities commissions (PUCs) were a major part of the water industry in Ontario for the better part of a century. Since 1996, their role has declined dramatically as a result of provincial reforms and municipal decisions to disband local public utilities commissions.[17]

Municipal councils were given the power to establish PUCs under the *Municipal Waterworks Act* of 1882. Public water supplies were relatively scarce in Ontario at the time.[18] Most people relied on wells, springs, cisterns, community pumps, private water carriers, and other sources for their water. One of the reasons for the establishment of PUCs was to allow local authorities to pay for water infrastructure directly, without provincial funding. Another purpose was to expand and consolidate newly installed water services across the municipality. Finally, PUCs were established to promote professional expertise and business principles in the operation of public utilities, and to separate that operation from the exigencies of municipal council politics.[19]

To ensure local accountability, PUCs were made up of elected three- or five-person commissions, including the head of council in an *ex officio* capacity. To promote expertise and business principles, there were specific provisions for

---

[17] In 1990, 124 out of 834 municipalities relied on public or water utility commissions to operate water facilities. By 2001, as a result of municipal amalgamations and the spinning off of electrical utilities, only 15 of 447 remaining municipalities continued to use commissions to operate water facilities. Sancton and Janik, p. 43.

[18] In 1882, for example, there were only 13 public water systems in the Province. See J. Benidickson, 2002, "Water supply and sewage infrastructure in Ontario, 1880–1990s: Legal and institutional aspects of public health and environmental history," Walkerton Inquiry Commissioned Paper 1, p. 11.

[19] N.B. Freeman, 1996, *Ontario's Water Industry – Models for the 21st Century*, report prepared for the Ontario Municipal Water Association, pp. 3, 14.

the autonomy of the utility through its separate administrative structure and its powers to raise funds directly from local revenue sources. PUCs operated on a transactional, fee-for-service basis; they had a distinct identity; and they were oriented to a specific public function.[20]

In 1996 the provincial government, in connection with reforms to the electricity sector, gave municipalities the authority to disband their public utilities commissions without first obtaining the assent of local electors, as had previously been required.[21] Most promptly did so, in many cases either taking over the operation of the system through a municipal department, or reconstituting the PUC as a municipally owned corporation with appointed – rather than elected – commissioners. There are probably a number of reasons for why this occurred. In many small towns, PUCs could not be justified for managing water alone following restructuring in the electricity sector. However, it is also suggested that some PUCs were disbanded because councils wanted direct control over water-related revenues to be able to cross-subsidize other municipal programs and services, especially following reductions in provincial subsidies.[22] To the extent this is the case, it is an unfortunate development.

The elected PUC is, in my view, a very attractive model because of the balance it achieves for accountability, expertise, and business autonomy.[23] It continues to be available as one of the alternatives open to municipalities to manage their water system. However, I recognize that the trend, for whatever reasons, appears to be strongly away from the use of PUCs for the management of water systems.

Municipally Owned Corporation

Proponents of the model of a municipally owned corporation argue that it provides a means to ensure effective management of the water system. Under

---

[20] Ibid., p. 1.

[21] From 1931 to 1998, the *Public Utilities Act* provided that the disbandment or sale of a utility could proceed only with the assent of the local electors. This requirement was removed with the passage of the *Savings and Restructuring Act* in 1996, amending the *Public Utilities Act*, R.S.O. 1990, c. P.52, ss. 38 and 67. See ibid., pp. 38–39.

[22] Strategic Alternatives, 2002a, p. 23; Sancton and Janik, p. 40; and Freeman, p. 2.

[23] As Freeman has commented, the PUC model allowed for the water system and other utilities to be governed with autonomy from municipal council to ensure service accountability to the public and financial separation from the municipality. The fact that public utilities commissioners were elected, rather than appointed, provided for direct accountability between the consumer, without compromising business autonomy. Freeman, p. 4.

this model, the corporation (whether for-profit or non-profit) operates the water system on behalf of municipal council. Its directors are appointed by municipal council and normally consist of persons with relevant expertise.

The Chair of the Peterborough Utilities Commission recommended to the Inquiry that all municipalities adopt this model by restructuring their PUC or water department as a non-profit company, as in the case of Peterborough.[24] He cited numerous benefits including competent oversight by the board of directors, dedicated revenues, and enhanced borrowing capacity without the need for private sector involvement. He also indicated that existing economies of scale can be maintained under this model by purchasing services from the municipality.

Another example of the corporate model is EPCOR, a municipally owned, for-profit corporation that offers water and electricity services. EPCOR was incorporated in 1995 by the City of Edmonton, out of the existing Edmonton power and water utility that had been in operation since 1902. The City is its sole shareholder. The City appoints the members of the board of directors, lays out the dividend policy, and approves the company's auditors. Under this structure, according to one of its managers, EPCOR has a great deal of financial and managerial independence.[25]

The corporate model offers the potential benefit of greater expertise in the oversight of the water system through the appointment of a qualified board of directors. In some cases, there may also be an advantage to having the corporation functioning independently of the pressures of local politics. However, as with the other models, municipalities will want to balance the benefits against the costs, in this case a reduction in direct accountability to local residents.[26] I also note that this model has emerged relatively recently in

---

[24] The Peterborough Utilities Commission has existed since 1914, and its municipal water commission since 1902. In 2000, it underwent significant changes as a result of restructuring in the energy sector. The Peterborough Utilities Commission has now been incorporated under the *Ontario Business Corporations Act* as a not-for-profit corporation owned solely by the City of Peterborough. The company is overseen by a board of directors appointed by the municipal council, which replaced the previously elected public utilities commissioners. See C. Maynes, Chair of the Peterborough Utilities Commission, Walkerton Inquiry Submission (e-mail to the Walkerton Inquiry, August 1, 2001).

[25] A. Davies, for OWWA/OMWA, Walkerton Inquiry Submission (Public Hearing, September 20, 2001), transcript pp. 24–26; and EPCOR <www.epcor.ca/EPCOR+Companies/ EPCOR+Group+of+Companies/default.html> [accessed April 14, 2002].

[26] The level of accountability will vary depending on the arrangement between the corporation and the municipality.

the context of water services, and municipalities may wish to evaluate the experience with this model as it unfolds in places like Peterborough.

10.2.4.2   *Regionalization*

Regionalization is a vehicle to improve the quality of the overall management and planning for a water system. It functions within a decision-making framework that allows for public accountability across the entire service region. As importantly, increasing the overall size of a water system allows for a higher level of expertise within the management and operation of the system. This also leads to greater financial strength and the ability to allocate resources to where they are most needed, whether to address infrastructure challenges or to improve source water and treatment requirements.[27] On the whole, regionalization generally improves the safety, reliability, and effectiveness of water services, while preserving a measure of direct accountability for participating municipalities.

The American Water Works Association (AWWA) defines a regional water system as

> a management or contractual administrative organization or a coordinated physical system plan of two or more community water systems using common resources and facilities to their optimum advantage.[28]

Regionalization may take different forms. In the words of AWWA, for example, it may take the form of "an urban complex of water systems with a plan to minimize duplication, identify future service areas ... and establish mutual aid pacts" or "a group of rural or suburban systems that could obtain economies of scale under a common management system."[29]

---

[27] A. Davies, 2001, for OWWA/OMWA, "Effective water utility management and organizational behaviour," Walkerton Inquiry Submission, p. 30, citing D.A. Okum, "State initiative for regionalization," *AWWA Journal* (May 1981). There may, of course, be limits to the benefits of regionalization, depending on the circumstances. See Association of Municipalities of Ontario, 2001, p. 28, citing S. Renzetti, 1998, "An empirical perspective on water pricing reforms," paper presented at the Workshop on Political Economy of Water Pricing Implementation, Washington, D.C., November 3–5.

[28] See J.A. MacDonald, 2001, for OWWA/OMWA, "Review of issue #8 – Production and distribution of drinking water," Walkerton Inquiry Submission.

[29] Ibid.

In Ontario, municipal amalgamations and the creation of regional governments have historically led to the consolidation of municipal water services, as discussed below.[30] However, municipalities also have the authority to enter into intermunicipal agreements for the delivery of water services. Intermunicipal agreements may provide for joint municipal ownership, joint operation, or both.[31] Each model provides different degrees of accountability. This choice is especially significant where a municipality wishes to retain some ongoing control over its water system beyond the provisions of a service contract with an external operating agency.[32]

The recent amalgamations of municipalities have in some cases brought different water systems under the authority of a single municipality.[33] In these cases, opportunities exist to consolidate the management of disparate water systems and thus achieve greater coordination of the water system across the entire region. I discuss one such example, Chatham-Kent, below.

The Chatham-Kent Public Utilities Commission

The Municipality of Chatham-Kent was created in 1997 following the amalgamation of 23 municipalities and 13 public utilities in Kent County. All of the pre-existing water systems in the region were integrated into a single utility for water, sewage, and hydro services: the Chatham-Kent Public Utilities

---

[30] Consolidation, short of the creation of a regional or amalgamated municipal government, has also occurred historically through various "area schemes" that were built by the provincial government to deliver shared water and sewage services to groups of municipalities. The Province divested the ownership of these area schemes to participating municipalities in 1997 under the *Water and Sewage Services Improvement Act*. See Strategic Alternatives, 2002a, pp. 25–28.

[31] *Municipal Act*, R.S.O. 1990, c. M.45, s. 207 and s. 210.1. Intermunicipal agreements of this nature are reportedly common. See Strategic Alternatives, 2002a, pp. 26–28.

[32] One model of regionalization, from Manitoba, is the Pembina Valley Water Cooperative Inc., an incorporated cooperative owned by 18 municipal governments, and serving about 40,000 people. The Cooperative is a not-for-profit organization with surplus revenue put into a reserve fund for infrastructure upgrades. Any surplus remaining after upgrades is paid back to the municipalities. The Cooperative is governed by an assembly of one representative from each participating municipality.

[33] From 1996 to January 2002, 566 municipalities were amalgamated into 198, and the total number of municipalities in Ontario was reduced from 815 to 447; Ministry of Municipal Affairs and Housing, "Restructuring *Flash*News" <http://www.mah.gov.on.ca/business/flashnews/flashnews-e.asp> [accessed April 3, 2002].

Commission (PUC).[34] The overall water supply system has, spread over the region, 10 wastewater treatment facilities, 9 water distribution systems, about 800 km of water lines, and about 330 km of sanitary sewers. The integrated system has a number of water sources, including wells, streams, small lakes, large lakes, and water purchased from municipalities outside the county.

Following the amalgamation, the Chatham-Kent PUC completed a master plan for how to service the needs of the amalgamated systems for the next 20 years. It consolidated 11 existing billing and collection systems into a single system. The PUC also terminated its existing operating contracts to gain full control over the financial management of the system, and to address the high interest rates on debt for some of the systems. Further, the PUC carried out a detailed mapping project of the entire system to assess the possibilities to standardize service levels and it did a rate study as to how to finance all the systems and a range of capital projects in the future. It is adopting a fully harmonized rate structure for all of Chatham-Kent, and a life-cycle reserve for the complete replacement costs of the existing system.

Overall, the amalgamation has led to significant cost savings.[35] On an annual basis, the PUC achieved overall savings in debt payments of $980,000,[36] savings in administrative costs of $430,000, savings in billing and collecting of $150,000, and savings in operations of $400,000. It is estimated that $2.5 million per year (out of an annual budget of $17 million) has been saved through staff realignment, operating efficiencies, and economies of scale.[37]

These cost savings have allowed the PUC to put more money back into the system, especially to meet infrastructure needs. The PUC has plans for about $160 million in water and wastewater projects over the next 20 years, to be financed from the newly harmonized water rate, and assuming no outside

---

[34] The manager of Water and Wastewater Services of the Chatham-Kent PUC, Jack Sonneveld, spoke about these reforms in a presentation to the Inquiry in Windsor on June 12, 2001. Unless otherwise indicated, the information in this section is adopted from his presentation.

[35] All figures were reported by Jack Sonneveld.

[36] At the time of amalgamation, the outstanding OCWA/MOE debt in the system was $4.9 million in water and $1.3 million in wastewater, with interest rates ranging from 8% to 14%. After amalgamation, the Chatham-Kent PUC paid out existing debts of over $5.6 million in debt with savings from the amalgamation, and refinanced at 5.25%, leading to the annual savings in debt payments of $980,000. This new borrowing was financed internally through the municipality because the PUC is not large enough to issue debentures.

[37] I note that amalgamation does not always lead to cost savings. There will usually be significant transitional costs, and in some cases costs may increase as a result of the harmonization of service levels or the harmonization of wages and salaries.

subsidies to offset the cost.[38] It has also established reserve funds of about $4.8 million for the water and wastewater systems. The water rate is reportedly comparable to others in the area.[39] According to the water manager of the Chatham-Kent PUC, "the cost of potable water is lower than high speed Internet, and this is a necessity of life."

In terms of staffing, the PUC has the same number of staff as before the amalgamation, although workloads have reportedly risen to address increased maintenance activities, increased sampling, work related to the new requirement for engineering reports, increased contracts to build and upgrade infrastructure, and a 20% increase in the service population. The salaries of PUC staff have been standardized; many wage levels increased while several positions were frozen. There were no strikes in the transition. In large part because of the consolidation, the PUC reportedly has a good cross-section of knowledge and skills across its workforce, allowing for cross-training and knowledgeable back-up staff.

Thus, the Chatham-Kent PUC has achieved higher standards of safety and has spread them throughout the service area at a common water rate. It has also maintained accountability to electors as part of the amalgamated municipality. An important part of the success of the consolidation, according to the water manager, was that the project was kept within manageable limits. Now that the management of the existing water systems has been consolidated, the PUC is at a stage where it can accommodate contracts with water systems from outside the municipality. Thus, as a regionalized entity, the PUC offers an option to neighbouring municipalities looking for an external operating agency to run their water systems.

Regional Governments and Shared Service Delivery

The establishment of 12 regional governments in Ontario between 1969 and 1975 is another example of how the management of water systems has been consolidated across a wide service area. The Regional Municipality of Waterloo submitted to the Inquiry that the consolidation of water services under regional governments has provided for "better planning, a critical mass for staffing,

---

[38] Among other projects, the PUC is constructing a new water treatment plant to replace two other plants, is going to micro-filtration technology, and will construct a new trunk water line to supply one small community.

[39] In July 2001, rates were about $38 for 30 cubic metres per month for water and sewage.

expertise in operations, and the ability to finance major works."[40] Also, it was submitted that regionalization has allowed for greater integration of the water system with other regional services, such as the public health programs of the Medical Officer of Health and his/her staff, who work within a regional department rather than a separate local health unit.[41]

In a few cases where regional governments were established, the responsibility for water is shared between the regional government and the lower-tier governments.[42] The regional government treats the water and sells it at a wholesale rate to the lower-tier governments, which in turn distribute it to consumers. The lower-tier governments also collect revenues from water rates.

Representatives of regional governments in Ontario recommended to me that, in these circumstances of shared responsibility, the provincial government should require lower-tier governments to transfer the water distribution systems to the regional government.[43] I have decided not to make a formal recommendation in this regard because I did not hear fully from the affected lower-tier municipalities about their positions and the possible implications to them. However, I am attracted to the idea for a number of reasons.

First, as discussed above, regionalization allows for greater economies of scale in the operation of water systems. Second, the regional government is in a better position to coordinate the management of distribution across the entire system; it is important to coordinate water treatment and distribution since decisions that relate to one frequently impact on the other. Third, the regional government is in a better position to implement common standards of service across the service region. Further, in cases where residents in different parts of a region have different levels of services at different costs, regional representatives are in the best position to decide how new or improved service should be allocated, and how the costs should be recovered. Finally, dividing the

---

[40] The Regional Municipality of Waterloo, Walkerton Inquiry (Town Hall Meeting, March 22, 2001), transcript p. 34.

[41] Ibid., p. 35.

[42] This is the case in the regional municipalities of Niagara, Waterloo, and York.

[43] The Regional and Single Tier CAOs of Ontario recommended that "future legislation identify the control of water treatment process and delivery be maintained under one roof, at the Regional or Upper Tier level where there is a two-tier system to maintain quality and consistent service delivery"; see A.B. Marshall, for the Regional and Single Tier CAOs of Ontario, Walkerton Inquiry Submission (letter to the Commissioner, November 28, 2001). The Regional Municipality of Waterloo made a similar recommendation.

responsibility for water services may discourage lower-tier municipalities from promoting conservation through full-cost pricing.[44]

In summary, it is my view that where the ownership and operation of a water system is shared between a regional and lower-tier municipality, there are significant advantages to coordinating the treatment and distribution of water under the direction of the regional government.[45] The provincial government may wish to consider requiring lower-tier municipalities to transfer ownership of their water systems to the upper-tier municipality.

10.2.4.3   *External Operating Agency*

Where a municipality decides not to operate its water system directly or join with other municipalities in a regional arrangement, it has the option to contract with an external operating agency, including the Ontario Clean Water Agency, a private company, or another municipality.[46] An overview of each of these options is presented below.

The Ontario Clean Water Agency

The Ontario Clean Water Agency is a provincial Crown corporation established under the *Capital Investment Plan Act* of 1993.[47] The Act sets out OCWA's objectives, including its mandate to provide operations and maintenance services to municipalities on a cost-recovery basis. Although OCWA's mandate has changed significantly since it was created, its primary purpose remains the

---

[44] This is because most of the savings arising from conservation go to the regional water wholesaler in the form of deferred treatment plant costs, as opposed to the lower tier retailer of the service. However, it is the lower-tier municipality that normally has the capability to implement full-cost pricing by adjusting the water rate structure.

[45] I note that the *Savings and Restructuring Act* allows an upper-tier municipality to pass a bylaw to provide for a service presently delivered at the lower tier, and if more than 50% of the lower-tier municipalities pass bylaws to the same effect, the service is moved to the upper tier for the whole municipality. *Savings and Restructuring Act*, S.O. 1996, c. 1, Schedule M, Part 1, s. 6, amending the *Municipal Act*, R.S.O. 1990, s. 209.2. See also Freeman, p. 51.

[46] The *Public Utilities Act*, R.S.O. 1990, c. P.52, s.11(2) specifies that contract terms for water supply may not exceed a term of 20 years; in practice, the duration of most such services contracts is much shorter, often in the neighbourhood of 5 years.

[47] *Capital Investment Plan Act*, S.O. 1993, c. 23. At the time it was created, OCWA assumed the operational (as well as financing) functions for water and sewage of the Ministry of the Environment.

same: to operate water systems under contract with the municipal owner.[48] OCWA offers an important alternative to other external operating agencies, especially for small or remote municipalities that have limited options to operate their own water systems or to pursue regionalization. Also, OCWA is a useful vehicle for the provincial government in circumstances where it finds it necessary to mandate the restructuring of "non-viable" municipal systems or to respond to emergency situations, as in the case of Walkerton. For these reasons, I see OCWA continuing to play an important role in the province's water industry.[49]

I discuss OCWA in more detail in 10.4.6 of this chapter; I discuss the issue of non-viable small systems in Chapter 14.

Another Municipality

Here I refer to the option of a municipality to enter into an agreement with another municipality to operate its water system. This differs from other types of intermunicipal agreements, discussed above, that provide for joint ownership or otherwise for direct accountability by all participating municipalities in the joint operation of their water systems. For some small municipalities it may be an attractive option to exchange direct local control for the assurance of a more effective operation.

During the course of the Inquiry, I spoke to the managers of several large water systems. All of them were very receptive to working out arrangements with smaller municipalities for the operation of the water systems in those communities. Such arrangements have the potential to benefit the larger municipality in terms of cost recovery, and the smaller municipality in terms of reduced costs, and greater safety and reliability.

Private Operating Agency

The private sector offers an option for municipalities seeking to contract with an external operating agency. There are a number of companies in Ontario

---

[48] In terms of the changes to its mandate, in May 1996 the Province transferred the administration of provincial water and wastewater grants programs from OCWA to the Ministry of the Environment. In 1997, the Province devolved the ownership of provincial water and sewage systems from OCWA to the municipalities served by those systems. See d'Ombrain, p. 48.

[49] I also envision OCWA becoming accredited like other operating agencies, as discussed in Chapter 11.

that are capable of operating all or part of a municipal water system. So long as an operating agency is accredited and regulated effectively, in my opinion the question of whether it is publicly or privately owned does not impact on issues of safety. Ensuring public accountability for the safety of drinking water is very important, however, and, in cases where a municipality decides to employ a private operating agency, the means to ensure accountability necessarily shifts to the contractual relationship with that agency. I discuss this issue in section 10.4 of this chapter.

10.2.5 Standard of Care

Recommendation 45: Given that the safety of drinking water is essential for public health, those who discharge the oversight responsibilities of the municipality should be held to a statutory standard of care.

In light of municipal ownership of water systems, municipal councils are responsible for ensuring the effective management and operation of their water systems. In some cases, councillors will assume this oversight responsibility directly; in others, they may delegate aspects of the oversight function. Given the importance of drinking water for public health, those responsible for discharging the oversight function of the municipality (e.g., the council or a committee of council)[50] should be held to a statutory standard of care that recognizes and formalizes their responsibilities. These individuals should be required under the *Safe Drinking Water Act* to act honestly and in good faith with a view to the protection of the safety of the consumer, and to exercise the care, diligence, and skill that a reasonably prudent person would exercise in comparable circumstances. This standard of care is similar to the standard of care for directors of corporations under the various corporations' statutes.

Depending on the circumstances, the types of oversight responsibilities to be discharged will include: adopting an overall policy for the system, hiring senior management or contracting with an external operating agency, and periodically auditing or evaluating the performance of the operating agency. Where those who are responsible lack the confidence in their expertise in a particular area, they would be expected to obtain outside expert advice. As with a board of directors of a corporation, obtaining and following proper expert advice can

---

[50] In order to maintain public accountability, it will be important that at least some publicly elected representatives be included in exercising oversight responsibility.

satisfy the statutory standard of care. Also, the fact that a municipality has an accredited operating agency will do much to satisfy the standard of care.[51]

The standard of care I recommend would apply to those discharging the owner's oversight function. I have not recommended a statutory duty of care for water managers and staff because the designated operator of a water system (the senior manager) is currently required, under Ontario Regulation 453/93, to ensure that the operation is safe and that the water is measured and monitored, to keep records, and to maintain the equipment. Also, under the provincial government's operator licensing program, the individual operator-in-charge is responsible for:[52]

- taking all steps reasonably necessary to operate the processes within his or her responsibility in a safe and efficient manner;

- ensuring that processes within his or her responsibility are measured, monitored, sampled, and tested in a manner that permits them to be adjusted when necessary;

- ensuring that records are maintained of all adjustments made to the processes within his or her responsibility; and

- ensuring that all equipment used in the processes within his or her responsibility is properly monitored, inspected, and evaluated and that records of equipment operating status are prepared and available at the end of every operating shift.

In my opinion, these duties, along with mandatory quality management and effective provincial oversight, are sufficient for the purposes of ensuring that managers and staff adhere to a minimum performance standard.

---

[51] In cases where a municipality has contracted with an external operating agency to run the water system, the municipal council is still responsible for ensuring effective oversight – including regular audits and evaluation – of the outside agency's performance.

[52] Water and Wastewater Utility Operator Licensing Program; See G. Samuel, 2001, for OWWA/ OMWA, "Training and accreditation of water supply professionals," Walkerton Inquiry Submission, Appendix 1.

10.2.6 The Role of the Provincial Government

Recommendation 46: The provincial government should provide guidance and technical advice to support municipal reviews of water systems.

The provincial government should support municipalities in their review of management and operating models, especially in the case of small and recently amalgamated municipalities. It should offer expertise from the Ministry of Municipal Affairs and Housing or the Ministry of the Environment about the available options – for example, by sponsoring workshops for municipal managers.

In addition, in connection with my recommendations for a statutory standard of care, the provincial government should produce a guidance manual giving direction to municipal officials about their roles and responsibilities.[53] In doing so, the provincial government should make clear that drinking water is essential to public health and that it is incumbent on the owner to take reasonable steps to ensure the competence of management. At the same time, the provincial government should indicate that this responsibility does not necessarily require specialized expertise in the operation of water systems, and that the standard of care should not deter dedicated individuals from running for municipal office.

10.3   Financial Issues

10.3.1 Overview

I turn now to financial planning for municipal water systems. In Ontario, municipalities raise money from local revenue sources – such as property taxes and water rates – to pay for operating and capital costs, according to provincial legislation.[54]

---

[53] In this regard, an appropriate approach might be for the Province to provide funding to OMWA or OWWA to develop a handbook oriented to the owners of municipal water systems – and municipal councilors in particular – akin to the *Municipal Electric Association Commissioners' and Senior Managers' Handbook* (Municipal Electrical Association [now the Electricity Distributors Association], 1998), which deals with the role and responsibilities of commissioners of electrical utilities.

[54] Under the *Municipal Act*, the *Public Utilities Act*, the *Development Charges Act*, and other statutes, municipalities are granted the power to levy taxes and charge fees in order to generate revenues from local residents to support local services and projects, such as the municipal water system.

I have dedicated a separate section to this topic because of the important relationship between financial issues and the capacity of a water provider to reliably deliver safe drinking water. The intent of this section is to show why and how municipalities, and local residents, need to ensure that adequate resources are available. I should note that it is unclear the extent to which municipalities are currently providing adequate resources to support their water systems. The assumption here is that not all municipalities are providing adequate resources[55] and that it would not be prudent to assume that they are without extensive research that this Inquiry is not in a position to conduct. The recommendations in this section are based on these assumptions.

10.3.2 The Proposed *Sustainable Water and Sewage Systems Act*

On December 12, 2001, the provincial government introduced Bill 155, proposing a *Sustainable Water and Sewage Systems Act, 2001*, for first reading.[56] If it is passed into law, the proposed Act would require all municipalities to submit to the Ministry of Municipal Affairs and Housing a written report on the full cost of providing water and wastewater services to the public (the "full-cost report").[57] In addition, the proposed Act would require municipalities to submit to the ministry, within six months of the approval of its full-cost report, a plan outlining how it intends to pay the full cost of water and wastewater services to the public (the "cost-recovery plan").

In my opinion, if passed into law, the Act will address many of the important issues concerning the financing of water systems that I discuss in this section. The requirements for a full-cost report and cost-recovery plan, as generally expressed in the proposed Act, are in my view appropriate. The regulations to be promulgated under the proposed Act will be critical since they will define "full cost" for the purposes of full-cost accounting and recovery, and outline standards to guide municipal financial planning, especially regarding asset management. I discuss these issues below.

---

[55] Based on the submissions of a number of parties and experts at the Inquiry.

[56] Bill 155, *An Act respecting the cost of water and waste water services*, 2d Sess., 37th Leg., Ontario, 2001 (1st reading, December 12, 2001); <www.ontla.on.ca/documents/Bills/37_Parliament/Session2/b155.pdf> [accessed April 10, 2002].

[57] As outlined in the proposed Act, the report would have to contain "such information as is required by regulation concerning the infrastructure needed to provide the water services, the full cost of providing the services and the revenue obtained to provide them and concerning such other matters as may be specified in the regulation." Bill 155, cl. 3(2).

10.3.3   The Requirement for a Financial Plan

Recommendation 47: The provincial government should require municipalities to submit a financial plan for their water system, in accordance with provincial standards, as a condition of licence for their water systems.

Municipalities need to ensure that their water systems are adequately financed. Over the long term, safety depends on stable and adequate financing to maintain the water system's infrastructure and its operational capacity to supply high-quality water consistently. Without adequate resources, corners will inevitably be cut, whether in the day-to-day operation of the facility, or in its long-term capital infrastructure. Ultimately, safety will be jeopardized.

Municipalities should therefore be required to submit a financial plan that lays out the resources required to run and sustain the water system, and how those resources will be raised. The plans should be filed and referred to by the provincial government in the course of provincial approvals of municipal water systems. As such, it should be a condition of a municipality's licence for its water system from the MOE that it have filed a financial plan. I leave it to the provincial government to determine the degree to which the government should review and approve such plans in detail, and whether they take the form of a policy or annual plan.

The plan would depend on two components: full-cost *accounting* and full-cost *recovery*. The former is a prerequisite for the latter. Once in place, municipalities should update their plan periodically, probably on an annual basis.

10.3.3.1   *Full-Cost Accounting*

Many municipalities in Ontario have worked to assess the costs of their water system in order to charge appropriate rates and generate sufficient revenues to sustain the system. In other municipalities, however, the costs of running the water system and, in particular, sustaining its infrastructure, may not be as well understood.[58] They may not be fully aware of the current state of the system

---

[58] OWWA/OMWA submitted at the Inquiry that most municipalities do have detailed inventory information on their system, although more detailed assessments of the condition and replacement value of the assets may not be carried out by all municipalities. See C.N. Watson and Associates, 2001a, for OWWA/OMWA, "Review of various papers submitted to the Walkerton Inquiry

infrastructure and its replacement value, or the costs arising from the operating requirements of the system. The municipality will not be in a position to put adequate resources into the system if municipal decision makers do not know what the full costs actually are. For this reason, the municipality needs to undertake a *full-cost accounting* of the water system. For consistency, this should be carried out in accordance with a provincial standard.

The proposed *Sustainable Water and Sewage Systems Act* would require municipalities to submit a full-cost report as follows:[59]

Report on Full Cost of Water Services

3. (1) Every regulated entity that provides water services to the public shall give a written report about those services to the Minister before the date specified by regulation.

Contents

(2) The report must contain such information as is required by regulation concerning the infrastructure needed to provide the water services, the full cost of providing the services and the revenue obtained to provide them and concerning such other matters as may be specified in the regulation.

...

Components of Full Cost

(4) The full cost of providing the water services includes the operating costs, financing costs, renewal and replacement costs and improvement costs associated with extracting, treating or distributing water to the public and such other costs as may be specified by regulation.

As proposed, the full-cost report represents an accounting of the full cost of the water system, including various operating and capital costs associated with the water system, as well as other costs that may be specified in the regulations.

Commission regarding financial matters on behalf of the Ontario Municipal Water Association and the Ontario Water Works Association," Walkerton Inquiry Submission, p. 3-3.
[59] Bill 155, cl. 3.

I discuss the types of costs that should be included in the definition of "full cost" below. I also discuss below the need for provincial standards in this area, especially in relation to sustainable asset management.

10.3.3.2   *Full-Cost Recovery*

Once the cost of safe water is known, a municipality must raise adequate funds to pay for it. In some municipalities, the pressure to keep water rates low may mean that sufficient revenues are not being generated in the first place. In other cases, the pressure to fund other municipal services and programs may lead council to redirect revenues from the water system to other purposes. Either scenario may result in underfunding of the water system. The purpose of a full-cost recovery plan is for a municipality to determine how it will pay for the full costs of its water system from its local revenue sources, including how it will raise the money to pay for future capital costs, whether from accumulated reserves or from borrowing.

The proposed *Sustainable Water and Sewage Systems Act* includes a requirement for a cost-recovery plan, based on the principle of full-cost recovery, as follows:[60]

Cost Recovery Plan for Water Services

9. (1) Every regulated entity that provides water services to the public shall prepare a plan describing how the entity intends to pay the full cost of providing those services.

...

Sources of Revenue

(4) The regulations may specify those sources of revenue that a regulated entity is, or is not, permitted to include in the plan and may impose conditions or restrictions with respect to different sources of revenue.

...

---

[60] Bill 155, cl. 9.

As in the case of the full-cost report, important aspects of the requirement for a cost-recovery plan await the regulations and the definition of provincial standards. I discuss these issues below.

10.3.4 The Definition of Full Cost

In connection with the proposed *Sustainable Water and Sewage Systems Act*, the Province will need to define in some detail the meaning of "full cost" for the purposes of full-cost accounting and recovery. Without a uniform definition, the requirement for a financial plan for municipal water systems would be undermined by divergent interpretations of the requirement. The definition of full cost was the subject of a great deal of discussion during the course of the Inquiry. In this section I offer my views about some of the more prominent positions that were advanced. I do so to provide background as to the definition that I envision under the proposed Act.

Defining full cost runs two competing risks. If the definition is too broad, municipalities may be forced to recover costs that are not legitimately part of the full cost of providing water, or that are too difficult to measure and account for effectively. For these reasons, one should be conservative in defining full cost to make the standard as accurate and practical as possible. However, if the definition is too narrow, one runs the risk of excluding costs that are integral to the delivery of safe water. Municipalities could have a financial plan, in accordance with provincial standards, and still fail to provide adequate resources. This would be a most unfortunate result.

For reasons of safety, full cost should be defined to include, at a minimum, all of the operating and capital costs of the system. I discuss these types of costs below.

Table 10.2 Outline of Operating and Capital Costs

Type of Cost	Description
Operating costs	• Salaries and benefits • Material and supplies, such as chemicals • Vehicles, tools, and other equipment • Maintenance • Monitoring and reporting • Accreditation and operational planning • Staff training • Utilities, such as electric power, gas, and telephone • Insurance for equipment and facilities • Sales and property taxes • Contracted or outsourced services, such as meter reading or water main repair • Administrative costs
Capital costs	• Upfront costs of infrastructure for supply, treatment, pumping, distribution, and storage • May include buildings, land, equipment, and vehicles • Upgrade, replacement, and growth costs

10.3.4.1   *Operating Costs*

Operating costs arise from running the system on an ongoing basis, including its operation, repair, and routine maintenance of physical assets, and general administration and billing. Examples are costs for labour, materials, energy, taxes, and contract services. Operating costs generally recur on an annual basis and are normally recovered during the year in which they are incurred.[61]

One of the most important operating costs is the cost of training for management and operating staff. Training is an investment in the quality of the people who run the water system. In the starkest terms, the safety of drinking water is a product of the expertise and commitment of those people. The cost of providing training, as required by the provincial government, is an operating cost that should be part of the full cost.

Administrative costs, or "overhead," are also a type of operating cost. In some cases, overhead costs of the water system are borne by the municipality rather than the operating agency.[62] Given that these are legitimately connected to water services, it is appropriate for the municipality to "charge back" the costs to the water system, although the amount charged back should be accurate to avoid unaccounted for cross-subsidization. In this regard, the provincial

---

[61] See Strategic Alternatives, 2002b, p. 48; and C.N. Watson and Associates, 2001b, for the Canadian Environmental Law Association, "Financial management of municipal water systems in Ontario," Walkerton Inquiry Submission, p. 4-2.

[62] These might include such administrative costs as for the chief administrative officer of the municipality, the accounting department, the planning department, or human resources.

government may wish to consider whether to prescribe a ceiling on charge backs for overhead costs under the proposed *Sustainable Water and Sewage Systems Act.*

Operating costs also include the cost of continuous monitoring of water quality, periodic sampling of raw and treated water, and reporting of results to regulatory agencies and to the public, in accordance with provincial standards. As such, since the closure of provincial testing laboratories in 1996 full cost also includes the cost of laboratory services.

Finally, it is reasonable to expect the cost of accreditation and operational planning, as recommended in Chapter 11, to be recovered from the water system. These costs include the cost to develop a quality management system and an operational plan according to a drinking water quality management standard for the industry, and to undergo third-party audit and peer review.

10.3.4.2   *Capital Costs*

Capital costs are incurred in the construction or replacement of a water system (e.g., including wells, treatment plants, reservoirs, and distribution systems). They represent the investments required to maintain a system that meets current and changing standards, meets customer needs, maintains the facilities, and provides for future growth.[63]

Capital costs include upfront costs for physical assets such as infrastructure, buildings, and equipment. They may also include costs for major rehabilitation or replacement of those assets.[64] Related items such as land and design work may also be considered capital costs. Because physical assets may need to be upgraded or replaced, it is necessary to maintain an asset inventory.

Capital spending tends to be "lumpy" in nature; that is, a major expenditure may be made one year, without a need for large investments for many years down the road. For this reason, municipalities commonly set aside reserve funds or borrow money to pay for capital costs. The annual cost of contributing to capital reserves, or of servicing debt incurred to pay for capital projects, is

---

[63] Strategic Alternatives, 2002b, p. 43.

[64] On the other hand, routine repair and maintenance costs are typically considered operating costs.

sometimes classified as an operating cost, but may also be reasonably viewed as a capital cost.

10.3.4.3   *Environmental Costs*

Water services include costs to the environment, some of which may not be accounted for in the financing of the water system. These costs result from the impacts of water takings and wastewater emissions in particular. Costs associated with these impacts are often considered "external" because they tend not to be incurred as actual expenditures by the municipality or its customers.[65]

Over the course of the Inquiry, there was a great deal of discussion about whether municipalities should recover an amount for environmental costs of water (and sewage) services, to support efforts to protect and clean up water sources. Many parties felt that they should, mainly because of the environmental benefits, but also because these costs are undeniably a part of the cost of our consumption of water and disposal of wastes into the environment. Other parties submitted that it is too difficult and contentious to assess and allocate environmental costs, and it would be unfair to charge water ratepayers without charging other users of the resource.

I do not consider it necessary for safety reasons to recommend that the provincial government require municipalities to incorporate environmental costs as part of the full cost of water systems. As I discuss in Chapter 4, however, municipalities should consider the option of raising funds from the water system to support at least part of the costs of implementing the measures I recommend relating to source protection.

10.3.5 Sustainable Asset Management

Sustainable asset management[66] entails both full-cost accounting and full-cost recovery for the costs of water infrastructure. Because water systems are capital-

---

[65] The costs are said to be "internalized" when the regulatory action of senior governments forces the municipality to adopt measures to prevent or offset the impacts or to compensate injured parties for their loss, or when the municipality otherwise takes the external costs into consideration. See Strategic Alternatives, 2002b, pp. 52–53.

[66] This is also described as "life-cycle costing." With respect to sustainable asset management and life-cycle costing, see respectively Pollution Probe, 2001, "The management and financing of

intensive, outlining capital costs is one of the most important parts of financial planning in this area. The purpose of sustainable asset management is to collect information about infrastructure so as to plan for its maintenance and eventual replacement over the lifetime of the asset.

Many municipalities presently face uncertainty with respect to their future costs to replace underground water infrastructure, stemming from the lack of information about it. In order to plan for future costs, information is required as to the size and location of system components, their anticipated lifespan, and their replacement value. All municipalities need to systematically compile this information and record it in a standard, accessible format as a basis for a comprehensive asset management plan.

I recognize that estimating an asset's lifetime is not necessarily straightforward.[67] However, asset management does not require an individualized assessment of every specific component in the system. It extrapolates conclusions about the system as a whole based on a sampling of information about the different component types. Still, the process may require a significant commitment of time and money, depending on the size, age, material of construction, and complexity of the system.

A number of Ontario municipalities[68] now have in place long-term infrastructure replacement programs, based on asset management plans; their experiences may prove useful to others.[69] In addition, the provincial government has a useful and important role to play in assisting municipalities to generate asset management plans. In particular, the provincial government should initiate and guide the development of a generic asset management standard for the water industry in Ontario, as discussed below.

---

drinking water systems: Sustainable asset management," Walkerton Inquiry Submission; and Watson and Associates, 2001b, p. 5-1.

[67] The anticipated lifetime and future costs for a water main, for instance, depends on a number of variables, such as its age, the original design, material used, the manner of construction, historical disturbances to the foundation, vibration, corrosion, the quality of maintenance over the years, and other local circumstances. Association of Municipalities of Ontario, 2001, p. 25.

[68] Such as in Aurora, Chatham-Kent, St. Thomas, Lincoln, and Halton Region. Watson and Associates, 2001b, pp. 5-9–5-10.

[69] OWWA/OMWA raised concerns about some of the practical problems associated with life-cycle costing and asset management, arguing that the assessments can be difficult, expensive, and unreliable, and that engineers who carry out the studies may overstate problems in the hope of winning bigger contracts to fix them. I anticipate that this can be addressed through the development of a provincial asset management standard with the involvement of the industry. OWWA/OMWA, Walkerton Inquiry Submission (Expert Meeting, June 20–21, 2001).

The Association of Municipalities of Ontario indicated that one difficulty associated with life-cycle costing and asset management is that some assets may have a much longer lifespan than the typically 10- to 20-year amortization periods for debt financing. In such circumstances, where the municipality borrows to pay for its capital costs, those customers who use the asset during its early years will bear a disproportionate share of its cost. To some extent, these concerns about intergenerational equity can be addressed through the municipal financial plan, based on the skilful use of both reserve funds and borrowing, to smooth the cost burden as much as possible over the lifetime of the asset. Also, in some cases, the costs will be offset by ongoing expansion.

However, where some assets have a lifespan of more than a few decades, some users will end up paying a higher share of the costs than others. Those generations who pay more in the future, or who have done so in the past, may have to accept this burden, either on behalf of those who came before them, or for those who will come after. The more municipalities invest today in careful financial planning to spread out the costs of long-term capital assets in an appropriate way, the less generational unfairness there will be in the future.

10.3.5.1   *The Extent of Future Capital Costs*

Capital costs appear to constitute the greatest cost for municipal water systems in future, calculated on an average basis for Ontario municipalities.[70] However, there is significant uncertainty about the extent of these future costs. Also, not all capital costs raise the same concerns in relation to drinking water safety.[71] The most that can be said is that future capital costs will be an important safety issue for some municipalities, and that all municipalities need to ensure they have a sustainable asset management plan as part of their financial plan.

---

[70] A number of parties at the Inquiry submitted that investments in water system infrastructure have been insufficient for several years. The downward trend corresponds with the reduction of water-related grants by the provincial and federal governments, according to AMO. See Association of Municipalities of Ontario, 2001, pp. 30–32. See also E. Doyle, 2002, "Production and distribution of drinking water," Walkerton Inquiry Commissioned Paper 8; Strategic Alternatives, 2002b, p. 85–86; and Watson and Associates, 2001b, p. 7-7.

[71] Capital costs are commonly divided into three categories: costs to address deficiencies in existing infrastructure and to bring the water system up to present standards, costs of replacement of existing infrastructure, and costs of infrastructure to accommodate growth. The first, "deficiencies," raises greater safety concerns than the other two categories because deficiencies in infrastructure will generally weaken the multi-barrier system that is in place to ensure drinking water safety. In contrast, the category of capital costs related to "growth" raises relatively few safety concerns. See generally Association of Municipalities of Ontario, 2001, pp. 25–26; and Watson and Associates, 2001b, p. 3-1.

Future capital costs will become fully apparent only after municipalities have done a comprehensive financial plan – including an asset inventory and sustainable asset management plan – for their water system. To assess future capital costs across the province, it would be helpful for the information reported in municipal "full-cost reports" under the proposed *Sustainable Water and Sewage Systems Act* to be consolidated into a provincial database and made available to municipal water providers, as recommended by OWWA/OMWA.[72] The priority should be for municipalities to assess capital costs that raise immediate or short-term safety concerns as part of a comprehensive financial plan. To facilitate this, the provincial government should provide guidance regarding what constitutes a safety-related water system deficiency, in association with the provincial asset management standard.[73]

Capital costs facing municipalities were described by some at the Inquiry as a provincial "infrastructure deficit." I am not in a position to say to what extent this may be the case. A legitimate reason for using this term is to highlight the importance of municipalities adequately investing in water infrastructure. Given that the extent of future capital costs is unclear, however, the term can also be misleading. For one, it conveys the message that all municipalities in the province have been underinvesting in their infrastructure, which is unfair to those that have effectively assessed and planned for their capital costs. In addition, not all future capital costs arise from past underinvestment in infrastructure. To the extent they relate to the replacement and expansion of existing infrastructure, capital costs are more appropriately viewed as normal expenditures to meet future needs.[74]

---

[72] I also note that the Ontario SuperBuild Corporation issued a number of contracts in 2001, including one that "will collect information on Ontario's water and sewer infrastructure assets and compile it into a comprehensive data base." Ontario, Ontario SuperBuild Corporation, 2001, "Request for proposals – #SSB-003505" (Toronto: Management Board Secretariat), Appendix A, p. 23.

[73] As the Ontario Water Works Association and the Ontario Municipal Water Association pointed out at the Inquiry, "deficiency" can be defined in many ways: source water quality, ability to treat the water, security of the water supply through the year, and so on. Different types of deficiency need to be addressed in different ways once they are understood. Watson and Associates, 2001b, pp. 1-1–1-2.

[74] To illustrate, a 1998 Canadian Water and Wastewater Association study identified $12.5 billion in water infrastructure needs for Ontario. Of this amount, only 9% related to deficiencies in the existing system. About 12% of the total needs related to ongoing replacement costs and a further 12% of the total needs to expanding the system to bring the entire service population onto municipal systems. The costs to expand the system to service new development over the next 15 years, based on a 30% increase in Ontario's population, was 65% of the total. Finally, 2% of the total estimated cost related to metering. Analysis for the Inquiry by Mike Loudon of data in Canadian Water and

The priority is for all municipalities to carry out comprehensive assessments of the current condition of their water system assets, the expected lifetime of those assets, and the anticipated maintenance and replacement costs over the long term. They will then be in a position to plan how to pay for those costs on a sustainable basis.

10.3.5.2   *Accounting Methods*

The starting point for asset management is to measure the value of assets and their rates of depreciation; to do this effectively, municipalities need to generate data regarding replacement value and depreciation. During the Inquiry, there was an involved discussion of accounting methods.[75] I do not think it necessary to make a recommendation regarding the accounting methods that should be adopted for water systems in Ontario. However, I would encourage the provincial government to consider this issue in relation to a generic asset management standard for the water industry.

10.3.6 The Role of the Provincial Government

The provincial government has an important role to play in supporting and overseeing the development of financial plans for municipal water systems. The provincial government's role is, in part, to establish common standards, where necessary, so that the requirements under the proposed *Sustainable Water and Sewage Systems Act* can be practically implemented by municipal water providers.[76] The provincial government will need to define "full cost" as it applies to mandatory cost recovery and develop a methodology for sustainable asset management. It should do so as part of a provincial standard. This process should involve municipalities and industry stakeholders. It should also involve the Ministry of Municipal Affairs and Housing and the Ministry of the Environment, given their joint interest in this area.

Wastewater Association, 1998, "Municipal water and wastewater infrastructure: Estimated investment needs, 1997–2012."

[75] For a discussion, see Strategic Alternatives, 2002b, pp. 99–112.

[76] I recognize that the Province has taken steps in this regard, such as the publication of the Ministry of Municipal Affairs and Housing, 2000, *Municipal Capital Budgeting Handbook* (Toronto: Queen's Printer) <www.mah.gov.on.ca/business/BudgHandbk/index-e.asp> [accessed April 10, 2002].

Under the proposed *Sustainable Water and Sewage Systems Act*, the Minister of Municipal Affairs and Housing would have the authority to approve, reject, or change both the full-cost report and the cost-recovery plan submitted by a municipality. The minister could also order a municipality to pay the full cost of water services by requiring it "to generate revenue in a specified manner or from a specified source to pay all or part of the cost of providing the services and to make specified or necessary amendments to existing contracts, resolutions or by-laws."[77]

It may very well be appropriate for these powers to rest with the Ministry of Municipal Affairs and Housing, given its historical role in relation to municipal financial affairs. However, the Ministry of the Environment may also have to play a role given that it will license municipalities in relation to their water systems and so that municipal water providers are not asked to satisfy disparate provincial requirements.

10.3.7 Paying for Future Costs

In this section, I discuss how municipalities can approach the issue of paying for the full cost of water services. The cost of water services in Ontario has risen since 2000 and will rise further if the recommendations of this Inquiry are implemented.[78]

Rising costs will put concurrent demands on local revenue sources, especially local water rates.[79] The question of how much water rates will rise depends on whether a given municipality has planned for the cost of its water system, especially capital costs. For municipalities that are not presently paying the full cost of their systems, especially in relation to infrastructure, the costs in future will be greater.

---

[77] Bill 155, cl. 21.

[78] To assist in planning for these costs, I have commissioned Strategic Alternatives to assess the cost implications of the recommendations in this report. Strategic Alternatives et al., 2002, "The costs of clean water: Estimates of costs arising from the recommendations of the Walkerton Inquiry," Walkerton Inquiry Commissioned Paper 25.

[79] In Ontario, water rates are the most common means for municipalities to recover the operating costs (excluding capital expenditures) of water services. In 1999, water rates accounted for 88% of revenues as a percentage of total revenue. In comparison, property taxes, other local charges, and grants accounted for 4.6%, 7%, and less than 1%, respectively. See Strategic Alternatives, 2002b, p. 15; and Association of Municipalities of Ontario, 2001, p. 36.

10.3.7.1   *Municipal Responsibility for Future Costs*

Recommendation 48: As a general principle, municipalities should plan to raise adequate resources for their water systems from local revenue sources, barring exceptional circumstances.

Since municipalities own their water systems and are accountable for the delivery of water services, and since the benefits of water services overwhelmingly go to local consumers, it is appropriate to expect municipalities to pay for the cost of their water system from local revenue sources,[80] within reasonable and clearly defined limits of affordability. The corollary to this is that it is generally not appropriate for senior governments to subsidize municipalities that have not planned effectively for the cost of water services, or that have underinvested in their system. Doing so would in effect penalize the residents of municipalities that have practised sound financial planning in the past.

I see two general exceptions to this. The first is where the additional costs of new regulatory requirements since the Walkerton outbreak, including those resulting from the recommendations of this report, overwhelm a municipality's ability to pay. This exception is discussed in Chapter 14. The second is where the residents of a municipality are unable to afford the future capital costs needed to ensure the safety of their drinking water. This exception is discussed in section 10.3.7.4 of this chapter.

10.3.7.2   *Household Affordability*

I would like to comment briefly on the prospect of rising water rates. At present, the average municipal water rate compares favourably to the cost of other household purchases such as Internet service or cable television. For the same cost as a bottle of spring water ($1.25) bought at the store, consumers receive several thousand glasses of tap water. Thus, there appears to be room for water rates to rise in cases where consumers are not paying the full cost of safe water. Ideally, water rates will rise as necessary to generate adequate resources for drinking water safety while remaining within reasonable boundaries of affordability. This should be possible in the large majority of municipalities.

---

[80] Own source revenues are total revenues minus transfers from other levels of government, transfers from reserves, and proceeds from the sale of property. Strategic Alternatives, 2002b, p. 21.

That said, the financing of water systems does not occur in isolation of other pressures on municipal budgets. In light of recent re-structuring in the municipal sector, especially the transfer of additional open-ended social service costs (e.g., welfare) to municipalities in 1998, there is currently some uncertainty about the ability of municipalities to finance all of the programs they are responsible for, including water services. Municipalities may be reducing spending (including borrowing) to plan for potential increases in social service costs. Although I consider it beyond my mandate to make a recommendation in this area, I encourage the Province to publicly review the program responsibilities and fiscal capability of municipalities in light of recent restructuring to ensure that the financial pressures on municipalities do not crowd out the adequate financing of water systems.[81]

I also recognize, however, that rising rates may constitute a significant burden for low-income families and individuals. I do not see it as being within my mandate to comment on the means by which this problem might be addressed. There are a variety of possible approaches. Suffice it to say that, since water is an essential need, it would be unacceptable for those who are unable to pay for safe water to go without. The provincial and municipal governments should ensure that this does not occur by whatever means they consider appropriate.

10.3.7.3 *Future Capital Costs*

The greatest future costs facing some municipalities, as discussed in section 10.3.4, appear to be for infrastructure. In light of my recommendation that municipalities, barring exceptional circumstances, pay for those costs from local revenue sources, I discuss here the financing options that are available.

Municipalities can raise funds for capital projects in three ways. First, they can pay for capital costs directly from water rates, or other revenue sources,[82] on a year-to-year basis. It usually does not make sense to pay for large-scale projects in this way, however, because of the sheer size of the costs involved. Municipalities can also raise money for capital spending on the longer term by

---

[81] See Association of Municipalities of Ontario, 2001, pp. 19–20; and Strategic Alternatives, 2002b, pp. 78, 93–96.
[82] Growth-related capital costs could be financed from development changes or construction by a developer, for example.

accumulating reserves (or reserve funds)[83] or by borrowing. Most municipalities rely on a mixture of annual revenues, reserves, and borrowing.

Municipal Reserves

Municipalities can put money away in a reserve fund each year to save for future capital projects. Thus, a portion of annual revenues is set aside in a special account and allowed to accumulate until withdrawn and used for a specific project.[84]

Financing capital projects through reserves is the reverse of financing through borrowing. Instead of repaying costs in the future, reserve funds pay for costs from past savings. The key advantage of using reserves is that it avoids having to go into debt and pay interest. If planned far enough in advance, life-cycle reserves can provide adequate financing for future capital costs.[85] Municipalities also develop reserve funds, according to the Association of Municipalities of Ontario, to cushion impacts in the case of an emergency and to help deal with unanticipated in-year expenses or potential overruns.[86]

On the other hand, the overuse of reserves may reflect an unduly conservative approach to financing. This appeared to be the case in Walkerton.[87] Reserves do not reflect the ideal in terms of intergenerational equity since those who put aside the money to pay for the asset may not be the ones who benefit from its use.[88] For this reason, it is reasonable and often preferable for municipalities to balance the use of reserves with borrowing for capital spending. Of course, some municipalities may simply find they have not put aside enough money to cover all capital costs necessary to address safety deficiencies. Where they have borrowing capacity available, as discussed below, those municipalities will

---

[83] There is a difference between municipal reserves and reserve funds, the former generally being permissive and at the discretion of municipal council, the latter being segregated for a specific purpose and established by statute (obligatory) or by municipal council (discretionary). For discussion here, both may serve the same ends of putting aside funds to pay for future capital costs, and I therefore use them interchangeably.

[84] Strategic Alternatives, 2002b, pp. 93–94.

[85] Watson and Associates, 2001b, p. 5-5.

[86] P. Vanini, for the Association of Municipalities of Ontario, "Presentation on municipal financing authority," Walkerton Inquiry Submission (Expert Meeting, June 20–21, 2002).

[87] The Walkerton Public Utilities Commission had a fiscally conservative approach to its water system. The PUC had roughly $347,000 in its reserve fund as of January 1, 2000.

[88] Strategic Alternatives, 2002b, p. 94.

have no choice but to borrow the necessary funds to invest adequately in the water system infrastructure.

Municipal Borrowing

Municipalities frequently finance major capital investment through borrowing. Municipalities are permitted to borrow for capital spending as long as they are within their borrowing limit as set out by the provincial government. This means a municipality's debt charges cannot exceed 25% of its local revenue sources without approval from the Ontario Municipal Board.[89] Most municipalities are well within this limit, and thus have room to borrow within provincial guidelines.[90] This estimated borrowing capacity would be available to finance future capital costs.[91]

10.3.7.4 *The Role of Provincial Subsidies*

Many of the parties in Part 2, including many with distinct interests, recommended that provincial subsidies for municipal water systems should only be available in exceptional circumstances. I agree. As I point out above, there are advantages, including from a safety standpoint, if municipal water systems are operated on a sound and sustainable financial basis. Experience indicates that relying on subsidies from senior levels of government can be unpredictable and, in some cases, can lead to delays in decision making about necessary capital expenditures.

Given that I did not address this issue in depth and that the full extent of future capital costs is as yet unknown, I do not consider it appropriate to make a definitive recommendation in this area. I do note, however, that in some situations where the amount of investment needed to address infrastructure

---

[89] Under O. Reg. 799/94 as amended by O. Reg. 75/97 and O. Reg. 155/99. See Association of Municipalities of Ontario, 2001, p. 15. *Municipal Act*, R.S.O. 1990, s. 187.

[90] On average, municipal debt charges do not exceed 5.1% of operating expenditures for any category of municipality. Water and sewage debt account for about 30% of the total debt incurred by Ontario municipalities and this proportion has remained roughly the same over the past ten years. Municipal borrowing in Ontario, on average, has reportedly fallen over the same time period, from about 18% of operating expenditures in 1989 to 13% in 1999. See Strategic Alternatives, 2002b, pp. 91–92, 114. Also, Watson and Associates, 2001b, Appendix A, provides a summary of the debt capacity of Ontario municipalities that deliver water services.

[91] See Watson and Associates, 2001b, pp. 1-6 and 3-8.

deficiencies to ensure the safety of drinking water overwhelms the ability of local residents to pay, the provincial government will have to make the necessary funds available. Many suggest low-interest loans rather than grants as the appropriate means for doing so.

I would suggest that such subsidies be made available (1) only in accordance with defined affordability criteria; (2) only to the extent necessary to bring the cost of water services within an affordable range; and (3) only after a municipality has reviewed available options for restructuring or has provided a reasonable timeline by which costs will be brought within an affordable range.

10.3.8 Methods of Cost Recovery

Many parties and members of the public made submissions to the Inquiry regarding the methods of cost recovery adopted by municipalities for their water (and sewage) systems. As I have indicated, so long as the full costs of water are accounted for, recovered, and put back into the water system, adequate resources will be available for safety. The related questions of how and from whom a municipality recovers those costs are not directly related to safety. Therefore, I do not make any recommendations in this regard. Similarly, decisions about the structure of water rates should also be left to municipalities and their operating agencies to determine, and I do not make any recommendations in this regard.[92]

I comment below, however, on methods of cost recovery and rate structures for municipal water systems. There are compelling arguments, for reasons of conservation and efficiency, to implement full-cost pricing and metering, to the extent they are appropriate in the local circumstances, in designing rate structures for water services. I also discuss other issues relating to cost recovery that were raised over the course of the Inquiry and that warrant a brief comment.

---

[92] The Ontario Water Works Association and the Ontario Municipal Water Association recommended that water service providers maintain the ability to use a variety of user fees and charges, and capital funding mechanisms. I accept that there are important advantages to retaining the existing flexibility in this regard. See Watson and Associates, 2001a, p. 5-1.

10.3.8.1   *Full-Cost Pricing and Metering*

The term "full-cost pricing" is based on the premise of user pay: those who benefit from water services should generally pay a price that reflects the full cost of providing those services. The reason to adopt full-cost pricing in the context of water services is to require people to pay the full cost of the water they use. Doing so gives them a better appreciation of the value of water, and encourages them to use it wisely. I encourage municipalities to adopt full-cost pricing in the context of the water system. Full-cost pricing generally means that most water system costs are recouped from the water rate; only water rates allow consumers to be charged according to the amount of water they use. However, it may be that some costs are appropriately recouped from other municipal revenue sources, such as using property taxes for fire protection and capital charges for system expansion.[93] Municipalities may also decide to adopt exceptions to full-cost pricing for reasons of household affordability, as discussed in section 10.3.7.2.

As in the case of full-cost pricing, the decision whether to meter the water system should be left to municipal water providers. I do note, however, that metering makes sense for reasons of conservation and efficiency. Even though installing meters can be expensive, the cost will normally be recovered in time through reduced water usage and lower infrastructure costs.[94]

10.4   Public-Private Issues

In section 10.2.3 of this chapter, I discussed the various models available to municipalities for the management and operation of their water systems. One of many options is to involve the private sector. A distinction can be made between different forms of "privatization" in relation to water systems. First, privatization can mean the engagement of a private operating agency to run the water system. Second, it can mean private ownership of the water system. The former type of privatization is discussed throughout this section; the latter is discussed separately in section 10.4.3.

---

[93] See Strategic Alternatives, 2002b, pp. 51–52; and Watson and Associates, 2001a, p. 3-2.

[94] One Canadian study estimated that metering reduces water demand by 15% to 20%, although estimates vary; D.W. Tate, 1990, "Water demand management in Canada: A state of the art review," Environment Canada, Soc. Sci. Ser. No. 23, p. 36. See also B. McGregor, Walkerton Inquiry (Town Hall Meeting, March 22, 2001), transcript p. 54; and R. Rivers, Walkerton Inquiry (Town Hall Meeting, April 10, 2001), transcript p. 191.

The issue of private sector involvement in providing drinking water has engendered a great deal of controversy in a sometimes emotional discussion. I have concluded that the so-called public-private debate has more to do with issues outside my mandate and less to do with the provision of safe drinking water. If implemented, the recommendations in this report should address safety concerns whether systems are operated by public or private entities. However, because of public interest and the prominence of the issue in the submissions to the Inquiry, I think it advisable to set out my analysis in some detail.

10.4.1 The Public-Private Dimension

During the past century and a half, water services have been handled in a variety of ways in industrialized countries. The roles of individuals, communities, and the private sector have shifted over time in response to changing circumstances, evolving community values, and altered understandings of relative costs and benefits.

During the nineteenth century there was a wide variety of family and community-based arrangements for providing water. As cities grew and scientific research established the link between disease and contaminated water, governments intervened, assuming broader regulatory and delivery roles to protect public health. Public ownership and operation of water systems became the pattern in most industrialized countries during much of the twentieth century.[95]

The past two decades, however, have seen significant changes in some countries, with the introduction of a larger role for private companies in the delivery of this vital public service.[96] In the water field, as elsewhere, there has been heated debate about the merits of the public sector and the private sector. The issue of the private sector's involvement in drinking water provision was extensively canvassed in Part 2 of the Inquiry. I will summarize below a number of the central contentions of the two positions.

---

[95] A significant exception to the case is France, which has traditionally organized the provision of these services with substantial private sector involvement. See, for example, J. Hassan, 1996, "France: Public Responsibility – Private Execution" in *The European Water Environment in a Period of Transformation*, J. Hassan et al., eds. (Manchester: Manchester University Press).

[96] The most radical reforms occurred in the United Kingdom, which turned over both ownership and management of water and sewage systems in England and Wales to private operators. No other industrialized state has privatized in this field to this extent; the normal practice is to retain public ownership of the assets and infrastructure.

Exponents of the private sector claim a number of significant benefits of private sector involvement, which include:

- greater access to financing and greater willingness to charge the full cost of the service;

- greater efficiencies in operation and management;

- greater technical and managerial expertise, and innovation;

- flexibility in terms of management, labour, and procurement;

- director expertise and legal liabilities;

- depoliticization of management decisions;

- stronger incentives to comply with standards; and

- transfer of risk to the private operator.

Overall, it is contended that private sector operators can provide competent service at lower cost than the public sector. The criticism that the drive for profit diverts revenue from reinvestment in future safety is countered by pointing out that the surplus can also be diverted from municipally operated utilities to other municipal services.

Promoters of the public sector argue that it has many advantages, including the following:

- priority of the public interest over shareholder interests;

- greater accountability and an obligation to keep the revenues in the municipality;

- greater transparency because of fewer confidentiality concerns;

- lower cost of capital (at least in the municipal sector in Ontario);

- comparable levels of efficiency, expertise, and innovation in well-run public utilities;

- better cooperation among agencies, greater concern with conservation, and higher sensitivity to social concerns (e.g., in rate setting); and

- capacity to restructure poor public sector performers.

In general, public sector advocates argue that public operations are at no disadvantage with respect to finance and capital investment, operational efficiency, and access to expertise and new technologies, while they display a marked advantage over the private sector in public accountability, equitable access to water and water services, and environmental protection and conservation.

10.4.2 Comments Regarding Private Operation

My first observation is to note that most of the arguments advanced on either side of the public-private debate touch only indirectly on the central matter confronting this Inquiry; namely, the safety and quality of drinking water. Although it is apparent that such things as compliance with standards, greater public accountability and transparency, adequate financing, and a higher sensitivity to social concerns are all likely to have a place in a water system that performs well, the achievement of high water quality as such is not typically a claim advanced by either side in the debate. Indeed, the quality management systems that have been designed to produce high-quality results generally do not either presuppose or exclude private sector operation.[97]

My second observation is that the private-public debate is frequently carried on at a level of abstraction far removed from the kinds of issues decision makers, confronted with the practical challenges of running a water system, normally have to face. There is rarely one big question for which there is one big answer, but rather a whole series of issues and decisions where sensible judgment will need to take into account a wide range of options and considerations. These include such things as the size of the operation, the existing weaknesses and strengths of the system, in-house capacity, the age and condition of the infrastructure, the regulatory framework, the relative cost of capital, the need

---

[97] Models of quality management are discussed in Chapter 11.

to gain access to the best expertise and technology, and the preferences of the local community.[98]

This brings me to my third point, namely, that it is not a matter of choosing between a "public system" and a "private system," pure and simple, but of deciding on the best mix of concrete arrangements in the circumstances at hand. Questions of ideological purity are less important than the day-to-day choices that need to be made in order to achieve the best operation of the water system. It is most unlikely that any system will be exclusively either private or public. Even in a radically privatized water system, such as exists in England and Wales, an elaborate, intrusive regulatory oversight role remains, as it must, with the public authority.[99]

In Ontario, on the other hand, public sector regulation, ownership, and management is the order of the day. The dominant pattern is provincial regulation, and municipal ownership and operation of water systems.[100] Municipalities have had the option of contracting with private actors to operate their water system, but have generally chosen not to. Yet, even in what would universally be acknowledged as a public system, the private sector has a notable presence.[101]

Let us suppose, for example, that a municipality with a public system decides to build and operate a new water treatment plant. If it chooses to float a

---

[98] See D. Cameron, 2002, "Drinking water safety: Do ownership and management matter?," Walkerton Inquiry Commissioned Paper 18, c. 4, for an account of the different ways in which three Ontario municipalities coped with the challenges they faced. The three municipalities reported on are the regional municipalities of York and Peel, and the amalgamated City of Hamilton.

[99] The *British Water Act* of 1989 removed regulatory functions from the water authorities and instituted three new agencies to regulate the industry. The Drinking Water Inspectorate (DWI) is responsible for ensuring that water companies supply water that meets all water quality regulations and is safe to drink. The Environment Agency (EA), formerly the National Rivers Authority (NRA), has responsibility for environmental regulation and implementation of European Community directives. These standards, to a large extent, determine the investment program necessary for the companies. OFWAT, the Office of Water Services, is the economic regulator for the water industry. All three report to the Water and Land Directorate of the Department of the Environment, Transport and the Regions (DETR), which works to coordinate the three and to set water policy. Ibid., p. 61–62.

[100] Strategic Alternatives, 2002a, pp. 14–15; and d'Ombrain, pp. 10–11.

[101] An example of the impact of the private sector on a public water system is the Regional Municipality of York. In making its decision to continue with direct public delivery, it was greatly aided by a highly productive relationship with the private sector. York reportedly came to understand its needs better, reached a grounded appreciation of its financial position, and learned about international norms and practices in part from its association with Consumer Utilities, a corporation created by North West Water and Consumers Gas. See Cameron, c. 4.

municipal debenture to finance the construction of this new facility, it will almost certainly rely on the expertise of a private financial services firm; engineers in a private firm will design the facility and lawyers will handle the legal process; engineering and construction firms will bid on the contract to build the structure; and private maintenance and service crews may assist in keeping it operating well once it is built. So the public-private distinction has more to do with an assessment of where the key functions and responsibilities are located than it has to do with a simple choice to make the system either entirely public or private.

Fourthly, as discussed in section 10.2.1 of this chapter, the provision of water services is almost a natural monopoly. It is not realistic to think of several service providers – governments or private actors – competing in the offering of some of the key services in question. Just as there can practically be only one electrical power grid in any given territory, there will be only one water system. Unlike electricity, however, which can have several electricity providers competing over a common grid, a water system doesn't usually accommodate multiple suppliers. This is because distinct lines of accountability for the quality and reliability of the water that is carried through the pipes is difficult.

It is thus more appropriate to speak of designated roles for the private sector in the water field, than it is to speak comprehensively about the wholesale "privatization" of water.[102] The latter suggests the existence of a market in a monopolistic industry in which, for the most part, there will be regulated service delivery by a single supplier, not market competition among multiple actors. To the extent that the advantages claimed for privatization rest on assumptions about the benefits of the market mechanism, therefore, they cannot be assumed to automatically exist in the largely monopolistic water industry. Normal market mechanisms simply do not apply, or apply only at specific points in the process, such as the bidding for a contract.

---

[102] According to Canadian Environmental Law Association/Canadian Union of Public Employees/ Ontario Public Sector Employees Union, 2001, "Water services in Ontario: For the public, by the public," Walkerton Inquiry Submission, p. 14:

> The ways in which private companies can be involved in the water supply and delivery systems vary. The most common are for municipalities to contract with private companies to design and build water treatment plant, to clean out water mains or carry out other maintenance activities, and to buy technologies from private companies for water filtration and other kinds of water treatment methods. These types of private sector involvement in the municipal water supply and delivery system are not considered to be forms of privatization because the municipality simply purchases a clearly defined service and maintains total ownership and daily control over operations.

Thus, the involvement of the private sector in the water field typically entails the competitive bidding of private firms for the chance: to offer a specific, time-limited service such as the construction of a pumping station ("competition in the market"); or to operate a part of the system as a tightly regulated monopoly in the water industry ("competition for the market"); or some combination of the two.[103]

10.4.3 Comments Regarding Private Ownership

Rarely does the discussion of privatization in the water industry in Ontario include the contention that the ownership of water facilities and infrastructure should be placed in private hands, and there was little argument during the Inquiry's hearings that Ontario municipalities should move in that direction.[104] Given that municipal responsibility and accountability flow from municipal ownership, I see no advantage for safety reasons to turning over ownership of municipal water systems to either the provincial government or to the private sector. Changes in the ownership regime for water systems would raise a number of significant issues in relation to the recommendations in this report. I have premised many recommendations on continued municipal ownership of water systems.

In not recommending the sale of municipal water systems to the private sector, my conclusion is based on several considerations: the essentially local character of water services; the natural-monopoly characteristics of the water industry; the importance of maintaining accountability to local residents; and the historical role of municipalities in this field. Given the wide range of circumstances, it does not seem desirable to formally exclude the possibility of a transfer of title in a particular case, but I see no reason, as a practical matter, why municipal ownership should not be continued. I would also note that, if a private firm actually owns some of the facilities in the monopoly components of a water system, then rate regulation would be required to establish fair and reasonable prices in the absence of competition.

---

[103] The use of terms has been adopted from Cameron, p. 9.

[104] The only party to recommend the privatization of ownership of municipal water systems was the Energy Probe Research Foundation. See E. Brubaker, 2001, for the Energy Probe Research Foundation, 2001, "The promise of privatization," Walkerton Inquiry Submission.

10.4.4 Implications for Safety

As in other countries, the water systems serving Canadians are made up of many different components and processes. My report in Part 1 of the Inquiry determined that multiple factors contributed to the contamination of Walkerton's water system. A review of other comparable situations and the information before the Inquiry confirms that high water quality is achieved when all the parts of a water system are working effectively together, and an organized procedure exists for identifying and correcting weaknesses when they occur. These are hallmarks of the quality management approach. The effectiveness with which the various elements of the system are connected to one another, the degree to which the right information circulates in a timely manner, and the extent to which multiple barriers bind the entire set of processes into a coherent whole, are all as important to the provision of safe water as is the quality or condition of any one of the components or parts. A community could endow itself with top-of-the-line pipes and pumping stations, but if staff are ill-trained or water quality monitoring is ineffective, the system as a whole will be at risk.

What impact does the introduction of private actors into a water system have on water quality? To begin, government is responsible for ensuring public health and safety. This means that public regulation of private actors whose conduct could put individual or community safety at risk is a primary function of government. Even in cases in which the regulatory function is devolved, for example, to an industry association, the ultimate accountability of public officials for the protection of health and safety remains. Water is a particularly sensitive resource, in view of its necessity to life, the absence of any alternatives, the wide range of uses to which it is put, and the risks of contaminated water harming large groups of people in short periods of time. As I discuss in Chapter 13, the provincial government should not devolve or transfer its regulatory function to third parties unless it is established that this will result in greater safety. Specifically, I propose that cost should not be the reason for any devolution.

Ultimately, the decision whether to engage a private company at a water system, and, if so, under what conditions, depends on a wide variety of considerations in the concrete circumstances of the case. These include: the legal and regulatory environment in which the transfer occurs; the professionalism of the public authority, and its ability to recruit expert assistance to support it in the negotiations; the integrity of the bidding process; and the existence of experienced private firms prepared to offer their services.[105] In terms of water safety, though, there are no simple answers. Both public and private operating agencies may perform well or badly. I am not convinced that either is uniquely able to operate a water system so as to achieve consistently high-quality drinking water.

10.4.5 The Decision to Engage a Private Operating Agency

The decision whether to engage an external operating agency is best left to municipalities to determine in light of local circumstances and because of their accountability to local residents. From the perspective of protecting water quality, the Province should adopt a position of neutrality with respect to the decision of municipalities to engage, or not to engage, private operating agencies to deliver water services. The provincial government should ensure that this neutrality is reflected in provincial legislation and regulations including Bill 46, *An Act Respecting the Accountability of Public Sector Organizations*, introduced into the Legislature in May 2001, as well as in the provision of SuperBuild funding for water systems.

Municipalities may invite the participation of private operating agencies in a variety of ways, or they may preserve to themselves, or to a public body that they create, the responsibilities for the operation of the system. Alternatively, they may choose to employ a provincial-level public contractor, such as the Ontario Clean Water Agency, as many of them do now. Whatever they choose to do, the regulatory framework outlined in this report is clear. All must be equally subject to the regulatory requirements elaborated by the provincial government with respect to water quality standards, licensing, training and accreditation, and the like. These are features of the Ontario system designed to protect the province's water; as such, they must be adhered to by all players in the system, public or private.

---

[105] One reason commonly cited for moving to privatization was to gain access to greater financing. However, the information presented to the Inquiry indicated that, if anything, the municipal sector in Ontario is able to borrow funds at lower cost than the private sector. See Strategic Alternatives, 2002b, pp. 96–99; and Watson and Associates, 2001b, pp. 7-1–7-11.

10.4.5.1   *The Importance of the Operating Agreement*

The public model aims to serve the public interest within a framework of public accountability where the elected representatives are held to account by their electors for their management of the system. A private company, on the other hand, pursues as its central objective the interest of the shareholders of the company; profit making and increasing shareholder value are the key indicators of success. Thus, the lines of accountability run back to the owners of the company.

The operating agreement, or contract, becomes "the means by which the public and private interest are brought together."[106] It effectively transfers responsibility for addressing a portion of the public interest to the private operator who is accountable for doing so only within the terms of the contract; the longer the term of the contract, the more this is the case.[107] As such, the operating contract between the public and private entities takes on a great deal of importance in terms of the municipality's responsibility for the system. It lays out the respective responsibilities, allocates the benefits, and assigns the risks between the two parties. Disputes will be resolved according to the contract or otherwise through the legal process.

Given the importance of the operating agreement, municipalities must ensure they are fully apprised of the legal implications in terms of future liability, financial responsibilities, information disclosure, dispute resolution, and enforcement.[108] Safety should be the primary principle governing the decision to contract with an external operator and the oversight of the operating agency once the operating agreement is in place. The municipality should include performance-based safety bonuses and penalties in the contract, and should have sufficient remedies if there is a default on safety issues. In the event of a major emergency, the onus will be on the municipality to show that safety was not compromised as a result of the operating arrangement.

Municipalities also have a legitimate interest in assessing the health and stability of the corporate structure of the private operating agency, since changes in ownership have the potential to generate instability with respect to the operating agreement. In the case of the City of Hamilton, for example, the ownership of

---

[106] Cameron, pp. 11–12, 146.

[107] Ibid., p. 146.

[108] This includes the implications of investment provisions under the North American Free Trade Agreement and other relevant trade agreements, a subject discussed at some length during Part 2.

the private operating agency has changed hands several times since the operating contract was signed at the end of 1994.[109]

10.4.5.2   *Municipal Accountability and Transparency*

Recommendation 49: Municipal contracts with external operating agencies should be made public.

Once an agreement with an external operating agency is signed, the orientation of the municipality shifts from direct-service delivery to ensuring contract compliance. The accountability of the municipality will be exercised as supervisor of the agreement, and the municipality will need to dedicate enough resources and personnel to fulfill this oversight role effectively. Although a municipality may engage an external operating agency, the municipality remains responsible for ensuring the safety of water delivered to consumers. The cost to a municipality of due diligence before entering a contract, and of compliance monitoring over the term of a contract, are an important part of its oversight responsibilities and, as such, the full cost of water services.

A municipality contemplating the engagement of an external operating agency to deliver water services should ensure that the proposed transaction is fully transparent. The concern for water quality justifies full publicity in the operation of a community's water system, whether it is run privately, by the public, or as a mixed system. Municipalities should actively solicit the views of residents before entering into such agreements so that the community can have a role in determining the preferred course of action. Also, the agreement should require the operating agency to report regularly and publicly on the achievement of water quality standards, on system performance, on financial results, and the

---

[109] The Regional Municipality of Hamilton-Wentworth entered into a contract in 1994 with Philips Utilities Management Corporation (PUMC) and its parent, Philip Environmental (later Philip Services Corporation), for the operation and maintenance of the city's water system. The collapse of the parent company, Philip Environmental, in 1998–1999, led to the subsidiary (PUMC), being sold in May 1999 to Azurix, a subsidiary of Enron Corporation. Azurix Corporation created Azurix North America, a wholly owned subsidiary of Azurix, which assumed responsibility for the contract with the now amalgamated City of Hamilton. Soon after, Enron, before it collapsed into bankruptcy, sold Azurix North America in the autumn of 2001 to American Water Works. Before the sale was completed, the German conglomerate RWE AG acquired American Water Works. At the time of preparing this report, therefore, the operating agreement rests with American Water Works, a subsidiary of RWE AG.

like. In some cases, operating contracts have been kept secret on grounds of commercial privacy; they should be made public.

10.4.6 The Ontario Clean Water Agency

The Ontario Clean Water Agency (OCWA) was established in 1993 as a Crown entity to assume the operational and financing functions for water and sewage of the Ministry of Environment. The Act establishing the agency[110] defined its mandate, which included the provision of operations and maintenance services to municipalities on a cost-recovery basis. In 1996, OCWA's administration of capital assistance programs for water and sewage facilities was transferred back to the Ministry of the Environment, and in 1997 ownership of water and sewage systems was shifted from OCWA to the municipalities those systems served. OCWA's central function remains the same, however: to operate water and wastewater facilities for those municipal authorities that choose to engage the provincial agency.

OCWA runs approximately 151 water treatment facilities in Ontario;[111] it has about 95% of the market of those municipalities that choose to outsource the operation of such facilities. It also provides project management services to municipalities seeking technical advice on planning, design, and construction of new and upgraded water and sewage treatment facilities.[112] The agency receives no funding from the Ontario government; it competes for municipal operating and maintenance contracts.

In addition to being one of the largest water operating agencies in the country, OCWA is unique in Ontario. As an "operational enterprise" (formerly, a schedule IV government agency) created under the *Capital Investment Plan Act*, it reports to the Minister of the Environment.[113] OCWA's chair and board of directors are Order-in-Council appointees, appointed in consultation with the minister.[114] The agency's approximately 675 staff are public servants and

---

[110] *Capital Investment Plan Act*, S.O. 1993, c. 23.

[111] Ontario, Ministry of the Environment, 2002, *Sewage and Water Treatment Program Database*. In all, OCWA runs over 400 water and sewage treatment plants. See <www.ocwa.com/fropsm.htm> [accessed April 17, 2002].

[112] d'Ombrain, pp. 48–49.

[113] Ontario Clean Water Agency, *Memorandum of Understanding*, March 31, 1994, s. 1.5. The Minister of the Environment has chosen on a number of occasions to extend the MOU without changes.

[114] Ibid., s. 3.1 (a), (b).

are hired pursuant to the *Public Service Act*, with bargaining unit employees represented by the Ontario Public Service Employees Union.

OCWA had operating expenses of just over $100 million for its 2000 fiscal year.[115] As a public corporation, it pays no corporate taxes, it is exempt from collecting GST on the fees it charges, and its clients do not normally require it to post performance bonds. In addition, its financial liability is backed by the province's guarantee.[116]

10.4.6.1   *Submissions Regarding OCWA*

Proponents of private sector involvement in the water industry criticize the privileged position of OCWA and argue that it should be forced to operate on a "level playing field" with private firms. For example, the Energy Probe Research Foundation states that OCWA should be disbanded, and, if it is not, it should be an arm's-length agency without subsidies, and it should be required through a dividend policy to turn over surplus cash to the public.[117] Other parties, however, submit that OCWA should be retained as a provincial Crown corporation, with a mandate to assist municipalities, especially small municipalities, to achieve self-sufficiency, to train municipal employees, and to act in water emergencies.[118]

OCWA itself reports that the fact it is clearly a government agency – operating under statute, possessing a public sector board appointed in consultation with the Minister of the Environment, and made up of employees who are public servants – provides some reassurance to local government decision makers who had to make important choices about how to deliver water services after the passage of Bill 107 in May 1997.[119] According to OCWA, this sense of comfort

---

[115] d'Ombrain, p. 49.

[116] Ibid.

[117] Energy Probe Research Foundation, 2001, "Recommendations for public hearings 7 and 8: The management of water providers," Walkerton Inquiry Submission, p. 2.

[118] Canadian Environmental Law Association/Canadian Union of Public Employees/Ontario Public Sector Employees Union, p. 52. The Ontario Public Service Employees Union also strongly favours the retention of OCWA, although it supports a clearer specification of its role as an "enterprise agency." Ontario Public Service Employees Union, 2001, "Recommendations and rationale concerning laboratories and drinking water providers," Walkerton Inquiry Submission, pp. 19–20.

[119] M. Brady, general counsel; L. Morrow Wickson, vice-president finance and corporate services; and N.Reid, vice-president business development; interviewed by D. Cameron and D. Whorley, June 13, 2001. See Cameron, p. 111. See also OCWA's *Memorandum of Understanding*, s. 3.1 that sets out the Minister of the Environment's responsibilities *vis-à-vis* the agency, and stipulates the

seems to have increased somewhat in the post-Walkerton environment in which municipalities have become more aware of their due diligence requirements, and the risks involved in the operation of water systems.[120]

After an organizational review in 1996, OCWA established its hub and satellite system. Prior to the review, the agency was responsible for what amounted to several hundred stand-alone operations and believed that there would be collective benefits available through reorganization. In the hub and satellite configuration, OCWA now has regional plants surrounded by smaller nearby satellite operations. The new configuration delivers economies of scale, introduces staffing flexibility, and facilitates information sharing that might not otherwise take place.[121] The agency suggests that smaller municipalities in particular seem to have benefited from the flexibility available through OCWA's organizational design. Smaller plants might, for example, only require a part-time staff person on-site for their operation. By folding the smaller plant's requirements into the hub plant's overall duties, OCWA has been able to meet the marginal requirement efficiently. In this respect, smaller municipalities buy into the expertise of the larger system, and the benefits of mutual assistance that it provides.[122]

There is some reason to believe that the types of benefits derived from contracting with OCWA differ based on the size of the contracting municipality. The larger municipalities are more likely to have in-house expertise on water systems and are therefore more likely to be aware of the risks and responsibilities associated with these operations. By comparison, smaller municipalities seem less likely to have resident expertise, and therefore may operate in a state of relatively higher uncertainty compared to larger centres. OCWA reports that, while cost considerations will also be important, smaller municipalities tend to be motivated by the desire to mitigate risk and obtain expertise.[123]

---

minister shall "assume accountability for the activities of the Agency at Cabinet or any of its committees as required."

[120] Cameron, p. 111.

[121] Ibid., p. 112.

[122] Ibid.

[123] Ibid., pp. 112–113.

10.4.6.2   *OCWA's Future Role*

A Crown corporation such as OCWA can perform a significant role in the provincial water supply system. It is a useful option for municipalities considering how best to discharge their responsibilities for the delivery of safe water. OCWA should continue to offer operational and maintenance services to Ontario municipalities, subject to the same safety, accountability, and transparency requirements as apply to all other external operating agencies in the province. Clearly, a publicly owned operating agency of this kind must accept the same accountability and transparency requirements as other actors in the system. Equally, it must be subjected to the same safety standards relating to accreditation, licensing, and enforcement that apply or will apply to other actors. As with private operating agencies, OCWA's contracts should be made public.

In addition to continuing its existing role as an external operator competing for municipal service contracts, it is apparent that OCWA offers the provincial government a useful instrument to assist in the reorganization of small water systems that would otherwise have great difficulty meeting contemporary safety and quality expectations. In addition, a formal emergency response mandate should be assigned to OCWA, so that the provincial agency is in a position to step in and offer needed support in times of crisis. In this regard, I note the crucial role that OCWA played in responding to the water contamination in Walkerton.

Recommendation 50: The role of the Ontario Clean Water Agency in offering operational services to municipalities should be maintained. The provincial government should clarify the Ontario Clean Water Agency's status and mandate. In particular, OCWA should be:

- an arm's-length agency with an independent, qualified board responsible for choosing the chief executive; and

- available to provide standby emergency capabilities.

Some clarification of the status and mandate of the Ontario Clean Water Agency would make sense at this juncture. This could be done by drafting a new Memorandum of Understanding and altering any other relevant instruments. By endowing the agency with greater operating independence, the province would more clearly separate the regulatory functions for which it is responsible from the operating mandate of OCWA.

The current board should be replaced by an independent board made up of persons with relevant experience, and the board should choose the agency's CEO. The new MOU should specify OCWA's mandate, setting out the objectives the government would expect it to meet. These objectives should include: offering water operating services on contract to municipalities; assisting small municipalities to achieve provincial standards of safety and quality management; and developing the capacity to provide emergency services when necessary. Board meetings and board minutes should be made public, with exceptions for bid strategies and other information reasonably related to OCWA's competitive position. As for other operating agencies, OCWA should be required to make its operating agreements[124] with municipalities, and ongoing water quality monitoring data, publicly available.

---

[124] I recognize that, in some cases, detailed financial and business information about an operating agency may be attached to bids or operating agreements and that it may be legitimately withheld. The MOE should have a process to review public complaints regarding non-disclosure by municipalities or operating agencies in this regard, and should have the authority to order disclosure where appropriate.

Chapter 11   The Management of Municipal Water Systems

Contents

Chapter 11   The Management of Municipal Water Systems

11.1   Introduction

In this chapter, I discuss the ways I envision bringing management and operating practices at water systems in Ontario to the highest standards possible. In particular, I recommend that municipal water providers[1] adopt a "quality management" approach, both through an accreditation program and through operational planning – including an emergency response plan – at all municipal water systems.

Ultimately, the safety of drinking water is protected by effective management systems and operating practices, run by skilled and well-trained staff. In Chapters 5 through 8, I discuss the technical barriers that protect the safety of drinking water. It is clear that the technology for treating and monitoring water quality to a high standard is well established. Failures in Walkerton, and elsewhere, appear to arise because of poor management or the inadequate implementation of good practices.[2]

The idea of quality management is that a water provider should continuously ensure that systems and processes are in place that take advantage of the available technology to design and implement effective multiple barriers. This approach expands the conventional focus and reliance on technological aspects of water systems to include the people responsible for managing and operating the system, and the strategies they adopt to ensure the safety of drinking water.

---

[1] The term "water provider" is intended to include both the owner and operator of a water system serving a municipality. The terms "owner" and "municipality" refer to the owner alone. The term "operating agency" refers to the entity assigned the direct responsibility for managing and operating the water system. Generally, legal requirements have been assigned to the owner/municipalities because they hold the title to the system, they have the statutory authority to raise revenues, they have the due diligence responsibilities discussed in Chapter 10, and the operating agency may change.
 This chapter focuses on municipal water systems for two reasons. First, most Ontarians are served by those systems. Second, private communal systems, private household wells, and other non-municipal water systems raise some different issues, which I discuss in Chapter 14.

[2] See S.E. Hrudey et al., 2002, "A fatal waterborne disease epidemic in Walkerton, Ontario: Comparison with other waterborne outbreaks in the developed world," proceedings at the Health-Related Water Microbiology Symposium, International Water Association World Water Congress, Melbourne, Australia, April 7–12.

There is one point I would like to make clear at the outset: the concept of quality management is not new, and I do not view it as antithetical to the current practices of water providers in Ontario. The water industry is moving to quality management in other jurisdictions, and many municipalities in Ontario have already adopted a managerial model that will comply with the requirements I am recommending here. As such, the recommendations are not intended to provoke a scramble to meet yet another level of operating standards; to do so could cause more harm than good. Rather, the recommendations are intended to give additional tools for water providers to build on and improve the many excellent management and operating practices that currently exist, and to spread those to the greatest extent possible across the province.

If the water industry meets this challenge, Ontario should be among the leading jurisdictions in terms of ensuring the safety of drinking water. In this regard, I am pleased by the support offered by the Ontario Municipal Water Association and the Ontario Water Works Association on behalf of their members for the quality management approach I am recommending. As these associations indicated at the Inquiry, quality management "has the ability to verify that industry best practices are being employed to produce water of the highest quality."[3]

11.1.1 Drinking Water Quality Management

The purpose of the quality management approach in the context of drinking water is to protect public health by achieving consistent good practice in managing and operating a water system. The hallmarks of this approach include

- the adoption of best practices and continuous improvement;

- "real time" process control (e.g., the continuous monitoring of turbidity, chlorine residual, and disinfectant contact time) wherever feasible;

- the effective operation of robust multiple barriers to protect public health;

- preventive rather than strictly reactive strategies to identify and manage risks to public health; and

---

[3] See A. Davies, for the Ontario Water Works Association/Ontario Municipal Water Association, 2001, "Effective water utility management and organizational behaviour: A report on selected issue 11 matters for the Walkerton Inquiry," Walkerton Inquiry Submission, p. 20.

- effective leadership.[4]

An important assumption of quality management is that, in evaluating or improving a management system, one should look at the process by which something is produced as well as the end product. In this way, one is able to adopt a preventive approach of improving the process before public health is put at risk. The focus on prevention distinguishes quality management from more reactive approaches to management or regulation, as exemplified by the traditional emphasis on compliance with numerical standards of water quality.[5] There are many conventional approaches to management and regulation that are geared to prevention – such as operator training and facilities approval – but the quality management approach can improve on them by promoting a comprehensive preventive strategy for drinking water safety.

11.1.2 Applying the Quality Management Approach

Quality management requires a commitment to seeking and implementing improvements at every level of the water provider's policy- and decision-making, from the policies of corporate management to the day-to-day decisions of those who have responsibility at the ground level. It begins with a commitment by the water provider, led by its owner and senior management, to improve the performance of the system continuously. But quality management must also be specific and clear from the perspective of operating staff. If it is not implemented in a practical and relevant way, in the context of the actual operation of a water system, then its value is limited.

---

[4] This summary is adapted from the various models summarized in section 11.2.

[5] In relation to regulation, the National Health and Medical Research Council of Australia has described this limitation to some of the conventional approaches as follows:

> In the past there has been a heavy reliance by many agencies on compliance monitoring as a mechanism for managing drinking water quality and notionally for the protection of public health. However, reliance on compliance monitoring has major limitations including the shortcomings of sampling and analytical techniques; inadequate consideration of the range of events that impact on drinking water quality; and failure to provide an effective response to contaminants without a prescribed numerical guideline value or established method of analysis.

See National Health and Medical Research Council of Australia, 2001, *Framework for Management of Drinking Water Quality – Background* <www.health.gov.au/nhmrc/advice/waterbkd.htm> [accessed April 3, 2002].

The Ontario Municipal Water Association, Ontario Water Works Association, Ontario Public Service Employees Union, and water industry experts all expressed similar reasons for adopting quality management in their submissions to the Inquiry.

The implications of quality management depend on the size and complexity of the water system, or network of water systems, for which an operating agency is responsible.[6] Large operating agencies, responsible for multiple water systems, will require a quality management system that is adaptable to a variety of situations. Smaller water providers, responsible for a single water system, may be able to develop a quality management system based on a relatively narrow set of circumstances.

In order to see how quality management should be applied, it is helpful to distinguish the corporate level of management from the operational level:

- The *corporate* management of an operating agency is responsible for an entire water supply system or network of water supply systems.

- The *operational* management of an individual water system, or of a specific component of that system (e.g., the treatment plant, distribution system, or monitoring system), is responsible for the day-to-day operation of that system or component.[7]

Managers and staff at both the corporate and the operational levels of a water system have a critical role to play in ensuring the provision of safe drinking water. Yet the means available to identify and realize opportunities for improvements will depend on the level of management in question.

11.1.2.1   *The Requirement for Accreditation*

I recommend below that all municipalities be required to have an accredited operating agency for their water system. Accreditation is intended to focus on the processes and systems that an operating agency puts in place at the corporate level to ensure that the entire organization is functioning effectively. Accreditation will be based on a drinking water quality management standard that has been developed by the industry, as well as other key stakeholders, and recognized by the provincial government.

---

[6] In large systems, there might be hundreds of individual operators, supervised by dozens of plant and system managers, who are under the direction of a large corporate head office and management team. In small systems, on the other hand, a single person might be responsible for the daily operation of the system as well for many aspects of its management.

[7] I discuss the role of individual operators, including the need for the certification and ongoing training of operators, in Chapter 12.

To be accredited, operating agencies would be required to adopt a quality management system and would be subject to independent audits by a certified accrediting body. The primary purpose is for senior management of the operating agency to be able to demonstrate to the owner of a water system that the system is being run effectively, so that the owner is confident that the system is capable of delivering safe drinking water. Having an accredited operating agency will do much to satisfy the owner's due diligence responsibilities and standard of care. I reiterate that many water providers have already adopted a managerial model similar to the type of quality management system I envision.

11.1.2.2   *The Requirement for an Operational Plan*

As part of its corporate quality management system, an operating agency will need to undertake operational planning at all of the individual water systems for which it is responsible. The safety benefits of the quality management approach make it desirable to formalize operational planning at the plant- or system-specific level as a regulatory requirement. Therefore, I recommend below that all municipalities be required to have an operational plan for their water system or, depending on the size and complexity, for each component of the system (e.g., the treatment plant, distribution system, and monitoring system). The plan should be public and should be subject to functional approval and review by the MOE, as I discuss in section 11.4.5.

I do not intend that the operational plan should become a whole new layer of paperwork for municipal water providers. Rather, I see it as a vehicle for management and staff to carefully outline, and periodically revisit, the barriers and strategies they have put in place to ensure safety. So that this requirement will not be overly bureaucratic, the general form of the operational plan should be left to the water provider to develop, and the MOE should provide model plans for assistance only. The existence of an accessible operational plan will also facilitate reviews of a water system by outside personnel, including MOE inspectors and consulting engineers.

11.2   Models of Drinking Water Quality Management

The examples of quality management plans outlined in the following sections are useful examples for both accreditation and operational planning in Ontario.

11.2.1 General Models

The quality management approach originated in general models such as ISO 9000, ISO 14000, and the HACCP (Hazard Analysis and Critical Control Point) system.[8] These models provide generic requirements for organizations carrying out a wide range of activities.

11.2.1.1   *ISO Standards*

ISO 9000 is an international standard adopted in 1987 by the International Organization for Standardization (ISO) setting specific criteria for documenting and establishing a quality management plan.[9] Its purpose is to show that a company documents its quality management principles and procedures, and that it operates according to them. Specific ISO standards have been designed and adopted in various industries, such as the aerospace, automobile manufacturing, and telecommunications industries. The European Union has begun to develop an ISO standard that is specific to the water industry.[10]

---

[8] See International Organization for Standardization, *The Magical Demystifying Tour of ISO 9000 and ISO 14000* <www.iso.ch/iso/en/iso9000-14000/tour/magical.html> [accessed April 3, 2002]; and Canadian Food Inspection Agency, 2001, *Food Safety Enhancement Program Implementation* manual <www.inspection.gc.ca/english/ppc/psps/haccp/manu/manue.shtml> [accessed April 2, 2002].

[9] The International Organization for Standardization was established in 1947 to develop common international standards in a range of areas. Its membership consists of national standards organizations from over 120 countries. For more information, see the ISO's Web site <www.iso.ch> [accessed April 3, 2002].

[10] International Organization for Standardization, AFNOR (France), 2001, "ISO/TS/P 194, 2001 – Standardization of service activities relating to drinking water supply and sewerage: Quality criteria of the service and performance indicators," proposal for a new field of technical activity, April 17, 2001.

11.2.1.2   *The HACCP System*

The HACCP (Hazard Analysis and Critical Control Point) system is a quality management plan that aims to apply a preventive approach to food production as a means of ensuring food safety. Briefly, HACCP is a systematic approach to the identification, evaluation, and control of food safety hazards. Rather than checking products after they are manufactured, the system identifies critical points in the production process and puts controls at these points to reduce the risk of food contamination.

11.2.2   Water Industry–Specific Models

ISO standards and the HACCP system are generally not specific to the water industry. The starting point for an accreditation standard in Ontario should naturally be the frameworks that are specific to the water industry. Examples of these water-specific models include

- the American Water Works Association QualServe program, Partnership for Safe Drinking Water, and International Water Treatment Alliance;

- the Australian *Framework for Management of Drinking Water Quality*; and

- the *Guidelines for Drinking-Water Quality Management for New Zealand.*

Each of these models should be assessed in relation to the development of operational plans for municipal water systems and the creation of an accreditation standard. The models differ in various ways, such as in the degree to which they focus on a particular component of a water system (especially treatment plants), the degree to which they focus on specific barriers rather than the overall management system, and the degree to which they are oriented to systems of different size and complexity. As such, they will have different strengths and weaknesses. In designing Ontario's standard, the goal should be to include all components of the system that relate to ensuring drinking water quality, to address both the corporate and the operational level of management, and to incorporate systems of varying size and complexity.

11.2.2.1   *American Water Works Association Programs*

The Partnership for Safe Drinking Water and the International Water Treatment Alliance: The membership of the American Water Works Association (AWWA) includes utilities from across both the United States and Canada – the Ontario Water Works Association (OWWA) is the provincial AWWA chapter. The AWWA Partnership for Safe Drinking Water is a cooperative effort of U.S. agencies to review operating practices at treatment plants, in which more than 200 utilities have been participating since 1995.[11] The International Water Treatment Alliance adapts this program to other countries; it has recently been implemented in Quebec with provincial funding. The International Water Treatment Alliance is a cooperative effort of the AWWA, water utilities, and in some cases foreign water organizations dedicated to safe drinking water.[12]

Both programs are part of a broader effort to improve operational aspects of water facilities. As outlined below in relation to the AWWA QualServe program, the approach is based on data collection and self-assessment, peer review, and optional outside assessment.

The QualServe Program: QualServe is a voluntary quality improvement program created by AWWA (representing water utilities) and the Water Environment Federation (representing wastewater utilities) in 1997.[13] Since its inception, the QualServe program has relied on two steps: self-assessment and peer review. In the first step, water providers and their staff are asked to fill out detailed questionnaires relating to all aspects of the management and operation of the water system. Their responses are then reviewed by a team of expert peers in the water industry who have undergone training in the QualServe

---

[11] The Partnership for Safe Drinking Water involves the American Water Works Association, the Association of Metropolitan Water Agencies, the U.S. Environmental Protection Agency, the National Association of Water Companies, the Association of State Drinking Water Administrators, and the American Water Works Research Foundation.

[12] E. Doyle et al., 2002, "Production and distribution of drinking water," Walkerton Inquiry Commissioned Paper 8, pp. 94–95; and J.A. MacDonald, for OWWA/OMWA, 2001, "Review of issue #8 – Production and distribution of drinking water," Walkerton Inquiry Submission, pp. 18–19.

[13] See QualServe, 1997, "Self-assessment and peer review for water and wastewater utilities" (Denver, CO: AWWA/WEA); and QualServe, 1998, "Program guidance part 1: Guidance for participating utilities" (Denver, CO: AWWA/WEA). See <www.awwa.org/qualserve> [accessed April 9, 2002].

program.[14] More recently, QualServe has expanded to a benchmarking program and an accreditation (described below). Overall, QualServe aims to assist utilities to achieve best practices in each of the processes involved in its operations and services, and to develop programs to improve performance on an ongoing basis.[15]

The AWWA Accreditation Program: The AWWA plans to integrate the existing QualServe program into a full accreditation program, based on third party audit and registration according to an accreditation standard.[16] An AWWA committee is developing an evaluation system that will confer accreditation based on water and wastewater utilities meeting defined operating and management standards. Under the program, a utility would be able to accredit to standards for the treatment plant, distribution system, source water, business and planning processes, communications, wastewater collection, wastewater treatment, wastewater pre-treatment monitoring, biosolids handling and management, and conservation and reclamation of water. However, the accreditation program is several years away from being fully operational.[17]

11.2.2.2 *The Australian* Framework for Management of Drinking Water Quality

The Australian *Framework for Management of Drinking Water Quality*[18] is intended as a template for best practices in the management and operation of water utilities, to support a more consistent national approach to drinking water quality.[19] The rationale of the document is:

to promote an understanding of the entire water supply system, the events that can compromise drinking water quality and the

---

[14] Peer review teams consist of three to five trained peers who share the tasks of examining the major areas of utility operations: customer relations, business operations, organizational development, water operations and/or wastewater operations. QualServe, 1997, p. 10.

[15] The program is designed for utilities to conduct self-assessments every two to four years, and peer reviews every four to seven years.

[16] See <www.awwa.org/qualserve/accreditation.htm> [accessed April 9, 2002]. See also MacDonald, p. 19.

[17] The American Water Works Association anticipates that all of its accreditation standards will be available in 2005.

[18] National Health and Medical Research Council of Australia/Agricultural and Resource Management Council of Australia and New Zealand Co-ordinating Group, 2001, *Framework for Management of Drinking Water Quality – A Preventative Strategy from Catchment to Consumer* <www.health.gov.au/nhmrc/advice/waterbkd.htm> [accessed April 3, 2002].

[19] Ibid.

operational control necessary for assuring the ongoing reliability and safety of drinking water supplies.[20]

The framework is organized into 12 elements: commitment to drinking water quality management, assessment of the drinking water supply system, planning-preventive strategies for drinking water quality management, implementation-operational procedures and process control, verification of drinking water quality, incident and emergency response, employee awareness and training, community involvement and awareness, research and development, documentation and reporting, evaluation and audit, review and continual improvement.

The development of the framework has been coordinated by the National Health and Medical Research Council of Australia under the auspices of the Agriculture and Resource Management Council of Australia and New Zealand. Although it has not yet been implemented as part of a national program in Australia, the framework is providing the primary basis for the 2002 restructuring and revision of the Australian Drinking Water Guidelines as a preventive, quality management approach to water quality.[21]

11.2.2.3   Guidelines for Drinking-Water Quality Management for New Zealand

Since 1993, public health "grading" of community water supplies in New Zealand serving more than 500 people is carried out by regional health authorities.[22] The grading system adopts a preventive, process-oriented approach to the multi-barrier protection of drinking water.[23]

---

[20] Ibid., p. 1.

[21] The framework was also reviewed in May 2001 by the Microbiology Working Group and the Protection & Control Working Group of the World Health Organization (WHO) in connection with development of the third edition of the *WHO Drinking Water Guidelines*, forecast for release in 2003.

[22] As part of the grading system, drinking water supplies are examined according to 33 aspects of the source and treatment of the water, and 22 aspects of the distribution system and treated water quality. All community water systems that serve more than 25 people for longer than 60 days a year are required to be registered on a national registry of community drinking water supplies. Government of New Zealand, Ministry of Health, 2001a, *Register of Community Drinking-Water Supplies in New Zealand* (Wellington: Ministry of Health), pp. 4, 9.

[23] Ibid., p. 9, which states in relation to the grading system: "There is a strong concern, not only about the quality of the end product, but also about whether adequate barriers to potential contamination are in place in the system."

The New Zealand Ministry of Health is currently examining options for further integrating public health risk management plans into New Zealand's drinking water grading system.[24] The Guidelines for Drinking-Water Quality Management for New Zealand have been incorporated as "background and supporting information" in New Zealand's Drinking Water Quality Standards in order to demonstrate how risk management principles can be applied for community water supplies.[25] The guidelines would require water suppliers to undertake critical point identification, risk assessment, risk management, contingency planning, and quality assurance.[26] The intent is to strengthen the existing *Health Act* as it applies to drinking water supplies by:

• placing duties on drinking water suppliers to take all practicable steps to comply with drinking water standards;

• requiring drinking water suppliers to introduce and implement public health risk management plans;

• providing for Ministry of Health officers to act as assessors to verify compliance with standards, the adoption and implementation of public health risk management plans, and the competence of water supply staff who carry out process and field analyses; and

• requiring designated assessors to have their competence accredited by an internationally recognized agency.[27]

To assist water suppliers in preparing for this requirement, the Ministry of Health has published a number of risk management planning guides covering various elements of the system, such as filtration, treatment, water storage, distribution, and staff training.[28] The guides provide useful models for

---

[24] K. Botherway, 2001, Office of the Parliamentary Commissioner for the Environment, New Zealand, e-mail to the Walkerton Inquiry, September 24.

[25] New Zealand, Ministry of Health, 2000a, *Drinking-Water Quality Standards for New Zealand 2000* (Wellington: Ministry of Health), p. 5.

[26] As proposed, these requirements would apply to four stages of water supply system: collection of raw water, treatment, distribution to consumers, and consumer storage and distribution. See New Zealand, Ministry of Health, 2000b, *Safe Drinking-Water: A Paper to Local Government* (Wellington: Ministry of Health), p. 10.

[27] New Zealand, Ministry of Health, 2001b, "Frequently asked questions about drinking water standards" <www.moh.govt.nz>.

[28] The risk management planning guides are available to water providers and to the public on the ministry's Web site <www.moh.govt.nz> [accessed April 3, 2002].

operational planning in Ontario water systems and are particularly helpful in terms of their application to small systems.

11.2.2.4   *Conclusion*

These examples of quality management design and implementation in other jurisdictions provide a strong basis for mandatory accreditation and operational planning in Ontario. There are other important examples of quality management, such as Ontario Clean Water Agency's (OCWA) Environmental Management System, which is based on ISO 14001.[29] OCWA's system may be useful not only because it originates in the Ontario context but also because it has been implemented by a large operating agency that is responsible for many small systems. As such, it has been implemented at both the corporate and the operational levels.

11.3   Accreditation

11.3.1   The Requirement for Accreditation

Recommendation 51: The provincial government should require all owners of municipal water systems, as a condition of their licence (see Recommendation 71), to have an accredited operating agency, whether internal or external to the municipality.

I am recommending the accreditation of operating agencies, which would require the operating agency to have a quality management system based on a drinking water quality management standard recognized by the Province. Although the quality management system would be adopted at the corporate level, the operating agency would have to demonstrate that it was implementing quality management at the water systems under its authority. Thus, the corporate quality management system would establish the organization's commitment to the quality management approach. It would also provide overarching direction about the implementation of operational planning to managers and staff at the plant- or system-specific level. A primary purpose of the quality management

---

[29] The Inquiry was limited in its ability to learn about OCWA's Environmental Management System because the provincial government did not permit Commission staff to meet or communicate directly with OCWA. General information about OCWA's system was provided to the Inquiry by the Ontario Public Service Employees Union and by experts outside the provincial government.

system is to enable senior management to demonstrate to the owner that its water system is being managed and operated to deliver safe drinking water on a reliable basis.

11.3.2 Independent Audits

Recommendation 52: Accreditation should be based on an independent audit and a periodic review by a certified accrediting body.

Accreditation should be verified by way of an external audit performed by an independent third party which itself must be approved for its competence and commitment. The role of the auditor is to visit and report on an operating agency's performance with respect to accreditation standards and to give a timeline for corrective action. Thus the auditor will review the agency's quality management system and examine how it has been implemented at the water system, or in a sampling of water systems, under the operating agency's responsibility.[30] Scheduled audits of an operating system should occur regularly. For reasons of accountability and transparency, audit results should be provided to the MOE and made available to the public. If the auditor finds a violation of a regulatory requirement, the auditor should report it to the Ministry of the Environment.

Auditors should be certified by a designated[31] accrediting organization. For accreditation to be useful, audits should be carried out by persons with experience in the water industry. It would not be appropriate to rely on persons who have only general expertise in quality management (such as ISO or HACCP) and who do not have substantial experience in the water industry. Persons certified as auditors should therefore be required to have experience and expertise in relation to the provision of drinking water, and I would suggest that most auditors be drawn from the relevant industry associations, so long as

---

[30] The Ontario Public Service Employees Union submitted to the Inquiry that accreditation be facility-based for three reasons: (1) so that non-conformity in one facility does not affect operating privileges of conforming facilities operated by the same operating agency, (2) to increase the likelihood that the consequences of non-conformity will be applied, and (3) because different plants will have different valid drinking water production processes that need to be individually considered. In terms of the first reason, I recommend below a variety of responses to non-compliance that will address this concern. In terms of the second and third reasons, I am satisfied that an appropriate balance between thoroughness and practicality of implementation will be struck by the dual accreditation and operational planning approach that I am recommending.

[31] By the Ministry of the Environment.

they are willing to play this role, complemented where necessary by staff from the MOE's Drinking Water Branch.

To ensure an adequate supply of auditors, members of the water industry – from within as well as from outside the province – should be encouraged to play a prominent role.[32] The provincial government, in concert with industry associations, should take steps to enable water providers to make their managers and employees available as auditors. If necessary for the accreditation system to function effectively, the provincial government should indemnify participating industry associations and water providers from potential liability arising from the participation of their members or staff.

11.3.3 The Development of a Drinking Water Quality Management Standard

Recommendation 53: The Ministry of the Environment should initiate the development of a drinking water quality management standard for Ontario. Municipalities, the water industry, and other relevant stakeholders should be actively recruited to take part in the development of the standard. The water industry is recognized as an essential participant in this initiative.

The provincial government should initiate forthwith the development of a drinking water quality management standard. The MOE should enter into an agreement with an appropriate body to manage the development of the standard.[33] The process must actively recruit key stakeholders, particularly experienced representatives of the water industry, in light of the important role that water providers must play in it.

The standard should be based on models of drinking water quality management and industry best practices from other jurisdictions, although no single model need drive the development of the Ontario standard. The standard should be universally applicable; that is, it should accommodate water providers of various

---

[32] During Part 2 of the Inquiry, I visited a number of water facilities that demonstrated some of the outstanding expertise that currently exists in Ontario; this expertise should be marshalled and directed to spreading good practices across the province.

[33] One option would be for the Province to contract with the Canadian Standards Association, a not-for-profit association that operates as part of the National Standards System coordinated by the Standards Council of Canada, to develop the standard.

sizes and complexity. To a reasonable extent, the process should also refer to the model operational plans developed by the MOE, as I recommend below.

The Ontario standard should not await the finalization of quality management standards in other jurisdictions. I do not consider it advisable, in particular, to await an AWWA or ISO accreditation standard.[34] Quality management is simply too important to rely on the expediency of actors outside the province. Enough progress has been made in developing the key concepts for drinking water quality management standards that Ontario can proceed expeditiously without awaiting cross-jurisdictional programs.

In light of the varying circumstances of water providers across Ontario, it is important that the drinking water quality management standard be adaptable, as appropriate, to water systems of different size and complexity. It should not exclude or discriminate against small water providers that are capable of effective operational planning according to the quality management approach. This is not an unrealistic expectation: quality management has been tailored to systems of varying size and complexity, including small systems, in other jurisdictions.[35]

In particular, accreditation should not demand so much organizational depth that it dooms all small water providers to extinction or causes a mass "shakeout" in the industry. The emphasis must be on the ability of any operating agency to assure the delivery of safe water. Larger, more complex systems will require greater management complexity, while smaller systems may have much more straightforward management and operating requirements. Although accreditation will no doubt lead many municipalities with small water systems to regionalize or engage an external operator, it is also desirable for well-run

---

[34] Further, the accreditation standard for water systems should not be delayed to incorporate wastewater systems, even though it is probably desirable to have both a water and wastewater accreditation program, as contemplated by the AWWA accreditation standard discussed in section 11.2.

[35] QualServe, for example, has been adapted for use by small water utilities, although its original focus was on large and medium-sized systems. Also, the AWWA initiative for capacity development for smaller utilities highlights quality management tools for small systems, such as information management, regular reporting, audits, performance analysis, peer review, and, assessments of options for restructuring. See J.A. Beecher and S.J. Rubin, 2001, "Ten practices of highly effective water utilities," *AWWA Opflow* (April), p. 6; and A. Davies, for OWWA/OMWA, Walkerton Inquiry Submission (Public Hearing, September 20, 2001), transcript p. 17. In addition, the Australian *Framework for Management of Drinking Water Quality* was developed by performing desktop trials by water providers, including some that operate many small water systems. Finally, the risk management planning guides developed by the New Zealand Ministry of Health have been designed for small systems.

small systems to be able to achieve accreditation. The provincial government should ensure that a number of capable small water providers participate in developing and implementing accreditation.

I have focused my comments here on small systems because they may present unique challenges in terms of the design of an accreditation standard. However, I recognize that municipalities of all sizes rely on a variety of arrangements for the management and operation of their water systems.[36] The accreditation standard will need to consider and accommodate these realities. I do not propose to be prescriptive in this regard. The details of accreditation are best left to those with the relevant experience and expertise in the industry.

11.3.4 The Role of the Water Industry

I have emphasized that the water industry must be actively recruited to participate in the standard development process, to allow those individuals who have the most expertise and experience in Ontario's industry to assume a leadership role in the process. Since the main reference points for defining due diligence are the best practices of the industry, leading water providers should be called on to play a central role in defining and implementing accreditation. It is they who are most familiar with how water systems can be organized to deliver water of the highest quality.

Industry leaders should welcome the opportunity to raise practices up to the best. Their common vision for ensuring the safety of drinking water will be essential to the successful implementation of accreditation and operational planning. The draft standard that emerges from the Ontario accreditation process should therefore not be recognized by the MOE without the approval and support of water industry representatives.

During the Inquiry, the concern was expressed that if the industry plays a prominent role in the standard development process, accreditation will emerge as a form of industry self-regulation and that somehow safety will be less

---

[36] For example, the municipality might contract out the operation of the treatment plant while retaining the operation of the distribution system; alternatively, the municipality might contract out the entire operation while retaining aspects of the overall management, such as billing and financial planning.

protected. I do not share this concern in light of the dual approach I am recommending – based on mandatory accreditation and operational plans – and because of the existence of much excellent practice in Ontario. Also, the goal of the water industry and the objective of accreditation are essentially the same: to maximize the safety of drinking water through the consistent use of good practices. By involving a diverse range of industry representatives and working in concert with government representatives, one would expect that best practices would be brought to the table and integrated into the standard. Moreover, experienced leaders in Ontario's water industry are in the best position to comment on how to design a standard that is practical and meaningful in relation to ground-level operational planning.

I also note that stakeholders from outside the industry, including consumer representatives and MOE personnel, should also be involved in the standard development process. Ultimately, it will be up to the provincial government to ensure that the standard that comes into force is appropriate from a safety perspective.

11.3.5 Peer Review

No matter how well it is run, an organization can benefit from constructive suggestions about its operation from people who do the same type of work in similar organizations. A benefit of mandatory quality management is that it will encourage the cross-fertilization of ideas and approaches from managers and operations staff of different water systems. This can be promoted through peer review, whereby management and staff obtain confidential and collegial feedback on their operations, and suggestions regarding any areas for improvement. In larger operating agencies, peer review opportunities may be available internally. Smaller water providers may need to participate in an external peer review program.

To support the implementation of mandatory accreditation and operational planning, therefore, the Province should contribute start-up funding for a formal peer review program. Such a program should be supported at least over the next few years, as municipalities develop their operational plans, as discussed in section 11.4. Participation in the program should be voluntary, but the provincial government should offer incentives to water providers, especially smaller ones, to participate. The AWWA's International Water Treatment Alliance (IWTA) is a good example of this type of self-assessment and peer review program, although its application is focused on water treatment plants.[37] The Ontario Water and Wastewater Association offered in its submissions to the Inquiry to implement the IWTA program in Ontario, provided that the provincial government provides start-up funding.[38] I agree with this approach, although I also consider it reasonable to expect water providers to pay for the costs of undergoing an external peer review as part of the program.[39]

11.3.6 The Role of the Ministry of the Environment

Recommendation 54: The Ministry of the Environment's Drinking Water Branch (see Recommendation 69) should have the responsibility for recognizing the drinking water quality management standard that will apply in Ontario and for ensuring that accreditation is properly implemented.

As I discuss in Chapter 13, accreditation is complementary to – not a substitute for – the regulatory role of the MOE. In addition, the water industry can and must play a central role. For these reasons, it is acceptable for the development and implementation of the accreditation standard to be contracted to a third party. The provincial government, however, remains responsible for the oversight of water systems in Ontario and, as such, it has a role to play in ensuring that accreditation serves its intended purpose.

The MOE should participate in the standard development process and should be responsible for recognizing the standard that emerges from that process. In addition, the MOE should ensure the proper implementation of accreditation, not by directly carrying out audits or administering the program, but by receiving and reviewing audit reports in conjunction with provincial approval and inspection of water systems. In this respect, the MOE should retain a residual audit capacity so that it can, if necessary, conduct an informed review

---

[37] Under the IWTA, peer review teams receive training from the AWWA that is oriented toward water or wastewater facilities of various sizes. Team members are drawn from experienced water and wastewater utilities' senior managers. All are volunteers who are reimbursed for travel expenses only. A number of municipal water providers in Ontario have taken part in the QualServe peer review program, including Fort Erie, Ottawa-Carleton, and Waterloo. For more information, see <www.awwa.org/qualserve> [accessed April 2, 2002].

[38] MacDonald, p. 19.

[39] If, for reasons of cost, the peer review program is not reasonably accessible to water providers, the MOE should compensate for this by making additional technical assistance available to those systems.

of an operating agency's quality management system, or verify the accuracy of an external audit.[40]

The MOE is the most appropriate ministry to assume the regulatory responsibility for developing the accreditation standard. Staff in the MOE's Drinking Water Branch, in particular, will have specialized expertise and experience in drinking water. Given their supervisory role, MOE staff should fully understand how the standard has evolved both before and after it comes into force. In light of the MOE's role, the accreditation standard should be based on models in which regulatory authorities may participate in accreditation activities to maintain their access to information about the process and to ensure that it is being carried out appropriately. Finally, following the adoption of the provincial standard, the requirement for owners of water systems to have an accredited operating agency should be a statutory requirement under the *Safe Drinking Water Act* that I recommend in Chapter 13.

It is appropriate for the start-up cost of developing the drinking water quality management standard to be borne by the provincial government so that the process proceeds expeditiously. Once accreditation is in place, the MOE should ensure that it is properly funded whether by the government or as a self-supporting program. It is appropriate for the cost of external audits and follow-up visits to be borne by the accreditee. However, the MOE should ensure that the cost of audits is not unreasonable in light of the size and complexity of an operating agency.[41]

11.3.7 Timeline for Implementation

Recommendation 55: The drinking water quality management standard should come into force by a date to be fixed by the provincial government. All municipalities should be required under the *Safe Drinking Water Act* (see Recommendation 67) to have an operating agency for their water system accredited within a specified time.

---

[40] If accreditation functions as I envision, with the industry playing a lead role, then I anticipate that the need for a residual audit capacity will be relatively small. Staff of the MOE's Drinking Water Branch who have appropriate expertise in the water industry should conduct or participate in the audits as required.

[41] If the market supply of external auditors does not allow for a reasonable cost, the Province could either set standardized fees or make sufficient MOE Drinking Water Branch staff available to carry out audits on a reasonable cost-recovery basis.

I have recommended that accreditation be implemented according to deadlines fixed by the Province. Based on information provided to the Inquiry, I suggest that the MOE endeavour to complete the standard development process for drinking water quality management, and that it come into force, by December 31, 2003. Further, I suggest that the MOE fix a date in 2006 as the final deadline for all municipalities to be required to have an accredited operating agency.

These are suggested deadlines. I recognize that, depending on the circumstances, the Province may find it necessary to adopt a different timeline. As I have mentioned above, it is important that accreditation not lead to a mass shakeout in Ontario's water industry; on the other hand, considering the energy that can be harnessed now in the aftermath of the Walkerton tragedy, the timeline should also be an expedited one.

It would make sense for accreditation to be phased in over time, beginning with larger operating agencies since many of them have already adopted a quality management system. Once the larger operating agencies become accredited, they will be in a better position to pursue options to regionalize or contract with smaller water providers and to make staff available for participating in the accreditation program as auditors. Adopting a phased approach also gives smaller municipalities more time to consider restructuring options, while still requiring them to develop an operational plan, as discussed below.

To help inform the planning for this implementation process, the following table is included to provide a rough approximation of the number of municipal water providers of different sizes in the province.[42]

---

[42] Table 11.1 summarizes the population served for each of the 265 municipalities identified in the Municipal Water Use Database (MUD). The table relies on the 1998 Sewage and Water Inspection Program (SWIP) database, as summarized in Doyle et al., the most recent complete information available.

Table 11.1 Summary of Municipal Water Providers by Size of Population Served

Population served	Number of municipalities	Total population served	Average population served
≥500	27	7,680	284
501–3,300	102	152,669	1,497
3,301–10,000	68	412,661	6,069
> 10,001–100,000	39	1,136,740	29,147
> 100,000	15	7,185,322	479,021
Missing	14		
Total	**265**	**8,895,072**	

11.4 Operational Planning

11.4.1 The Requirement for an Operational Plan

Recommendation 56: The provincial government should require municipalities to have operational plans for their water systems by a date to be fixed by the provincial government.

As part of its quality management system, an operating agency will no doubt engage in comprehensive operational planning at the individual water systems for which it is responsible. However, in light of the importance of strategies and decisions at the operational level to the ultimate safety of drinking water, all municipalities should be required under the *Safe Drinking Water Act* to have operational plans[43] for their water systems. This requirement would be in addition to other conditions of the owner's licence for municipal water systems (e.g., Certificate of Approval, Permit to Take Water, and financial plan), as discussed in Chapter 13.

---

[43] The size and complexity of the water system may determine whether a municipality requires a separate plan for distinct components of the system (e.g., the treatment plant, distribution system, or monitoring system).

The requirement for an operational plan applies at the level of the individual water system[44] and is based on plant- and system-specific measures. The purpose of the operational plan is to outline the current capability of a water provider's management and operating system for providing safe drinking water, to identify areas where improvement is needed, and to implement corrective action. Based on the quality management approach, the plan should include:

- the comprehensive self-assessment and implementation of effective multiple barriers;

- the identification of activities and processes considered essential for the control of water quality ("critical control points"); and

- the establishment of mechanisms to provide operational control at critical control points, including methods that will monitor performance and trigger corrective action where required.[45]

The operational plan should be implemented as part of a formal program to ensure that all processes and activities are carried out effectively, including adequate skills and training for operations staff. The plan should be reviewed regularly to ensure that the preventive strategies are adequate and are being implemented, and to identify new opportunities for improvement. It should also be available to the public for inspection.[46]

What the operational plan should *not* be is a mere collection of the design and operating specifications of the system's equipment.[47] This approach would be too narrow and detailed to be of use. Most importantly, it would not reflect a

---

[44] Use of the term "water system" is intended to include all of the physical components of a water supply system, including the water intake, treatment facilities, the distribution network, storage reservoirs, pumping stations, etc., serving a defined population. The issue of how to delineate a particular system, and whether to adopt a distinct operational plan for the various components of that system, will depend on the circumstances. In a large system, it might make sense to adopt a distinct operational plan for each treatment plant and an additional plan for the distribution system. In a smaller system, a single operational plan for the entire system might suffice. The goal should be to design the operational plan that is comprehensive, but also practically useful and accessible.

[45] Adapted from National Health and Medical Research Council of Australia.

[46] This is consistent with the public information requirements under O. Reg. 459/00, ss. 11–12.

[47] The "operating manual" for a water system, as currently required under O. Reg. 453/93 and Certificates of Approval, is typically detailed, dense, and not very accessible. The operational plan I have in mind is a more accessible summary of the critical information needed regarding the multiple barriers in place to ensure drinking water safety.

careful assessment of the role of the multiple barriers and operating processes in addressing specific threats to drinking water quality.

11.4.2 The Process of Operational Planning

Although the owner of a water system will be required to have an operational plan, the operating agency (whether municipally owned or not) will normally be responsible for developing, implementing, and updating the plan.[48] These activities will demonstrate the effectiveness of the agency's management and operating practices to the owner. Some operating agencies in Ontario have already adopted comprehensive operational planning, based on the quality management approach, although sometimes with a disproportionate focus on treatment plants. For industry leaders, all that may be needed is to review and formalize the operational plan, undergo peer review as necessary, submit the plan to the MOE, and establish an internal process to address any areas for improvement on an ongoing basis.

For other water systems, however, existing practices may not be adequate to generate an operational plan that addresses the full range of drinking water quality issues. Moreover, the existing management arrangements may not be structured, documented, or subject to external review. In these cases, there is no assurance that management is functioning effectively or that it is oriented to continuous improvement. Further, there may be a need to expand the quality management approach to all components of the water system. In these circumstances, it will be necessary to invest time and resources to develop the operational plan. The organizational culture of the water provider may need to change considerably.

In developing an operational plan, the first step is for the operating agency to assess the current management and operation of the water system.[49] This *self-assessment* should systemically engage both the operational management and staff, on a collaborative basis, in:

---

[48] Unlike the current requirements for engineer's reports under O. Reg. 459/00, it should be permissible for operational plans to be prepared by employees of a municipal water provider.

[49] This will entail a review of existing operating practices, operating manuals, Certificates of Approval, regulatory requirements, and other relevant material to determine how the operation of the system will effectively ensure drinking water safety.

- reviewing the multiple barriers in the water system;

- identifying critical activities in the system where, in the event of a breakdown, safety would be threatened; and

- implementing strategies to ensure multi-barrier protection and, specifically, to control any critical control points.[50]

Given the changing nature of the multiple barriers that are in place, the understanding of risks, and the options for mitigation, the operational plan will necessarily be a working document.

11.4.3 The Relationship to Certificates of Approval

At present, municipalities are required to obtain a Certificate of Approval from the MOE for their water system. As I discuss in Chapter 13, the Certificate of Approval applies to "water works," which may be a treatment plant, reservoir, pumping station, distribution system, or other element of the overall water system. Historically, the MOE approvals process for Certificates of Approval involved a detailed review of the design and construction of the facilities and the hardware of a water system. The orientation was not to the system's operating conditions and requirements.

Since the early 1990s, the MOE has attached operating conditions to Certificates of Approval. These conditions include requirements to properly operate and maintain equipment (such as requirements for effective performance, adequate operator staffing and training, adequate funding, and adequate laboratory and process controls); to establish contingency plans and notification procedures; to prepare an operations and maintenance manual; and to establish procedures for responding to complaints.[51] They also include performance requirements in relation to water quality standards and the requirement for a comprehensive monitoring program.

---

[50] The process is not intended to be a massive exercise in data collection. Rather, it should involve "the characterisation of the system at an appropriate level of detail to provide a useful information base from which to make effective decisions," as described in National Health and Medical Research Council of Australia, p. 12.

[51] See Ontario, Ministry of the Environment, 1992, *Review Procedures Manual for Approval of Municipal and Private Water and Sewage Works*, Appendix B.

The imposition of these requirements has been a step in the right direction. In my view, however, managerial and operating aspects are important enough to be outlined in a distinct document from the Certificate of Approval. This will allow a greater focus on the water providers' processes and practices at the plant- and system-specific level, and more readily permit improvements. Thus, municipalities should be required to have in place a comprehensive operational plan, oriented to the multiple barrier protection of public health, in addition to the Certificate of Approval, which should focus on the facilities and hardware of a system.

11.4.4 The Relationship to Engineering Reviews

Municipalities are currently required under Ontario Regulation 459/00 to engage a professional engineer to prepare a report for their water system for submission to the Ministry of the Environment. The engineer's report must follow terms of reference prepared by the ministry.[52] As currently outlined, its principal objectives are to assess the potential for microbiological contamination, and to identify operational and physical improvements necessary to mitigate this potential using multiple barrier concepts.

Although engineers' reports currently include recommendations on both operational and physical aspects of the system, the most appropriate focus of these reviews is on physical aspects, as a companion document to the Certificate of Approval. Managerial and operational aspects should be dealt with as part of a distinct operational plan. The MOE should define the requirements for engineer's reports and operational plans so that they are complementary. From a cost standpoint, it is important that there not be significant duplication between the engineer's report and the operational plan.

11.4.5 The Role of the Ministry of the Environment

Recommendation 57: Operational plans should be approved and reviewed as part of the Ministry of the Environment approvals and inspections programs.

---

[52] See Ontario, Ministry of the Environment, 2000, *Terms of Reference – Engineers' Reports for Water Works* <www.ene.gov.on.ca/envision/gp/4057e.pdf>.

Municipalities should be required to file their operational plans with the MOE as a condition of their owner's licence. Because operational plans are oriented to individual water systems, it is appropriate that they be subject to MOE approval, in connection with the Certificate of Approval, and to MOE inspections. Given that staff of the MOE's Drinking Water Branch will have specialized expertise in managing and operating water systems, they should be assigned these responsibilities.

In terms of MOE approval, I do not envision a detailed engineering review of operational plans, as was historically the case for Certificates of Approval. Rather, I envision a general or functional review of whether the operational plan is adequate for the purposes of documenting the management systems and operating practices that are in place to protect public health. The purpose is to provide a reference document to assess whether the system is being operated appropriately, has achieved its performance goals, and has complied with provincial requirements. The operational plan will also draw the attention of MOE inspectors to those aspects of the water system that are of the highest priority in relation to drinking water safety. Overall, operational planning is intended to improve the existing structure and effectiveness of regulatory oversight, not to merely impose a new layer of paperwork on water systems.

To support municipal water providers in developing operational plans, the MOE should provide guidance and technical assistance about how to develop and implement operational plans in different circumstances. The MOE should look to other jurisdictions, particularly New Zealand, in this regard.[53]

In particular, the MOE should make available guidelines and models for operational plans that apply to different circumstances (e.g., size and complexity) and components (e.g., treatment plant, distribution system, monitoring system) of a drinking water system. These models should be designed to support, not prescribe, operational planning by municipal water providers. As such, water providers should be allowed to work from an MOE model or to develop their own plans, independent of MOE models.[54]

---

[53] The New Zealand Ministry of Health has developed model risk management plans for water supply owners. The plans are tailored to small systems. Owners may also develop their own plans. Individual plans must be developed for each water supply. See New Zealand, Ministry of Health, 2000b, p. 10.

[54] The plan would be subject to MOE approval and inspection in either case.

A logical starting point would be for the MOE to work with a manageable number of exemplary facilities, large and small, to prototype operational plans and develop expertise in their implementation. At the same time, it might require all municipalities to supply basic information (e.g., thorough description of the entire system from source to consumer and a description of all personnel and their relevant experience) to lay the foundation for the operational plan.

11.4.6 Timeline for Implementation

I recommend above that the Province require municipalities to develop operational plans by a date to be fixed by the MOE. I would suggest that the MOE adopt December 31, 2003, as the deadline for municipalities to submit their operational plans to the MOE. The MOE should endeavour to make available model operational plans by December 31, 2002, to allow water providers at least one year to develop their plans. These model plans, in combination with MOE technical assistance and a peer review program, will provide a support package for small water providers.

I do not think that it is necessary to wait for the development of the drinking water quality management standard, discussed above, before requiring municipalities to submit operational plans. There will be ample opportunity for the plans to be adapted within the quality management systems adopted by operating agencies as part of accreditation. Thus, municipalities can and should carry out operational planning while the drinking water quality management standard is being developed.

Table 11.2 provides a general guide to how I see mandatory quality management – including both accreditation and operational planning – being implemented by the provincial government and by municipal water providers. I reiterate that the deadlines in the table are only suggestions.

Table 11.2 The Implementation of Mandatory Quality Management

Transitional Step	Timing of Implementation
Development of a drinking water quality management standard	MOE should initiate immediately. Target date for the standard to come into force: December 31, 2003.
Design and implementation of quality management systems	Water providers should initiate as soon as they deem it appropriate. Target date for municipalities to be required to have an accredited operating agency: 2006.
Implementation of a formal peer review program such as that of the International Water Treatment Alliance	MOE should begin discussions with industry associations immediately. Target date for peer reviews to begin: December 31, 2002.
Design and publication of MOE model operational plans	MOE should initiate immediately. Target date for publication: December 31, 2002.
Design and submission of operational plans	Water providers should initiate as soon as they deem it appropriate, with reference to MOE models, if necessary, once they are available. Target date for all municipalities to submit operational plans to the MOE: December 31, 2003.
Governance reviews	Municipalities should initiate as soon as they deem it necessary in relation to accreditation, operational planning, and other relevant recommendations of this Inquiry.

11.5   Other Considerations

11.5.1 Relationship to Municipal Governance Reviews

In Chapter 10, I encourage municipalities to conduct a governance review in relation to their water system. The governance reviews should consider the future requirements for accreditation and operational planning. I also reiterate that a key reason for these quality management measures is to put operating agencies in a stronger position to inform owners about the effectiveness of the management and operation of the water system, in connection with the owner's due diligence responsibilities.

11.5.2 Application to Municipal Water Systems

I have recommended that the requirements for accreditation and operational planning apply to municipal systems, rather than private communal systems (e.g., small subdivisions, retirement communities, trailer parks) or other non-municipal systems serving the public (e.g., service stations, rural restaurants, rural schools).

It would obviously be preferable for quality management to be employed by all water systems in Ontario. However, the prospect of requiring all private communal systems and other non-municipal systems to carry out quality management is a daunting one. I have opted to recommend, for the time being, that the requirement only apply to municipal water systems. Once these measures are well established for municipal water systems, the provincial government should review the question of whether to require accreditation, and especially operational planning, in the circumstances of non-municipal systems.

I discuss the approach I envision for ensuring drinking water safety at non-municipal systems in Chapter 14.

11.5.3 Confidentiality Concerns

Confidentiality concerns that arise in relation to accreditation or operational planning should be resolved by the Province so as not to compromise the thoroughness and transparency of either accreditation audits or MOE approvals and inspections. An exception to this is the formal peer review program, the primary goal of which should be to resolve any confidentiality concerns in a way that does not compromise the confidentiality and collegiality of the peer review.

11.5.4 Relationship to Benchmarking

Benchmarking compares performance on the basis of numerical and process-related criteria.[55] Benchmarking may complement the process of self-assessment and peer review by allowing municipalities and operating agencies to compare

---

[55] In particular, the Inquiry heard submissions about the Canadian CAO Benchmarking Initiative, a process under development whereby municipalities create performance indicators in a number of different areas, including for water and wastewater services. See Ontario Municipal CAO's Benchmarking Initiative, 2001, "A Summary of Phase 1 and Phase 2 Pilot Projects" <www.caobenchmarking.ca/docs/newsinfo.asp> [accessed April 2, 2002]; and Strategic Alternatives, "Governance and methods of service delivery for water and sewage systems," Walkerton Inquiry Commissioned Paper 17, p. 17.

their performance with that of other water systems. The aim is to support continuous improvement by water system operating agencies.

In Ontario, benchmarking has been tied to municipal report cards mandated by the provincial government's Municipal Performance Measurement Program (MPMP), which was initiated by the Ministry of Municipal Affairs and Housing in 2000.[56] The stated purpose of the program is to determine the efficiency and effectiveness of municipal services, including water and sewage services.[57] In contrast to other benchmarking programs in Canada, the results of MPMP comparisons are to be made public. Concerns were expressed at the Inquiry that the performance comparisons would not allow for accurate comparisons of different water systems; however, they are also viewed as an important starting point for improving performance.

In my view, benchmarking can be complementary, but it is not integral, to accreditation and operational planning. Given the difficulties in achieving common measurements or benchmarks that will apply on a universal basis to all utilities, and the skepticism with which benchmarking may be viewed in some quarters of the industry, I suggest that performance comparisons be done by the operating agency itself, subject to review by the owner as part of its oversight duties. To encourage participation by a wide range of municipalities and operating agencies in the quality management initiatives I am recommending, they should not be used by the Province, or required as public measurements, in conjunction with the requirements for accreditation and operational planning.

As benchmarking becomes more widely accepted in the water industry, the Province may wish to incorporate the process as a part of the accreditation program, provided that there are assurances that the bases of comparison are fair and accurate. Developing and implementing mandatory quality management should not be delayed, however, for reasons related to the development of benchmarking generally or to the Municipal Performance Measurement Program.

---

[56] Ontario, Ministry of Municipal Affairs and Housing, 2002, "Municipal Performance Measurement Program – Year 2" <www.mah.gov.on.ca/business/mpmp/mpmp-e.asp> [accessed April 2, 2002]. Also see Strategic Alternatives, ibid., pp. 11–12.

[57] For water and sewage services, this will include criteria for operating costs for water treatment and distribution, approximate water loss, test results, water leaks, boil water advisories, operating costs for sewage collection and treatment, sewage-main back-ups, test results, and untreated sewage released.

11.6   Emergency Response Planning

This section deals with emergency response planning. In the chapter thus far I have discussed the need for municipal water providers to have an operational plan. A critical component of an operational plan is an emergency response plan focused on events capable of affecting drinking water safety. Because of the importance of emergency response planning, I thought it useful to address this subject in some detail and in a separate section of this chapter.[58]

In this section, I recommend that a generic emergency response plan for water providers be developed and that emergency response planning be a required element of accreditation and operational planning. In addition, I discuss the elements of an effective emergency response plan for water providers including the need for a guideline for the issuance of boil water advisories. The American Water Works Association (AWWA) has done a great deal of useful work in this area and I draw on their experience.

11.6.1 Defining Emergencies for Water Providers

According to AWWA, a water emergency is "an unforeseen or unplanned event that may degrade the quality or quantity of potable water supplies available to serve customers."[59] Emergencies may be minor; that is, a fairly routine, normal, or localized event that affects few customers. Emergencies may also be major; that is, a disaster that affects an entire or large portion of a water system, lowers the quality and quantity of water, or places the health and safety of the community at risk.[60] In this section I am addressing only major emergencies.

The *Emergency Plans Act*[61] currently provides the formal legal structure for municipal and provincial emergency response plans and authorizes Emergency

---

[58] By devoting a separate section to emergency response planning, I do not intend to suggest that the many other components of an operational plan are not equally important.

[59] American Water Works Association, 2001, *Emergency Planning for Water Utilities, Manual of Water Supply Practices M19*, 4th ed. (Denver, CO: AWWA), p. 4.

[60] Ibid. The urgency and severity of any emergency will depend on many factors including the magnitude of the changes arising and their capacity to cause harm, the lead time of any warning, the time available from first recognition of imminent danger for corrective action to be taken, and the duration over which harm may occur.

[61] The *Emergency Plans Act*, R.S.O. 1990, c. E.9, defines "emergency" as "a situation or an impending situation caused by forces of nature, an accident, an intentional act, or otherwise, that constitutes a danger of major proportions to life or property."

Measures Ontario[62] to be the provincial agency responsible for monitoring, coordinating, and assisting in the formulation and implementation of provincial emergency plans, and ensuring that provincial plans are coordinated with municipal and federal emergency plans. A new *Emergency Readiness Act* has been introduced to the Ontario legislature[63] that will require municipalities to undertake a risk assessment and critical infrastructure identification process in developing their emergency program. Although a recent survey found that approximately 91% of Ontario municipalities have an emergency plan, fewer than 50% have a training program in place or have held regular exercises of their plan.[64] The value of any emergency response plan is very limited unless key personnel are well trained in the implementation of the plan.

11.6.2 Steps in Water Emergency Planning

Recommendation 58: The Ministry of the Environment should work with Emergency Measures Ontario and water industry associations to develop a generic emergency response plan for municipal water providers. A viable and current emergency response plan, and procedures for training and periodic testing of the plan, should be an essential element of mandatory accreditation and operational planning.

The experience and proposals of AWWA are particularly useful and instructive. They have proposed five steps for planning for emergencies affecting a drinking water provider: hazard identification and summary, vulnerability assessment, mitigation actions, preparedness planning (development of an emergency plan), and emergency response, recovery, and training.[65]

---

[62] Emergency Measures Ontario <www.sgcs.gov.on.ca/english/public/emo.html> [accessed April 9, 2002].

[63] Bill 148, *Emergency Readiness Act*, 2d Sess., 37th Leg., Ontario, 2001 (1st reading December 6, 2001).

[64] See <www.newswire.ca/government/ontario/english/releases/December2001/06/c4494.html> [accessed April 7, 2002].

[65] American Water Works Association.

11.6.2.1 *Hazard Identification and Summary*

A number of conditions can become drinking water emergencies and these can arise from natural or human-made hazards, or some combination of both, such as waterborne outbreaks, flooding, forest fires, construction accidents, power failures, nuclear power plant or major industrial incidents, hazardous material release, or source water contamination by any cause, vandalism, and terrorism.

Waterborne outbreaks are clearly the most common indicator of a major emergency and usually cause the most severe health consequences. In particular, waterborne outbreaks have been found in a recent review to correlate strongly with heavy precipitation.[66] Consequently, a drinking water emergency plan must thoroughly and explicitly address all conceivable means by which such plausible hazards could lead to a disease outbreak, and how the corresponding risks can be detected and potential consequences reduced.

11.6.2.2 *Vulnerability Assessment*

An assessment of the vulnerability of any water system to the hazards identified should follow a logical sequence of steps and evaluation, including:[67]

1. Identify the major system components.[68]

2. Evaluate the plausible effects of likely disaster hazards on system components, such as personnel shortages, contamination of water supplies by any means, contamination of air, well and pump damage, pipeline breaks and associated equipment damage, damage to structures, equipment and material damage or loss, process tank damage, electrical power outage, communications disruption and transportation failure.

---

[66] Of 548 waterborne disease outbreaks in the U.S. Environmental Protection Agency database, 51% were preceded by precipitation events above the 90th percentile in severity; F.C. Curriero et al., 2001, "The association between extreme precipitation and waterborne disease outbreaks in the United States, 1948–1994," *American Journal of Public Health* 91, p. 1194.

[67] American Water Works Association, p. 5.

[68] These may be grouped into the major features of the water supply, such as: administration and operations, source water supply, raw water transmission system, treatment facilities, storage facilities, distribution system, electrical power, transportation, and control systems/communications.

3. Decide on performance goals and determine acceptable levels of service for the system under stress.[69]

4. Identify the vulnerability of system components that pose the greatest risk of failure or reduced performance as a result of each hazard identified.[70]

11.6.2.3 *Mitigation Actions*

A variety of measures can be proposed to improve the ability of the water provider to respond to the identified hazards. The following questions have been suggested as the first step in screening any proposed mitigation actions:[71]

- How critical is the component to the system?

- What is the age of the component?

- What are the present and projected expansion, replacement, or construction programs?

- What is the cost of the mitigation action?

Major categories of the system that should be reviewed to determine what mitigation actions could reasonably be taken would include: personnel and likely shortages during an emergency; source water and transmission; treatment; equipment, chemical storage and piping; process basins or tanks; storage tanks; distribution system; system control; interagency coordination; and administration, transportation, and communications.

---

[69] Provision of water to satisfy public health needs is clearly a high priority, but the urgency of demands varies with different uses. Also, the quantities of water likely to be demanded under different disaster scenarios should be estimated so that the likely challenges and needs for priority rationing can be preplanned.

[70] Such forecasting exercises will always be speculative, but the process of attempting to predict component vulnerability should identify practical measures that can reduce the likelihood of complete system failure.

[71] American Water Works Association, p. 39.

11.6.2.4   *Developing an Emergency Plan*

The critical issue for any emergency plan is that it must represent a process rather than a product.[72] Like the operational plan for a water system, an emergency plan cannot be a document that is written only to be filed. It must represent a continuing process to maintain readiness to respond when the need arises. Continuing actions to keep the process alive include training in the response procedures, testing to determine the effectiveness of procedures, revision to improve procedures found to be ineffective, additional training in revised procedures and re-testing.

An effective emergency plan should reference existing resources, be concise and logical, and be coordinated with other agencies. It should include:[73]

- a clear statement of purpose;

- identification of a control group that will deal with the emergency indicating its members, support personnel, legal authority, implementation procedures, and clearly identified responsibilities;

- a system for notifying the control group, and officials and agencies who must respond;

- a description of emergency operations procedures;

- a description of the communications systems that will be used;

- an address and telephone directory of vital services;[74]

- plans for requesting provincial or federal assistance;

- provisions for dealing with the media and for notifying the public; and

---

[72] Emergency Measures Ontario, 1999, *Emergency Planning: A Guide to Emergency Planning for Community Officials* (Toronto: Queen's Printer) <www.sgcs.gov.on.ca/english/public/emoguide/emo.html> [accessed April 8, 2002].

[73] American Water Works Association; and Emergency Measures Ontario, pp. 54–68.

[74] The local Public Health Unit, fire department, police, ambulance service, hospitals, nursing homes, retirement homes, water system operator, electricians, pump specialists, and soil excavators are examples.

- a list of recipients of the most recent edition of the plan.

11.6.2.5   *Emergency Response, Recovery, and Training*

When an emergency arises, the plan can only be effective if its implementation involves a series of rational steps. These steps include: analyzing the severity of the emergency, providing emergency assistance to save lives, reducing the probability of additional injuries or damage, performing emergency repairs based on priority demand, returning the system to normal levels, evaluating the emergency plan, and revising the emergency plan as necessary.[75]

An important consideration during any water contamination episode is the degree of advance warning of the hazard that a water provider can obtain to allow appropriate responses, ranging from increased monitoring and treatment to complete system shutdown. Early warning systems for water providers have received increasing attention in recent years and continuous monitoring technologies have improved substantially. However, there are no universal early warning systems currently available that are capable of rapidly and reliably detecting the full range of hazards that any major water provider currently faces.[76] Thus, effective and adaptive responses are a critical aspect of protecting public health.

Effective personnel response to emergency situations requires proper training of water system operators. I make recommendations regarding operator training in Chapter 12.

11.6.3 Roles in Drinking Water Emergencies

11.6.3.1   *Ministry of the Environment and Emergency Measures Ontario*

As the provincial regulator of water systems, the Ministry of the Environment (MOE) is chiefly responsible for specifying an adequate level of drinking water emergency preparedness. Emergency Measures Ontario (EMO) is assuming increasing responsibility for requiring emergency response planning by Ontario

---

[75] American Water Works Association, pp. 54–68.
[76] T. Brosnan, 1999, *Early Warning Monitoring to Detect Hazardous Events in Water Supplies,* ILSI Risk Science Institute Workshop Report (Washington, DC: International Life Sciences Institute), pp. 24–26.

municipalities and the provincial government. Logically, there should be close cooperation and collaboration between the MOE and EMO in specifying the emergency planning requirements for drinking water providers. EMO can provide a general perspective regarding the content of emergency plans under Ontario's conditions. The MOE can provide the specific perspective of drinking water supply systems in Ontario. The development of this reference document should involve the participation and input from the larger water providers in the province, perhaps by means of a workshop to share experience and insight.

11.6.3.2 *Municipal Water Providers*

Every municipality in Ontario will be obliged to have an emergency plan under the provisions of the proposed *Emergency Readiness Act*. Clearly, drinking water safety must be an essential element of these plans. However, it would not be feasible for the general municipal plan to consider all the details that should be contained in the emergency plan prepared specifically for the water system. Ultimately, each municipal water provider should be required to prepare and evaluate an adequate, site-specific emergency response plan as part of its operational plan. The overall municipal plan should be focused on assuring effective coordination with this site-specific water emergency response plan.

11.6.3.3 *Medical Officers of Health*

Because public health will always be a concern in a water emergency, the Medical Officer of Health must be a central player in the emergency response plan for any water provider. In particular, boil water advisories and boil water orders will be a key consideration in dealing with any water contamination episode.[77]

As I recommended in the Part 1 report of this Inquiry, the Public Health Branch of the Ministry of Health should develop a Boil Water Protocol in consultation with Medical Officers of Health, municipalities, and the MOE. This protocol should outline the circumstances in which a boil water advisory or a boil water

---

[77] There is a distinction between boil water advisories and boil water orders. A boil water advisory is generally issued by the Medical Officer of Health to advise consumers not to drink the water. A boil water order is issued by a Medical Officer of Health or a public health inspector to direct certain institutions to boil water before providing it to consumers, pursuant to the *Health Protection and Promotion Act*, R.S.O. 1990, c. H.7, s. 13.

order should be issued. It should also provide guidance as to an effective communications strategy for the dissemination of a boil water advisory or order.

In the spring of 2001, the Public Health Branch developed a draft boil water advisory protocol.[78] In reviewing the draft protocol, it would appear that it does not address the following issue that is integral to effective emergency response. The Boil Water Protocol should emphasize the importance of establishing an effective relationship among the water provider, the MOE, and the Medical Officer of Health in advance of any problems that might give rise to the need for a drinking water advisory. It is not possible to anticipate all possible adverse water quality conditions in advance. Therefore, effective communication and a common understanding of the water quality problem are important to assure the most effective public health response.

Municipal water providers must recognize the statutory obligations of the Medical Officer of Health to protect public health, while the Medical Officer of Health should recognize the benefit of informed discourse about water quality problems in forming a sound judgment about potential health risks. In most cases, close cooperation between the Medical Officer of Health, the water provider, and the MOE will allow for much more effective communication with the public. This cooperation, developed in advance of a crisis, is also of great importance where it becomes necessary to issue a boil water advisory. The Boil Water Protocol should address the need for this continued cooperation, including the need for water providers to develop guidelines relating to the issuance of boil water advisories, as discussed below.

Cooperation among the parties will be particularly important in cases that are not as clear as those in which there is a finding of *E. coli* or fecal coliforms in treated water. In these cases, sound judgment is required to determine the balance between failing to take action when it may be required and the issuance of false alarms that may lessen the credibility of future warnings. The communication among parties will be particularly important for cases of advisories for non-microbial contamination. For example, the proposal to issue an advisory to the public whenever any water quality parameter exceeds, by any margin, a maximum acceptable parameter concentration deserves more careful consideration.

---

[78] Ontario, Ministry of Health and Long-Term Care, 2001, "Protocol for the issuance of a boil water and a drinking water advisory (draft)" <www.gov.on.ca/health/english/pub/pubhealth/boil_water/boil_water_advisory.doc> [accessed April 15, 2002].

As stated above, the Medical Officer of Health cannot issue a boil water advisory effectively without cooperation from the water provider and the MOE. Without such cooperation there will inevitably be delays in action and decisions made on less complete information than should be available. Therefore, as part of an emergency response plan, water providers should develop a guideline relating to the issuance of boil water advisories and orders in cooperation with the local Medical Officer of Health and the local MOE office, based on the Boil Water Protocol developed by the Public Health Branch. The guideline should acknowledge the legal authority of the Medical Officer of Health to declare a boil water advisory, and should also outline the notification process, information exchange, and other procedural details to ensure that such advisories are issued as quickly and efficiently as possible, based on the best available information.

The guideline should also include a communications strategy between the water provider and the local Medical Officer of Health to ensure that the most effective means of informing consumers will be followed in the event of any drinking water emergency.

The importance of having a boil water protocol was illustrated in Sydney, Australia, in 1998. The Sydney water crisis provided a severe example of a major media event with considerable misinformation, largely because of an avoidable conflict between Sydney Water and the New South Wales Health Department over the interpretation of water quality monitoring results and the need for a boil water advisory. A subsequent Commission of Inquiry criticized the poor communications between the water provider and the health regulator.[79]

An interesting contrast was an incident in Edmonton, one year earlier during the spring of 1997, when *Cryptosporidium* cysts were detected in treated water by Edmonton's water provider, Epcor Water Services (named Aqualta at that time). In this case, there was a reasonable level of collaboration between Epcor Water Services and the Medical Officer of Health of the Capital Health Authority. As a result of this experience, a very detailed boil water protocol has been jointly developed by Epcor Water Services, the Capital Health Authority, and Alberta Environment. This protocol offers a useful template for

---

[79] P. McClellan, 1998, *Sydney Water Inquiry* (Sydney, Australia: New South Wales Premier's Department) <www.premiers.nsw.gov.au/pubs.htm> [accessed April 9, 2002].

coordination between Ontario municipal water providers, Medical Officers of Health, and the Ministry of Environment.[80]

11.6.3.4   *Public Information and Risk Communication*

The ability to communicate efficiently and effectively, especially during a crisis, is of critical importance. As mentioned in section 11.6.2.4, an emergency plan should clearly identify the responsibilities of a control group, including identification of the member who will take the lead with respect to communications. During a crisis, the members of the control group responsible for communications will need to provide ongoing and in-depth notification to several stakeholders including the medical community, media, consumers and the general public, and appointed or elected officials.[81]

Communications about risk are difficult to produce for a number of practical reasons related to the complexity and uncertainty that surrounds risk. Effective risk communication seeks to address these issues in the following ways. First, the public's communication needs about a specific set of risks (such as drinking water safety), and the information base available to the public, should be assessed periodically. Second, key messages should represent the latest consensus of expert knowledge on the subject. Third, technical terminology should be translated into clear language that is understandable to the public and free of ambiguity.

A number of steps can be taken to plan communications strategies before an emergency arises. These include: discussions between decision makers and the public about drinking water risks; the elaboration of standard operating procedures and training of key people in the case of emergency situations; the development of guidelines for communicating with the public; and periodic informal and personal contacts among experts, planners, decision makers, and the media.

In developing a communications strategy, a list of local and regional media should be compiled, including phone numbers and other contact information. The information should be given to municipal officials and the Medical Officer

---

[80] L. Gammie, D. Pelletier, and N. Fox, 2001, "Development of a Boil water emergency response plan for a water utility," proceedings at the 9th National Conference on Drinking Water, Regina, Saskatchewan, May 16–18, pp. 50–65.

[81] J. Mainiero, *Waterborne Gastrointestinal Disease Outbreak Detection* (Denver, CO: AWWA Research Foundation), pp. 39–47.

of Health, and should be updated at least annually. To protect public health, consumers need to receive, understand, and comply with a risk message. To communicate a risk message to the public effectively, several goals need to be achieved, including: rapid decision making to allow timely notification; rapid communication with a target audience; and avoidance measures to be undertaken. Although only the Medical Officer of Health has the authority to issue a boil water advisory, once this is done, others can be brought in to draw attention to the announcement.

The announcement itself must be simple, direct, and unqualified. It should describe the risk and provide information on what members of the public should do. If possible, the Medical Officer of Health should make the announcement. Elected representatives, such as mayors and councillors, should speak for themselves. Local media have a strong sense of community responsibility and like to pitch in with news coverage during a crisis. Sometimes officials are fearful of creating panic if they approach the media. There may be exceptions, but generally media will report on an emergency in a responsible way if given the information.

Chapter 12   The Certification and Training of Operators

Contents

Chapter 12   The Certification and Training of Operators

12. 1   Overview

There is no question that competent water operators are an essential element of a safe drinking water system. The evidence in Part 1 of the Inquiry pointed out the dangers of unqualified operators. The system now in place in Ontario satisfies many of the requirements in this area. Currently, the certification of operators is mandatory, and operators are required to receive continuous training. There is, however, room for improvement, and in this chapter I make several recommendations that I believe will achieve the goal of ensuring that water system operators are fully knowledgeable and capable of carrying out those tasks that are necessary to provide safe water to the communities they serve.

In 1993, the provincial government implemented mandatory certification. This is an essential component of a safe drinking water system. I specifically recommend its continuance. As well, I recommend that the use of grandparented operators – those experienced operators who were certified without examination – be phased out.

Regarding continuous operator training, I recommend that the Ministry of the Environment (MOE) consult with the drinking and wastewater industry to develop a curriculum focused on water safety and public health issues. Decisions regarding the number of hours of training and the content of the curriculum are best left to that consultation process. I also recommend that the government take steps to ensure that the necessary training is available for operators located in small and remote communities. Finally, I am of the view that the government should assist in the development of training materials and courses for water system operators.

12.2   Mandatory Certification

Recommendation 59: The Ministry of the Environment should continue to require the mandatory certification of persons who perform operational work in water treatment and distribution facilities. Education, examination, and experience are essential components of ensuring competence.

In June 1993, Ontario Regulation 435/93 was passed pursuant to section 75 of the *Ontario Water Resources Act*[1] and the certification of operators became mandatory. The administration of the certification program was transferred from the MOE to the Ontario Environmental Training Consortium (OETC).

The mandatory certification program for operators in Ontario seeks to

- provide safe drinking water to the residents of Ontario;

- ensure that operators have the required knowledge and experience to perform their duties safely and efficiently; and

- promote professionalism and establish and maintain standards for operators.[2]

Five provinces have established or are establishing mandatory operator certification requirements.[3] Many U.S. states have established mandatory certification for waterworks operators.

Each waterworks facility that is capable of supplying water for human consumption at a rate greater than 50,000 L daily must be classified into one of four classes. Classification is based on the complexity of the facility, its source water quality, and the size of the population it serves.

Ontario Regulation 435/93 requires operators to be certified for the class of facility in which they work. The owner must ensure that every operator holds the appropriate licence applicable to the class of facility. Copies of the licences of each operator are to be posted by the owner at the facility.[4]

An individual at the beginning of a career as a waterworks operator must obtain an operator-in-training licence. A Grade 12 education is required, and the operator-in-training must pass an examination. Table 12.1 outlines the education, experience, and examination requirements that must be fulfilled for each class of licence.[5]

[1] R.S.O. 1990, c. O.40.
[2] A. Castel, Assistant Deputy Minister, 1993, memorandum to the Honourable C.J. Wildman, June 16.
[3] B. Gildner, testimony, Walkerton Inquiry (Part 1 Hearing, June 7, 2001), transcript p. 60.
[4] O. Reg. 435/93, s. 9.
[5] See ibid., s. 2; and Ontario Environmental Training Consortium, 2002, *Water and Wastewater Operator Licensing and Facility Classification Program Guide* <www.oetc.on.ca/programguide.htm>.

Table 12.1 Licence Requirements for Waterworks Operators in Ontario

	Education	Experience	Exam	Other
Operator-in-training	Grade 12 or equivalent	N/A	70% on operator-in-training exam	Cannot be in charge of a facility
Class 1	Grade 12 or equivalent	1 year of experience	70% on class 1 exam	
Class 2	Grade 12 or equivalent	3 years of experience	70% on class 2 exam	Must hold a class 1 licence
Class 3	Grade 12 or equivalent + 2 years of additional education or training	4 years of experience with at least 2 years as "operator-in-charge"	70% on class 3 exam	Must hold a class 2 licence
Class 4	Grade 12 or equivalent + 4 years of additional education or training	4 years of experience with at least 2 years as "operator-in-charge"	70% on class 4 exam	Must hold a class 3 licence

Licences must be renewed every three years.[6] If the operator has not had experience operating a waterworks in the past five years, he or she is required to pass an examination as a condition of renewal of the licence.

As a result of the 1998 amendments to Ontario Regulation 435/93, a conditional licence can be granted if the owner of the facility cannot readily obtain the services of an operator licensed for that class of facility and undertakes to facilitate compliance with the conditions prescribed in the licence. This situation may occur if the facility's classification is upgraded, and the existing operators are not certified for that class of facility. A conditional licence may also be granted in small, isolated communities if an individual with proper qualifications is not available. The conditional licence is limited to the particular facility and is subject to the conditions prescribed by the director. It expires three years after it is issued, or earlier if that is specified in the licence.

Certification has three essential components: formal education, experience, and the successful completion of an examination. A formal education is necessary to ensure that the individual is literate, has problem-solving abilities, and possesses mathematical and other skills required to perform as an operator. In the past, people have been permitted to substitute training for a high school diploma. The successful completion of a high school diploma or equivalent education is a precondition to competency and should be enforced. Experience

---

[6] O. Reg. 435/93, s. 6(7).

is also important for the operator to know how to respond appropriately to a variety of operating conditions. Finally, passing an examination helps ensure that the operator has the knowledge required to carry out his or her duties.

The government should continue to require mandatory certification of persons who perform operational work in water treatment and distribution facilities. The requirements for education, examination, and experience, are essential components of competency.

The government should also ensure that the certification program is adequately funded and staffed and has the necessary resources to support the program.

In the past several years, the MOE's certification program, administered by the OETC, has not been self-supporting and has operated at a deficit. Between 1996 and 1999, for example, the average annual expenditure for the certification program was approximately $450,000. However, because revenues from applications for certification, renewals of licence, examination fees, and study materials have been approximately $275,000, the program has operated at an annual deficit of $175,000.[7] Although the MOE has made some monetary contributions to the program, it continues to operate at a deficit. Both the Association of Boards of Certification (ABC), an organization that provides resources and guidance to certification authorities in the United States and Canada, and the U.S. Environmental Protection Agency (U.S. EPA) take the position that governments must provide sufficient resources to adequately fund and sustain the operator certification program.[8]

Moreover, the Ontario certification program does not have an adequate number of staff, according to the ABC standards. Ontario has approximately 6,500 certified operators and 4,000 individuals who hold operator-in-training certificates. The Ontario certification program has five full-time staff. According to the ABC standards, the certification program in Ontario should have a staff of eight.[9]

---

[7] G. Samuel, for the Ontario Water Works Association and the Ontario Municipal Water Association, 2001, "Training and accreditation of water supply professionals," Walkerton Inquiry Submission, pp. 22–23.

[8] Ibid.

[9] Ibid.

12.3   Grandparented Operators

Recommendation 60: The Ministry of the Environment should require water system operators who currently hold certificates obtained through the grandparenting process to become certified through examination within two years, and it should require operators to be recertified periodically.

The MOE introduced a voluntary certification program for operators in the waterworks industry in 1987.[10] The purposes of certification were to impart the necessary knowledge and skills to operators in the performance of their duties, to assure the safety of drinking water in Ontario, to establish operator standards, and to promote professionalism.

The certification standards of the ABC, which included the three components of education, experience, and examination, were adopted by the Ontario government.[11] It was hoped that the licence would become the standard expectation of Ontario operators and that, as a result, operators would voluntarily seek certification and owners would gradually require employees to be licensed.

In support of the voluntary program, the provincial government in 1987 developed the "Water and Wastewater Utility Operator Certification Program Guidelines"[12] pursuant to the *Ontario Water Resources Act*. A grandparenting provision was included in the guidelines in section 14(4) which stated that the Ontario Advisory Board of Certification for operators of water and wastewater utilities

> may, at its discretion until April 1, 1990, waive the examination and/or education requirements for those operators who have demonstrated, through their past performance, their ability to operate, repair and maintain the utility, meet the experience requirements and have been recommended for certification by the owner or his representative.

The deadline for application was extended to October 1990.

---

[10] Gildner, testimony, p. 17; Samuel, p. 2.

[11] Samuel, pp. 2–3.

[12] The guidelines were dated February 9, 1987.

Pursuant to the voluntary grandparenting program, an operator who satisfied the experience requirements could receive a licence without writing the certification exam or satisfying the education requirement. The operator was eligible for the level of licence at which the facility in which he or she worked had been classified; for example, if the operator worked in a class 3 facility, he or she would receive a class 3 licence.

Initially, the licence obtained under the voluntary certification program was restricted to the facility in which the operator worked; it was not valid if the operator sought employment or was transferred to another facility. This restriction was removed in 1991 because of concern among stakeholders that it unduly restricted operators from working in other facilities, particularly in circumstances in which a municipality had several water treatment or wastewater treatment facilities.[13]

The grandparenting provision was included for a number of reasons. It was intended to serve as a transition provision in the move from a non-regulated to a regulated industry. The purpose of voluntary certification was to make the licence the standard expectation of operators and owners; it was hoped that new operators would voluntarily seek certification and that owners would gradually begin to require licensing as a condition of employment. Another purpose of the grandparenting provision was to allow experienced operators to maintain their employment. Finally, the provision was included to ensure that there would be a sufficient number of experienced operators to meet Ontario's demands once certification became mandatory.[14]

When the mandatory certification of operators was introduced in 1993, there was another opportunity to apply for certification under a grandparenting provision. The deadline was February 1, 1994. Again, the operator could receive a class of licence equal to the facility in which he or she worked without writing a certification exam. However, unlike the 1987 provision, the operator was required to successfully complete the exam in the three-year period in which his or her licence was renewed. If the operator did not pass the exam, his or her level of licence was lowered by one class.[15]

---

[13] Gildner, testimony, pp. 33–37.
[14] M. Christie, testimony, Walkerton Inquiry (Part 1 Hearing, June 7, 2001), transcript pp. 34–35.
[15] Gildner, testimony, pp. 49–51.

The requirement for writing an examination was applied differently for operators who had been grandparented in the 1987–90 period. These operators were not required to pass an examination as a condition of the renewal of their licences. They continued to be certified without ever having passed an examination. Approximately 5,000 licences were granted under the 1987 and 1993 grandparenting programs;[16] the Inquiry heard that a significant number of certified operators remain who have never been required to pass an examination.

Grandparenting makes a good deal of sense as a transitional measure when moving to a mandatory certification model. It ensures a continued supply of operators for water providers and avoids the prospect of abruptly terminating many long-standing employees. Several jurisdictions introduced the concept of grandparenting when they first established an operator certification program. Alberta had a provision for grandparenting when it introduced mandatory certification in 1993. Most U.S. states and all the other Canadian provinces except Quebec resorted to the concept of grandparenting in their voluntary certification programs.[17]

However, for reasons of public safety and to ensure that operators are properly qualified to carry out their duties, it is important that over time all Ontario operators be required to pass a certification examination. Individuals who were grandparented in the 1987–90 period should be required to successfully complete the qualifying examination. It has now been nearly 14 years since voluntary certification was first introduced, and nearly 9 years since certification was made mandatory in Ontario. It is time to move ahead. Efforts should be made to ensure that the examination process accommodates any study or exam-writing difficulties that long-standing employees may have. At the same time, efforts should be made to ensure that these employees have the knowledge required to protect public health and safety. This approach is in conformity with the guidelines of the United States Environmental Protection Agency, which require that within a specified time, grandparented operators meet all the requirements for certification.[18]

---

[16] Samuel, p. 3.

[17] Gildner, testimony, pp. 60–61.

[18] Ibid.; and United States Environmental Protection Agency, 1994, "Final Guidelines for the Certification and Recertification of the Operator of Community and Nontransient Noncommunity Public Water Systems" <www.epa.gov/ogwdw/opcert/opguide.html> [accessed May 6, 2002].

Requiring all operators in Ontario to successfully complete the certification exam will help ensure that these individuals have the knowledge, skills, and judgment to perform their jobs and in turn help ensure the safety of drinking water in the province. Operators who received licences under the voluntary grandparenting program should be required to meet the same standards as other certified operators.

It is also important that licences received under the grandparenting program be site-specific and non-transferable. If grandparented operators choose to work for another water system, they should be required to meet the certification requirements for that system. I note that the U.S. EPA also recommends that licences received under grandparenting be site-specific and non-transferable.[19]

12.4   New Operators

Recommendation 61: The Ministry of the Environment should require all applicants for an operator's licence at the entry level to complete a training course that has a specific curriculum to ensure a basic minimum knowledge of principles in relevant subject areas.

Individuals who wish to become operators of a water utility are required to have a high school diploma and pass an examination. Candidates prepare for the examination by obtaining materials from the OETC Web site or from other sources. At present, it is not necessary for a prospective operator to complete a training course that has a specific curriculum. It is possible for an individual to pass the certification exam with no knowledge of, or experience in, one or more specific subjects. Currently, training is required only after the individual has been certified.

The importance of acquiring information at the entry level in particular areas is essential for ensuring the safety of drinking water. For this reason, an entry-level mandatory training course should be developed to ensure that all certified operators have been exposed to, and have demonstrated knowledge of, the basic principles underlying the provision of safe drinking water. This course should include information on the treatment and monitoring of drinking water, the health risks associated with drinking water, the statutes and regulations pertinent to the protection of drinking water, the impact on public health of

---

[19] Gildner, testimony, p. 62; and U.S. EPA.

the failure to properly treat and monitor the water, and contingency or emergency procedures. After successfully completing the mandatory entry-level training course and the certification examination, operators-in-training should be "shadowed" by an experienced individual to ensure that they perform their duties correctly and safely.

12.5   The Training of Certified Operators

Recommendation 62: The Ministry of the Environment should develop a comprehensive training curriculum for operators and should consolidate the current annual training requirement in Ontario Regulation 435/93 and the proposed requirement of ministry-approved training into a single, integrated program approved by the Ministry of the Environment.

In the Part 1 report of this Inquiry, I made several recommendations regarding operator training. The above recommendation and the following discussion include the substance of those recommendations.

Section 17(1) of Ontario Regulation 435/93 requires the owner of a facility to take measures to ensure that each operator employed in the facility receives a minimum of 40 hours of training each year. The purpose of the annual training or professional development is to ensure that operators continuously refresh their skills and acquire knowledge about new developments in their field, remain aware of risks to public health, and understand the measures that must be taken in the event of an emergency. Section 17(2) of the regulation provides examples of types of training that may satisfy the 40-hour requirement, such as training in new or revised operating procedures, reviewing existing operating procedures, safety training, and studying information and acquiring technical skills related to environmental issues.

Several problems have arisen in the context of the 40 required hours of operator training. One problem is the broad description of "training" in the regulation. The definition of training is largely within the discretion of the owner of the facility. Evidence at the Part 1 hearings suggested that spending the entire 40 hours of training on workplace safety would not contravene the regulation.[20] There is currently no requirement that training focus on technical issues involving water treatment or human health, such as the significance of pathogens

---

[20] Gildner, testimony, pp. 160–161.

in drinking water. In addition, there is no requirement that training be tailored to the class of facility in which the operator works.

A further problem is that the Ontario government has inconsistently enforced this provision. For example, as was discussed in the Part 1 report of this Inquiry, operators of the Walkerton Public Utilities Commission did not receive the appropriate training. The manager and the foreman of the Walkerton waterworks did not take the required hours of training. Moreover, the training that they did take did not address water safety or public health issues. The manager considered training to include the time he spent with an MOE inspector in the 1998 inspection of the Walkerton facility as well as the explanation of the water system to a new employee.

The MOE is unaware whether operators in a facility are satisfying the requisite training hours from year to year; only during the three-year inspection of the facility do MOE officials generally verify whether the requirement of section 17(1) of the regulation has been met. Although section 17(4) states that owners shall provide copies of summaries of training records to the director "when requested to do so," this rarely occurs.

The government has proposed that Regulation 435/93 be amended to include a provision that requires an operator to obtain 36 hours of MOE-approved training every three years as a condition of licence renewal. It is the operator's responsibility to acquire the requisite number of hours of continuing education. A prescribed number of hours of annual continuing education is endorsed by both the Association of Boards of Certification and the United States Environmental Protection Agency.[21]

It is contemplated that the 36 hours of continuing education will consist of formal courses, that the courses will be taught by qualified instructors, and that operators will be tested or evaluated at the conclusion of the course. The continuing education courses must be approved by the government. The purpose of such a requirement is to ensure that operators are knowledgeable in such areas as the applicable statutory and regulatory provisions on drinking water, emerging pathogens, the importance of the treatment and monitoring of drinking water to public health, and the measures to be taken in the event of an emergency.

---

[21] Ibid., p. 228.

In my view, the MOE should develop a comprehensive training curriculum for each class of operator and consolidate the current training requirements in Ontario Regulation 435/93 with the proposal of MOE-approved continuing education for operators. It should prescribe the particular type of training required for class 1 to 4 operators. It should designate and approve both the courses that must be taken in the various subject areas and the number of hours of training required annually. The mandatory training program should focus on the protection of public health and the safety of drinking water systems and should prescribe the number of hours to be devoted to such issues as the risk of pathogens in water, the treatment and monitoring of drinking water, and measures designed to lessen risks to public health.

To ensure that the training requirements are met, the MOE should require that annual records be forwarded to them that specify the particular training taken by each operator at a facility. To facilitate the enforcement of mandatory training, the MOE should develop a standardized form that lists the name and position of operators who attended training sessions, the dates and duration of the sessions, and the subjects covered at each session. This will assist MOE officials and inspectors in assessing compliance with the training requirements.

12.6   The Training of Operators in Small and Remote Communities

Recommendation 63: The Ministry of the Environment should take measures to ensure that training courses are accessible to operators in small and remote communities and that the courses are tailored to meet the needs of the operators of these water systems.

Operators of water systems in small and remote communities must satisfy the annual 40-hour professional development requirement prescribed in section 17 of Ontario Regulation 435/93. It is also proposed that they should be obliged to fulfill the required hours of MOE-approved continuing education when this regulation comes into effect. A number of operators have not been fulfilling the 40-hour requirement stipulated in the regulation.[22] Travel to and from, and participation in, training courses may require operators to be away from their communities for several days. Those in small and remote communities

---

[22] E.E. Geldreich and J.E. Singley, 2002, "Ontario water suppliers: Two experts' assessments," Walkerton Inquiry Commissioned Paper 24, p. 5.

have difficulty obtaining the required training because few individuals are available to replace them during their absence from the facility. In addition, owners of such facilities have been reluctant to fund this training because of the cost of the courses, transportation, and accommodation.

It is important that training courses be accessible to operators in these communities and that courses be designed to address operator information and operational needs. In contrast to operators in large municipalities, who may perform a narrow range of tasks, operators in water systems in small communities are generally involved in all aspects of operating the system. Training courses should be developed to address the knowledge required to safely and efficiently operate these systems. CD-ROM training packages, video-teleconferences, and online courses, such as those that have been developed in the United States by the American Water Works Association and the Water Environment Federation, should be evaluated and, if suitable, introduced or developed to improve the access of operators in small and remote communities to continuous education and training courses.

12.7   Training Materials

The existence of good training materials for operators will help ensure the delivery of safe drinking water to the residents of Ontario. Some of the existing materials have been criticized for focusing on examination preparation rather than on job performance. It has also been said that some of the materials emphasize what must be done rather than providing reasons for following particular procedures. Training materials for each class of operator should be assessed to ensure that the necessary information is conveyed, and they should be updated continuously to reflect new statutory and regulatory provisions, discoveries of new pathogens and public health risks, new methods for treating and monitoring drinking water, and new technological developments.

12.8   Providing Quality Training Courses on Diverse Subjects

Recommendation 64: The Ministry of the Environment should meet with stakeholders to evaluate existing training courses and to determine the long-term training requirements of the waterworks industry. The ministry should play an active role in ensuring the availability of an array of courses on the subjects required to train operators.

Providing an adequate number of courses that offer quality training in various regions of Ontario is essential for ensuring that operators in the water industry have the requisite skills, knowledge, and judgment to perform their work. The provincial government was involved in training from the 1960s to the 1990s. This involvement has dissipated with the result that an insufficient number of quality courses are available to operators in Ontario. Neither the private sector nor community colleges have completely filled the void.[23]

The Ontario Water Resources Commission, the predecessor to the MOE, began to offer training courses to operators in 1959. Courses were further developed by the provincial government in the 1960s, and in 1970 a training centre was established in Brampton.[24] The courses at that time were primarily operational and were intended to impart information on the functioning of water systems.

As a result of the introduction of voluntary certification in 1987 and the anticipated need for more training courses, the MOE established the Ontario Environmental Training Consortium (OETC). The main purposes of the OETC were to increase training opportunities for operators in the province, to relieve pressure on the Brampton facility, and to create linkages between the MOE and community colleges.[25] A dual approach was endorsed: the MOE retained the training centre in Brampton, and community colleges offered courses to operators in other parts of the province.

Between 1974 and 1995, more than 17,600 people attended courses at the MOE training centre in Brampton. From 1990 to 1995, an additional 1,450 people participated in OETC courses offered through community colleges.[26] The OETC did not directly provide the training; rather, it served as an administrative or coordinating body for the community colleges. Sixteen colleges, from Thunder Bay to Ottawa, offered courses that were audited by the MOE. Drinking water specialists and MOE officials taught courses on various subjects, including water treatment, distribution systems, surface water, gas chlorination, hypochlorination, small water systems, and laboratory skills for plant operators.

---

[23] Samuel, p. 24.
[24] Gildner, testimony, p. 121.
[25] Samuel, p. 5.
[26] Gildner, testimony, p. 124.

Before 1990, the courses offered by the MOE were heavily subsidized. However, to ensure that the community colleges could provide the courses, the subsidy for the MOE courses was no longer available after 1990. The cost of training courses increased from approximately $60 to $500/$600, and many public utilities were unable or reluctant to absorb the course fees for operators in their facilities. Large municipalities began to develop their own training programs, and courses in the private sector became available. As a result, the number of operators enrolled in the courses decreased.[27]

In 1995, the Brampton MOE training centre was closed and the OETC stopped coordinating the courses offered by the community colleges. The MOE transferred the responsibility for the training of operators to the Ontario Clean Water Agency (OCWA). However, by 1999, the OCWA restricted its courses to its own staff, and municipal operators were precluded from attending the OCWA training courses.[28]

Some community colleges continue to offer courses based on demand. They do not, however, provide the array of courses previously available, when the OETC coordinated the program. Although private sector training does exist, the quality of some courses has been questioned. No process currently exists to systematically evaluate the quality of operator training courses offered in Ontario.

Although I do not consider it essential for the MOE to offer training courses directly to water system operators, the ministry should, in consultation with the industry, community colleges, and private sector training organizations, ensure that adequate courses are available. There is little point in requiring MOE-approved training for certified operators if the courses necessary to fulfill the requirement are not available.

On the subject of training, I received submissions from the Centre for Water Quality Committee (CWQC) regarding the establishment of a Walkerton Centre for Water Quality. One of the purposes of the centre would be to coordinate training for water system operators. In my view there is merit in a coordinating body and I suggest that the province examine carefully the proposal made by CWQC.

---

[27] Christie, testimony, p. 126; Gildner, testimony, pp. 128–129.
[28] Samuel, p. 6.

Chapter 13   The Provincial Government Role in Overseeing Drinking Water Systems

Contents

Chapter 13   The Provincial Government Role in Overseeing Drinking Water Systems

13.1   Overview

In this chapter I deal with the government's role in overseeing a safe drinking water system. The topic of government oversight was introduced in Chapter 2 with a summary of constitutional responsibilities, a review of the province's current approach to oversight, and a review of and comments on the recommendations regarding oversight made in the Gibbons Report.[1] The chapters following that introduction focused on the mechanics of the delivery of safe drinking water but included liberal reference to the oversight function. In this chapter I develop recommendations in respect of the oversight function as well as bring together oversight recommendations made in earlier chapters and in the Part 1 report of this Inquiry.

The intent of the recommendations in this area is to strengthen provincial oversight of water delivery systems. In the Part 1 report, I found several failures in the way the provincial government exercised its oversight role in relation to Walkerton and I made a number of specific recommendations to address those failures. Taken together, the recommendations in the two reports will, in my view, improve the quality of provincial policy and provide effective oversight across the province.

As to policy, I recommend that the government develop a comprehensive, source to tap, government-wide drinking water policy and that it enact a *Safe Drinking Water Act* embodying the important elements of that policy. I also propose that the Ministry of the Environment (MOE) be the lead ministry for the development and implementation of the policy.

I recommend that two new branches be created within the Ministry of the Environment. The first, the Watershed Management Branch, would be responsible for the oversight of the watershed-based planning process described in Chapter 4. It is important that the responsibilities of the provincial

---

[1] Executive Resource Group, 2001, *Managing the Environment: A Review of Best Practices* (Toronto) [hereafter Gibbons Report].

In reviewing the province's current approach to oversight, I relied heavily on the following: N. d'Ombrain, 2002, "Machinery of government for safe drinking water in Ontario," Walkerton Inquiry Commissioned Paper 4; J. Merritt and C. Gore, 2002, "Drinking water services: A functional review of the Ontario Ministry of Environment," Walkerton Inquiry Commissioned Paper 5.

government for watershed management be coordinated in one place where there is sufficient expertise to manage the process. This new branch would be responsible for developing the framework for watershed planning, participating in the locally based process for the development of plans, and approving draft plans. In the event that draft plans are not developed as required at the local level, this branch of the MOE would step in and take charge of the process. A dedicated centralized branch in the MOE should promote consistency in planning across the province and provide the necessary expertise and support to ensure that good plans are developed.

I also propose the establishment of a specialized Drinking Water Branch within the MOE responsible for the oversight of drinking water treatment and distribution systems. The skills and knowledge needed to regulate and oversee drinking water providers and systems differ significantly from those required to perform most of the other responsibilities of the ministry. Within this branch I recommend creating a new position, the Chief Inspector – Drinking Water Systems, responsible for the inspections program. I suggest that individual inspectors should have the same or higher qualifications as the operators of the systems they inspect. The Drinking Water Branch would assume oversight and responsibility for the proposed quality management accreditation program discussed above. The Drinking Water Branch would also be responsible for granting most approvals necessary for operating a drinking water system. I recommend a new form of approval – an owner's licence – that will collect in one set of documents all approvals and conditions which are necessary to operate a waterworks.

To date, the MOE has conducted investigations and prosecutions of those suspected of non-compliance with regulatory requirements through its Investigations and Enforcement Branch (IEB). I am satisfied that the IEB of the MOE should remain as presently constituted, a separate branch within the ministry. For the most part, it has worked well and, in my view, the necessary independence from inspections and abatement can be maintained without the need to establish a new agency outside the ministry. However, I do recommend that the new provincial policy on drinking water provide for strict enforcement of drinking water regulations and that it be equally applied to all municipal water systems in Ontario, whether they are run by OCWA, a municipality, or a private operator.

Finally, I urge the government to proceed with the proposed Integrated Divisional System and that it include in one database, or provide central access to, information related to source protection, each drinking water system in Ontario, and all data reasonably required by the drinking water branch and the local boards of health.

I discussed in some detail in the Part 1 report the budget reductions in the MOE. A number of the recommendations I make in this report will involve expenditures to ensure that the MOE is able to fully and effectively carry out its oversight role. It will be essential for the Province to provide sufficient resources, financial and otherwise, to implement these recommendations.

The chapter deals with the following topics: government policy, required legislative changes, required institutional and structural changes, the government's operations function, the role of ministries other than the Ministry of the Environment (MOE), the need for resource management, and transparency.

On the issue of government oversight of treatment facilities, my focus in this chapter is on water treatment and I do not devote much discussion to sewage and wastewater treatment. Although sewage treatment is an important element of source protection and is discussed in that context in Chapter 4, I do not interpret my mandate as including the management and oversight of sewage and wastewater treatment facilities. Nevertheless, there are obvious similarities in both management and oversight between water treatment and sewage treatment facilities, and much of what is set out below in regard to government oversight of water treatment has application to sewage treatment as well.

13.2   Government Policy

13.2.1 Current Practice

One of the most common submissions I heard from the parties who participated in Part 2 of this Inquiry was that the provincial government needed to develop a comprehensive policy covering all aspects of drinking water oversight from source protection through to the return of treated wastewater to the environment.

A number of parties expressed the view that prior to the tragedy in Walkerton, the government did not have a coherent and comprehensive drinking water policy that linked all elements of the drinking water system. It was argued that, while the absence of a coherent policy was a general problem, the most significant deficiency is the absence of a clear link between source protection and safe drinking water. Although the government recognizes that these two areas are interrelated, government policies dealing with each have not been integrated. I agree with the need for a comprehensive drinking water policy.

Even the government's policy relating to source protection is fragmented in that source protection from contamination due to agriculture is, to a significant extent, carved out of the rest of the province's environmental protection regime and treated differently. Illustrations of this separation include exemptions from environmental prohibitions on the basis that an activity is a "normal farm practice," as well as the fact that the environmental regulation of farms is overseen by the Ontario Ministry of Agriculture, Food and Rural Affairs (OMAFRA) and not the MOE.

Fragmentation is also evident in relation to drinking water treatment and distribution. For example, as the inquiry into the events in Walkerton showed, there was confusion as to what the respective roles of the MOE and the local Medical Officer of Health should be in responding to adverse test results, or to deficiencies found during an MOE inspection.[2]

Although the provincial government has toughened regulations and enforcement and committed more resources to drinking water safety since the Walkerton tragedy, there is still little evidence of the emergence of a coherent and comprehensive safe dinking water policy or strategy. A similar observation was made in the Gibbons Report, where it was recommended that the MOE develop a high-level, government-wide vision with respect to its regulation of the environment in general.[3] In my view, the point is also applicable to the narrower issue of drinking water safety.

---

[2] See Ontario, Ministry of the Attorney General, 2002, *Report of the Walkerton Inquiry, Part 1: The Events of May 2000 and Related Issues* (Toronto: Queen's Printer). See also section 13.6.1 of this chapter.

[3] Gibbons Report, Executive Summary, pp. 3–4.

13.2.2 Recommendations and Comments

13.2.2.1   *Comprehensive "Source to Tap" Drinking Water Policy*

Recommendation 65: The provincial government should develop a comprehensive "source to tap" drinking water policy covering all elements of the provision of drinking water, from source protection to standards development, treatment, distribution, and emergency response.

It is appropriate that my first recommendation with respect to government oversight relate to the development of a comprehensive policy because in my view, the necessary first step in achieving safe drinking water is to develop a government strategy or policy for doing so.[4] Such a strategy must identify all elements of the drinking water delivery process, develop and set out an approach to each element, and assign responsibility for each element. The main elements of the drinking water process are the barriers that have been discussed in this report: source protection, treatment, monitoring, distribution, and emergency response. All of these elements should be supported by the clear assignment of responsibility, competent operators and management, and effective regulation and provincial oversight.

This report can be viewed as a recommended framework for such a comprehensive policy. However, in this regard it should be seen as the beginning rather than the end of the policy-making process. Many details remain to be worked out. I discuss the policy-making process further under Recommendation 66.

Once developed, the government's strategy should, to the extent possible, be codified into a policy manual. Codification of the policy serves a number of useful functions. First, it helps to ensure consistency. A policy set out in clear language helps avoid the inconsistency in application that often arises from vague concepts. Second, it serves an educational and motivational function. The policy should be set out in a way that will motivate employees and should become required reading for all management personnel involved in the system.

---

[4] In defining policy, d'Ombrain states at p. 127: "Governments require a capacity to identify the character and scope of their responsibilities and the means of carrying them into effect. This is the policy function and must be present within government and capable of providing the coordination necessary to fulfill government-wide responsibilities and to develop appropriate legislation."

Codification of the policy also enhances the transparency of the government oversight function in that it informs interested members of the public what the government's overall approach and strategy is intended to be. This is not to say that every last detail of the government's oversight function needs to be set out on paper. It is possible to become overly prescriptive, which would not be helpful. What I envision is a document that sets out the government's goals and approach to safe drinking water with reference to the five barriers as well as to the principles of clear responsibility, competent operators and management, effective regulation, and provincial oversight.

13.2.2.2   *The Leadership Role of the Ministry of Environment*

Recommendation 66: The Ministry of the Environment should be the lead ministry responsible for developing and implementing the "source to tap" Drinking Water Policy.

Many ministries and agencies in the provincial government play a role in matters that are related to drinking water. In addition to the MOE, other entities include the Ministry of Health and Long-Term Care (Ministry of Health); local medical health offices; the Ministry of Agriculture, Food and Rural Affairs (OMAFRA); the Ministry of Natural Resources (MNR); and the Ministry of Municipal Affairs and Housing (MMAH). Although it is appropriate for a variety of ministries and agencies to play a role, it is in my view important that prime responsibility reside in a single lead ministry. A lead ministry will greatly assist in the development of a uniform comprehensive drinking water policy. The lead ministry's primary role should be to coordinate government efforts in enforcing and implementing the drinking water policy and to serve as the focus of accountability for the performance of the policy.[5]

Two plausible candidates exist for the leadership role in relation to drinking water: the MOE and the Ministry of Health. Upon initial consideration, the Ministry of Health emerges as a good choice. The safety of drinking water is associated in the public's mind with the maintenance of public health in the province. In some jurisdictions, the lead role in drinking water safety has been given to a health ministry or department.[6] Even in Ontario, safe drinking water

---

[5] For a further discussion of the importance of leadership as well as the Ontario government's current approach, see d'Ombrain, pp. 126–131, 137–143.

[6] See ibid., p. 140, and the brief discussion of the approaches taken in New York and California. Drinking water initiatives in the Canadian federal government are also led by the health department.

grew out of the health function; not until the 1970s and the creation of the MOE did responsibility begin to shift.[7]

The other possible choice for the leadership role is the MOE, the current leader by default. I recommend that the leadership role be expressly assigned to the MOE. My recommendation is based partly on the fact that the Ministry of Health would not be an ideal choice. First, the Ministry of Health has since the 1970s had only a relatively minor (albeit important) role to play in the drinking water process. It would be a dramatic change to shift responsibility for the whole process. One of the principles to which I have attempted to adhere in making my recommendations in this Inquiry is to make major institutional changes only if necessary and only if clear benefits outweigh the inevitable substantial costs. The MOE has historically had a substantial involvement in drinking water. Although it has had problems in performing this role, I believe they can be resolved.

A second reason for not choosing the Ministry of Health is that it already has a number of important and sometimes controversial matters within its responsibility. Especially in view of the difficulties with our drinking water system, it is critical that lead responsibility go to a ministry that can devote substantial attention to it. Given the current public focus on health care in general, I believe that the MOE is more likely to be able to devote substantial attention to this issue. Finally, I think it is beneficial that the MOE also has a historical connection with source protection. This underscores the importance of source protection to ensuring safe drinking water.

In supporting a leadership role for the MOE, I am not recommending a continuation of the status quo. In my view, although the MOE may have been the leader by default up to the present, it has not performed the role particularly well. For it to be effective, the government must clearly and unequivocally identify the MOE as the lead ministry and must give it the mandate to develop policy beyond its present regulatory and operational reach. As I have noted in Chapter 4, this includes a mandate to influence issues that have traditionally been within the purview of OMAFRA, MMAH, and MNR. The MOE also requires adequate resources to carry out this mandate.

---

[7] Ibid., p. 140. See also J. Benidickson, 2002, "Water supply and sewage infrastructure in Ontario, 1880–1990s: Legal and institutional aspects of public health and environmental history," Walkerton Inquiry Commissioned Paper 1.

13.2.2.3   *The Role of Other Ministries*

By recommending a leadership role for the MOE, I do not suggest that it alone should handle all aspects of the government's drinking water policy. In regard to the development, review, and implementation of the policy, it is critical that the MOE consult with other ministries and stakeholders. As noted earlier in this section, issues relating to drinking water affect and will continue to affect a number of ministries. Even in areas where I have recommended a change in responsibilities, consultation with the original ministry may nonetheless be advisable. A good example of this is OMAFRA. Although I have recommended that most elements of the environmental regulation of agriculture be moved from OMAFRA to the MOE, OMAFRA should continue to be consulted and have significant input into the development of a drinking water policy.[8]

Consultation with other governments will also be important. For example, in certain areas, including source protection, consultation with the federal government – which exercises considerable jurisdiction over environmental matters – is clearly necessary. Consultation with the federal government will also be necessary in regard to standard setting.

Of particular importance to issues relating to drinking water is consultation with municipalities. Virtually all aspects of a drinking water policy will have some impact upon municipalities. During the Part 2 expert meetings and public hearings, the Association of Municipalities of Ontario (AMO), the Ontario Water Works Association (OWWA)/Ontario Municipal Water Association (OMWA), and Conservation Ontario all agreed that there needs to be more consultation between the provincial government, municipalities, and conservation authorities. AMO, in particular, argued that as a result of a combination of cost-cutting and downloading, municipalities were left with responsibilities that they had no clear idea how to fulfill. It is essential that the relationship between the province and municipalities, as it relates to safe drinking water, be cooperative and non-confrontational. Municipal involvement in the

---

[8] Although I do not consider it to be part of my mandate to dictate to government who within a ministry should be consulted, I support OPSEU's recommendation that consultation should include front-line staff. From my experience in this Inquiry, I can state that I found the perspective of front-line staff, as represented by OPSEU and the Canadian Union of Public Employees (CUPE), to be helpful in advancing my understanding of the issues. Ontario Public Service Employees Union, 2001, "Submissions concerning recommendations about provincial government operations and resources (Public Hearings 2 and 3)," Walkerton Inquiry Submission, pp. 20–22.

development of the province's policy will help to promote a healthy working relationship.

Finally, consultation should also take place with other parties that have an interest in any element of the policy. They include land users (including farmers), water systems operators, and the public, in its important role of drinking water consumer.

13.3 Required Legislative Changes

Certain legislative changes will be necessary to effect my recommendations. In making changes to legislation, I have also attempted to simplify the legislative and regulatory regime.

13.3.1 Current Practice

A number of existing Acts and regulations affect the safety of drinking water. I have set out the existing legislative framework in Chapter 2 of this report and have discussed the most significant pieces of legislation in those chapters to which they are relevant.[9]

A number of parties submitted that the volume of legislation in relation to drinking water safety can lead to confusion. For example, the Canadian Environmental Law Association (CELA) suggested that the legislation and regulatory provisions that relate to drinking water "are scattered across a number of different statutes and regulations that are administered by different Ministries, agencies or institutions whose mandates, resources, and degrees of expertise in drinking water matters vary greatly."[10] To rectify this situation, CELA recommended that all regulations relating to drinking water safety (or at least as many as is reasonably possible) be put into a single *Safe Drinking Water Act*. It went further in recommending that a single commission, under a drinking water commissioner, be responsible for administering the new Act.

---

[9] These include the *Environmental Protection Act*, the *Ontario Water Resources Act*, the *Farming and Food Production Protection Act*, the *Planning Act*, and the *Municipal Act*.

[10] Canadian Environmental Law Association, 2001, "Tragedy on tap: Why Ontario needs a Safe Drinking Water Act," vol. 2, Walkerton Inquiry Submission, p. 95.

I agree with many of CELA's very helpful comments, although I am not in complete agreement with all the recommendations made. There are advantages to including all legislation relating to drinking water in a single Act. Questions could be answered by looking at a single source, and the potential for conflict among statutes and lack of clarity would be reduced. A single Act would help to underscore the notion of a uniform "source to tap" drinking water policy. It would also raise the profile of, and help to maintain the priority of, drinking water safety.

On the other hand, drinking water covers a broad range of factors. Some of these factors, while important to drinking water safety, also have much wider ramifications. A good example is my recommendation of watershed-based source protection planning. As I discuss in Chapter 4 of this report, it makes sense to do such planning in the context of province-wide watershed management planning. If implemented, such plans will be a very important element of the first barrier in a safe drinking water system – source protection. However, they also potentially have a much broader impact on environmental regulation in general. Although I have not dealt with the details of watershed management plans beyond the needs of drinking water protection, I recognize that such plans could form the basis for virtually all environmental regulation of water. For this reason they are probably most effectively dealt with in general environmental legislation such as the *Environmental Protection Act* (EPA).

While I do not believe that it is practical to have a single Act covering all matters related to drinking water, I do recommend some consolidation and simplification. Legislation related to drinking water, as well as virtually all of the recommendations in my report, should be put into four pieces of legislation, together with relevant regulations thereunder: a new *Safe Drinking Water Act*, containing provisions dealing with the treatment and distribution of drinking water; amendments to the EPA and regulations thereunder, containing provisions necessary to bring my source protection recommendations into effect; an act or regulation dealing with drinking water protection on farms; and an Act governing asset management in relation to municipal water systems.

13.3.2 Recommendations and Comments

13.3.2.1   Safe Drinking Water Act

Recommendation 67: The provincial government should enact a *Safe Drinking Water Act* to deal with matters related to the treatment and distribution of drinking water.

The purpose of the *Safe Drinking Water Act* (SDWA) is to gather in one place all legislation and regulation relating to the treatment and distribution of drinking water. As such, it should include those matters in the *Ontario Water Resources Act* (OWRA) and in my recommendations relating to treatment and distribution. Most of my recommendations for inclusion in the SDWA are dealt with in detail elsewhere in this report and, in those cases, I set out below only a general description of the subject matter to be included. In a few cases, a subject is introduced for the first time and, as a result, is discussed in greater detail.

Recognition that the Public Is Entitled to Expect that the Drinking Water Coming Out of Their Taps Is Safe

Certain parties have urged that I create a new statutory cause of action for safe drinking water. The cause of action would enable a member of the public to take the government to court for breaches of a right to safe drinking water. I have considered this issue very carefully and decided against the creation of a right. Instead, I recommend that the SDWA include recognition that people in the province are entitled to expect their water to be safe[11] and that there be a legislative and regulatory scheme put in place to ensure its safety. In my view, this is the ultimate goal of the drinking water system, and it is important to recognize this goal in one of the central pieces of legislation on the subject.

I have carefully chosen the words "entitled to expect" to convey the notion that it is reasonable for all those in Ontario to expect that the government will do all it reasonably can to support a safe drinking water system, *but without* creating a new substantive right. Safe drinking water is clearly a necessity of life, and it is trite to say that a healthy population could not exist without it. It is, however,

---

[11] As set out in Chapter 3 of this report, "safe" in this context means that the level of risk associated with drinking water is so minimal that a reasonable and informed person would feel safe drinking the water. See also the discussion under "Standards" in Chapter 5 of this report.

not the only such necessity. Other examples include clean air, sufficient food, and shelter. Although it can be said that the public is entitled to expect the government to take reasonable steps to ensure fair access to each of these basics, they have not, generally, been the subject of substantive rights.

To date, governments have accepted the entitlement of citizens to expect the provision of basics. Citizens may express their views on a government's success or failure to meet such expectations at the ballot box. Although governments are not always perfect in advancing such matters, I do not detect a need for the declaration of a right. This is not a situation akin to human rights or civil liberties, in which there are concerns about the tyranny of the majority. Almost all members of the public have the same interest in safe drinking water.

I am satisfied that the existing causes of action, such as negligence, nuisance, and breach of statutory duty, provide sufficient access to the courts to compensate those who suffer damages from consuming unsafe drinking water. In my view, the primary tools for ensuring the safety of drinking water lie in protecting water sources, managing water systems competently, and regulating those systems effectively. I do not think that creating new routes of access to the courts is the most effective way to advance these goals. Indeed, I would be concerned that a significant increase in legal actions would divert money and time away from those activities that are better able to address the safety of drinking water.

Identification of a Lead Ministry for the Purposes of the *Safe Drinking Water Act*

I think that it is important that the SDWA identify a lead ministry. For the reasons set out above in my discussion on government policy, the MOE should be designated as the lead ministry for the purpose of the SDWA and for the development and implementation of the province's drinking water policy.

Owner's Licences

As discussed in Chapter 11 and section 13.5.1.2, the provincial government should require water system owners to obtain licences. In order to obtain a licence, an owner will have to have a Certificate of Approval for the facility, a

Permit to Take Water, an approved operational plan, an approved financial plan, and an accredited operator. The concept of a licence and its elements should be set out in the SDWA.

Standard of Care

The SDWA should include the standard of care to be applied to those who exercise the municipal oversight functions, which is discussed in Chapter 10.

Approvals

The SDWA should set out the requirement for Certificates of Approval, Permits to Take Water, and operational plans in accordance with the recommendations and comments I have made in both this report and the Part 1 report of this Inquiry.[12]

Operating Agencies

In regard to operating agencies of municipal water systems, the SDWA should:

- set out a requirement that by a date to be fixed, all operating agencies of municipal treatment and distribution systems be accredited;

- require the promulgation of regulations that designate a body to design and oversee an accreditation system, set out certain minimum standards for the accreditation system (regarding classes of operator, biannual audits, and so on), and provide for government oversight of the process; and

- require that contracts with external operating agencies be made public.

Certification and Training of Operators

The SDWA should set out, or authorize regulations setting out, the

---

[12] See the Part 1 report of this Inquiry, section 9.2. See also Part 2 of this report, Chapter 11 and section 13.5.1.

recommendations I make in Chapter 12 relating to the certification and training of operators.

Standard Setting

In respect of standard setting, the SDWA should:

- provide for the creation of an advisory council on standards; and

- require regulations setting out standards for drinking water quality.

I have recommended in relation to drinking water quality standards (Chapter 5) and elsewhere that there be a requirement or authority for making regulations. In making this recommendation, I am mindful of the submissions of some parties that as much of the regulatory detail as possible be set out in the SDWA itself.[13] The rationale for this submission is that legislation is more difficult for a government to change, and therefore less likely to be interfered with, should the government's financial position deteriorate. Although certain elements of the government's strategy (e.g., drinking water quality standards) should have the force of law and consequently should be more than guidelines or objectives,[14] it is not always practical to set them out in legislation. In the case of drinking water quality standards, for example, the ever-expanding scope of knowledge and understanding regarding pathogens and other contaminants makes it likely that the standards will have to be amended regularly. This is much more easily accomplished in a regulation.

The contents of a standards regulation, including a critique of Ontario Regulation 459/00, are discussed in some detail in Chapters 6 and 7.

Treatment, Distribution, and Monitoring

The SDWA should require regulations setting treatment, distribution, and monitoring requirements for both municipal and private drinking water systems as discussed in Chapters 6, 7, 8, and 14 of this report. The SDWA (or the

---

[13] See, for example, Canadian Environmental Law Association.

[14] For example, prior to August 2000, the Ontario Drinking Water Objectives (ODWO) did not have the force of law.

relevant regulations passed pursuant to it) should clearly define the systems to which it applies. The SDWA should also set out the criteria and procedure for obtaining a variance in respect of treatment or monitoring standards as discussed in Chapter 14.[15]

Laboratories

The SDWA (or the relevant regulation passed pursuant to it) should set out requirements dealing with government oversight of environmental laboratories as I discuss in Chapter 9.

Inspections

In regard to inspections, the SDWA should:

- create the Office of Chief Inspector – Drinking Water Systems;

- set out a requirement that if in the course of an inspection or an accreditation audit a deficiency is found, a follow-up inspection must take place within one year;

- require regulations dealing with the frequency of inspections and the actions required and response time in the event of a deficiency; and

- authorize regulations for various abatement tools.[16]

My comments on the inspection function are discussed in detail later in this chapter.

Enforcement

In regard to investigations and enforcement, the SDWA should:

---

[15] See Recommendation 82.
[16] See the discussion in section 13.5.3.

- maintain the investigation and enforcement function in a separate Investigation and Enforcement Branch (IEB) of the MOE; and

- authorize regulations regarding procedures and protocols for investigations and enforcement.[17]

I also deal with enforcement in greater detail below.

13.3.2.2   *Amendments to the* Environmental Protection Act

Recommendation 68: The provincial government should amend the *Environmental Protection Act* to implement the recommendations regarding source protection.

As noted above, it makes sense to separate the source protection function from the treatment and distribution function for the purpose of legislation. For this reason, I would take the source protection provisions currently in the *Ontario Water Resources Act* (OWRA) and put them in the *Environmental Protection Act* (EPA). I do not see how the OWRA provisions add much to what is already in the EPA. Consequently, it may not be necessary to duplicate all provisions.

The EPA should also be amended to bring the watershed-based source protection planning process I recommend in Chapter 4 into being. This will include provisions that:

- empower the conservation authorities to oversee the creation of draft watershed-based source protection plans;

- make watershed-based source protection plans mandatory and require the Watershed Management Branch (discussed later in this chapter) to develop the plans where a conservation authority is unwilling or unable to do so;

- require MOE approval of all watershed-based source protection plans;

- set out the legal effect of watershed-based source protection plans; and

---

[17] See the discussion in section 13.5.4.

- authorize regulations regarding process, including parties that have a right to be involved in the process.

These provisions are dealt with in detail in Chapter 4. I also note my comments in Chapter 4 that a legislative review be undertaken to ensure the effective implementation of the watershed-based source protection plan concept. The goal of this review should be to eliminate inconsistency and ensure that the tools needed to implement the scheme are available.

13.3.2.3   *Agriculture*

In Chapter 4, I make a number of recommendations concerning source protection and agricultural operations including minimum standards for farming operations and individual farm water protection plans. The legislative provisions necessary to effect these recommendations could be included in the EPA. As discussed in Chapter 4, they could also be included in the proposed *Nutrient Management Act*, so long as the scope of that proposed legislation is broadened sufficiently to cover the recommendations. Any such legislation should be included within the authority of the MOE.

13.3.2.4   *Asset Management*

As discussed in Chapters 2 and 10 of this report, the provincial government has introduced a *Sustainable Water and Sewage Systems Act* to deal with asset management and cost recovery. I strongly support the implementation of asset management and full-cost recovery plans in relation to drinking water treatment and distribution systems.[18] I had originally envisioned that the oversight responsibility for such activities would reside in the MOE (with legislation and regulations contained in or under the SDWA). Upon reflection, it may well be appropriate for financial plans to be approved by the Ministry of Municipal Affairs and Housing (MMAH), which has historically had a close relationship with municipalities and greater experience with municipal financial affairs. Given my recommendation that water system owners obtain a licence for their water systems from the MOE[19] and that an asset management plan and a full-cost recovery plan (now to be approved by MMAH) is a requirement

---

[18] Although I do not deal with sewage treatment extensively in this report, such plans would be of obvious merit in that area as well.

[19] See Chapter 10 and Recommendation 71.

of such a licence, I am satisfied that the MOE retains sufficient involvement in the process.[20] Since the provincial government currently envisions the asset management process is to be managed by MMAH, it makes sense that a separate Act be created.

13.4   Government Structure

In this section I recommend changes to government structure that will, in my view, help to improve the government's oversight function.

13.4.1 Current Practice

As discussed in Chapter 2, the government oversight function is currently carried out primarily within the MOE. I will not repeat the details of the structure here except to note that it was the product of a reorganization in 1998. The philosophy of that reorganization was to organize around three broad functions: "Plan, Do/Deliver, and Measure." The planning and policy function takes place within the Integrated Environmental Planning Division, which is divided into three branches: land use, air, and water. The "Do/Deliver" function takes place within the Operations Division. For the purpose of safe drinking water, relevant branches within this division include the Investigations and Enforcement Branch, the Environmental Assessment and Approvals Branch, and the Spills Action Centre. As noted in Chapter 2, the Operations Division is divided into five geographic regions, which are in turn responsible for the district offices and area offices within the region. The regions are involved in a broad range of activities, including dealing with complaints, public education, abatement, and inspections. A third function relevant to drinking water that is performed by the MOE – measurement – includes setting standards, testing, research, and monitoring financial performance. This function includes the Environmental Sciences and Standards Division, which includes the Laboratory Services Branch, the Environmental Monitoring and Reporting Branch, the Standards Development Branch, and the Environmental Partnerships Branch.

From the perspective of creating an ideal safe drinking water system, the difficulty with the current structure is that it does not focus directly on drinking

---

[20] Note as well my recommendation that the MOE, because of its technical expertise in water systems, be required to approve any provincial funding.

water issues.[21] The MOE has a broad mandate and is responsible for many issues other than safe drinking water. The current structure is not designed to avoid losing drinking water issues "in the crowd." While the move away from a media-based approach that was intended by the 1998 reorganization may have achieved certain efficiencies, it has also had a cost, in the form of less focused attention on particular areas, such as drinking water. This lack of focus allowed government functions relating to drinking water to slip down – and eventually off – the priority list. It allowed a situation to develop in which inspections occurred less frequently than they should have, and in which follow-up was not done. A safe drinking water system is of sufficient importance to merit more focus.

Importantly, the expertise required to oversee and regulate the safety of drinking water is often quite different from that involved in carrying out other MOE functions. For example, the knowledge and experience required to oversee water treatment, monitoring, distribution, and the competent management of a water system are different from the knowledge and expertise needed to prevent the contamination of the natural environment. As it is now, MOE officers who are responsible for inspections, abatement, and enforcement are asked to perform both functions.

A number of parties submitted to me that it would be helpful to create a drinking water commission that would have a semi-autonomous existence outside of the MOE and would be responsible for the government oversight of the treatment and distribution functions.[22] It was argued that the advantages of an independent commission include: the ability to focus solely on drinking water issues, free from the distractions of the other demands of the MOE, a greater likelihood that there will be a uniform comprehensive approach to drinking water safety, and the separation (to some extent), of drinking water issues from the political influences of the day.[23]

I agree that increased focus and greater uniformity are desirable goals. I also recognize that benefits arise from separation from the political sphere. In addition, as I set out in the Part 1 report, the MOE has in the past not done a particularly good job of overseeing the drinking water system in Ontario.

---

[21] As noted in the Part I report of this Inquiry, there was evidence that in May–June 1995, senior managers in the Operations Division were polled and responded that communal water was not a core program of the MOE. It was clear that there was not much focus on drinking water.

[22] I note that none of the parties advocated an equivalent entity for source protection.

[23] Canadian Environmental Law Association, pp. 109–111.

However, I have decided not to recommend a separate commission. Although drinking water is critically important to the quality of life in Ontario, it is no more important than such things as clean air, land, and food. Strong arguments can be made for the special status of other "needs." If a water commission were to be seen as the beginning of a trend for ways of dealing with important needs of the population, the structure of government could be changed dramatically.

In addition, the other effect of increased independence from political influence which has been advocated by some parties, is a decrease in political accountability. If responsibility is passed on to a commission, the government will find it easier to deflect blame when something goes wrong. So long as processes are in place to promote transparency, political accountability can be a powerful democratic tool.

As I develop below, I am satisfied that the focus and expertise that would result from a dedicated entity such as a commission can be achieved by the creation of a new separate Drinking Water Branch in the MOE.

13.4.2 Recommendations and Comments

13.4.2.1   *Drinking Water Branch*

Recommendation 69: The provincial government should create a Drinking Water Branch within the Ministry of the Environment to be responsible for overseeing the drinking water treatment and distribution system.

The Drinking Water Branch should perform almost all of the drinking water treatment and distribution functions currently performed by the MOE. The only exception is the enforcement function, which should remain in a separate Investigations and Enforcement Branch.[24] The functions of the Drinking Water Branch would include:

• assisting in developing drinking water policy;

• developing and maintaining sufficient technical expertise, including access to outside expertise, to enable the branch to effectively oversee the regulation of drinking water treatment and distribution;

---

[24] This is discussed in detail in section 13.5.4 below.

- participating in drinking water standards development and implementation;

- granting approvals for water takings and for municipal water systems;

- issuing owner's licences for municipal water systems;

- monitoring the accreditation program for operating agencies;

- performing inspection and abatement duties;

- carrying out emergency response; and

- providing public education.

I recognize that a separate branch focused solely on drinking water goes against the recent trend toward a multi-media approach at the MOE. I further recognize that a multi-media approach results in certain efficiencies that will not be available to the branches I recommend. On the other hand, the creation of a Drinking Water Branch results in a number of advantages that outweigh any disadvantage.[25]

The first advantage is that the creation of this branch increases the profile of drinking water within the government. The existence of a branch, the sole focus of which is drinking water, will help ensure that drinking water safety does not fade into the background when other competing issues begin to demand the attention of the senior public servants or the minister.

Second, this branch can be very useful in maintaining accountability. A branch that is assigned the responsibility of drinking water safety will help to eliminate confusion about who is responsible for what. However, since the branch remains under the direct authority of the minister, direct political accountability remains intact as well. This is to be contrasted with a commission or other arm's-length entity that enables the government of the day to be shielded to some extent from responsibility.

---

[25] I note as well that the concept of a Drinking Water Branch and a Watershed Management Branch received widespread support from the parties in Part 2. I invited all participants to comment on the concept and received no negative comments.

Finally, a branch is conducive to the formation and maintenance of an expertise in drinking water safety. I have noted that the government's level of expertise in matters of drinking water safety must be increased. For example, I recommend in Recommendation 73 that water treatment plant inspectors should have qualifications that are the same as or better than those of water treatment plant operators. This leads to the development of a team of inspectors dedicated to treatment plants.

The need for the development of a body of expertise goes well beyond inspections. Even in areas where the relevant function, such as accreditation, will be carried out by entities outside of the provincial government it is in my view essential that the MOE have sufficient expertise to be able to effectively monitor and evaluate the system. The need for expertise within the MOE will be particularly great during the transition period between the present and the final implementation of the new quality management system that I have recommended. During this period, municipalities will be faced with very important decisions, such as whether to combine their systems with those of other municipalities and whether to contract out the operation of their systems or to seek accreditation themselves. In my view, it is very important that they be given assistance and guidance in respect of these decisions.[26]

In summary, in my view the provision of safe drinking water is a function of sufficient importance to warrant a separate branch. The specific contents of the functions listed in the recommendations are dealt with elsewhere in this report.

13.4.2.2   *Watershed Management Branch*

Recommendation 70: The provincial government should create a Watershed Management Branch within the Ministry of the Environment to be responsible for oversight of watershed-based source protection plans and, if implemented, watershed management plans.

In Chapter 4, I recommend the implementation of watershed-based source protection plans and also endorse the concept of watershed planning generally.

---

[26] The development of a body of expertise within the Drinking Water Branch does not mean that the branch should do it all alone. As noted elsewhere in this report, I encourage the MOE to make use of expertise that exists elsewhere, including at universities and within organizations such as the OWWA, the OMWA, and the AWWA.

I did not make a recommendation for the implementation of watershed management plans because I recognize that they have broad implications that take me beyond my mandate. However, they do appear to me to constitute a sensible way for the province to proceed. Whether the Province proceeds only with watershed-based source protection plans or with watershed management plans as well, in my view the MOE should carry out the function through a separate branch.

Although source protection plans are directly related to drinking water, they involve implications that go much further. Indeed, they seem to me to have the potential of being a cornerstone of environmental management in general. Over time, it will be critical for the MOE to build a body of expertise dedicated to the planning process. These factors lend themselves to the creation of a separate branch.

The responsibilities of the Watershed Management Branch should include:

- providing assistance in developing the Province's Drinking Water Policy as well as broader environmental policy;

- overseeing the creation and implementation of watershed-based source protection plans and watershed management plans;

- approving draft watershed-based source protection plans;

- developing and maintaining sufficient technical expertise, including access to outside expertise, to enable the branch to oversee the creation and implementation of watershed-based source protection plans;

- providing technical support for conservation authorities;

- running the watershed-based source protection plan process in areas where there is no conservation authority or where the conservation authority is unwilling or unable to do so; and

- overseeing farm drinking water protection plans.

I stress that for the government's overall drinking water strategy to be effective, it is necessary that there be a close relationship between the Watershed Management Branch and the Drinking Water Branch. As noted in the policy section above, one of the important functions of the Minister of the Environment will be to foster a culture within the MOE that is based on a source to tap drinking water policy.

13.5   Operations

Operations has been referred to as the "Do/Deliver" function within the MOE. Although it includes a fairly broad range of responsibilities, those most relevant to safe drinking water are approvals, inspections, abatement, and investigations and enforcement. I have recommended that these functions, with the exception of investigations and enforcement, be the responsibility of the Drinking Water Branch.

All four functions, as they related to the tragedy in Walkerton, were important themes in Part 1 of this Inquiry. They were repeated and in some cases expanded upon during the Part 2 process. It was generally recognized by the parties and the commissioned issue paper authors who dealt with the subject that although these functions play a vital role in the overall strategy for safe drinking water, significant shortcomings exist.

A number of issues were raised repeatedly in both parts of the Inquiry. The most significant of these were the contents of Certificates of Approval, the frequency of inspections, the desirability of unannounced inspections, the need for more direction on the scope of inspections, the need for more attention to follow-up on identified deficiencies, the need to improve the training and qualifications of MOE staff, a more creative use of abatement tools, and the need for a strict enforcement policy.

As in other areas, I was able to take comfort from the fact that many of the parties identified the same shortcomings of the approvals, inspection, abatement, and enforcement functions, at least in general terms. Not surprisingly, there was not the same level of unanimity regarding possible solutions.

In sections 13.5.1 to 13.5.4 below, I begin with a brief description of the current system (both before and immediately after the Walkerton tragedy) followed in each section by my recommendations for ensuring that these important government oversight functions work effectively to help ensure the safety of drinking water in Ontario. In section 13.5.5, I deal in general terms with the issue of government oversight of accredited bodies.

13.5.1 Approvals

The focus in this section is on two existing types of approvals: Certificates of Approval for waterworks and distribution systems, and Permits to Take Water (PTTW). Included among my recommendations in this section is a new form of approval relevant to treatment and distribution systems – the owner's licence.

13.5.1.1 *Current Practice*

Certificates of Approval: The concept of a Certificate of Approval dates from the nineteenth century and was originally issued under provincial public health legislation. Currently, the Environmental Assessment and Approvals Branch (formerly the Approvals Branch) of the Operations Division issues Certificates of Approval for waterworks under the OWRA. The owner of the waterworks (including distribution systems) must obtain approval for the construction and operation of the works.[27] At the time of the Walkerton tragedy, Certificates of Approval remained valid until they were rescinded.

Certificates of Approval were initially similar to building permits and were approvals to build a municipal water system with specific machinery. The MOE began to attach operating conditions to Certificates of Approval, including conditions relating to water treatment and monitoring, in the mid-1980s. Since such conditions were released by the MOE only as non-binding guidelines (the Ontario Drinking Water Objectives (ODWO)), their inclusion in a Certificate of Approval provided the district offices with a mechanism for enforcing treatment and monitoring requirements. The practice of attaching conditions evolved slowly and sporadically, on a site-specific basis, and in time moved to the inclusion of model conditions in new or amended Certificates of Approval. By 1992, the MOE had developed a set of model operating conditions ("Model Terms and Conditions") that were attached to new Certificates of Approval for municipal water systems. Unfortunately, there was no effort to reach back in a systematic way to determine whether conditions should be attached to existing certificates.

Initially, the ODWO formed the basis for the express conditions attached to newly issued Certificates of Approval for waterworks. Adherence to the ODWO

---

[27] Ontario, Ministry of the Environment, November 1999, *Guide to Applying for Approval of Municipal and Private Water and Sewage Works* <www.ene.gov.on.ca/envision/gp/30700le.pdf>. Sections 52 and 53, *Ontario Water Resources Act*, R.S.O. 1990, p. 1.

was often mandated through the inclusion of a condition requiring the applicant to "comply with the requirements of the Ontario Drinking Water Objectives, as amended from time to time." Over time, however, Approvals Branch staff developed generic conditions that were included in the guide used by engineers who were reviewing applications for approval. In September 1992, the branch issued its *Review Procedures Manual for Approval of Municipal and Private Water and Sewage Works*, which contained model conditions for waterworks Certificates of Approval. In June 1996, the MOE published a document titled *Approval Process and Drinking Water Sampling and Monitoring*, which further refined the model conditions to be attached to waterworks Certificates of Approval.[28]

Partly as a result of their evolutionary development, the current state of Certificates of Approval is extremely confusing. For example, some certificates have conditions, some do not. They are a strange hybrid of building permit and operating licence, and a single treatment and distribution system can have tens and even hundreds of Certificates of Approval attached to it. In addition, as noted in the Part 1 report of this Inquiry, it is difficult for MOE staff, let alone the public, to access much of the information related to Certificates of Approval.

Since the Walkerton tragedy, the MOE has taken some steps to improve the approvals process:

- All Certificates of Approval for municipal water treatment plants must now be renewed every three years.

- Municipalities are now required to submit a professional engineer's report to the MOE in relation to each waterworks every three years.[29]

- The MOE is intending to consolidate all past approvals into a single document with appropriate conditions of approval for each of the 700

---

[28] These model conditions included requirements for maintaining a total chlorine residual of 0.5 mg/L after 15 minutes of contact time and for the water system owner to notify the district manager and the local Medical Officer of Health when results failed to meet the ODWO standards or when unchlorinated water was introduced into the distribution system. MOE staff testified that the former condition could be appropriate when (as was the case with Well 5 in Walkerton) the water source had a known history of bacterial contamination or in cases where there was relatively direct communication between the aquifer and the surface. The latter condition would likely have been included in all new Certificates of Approval for facilities with chlorinated groundwater.

[29] O. Reg. 459/00, s. 13.

municipal water supplies. The new certificate will also indicate the physical upgrades that are necessary to ensure compliance with Ontario Regulation 459/00.[30]

- The MOE is implementing a data system to store such documentation related to Certificates of Approval.

Only since the Walkerton outbreak, has the absence (or inconsistency) of operating conditions in existing Certificates of Approval been comprehensively addressed by the MOE. Prior to that, however, problems with Certificates of Approval did not escape comment. Citing the lack of "enforceable criteria or certificate of approval limits with which to regulate and ensure compliance for most ... water facilities," the 1992 report of the provincial government's Sewage and Water Inspection Program (SWIP) proposed either the enactment of a legally binding regulation regarding the operation of sewage and water treatment facilities, or the issuance of a new Certificate of Approval to every facility.

Further, in a report finalized in March 2000 but not issued until October 2000, the Provincial Auditor found that the MOE did not have an adequate system for reviewing the conditions of existing Certificates of Approval in order to ensure that they met current environmental standards. As I noted in the Part 1 report, the MOE also failed to put in place a program to examine the water sources supplying existing wells to determine whether a condition requiring continuous monitoring should be added to their Certificates of Approval.

Permits to Take Water: Permits to Take Water (PTTW) are of more recent origin than Certificates of Approval. They were introduced in 1961, when the OWRA was amended to authorize the regulation of water taking after disputes arose over the taking of water to irrigate tobacco crops. Any facility capable of drawing 50,000 or more litres of water per day requires a permit under the OWRA.[31] Permits are issued by the MOE's regional offices.[32] Decisions to grant PTTW are subject to the notification and public consultation provisions

---

[30] Ontario, Ministry of the Environment, 2002, "Operation clean water," Fact Sheet <http://www.ene.gov.on.ca/envision/news/2002/011801fs.htm> [accessed January 2002].

[31] OWRA, s. 34 (3).

[32] According to the OWRA, s. 34(6), a director may in his or her discretion issue, refuse to issue, or cancel a permit, may impose such terms and conditions in issuing a permit as he or she considers proper, and may alter the terms and conditions of a permit after it is issued.

of the *Environmental Bill of Rights*. PTTW are concerned with water *quantity* rather than water quality.

13.5.1.2   *Recommendations and Comments*

13.5.1.2.1   Owner's Licence

Recommendation 71: The Ministry of the Environment should require the owners of municipal water systems to obtain an owner's licence for the operation of their waterworks. In order to obtain a licence, an owner should have:

- a Certificate of Approval for the facility;

- a Permit to Take Water;

- approved operational plans;

- an approved financial plan; and

- an accredited operating agency.

I strongly favour a requirement that owners obtain a licence for each municipal water treatment system that they own. In order not to overcomplicate the matter, I recommend that initially licences be restricted to treatment plants and distribution systems. The licence requirement should eventually be extended to wastewater treatment systems. For reasons of practicality, it will also likely be important that a separate licence be obtained for each municipal water system. Some municipalities will therefore require several licences.[33]

The licence will enable the province to both consolidate and simplify the current array of approvals and will function as a means of setting out in one place all the obligations of the owner in respect of the plant to which it relates. The owner's licence should be renewed every three to five years, at which time the MOE should be obliged to review each component as well.[34]

---

[33] In case of a multi-plant municipality, the licences will obviously have to be coordinated.

[34] In Part 1, I recommended that Certificates of Approval be subject to renewal every five years. The current recommendation is made to accommodate my expansion of the traditional certificate of approval into a licence.

Most of the components of the licence are discussed in detail in Chapter 10 of this report. However, the Certificate of Approval that I envision is somewhat different from the one currently in existence and requires some elaboration. The primary focus of the new Certificate of Approval[35] I have in mind will be on the physical and technical capabilities of the municipal water system. Its purpose is to certify that the system is technically capable of achieving what it is intended to achieve. There should only be one certificate per water system. I recognize that the certificate may have to encompass a relatively large number of separate pieces of equipment, but I do not see that as an obstacle to consolidation. Where under the old system an operator would have to obtain a new Certificate of Approval when a new pump was obtained, the certificate I envision would require the amendment of the system certificate to take the new pump into account. Consideration should also be given to the question of whether every change to the system should require an amendment to the Certificate of Approval. For example, it seems to be reasonable that the replacement of an existing pump with a new pre-approved model would not require an amendment. This could be achieved if the original certificate provided for a range of options.

The water system certificate would likely not contain operating conditions or performance criteria. Any such conditions and requirements that are not set out in the legislation or regulations should be incorporated in the operational plan, which is also required as part of the licence.

In relation to physical and technical capabilities, it is important that the MOE approve systems and any significant modifications to systems in order to ensure that each system is capable of meeting minimum requirements and that it does not wildly exceed what would reasonably be required. The latter concern is particularly important in view of my recommendation of full-cost recovery.

13.5.2 Inspections

Inspections are another critical element in the government's oversight function. The most significant inspection issues raised in the Inquiry were the frequency of inspections, the desirability of unannounced inspections, the need for more direction on the scope of inspections, the need for more attention to follow up

---

[35] Given the historical baggage associated with the term "Certificate of Approval," it may be appropriate to change the name of this instrument.

on identified deficiencies, and the need to improve the training and qualifications of inspectors.

13.5.2.1   *Current Regime*

As noted in the Part 1 report, inspections of water treatment plants have occurred since the time of the Ontario Water Resources Commission (OWRC).[36] They were initiated to ensure that plants were operated in a manner that provided potable water. In 1972, the functions of the OWRC were assumed by the newly created MOE. The MOE decentralized in 1974, and the district offices became responsible for water treatment plant inspections. Thereafter, the function alternated between the regional and district offices. The policy-making function, including decisions about the scope and frequency of inspections, has remained a centralized ministry function.

Although there was no prescribed frequency for inspections between 1974 and 1988, inspections of water treatment plants were conducted on a regular basis prior to 1980.[37] The number of formal inspections diminished substantially in the 1980s; some plants received only one inspection during the entire decade.[38]

The low frequency of inspections of any kind and the total absence of scheduled inspections during the 1980s were noted by the Provincial Auditor in his 1988 report. Finding a number of deficiencies with the function, he noted that during the 1980s the approach to inspections was primarily reactive and he recommended a shift in focus to make them primarily preventive and proactive. To facilitate this shift, the Provincial Auditor recommended scheduled annual inspections of all water treatment plants.

In response to the Provincial Auditor's 1988 report, the MOE established the Sewage and Water Inspection Program (SWIP), under which, after an initial inspection, water facilities were to be inspected every two years. Initially SWIP was administered by the regional offices and between 1990 and 1994, a two-

---

[36] The OWRC took the lead in the regulation and operation of water and sewage facilities from 1956 to 1972.

Much of the information about inspections found in this section is taken from the Part 1 testimony of R. Shaw (Exhibit 287A, Table 1, p. 2).

[37] Many plants were annually inspected.

[38] In Walkerton, after the 1980 inspection, the MOE did not conduct a formal structured inspection again until 1991. There were, however, periodic drop-ins by abatement officers.

year inspection schedule for water and sewage treatment plants was maintained. In 1994, the responsibility for determining the frequency of inspections under SWIP was transferred back to the district offices. After this transfer, the frequency of inspections varied, but SWIP placed emphasis on the need to inspect more often those facilities that had historical problems or significant deficiencies. From 1994 to 2000, the Operations Division work plan set out that inspections of water treatment plants were to be completed once every four years. However, if a significant deficiency was found, that plant was to be inspected again in the following year. In 1998, in response to budget cuts, water treatment plant inspections were put into the "optional" category to distinguish them from other inspections, those in the "mandatory" category, which were given priority.

The nature of water treatment plant inspections has also changed over time. At the time of the OWRC, much of the expertise relating to the operation of a water treatment plant lay with the OWRC and an important function of inspections was to facilitate the transfer of knowledge to the operators. At that time, inspections were informal and consultative in nature. Although reports were prepared, they had no standardized format. The reports were sent to the relevant municipality, the operating authority and, if adverse bacteriological results were found, to the Medical Officer of Health. The same general approach was followed after the establishment of the MOE in 1972 and the assignment of the inspections function to the district offices in 1974.

The nature of inspections changed significantly after the creation of the SWIP program in 1990. In response to the concerns expressed in the Provincial Auditor's 1988 report regarding the lack of scheduled inspections and the absence of the reports on whether the health and aesthetic requirements of the ODWO were being met, inspections became regularly scheduled and focused on compliance and conformance issues. Although they still had an educational component, this was no longer the focus of inspections. During this period, inspection reports were standardized. Copies of the reports were sent to the municipal operating authority and the local Medical Officer of Health. Action plans were requested from operators to deal with any deficiencies, and voluntary (rather than mandatory) compliance was the preferred MOE response to deficiencies. Internal reports were prepared summarizing the inspection findings for 1990–1992 and 1992–1994. The 1992–1994 report identified inadequate sampling at 51% of the plants inspected and a failure to meet PTTW requirements at 18% of the plants that had permits.

As noted above, in the 1994–2000 period, responsibility for SWIP shifted back to the district offices. During this period, the focus in inspections continued to be on compliance/conformance with Certificates of Approval, PTTW, licensing, the ODWO, and Procedure B13-3 (Chlorination). The 1994 Provincial Auditor's report made two significant recommendations dealing with inspections: that priority be given to following up at plants that had significant compliance issues, and that enforcement actions should be strengthened to include mandatory orders.

An internal MOE evaluation of the district inspection function (including water treatment plant inspections) undertaken in 1999 included the following observation: problems disclosed in an inspection were not rigorously followed up; the tracking of deficiencies was not readily accessible to decision makers; and follow-up inspections were not undertaken.

As noted in the Part 1 report, the experience in Walkerton demonstrated significant difficulties with the inspection process in the late 1990s. In Chapter 9 of that report, I provide details about the lack of instructions to inspectors for reviewing MOE files, the lack of clarity in instructions with respect to the review of operator records, the inadequacy of follow-up procedures, and the need for unannounced inspections. I will not repeat those comments here, except to note that they provide useful background for the recommendations I make below.

A number of changes were made to the inspections program after the *E. coli* outbreak in Walkerton. All water treatment plants were inspected between June and December 2000 and again in 2001. Currently, the goal of the MOE is to inspect all plants annually. Table 13.1 shows the number and percentage of plants inspected in each year since 1990.

Responsibility for inspections remains with the district office. Since May 2000, the focus of inspections continues to be on compliance. This now requires compliance with Ontario Regulation 459/00, which includes several new requirements and gives the force of regulation to matters that were previously guidelines.[39]

---

[39] Prior to August 2000, the ODWO (guidelines) were often incorporated as requirements in Certificates of Approval, thereby making them mandatory.

Table 13.1 The Communal (Municipal) Water Inspection Program, 1990–2001

Period (Total No. of Plants)	No. Inspected	% Inspected
1990–1992 (607)	607	100
1992–1994 (607)	532	86
1994–1995 (630)	378	60
1995–1996 (630)	188	30
1996–1997 (630)	224	35
1997–1998 (630)	186	30
1998–1999 (630)	152	24
1999–2000 (630)	185	29
2000–2001 (659)	659	100

Among the new requirements, owners of water treatment plants and distribution systems are required to prepare quarterly reports. These reports must:

- describe the water system, the operation of the system, and the sources of the water collected, produced, treated, stored, supplied, or distributed by the system;

- describe the measures taken to comply with Ontario Regulation 459/00 and the Ontario Drinking Water Standards (ODWS) during the quarter;

- summarize the analytical results for water sampling obtained during the quarter for water sampling and the notices of adverse water quality sent to the Medical Officer of Health and the MOE in accordance with regulation 459/00.[40]

In addition, owners are also required to prepare engineer's reports every three years.[41] An engineer's report is to include:

---

[40] O. Reg. 459/00, s. 12(1)(a)–(c). Section 12(d) provides that the owner must also provide information referred to in s. 12(1)(a)–(c) relating to previous quarters if the information only became known during the quarter for which the report is prepared.

[41] O. Reg. 459/00, s. 13(1), (2). Reports under this section must be prepared by a professional engineer (as defined in the *Professional Engineers Act*, one who has experience in sanitary engineering related to drinking water supplies and who is not an employee of the owner) in accordance with the MOE publication "Terms of reference for engineers' reports for water works," originally dated

- a description of the waterworks;

- a compilation of Certificates of Approval for the works that is available within the municipality;

- an assessment of the potential for microbiological contamination;

- a characterization of the raw water supply source;

- an assessment of operational procedures and recommendations;

- an assessment of existing physical works and recommendations;

- recommendations for a monitoring regime for the entire waterworks system to ensure compliance with the ODWS and Ontario Regulation 459/00.[42]

Quarterly reports and engineer's reports are intended to assist the inspection process.

The Environmental SWAT Team is another recent addition to the MOE's Operations Division. Environmental officers and investigation officers conduct inspection sweeps of sectors that have high non-compliance rates and/or present a high risk to public health. None of the sectors currently being inspected by the Environmental SWAT Team is directly related to drinking water.

13.5.2.2   *Recommendations and Comments*

13.5.2.2.1   Who Should Perform the Inspection Function?

Most parties in Parts 1 and 2 of the Inquiry advocated keeping the inspection function within the MOE. There is, however, a suggestion in the Gibbons

August 2000. The specifics of submitting the reports depend on whether the system is listed in the MOE publication "Drinking water submission dates for first engineer's report," dated August 2000. Under O. Reg. 459/00, s. 13(1), the requirement applies if: (a) the system is owned or operated by a municipality or by OCWA; (b) a municipality or OCWA has contracted with the owner of the system to obtain water from the system; or (c) reports under this section are required by an approval or by an order or direction under the Act.

[42] Ontario, Ministry of the Environment, 2000, "Engineers' reports for waterworks – technical brief, Ontario," August, p. 1.

Report that inspections are a type of function that may be appropriate for alternative service delivery. Inspections are an operational rather than a policy function. The Gibbons Report recommends that "at some point in the future" the government should consider creating an arm's-length operating agency to fulfill the MOE's "operational/program delivery" functions.[43] While the report stops short of advocating such a move at this time, the clear impression is that the authors consider the assignment of such function to an arm's-length independent body to be a "best practice." In my view, any such move would have several disadvantages and should in no circumstances be undertaken unless and until it can be established to have no negative impact on safety.

I recognize that my findings in the Part 1 report show that the MOE has not done a good job in recent years in conducting inspections. That, however, does not in my view lead necessarily to the conclusion that the government should transfer these functions to others. First, I do not accept that the MOE, with proper funding, training, and direction, cannot carry out this function as effectively as any third party. Accepting, as I do, that the oversight of drinking water is of such public importance that the government should perform the oversight role itself, I think we would have arrived at a very sorry state of affairs if we were to conclude that the government, even with proper direction and resources, is unable to fulfill its function.

The reason commonly given for outsourcing government functions is cost savings, and there is no doubt that outsourcing the inspections function may provide cost savings to the government. Cost is always important, but some government functions are of such a nature that the potential for cost savings alone should not lead to a decision to transfer all or part of the government regulatory function to a third party. In my view, the oversight of the safety of Ontario's drinking water is such a function.

There are two primary reasons why I favour retaining the inspections of drinking water systems in the MOE. The first is political accountability. I have already, in the context of the suggestion that there be a separate drinking water commission, expressed the view that it is essential for direct and immediate political accountability to exist regarding the safety of our drinking water. The Walkerton *E. coli* outbreak presents an excellent example of the importance of this accountability. This Inquiry has not only exposed the failure of the government's oversight and regulatory role, but has made clear the responsibility

---

[43] Gibbons Report, p. 24.

that must be borne for those failures by the government. Even before the delivery of the Part 1 report, the government responded quickly and strongly to address what it saw as the weaknesses in the way its oversight role had been exercised. That response was no doubt dictated both by the concerns about what happened in Walkerton and by the public outcry and concern about the safety of drinking water across the province. I question whether, if the inspections and oversight role at the time of the Walkerton outbreak had been exercised through an independent third party, the government would have been under the same need to be accountable for what took place or would have taken the immediate action that it did. Immediate and direct political accountability for the regulatory and oversight role is an important safeguard for the people of Ontario to ensure the safety of their drinking water.

I also have concerns about the potential for real and perceived conflict of interest if the inspection function is transferred to a body made up of industry representatives. It is essential that Ontario's drinking water be safe and that the reasonable public be confident about the safety of its drinking water. A self-regulating organization composed in whole or in part of industry representatives responsible for the operations management of water systems may raise the perception of a lack of independence. I note that in the United Kingdom, where the water systems are privately owned and operated, the government has rejected the concept of an industry self-regulating organization to carry out the inspections and regulatory role. Instead, the government has created an inspectorate that is accountable to the minister responsible for the delivery of safe drinking water. This inspectorate has been provided with a strong mandate and strong powers to ensure that those operating and managing water systems comply with government regulations.

I also agree with a point made by Professor Nicholas d'Ombrain in his paper commissioned by the Inquiry. He raises the question of "the viability of what would be left of the Ministry of the Environment if the regulatory and enforcement functions were removed."[44] He is referring here to the risk that the ministry would eventually lose all operational expertise if it were not involved in either the operational or the oversight function. This loss would critically

---

[44] d'Ombrain, p. 145.

hamper the MOE in its policy development role as well as its overall responsibility for the safety of the system.

In summary, while I do not foreclose the possibility of transferring the inspection function to an arm's-length entity at some point in the future, in light of the many potential disadvantages, I suggest that the government proceed cautiously. Further, because the primary concern in regard to drinking water delivery is safety, delegation to a non-government third party should not occur unless it is clearly established that the proposed system is just as – and preferably more – safe.

13.5.2.2.2 Chief Inspector – Drinking Water Systems

Recommendation 72: The provincial government should create an office of Chief Inspector – Drinking Water Systems.

The inspection program for water treatment plants would benefit enormously from the creation of the office of Chief Inspector – Drinking Water Systems. Someone of sufficient expertise and stature to obtain the respect of the operators' community should be appointed to the position.

My impression of the current inspection program is that it lacks clear direction and consistency of practice. As discussed below, there is no accepted protocol for carrying out all inspections. Practices, as well as the frequency of inspection, differ from district to district. Although it is acceptable for the actual inspection function to be carried out from the district or regional offices, there is a need for a centralized position responsible for implementing the program across the province.

The position of Chief Inspector should be located within the Drinking Water Branch. The Chief Inspector should have input into the content of the MOE's inspection policy and should be responsible for ensuring that the policy is implemented. On a more practical level, the Chief Inspector should be responsible for: developing and then updating the inspection protocol (discussed below); developing, updating, and (possibly) implementing the inspection training program; monitoring the overall frequency and adequacy of inspections; and reporting to the public about the overall performance of Ontario's water supply systems and the inspection program.

One benefit of giving the Chief Inspector a public reporting function is that it would increase the public awareness of the inspection function. This, in turn, would increase the effectiveness of the inspection program. I envisage a Chief Inspector who operates in a manner analogous to that of the Chief Medical Officer of Health.

13.5.2.2.3   Inspector Qualifications

Recommendation 73: Inspectors should be required to have the same or higher qualifications as the operators of the systems they inspect and should receive special training in inspections.

It is clearly important that inspectors receive training. Below, I discuss the scope of inspections and the development of an inspections protocol. Inspectors should be trained to understand and implement this protocol. In addition, it is in my view equally important that inspectors have a good understanding of what they are inspecting. This is necessary in order for them to perform satisfactorily. For example, in weighing the significance of a deficiency and then deciding what follow-up action to take, an inspector must appreciate the practical consequences of the deficiency. Such appreciation is more likely to come about if the inspector has obtained the same technical qualifications as an operator has. Qualification as an operator should ensure that an inspector is able to fully understand the practices of the operator who is being inspected and the significance of those practices to the provision of safe drinking water. In addition, qualification as an operator will also assist the inspector in obtaining the respect and cooperation of operators, another desirable outcome. In order to achieve the appropriate level of expertise, it may be desirable for inspectors to be dedicated to inspections within their area of expertise.

13.5.2.2.4   Scope and Content of Inspections

In the Part 1 report of this Inquiry, I made the following recommendations in response to certain deficiencies I observed in the inspections performed in Walkerton:

The Ministry of the Environment should develop and make available to all Ministry of the Environment inspectors a written direction or protocol, for both announced and unannounced inspections:

- *Outlining the specific matters to be reviewed by an inspector in preparing for the inspection of a water system;*

- *Providing a checklist of matters that an inspector is required to review, as well as matters that it may be desirable to review, during an inspection of a water system, and providing guidance concerning those matters to be discussed with the operator of a waterworks facility during an inspection.*

In particular, I was very concerned that none of the inspections conducted in Walkerton in the 1990s addressed the vulnerability of Well 5 to surface water contamination despite the fact that information about this vulnerability was contained in the MOE's files.[45] Similarly, it was unfortunate that in 1998, the inspector did not go beyond the current month's operating sheets. Had she done so, she would likely have noticed that the usual practice in Walkerton was to record only chlorine residuals of either 0.5 or 0.75 mg/L, a fact that would likely have raised suspicions. Some of the inspectors who gave evidence in Part 1 would have looked at earlier data, but there was no consistent practice. Such problems are not restricted to Walkerton. For example, while a protocol was included in the *Report on Municipal Sewage and Water Treatment Plant Inspections*,[46] the evidence in Part 1 was that it was not circulated widely and that even experienced inspectors had never seen the document.

The development, distribution, and enforcement of a protocol will help to ensure the uniformity and adequacy of inspections. I do not propose to draft such a protocol for this report, but I note that much can be learned from the lessons of Walkerton and from my comments about the shortcomings of the process discussed there.

In my view, among the things that an inspector should be required to review, before beginning an inspection, are data relating to the quality of source waters and circumstances relating to changes in land users or surrounding water. Further, inspections should identify any problems and should recommend the steps required to correct such problems. A copy of this report should be provided to the local conservation authorities.

---

[45] This highly relevant fact had been known since the well was constructed in 1978. Critical information in this regard was contained in the MOE's files and storage areas. However, the inspections were not directed to examine those materials; nor, indeed, were all these materials accessible to them. See Recommendations in section 13.7.3.1 below regarding access to and organization of information.

[46] Ontario, Ministry of the Environment, 1989, *Report on Municipal Sewage and Water Treatment Plant Inspections*. The report resulted in the establishment of SWIP.

I raise one point of caution in regard to the protocol. In designing it, the Drinking Water Branch should be careful not to create a mere checklist. I do not advocate turning inspections into an exercise of putting tick-marks on a form. The protocol I envision is a more detailed, thoughtful review of what an inspection should cover.

13.5.2.2.5   Frequency of Inspection

In Part 1, I made the following recommendations about the frequency of inspections:

- *The Ministry of the Environment's inspections program for municipal water systems should consist of a combination of announced and unannounced inspections. The inspector may conduct unannounced inspections when he or she deems it appropriate, and at least once every three years, taking into account such factors as work priority and planning, time constraints, and the record of the operating authority.*

- *As a matter of policy, inspections of municipal water systems, whether announced or unannounced, should be conducted at least annually. The government's current program for annual inspections should be continued.*

- *There should be a legal requirement that systems with significant deficiencies be inspected at least once per year. Ontario Regulation 459/00, also known as the Drinking Water Protection Regulation, should be amended to require that an inspection be conducted within one year of any inspection that discloses a deficiency as defined in the regulation. In this regard, deficiencies include any failure to comply with the treatment, monitoring, or testing requirements, or with specified performance criteria, set out in the regulation or in the accompanying drinking water standards.*

As noted at the beginning of this section, the frequency of inspections has varied substantially over the past 20 years. During certain periods, at various plants, years passed without an inspection. More troubling is the fact that follow-up inspections were not conducted at plants with known, serious deficiencies – including the Walkerton plant. Fortunately, this practice has changed since the tragedy in Walkerton. In my view, the current practice of annual inspections is appropriate in the circumstances. I am concerned, however, that the current attitudes toward inspections will change as the memory of the Walkerton outbreak fades. When budget-cutting pressures return in the future, for example, there may be pressures to reduce inspection frequency. Although frequent inspections have an impact on safety generally, they are particularly important with respect to problem systems. For these reasons, it is advisable to set out a statutory requirement that a follow-up inspection be carried out within 12 months if an inspection discloses that an operator has failed to comply with treatment, monitoring, or testing requirements.

The need for annual MOE inspections when follow-up is not required by statute may be affected by the implementation of accreditation and biannual audits for operating agencies of municipal water systems. Accreditation audits and the inspections will overlap to some extent, and, in some circumstances, it may be appropriate for the MOE to reduce the frequency of inspections. Specifically, once accreditation is implemented, it should be reasonable for the MOE to aim for inspections every two to three years of those systems that are trouble-free and have a history of sound management. The audit reports should be provided to the MOE and if deficiencies are noted in either an audit or an MOE inspection, the 12-month statutory follow-up requirement should be triggered.

In my view, not all inspections should be regularly scheduled inspections. There is much merit in unannounced inspections. As I noted in my Part 1 report, unannounced inspections enable an assessment to be done under normal working conditions rather than in a situation possibly structured to accommodate the inspection. They can also eliminate the effect that preparation may have upon an accurate view of the operation.[47] As a result, I recommend that the MOE should immediately alter its practice and should have a mix of scheduled and unannounced inspections.

13.5.2.2.6   Timeliness of Follow-Up

In Part 1, I recommended:

- *The Ministry of the Environment should establish and require adherence to time lines for the preparation and delivery of inspection*

---

[47] See my discussion in the Part 1 report, pp. 321–322, of the likelihood that Stan Koebel altered chlorine residuals in preparation for Michelle Zillinger's February 1998 inspection.

reports and operator responses and the delivery of interim status reports regarding remedial action.

It is perhaps obvious to note that inspections are of limited or no utility in the absence of a follow-up mechanism to help ensure that deficiencies are addressed and eliminated. The experience in Walkerton shows that in a number of respects, the MOE's follow-up to inspections was faulty. I have set out detailed findings in section 9.3.5 of my Part 1 report. For present purposes it is sufficient to note that in the 1990s the inspections of the Walkerton plant revealed compliance deficiencies. In each case, the general manager of the Walkerton Public Utilities Commission stated that he would comply, but he never did.

As was the case with inadequate inspection procedures, the information before me suggests that this problem was not restricted to Walkerton. An internal evaluation of the district inspection function, including water treatment plant inspections, conducted in 1999 found as a general problem that follow-up on deficiencies noted during inspections was not being rigorously pursued and that the subsequent inspections required in the work plan were not being undertaken.

The MOE must take steps to correct this situation. The mandatory 12-month follow-up inspection that would occur when deficiencies are found is an important element of a better approach. Follow-up can also be improved in other ways. First, the MOE must ensure that its own reports are completed and delivered within a reasonable period of time. If deficiencies are found, the operator should be required to respond with an action plan that will address those deficiencies, also in a reasonable time. The action plan should be approved by the MOE. Once the plan is approved, the operator should be required to deliver interim status reports on any remedial action. This follow-up procedure should have the same effect as an order, so that any breach is subject to enforcement proceedings.

When the accreditation system for operating agencies that I have recommended in Chapter 11 takes effect, deficiencies found in the biannual audits will have to be integrated as well. In addition to whatever "accreditation" actions result from such deficiencies, they should also be reported to the MOE, whereupon the same procedure should apply, as if they had been discovered in an MOE inspection.

13.5.2.2.7   Additional Comments

An additional matter relating to inspections, although not appropriate for a recommendation, does merit comment. This is the principle by which inspection decisions should be guided. My recommendation regarding the scope of inspections involves the development of an inspection protocol. I have suggested a number of elements of such a protocol, both in this report and in the Part 1 report, but I leave the protocol's development and evolution to the MOE. Even when a protocol has been developed, it is not realistic to expect that it will provide instructions on all aspects of the inspection process. Of necessity, some matters will be left to the discretion of the inspector or other MOE personnel. In these circumstances it is useful to develop a set of principles to guide the development of protocols and the exercise of individual discretion.[48] These decisions should be guided by the following principles: effectiveness, a precautionary approach, consistent application, independence from outside influence, transparency, and adequate resources.

The first principle, effectiveness, is best understood as the overall goal of the inspections program. An effective program will identify deficiencies in an operation and react so as to minimize the reoccurrence of deficiencies in the future. Effectiveness requires the regular review and analysis of the outcomes (the performance of the systems) and the adjustment of existing practices when improvement is required.

The second principle, a precautionary approach, flows from my view that decisions should be made with a view to the significant health risks that can result from improperly treated drinking water. Since decisions affecting the inspection of water treatment plants have a potentially serious effect on human health, decision-makers should err on the side of caution. Operators should not be given the benefit of the doubt. If there is any doubt, the safer approach should be adopted.

Decisions regarding inspections should also be made without regard to the identity of the operator. Private operating agencies, municipalities, and the OCWA should be treated alike. During Part 1 of the Inquiry it was suggested that the MOE was reluctant to prosecute municipalities – that they were viewed as being "children of the province."[49] The data on enforcement practices lends

---

[48] I have made a similar recommendation in regard to enforcement.

[49] This allegation was repeated in Part 2 of the Inquiry by Energy Probe.

some support to this allegation. I do not need to deal with this allegation beyond stating the obvious: inspections should be approached in the same way, no matter who the operator is. The chief inspector should have a specific mandate to ensure that all operators are treated equally insofar as inspections and enforcement are concerned.

The principle of independence from outside interests flows from the equal application principle. Inspections should be used as a means of determining how well operators are performing their functions in an effort, ultimately, to protect public health and safety. They should not be used for any other purpose. Here I am referring primarily to the potential use of inspections to aid the enforcement function. I will deal with this in more detail in the enforcement section of this chapter. For present purposes, it is sufficient to note that for reasons of procedural fairness, it is important that the inspection function remain separate from the Investigations and Enforcement Branch.

The fifth principle, transparency, requires that all those with an interest in the process – including the operator, the municipality, and the public – have access to the inspection process and results. When deficiencies are noted, these parties should be made aware of the plans for follow-up inspections as well as the results of each of these inspections.

Finally, it is important that the inspection program have adequate resources. Adequacy of resources for all government initiatives and responsibilities is the subject of another section in this chapter. As a general proposition, where health is concerned, budgets should not be cut at random, leaving those responsible to "make do" with what they have. The government should decide what programs to offer and what the content of such programs should be. Once this decision has been made, the government should provide adequate resources. In the context of inspections, the MOE is free to decide the frequency, form, and scope of inspections. Once the program has been decided, however, it should be realistically costed, and sufficient funds should be made available to run it.

13.5.3 Voluntary versus Mandatory Abatement

For the purpose of this chapter I use the term "abatement tools" to refer to the measures used to help bring operators back into compliance. Traditionally, the debate in this area has focused on whether to use mandatory or voluntary means to attempt to achieve compliance. In my view, the MOE must take action to use mandatory abatement more often than has been the case in the past. Legally enforceable orders should be issued whenever a deficiency is noted relating to the safety of drinking water.

Mandatory abatement should not be restricted to issuing orders that, if breached, result in enforcement proceedings. The MOE should continue with abatement mechanisms such as administrative orders.

In addition to using mandatory abatement to achieve compliance with standards, it is also appropriate for the MOE to use voluntary abatement techniques to improve performance beyond minimum requirements. Voluntary abatement is particularly useful in regard to source protection. To avoid confusion, I will refer to this latter form of abatement as "technical assistance."

13.5.3.1 *Current Regime*

The current practice of the MOE is to rely on a combination of voluntary and mandatory abatement measures. Voluntary abatement describes the process under which the MOE, without resorting to legal compulsion, asks or directs an operator to take certain measures. Voluntary abatement may take a variety of forms: a letter, a violation notice, a recommendation in an inspection report, a phone call, or even an oral instruction during a field visit.[50] Depending on the nature of the problem, voluntary abatement could involve establishing a program to be undertaken by a water utility within prescribed time limits.

The MOE's Compliance Guideline of 1995 has several criteria for pursuing mandatory abatement, including an unsatisfactory compliance record, deliberate non-compliance, repeated violations, and unsatisfactory progress in a voluntary program. The guideline suggests that when these situations occur, mandatory abatement should be pursued unless it is decided that a voluntary program should be followed.[51] The reasons for this decision are to be documented in an occurrence report. The guideline also provides that the MOE will issue no more than two written warnings before mandatory abatement is initiated, and

---

[50] Ontario, Ministry of the Environment, 1995, "Compliance guideline," June 16, s. 5.0.
[51] Ibid., s. 4.4.

that unsatisfactory progress on a voluntary abatement program should not be tolerated for more than 180 calendar days.[52]

The hallmark of mandatory abatement, whatever form it takes, is that the required measures are compelled by a legal obligation and are subject to enforcement proceedings. The MOE may issue a control document[53] – either a Director's Order or a Field Order under the OWRA, requiring the operator to carry out the desired measures. Alternatively, the MOE may choose to amend an authorizing document,[54] such as a Certificate of Approval, to direct the operator to do what is required. Therefore, mandatory abatement can convert a requirement under a government guideline or policy into a legally enforceable prescription, similar to a provision in legislation or a regulation.

There are more than 60 control documents and authorizing documents available to the MOE. The most common documents invoked are various kinds of orders. The provincial officer may issue an order (often called a Field Order[55]) if there has been a contravention of a provision of the OWRA or the regulations; a provision of an order, notice, direction, requirement, or report made under the OWRA; or a term or condition of a licence, permit, or approval made under the OWRA.[56] An order is an enforcement instrument issued to "legally encourage" operators to take corrective action.

If an order is issued, it may require the person to whom it is directed to comply with any directions set out in the order within the time specified. For example, orders may relate to:

- the repair, maintenance, or operation of waterworks in such a manner and with such facilities as are specified in the order;

---

[52] Ibid., s. 5.6. This period relates to any one period of unsatisfactory progress and not to the length of the program.

[53] Ibid., s. 1, defines control documents as "documents which are authorized by statute such as control order, stop orders, etc., which have specific requirements." They are binding upon the recipient and can be directly enforced by prosecution.

[54] Ibid, s. 1, defines authorizing documents as "documents which are authorized by statute such as certificates of approval, licences and permits which may have conditions." These documents permit and control the manner in which activities are carried out. They are binding on the recipient and are directly enforceable by prosecution.

[55] Ibid., s. 1, defines a Field Order as "a control document issued by a Director who has been appointed for the purposes of field orders."

[56] OWRA, s. 16(1).

- sampling, analysis, or reporting with respect to the quality or quantity of any waters;

- monitoring and recording in relation to the natural environment and waters and reporting on the monitoring and recording (e.g., an officer might use a Field Order to instruct an operator to conduct proper sampling or chlorination).[57]

Field Orders, unlike Director's Orders, are used to address immediate problems in situations when time may be of the essence (e.g., in the case of a stop order). However, in the case of longer-term problems, such as a situation where a water treatment facility was in need of a new chlorinator, a Director's Order would be used.

The issuance of orders is usually followed by assistance with compliance. Environmental officers work with waterworks owners and operators to correct problems that are brought to the MOE's attention. If the operator does not comply with the issued order or take corrective action, it can be prosecuted for violating the statute, regulation, Certificate of Approval, permit, or order.[58]

The 1994 Provincial Auditor's report found that the MOE was placing too much emphasis on voluntary abatement and recommended that enforcement actions be strengthened to include the increased issuance of orders. Partially in response to this criticism, the MOE issued the 1995 Compliance Guideline. Despite the fact that this guideline set out circumstances in which mandatory abatement was to occur, MOE staff continued to use voluntary measures in circumstances where mandatory measures would have been a better choice.

In Part 1 of the Inquiry, I heard evidence suggesting a continued reluctance on the part of MOE staff to use mandatory abatement measures.[59] As noted in the Part 1 report, this reluctance gradually began to change, beginning in 1997.[60] In March 2000, the MOE issued a directive to follow a mandatory abatement approach.

---

[57] OWRA, s. 16(3).
[58] OWRA, s. 107.
[59] See the Part 1 report of the Inquiry, section 9.4.2.3.
[60] Ibid., section 9.4.2.4.

Since the tragedy in Walkerton, the MOE has introduced policies strongly focusing on mandatory abatement. The statistics suggest an increased propensity to issue Field Orders (now Provincial Officers' Orders) and to follow up on such orders and other deficiencies.[61] Of the 659 plants inspected in 2000, a total of 367 were identified with one or more of the following deficiencies:

- inadequate sampling programs (267);

- inadequate disinfection procedures or practices (111);

- a failure to meet minimum treatment standards (76); and

- improperly certified operators (63).[62]

In total, 341 Field Orders were issued, all of which were followed up on by their respective expiry dates.

Although they are not part of the evidence before me, I have heard of complaints about MOE staff who issued orders, where none were required, solely in order to improve statistics. Specifically, the complaint was that an order was issued regarding a practice in respect of which the operator was already in compliance, thereby inflating statistics concerning the number of orders issued and, subsequently, concerning the numbers of operators brought into compliance. If this occurred, it is obviously not an acceptable practice.

Since May 2000, the MOE has also made important inroads in the area of administrative actions. Administrative actions are a potentially useful alternative to enforcement proceedings and go hand-in-hand with mandatory abatement. They give MOE officers the power to impose penalties or take action, including issuing stop orders on the spot. These powers were increased significantly in 2000 by the *Toughest Environmental Penalties Act, 2000* – an Act that amends the OWRA, the EPA, and the *Pesticides Act*.

This Act provides for significant new powers for provincial enforcement officers, particularly in the area of administrative actions. Administrative monetary penalties will enable abatement officers to issue tickets of up to $10,000 for

---

[61] There were 1,265 such orders issued in 2000, compared with 307 in 1999. This has been attributed to being a response to the Provincial Auditor's report of 2000. Ontario, Hansard, Standing Committee on Public Accounts, April 26, 2001.

[62] R. Shaw, testimony, Walkerton Inquiry (Part 1 Hearing, April 17, 2001).

pollution offences. Administrative penalties reduce the time and expense of enforcement by allowing for summary convictions without a lengthy investigation and trial, but they do not carry the stigma of a conviction. However, regulations under the Act are yet to be passed before it can have any effect on enforcement efforts.

13.5.3.2   *Recommendations and Comments*

13.5.3.2.1   Mandatory Orders and Strict Enforcement

Recommendation 74: The Ministry of the Environment should increase its commitment to the use of mandatory abatement.

Mandatory abatement should be the only option to address anything other than technical violations of operations requirements. Mandatory orders carry greater force than do voluntary measures. If they are breached, they can result in the commencement of enforcement procedures or, as discussed below, an administrative penalty. Voluntary abatement tools, on the other hand, can result in confusion. The clear message behind them is that the deficiency is not as serious as one that would merit a mandatory order. In times of pressure on available resources, it would not be surprising to see voluntary measures slide down the priority list. As such, while voluntary abatement may be sufficient for minor problems,[63] it is not appropriate for any deficiency that affects the safety of drinking water.

A greater use of mandatory abatement received the support of a number of parties in the Part 2 process of the Inquiry. The Ontario Public Service Employees Union (OPSEU), for example, submitted that the increased use of mandatory compliance was necessary to restore "public trust and confidence in the supervisory role of the Ministry of Environment."[64] The Canadian Environmental Law Association (CELA), Canadian Environmental Defence Fund (CEDF), and the Ontario Water Works Association (OWWA)/Ontario Municipal Water Association (OMWA) also made very strong submissions for the implementation of a broad range of mandatory abatement tools.

---

[63] I understand that deficiencies measured in the 2000 inspection included such minor matters as improper signage. Such matters do not require a mandatory order.

[64] Ontario Public Service Employees Union.

13.5.3.2.2 Additional Abatement Tools

I support the recent trend toward the expansion and development of new tools to assist mandatory abatement. Such tools include administrative penalties and various forms of administrative orders, including stop orders and administrative orders. These remedies need to be studied more carefully. I agree with OPSEU's observations that the MOE needs to study the effect of such tools and develop a policy for their use. Although it is conceivable that a penalty of $10,000 per occurrence would have a positive effect on compliance for water treatment operators, effectiveness – one of the guiding principles I referred to earlier – requires that the penalties be reviewed and assessed regularly to determine whether they have an effect on compliance.

13.5.3.2.3 Government Assistance

The strict enforcement of standards and requirements is an essential component of a safe drinking water system, but there is also room for government assistance in a range of options, from financial and technical assistance to education programs.

In regard to source protection, the recommendations I have made in respect of minimum standards for farms and individual farm water protection plans, for example, should provide significant protection for the environment. Clearly, though, there is room for further improvement. As discussed in Chapter 4, the MOE and OMAFRA should develop programs and incentives that encourage farmers to do even better.

A number of forms of technical assistance would also be useful in respect of the treatment and distribution system. The concept of circuit riders was recommended by a number of parties in Part 2. Circuit riders would be trained and experienced individuals who offer assistance to operators. They would be especially useful for small operations and in the interim period leading up to mandatory accreditation. However, even after that period, they would continue to serve a useful purpose in assisting small and medium-size operations as well as ensuring that the MOE retained sufficient operational and technical expertise.

13.5.4 Investigation and Enforcement

Breaches of legally enforceable requirements – whether they are set out in legislation, regulations, ministry orders, or authorizing documents – are subject to enforcement proceedings. In the MOE, these proceedings are handled by the Investigations and Enforcement Branch (IEB).

The operation of the IEB was not directly called into question in Part 1 of the Inquiry because no mandatory orders were issued to the Walkerton Public Utilities Commission before May 2000, when the tragedy occurred. In Part 2, the primary criticism I heard with respect to inspections was that enforcement was not sufficiently strict. In support of this assertion, a number of parties relied on the see-sawing numbers of enforcement procedures and penalties obtained through the 1990s. Table 13.2 was cited by the CEDF in their written submissions to the Inquiry.

Although the numbers rebounded from a low in 1995, many parties argued that the MOE's general approach to enforcement still needs to be toughened.

13.5.4.1 *Current Regime*

The IEB investigates suspected violations of environmental legislation and is responsible for all aspects of environmental enforcement.[65] Investigation officers in the branch collect the evidence and lay the charges for environmental prosecutions. The IEB is usually made aware of information about a violation through an occurrence report. If deemed necessary, an IEB (provincial) officer will start an investigation to determine whether there are reasonable and probable grounds to lay charges.

If an investigation is warranted, the supervisor will assign an IEB officer "for the purpose of conducting an investigation to determine whether reasonable and probable grounds exist for laying charges."[66]

The Compliance Guideline outlines what IEB staff should consider in order to reach an "informed judgment" as to whether a prosecution should be initiated.

---

[65] The IEB was created in 1985 because of a perceived delivery conflict with the local district officers playing the role of inspector as well as enforcer.

[66] Ontario, Ministry of the Environment, 1995, s. 9.1.

Table 13.2 Annual Enforcement Summary, 1992-1998

This chart compares statistics as enforcement activities for the calendar years 1991 to 1998.

Activity	1991	1992	1993	1994	1995	1996	1997	1998
Assigned Investigations	1,569	1,502	1,605	1,452	1,372	821	874	1,045
Prosecutions Initiated	309	322	289	289	170	128	142	208
Charges Laid	1,896	2,158	1,570	1,640	1,045	758	951	805
Individuals Charged					158	110	102	159
Companies Charged					125	104	130	270
Charges against Individuals					615	342	488	353
Charges against Companies					430	416	463	452
Cases with Convictions	299	266	211	237	188	121	136	137
Cases Withdrawn	30	21	17	27	35	20	8	15
Cases Dismissed	52	31	21	34	18	7	5	12
Individuals Convicted	166	426	248	362	255	182	205	105
Companies Convicted	388	352	246	284	218	148	225	183
Number of Fines	674	686	464	551	387	273	262	391
Charges with Convictions	757	768	512	652	504	365	418	414
Companies with Convictions					230	162	215	243
Individuals with Convictions					274	204	203	171
Fines against Individuals					$1,845,279	$750,535	$760,100	$622,325
Fines against Individuals					$1,220,225	$453,499	$195,760	$241,515
Jail Terms	0	0	10 d	0	7-1/2 m	490 d	5 m	
Other Penalties	$687k	$266k	$48k	$373k	$2.7m	$298k	$385k	
Fines Imposed	$2.5m	$3.4m	$2.1m	$2.4m	$3.0m	$1.2m	$95k	$863k

Please Note: These figures are subject to change when or if new information is received, e.g., appeal.

The considerations include:

- the seriousness of the violation itself, including whether the violation poses a significant risk to, or will have an adverse effect on, human, plant, or animal life, property, or the environment;

- the seriousness of the violation in the context of the ministry's overall regulatory scheme, including a consideration as to whether the pollution emitted as a result of the violation is a serious obstacle to achieving the ministry's air quality and water quality objectives;

- whether the violation appears to have been deliberate;

- whether due diligence exists; and

- the offender's compliance record.[67]

If the IEB officer recommends prosecution, the officer prepares a written brief and submits it to the IEB supervisor. The IEB supervisor and manager will review the brief and then forward it to the IEB director or designate; that person reviews the brief and forwards it to the Legal Services Branch.[68] Once a prosecution brief has been prepared, the Assistant Deputy Minister's Office (Operations Division), the district office, and others (where appropriate) will be notified of the recommendation to initiate a prosecution.[69]

The Legal Services Branch becomes involved after the investigation and the preparation and circulation of the prosecution brief. The director of the Legal Services Branch or his/her designate will consult with staff lawyers about whether the evidence obtained is adequate and about whether prosecution would be "in the interests of the administration of justice." There may also be consultation with staff of the Ministry of the Attorney General. The Legal Services Branch may choose not to proceed, but it will first make contact with and consider any additional information provided by the IEB.[70] Ultimately, the decision and authority regarding whether a prosecution will proceed rests with the Attorney General.[71]

---

[67] Ibid., s. 10.
[68] Ibid., s. 9.3.
[69] Ibid., s. 9.4.
[70] Ibid., s. 9.5.
[71] Ibid., s. 9.6.

When a formal prosecution proceeds, either there will be a guilty plea and settlement, or the matter will proceed to trial. Often, a central issue in any trial is the alleged violator's due diligence – based on some of the "informed judgment" factors referred to above. If the alleged violator took all reasonable precautions, it is unlikely that the prosecution will go forth or be successful.

The OWRA states that every person that contravenes the Act or regulations, that fails to comply with an order, notice, requirement, or report made under the Act, or that contravenes a term or condition of a licence, permit, approval, or report made under the Act is guilty of an offence.[72] The OWRA identifies the penalties that both individuals and corporations are liable for.

Every individual convicted of an offence under the Act is liable to fines and/or imprisonment. Similarly, every corporation convicted of an offence under the Act is liable, and fines (and, in the case of officers and directors who have acted improperly, imprisonment terms), are specified.[73] The *Toughest Environmental Penalties Act, 2000* recently amended the penalty structure of the OWRA, the EPA, and the *Pesticides Act* by increasing the amount for fines and lengthening terms of imprisonment.

More severe fines and terms of imprisonment apply to certain offences under the OWRA (as they did prior to the new Act), including any act that "impairs the quality" of any waters and any act that contravenes a provision of the regulations that relates to water treatment or distribution systems with specific requirements.[74]

13.5.4.2   *Recommendations and Comments*

13.5.4.2.1   Location of the Investigation and Enforcement Function

During the Inquiry, some concern was expressed about the status of the Investigations and Enforcement Branch (IEB) within the MOE. Specifically, the Energy Probe Research Foundation (EPRF) argued strenuously that the IEB function should be moved out of the MOE to the Ministry of the Solicitor General. It argued that the co-existence of policy-making, operations, abatement, and enforcement within one ministry leads to conflicts of interests

---

[72] OWRA, s. 107. "Person" is defined to include a municipality.
[73] OWRA, s. 108.
[74] OWRA, s. 109 (3.1).

and diminishes "the effectiveness of the enforcement function." The EPRF further argued that the transfer of the IEB function out of the MOE would reduce the risk of a successful challenge in an enforcement proceeding on the grounds of "abuse of process" and "officially induced errors."[75] Finally, the EPRF argued that moving the function would reduce concerns over bias or favouritism that have arisen in connection with enforcement against OCWA or the municipalities.[76]

Other parties have argued that significant benefits attach to having some interaction between IEB and other MOE functions such as policy-making, abatement, and inspection. This position was advanced by the MOE "front-line workers," as represented by OPSEU, which argued that although the IEB should remain in a separate branch and procedural protections should be put in place, a good working relationship must exist between abatement (including inspections) and the IEB.[77] A good analogy is found in many professional governing bodies where there are separate departments for handling complaints, inspections, and audits that do not necessarily lead to proceedings for the discipline or prosecution branch. OPSEU recognizes the potential conflict between the two types of functions and concedes that it is important for the IEB to have a quasi-independent status.[78]

While I am mindful of the concerns raised by EPRF, I am in general agreement with the position advanced by OPSEU. Specifically, I agree with EPRF (and many other parties) that there needs to be a strong, strict enforcement policy that applies equally to all operators – municipal, provincial, or private. I also agree that the process must function in such a way to avoid successful challenges based on abuse of process, officially induced error, or other administrative unfairness problems. I am not persuaded, however, that it is necessary to move the IEB out of the MOE to achieve these objectives.

---

[75] Energy Probe Research Foundation, "Energy Probe Research Foundation's recommendations for public hearings no. 2 & 3: Provincial government: functions and resources," Walkerton Inquiry Submission (Public Hearing, July 24, 2001), p. 3.

[76] In their submissions, representatives of EPRF stressed evidence heard in Part 1 to the effect that the IEB considered municipalities to be the "children of the province," the implication being that it would be difficult to prosecute one's own children. Note that the CEDF also referred to the lack of enforcement against municipalities but not in support of an argument from the MOE to relocate the functions of the IEB.

[77] Ontario Public Service Employee's Union, 2001, "Submissions to Part 2 of the Walkerton Inquiry concerning public hearing no. 1: Guiding principles and government structure," Walkerton Inquiry Submission, pp. 37–38.

[78] As OPSEU pointed out, Jim Merritt testified on April 12, 2001 at p. 40 that the IEB was created to separate the enforcement and abatement functions and to avoid potential conflicts between them.

Throughout this chapter I have stressed that in future the MOE must take a stricter approach to deficiencies at water treatment plants. Voluntary abatement practices for serious deficiencies in water treatment operations can no longer be tolerated. This strict enforcement of regulations and orders must also apply within the IEB. I will deal with this point again under the next recommendation. However, in my view, the strict enforcement policy can be implemented in an IEB that exists within the MOE. There are many examples in Ontario of policy, abatement, and enforcement functions existing successfully within the same ministry or entity.[79] Having the various functions co-exist successfully within the same ministry requires both an acceptance of the principle that strict enforcement is necessary and an assurance of procedural fairness.

I want to deal briefly with the procedural fairness point. The concern – which can be characterized as a breach of procedural fairness or an abuse of administrative discretion under section 8 and possibly section 7 of the *Canadian Charter of Rights and Freedoms*[80] – comes down to a concern that routine inspections could be turned into covert investigations that would otherwise require the use of search warrants or other procedural protections. When inspectors are truly acting as investigators, they are required to adhere to the stricter procedural requirements of the investigation process.[81]

Although the determination of whether an individual is acting as an inspector or an investigator can be factually difficult, the problem can be avoided by a clear separation of functions and personnel. So long as inspectors function solely as inspectors and do not also participate in the investigation process, and so long as investigators stick to investigations and do not improperly use inspection powers to assist, it is difficult to see how *Charter* or procedural fairness problems will arise. For these reasons, it is important that the investigation and enforcement function be kept separate from other functions within the MOE. This does not mean that there cannot be communication between inspectors and investigators. So long as the lines of communication

---

[79] For example, the Ontario Securities Commission, the Toronto Stock Exchange, the Law Society of Upper Canada, and the College of Physicians and Surgeons of Ontario.

[80] Section 7 of the *Charter* states that "Everyone has the right to life, liberty and security of the person and the right not to be deprived thereof except in accordance with the principles of fundamental justice." Section 8 provides that "Everyone has the right to be secure against unreasonable search or seizure."

[81] See, for example, *R. v. Inco Ltd.* (2001), 54 O.R. (3d) 495 (C.A.), which turned on the issue of whether an MOE officer was acting on reasonable grounds that a violation had occurred (in which case he would have required a search warrant) or had no such reasonable grounds (in which case he could have relied on statutory inspection powers).

remain formal, so that the functions of the two groups are not seen to meld, the procedural rights of those being regulated can be protected.

13.5.4.2.2   Enforcement Principles

Recommendation 75: The Ministry of the Environment should increase its commitment to strict enforcement of all regulations and provisions related to the safety of drinking water.

In a previous section, I discussed the development and adoption of a set of guiding principles to assist with decision making relating to inspections. I believe that a similar set of principles would assist in the investigation and enforcement function.[82] The principles are very similar, and any differences between them are in response to the different contexts of the functions:

- strict enforcement;

- effectiveness;

- consistent application to all operators;

- independence from all non-IEB influence;

- transparency of decision making; and

- adequate resources including staff with knowledge and training.[83]

Strict enforcement is the primary principle in relation to enforcing statutes and regulations dealing with the safety of drinking water. This was one of the most oft-repeated submissions I heard in Part 2 of the Inquiry. Virtually all parties felt, and I strongly agree, that those involved in the provision of drinking water must understand that deviation from the regulations and lapses in safety will not be tolerated. This message is best reinforced by a strict enforcement policy, in which the failure to follow the requirements of the system will be prosecuted and will have serious adverse consequences for those responsible.

---

[82] Because of my mandate, these principles are focused on drinking water issues.

[83] I asked the parties to comment upon the first four principles listed during the Part 2 public hearings. They received broad endorsement from most of the parties. Transparency and effectiveness were suggested by the parties, and I agree that they should be added to the list.

This is not to say that strict enforcement is the only tool to be used to achieve safe drinking water. As noted elsewhere in this report, other tools must also be used. With regard to source protection, for example, a combination of education, financial incentives, and regulation can be beneficial.[84] In my view, however, the strict enforcement of existing regulations is the necessary foundation on which such programs and incentives must be based.

The second principle is effectiveness. As I noted in relation to inspections, effectiveness is best understood as the overall goal of the IEB to minimize the occurrence, specifically the reoccurrence, of breaches of the regulatory framework governing safe drinking water. Effectiveness will hopefully result from the application of the other principles. As I noted above, it involves pausing at regular intervals to review the consequences of previous work – to identify what works and what does not work – and to adjust practice to achieve the desired results.[85]

The principle of consistent application applies to enforcement decisions as it does to inspection decisions. For the system to be effective, it is critical that enforcement apply equally to all. In relation to water treatment plant operators, it should apply equally to municipalities who operate their own systems, to OCWA, and to private operators. Similarly, in relation to source protection, enforcement should be applied in the same way to municipalities, to agriculture, and to industry.

Independence from non-IEB influence is another principle that, it is hoped, does not require much elaboration. Enforcement should not be used as a tool to achieve objectives not related to the delivery of safe drinking water. There should not be a policy of leniency in response to an infraction because the activity it relates to has other benefits. Similarly, the function should be free from political influence. The permanent instruction to the IEB should be: "strict enforcement, consistently applied."

---

[84] M.J. Goss, K.S. Rollins, K. McEwan, J.R. Shaw, H. Lammers-Helps, 2002, "The management of manure with respect to water quality," Walkerton Inquiry Commissioned Paper 6, p. 28.

[85] I am in complete agreement with the comments made by OWWA/OMWA that effectiveness should not be measured solely by the number of successful prosecutions, but also by effect on compliance rates, repeat offender rates, and improvement in drinking water quality or environmental quality. Ontario Water Works Association/Ontario Municipal Water Association, "Final submission related to the provision of safe drinking water in Ontario," Walkerton Inquiry Submission (October 2001).

The final two principles, transparency and adequate resources, also apply to the inspection function. Both principles are the subject of further analysis later in this chapter.

13.5.4.2.2   Public Enforcement Rights

Recommendation 76: The Ministry of the Environment should initiate a process whereby the public can require the Investigations and Enforcement Branch to investigate alleged violations of drinking water provisions.

CELA and CEDF each made forceful and persuasive arguments for broadening and strengthening the public's enforcement rights. CELA, for example, argued for the creation of a "citizen's suit" mechanism that "allows Ontarians to enforce drinking water requirements in civil court."[86] At its broadest, this recommendation would allow each citizen to step into the shoes of the IEB and the Ministry of the Attorney General and enforce the regulatory framework.

In my view, the enforcement of provincial regulation should primarily be the responsibility of the provincial government. Certainly, in respect of water treatment operations, if the IEB is functioning properly, it is difficult to imagine the need for citizen enforcement rights. I am also concerned that an increase in actions commenced by the public will divert time and money from the operation of the system. Consequently, in regard to water treatment plant operations, I am not inclined to recommend such a right.

On the other hand, I do favour a mechanism by which members of the public can report suspected violations resulting in a requirement that the IEB inspect these alleged violations within a reasonable time. After such an investigation, if the IEB does not initiate an action, it should provide publicly available reasons for not doing so. So long as the IEB's decisions and actions are transparent and accountable, the preferable course is to maintain enforcement as an IEB responsibility. The IEB's failure to act properly can in turn result in an appropriate public response.

Circumstances may be different in respect to other environmental offences, including those arising in the source protection context. The higher volume of potential offenders and the almost infinite number of potential infractions means that enforcement is a never-ending task. For such offences, I suggest

---

[86] Canadian Environmental Law Association, pp. 146–149.

that the government consider the implications of providing that violations of source protection regulations should be included as a matter covered by the right to sue for harm to a public resource, as contemplated by sections 82 to 102 of the *Environmental Bill of Rights*.

13.5.5   Regulation of Accredited Bodies

In matters relating to the safety of drinking water, the distinction between accreditation and regulation becomes relevant in at least two contexts: the operation of environmental laboratories and the operation of water systems. Under Ontario Regulation 459/00, environmental laboratories that test drinking water samples are now required to be accredited. The Canadian Association of Environmental Analytical Laboratories (CAEAL) is the accrediting body. I discuss this arrangement in Chapter 9.

In terms of the operation of water systems, I recommend two things. First, that the government require the owners of municipal water systems to have an accredited operating agency. Second, I recommend that owners be required to have an operational plan in place for their system, for functional approval and review by the MOE.[87] These recommendations are discussed in Chapter 11, and in the current chapter as they relate to MOE approval of municipal water systems.

The purposes of accreditation and regulation should not be confused. The purpose of accreditation is to ascertain whether an organization has appropriate systems and personnel in place to perform effectively, with periodic audits to ensure continued competency. The purpose of regulation, on the other hand, is to set out standards within which water providers must function and to ensure there is adequate oversight and enforcement in relation to those standards, that is, regulatory compliance. Although there may be some overlap between accreditation and regulation, it is important to be clear that accreditation is not a substitute for regulatory oversight.

---

[87] No doubt, water providers will want to develop effective operational plans as part of their overall quality management system. However, I recommend that this be made a formal requirement in order to separate operational aspects of the water system from the Certificate of Approval, and to allow for greater focus by MOE personnel on the multi-barrier strategies that are adopted at the plant – or facility – level.

How the government carries out its regulatory role will, of course, evolve once accreditation is well established. If accreditation is successful in raising capability across the industry, regulators will be able to focus their attention on a smaller number of more specifically defined compliance problems. From a practical point of view, MOE inspections of water systems run by an operating agency with a proven quality management system would not need to be as frequent as for other water systems. Further, it is not realistic to expect regulatory staff to have the same level of detailed knowledge and experience with water systems as do the leading members of the water industry, or to expect them to specify precisely what water providers need to do to improve performance. On the whole, accreditation should be designed and implemented so as to make regulatory assessment of compliance more effective. In terms of the concern expressed by some parties at the Inquiry that accreditation would create an alternative regime that would, in time, undermine the provincial regulatory system, the Province simply should not allow this to happen.

Let me repeat a point I made earlier. I consider the government's regulatory role to be essential. Some argue that the government in the past has not exercised this role well – the Walkerton tragedy being the prime example. Indeed, I was very critical in the Part 1 report about the manner in which the government's regulatory role was exercised in relation to Walkerton. I have no doubt that improvements are required.

However, I do not accept that the government is not capable of competently carrying out its regulatory role. On the contrary, I am satisfied that with leadership, the allocation of adequate resources, and a recognition that the safety of Ontario's drinking water is of prime importance, the government can put in place the necessary people and programs to regulate the operation of water systems and environmental testing laboratories effectively. In my view, if the government implements the recommendations in this report and those in the Part 1 report, it will be able to fulfill its regulatory and oversight responsibilities.

13.6 The Role of Other Ministries

Up to this point, the focus of my comments on government oversight has been on the MOE. However, although the MOE has had the largest part of the oversight role in regard to drinking water safety and although I have recommended that it continue to have the role of lead ministry, significant roles have been played and will continue to be played by other ministries. Most significant among them are the Ministry of Health and Long-Term Care (Ministry of Health) and the Ministry of Agriculture, Food and Rural Affairs (OMAFRA). Important roles are also played by the Ministry of Municipal Affairs and Housing (MMAH) and the Ministry of Natural Resources (MNR). I will deal with each of these in turn.

13.6.1   The Ministry of Health and Long-Term Care

As was evident from a review of the facts surrounding the tragedy in Walkerton, the Ministry of Health plays a significant role in the delivery of safe drinking water. I have discussed this role both in general and in relation to the events in Walkerton in the Part 1 report of this Inquiry.[88] I will not repeat that discussion in any detail, but I summarize the central point for ease of reference here:

- For matters of drinking water safety, the relevant part of the Ministry of Health is the Public Health Branch, headed by a director who is also the Chief Medical Officer of Health of Ontario.

- The role of the Public Health Branch is threefold:

    - to manage funding for public health programs;

    - to advise the Minister of Health on matters relating to public health; and

    - to provide advice and assistance to local health units.

- Each local health unit[89] must have a board of health which is administered by a local Medical Officer of Health (MoH).

- The office of the MoH is established under the *Health Protection and Promotion Act*. The appointment of the MoH (approved by the Minister of Health) is made by the Governor-in-Council. The MoH reports to the local board of health. The independence of the office is protected by a

---

[88] See the Part 1 report of this Inquiry, pp. 246–263.

[89] Health units are local health agencies established by a municipality (e.g., Toronto Public Health) or a group of municipalities to provide community health programs. They are funded by the province and relevant municipalities.

provision that an MoH can only be dismissed with the written consent of two-thirds of the members of the local Board of Health, as well as that of the Minister of Health.

• Among the programs administered by local health units, two are relevant to drinking water: the Control of Infectious Disease Program and the Safe Water Program. The Ministry of Health sets minimum standards in respect of both programs.

• Pursuant to the Safe Water Program, health units are required to:

  - maintain an ongoing list of all drinking water systems;

  - receive reports of adverse drinking water test results from the systems;

  - have a written protocol for dealing with adverse results; and

  - "act immediately" in accordance with the ODWO (now ODWS) "to protect the health of the public whenever an adverse drinking water result is received."

• The traditional role of the local health unit and the MoH in relation to drinking water has arisen after the point where drinking water leaves a tap. In other words, the MoH's main responsibilities have arisen when there is a potential that people will become sick from the water.

• Health units did receive notice of reports of adverse water quality as well as MOE inspection reports. However, as I found in Part 1, there was some confusion and a lack of direction to local units regarding how to respond to such reports.

• Health units generally do not consider it part of their mandate to oversee the operation of water treatment and distribution systems within their jurisdiction.

• Once a potential public health outbreak is reported, the health unit investigates; if drinking water is found to be the cause, the health unit has the power to issue a boil water advisory.[90]

---

[90] *Health Protection and Promotion Act*, s. 13 [hereafter HPPA].

- There is currently no protocol in place to provide guidance regarding when to issue a boil water advisory.[91]

Local health units play another function that was not directly relevant to the events in Walkerton but is important to the safety of drinking water. In regard to private water systems, they interpret water analysis reports, provide information regarding the potential health effects, and provide information about the health-related parameters in the Ontario Drinking Water Standards (ODWS). This is an important function: Ministry of Health laboratories and local boards of health were swamped with inquiries from private well owners after the Walkerton tragedy.

Ontario's public health system has undergone a significant evolution in the past 20 years, from being a fragmented system of about 800 boards of health to becoming a more organized and coordinated system composed of 37 health units. These units vary significantly in terms of the numbers of people they serve, from 40,000 at the low end to more than 2.6 million in the City of Toronto.

Both the Association of Local Public Health Agencies (ALPHA) and the Ontario Medical Association (OMA) made submissions regarding local boards of health. Their submissions focused on two issues: the need to ensure adequate resources to allow boards of health to fulfill their functions, and the need to clearly set out the roles and responsibilities of public health boards. Although the information before me was not extensive, both submissions are supported by the information and evidence brought to my attention. On the question of funding, the Ministry of Health has, since the early 1990s, increased the responsibility of boards of health without increasing the funding required to fulfill those responsibilities.[92] The result has been that boards' compliance with ministerial requirements has decreased. A 1999 compliance survey carried out by the ministry found that compliance with the Mandatory Health Programs and Services Guidelines was only 75%.[93] On the point of clearer roles and

---

[91] The Province has developed a draft protocol: Ontario, Ministry of Health and Long-Term Care (Public Health Branch), 2001, "Protocol for the issuance of a boil water or a drinking water advisory." See also section 11.6.3.3 of the report of the Walkerton Inquiry, Part 2, for a discussion of the draft protocol.

[92] The OMA has cited the example of the new provincial requirement that all school children be given a two-step measles vaccination. Because no funding was given, boards of health had to suspend or cut back other programs. Ontario Medical Association, 2001, "Protecting the public's health," Walkerton Inquiry Submission, p. 3.

[93] Ibid.

guidelines, the evidence in Part 1 of the Inquiry suggested that there was confusion about what the role of the Ministry of Health was or should be in relation to drinking water. This was particularly the case in regard to the issue of what action the Ministry of Health should take in the face of adverse test results and unsatisfactory inspection reports received from the MOE.

13.6.1.1 *Recommendations and Comments*

13.6.1.1.1   Role of the Local Health Units

In the Part 1 report of this Inquiry, I made three recommendations aimed at clarifying and improving the role of the Board of Health in relation to drinking water safety:

- *The* Health Protection and Promotion Act *should be amended to require boards of health and the Minister of Health, acting in concert, to expeditiously fill any vacant Medical Officer of Health position with a full-time Medical Officer of Health (MoH).*

- *The role of local Medical Officers of Health and health units in relation to public health issues concerning treated and untreated municipal water systems should be clarified and strengthened. In particular, clarification is required as to whether local Medical Officers of Health are required to implement a proactive approach to responding to adverse drinking water sample test results upon receiving notification of those results.*

- *Written guidance – developed in cooperation with local Medical Officers of Health and the Ministry of the Environment – should be provided to the local Medical Officers of Health by the Public Health Branch. It should include steps to be taken by Medical Officers of Health upon receipt of Ministry of the Environment inspection reports and adverse drinking water sample test results.*

In regard to the Medical Officer of Health (MoH) position, section 62 of the *Health Protection and Promotion Act* (HPPA) requires every board of health to have a full-time MoH. I heard evidence in Part 1 and submissions were made in Part 2 that a significant number of boards of health had MoH positions vacant. This is particularly an issue for boards that are not near a major urban centre. In addition, while the HPPA permits the appointment of an acting MoH where there is no MoH or associate MoH, there is no requirement that the acting MoH have any of the skills required for the position and there is no time limit within which a permanent MoH must be appointed.[94]

The MoH plays a vital role in maintaining public health in general, including preventing or limiting the spread of illness resulting from drinking water. It is not a position that a community should do without for any substantial length of time. If the position is difficult to fill because of a structural issue (e.g., more pay is required to have professionals agree to work in remote communities), the Ministry of Health should correct these problems.

The second and third recommendations arose from shortcomings identified in Part 1 of the Inquiry. In Walkerton, inspection reports and adverse water quality reports were received by the health unit, which did little if anything in response to such reports. As noted in Part 1, I do not fault the health unit staff for this lack of action. They were given no direction from either the ministry or the management of the health unit about what to do in these circumstances. To rectify this shortcoming, I recommend that a protocol be developed. The protocol will require further development after consultations among the MOE, the Ministry of Health, and the local health units, but its basic elements should include the following:

- Prime responsibility for treatment and distribution facilities, including responsibility for ensuring that they are compliant, should remain with the MOE. (I do not want to create a system of overlapping roles, in which confusion may arise about who is ultimately responsible.)

- The receipt of either an inspection report noting a deficiency or an adverse sample report should "engage" the health unit.

- The relevant water treatment plant should immediately be posted conspicuously at the health unit so that if illness is reported, drinking water is immediately identified as a potential cause that has a higher than normal likelihood of possibility.

- The health unit should maintain regular contact with the local MOE office and should take the system in question off "posted" status only

---

[94] HPPA, s. 69.

when the deficiency is corrected or when results return to normal for a reasonable period of time.

- In cases of chronic problems with any system, the health unit should embark on an education campaign that is aimed particularly at vulnerable elements of the population.

In addition, I have one further recommendation regarding the role of the local health units.

Recommendation 77: A steering group should be established within each public health unit area in the province, comprised of representatives of affected local hospitals, municipalities, local Ministry of the Environment offices and local boards of health, for the purpose of developing in a coordinated fashion emergency response plans for the control of, or the response to, infectious diseases and public health hazard outbreaks.

Local medical officers of health should have input into and help facilitate the development of public health aspects of emergency response plans for municipalities and hospitals within their geographical area of responsibility. I have included in section 11.6 the requirements of an emergency response plan for water providers. I think it would be useful, as well, for there to be a response plan on a community-wide basis.

13.6.1.1.2   Health Unit Resources

It was submitted in both Parts 1 and 2 of the Inquiry that local boards of health had insufficient resources to fulfill their mandates. This Inquiry has not focused on public health boards, and I do not have enough information to make specific recommendations about the adequacy of resources. I note, however, that from the evidence I have heard, including the compliance rates discussed earlier, there is a clear need for further study by the government. I recommend that the Ministry of Health take steps to obtain better information and, when conclusions can be reached, make the required adjustments. I note that the Ontario Medical Association has submitted that such adjustments should not necessarily be limited to increasing resources. For example, it may be appropriate to reorganize boards so that all have viable population bases. I will not comment on the need for reorganization, but I agree that all options should be explored. In the end, however, if further resources are required to enable local boards of health to fulfill their mandate as it relates to safe drinking water, the provincial government should ensure that a system is in place to make such resources available. There is no room to compromise the important role played by the local boards of health.

13.6.1.1.3   Information Available to Health Units

In the Part 1 report of this Inquiry, I made two recommendations about the need to improve the information made available to local boards of health.

- *Regular meetings should be scheduled between the local Ministry of the Environment office and local health unit personnel to discuss public health issues, including issues related to waterworks facilities as documented in Ministry of the Environment inspection reports. Any affected operator or laboratory should be invited to attend the meeting.*

- *Upon the implementation by the Ministry of the Environment of the Integrated Divisional System (management information system), access to it should be made available to local health units and, where appropriate, to the public. This should include access to profiles of municipal water systems and to data concerning adverse drinking water quality sample test results, as included in that database.*

I was fortunate to be able to tour a number of treatment and distribution systems during the Inquiry. I was very impressed and took great comfort from those municipalities where the local MoH had a good understanding of the system. I think that an understanding of the local systems is critical to the role of an MoH. I recognize that it will be easier to fulfill this role in larger urban centres that have relatively few treatment and distribution systems in the area covered by the local health unit. In such areas, meetings might be site-specific. Unfortunately, the need for the MoH to have a good understanding of systems is probably the greatest in more sparsely populated areas, where regular site visits are likely to be impractical. In such areas, it is particularly important that the local health unit have regular meetings with the MOE to be briefed on the problems or idiosyncrasies of each system.

The ability of the local health unit to perform its role will also be enhanced by granting it access to the Integrated Divisional System when it is operational.

13.6.2 The Ontario Ministry of Agriculture, Food and Rural Affairs

As discussed in Chapter 4, the Ontario Ministry of Agriculture, Food and Rural Affairs (OMAFRA) plays a significant role in regard to the environmental regulation of farmers. As I set out in detail above, in my view, elements of this function, including possible new initiatives like individual farm water protection plans, should be moved to the MOE. An approach has developed within the provincial government that separates the environmental impact of farming operations from all other environmental impacts. I do not think that this separation has been helpful to the ultimate goal of source protection. In my view, source protection measures should be aimed at all land users equally. This is not to say that agriculture does not have unique considerations; it clearly does. However, the likelihood of achieving an effective comprehensive policy increases when it is created and implemented by an entity the primary focus of which is the environment. Obviously, OMAFRA has and will continue to have expertise in regard to agriculture. For this reason, it is important that there be clear channels of communication between the two ministries. In addition, it will be important for the MOE to develop or, if possible, inherit an agricultural expertise.

My recommendation is not intended to result in the elimination of any role for OMAFRA. I have included a number of recommendations in Chapter 4 that involve assistance from that ministry.[95]

13.6.3 Other Ministries

As set out in Chapter 2, the Ministry of Natural Resources (MNR) and the Ministry of Municipal Affairs and Housing (MMAH) currently play peripheral roles in relation to drinking water safety.

I do not envisage a markedly different role for the MNR as a result of my recommendations. I think it is appropriate that it continue to function as the lead ministry for programs related to water quantity. However, my comment must be taken in the context of what I have recommended at the outset of this chapter – that the MOE should be given the lead role in developing and implementing the government's policy for safe drinking water. As a result, there must be consultation between the MOE and the MNR; and MNR programs,

---

[95] See Recommendations 11, 15, and 16.

to the extent that they affect the safety of drinking water, must be tailored to the overall policy.

In regard to conservation authorities, I see no difficulty in their continuing to fulfill their functions, other than those related to watershed planning, under the auspices of the MNR. However, the watershed planning process should be under the oversight of the MOE. I suspect that the watershed planning function will occupy a large part of the conservation authorities' time and resources. The provincial government should consider whether it makes sense to transfer the oversight of conservation authorities to the MOE.

The government has proposed a new role in sustained asset management for the MMAH. I have recommended a similar role in Chapter 11. As noted earlier, the asset management function must be performed in close cooperation with the MOE. If my recommendations are adopted, the MOE will have the expertise necessary to assess the technical viability of an asset management plan. This must be coordinated with MMAH's expertise in municipal financing.

13.7   Resource Management

The topic of resource management invokes three issues that transcend the entire government oversight function: the need to provide adequate financial resources, the need to improve human resource management, and the need to improve the management of information. Each issue arises repeatedly, both in this chapter and elsewhere in this report.

13.7.1   Financial Resources

Limited financial resources have become a reality of modern-day government. In the past decade, governments were elected on platforms based primarily on cost-cutting and tax-cutting. The overall merits of cost-cutting takes me well beyond my mandate, but what is relevant to the issues directly before me is the effect that inadequate resources or insufficiently considered cost-cutting measures have on the safety of the drinking water system. A number of parties in both Part 1 and 2 of the Inquiry commented on the effects of budget cuts and the lack of sufficient resources to effectively carry out the government oversight functions. I have already commented on this issue, specifically in relation to inspections, enforcement, and local health units. In addition, I concluded in the Part 1 report of this Inquiry that budget cuts at the MOE had both a direct effect and an indirect effect on the events in Walkerton. The direct effect was the failure to enact a regulation mandating testing laboratories to follow a notification protocol at the time of the privatization of laboratory testing services. The indirect effect was that budget cuts made it less likely that approvals or inspections programs would have led to the discovery of problems at Walkerton.[96]

13.7.1.1 *Recommendations and Comments*

Recommendation 78: The provincial government should ensure that programs relating to the safety of drinking water are adequately funded.

In my view, questions relating to the adequacy of financial resources, particularly in regard to drinking water, must be made in the context of the effect such decisions have upon safety. This applies equally to questions of whether a program should be offered in the first place, whether it should be scaled back, or whether it should be eliminated altogether. In the face of such decisions, the government should conduct a risk assessment in which the risks that might result from the decision are identified and assessed. As I have noted elsewhere in this report, the approach to risk assessment should be precautionary in always erring on the side of caution.

The Government of Ontario should also conduct a review of all current programs that are concerned with the safety of drinking water to assess whether those programs are adequately financed. Financial strains exist in a number of programs, including inspections, enforcement, and the local public health function. Concern about the adequacy of resources has also been raised by the municipalities. In each case, the provincial government should conduct a review of the program to determine the level of risk and the impact on safety that the current level of funding presents. Resourcing decisions should be based on the results of this analysis.

Some parties, including OPSEU, have submitted that I should recommend that MOE funding be restored to some earlier level. Their view is that this would help to bring the MOE back to a level of service that was considered superior. In my view, while I agree that increased funding is necessary, this is

---

[96] See the Part 1 report of this Inquiry, pp. 412–413.

not the appropriate way to proceed. In fact, in its random nature, it has the same flaw that some of the cutbacks had. I prefer the approach I have discussed above.

13.7.2 Human Resource Management

Related to the subject of adequate financial resources is adequate human resource management. In addition to the obvious point that greater financial resources will allow the government to employ more human resources, two general themes emerged from Part 1 of the Inquiry and were emphasized in Part 2: the need to improve morale in the public service and the need to ensure that civil servants have the required expertise and training.

As I found in Part 1, the budget cuts and staff reductions of the 1990s had a negative impact on staff morale. The same point was argued in Part 2, particularly in the submissions of OPSEU and also in the issue paper prepared by Mr. d'Ombrain.[97] OPSEU, with particular reference to the MOE, argued that at the root of the morale problem is the fact that the public service has lost some of its sense of purpose. I have not conducted an investigation into staff morale in the Ontario public service and am unable to comment extensively in this regard. However, the evidence in Part 1 and the submissions made in Part 2 provide significant support for the existence of a morale problem, especially within the MOE. It is perhaps obvious to note that good morale is important to an effective public service and that poor morale can hamper the government's oversight function. The provincial government should become proactive with respect to morale and should take steps to improve it.

The second important issue with respect to human resource management is the need to ensure adequate expertise and training. I have dealt with the topic of operator training in Chapter 12 . A similar need to improve training and expertise exists within the government. As I discussed above in connection with inspections, there is evidence that the inadequate training of environmental officers, particularly inspectors, may have played a role in the tragedy in Walkerton.

---

[97] See d'Ombrain, pp. 113–114.

13.7.2.1   *Recommendations and Comments*

I repeat the recommendations I made with respect to the training of MOE staff in the Part 1 report of this Inquiry:

- *A full needs assessment for training should be undertaken for Ministry of the Environment technical staff, and a component of that assessment should focus on communal drinking water.*

- *The Ministry of the Environment, on the basis of the needs assessment, should develop and maintain both introductory and advanced mandatory courses for environmental officers pertaining to communal drinking water systems. These courses should emphasize science and technology, including all matters that could present a risk to public health and safety; emergency pathogen risks; existing, new, and emerging treatment technologies; the limits of particular technologies; and the proper interpretation and application of government regulations, guidelines, and policies.*

- *The Ministry of the Environment should devote sufficient resources to technical training to allow the ministry to meet the challenges outlined in its "Human Resources Business Plan and Learning Plan for Fiscal Year 2000–2001."*

13.7.3 Data Management

I have commented extensively in the Part 1 report about the problems experienced in attempting to access relevant data.[98] This concern was echoed throughout the Part 2 expert meetings and public hearings. Problems from inadequate access to data arise in connection with almost all aspects of the drinking water regime from source protection to the obligations of the local boards of health. The problem is not so much that relevant information is not collected but that this information is not stored in a central, easily accessible location. During the Part 2 Public Hearings, I was informed by representatives of the province that the province is committed to the development and implementation of an Integrated Divisional System. This system, I was told, would eventually include the storage of all data related to the regulation of

---

[98] See the Part 1 report of this Inquiry, pp. 347–350.

drinking water safety and would allow access to all relevant databanks by all players in the drinking water system, including – where appropriate – the public.[99]

13.7.3.1   *Recommendations and Comments*

Recommendation 79: The Ministry of the Environment should create an Integrated Divisional System that provides central electronic access to information:

- relevant to source protection;

- relevant to each drinking water system in Ontario (including a description of the system, trend analyses, water quality, and systems data);

- required by the Drinking Water Branch (including for approvals and inspections); and

- required by local boards of health.

The need for better organization of and access to information is important in many areas related to the delivery of safe drinking water. In regard to source protection, there is a wealth of data both in existence and to be collected that is relevant to the recommendations I have made. The problem is that those entities that need it, including conservation authorities, do not always have access to it. If the watershed-based source protection planning process that I recommend is to be effective and efficient, it is important that conservation authorities be given full and free access to all needed information.

As I noted in the Part 1 report, there is also a need for improved access to data in regard to the MOE approval and inspections functions. In Walkerton, MOE employees did not have easy access to information about prior approvals and inspections of the local drinking water system, and that may have made a difference to the actions that were taken or not taken closer to the tragedy. As noted in an earlier section of this chapter, similar improvements are required with respect to access to information by local boards of health.

---

[99] R. Breeze, Walkerton Inquiry Submission (Public Hearing, July 23, 2001), transcript pp. 200–215.

13.8   Transparency and Public Access to Information

As a final point in this chapter, I would like to comment briefly on the importance of transparency and public access to information. This theme echoes throughout this report, and I do not need to go into detail about it here. The main point is that because of the importance of the safety of drinking water to the public at large, the public should be granted external access to information and data about the operation and oversight of the drinking water system. In my view, as a general rule, all elements in the program to deliver safe drinking water should be transparent and open to public scrutiny. The only caveat I make, which also relates to public safety, is that the operators and the government must be mindful of the possibility of terrorist attacks on and the vandalism of water systems. With this in mind, the public should, with relative ease, be able to access enough information to satisfy a reasonable person about the safety of the drinking water.

I have commented on the desirability of consumer confidence reports in Chapter 8. Such reports are an excellent means of disseminating relevant information to the public. They should be prepared by the system owner and operator and should set out basic information about the system and provide an annual update on its operation. A consumer confidence report would include information about any deviation from the required standards, the reason for such deviation, and the action taken to correct the problem. The reports could be included, once a year, with the local water bill.

Some parties in Part 2 recommended that continuous on-line monitoring be available to the consumer so that any member of the public could access monitoring information on the Web. Such Web sites are available in the United States.[100] While I have no objection to such systems, I am not recommending that they be implemented. Although such systems contain a good deal of information, in my view they will not be of much use to the average consumer. The combination of consumer confidence reports, an effective emergency response plan, and the annual province-wide reports I have recommended below will give consumers a more digestible, and ultimately more useful, package of information.

---

[100] See, for example, the Des Moines, Iowa, water works Web page: <http://www.dmww.com/empact.asp>.

13.8.1 Recommendations and Comments

Recommendation 80: The Drinking Water Branch should prepare an annual "State of Ontario's Drinking Water Report," which should be tabled in the Legislature.

To ensure transparency and keep the public apprised of the state of Ontario's drinking water system, including the state of the government's oversight role, a report should be prepared by the Drinking Water Branch and presented by the Minister of Environment to the legislature every year. The report should review, on a province-wide basis:

- the quality of source water and a review of source protection initiatives;

- drinking water standards, including discussions of new and emerging pathogens;

- the results (pass/failure rates) of inspections and accreditation audits; and

- a summary of enforcement activities.

The reports would not provide the same level of individual system details that consumer confidence reports do, but they should provide sufficient detail to allow an educated member of the public make an assessment of the government's performance of its oversight function.

Chapter 14   Small Drinking Water Systems

Contents

Chapter 14   Small Drinking Water Systems

14.1   Introduction

This chapter discusses some of the problems that confront small drinking water systems. Small systems lack economies of scale, and as a result it may be more expensive, on a per capita basis, for them to meet regulatory requirements. In addition, they may have difficulty attracting, retaining, and affording the expertise they need.[1]

The challenge lies not in making small systems safe; technically, this is rarely difficult. Rather, the challenge lies in doing so affordably. In this chapter, I make recommendations regarding the minimum safe operating requirements for three categories of small systems and point to some ways in which technology and good management can keep costs to a reasonable level. The three categories of small systems are those that come within the purview of Ontario Regulation 459/00, those that do not come within the regulation but provide water to the public, and private systems operated for private use.

14.2   Systems Regulated by Ontario Regulation 459/00

The starting point for determining whether a system is regulated under Ontario Regulation 459/00 is section 52 of the *Ontario Water Resources Act*,[2] which requires all waterworks to have the approval of the Ministry of the Environment (MOE) unless they fall under one of the following exemptions:

- They are used only to supply water for agricultural, commercial, or industrial purposes and not for human consumption.

- They are incapable of supplying more than 50,000 L per day.

- They are privately owned waterworks that supply water to five or fewer private residences.

---

[1] See American Water Works Association, 1995, "White paper on building water system viability" in J.A. MacDonald, for the Ontario Water Works Association/Ontario Municipal Water Association, 2001, "Review of issue #8 – Production and distribution of drinking water," Walkerton Inquiry Submission.

[2] R.S.O. 1990, c. O.40.

- They are exempted by the regulations under the Act.

Ontario Regulation 459/00 applies to water systems for which approval is required under section 52, with two additional exemptions:

- They supply 50,000 L of water or less on 88 days in every 90-day period, unless they serve more than five private residences.

- They are not capable of supplying water at a rate greater than 250,000 L per day, unless they serve more than five private residences.

Recommendation 81: Ontario Regulation 459/00 should apply to any system that provides drinking water to more than a prescribed number of private residences.

Using pumping capacity or actual use as criteria for determining the applicability of Ontario Regulation 459/00 is unnecessarily confusing. The important issue is the number of families, households, or private residences (a matter to be defined in the regulation) that should serve as the cut-off point for a communal system falling under the regulation. Currently that number is five. I recognize that a line has to be drawn somewhere, and I have no reason to disagree with this number.

14.3 Variances from Ontario Regulation 459/00

During the Inquiry, I heard from a number of parties that the requirements of Ontario Regulation 459/00 were financially onerous for some small systems. This was said to be true whether the systems were municipally or privately owned, although the private owners who appeared before the Inquiry were rural subdivisions, not the nine industrial owners of communal drinking water systems. The recommendations in this report relating to accreditation would raise costs further for municipally owned systems.

The underlying principle is that communal water systems should be safe, in the sense of the goal I set out in Chapter 1.[3] I would therefore not propose that variances from the requirements of Ontario Regulation 459/00 or the

---

[3] The overall goal of the recommendations is to ensure that drinking water systems in Ontario deliver water with a level of risk so negligible that a reasonable and informed person would feel safe drinking from the tap.

recommendations of this report be granted simply on the basis of cost. The test should be based solely on an assessment of risk.

Recommendation 82: The Ministry of the Environment should establish a procedure under which owners of communal water systems may apply for a variance from provincial regulations only if a risk analysis and management plan demonstrate that safe drinking water can be provided by means other than those laid down in regulations.

Ontario Regulation 459/00 was created quickly in the wake of the tragic events in Walkerton. The commendable result was that the standards for quality and sampling that had previously been mere guidelines or objectives were made enforceable in law. In so doing, the regulation stiffened some requirements and imposed new costs on municipalities. It may also have made a few matters more rigid and universal than they need to be.

The main changes introduced by Ontario Regulation 459/00 that carried cost implications, for at least some of the smaller systems, are as follows:

- Groundwater must be disinfected – in practice, with chlorine (s. 5).

- Surface water must have chemically assisted filtration and disinfection or, in the view of the MOE director, receive equivalent or better treatment (s. 5).

- An exemption can be made from disinfection and chlorination, but only after a lengthy and expensive process, and only if the equipment and chemicals for disinfection are installed and available for instant use if needed (s. 6).

- A more onerous sampling regime (s. 7) requires, among other things, that testing be done either in a laboratory accredited for the particular test by the Canadian Association of Environmental Analytical Laboratories (CAEAL), operating under the aegis of the Standards Council of Canada (SCC) (s. 2), or by staff certified for the procedure in question (s. 7).

- Notification requirements are formalized, and requirements to take any necessary corrective action and to inform the public are introduced (ss. 8–11).

- Exhaustive quarterly public reports of test results and actions taken must be made available to the public (s. 12).

- Consulting engineers must be retained every 3 years to make a detailed examination of the works and to prepare reports according to an MOE outline.

Small communities are now faced with new requirements for qualified and certificated staff and with the logistics and costs of having regular sampling done. Information management systems must be improved. Some communities must acquire chlorinators and deal with the resulting materials-handling and qualified-labour expenses.

The costs of the new testing and chlorination requirements are most burdensome in some rural subdivisions, villages, and other very small drinking water systems. Many of these systems have never had problems with their water. Thus it seems to me that it is reasonable to relax some requirements of Ontario Regulation 459/00 in cases where the water supply comes from wells of long-established safety or where an assessment of the risks indicates that certain standards are not necessary. The test for granting a variance, however, should be based solely on an assessment of risk, not of cost.

Assessing risks may reduce the burden of costs for some communities, but not for all. With this in mind, I make two further recommendations.

Recommendation 83: The provincial government should not approve water systems that would not be economically viable under the regulatory regime existing at the time of the application.

This recommendation can prevent the creation of further problems. Often, when an applicant seeks approval for a water system, it is faced with making choices about the manner in which the system will be managed and the technology that will be used. To save costs, small communities may involve others in the management and operation of their water systems through consolidation or contracting, build for present rather than distant future requirements, or choose less expensive technologies as a condition of provincial approval. The Province should not, however, after approving a system, be confronted with the dilemma of either reducing regulatory standards to an unacceptable level or facing demands for financial assistance to ensure the system's compliance. The applicant should confront the economic problems before approval is granted.

Recommendation 84: Approved systems that are not economically viable under the improved regulatory scheme should be required to explore all managerial, operational, and technological options to find the most economical way of providing safe drinking water. If the system is still too expensive, the provincial government should make assistance available to lower the cost per household to a predetermined level.

The difficulty here is that the Province has approved some systems and has imposed or will be imposing, for safety reasons, regulatory requirements that are more costly than those existing at the time of approval. The first step in these situations must be to consider less expensive alternatives for safely managing and operating the system, including making improvements in the use of technology.

A number of avenues exist to upgrade the quality of the small systems' water operations. These systems may move related functions under one administrative roof, thus increasing the scope and skill of management and other specialized services. They may seek cooperative or contractual arrangements with a larger nearby municipality. They may consolidate their operations with those of other municipalities in the region who have similar concerns, or they may gradually upgrade their own staff, through training. In addition, they may contract their operations to a suitably competent operator, such as the Ontario Clean Water Agency (OCWA), or to the private companies that may bid for the business.

When all these options fail to reduce the cost of drinking water to a predetermined level, the Province may determine that the system is not economically viable. In these cases, the Province should provide enough assistance to reduce the cost to the predetermined level. Although I do not have figures to indicate the costs of such assistance, my impression from the somewhat fragmentary evidence given in presentations to the Inquiry is that the aggregate subsidy would not be large. Situations requiring subsidies should be dealt with as the need arises, rather than cause a departure from the high standards of drinking water safety that Ontario residents expect.

14.4   Other Systems Serving the Public

Ontario Regulation 459/00 does not apply:

- to systems that do not have the capacity to supply more than 50,000 L per day (because of the exemption in section 52(8)(b) of the *Ontario Water Resources Act*); or

- to private systems that have a capacity of less than 250,000 L per day and that do not serve more than five private residences; or

- to private systems that actually deliver less than 50,000 L per day for 88 out of any 90 days and do not serve more than five private residences.

Whether or not the volumetric criterion is dropped, as I recommend, there are many types of systems not covered by Ontario Regulation 459/00 that serve water to the public. Here I refer to water providers such as rural schools, hospitals, churches, retirement homes, hospitals, restaurants, gas stations, daycare centers, campgrounds, summer camps, resorts, and golf courses that rely on their own water supply.

Ontario has begun to address this situation with the passage of Ontario Regulation 505/01, which requires designated types of small private water systems to meet certain treatment requirements. This regulation applies only when Ontario Regulation 459/00 does not. The designated systems include those that provide water to at-risk groups, such as the young, the elderly, and the infirm.

Systems regulated under Ontario Regulation 505/01 that use groundwater are required to disinfect the water,[4] and those that use surface water or groundwater that is within 15 m of surface water must either follow the surface water treatment requirements of the Chlorination Procedure or provide equivalent filtration and disinfection.[5] The regulation also contains provisions regarding

---

[4] Disinfection must be able to inactive 99% of waterborne viruses and provide *CT* to a prescribed level.

[5] Treatment must be able to achieve 4-log inactivation of waterborne viruses and 3-log inactivation of *Giardia*, and it must be as reliable and as free of disinfection by-products as the systems recommended in the Chlorination Procedure: Ontario, Ministry of the Environment, 2001, "Procedure B13-3 Chlorination of Potable Water Supplies in Ontario" (updated January 2001).

the need for residual disinfection in the distribution system, monitoring and reporting obligations, and responding to adverse test results.

However, Ontario Regulation 505/01 does not apply to many of the types of private systems mentioned above that have a commercial or institutional interest in providing water for human consumption to the public. There is a need, in my view, for additional protection.

Recommendation 85: The application of Ontario Regulation 505/01 should be broadened to include all owners of water systems that serve the public for a commercial or institutional purpose and that do not come within the requirements of Ontario Regulation 459/00.

In my view, where a person has a commercial or institutional interest in supplying water to another, the supplier is bound to ensure that the water being supplied is safe and that the people who put their trust in the supplier are justified in doing so. Such a person should act with the prudence of any reasonable person. The Province has established a standard for this circumstance by enacting Ontario Regulation 505/01, the requirements of which seem to me to cover these situations reasonably.

However, it is not necessary for all such establishments to provide potable water to the public. While I agree that those institutions to which Ontario Regulation 505/01 currently applies must provide potable water and therefore must meet the treatment requirements laid out in the regulation, the newly captured establishments should be given an option of either complying with the current requirements of Ontario Regulation 505/01 or posting notices at every tap that inform water users that the water is not potable. Depending on the circumstances, water suppliers who choose to post non-potable water signs may wish to provide an alternative supply of bottled or bulk drinking water.

14.5   Private Systems

At present, owners of private water systems that do not come within the application of Ontario Regulation 459/00 or Ontario Regulation 505/01 are not required to meet any regulatory standards to ensure the safety of the water. I recommend above that this be changed for those who provide drinking water to the public as part of their institutional or commercial business. I do not recommend, however, that private owners who do not supply water to the public be required to meet regulatory requirements. I am suggesting that private water system owners not serving the public continue to be responsible for the safety of their own water. I do think, however, that the Province can assist private owners in providing safe water.

Recommendation 86: With regard to private drinking water systems that are not covered by either Ontario Regulation 459/00 or Ontario Regulation 505/01, the provincial government should provide the public with information about how to supply water safely and should ensure that this information is well distributed. It should also maintain the system of licensing well drillers and ensure the easy availability of microbiological testing, including testing for *E. coli.*

Present regulations use five residential units as the cut-off point to distinguish the systems to which Ontario Regulation 459/00 applies from those to which it does not. Ontario Regulation 505/01, even amended as I propose, would apply only to private systems serving the public.

Whatever the number of residences to which Ontario Regulation 459/00 applies, I do not consider it practical to impose the whole regulatory and testing regime of Ontario Regulations 459/00 and 505/01 on private systems that are smaller than a certain size and that do not serve the public. The inspections would be costly and intrusive, and the costs of implementing compliant systems would, for many, be prohibitive. Fortunately, developing technologies such as UV radiation and membrane treatment techniques are becoming economically viable for single houses and small systems. Since owners of private systems do not pay for water from treated communal supplies, they should be able to pay for their own treatment technology.

One important contribution for the provincial government in this area lies in providing information to the public on such topics as wells and their protection, water treatment options, and good sanitation practices. Much of this information exists in some form, but improvements in presentation are required, as are more technical resources to complement simplified consumer information.

Rural households have a corresponding obligation to construct and decommission wells properly and to supply the information necessary for the assessment of common resources. This obligation is laid out in Regulation 903 under the *Ontario Water Resources Act,* which also requires all well drillers and technicians to be licensed.[6] The proper construction of water wells is best accomplished by thoroughly applying existing licensing systems. Ontario Regulation 903 should be reviewed and updated if necessary to ensure that it requires best construction practices.[7]

The Province can also assist in the area of drinking water testing. The Ministry of Health commendably now offers free bacteriological testing, which should be available to all owners of private wells. Consumers would, of course, be free to test more frequently, or for other parameters, at their own expense.

14.6   Technology

Some recent technical developments may be of use to small communal water systems, private water systems, and small waste treatment systems.

14.6.1 Technology for Small Communal Systems

New technology can play an important role in assisting small systems to provide reliable safe water at a reasonable price. The problem arises with the application of big-system standards – including chemically assisted filtration and chlorination – to small communal water systems.

Small communal systems also have problems that transcend regulations. From a technical point of view, one is the variation in demand over time. Water treatment technologies, with the partial exception of membrane and UV systems, perform best under relatively stable flows and with unchanging source water quality. As a result, water in small systems may have to be treated and stored rather than treated on demand.[8] Another challenge facing small communal systems lies in designing an affordable treatment process capable of responding to changing raw water conditions. The stability of raw water quality should be of particular concern, because the complex treatments for dealing

---

[6] R.R.O. 1990, Reg. 903.

[7] The government has recently proposed changes to the way it regulates wells. I am not in a position to comment on the proposed changes because they have been introduced only recently. Ontario, Ministry of the Environment, 2002, "Government toughens well construction rules to protect drinking water," press release, April 5 <www.ene.gov.on.ca/envision/news/20021040501.htm> [accessed April 23, 2002].

[8] K. Faller, ed., 1999, *Design and Construction of Small Water Systems*, 2nd ed. (Denver: American Water Works Association), p. 8.

with varying quality can quickly drive costs to unaffordable levels. On the regulatory side, the problem may lie less in designing a system to meet today's standards than in designing the one that will be able to meet future standards.[9]

In general, capital and operating costs can be significantly higher per customer for small systems [10] and the availability of trained staff and management may be a fundamental constraint. There is no getting around the fact that the technical systems needed to ensure safety demand trained specialists, who are in short supply and who may not be needed full-time in smaller places. As drinking water standards become more stringent, small systems will have to develop new strategies.

Appropriate technologies for these systems include traditional filtration and disinfection systems, as well as membrane and UV treatment. All these technologies remove pathogens. Membrane technologies also remove sediment and many contaminants, and the only other treatment required for membrane technologies is a disinfectant residual for the distribution system, if there is one. It is also possible to install ultrafiltration units sized to an individual household.

UV treatment, which requires filtration and a chemical residual, may also require specialized treatment processes such as granular activated carbon (GAC) for taste and odour removal. The advantages of these technologies for small systems include compactness, reasonable capital expenditures, and low maintenance and operating costs. Packaged conventional treatment facilities are another alternative for small systems with good-quality source water. These self-contained units are delivered to a site and hooked up to the source water and distribution systems. They treat the water while requiring little maintenance.

Innovations in management and technology will provide more fruitful avenues for smaller systems than will the relaxation of standards.

---

[9] Canada, Department of National Health and Welfare, Health Protection Branch, 1993, *Water Treatment Principles and Applications* (Ottawa: Canadian Water and Wastewater Association), p. 31.

[10] Costs decline dramatically with the scale of operation, typically levelling off in the 40 ML/d range, according to U.S. Environmental Protection Agency work reported in W.B. Dowbiggin, 2001, "Advanced water treatment without advanced treatment costs," proceedings at the AWWA Annual Conference, Washington, June 18, 2001.

14.6.2 Technology for Small Private Systems

Two types of water treatment devices are available for private individual systems: point of entry (POE) and point of use (POU) devices. POE technologies treat water as it enters a house; water flowing to all outlets in the house is therefore treated but not necessarily chlorinated. Both UV and membrane technology devices are POE treatments. POU devices treat water as it leaves the tap. Faucet filters and fridge filters are in this category. According to Statistics Canada, in 1994, 19.5% of Canadians and 24.9% of Ontarians had a filter or purifier system for drinking water in their homes.[11]

Cartridge filters, which are traditional POU devices, can be used for membrane pre-treatment as well. Filter media include membranes, fabrics, string, and porous ceramic filter elements. Viruses and bacteria can pass through most of these filters – a problem exacerbated by the ability of protozoan cysts and oöcysts to deform to a certain extent and pass through smaller pore sizes than might be anticipated. Thus, it may be necessary to use pre-treatment to remove larger sediments and disinfection to prevent microbial growth.[12] Once the system reaches a certain pressure drop or headloss, the cartridge is discarded rather than cleaned. If the cartridge is not replaced at the appropriate time, highly concentrated contaminants may break through, into the filtered water, and lower water quality.

This type of occurrence highlights the greatest problem with the use of POE and POU treatment systems: the user is responsible for their operation and maintenance. If the equipment is not cared for and the filters are not replaced when necessary, the systems can *reduce* water quality. As well as experiencing filter breakthrough, POE and POU systems can provide an attractive host environment for bacterial growth. Thus they require a method of monitoring use or contaminant build-up, as well as foolproof warning systems. For example, one manufacturer has introduced a pressure-sensitive dial that indicates the appropriate time to change the filter.

A further problem with POU devices is the lack of certification for different products. It is difficult to know how effective some of these devices are, if at all, against various water contaminants. The Canadian Standards Association (CSA)

---

[11] Statistics Canada, 1995, "Households and the environment survey 1994," Cat. no. 11-526, Table 12, p. 41.

[12] HDR Engineering Inc., 2001, *Handbook of Public Water Systems*, 2nd ed. (New York: John Wiley & Sons), p. 354.

certifies devices by using relevant American National Standards Institute (ANSI) standards, but this certification is not mandatory. Although independent laboratories can assess the validity of claims made, their approval is not mandatory.

An alternative for some small communities and individual homeowners is to have drinking water delivered in bulk. This area of drinking water supply is presently unregulated. Although I have not looked into this issue in detail, I encourage the Province to do so and to develop an appropriate regulatory framework as necessary.

Recommendation 87: The provincial government should review the current practices for the delivery of drinking water in bulk and the need for a regulatory framework in this area.

14.6.3 Waste Treatment Techniques for Small Systems

Small-scale wastewater treatment devices, such as septic tanks, have great potential to pollute source waters. This is primarily because of their large numbers, the lack of certification and monitoring, and a frequent lack of maintenance that leads to the premature release of undigested matter. Although regulated under both the Ontario Building Code and Ontario Regulation 122/98, septic tanks tend to be built and forgotten. As a result, substantial groundwater pollution can occur before it is obvious or visible. The Ministry of Municipal Affairs and Housing has developed a guide to septic tank operation and maintenance.[13] It also provides a list of approved systems to meet the secondary effluent quality criteria of the Ontario Building Code.

Packaged systems for the private treatment of wastewater are increasingly available. They are based on either conventional digestion, composting, or incineration. In general, they are delivered in a self-contained unit and maintained by an authorized contractor, and they may include built-in monitoring devices that draw immediate attention to system failure. Current warning systems for septic tanks use a float system hooked up to a klaxon and light warning panel. Their prices range from $150 to $450.

---

[13] See, for example, Ontario, Ministry of Municipal Affairs and Housing, n.d., "A guide to operating and maintaining your septic system" <www.obc.mah.gov.on.ca/septic.htm/new_sept.pdf> [accessed April 7, 2002].

The treatment capacity of self-contained conventional wastewater treatment units ranges from single homes to small municipalities of up to 2,000 people. This capacity can be increased by using multiple units. The units provide settling, biological oxidation, final settling, and sludge storage. Advanced options such as tertiary filtration, denitrification, disinfection, and phosphorus reduction can be integrated into the units.

Composting toilets are an alternative method of treating wastewater. Some composting toilets do not require water or use only small amounts; other designs use foam instead of water. Typically, systems that use water will be part of a total wastewater treatment system. If a home does not have central wastewater services, a composting toilet may be practical. Coupled with a subsurface grey-water irrigation system, a composting toilet can make the installation of a black-water septic system unnecessary. Commercially available composting toilets range in price from $1,000 for simpler units to more than $10,000 for fully integrated wastewater/composting systems.[14]

On-site composting can be done on any scale, to serve either individual users or 10,000 people a day at a beach. Municipalities can use composting as part of their wastewater treatment and may even do so profitably, if the product can be sold as fertilizer, as it is in Austin, Texas. Closer to home, the C.K. Choi Building at the University of British Columbia, a 3,000-m^2 office complex that houses the Institute of Asian Research, is not connected to the city's sewer system. Instead, it composts its sewage and recycles its grey water for on-site irrigation. [15]

[14] See <http://www.greenbuilder.com/sourcebook/CompostToilet.html-Implement> [accessed April 7, 2002].

[15] City Farmer, n.d., "Composting toilets, Urban agricultural notes" <www.cityfarmer.org/comptoilet64.html> [accessed April 16, 2002].

Chapter 15   First Nations

Contents

Chapter 15   First Nations

15.1   Aboriginal Ontario

The water provided to many Métis and non-status Indian communities and to First Nations reserves is some of the poorest quality water in the province. Submissions by the Ontario Métis Aboriginal Association[1] and the Chiefs of Ontario,[2] as well as the federal government's reports about the quality of water on reserves,[3] make it clear that water is not provided for aboriginal people at the standards that generally prevail throughout Ontario. In summary:

- infrastructure is either obsolete, entirely absent, inappropriate, or of low quality;

- not enough operators are adequately trained or certified;

- testing and inspection are inadequate;

- microbial contamination is frequent; and

- distribution systems, especially on reserves, are sized to deliver about half the water available per capita to other Ontarians.

This is not acceptable. Aboriginal Ontarians, including First Nations people living on "lands reserved for Indians," are residents of the province and should be entitled to safe drinking water on the same terms as those prevailing in other similarly placed communities. Métis and non-status Indian communities are addressed as part of the other recommendations in this report; the focus of the present chapter is on drinking water systems on Indian reserves in Ontario.

---

[1] Ontario Métis Aboriginal Association, 2001, "Safety of drinking water supplying off-reserve aboriginal peoples in Ontario," Walkerton Inquiry Submission.

[2] Chiefs of Ontario, 2001, "Drinking water in Ontario First Nation communities: Present challenges and future directions for on-reserve water treatment in the province of Ontario," Walkerton Inquiry Submission.

[3] Canada, Health Canada and Department of Indian Affairs and Northern Development, 1995, *Community Drinking Water and Sewage Treatment in First Nation Communities* (Ottawa).

15.2   First Nations: The Mandate of This Inquiry

This is a provincial Inquiry under the Ontario *Public Inquiries Act.* There are therefore limits to how far I should comment on matters outside the responsibility of the province and provincially constituted institutions such as municipalities. It might be argued that all matters within the jurisdiction of the First Nations and the federal government should be beyond comment. Other provincial commissions, however, have not adopted so strict a guideline.[4]

In the present case, there are two compelling arguments for making observations and recommendations relating to the quality of drinking water provided on First Nations reserves. First, water is a mobile resource that does not respect political boundaries. One person's sewage disposal system may affect someone else's water supply. Simple geography argues for the joint management of a commonly shared resource. Second, and even more compelling, is the argument of equity. There is no justification for permitting lower public health standards for some residents of Ontario than those enjoyed by others. Members of First Nations are also residents of Ontario. There can be no justification for acquiescing in the application of a lesser public health standard on certain residents of Ontario than that enjoyed by others in the province. This is especially true when there is ample evidence that the water provided in First Nations communities falls well short of the standards of safety and adequacy that are considered acceptable in other parts of the province.

It seems to me, therefore, that recommendations that do not address the social and geographical unity of Ontario would be short of the mark. That said, I recognize the constitutional reality relating to First Nations reserves, and I have tried to craft my analysis and recommendations in appropriate language so as not to tread on the constitutional territory of others.

It is important to note that the First Nations themselves have encouraged me to make certain recommendations relating to their drinking water situations.

---

[4] Commissioner J.E.J. Fahlgren, for example, addressed some recommendations to Indian communities, and in another case urged the Government of Ontario to urge the federal government to undertake reforms: Ontario, Royal Commission on the Northern Environment, 1985, *Final Report and Recommendations of the Royal Commission on the Northern Environment* (Toronto). Commissioner the Hon. John P. Robarts, P.C., C.C., Q.C., took account of federal–provincial–municipal fiscal relations and addressed one recommendation to a federal body, the Toronto Harbour Commissioners: Ontario, Royal Commission on Metropolitan Toronto, 1977, *Report*, vol. 2, *Detailed Findings and Recommendations* (Toronto).

In August 2000, the Chiefs of Ontario applied for standing under Part 2 of this Inquiry and subsequently prepared a very helpful paper for the Inquiry. Although the federal government has not participated formally in the work of the Inquiry, it has gone some distance to assist that work, and undoubtedly recognizes the importance of improving drinking water conditions on reserves.

It is difficult to measure precisely the state of drinking water systems on First Nations reserves in Ontario. All indications are that a high proportion of reserves have high-risk systems. For example, in 1995 Health Canada and the Department of Indian Affairs and Northern Development undertook a survey of drinking water quality on Indian reserves across the country.[5] The results were disturbing – one-quarter of the reserves were not up to basic safety standards. In response, the federal government doubled its allocation to water and sewage capital for reserve water systems to $250 million per year. A mid-2000 update showed improvement and produced the results shown in Table 15.1.

The survey demonstrates that progress is being made, but slowly. The 22 communities identified as "high risk" in September 2000 do not include those needing capital upgrades, backup equipment, operator training, emergency procedures, safety equipment, or operating manuals. Clearly, much remains to be done.[6]

Table 15.1 Ontario First Nations Water Systems, 2000

Number of systems (1995):	179
Number of high-risk systems in 1995:	40
Number of high-risk systems in September 2000:	22

Source: Canada, Department of Indian Affairs and Northern Development, 2000, memo from P. Chabot to B. Labrador, Ottawa, December 21.

The definition of "high risk" used in the 2000 survey was "systems with potential health and safety concerns such as repetitive water boiling advisories, not meeting the [MAC] parameters specified in the *Guidelines for Canadian Drinking Water Quality*, and other issues of a similar nature. Deficiencies identified under this

---

[5] Canada, Health Canada and Department of Indian Affairs and Northern Development.

[6] Ontario First Nations are not alone: 105 communities were at high risk across Canada in June 2000: Canada, Department of Indian Affairs and Northern Development, 2000, memo from P. Chabot to B. Labrador, Ottawa, December 21.

category may pose an immediate health risk." The survey provided some examples of deficiencies:

- a main component of water treatment equipment is dysfunctional and requires immediate replacement of a part such as a chlorination unit, filter, or chlorine feed pump; ...

- an operator does not have formal training and, at ... minimum, background knowledge of the system that he or she operates;

- the quality of the raw water source is poor and there is no appropriate treatment in place;

- bacteriological tests of the drinking water indicating the presence of coliform organisms;

- a lack of regular testing and maintenance of records.[7]

15.2.1 The Federal Role

In response to a request from the Inquiry,[8] the federal government described the roles and responsibilities for drinking water on reserves as follows:

> Responsibility for drinking water on reserves is shared among First Nation Band Councils, Health Canada, and Indian and Northern Affairs Canada (INAC). INAC provides funding to First Nations to assist them in the provision of water services within reserve communities and monitors the design, construction and maintenance of the facilities. Funding is provided for capital construction, or upgrading, as well as for the operation and maintenance of the water facilities. Generally, First Nations Band Councils are responsible for ensuring that water facilities are

---

[7] Canada, DIAND, Terms of Reference, June 7, 2001.

[8] A request for a statement of federal compared with First Nations roles and responsibilities was first made to the-then Deputy Minister of Indian Affairs and Northern Development in October 2000 and was followed up in correspondence dated June 5, 2001. A response was received on July 5, 2001. The Inquiry has been informed that a more detailed policy-oriented paper has been prepared but is still under review in the Prime Minister's Office. Informal discussions with federal officials have aided my understanding, however.

designed, constructed, maintained and operated in accordance with established federal or provincial/territorial standards, whichever are the most stringent. Health Canada provides assistance to water quality monitoring and surveillance programs in First Nations' communities.[9]

...

With respect to Indian reserves, the policy of Indian and Northern Affairs Canada (INAC) is that all new or upgraded systems are to be designed and constructed to meet the *Guidelines for Canadian Drinking Water Quality* or provincial/territorial standards, whichever are more stringent.[10]

I would make three observations about this situation. First, there are no legally enforceable federal or provincial standards relating to drinking water on First Nations reserves. First Nations band councils have the responsibility for ensuring that water facilities are designed, constructed, and maintained, and operated within the more stringent of the federal or provincial standards. Contracts and funding arrangements may require compliance with these standards. However, absent a band bylaw conferring authority on Health Canada or its officers, who are asked to provide assistance on water quality and surveillance programs, the system must work by goodwill and cooperation. Elsewhere in this report, I recommend legally enforceable standards for all water treatment and delivery systems in the province.

Second, Ontario now imposes higher standards than do the *Guidelines for Canadian Drinking Water Quality* for sampling, testing, and reporting on water quality. It was reported to me that the federal government has not yet adopted these standards for First Nations reserves of applying the more stringent of the federal or provincial standards despite the stated policy. If this is indeed the case, it should be addressed.

Third, other than the possibility of a First Nation band council adopting provincial standards, the position as stated by the federal government makes

---

[9] J. Weiner, Health Canada, and J. Mills, Environment Canada, 2001, letter to Dr. H. Swain, Walkerton Inquiry, July 5, p. 1.
[10] Ibid., appendix to letter, p. B-1.

no provision for a role, even a voluntary one, for the province for ensuring the safety of drinking water on First Nations reserves. As I set out below, I believe that the province, if asked, has much to contribute.

15.2.2 Ontario's Views

The provincial government correctly takes the view that "Indians and lands reserved for Indians" are matters for the federal government and the First Nations. It does not assert that Ontario Regulation 459/00 applies to First Nations reserves, and it does not provide training, inspection, mechanisms for joint planning, or (through the Ontario Clean Water Agency) operations and maintenance of on-reserve systems.[11] Certificates of Approval are not provided for waterworks, although "if requested, technical comments may be provided by MOE if resources [are] available."[12] Should a part of the works lie outside the reserve, normal conditions apply, with the exception that the Certificate of Approval will contain a condition that it be revoked if the land on which the facility lies becomes reserve land. If the MOE is aware of a situation that may be environmentally significant, "a request may be made that the Minister of Indian and Northern Affairs consider provincial requirements when issuing a permit." However, the minister does not issue permits.

In fact, there is some involvement by the province in drinking water matters for some First Nations. For example, the MOE monitors water quality at Walpole Island and at Ohsweken, two substantial Southern Ontario aboriginal communities whose traditional drinking water resources have been seriously polluted by their neighbours. The province has also provided technical advice regarding nitrosodimethylamine (NDMA) pollution at Ohsweken.[13]

Formally, Ontario seeks to avoid new and potentially expensive responsibilities in this area. The opportunities for both aboriginal and non-aboriginal Ontarians are large, however, and I sense that if requested, the province would be willing to assume a much more active role. After all, water does not respect political boundaries. A variety of informal cooperative arrangements already exist in the area of water as well as in broader environmental fields. A good way to start

[11] Curiously, OCWA sometimes advertises in the *Bulletin* of the Aboriginal Water Works Association of Ontario. OCWA was reported to be undertaking a survey of reserve water facilities in Ontario for the Ontario First Nations Technical Services Corporation: Chiefs of Ontario, p. 55.
[12] Ontario, Native Affairs Secretariat, 2000, "Water quality on Indian reserves."
[13] Ibid.

would be to have First Nations, where appropriate, involved in the watershed-based source protection planning process recommended in Chapter 4 of this report.

15.2.3 First Nations' Views on Government Roles

The view of the Chiefs of Ontario has been set out clearly in their submission to this Inquiry.[14] They point out that the provincial water regulation regime does not apply to Indian reserves. They agree, however, that cross-border issues require "that First Nations cannot afford to be oblivious to provincial requirements."[15] The Chiefs of Ontario also say that "the question of 'which law applies' is inherently uncertain for most activities that take place on reserve because of the judicially undefined scope of aboriginal rights and the vague and subjective tests which govern the division of powers impacting on 'Indianness.'"[16]

There is another view, also referred to in the Chiefs of Ontario brief, that provincial or federal laws of general application apply on reserve to the degree they do not impinge on aboriginal, treaty, or specific statute rights – in other words, on the essence of aboriginality.[17] Thus, for example, the *Criminal Code* applies on reserve lands, as do some other statutes insofar as their provisions do not contradict sections 86 or 88 of the *Indian Act*. There is an argument that the same may apply to public health and other social standards, though the Chiefs of Ontario would disagree.[18]

The Chiefs of Ontario also take the position that there is a federal fiduciary obligation to provide resources to the First Nations so that they have the capacity to provide for themselves.[19]

---

[14] Chiefs of Ontario, c. 2.

[15] Ibid., p. 24.

[16] Ibid., p. 28.

[17] Ibid., c. 2; R. Foerster, 2002, "Constitutional jurisdiction over the safety of drinking water," Walkerton Commissioned Paper 2.

[18] Chiefs of Ontario, pp. 36–37.

[19] Ibid.

The Chiefs of Ontario brief concludes its analysis of responsibilities by saying that nothing prevents

> the establishment of an effective tripartite relationship between DIAND, First Nations and provinces such as Ontario which may well be better equipped than the federal government to provide some of the mechanisms to build First Nation capacity to operate and maintain effective water treatment systems. However as a further incident of the fiduciary relationship between Canada and First Nations, capacity-building solutions must not be unilaterally imposed on First Nations, particularly by a federal-provincial agreement to which First Nations are not a party.[20]

This is a sensible conclusion. The First Nations face a serious public health problem, and nothing should impede all three parties from exercising their best efforts, and their comparative advantages, in together improving conditions on reserves. Accepting for purposes of discussion that the province has no obligation to bear any unrecovered costs, that should be no bar to access on a fee-for-service basis to the training, certification, licensing, laboratory, inspection, and even enforcement resources of the Province. The question as to who – among residents, First Nations, and the federal government – should pay the costs is separate from the question of the willingness of Ontario to offer assistance in helping its First Nations citizens improve their drinking water supplies.

15.3   Issues and Recommendations

There are many areas for improvement with respect to the water supplies of Ontarians living on reserves. My discussion has focused on communities subject to the *Indian Act*, but a number of First Nations are moving toward self-government – in principle, "special Act" status that will define a new relationship between a freestanding First Nation government and the existing orders of government. One commentator suggests that the negotiators' briefs contain

---

[20] Chiefs of Ontario, p. 39.

nothing specific about the exacting business of delivering safe drinking water, and I note his concern on this point.[21]

Below I set out a number of recommendations. When they are directed to the First Nations or the federal government, these recommendations are simply suggestions that I make respectfully recognizing the constitutional limits of my mandate.

15.3.1 Planning

Recommendation 88: Ontario First Nations should be invited to join in the watershed planning process outlined in Chapter 4 of this report.

Elsewhere I have recommended that multi-stakeholder planning on a watershed basis is the key to source water protection. It is vital that First Nations be at the table when the resources they share with the rest of the community are at issue. Waters flow onto reserve and off, carrying their particular loads of contaminants. No one in a watershed should be required to import a problem from or be able to export a problem to a neighbour.

15.3.2 Standards

On the important issue of what standards should apply on reserve, no one would argue that First Nations should have a lower standard of health-related standards than others in the province.

Recommendation 89: I encourage First Nations and the federal government to formally adopt drinking water standards, applicable to reserves, that are as stringent as, or more stringent than, the standards adopted by the provincial government.

This suggestion has two parts. The first is the need to have the same or a higher level of standards on reserve as off reserve, including standards such as those found in Ontario Regulation 459/00 relating to the treatment, sampling, testing,

---

[21] J. Graham, 2001, "Rethinking self-government agreements: The case of potable water," Policy Brief No. 12, November (Ottawa: Institute on Governance). Graham thinks it unrealistic to expect small, isolated communities to set standards for and deliver on matters that evidently stretch the capacities of much larger entities.

and reporting of water quality. The second part is that the First Nations and the federal government should explore ways to make these standards legally enforceable. In the Part 1 report, I discussed at some length the disadvantages of using guidelines rather than legally enforceable standards in this critical public health area. Because the risks of unsafe drinking water are so high, it is important to have legal mechanisms that will respond to unsafe conditions.

Finally, I would include as a health matter the suggestion that First Nations water systems be constructed to provide the quantities of water normally provided for households in similar geographical conditions. The consequence of too meagre a supply encourages informal arrangements that carry a higher risk.[22]

15.3.3 Ensuring Safety

In Chapter 11 of this report, I recommend the development of quality management standards for Ontario drinking water systems. I recognize that adopting these standards on reserves may be problematic in the near future because of the lack of resources and trained operators of sophisticated water supply organizations. However, I consider quality management standards to be at the heart of providing safe drinking water.

Recommendation 90: I encourage First Nations and the federal government to consider moving to a quality management standard over time, even if the consequence is that several communities, perhaps both reserve and non-reserve, might collaborate on a regional basis, or that First Nation communities might choose to contract with others to manage their water supply systems.

I am not suggesting that the attainment of quality management accreditation would be easy. Rather, it is a goal worth striving for – one that might in some situations be more easily approached through the consolidation, regionalization, or outsourcing that is available to other Ontario communities.

There are questions about how reasonable it is to expect small and generally remote communities to exercise powers in technical areas that do not impinge

---

[22] The Inquiry heard informally about one reserve where a consequence of low supply was low pressure, which encouraged residents to connect hoses directly to fire hydrants. The Northern Ontario winter then destroyed the hydrants and allowed contamination to enter the mains.

on community identity.[23] Under the *Indian Act*, the federal government has long assumed both funding and residual responsibility for on-reserve water supplies. However, the most effective way of achieving quality management may lie in engaging in joint management with others with experience and expertise in delivering safe water. Where negotiations for self-government take place, negotiators of these agreements should take care not to impede opportunities for the same sort of consolidation, regionalization, or contracting out that is available to other Ontario communities.

Recommendation 91: The provincial government should require the Ontario Clean Water Agency (OCWA) to offer its services to First Nations band councils for operating on-reserve water systems on a normal commercial basis.

15.3.4 Training

Recommendation 92: The provincial government should actively offer, on a cost-recovery basis, its training facilities and curriculum to First Nations water system operators.

In Chapter 12, I recommend improvements to Ontario's current approach to operator training. I would encourage these facilities to be made available to First Nations operators, perhaps in cooperation with the Aboriginal Water Works Association of Ontario (AWWAO). Competent people and good equipment are necessary for safe drinking water. In regard to the former, I note that Health Canada has been funding the Circuit Rider program operated by the First Nations Technical Institute, which seeks to upgrade the qualifications of the people operating on-reserve water systems. AWWAO is a professional organization seeking the same end. It is not clear, however, that connections between these programs and the resources available to Ontario or such major professional organizations as the Ontario Water Works Association (OWWA) are utilized to the extent possible. I would encourage a closer connection between OWWA and AWWAO and, as mentioned, the full opening of Ontario training and certification processes to operators of on-reserve systems. Band councils,

---

[23] J. Graham. The author is alarmed at the accelerating pace of self-government negotiations that make no realistic provisions for safe water.

supported by DIAND funding, should take full advantage of these opportunities, as well as those freely available from other sources.[24]

15.3.5 Testing, Inspection, and Enforcement

Recommendation 93: As a matter of principle, the provincial government should make technical assistance, drinking water testing, inspection, and enforcement available to First Nations communities on a cost-recovery basis, if requested.

Although Canadian Association of Environmental Analytical Laboratories (CAEAL)–certified private laboratories are available to First Nations water providers, many communities are too remote for easy sample preservation. Where Ontario has laboratory facilities available, their services should be available to First Nations on a reasonable cost-recovery basis. It should also be open to First Nations applying the Ontario Regulation 459/00 water quality standards to contract for professional inspection, and possibly even enforcement, from the MOE. Arrangements that would not pose new net costs for Ontario and that preserved the present structure of liability and jurisdictional authority can surely be made among willing parties.

---

[24] The splendid course materials available from the U.S. Environmental Protection Agency are freely available to all through the EPA's Web site <www.epa.gov/safewater/dwa.html>.

Chapter 16   The Process of Part 2 of the Inquiry

Contents

Chapter 16   The Process of Part 2 of the Inquiry

16.1   Introduction

In Chapter 14 of the Part 1 report of this Inquiry, I described the process by which I addressed the broad mandate and the dual roles of the Inquiry: to report on what happened in Walkerton and why, and to make recommendations to ensure the safety of drinking water across the Province in the future. It is not unusual for public inquiries to have both an adjudicative-type role, to determine why a particular tragedy occurred, and a forward-looking policy function, to make recommendations so that a similar tragedy will not occur again. What is somewhat unusual about the mandate of this Inquiry is that the second part of the exercise goes far beyond making recommendations arising solely from the events of Walkerton. Indeed, many of the issues that arise in the course of looking into what is necessary to ensure the safety of Ontario's water system have little to do with what occurred in Walkerton.

Given the dual roles of the Inquiry, one of the first decisions was to divide the Inquiry into two parts, Part 1 and Part 2, which allowed the development of a separate process for each part. I proceeded with both parts simultaneously.

16.2   Principles

In the Part 1 report, I set out four principles that guided the process: thoroughness, expedition, openness to the public, and fairness. These four principles also guided the process in Part 2, although in the context of a broader set of questions they called for a different process. In Part 2, I also considered the proximity of the issues to the safety of drinking water.

16.2.1   Thoroughness

In the aftermath of Walkerton, there was a widespread concern in Ontario about the safety of drinking water. One objective of Part 2 is to restore the public's faith in their drinking water systems. In order to do that, and to ensure that the Inquiry was fair and complete, it was important to examine all the issues that may have an impact on the safety of drinking water. I considered every suggestion made concerning issues that might even remotely be connected to the mandate. In the end, some issues that were examined were not sufficiently connected to the mandate to warrant recommendations. Other issues, such as the standards applicable to specific water contaminants, were too broad to address comprehensively and in detail; instead, the relevant standard-setting processes were reviewed. In several places in this report, I point out where I conclude that certain matters on which I heard submissions were beyond my mandate.

16.2.2   Expedition

To remain relevant, a public inquiry should be expeditious. Expedition in the conduct of an inquiry makes it more likely that members of the public will be engaged by the process and that they will feel confident that the issues are being appropriately addressed. When the mandate involves issues concerning public health and safety, it is especially important to proceed as quickly as possible. With this in mind, I established two processes, largely with separate teams of staff, for Parts 1 and 2. The two parts were carried on simultaneously. Although the evidence heard in the Part 1 hearings was useful to my consideration of some of the Part 2 issues, I found that the two processes were by and large able to proceed apace and somewhat independently of each other. This resulted in a considerable saving in time and likely also in expense. Although this approach entailed the expense of two separate teams of staff, even more expense would probably have been incurred if the processes had been run consecutively rather than concurrently.

16.2.3   Openness

In Part 1, I sought to ensure that the public had full access to the Inquiry. There was a similar need for openness in Part 2. In Part 2, it was important to ensure that there was not only ample opportunity for the public to see and scrutinize the process, but also to participate meaningfully. The expert meetings and the public hearings were open to the public. The town hall meetings across the province were widely advertised and, with one exception, were televised. In addition, the Inquiry's Web site was kept current and the various papers and records of proceedings were made available to the public.

16.2.4 Fairness

Section 5 of the *Public Inquiries Act* provides that any party with a substantial and direct interest in an inquiry should be granted the opportunity to provide evidence and to examine or cross-examine witnesses.[1] It also provides that an inquiry cannot make any findings of misconduct against a person without giving that person notice of the substance of the alleged misconduct and the opportunity to be heard in person or through counsel. These requirements had strong implications for the Part 1 process. The nature of Part 2 was such that section 5 of the Act, particularly the second provision of the section, was not engaged. That said, in some cases parties in Part 2 had radically differing points of view about what should be done to ensure drinking water safety in Ontario. Fairness in Part 2 therefore required that I ensure that all of those who wished to participate could and that parties with differing points of view had equal opportunity to be heard.

16.2.5 Proximity to the Issue of Drinking Water Safety

It quickly became apparent as I considered the safety of drinking water in Ontario that with a little creativity, a wide array of issues could be linked to the topic. I did not make a hard and fast rule about how to determine whether an issue was closely enough related to the safety of drinking water to merit consideration, but rather relied on the advice of experts, researchers, parties in Part 2, and ultimately my own judgment. These determinations led to the different degrees of emphasis given to topics in this report and the specificity of some recommendations. Where an improvement in the existing system is considered essential, the language of this report is intended to make that clear; where change might be helpful, or be more closely related to objectives other than safety – such as conservation, efficiency, and equity – the language becomes less imperative and the discussion more brief.

16.3   The Internet

Throughout Part 2, the Inquiry made extensive use of the Internet as the principal means of communication with parties and with the public. Without

---

[1] R.S.O. 1990, c. P.41.

instant electronic communication, the work of Part 2 would have taken much longer.

All the issue papers commissioned by the Inquiry, nearly all of the submissions from the Part 2 parties, and many public submissions were posted on the Inquiry's Web site, as were notices and agendas concerning upcoming meetings and other public notices. Drafts of papers, comments and suggestions, references to literature, and sometimes the literature itself, circulated rapidly among the participants. This use of the Internet proved to be highly effective and provided the additional benefit of being completely transparent to the public.

16.4 The Research Advisory Panel

Early in the Part 2 process, I appointed a Research Advisory Panel consisting of leading practitioners and academics in fields relating to the issues being examined by the Inquiry. In selecting members of the panel, I attempted to ensure that they would represent a diversity of expertise and perspective to help me in fulfilling the mandate. The panel's first task was to assist in determining the subjects to be addressed in the commissioned papers and in deciding who should prepare them, a job that they performed admirably. I met with the panel regularly, and their expert assistance in many areas regarding both parts of the Inquiry was invaluable. I am deeply appreciative of the time and effort that the panel devoted to their task.

The Panel consisted of the following individuals:

Harry Swain, Ph.D. (Chair), a partner in the consulting firm Sussex Circle and a former deputy minister in the federal government. As Deputy Minister of Industry, he was responsible for science policy advice for the Government of Canada. Educated in urban and economic geography, Mr. Swain taught at the Universities of Toronto and British Columbia and was a project leader at the International Institute for Applied Analysis in Laxenburg, Austria. He holds a doctorate from the University of Minnesota and was awarded an honorary degree by the University of Victoria. From 1996 to 1998, he was a director of Hambros Bank Limited, a U.K. merchant bank, and CEO of its Canadian subsidiary.

Prof. George E. Connell, OC, FCIC, FRSC, is a biochemist who became one of Canada's leading academic administrators and, from 1991 to 1995, was chairman of the National Round Table on the Environment and the Economy. Prof. Connell also served, from 1990 to 1993, as vice-chair of the Environmental Assessment Board of Ontario. He has served on numerous boards, inquiries, and public policy bodies, including the Corporate Higher Education Forum; as chair of the Task Force on Human Resource Management and the Status of Higher Education; as senior policy adviser, Canada Foundation for Innovation; and as chair of the 1995 Ontario Task Force on Funding and Delivery of Medical Care. His administrative posts included terms as president of both the University of Western Ontario and the University of Toronto.

Prof. Steve E. Hrudey is professor of environmental health in the Faculty of Medicine at the University of Alberta and a member of the Alberta Environmental Appeal Board. A specialist in public health engineering, Prof. Hrudey chaired the 1985 inquiry into the safety and quality of Edmonton's drinking water. Recently he has been collaborating with the Australian Health and Medical Research Council in revising the framework of the Australian drinking water guidelines. The author of numerous scientific contributions to environmental quality, health risk assessment, and management, he holds an M.Sc. and Ph.D. from Imperial College, University of London, in public health engineering. His awards include the Alberta Emerald Award from the Alberta Foundation for Environmental Excellence.

Prof. William Leiss, president of the Royal Society of Canada, has a wide-ranging background in the social sciences, public policy, and environmental risk issues. He is professor in the School of Policy Studies at Queen's University and also currently holds the NSERC/SSHRC Industry Research Chair in Risk Communication and Public Policy at the University of Calgary's Faculty of Management. He has taught political science, environmental studies, and sociology at the University of Regina, York University, and the University of Toronto. He has served as vice-president, research, at Simon Fraser University, where he also served as department chair in the School of Communications. In 1994, he was awarded the Eco-Research Chair in Environmental Policy at the School of Policy Studies at Queen's University. He has written extensively. He co-authored *Mad Cows and Mother's Milk*, which contains seven case studies of failure in risk communication. For the past 15 years, Dr. Leiss has worked as a consultant, mostly with the federal government, on health and environmental risk issues.

Douglas Macdonald, Ph.D., is a lecturer in the Environmental Studies Program, Innis College, University of Toronto. His area of specialty is Canadian environmental politics and policy. He has been active in a number of environmental non-governmental organizations and from 1982 to 1988 served as executive director of the Canadian Institute of Environmental Law and Policy. Scholarly and professional publications include *The Politics of Pollution* (1991), an examination of the environmental regulatory system, and a number of articles and applied research studies on various aspects of environmental policy. He is currently writing a book on the role of business in environmental policy.

Dr. Allison J. McGeer is a specialist in infectious diseases, public health, and internal medicine. She is a staff microbiologist and director of infection control at Mount Sinai Hospital in Toronto and is associate professor in the Departments of Pathobiology and Laboratory Medicine and Public Health Sciences at the University of Toronto. She has published extensively in the scientific literature on disease prevention and public health. Her many honours include the Louis Weinstein Award for best paper on clinical infectious diseases and the Family and Community Medicine Research Award.

Prof. Michèle Prévost is an internationally recognized expert in environmental engineering whose career spans academic research and executive assignments in the private sector. She is a professor in the Department of Civil Engineering at the Ecole Polytechnique de Montréal, where she holds the Natural Science and Engineering Research Council of Canada Industrial Chair on Drinking Water. Prof. Prévost also advises Vivendi Water, North America on its research and development program. Her past projects include directing a study on the internal corrosion of drinking water distribution systems, a collaborative effort with the Université Libre de Bruxelles, funded by the Québec and federal governments as well as the City of Laval. She has also served on numerous advisory committees, including the technical advisory committee for the Greater Vancouver Regional District drinking water program.

16.5 Key Rulings

16.5.1 Standing

In Part 2, I granted standing to parties who I felt either had a direct interest in the outcome of Part 2 (i.e., those who might be directly affected by the recommendations) or represented a distinct viewpoint that needed to be separately represented in Part 2. I wanted to hear as broad a cross-section of opinion as possible, so I erred on the side of inclusion, granting standing to all parties that I believed would assist me in my mandate. This included parties from a broad political spectrum and from diverse backgrounds. A list of the 36 parties granted standing in Part 2 is provided as section 16.5.3. A review of the list shows that all relevant interests and areas of expertise were represented.

Standing in Part 2 included the following:

1.   access to documents collected by the Commission that related to Part 2, subject to the Rules of Procedure and Practice;

2.   the opportunity to make submissions on any matter relevant to the Commission's mandate in Part 2, including submitting papers to respond to the commissioned papers;

3.   the opportunity to participate directly in one or more public meetings, where such participation would make a contribution to the subject matter of the meeting; and

4.   the opportunity to apply for funding to participate in Part 2.

Parties with standing also received most correspondence from the Commission by direct e-mail, rather than by having to visit our Web site.

It should be noted that the public were also free to provide submissions in writing and to participate in any of the Inquiry's public processes. The principal difference between parties with standing and the public was access to some of the documents collected by the Commission and the ability to apply for funding.

16.5.2 Funding for Parties with Standing

I recommended that the Attorney General grant funding to parties with standing in Part 2 for one of two purposes: the preparation of papers presenting the party's position on issues in Part 2, and participation in the Part 2 meetings and hearings. In order to be eligible for funding in Part 2, parties had to demonstrate that their participation would be of assistance in making my recommendations and that without funding, this participation would not have been possible. Since many of the parties in Part 2 were advocacy groups whose mandates include participation in exercises like this Inquiry, I set the bar quite high in determining when participation would not have been possible without funding. That said, many of the parties did receive funding for both of these types of participation.

To apply for funding, a party made a written request setting out the nature of the proposed submission or participation and explaining how it would help the work of the Inquiry and why the work could not be done without funding. If I considered that the proposal would be helpful and agreed that the party could not participate without assistance, I wrote to the Attorney General recommending that the party receive funding. I am pleased to say that the Attorney General accepted all of these recommendations and provided funding in the form of grants. This process was, in general, smooth and successful in ensuring the participation of the parties.

The assistance I received from the parties with standing was, almost without exception, of a very high quality and was extremely helpful to me in making my recommendations. In my view, this funding was money well spent.

16.5.3 Parties Granted Standing in Part 2

1   ALERT/Sierra Club Coalition

2   Association of Local Public Health Agencies

3   Association of Municipalities of Ontario

4   Azurix North America (Canada) Corp.

5   Bruce-Grey-Owen Sound Health Unit

6   Canadian Environmental Defence Fund and Pollution Probe Coalition

7   Canadian Union of Public Employees

8   Christian Farmers Federation of Ontario

9   Concerned Walkerton Citizens/Canadian Environmental Law Association

10   Conservation Ontario and the Saugeen Valley Conservation Authority

11   Dairy Farmers of Ontario

12   Ducks Unlimited Canada

13   Energy Probe Research Foundation

14   Government of Ontario

15   Grand River Conservation Authority

16   Indian Associations Coordinating Committee of Ontario Inc. (Chiefs of Ontario)

17   Dr. Murray McQuigge

18   Office of the Chief Coroner of the Province of Ontario

19   Ontario Cattle Feeders Association

20   Ontario Cattlemen's Association

21   Ontario Farm Animal Council

22   Ontario Farm Environmental Coalition

23   Ontario Federation of Agriculture

24   Ontario Medical Association

25   Ontario Métis Aboriginal Association

26   Ontario Municipal Water Association

27   Ontario Pork Producers' Board

28   Ontario Public Service Employees Union

29   Ontario Society of Professional Engineers

30   Ontario Water Works Association

31   Professional Engineers and Architects of the Ontario Public Service

32   Professional Engineers of Ontario

33   Sierra Legal Defence Fund Coalition

34   Uxbridge Conservation Association

35   Walkerton and District Chamber of Commerce

36   Walkerton Community Foundation

16.6 Research

16.6.1 The Commissioned Papers

Under the guidance of the Research Advisory Panel, I commissioned 25 research papers addressing what were initially 15 topics.[2] These papers were written by outside experts, not Commission staff, and were intended to provide a sound understanding of the basic issues involved in providing safe drinking water.

Authors were instructed to provide a descriptive overview of their topics, to describe the state of the art, and to compare approaches in various jurisdictions. They were specifically instructed not to reach normative conclusions. It was my intention to create a baseline level of understanding within the Commission and among the parties with standing and the public, on which debate about the future of drinking water safety in Ontario could take place.

As a quality control measure, the commissioned papers (also known as "issue papers") were peer reviewed, and I owe a debt of thanks to the reviewers, many of whom undertook highly detailed reviews of lengthy and dense materials. I also wish to thank the capable team of editors who edited the papers. These papers now stand as a substantial and up-to-date library of information about the state of the art of protecting drinking water safety.

---

[2] The Commission's issue papers are available on the Walkerton Inquiry CD-ROM or on the Inquiry's Web site at <www.walkertoninquiry.com>.

16.6.2   Other Staff Research

In addition to the research done by commissioned paper authors, there was a need for substantial research capacity within the Commission itself. This need was identified early and grew as the Inquiry proceeded, particularly through the drafting phase as I identified areas where additional information was needed. There is a wealth of academic research and government resources concerning all facets of drinking water management. Staff researchers have now assembled an extensive library of information about drinking water source protection, treatment, distribution, monitoring, pathogens, and a variety of other related topics.

16.6.3   The Expert Tour

In addition to the issue papers and submissions from parties with standing, I felt it was important to obtain expert opinions from drinking water veterans who had no stake in the Ontario system. Dr. Edwin E. Geldreich and Dr. J. Edward Singley are two of the leading American experts in water treatment systems.

Dr. J. Edward Singley

Dr. J. Edward Singley has had 42 years' experience in the drinking water industry as a process and operations consultant. He served as president of AWWA in 1991–92 and as the director of the operator-training centre in Florida for water and wastewater operators. He has consulted on water treatment problems for many utilities and has published over 100 peer-reviewed technical papers, hundreds of other papers, and chapters in several books.

Dr. Edwin E. Geldreich

Dr. Geldreich's 46 years of experience as a research microbiologist includes the pioneering development of the membrane filter technique for use in sanitary microbiology, the origination of the fecal coliform concept, and the writing of over 125 publications in peer-reviewed publications as well as three books. He has carried out numerous assignments, including reviews of standards development and laboratory certification, and he has been involved in a number of outbreak investigations around the world.

Dr. Geldreich and Dr. Singley, accompanied by one member of the Commission staff, toured 27 water facilities around Ontario. They met plant managers and workers and discussed issues relating to the safety of drinking water on an informal, collegial basis. This process was very useful in developing a picture of the current state of water treatment at the plant level in Ontario. The report of what became known as the "Two Eds Tour" is included in the commissioned papers.

16.7   Submissions from the Parties with Standing

The parties in Part 2 were invited to make submissions about what should be done to protect the safety of drinking water in Ontario. Many of the parties made substantial written submissions in this regard. These submissions generally took two forms. One type of submission was much like an issue paper, providing a substantial amount of background information about topics the parties considered relevant; the difference, however, was that these submissions reached conclusions about what should be done. The second type of submission was provided prior to the public hearings. In these submissions, the parties were encouraged to provide suggestions regarding specific recommendations that they felt I should make regarding the topic of the particular public hearing.

The parties helped to augment the background information provided in the issue papers. But more importantly, they brought their informed and considered opinions about what should be done. Their submissions helped to develop many of the recommendations I have presented in this report.

16.8   Public Submissions

Members of the public also provided numerous submissions. Many of these contributions reflected much careful consideration and hard work, and they were a useful addition to the work of the Inquiry.

Some of the public submissions came from groups who could or arguably should have had standing in Part 2, but who did not apply. These groups were generally treated as parties, although they were not eligible for funding.

Taken together, I think that the commissioned papers, the submissions from parties with standing, the submissions from the public, and the discussions held have created a complete and in-depth picture of the water systems of Ontario and have outlined the full range of alternatives regarding what should be done to ensure drinking water safety.

16.9   Consultations

I considered it important to provide opportunities for active debate among those concerned with the various issues. I also wanted to ensure that I had the opportunity to engage directly with the parties in Part 2 and the public to discuss their views, research, and recommendations. I therefore established three types of meetings in Part 2: town hall meetings, expert meetings, and public hearings. In all cases, a complete schedule of the meetings was available on the Inquiry's Web site. All meetings were open to the public, and although participation from the general public was encouraged to occur through the town hall meetings and written submissions, anyone who wished to participate in any of the expert meetings or public hearings was permitted to do so.

16.9.1   Town Hall Meetings

The town hall meetings were a series of public meetings held in locations across Ontario. They were advertised in local media several weeks in advance, and submissions from the public were solicited. People who wished to make a presentation were asked to provide a written submission describing what they wanted to discuss, although some time was allocated for last-minute presenters.

I was impressed by the level of commitment demonstrated by the presenters, including municipal officials, technicians, scientists, academics, advocacy groups, farmers, and the public at large. These people put a great deal of work into their presentations, and I thank them for their efforts. The presentations were most useful, and helped me to understand the issues that were being faced by people in cities, towns, and rural areas around Ontario.

In each city or town that we visited, Commission staff and I met local water managers and toured the water facilities. This exercise helped to develop a better understanding of water treatment and distribution systems and the challenges faced by various types of systems.

16.9.2 Expert Meetings

The expert meetings were a series of meetings held in Toronto that were chaired by Commission staff or members of the Research Advisory Panel. These meetings provided a forum for discussion among Commission staff, issue paper authors, parties with standing in Part 2, invited experts, and members of the public. The purpose of the meetings was to ensure a complete and open discussion of the issues and to canvass the diversity of opinion among the people attending.

The discussions at the expert meetings were not transcribed, but a team of graduate students was engaged to take comprehensive notes. The meetings were also recorded. At the end of each meeting, the note-takers prepared a summary of the meeting. These summaries were vetted by the participants in the meeting and Commission staff. They were then published on the Inquiry's Web site.

16.9.3 Public Hearings

The public hearings provided the opportunity for parties with standing and some other groups and members of the public to present their suggestions for recommendations in Part 2 directly to me.

These meetings were not as formal as the Part 1 hearings in Walkerton, but I considered it necessary to engage with the presenters one group at a time, rather than permitting the relatively open discussions that characterized the expert meetings. In order to ensure that presenters would have the opportunity needed to rebut points made by others, I made two stipulations. The first was that all those who wished to present at the public hearings should provide a written outline of what they wished to discuss prior to the hearing, for posting on the Web site. Second, I allowed a round of rebuttal after all of the presenters had been given their initial time for presentation.

Prior to each public hearing, a list of what I considered to be essential questions was circulated to the parties with standing and posted on the Web site. The list of questions was helpful in provoking written responses from many of the presenters and in focusing the discussions at the hearings.

16.10 Expert Advice

Throughout the process of Part 2, I often required expert advice on specific issues. In general I tried to rely on the Research Advisory Panel members for this advice, but from time to time it was necessary to seek outside advice from consultants in the relevant fields.

16.11 Budget

In August 2000, approximately six weeks after the beginning of this Inquiry, I provided a budget estimate to the Government of Ontario. The total amount of that estimate was $6,982,200, which included $3,928,100 for the 2000/2001 fiscal year, and $3,054,100 for 2001/2002. The figure for 2001/2002 was little more than a guess at that time, because the scope of the mandate and the processes that would be developed to achieve it were only just being developed.

In May 2001, a second budget estimate was provided to the government based on a much-improved understanding of the amount of work involved. Our expenditures in the 2000/2001 fiscal year had been $3,931,300, just $3,200 more than projected in August 2000. The final budget for 2001/2002 was $5,026,900. In October 2001, I also requested a contingency amount of $300,000–$500,000 for 2002/2003, in case the Commission continued past the end of the 2001/2002 fiscal year. Thus, the final budget estimate provided to the government in October 2001 was for a total of approximately $9,458,200.

The final figure for the expenditure of this Inquiry is not yet available. However, I expect that the total amount spent by the Inquiry will be less than the final budget. It is difficult to allocate costs between Part 1 and Part 2 with complete precision, but a rough estimate is that costs were equally divided between the two parts.

16.12 Appreciation

A great number of people have provided assistance to me during Part 2 of the Inquiry. I am indebted to all of them for their conscientious and diligent work. I would like to formally thank those who were most deeply involved in the Part 2 process.

First, I would like to thank Harry Swain, who is the Chair of the Research Advisory Panel, and who, along with James Van Loon, his Executive Assistant, did an excellent job of organizing and managing the work of Part 2.

I would also like to thank the Research Advisory Panel: Professor George Connell, Professor Steve Hrudey, Professor William Leiss, Dr. Douglas Macdonald, Dr. Allison McGeer, and Professor Michèle Prévost. As I mentioned above, their assistance was invaluable throughout both parts of the Inquiry.

I was greatly helped by two senior Commission Counsel, David Stockwood and Ronald Foerster, and by my Executive Assistant, Gus Van Harten.

In addition, I am indebted to the very dedicated staff who helped with the organization, research, and drafting of the report. Here I speak of Ronda Bessner, Bay Ryley, Corinne Wallace, Robert Rishikof, Nimali Gamage, Nirupama Kumar, and Arlette Al-Shaikh.

Peter Rehak, the media consultant, provided excellent advice throughout the Inquiry and, along with Nicole Caron and Debora Harper, was critical to ensuring the success of the town hall meetings. Djordje Sredojevic and Ljiljana Vuletic, our Web masters, were extremely responsive and frequently worked under tight deadlines to ensure that materials were posted in a timely fashion.

Commission Counsel for Part 1, Paul Cavalluzzo, Brian Gover, and Freya Kristjansen were also very generous with their time and advice in assisting during the Part 2 process.

I would also like to express my appreciation to those involved with the administration of the Inquiry: David Henderson, the Chief Administrator, and Kathleen Genore, the Financial Manager. As administrative assistants, Pat Hall and Abbie Adelman contributed greatly to the smooth running of the office and the production of the report.

As she did in Part 1, Joyce Ihamaki performed her duties as the Registrar with care and efficiency.

A huge amount of research was completed by our issue paper authors, who developed excellent papers under tight deadlines and were key participants in the expert meetings. I would like to single out the following authors who not only contributed excellent papers but also made themselves available time and time again to provide the Commission with additional advice and assistance: David Cameron, Nicholas d'Ombrain, Jim Merritt, and Jim Joe and his colleagues from Strategic Alternatives.

I am greatly appreciative of Dr. Edwin E. Geldreich and Dr. J. Edward Singley, leading American experts in water treatment systems. They toured 27 water facilities in Ontario and reported their findings. I thank Wayne Scott, formerly of the MOE, for coordinating the tour.

Carolyn Johns, another one of the issue paper authors, also led the team of graduate students who took excellent notes at the expert meetings. The students were Sarah Hartley, Rachel Melzer, Judith Muncaster, and Sarah Wolfe.

I would like to thank the parties with standing in Part 2. Without their participation, this Inquiry could not have reached its objective. Many of the parties dedicated tremendous resources of their own to assisting the Inquiry and produced work of a depth, quality, and relevance greater than I could have hoped for. For that I am deeply thankful.

Although I do not wish to single out particular parties here, there was one special subclass of the parties who deserve mention. The provincial government staff who attended and participated in our expert meetings and public hearings have my sincere thanks.

In the Part 1 report, I expressed my appreciation to the Chief Coroner for his assistance. Several of the recommendations in this report result from recommendations made by the Chief Coroner. I reiterate my thanks for the support that he has provided to the Inquiry.

Several of the experts who were helpful in Part 1 also aided the Part 2 process. These included Prof. Michael Goss of the University of Guelph, and Professors Peter Huck and Robert Gillham of the University of Waterloo.

I would like to thank all of the people who made presentations at the town hall meetings. Evident in most of those presentations was a tremendous amount of effort, for which I am very thankful. The perspectives presented to me at town hall meetings were very helpful in developing my understanding of the problems facing drinking water systems in Ontario.

I also thank all of the municipal staff and other people who helped to arrange the tours we took in each city or town we visited.

Finally, I would like to thank the editors, proofreaders, and layout designers of the commissioned papers and the report. The Part 2 report was prepared by John Eerkes-Medrano, Brian Grebow, Riça Night, Pamela Erlichman, and Maraya Raduha. Riça Night and Brian Grebow also prepared the index. The issue papers were prepared by a team of editors, proofreaders, and designers led by Sheila Protti. Her team consisted of Elizabeth d'Anjou, Frances Emery, Brian Grebow, Marie-Lynn Hammond, Anne Holloway, Bernard Kelly, Madeline Koch, Doug Linzey, Dennis A. Mills, Georgina Montgomery, Robyn Packard, Iris Hossé Phillips, Rosemary Tanner, and Kathy Vanderlinden. All of these people worked on difficult material under tight time constraints, and I thank them.

Appendix A   An Interjurisdictional Comparison of Water Quality Standards

Contents

Water Quality Standards: Contaminant Standards Required in the Ontario Drinking Water Regulation Compared to Canadian Guidelines and the United States, Australia and the World Health Organization

Table A.1. Chemical/Physical Standards and Objectives (mg/L)

Parameter	Ontario	Canada	US	Australia	WHO[1]
Acephate				0.01a	
Acrylamide	0.005b		0b[2]	0.0002a	0.0005a
Alachlor			0.002a[3]		0.020a
Aldicarb	0.009a	0.009a[3]	0.007ab[4]	0.001ab	0.010a
Aldrin + Dieldrin	0.0007a	0.0007a		0.00001b[5]	0.00003a
Ametryn				0.005b[6]	
Amitrole				0.001b[7]	
Antimony		0.006b	0.006ab	0.003a	0.005b
Arsenic	0.025b	0.025b	0.05a[3]	0.007a	0.01b
Asbestos			7ab[8]	Insufficient data	Unnecessary[9]
Asulam				0.05b	
Atrazine + N-dealkylated metabolites	0.005b	0.005b	0.003ab[10]	0.0005b[11]	0.002a[12]
Azinphos-methyl	0.02a	0.02a		0.002b[13]	

[1] Some values have been converted from mg/L for consistency

[2] TT – the combination (or product) of dose and monomer level shall not exceed that equivalent to a polyacrylamide polymer containing 0.05 % monomer dosed at 1 mg/L

[3] Aldicarb + metabolites

[4] The lifetime Health Advisory value or the MCL/MCLG value for any combination of two or more of the chemicals aldicarb, aldicarb sulfone and aldicarb sulfoxide should remain at 0.007 mg/L because of a similar mode of action

[5] Health value is 0.0003

[6] Health value is 0.05

[7] Health value is 0.01

[8] Units are MFL – million fibers per liter

[9] The WHO finds that it is unnecessary to recommend a health-based guideline for this compound because it is not hazardous to human health at concentrations normally found in drinking water.

[10] Atrazine only and under review

[11] Atrazine only and the health value is 0.2

[12] Atrazine only

[13] Health value is 0.003

Table A.1. continued

Parameter	Ontario	Canada	US	Australia	WHO[1]
Barium	1.0a	1.0a	2ab	0.7a	0.7a
Bendiocarb	0.04a	0.04a			
Benomyl				0.1a	
Bentazone				0.03a	0.300a
Benzene	0.005a	0.005a	0.005a[a]	0.001a	0.010a
Benzo(a)pyrene	0.00001a	0.00001a	0.0002a[a]	0.00001a	0.0007a
Beryllium			0.004ab	Insufficient data	Inadequate data
Bioresmethrin				0.1a	
Boron	5.0b	5.0b		0.3a	0.5b
Bromacil				0.1b[14]	
Bromate		0.01b	0.010a[a]	0.02a	0.025b
Bromodichloromethane (THM)			0.080a[ab]		0.060a
Bromoform (THM)			0.080a[ab]		0.100a
Bromophos-ethyl				0.01a	
Bromoxynil	0.005b	0.005b		0.03[a]	
Cadmium	0.005a	0.005a	0.005ab	0.002a	0.003a
Carbaryl	0.09a	0.09a		0.005b[15]	
Carbendazim				0.1a	
Carbofuran	0.09a	0.09a	0.04ab[16]	0.005b[17]	0.007a
Carbon Tetrachloride	0.005a	0.005a	0.005a[a]	0.003a	0.002a
Carbophenothion				0.0005a	

[14] Health value is 0.3
[15] Health value is 0.03
[16] Under review
[17] Health value is 0.01

Table A.1. *continued*

Parameter	Ontario	Canada	US	Australia	WHO[1]
Carboxin				0.002b[18]	
Chloral hydrate					0.010b
Chloramines	3.0a	3.0a			
Chlordane (total)	0.007a		0.002a[a]	0.00001b[19]	0.0002a
Chlorfenvinphos				0.005a	
Chlorine			4ab	5.0a[20]	5a
Chlorine Dioxide			0.8ab	1.0a[21]	[22]
Chlorite			1.0a[23]	0.3a	0.200b
Chloroacetic acids				0.15a	
Chlorobenzene			0.1ab	0.3a[24]	
Chloroform (THM)			0.080a[ab]		0.200a
2-Chlorophenol				0.3a[25]	Inadequate data
Chlorothalonil				0.0001b[26]	
Chlorotoluron					0.030a
Chloroxuron				0.01a	
Chlorpyrifos	0.09a	0.09a		0.01a	
Chlorsulfuron				0.1a	
Chlopyralid				1ab	

[18] Health value is 0.3
[19] Aesthetic value is 0.0001
[20] Aesthetic value is 0.6
[21] Aesthetic value is 0.4
[22] The WHO states: "A guideline value has not been established because of the rapid breakdown of chlorine dioxide and because the chlorite guideline is adequately protective for potential toxicity from chlorine dioxide."
[23] MCLG is 0.8
[24] Aesthetic value is 0.01
[25] Aesthetic value is 0.0001
[26] Health value 0.03

Table A.1. *continued*

Parameter	Ontario	Canada	US	Australia	WHO[1]
Chromium	0.05a	0.05a	0.1ab	0.05a	0.05b
Copper			1.3bc	2a[27]	2b
Cyanazine	0.01b	0.01b			0.0006a
Cyanide	0.2a	0.2a	0.2ab	0.08a[28]	0.070a[29]
Dalapon (sodium salt)			0.2ab		
2,4-DB					0.090a
Di(2-ethylhexyl)adipate			0.4ab	Insufficient data	0.080a
Di(2-ethylhexyl)phthalate (PAE)			0.006a[a]	0.01a	0.008a
Diazinon	0.02a	0.02a		0.001b[30]	
1,2-dibromo-3-chloropropane					0.001a
1,2-dibromoethane					0.0004-0.015b
Dibromoacetonitrile				Insufficient data	0.100b
Dibromochloromethane			0.080a[b][31]		0.100a
Dibromochloropropane (DBCP)			0.0002a		
Dicamba	0.12a	0.12a		0.1a	
Dichlobenil				0.01a	
Dichloroacetic acid			0.060a[ac]	0.1a	0.050b
Dichloroacetonitrile				Insufficient data	0.090b
Dichlorobenzene o-			0.6ab		
Dichlorobenzene p-			0.075ab		

[27] Health value is 0.3
[28] Cyanogen chloride (as cyanide)
[29] Cyanogen chloride (as cyanide)
[30] Health value is 0.003
[31] MCLG is 0.06

Table A.1. *continued*

Parameter	Ontario	Canada	US	Australia	WHO[1]
1,2-Dichlorobenzene	0.2a[32]	0.20a[33]		1.5a[34]	1.000a
1,4-Dichlorobenzene	0.005a[35]	0.005a[36]		0.04a[37]	0.300a
Dichlorodiphenyltrichloroethane (DDT) + metabolites	0.03a			0.00006b[38]	0.002a
1,2-Dichloroethane	0.005b	0.005b	0.005a[a]	0.003a	0.030a
1,1-Dichloroethene				0.03a	0.030a
1,2-Dichloroethene				0.06a	0.050a
1,1-Dichloroethylene (vinylidene chloride)	0.014a	0.014a	0.007ab		
Dichloroethylene (cis-1,2-)			0.07ab		
Dichloroethylene (trans-1,2-)			0.1ab		
Dichloromethane	0.05a	0.05a	0.005a[a]	0.004a	0.020a
2-4-Dichlorophenol	0.9a[39]	0.9a[40]		0.2a[41]	Inadequate data
2,4-Dichlorophenoxy acetic acid (2,4-D)	0.1b	0.1b	0.07ab	0.0001b[42]	0.030a
Dichloropropane (1,2-)			0.005a[a]		0.040a
1,3-dichloropropene					0.020a
Dichlorprop					0.100a
Dichlorvos				0.001ab	
Diclofop-methyl	0.009a	0.009a		0.005a	

[32] Aesthetic objective is 0.003
[33] Aesthetic objective is ≤ 0.003
[34] Aesthetic value is 0.001
[35] Aesthetic objective is 0.001
[36] Aesthetic objective is ≤ 0.001
[37] Aesthetic value is 0.0003
[38] DDT only and health value is 0.02
[39] Aesthetic objective is 0.0003
[40] Aesthetic objective is ≤ 0.003
[41] Aesthetic objective is aesthetic value
[42] Health value is 0.03

Table A.1. *continued*

Parameter	Ontario	Canada	US	Australia	WHO[1]
Dicofol				0.003a	
Difenzoquat				0.1a	
Dimethoate	0.02b	0.02b		0.05a	
Dinoseb	0.01a	0.01a	0.007ab		
Dioxin and Furan	0.000000015b[43]		0.00000003a[44]		
Diphenamid				0.002b[45]	
Diquat	0.07a	0.07a	0.02ab	0.0005b[46]	0.010b
Disulfoton				0.001b[47]	
Diuron	0.15a	0.15a		0.03a	
DPA (2,2-DPA)				0.5a	0.020a
EDB				0.001ab	
Endosulfan				0.00005b[48]	
Endothal			0.1ab	0.01b[49]	
Endrin			0.002ab		0.020a
Epichlorohydrin			0.0b[50]	0.0005a	0.0004b
EPTC				0.001b[51]	
Ethion				0.003a	
Ethoprophos				0.001ab	

[43] Total toxic equivalents when compared with 2,3,7,8-TCDD (tetrachlorodibenzo-p-dioxin)
[44] Dioxin (2,3,7,8-TCDD) only
[45] Health value 0.3
[46] Health value 0.005
[47] Health value is 0.003
[48] Health value is 0.03
[49] Health value 0.1
[50] TT – the combination (or product) of dose and monomer level shall not exceed that equivalent to a polymer containing 0.01 % monomer dosed at 20 mg/L
[51] Health value is 0.03

Table A.1. *continued*

Parameter	Ontario	Canada	US	Australia	WHO[1]
Ethylbenzene			0.7ab	0.3a[52]	0.300a
Ethylenediamine tetraacetic acid (EDTA)				0.25a	0.600a
Ethylene dibromide			0.00005a[a]		
Etridiazole				0.0001b[53]	
Fenamiphos				0.0003a	
Fenarimol				0.001b[54]	
Fenchlorphos				0.03a	
Fenitrothion				0.01a	
Fenoprop				0.01a	0.009a
Fensulfothion				0.01ab	
Fenvalerate				0.05a	
Flamprop-methyl				0.003a	
Fluometuron				0.05a	
Fluoride	1.5a[55]	1.5a	4ab	1.5a	1.5a
Formaldehyde				0.5a	0.900a
Formothion				0.05a	
Fosamine				0.03a	
Glyphosate	0.28b	0.28b	0.7ab	0.01b[56]	Unnecessary[57]

[52] Aesthetic value is 0.003
[53] Health value is 0.1
[54] Health value is 0.03
[55] Where fluoride is added to drinking water, it is recommended that the concentration be adjusted to 1.0 +/- 0.2 mg/L the optimum level for control of tooth decay. Where supplies contain naturally occurring fluoride at levels higher than 1.5 mg/L but less than 2.4 mg/L the Ministry of Health and Long Term Care recommends an approach through local boards of health to raise public awareness to control excessive exposure to fluoride from other sources. Levels above the MAC must be reported to the local Medical Officer of Health.
[56] Health value is 1
[57] The WHO finds that it is unnecessary to recommend a health-based guideline for this compound because it is not hazardous to human health at concentrations normally found in drinking water.

Table A.1. *continued*

Parameter	Ontario	Canada	US	Australia	WHO[1]
Haloacetic Acids			0.060a[c]		
Heptachlor + Heptachlor Epoxide	0.003a		0.0004a[58]	0.00005b[59]	0.00003a
Hexachlorobenzene			0.001[a]		0.001a
Hexachlorobutadiene				0.0007a	0.0006a
Hexachlorocyclopentadiene			0.05ab		
Hexaflurate				0.03a	
Hexazinone				0.002b[60]	
Iodide				0.1a	
Iodine				Insufficient Data	Inadequate Data
Isoproturon					0.009a
Lead	0.01a[61]	0.01a	0.015c[a]	0.01a	0.01a
Lindane (total)	0.004a		0.0002ab	0.00005b[62]	0.002a
Malathion	0.19a	0.19a			
Maldison				0.05a	
Manganese				0.5a[63]	0.5b
MCPA					0.002a
Mecoprop					0.010a
Mercury	0.001a	0.001a	0.002ab[64]	0.001a	0.001a[65]
Methidathion				0.03a	

58 This applies to Heptachlor only. Heptachlor epoxide has an MCL of 0.0002 and an MCLG of zero.
59 Aesthetic value is 0.0003
60 Health value is 0.3
61 This standard applies to water at the point of consumption.
62 Health value is 0.02
63 Aesthetic value is 0.1
64 Inorganic
65 Total

Table A.1. *continued*

Parameter	Ontario	Canada	US	Australia	WHO[1]
Methiocarb				0.005ab	
Methomyl				0.005b[66]	
Methoxychlor	0.9a	0.9a	0.04ab	0.0002b[67]	0.020a
Metolachlor	0.05b	0.05b		0.002b[68]	0.010a
Metribuzin	0.08a	0.08a		0.001b[69]	
Metsulfuron-methyl				0.03a	
Mevinphos				0.005ab	
Microcystin-LR					0.001b
Molinate				0.0005b[70]	0.006a
Molybdenum				0.05a	0.07a
Monochloramine				3a[71]	3a
Monochloroacetic acid			0.060a[ac]		Inadequate Data
Monochlorobenzene	0.08a[72]	0.08a	0.1ab		0.300a
Monocrotophos				0.001a	
Napropamide				0.001b[73]	
Nickel				0.02a	0.02b
Nitralin				0.5a	
Nitrate (as Nitrogen)	10.0a[74]	45a[75]	10ab		

[66] Health value is 0.03
[67] Health value is 0.3
[68] Health value is 0.3
[69] Health value is 0.05
[70] Health value is 0.005
[71] Aesthetic value is 0.5
[72] Aesthetic objective is 0.03
[73] Health value is 1
[74] Where both nitrate and nitrite are present, the total of the two should not exceed 10 mg/L (as nitrogen)
[75] Equivalent to 10 mg/L as nitrate-nitrogen. Where nitrate and nitrite are determined separately, levels of nitrite should not exceed 3.2 mg/L

Table A.1. continued

Parameter	Ontario	Canada	US	Australia	WHO[1]
Nitrate (as Nitrate)				50a	50a
Nitrite (as Nitrogen)	1.0a[76]		1ab		
Nitrite (as Nitrite)				3a	3a[77]
Nitrate + Nitrite (as Nitrogen)	10.0a[78]		10ab	0.2a	0.200a
Nitrilotriacetic Acid (NTA)	0.4a	0.4a			
Nitrosodimethylamine (NDMA)	0.000009b				
Nitrotriacetic acid				0.2a	
Norflurazon				0.002b[79]	
Oryzalin				0.3a	
Oxamyl (Vydate)			0.2ab	0.005b[80]	
Paraquat	0.01b	0.01b[81]		0.001b[82]	
Parathion	0.05a	0.05a		0.01a	
Parathion methyl				0.0003b[83]	
Pebulate				0.0005b[84]	
Pendimethalin				0.3a	0.020a
Pentachlorophenol	0.06a[85]	0.06a[86]	0.001a[a]	0.00001b[87]	0.009b
Permethrin				0.001b[88]	0.020a

[76] Where both nitrate and nitrite are present, the total of the two should not exceed 10 mg/L (as nitrogen)
[77] Nitrate and nitrite values refer to acute. A chronic provisional guideline for nitrite is 0.2
[78] Where both nitrate and nitrite are present, the total of the two should not exceed 10 mg/L (as nitrogen)
[79] Health value is 0.05
[80] Health value is 0.1
[81] Paraquat as dichloride, equivalent to 0.007 mg/L for paraquat ion
[82] Health value is 0.03
[83] Health value is 0.1
[84] Health value is 0.03
[85] Aesthetic objective is 0.03
[86] Aesthetic objective is ≤ 0.03
[87] Health value is 0.01
[88] Health value is 0.1

Table A.1. *continued*

Parameter	Ontario	Canada	US	Australia	WHO[1]
Phorate	0.002b	0.002a		0.3a	
Picloram	0.19b	0.19b	0.5ab	0.1a	
Piperonyl butoxide					
Pirimicarb				0.005a	
Pirimicarb-ethyl				0.0005a	
Pirimicarb-methyl				0.05a	
Polychlorinated Biphenyls (PCB)	0.003b		0.0005a		
Profenofos				0.0003a	
Promecarb				0.03a	
Prometryne	0.001b				
Propachlor				0.001b[89]	
Propanil				0.0001b[90]	0.020a
Propargite				0.05a	
Propazine				0.0005b[91]	
Propiconazole				0.0001b[92]	
Propyzamide				0.002b[93]	
Pyrazophos				0.03a	
Pyridate					0.100a
Quintozene				0.03a	
Selenium	0.01a	0.01a	0.05ab	0.01a	0.01a
Silver				0.1a	Unnecessary[94]

89 Health value is 0.05
90 Health value is 0.5
91 Health value is 0.05
92 Health value is 0.1
93 Health value is 0.3
94 The WHO finds that it is unnecessary to recommend a health-based guideline for this compound because it is not hazardous to human health at concentrations normally found in drinking water.

Table A.1. *continued*

Parameter	Ontario	Canada	US	Australia	WHO[1]
Simazine	0.01b	0.01b	0.004ab	0.0005b[95]	0.002a
Styrene			0.1ab	0.03a[96]	0.020a
Sulphate				500a[97]	
Sulprofos				0.01a	
2,4,5-T				0.00005b[98]	0.009a
2,3,7,8-TCDD (Dioxin)			0.00000003a[a]		
Temephos	0.28b			0.3ab	
Terbacil				0.01b[99]	
Terbufos	0.001b	0.001b		0.0005ab	
Terbuthylazine (TBA)					0.007a
Terbutryn				0.001b[100]	
Tetrachloroethane					
Tetrachloroethene				0.05a	0.040a
Tetrachloroethylene (perchloroethylene)	0.030a	0.03a	0.005a[a]		
2,3,4,6-Tetrachlorophenol	0.10a[101]	0.1a[102]			
Tetrachlorvinphos				0.002b[103]	
Thalium			0.002a[104]		

95 Health value is 0.02
96 Aesthetic value is 0.004
97 Aesthetic value is 250
98 Health value is 0.1
99 Health value is 0.03
100 Health value is 0.3
101 Aesthetic objective is 0.001
102 Aesthetic objective is ≤ 0.001
103 Health value is 0.1
104 MCLG is 0.0005

Table A.1. *continued*

Parameter	Ontario	Canada	US	Australia	WHO[1]
Thiobencarb				0.03a	
Thiometon				0.003a	
Thiophanate				0.005a	
Thiram				0.003a	
Toluene			1ab	0.8a[105]	0.700a
Toxaphene			0.003a[a]		
2,4,5-TP (Silvex)			0.05ab		
Triadimefon				0.1b[106]	
Triallate	0.23a				
Tributylin oxide				0.001	0.002a
Trichloroacetaldehyde				0.02a	
Trichloroacetic acid			0.06a[c][107]	0.1a	0.100b
Trichloroacetonitrile				Insufficient data	0.001b
Trichlorfon				0.005a	
1,2,4-Trichlorobenzene			0.07ab		
Trichlorobenzene (total)				0.03a[108]	
1,1,1-Trichloroethane			0.2ab[109]	Insufficient data	0.020a
1,1,2-Trichloroethane			0.005a[110]		2.000b

[105] Aesthetic value is 0.025
[106] Health value is 0.002
[107] MCLG is 0.3
[108] Aesthetic value is 0.005
[109] MCLG is 0.20
[110] MCLG is 0.003

Table A.1. *continued*

Parameter	Ontario	Canada	US	Australia	WHO[1]
Trichloroethene					0.070b
Trichloroethylene	0.05a	0.05a	0.005a[a]	Insufficient data	
2,4,6-Trichlorophenol	0.005a[111]	0.005a[112]		0.02a[113]	0.200a
2,4,5-Trichlorophenoxy acetic acid (2,4,5-T)	0.28a[114]				0.009a
Triclopyr				0.01a	
Trifluralin	0.045b	0.045b		0.0001b[115]	0.020a
Trihalomethanes	0.100a[116]	0.1b	0.080a[b]	0.25a	[117]
Turbidity	1.0a[118]	1.0a[119]			
Uranium	0.10a	0.02b			0.002b
Vernolate				0.0005b[120]	
Vinyl Chloride	0.002a	0.002a	0.002a[a]	0.0003a	0.005a
Xylenes (total)			10ab	0.6[121]	0.500a

[111] Aesthetic objective is 0.002
[112] Aesthetic objective is ≤ 0.002
[113] Aesthetic value is 0.002
[114] Aesthetic objective is 0.02
[115] Health value is 0.05
[116] This standard is expressed as a running annual average of quarterly samples measured at a point reflecting the maximum residence time in the distribution system.
[117] The sum value of the ratio of the concentration of each to its respective guideline value should not exceed 1.
[118] A MAC for turbidity of 1.0 NTU (Nephelometric Turbidity Unit) in drinking water leaving the treatment plant was established to ensure the efficiency of the disinfection process. To ensure that the aesthetic quality is not degraded, an AO for turbidity at the free flowing outlet of the ultimate consumer has been set at 5 NTU.
[119] A MAC for turbidity of 1.0 NTU (Nephelometric Turbidity Unit) and an aesthetic objective of ≤ 5 NTU at point of consumption
[120] Health value is 0.03
[121] Aesthetic value is 0.02

a – MCLG is zero
b – the total for THMs is 0.080 mg/L (1998 Final Rule for Disinfectants and Disinfectant Byproducts)
c – the total for the five haloacetic acids is 0.060 mg/L (1998 Final Rule for Disinfectants and Disinfection Byproducts Rule)

Table A.2. Microbiological Standards – Health Related

Parameter	Ontario[122]	Canada[123]	US	Australia[124]	WHO
Cryptosporidium	none[125]		99% removal/ inactivation c	Insufficient data	
Escherichia coli and/or Fecal Coliforms		none	none	none[126]	none[127]
General Bacterial Population	Less than 500 colonies per ml[128]	Less than 500 colonies per ml or less than 200 background coliforms on a total coliform membrane filter	Less than 500 colonies per ml		
Giardia lamblia			99.9 % removal/ inactivation c	Insufficient data	
Legionella			No limit C[129]	Insufficient data	

[122] MAC (per 100 ml)
[123] Currently there are no guidelines for viruses or protozoa. Viruses are currently under consideration. However, it is desirable that no viruses or protozoa are detected.
[124] Australia lists selected bacteria, viruses and protozoa which, if detected in water, require advice to be sought from the relevant health authority.
[125] E coli is a more definitive indicator of faecal contamination than total coliforms or faecal coliforms.
[126] Minimum sample 100 ml
[127] E. coli or thermotolerant coliform bacteria must not be detectable in any 100 ml sample in all water intended for drinking, treated water entering the distribution system or treated water in the distribution system.
[128] At elevated levels, general bacterial population may interfere with coliform detection. The detection of E coli or faecal coliforms and elevated general beacterial population levels are indicators of adverse water quality (Section 4.2.2.of the Ontario Drinking Water Standards) and require immediate corrective action (increase chlorine dose and flush system).
[129] US EPA believes that if Giardia and viruses inactivated, Legionella will also be controled

Table A.2. *continued*

Parameter	Ontario[122]	Canada[123]	US	Australia[124]	WHO
Total Coliforms	[130]	3000 per 100 ml[131]	≤ 5 %[132]	none[133]	none[134]
Turbidity			≤ 5 NTU c		
Viruses			99.9 % killed/ inactivated c		

[130] Referred to section 4.2.2 of the Ontario Drinking Water Standards titled "Indicators of Adverse Water Quality, Notification and Procedure and Corrective Actions." This states that if total coliforms are detected in any required sample other than from raw water, resampling and corrective action are required.

[131] However, because coliforms are not uniformly distributed in water and are subject to considerable variation in enumeration, drinking water fulfilling the following conditions is considered to be in compliance with the coliform MAC: no sample should contain more than 10 total coliform organisms per 100 ml with no fecal coliforms; no consecutive sample from the same site should show the presence of coliform organisms; and, for community distribution drinking water systems, not more than one sample from a set of samples taken from the community on a given day should show the presence of coliform organisms and not more than 10 % of samples based on a minimum of 10 samples should show the presence of coliform organisms.

[132] No more than 5 % total samples total coliform positive in a month. Positive tests must be analyzed for fecal coliforms. No fecal coliforms are allowed.

[133] Minimum sample 100 ml

[134] Total coliform bacteria must not be detectable in any 100 ml sample in treated water entering the distribution system or treated water in the distribution system. In the case of large supplies where sufficient samples are examined, they must not be present in 95 % of samples throughout any 12 month period.

Table A.3. Radionuclide Standards – Health Related
Natural Radionuclides[135]

Parameter		Parameter		Parameter	
Beryllium-7	4000	Radium-226	0.6	Thorium-234	20
Bismuth-210	70	Radium-228	0.5	Uranium-234	4
Lead-210	0.1	Thorium-228	2	Uranium-235	4
Polonium-210	0.2	Thorium-230	0.4	Uranium-238	4
Radium-224	2	Thorium-232	0.1		

Artificial Radionuclides[136]

Parameter		Parameter		Parameter	
Americium-241	0.2	Iodine-125	10	Selenium-75	70
Antimony-122	50	Iodine-129	1	Silver-108m	70
Antimony-124	40	Iodine131	6	Silver-110m	50
Antimony-125	100	Iron-55	300	Silver-111	70
Barium-140	40	Iron-59	40	Sodium-22	50
Bromine-82	300	Managnaese-54	200	Strontium-85	300
Calcium-45	200	Mercury-197	400	Strontium-89	40
Calcium-47	60	Mercury-203	80	Strontium-90	5
Carbon-14	200	Molybdenum-99	70	Sulphur-35	500
Cerium-141	100	Neptunium-239	100	Technetium-99	200
Cerium-144	20	Niobium-95	200	Technetium-99m	7000
Cesium-133	2000	Phosphorous-32	50	Tellurium-129m	40
Cesium-134	7	Plutonium-238	0.3	Tellerium-131m	40
Cesium-136	50	Plutonium-239	0.2	Tellurium-132	40
Cesium-137	10	Plutonium-240	0.2	Thallium-201	2000
Chromium-51	3000	Plutonium-241	10	Tritium	7000
Cobalt-57	40	Rhodium-105	300	Ytterbium-169	100
Cobalt-58	20	Rubidium-81	3000	Yttrium-90	30
Cobalt-60	2	Rubidium-86	50	Yttrium-91	30
Gallium-67	500	Ruthenium-103	100	Zinc-65	40
Gold-198	90	Ruthenium-106	10	Zirconium-95	100
Indium-111	400				

[135] MAC Becquerel per litre (Bq/L)
[136] MAC (Bq/L)

US		Australia		WHO	
Parameter		Parameter			
Alpha Particles	15 pCi/La[a]	Gross alpha activity	0.1 Bq/L		0.1 Bq/L
Beta Particles and photon emitters	4 mrem/year a[a]	Gross beta activity	0.5 Bq/L		1 Bq/L
Radium 226 and Radium 228 (combined)	5 pCi/La[a]				
Uranium	30 mg/L[b]				

[a] MCLG will be zero as of 12/08/03
[b] MCL as of 12/08/03 and MCLG will be zero as of 12/08/03

Table A.4. Chemical/Physical Objectives (mg/L) – Not Health Related

Parameter	Ontario	Canada	US	Australia	WHO[137]
Alkalinity (as CaCO3)	30-500c				
Aluminum (Aluminium)	0.10c		0.05-0.2d	0.2d	0.2
Ammonia				0.5d	1.5
Chloride	250d	≤ 250d	250d	250d	250
Chlorine					0.600-1.000
2-chlorophenol					0.0001-0.010
Colour	5 TCUd[138]	≤ 15 TCUd	15 Cu d[139]	15 Hazen Units d	15 TCU
Copper	1.0d	≤ 1.0[140]	1.0d	1d	1
Corrosivity			Non-corrosive		
1,2-Dichlorobenzene					0.001-0.010
1,3-Dichlorobenzene					
1,4-Dichlorobenzene					0.0003-0.030
2,4-dichlorophenol					0.0003-0.040
2,4,6-dichlorophenol					0.002-0.300
Dissolved Organic Carbon	5.0d				
Dissolved Oxygen				> 85 % d	
Ethylbenzene	0.0024d	≤ 0.0024d			0.002-0.200
Fluoride			2.0d		
Foaming agents			0.5d		
Hardness (as CaCO3)	80-100c			0.05d	
Hydrogen Sulphide					0.05
Iron	0.30d	≤ 0.3d	0.3d		0.3
Manganese	0.05d	≤ 0.05d	0.05d		0.1

137 Level at which likely to give rise to consumer complaints. As such, this represents the upper limits, rather than a maximum value.
138 Total colour units (TCU)
139 15 colour units
140 At point of consumption

Table A.4. continued

Parameter	Ontario	Canada	US	Australia	WHO[137]
Methane	3L/m3d				
Monochlorobenzene					0.010-0.120
MtBE			0.040/0.020[141]		
Odour	Inoffensive d	Inoffensive d	3[142]	Acceptable to most people d	Should be acceptable
Organic Nitrogen	0.15c				
pH[143]	6.5-8.5c	6.5-8.5d	6.5-8.5d	6.5-8.5d	<8[144]
Silver			0.1d		
Sodium	200d[145]	≤ 200d		180d	200
Styrene					0.004-2.600
Sulphate	500d[146]	≤ 500d[147]	250d		250
Sulphide	0.05d	≤ 0.05d			
Taste	Inoffensive d	Inoffensive d		Acceptable to most people d	Should be acceptable
Temperature	15°Cd	≤ 15°Cd			Should be acceptable
Toluene	0.024d	≤ 0.024d			0.024-0.170
Total Dissolved Solids	500d	≤ 500d	500d	500d	1000
Trichlorobenzenes (total)					0.005-0.050
Turbidity				5 NTU d	5 NTU
Xylenes	0.30d	≤ 0.30d			0.020-1.800
Zinc	5.0d	≤ 5.0d	5.0d	3d	3

[141] Taste and odour threshold respectively in the consumer acceptability advisory table
[142] Units are threshold odor numbers
[143] No units
[144] For effective disinfection with chlorine
[145] The local Medical Officer of Health should be notified when sodium concentration exceeds 20 mg/L so that the information can be communicated to local physicians for their use with patients on sodium restricted diets
[146] Higher sulphate levels than this may have a laxative effect on some people
[147] Ibid

Ontario and Canada: a = MAC; b = IMAC; c = OG; d = AO
US: a = MCL; b = MCLG; c = TT; d = SDWR
Australia: a = health value; b = guideline; d = aesthetic value
WHO: a = guideline; b = provisional guideline

MAC is a Maximum Acceptable Concentration
IMAC is an Interim Maximum Acceptable Concentration
OG is an Operational Guideline
AO is an Aesthetic Objective

MCL is a maximum contaminant level
MCLG is a maximum contaminant level goal
TT is a treatment technique, which is a required process intended to reduce the level of a contaminant in drinking water
SDWR is a secondary drinking water regulation that is a non-enforceable federal guideline regarding cosmetic or aesthetic effects

Although the US does not have as many standards for chemical contaminants, they have many more chemicals listed with Health Advisories outlined for children and adults as well as daily, 10-day and lifetime exposure rates. The chemicals are further rated for cancer risk and group

Sources:
Australian Guidelines, 2001, http://www.nhmrc.gov.au/publications/pdf/eh19_2001.pdf
Australian Standards document, http://www.pc.gov.au/research/benchmrk/drinkw/finalreport/drinkw.pdf
Canada Guidelines, 1996, http://www.hc-sc.gc.ca/ehp/ehd/catalogue/bch_pubs/summary.pdf
Ontario Drinking Water Standards, 2000
US Standards, 2002, http://www.epa.gov/safewater/mcl.html
WHO, 1998, http://www.who.int/water_sanitation_health/GDWQ/Summary_tables/Sumtab.htm

List of Abbreviations

ABC   Association of Boards of Certification

ALPHA   Association of Local Public Health Agencies

AMO   Association of Municipalities of Ontario

ANSI   American National Standards Institute

AWWA   American Water Works Association

AWWAO   Aboriginal Water Works Association of Ontario

AWWARF   American Water Works Association Research Foundation

BAC   Biologically Activated Carbon

BCCDC   B.C. Centre for Disease Control

BOD   Biochemical Oxygen Demand

CAEAL   Canadian Association of Environmental Analytical
               Laboratories

CCIL   Canadian Council of Independent Laboratories

CCL   Contaminant Candidate List

CELA   Canadian Environmental Law Association

CEDF   Canadian Environmental Defence Fund

CEOH   Committee on Environmental and Occupational Health

CITAC   Canadian Infrastructure Technology Assessment Centre

COMELG   Central Ontario Municipal Environmental Laboratories
               Group

CSA   Canadian Standards Association

CT   Concentration x Contact Time

CUPE   Canadian Union of Public Employees

CWQC   Centre for Water Quality Committee

DBP   Disinfection By-Products

DST	Defined Substrate Technology
DVGW	Deutche Vereinigung des Gas-und Wasserfaches
DWCC	Drinking Water Coordination Committee
DWSP	Drinking Water Surveillance Program

EBR	*Environmental Bill of Rights*
EFP	Environmental Farm Plan
EMO	Emergency Measures Ontario
EPA	*Environmental Protection Act*
EPRF	Energy Probe Research Foundation
ESSD	Environmental Sciences and Standards Division [MOE]
ETV	Environment Technology Verification program

| FC | Fecal Coliform |
| FFPPA | *Farming and Food Production Protection Act* |

| GAC | Granular Activated Carbon |
| GRCC | Grand River Conservation Commission |

HACCP	Hazard Analysis and Critical Control Point
HPC	Heterotrophic Plate Count
HPPA	*Health Protection and Promotion Act*
HUS	Hemolytic Uremic Syndrome

IAETL	International Association for Environmental Testing Laboratories
IDS	Integrated Divisional System
IEB	Investigations and Enforcement Branch
IEC	International Electrotechnical Commission
IMAC	Interim Maximum Acceptable Concentration

ISO	International Organization for Standardization
IWTA	International Water Treatment Alliance
LCR	Lead and Copper Rule [U.S.]
LT2ESWTR	Long-Term 2 Enhanced Surface Water Treatment Rule [U.S.]
MAC	Maximum Acceptable Concentration
MCL	Maximum Concentration Limit
MCLG	Maximum Contaminant Level Goal
MLSS	Mixed-Liquor Suspended Solids
MMAH	Ministry of Municipal Affairs and Housing
MNR	Ministry of Natural Resources
MOE	Ministry of the Environment
MoH	Medical Officer of Health
MRA	Mutual Recognition Arrangement
MRSP	Minimum Recommended Sampling Program
NDMA	nitrosodimethylamine
NFPA	National Food Processors Association
NOM	Natural Organic Matter
NRC	National Research Council
NSERC	Natural Sciences and Engineering Research Council
NTU	Nephelometric Turbidity Unit
NWRI	National Water Research Institute
OCETA	Ontario Centre for Environmental Technology Advancement
OCWA	Ontario Clean Water Agency
ODWO	Ontario Drinking Water Objectives

ODWS	Ontario Drinking Water Standards
OETC	Ontario Environmental Training Consortium
OFA	Ontario Federation of Agriculture
OFEC	Ontario Farm Environmental Coalition
OMA	Ontario Medical Association
OMAFRA	Ontario Ministry of Agriculture, Food and Rural Affairs
OMWA	Ontario Municipal Water Association
OPSEU	Ontario Public Service Employees Union
ORIS	Occurrence Reporting Information System
OWRA	*Ontario Water Resources Act*
OWRC	Ontario Water Resources Commission
OWWA	Ontario Water Works Association

PAC	Powder Activated Carbon
PCR	Polymerase Chain Reaction
PEGO	Professional Engineers and Architects of the Ontario Public Service
PFGE	Pulsed-Field Gel Electrophoresis
PHERO	Public Health and Epidemiology Report Ontario
POE	Point of Entry
POU	Point of Use
PPS	Provincial Policy Statement
PTTW	Permit to Take Water
PUC	Public Utility Commission

| RICT | Regulatory Impact and Competitiveness Test |

SAC	Spills Action Centre [MOE]
SCADA	Supervisory Control And Data Acquisition
SCC	Standards Council of Canada

SWIP   Sewage and Water Inspection Program

TC   Total Coliform
TCE   trichloroethylene
THM   trihalomethane
TOC   Total Organic Carbon
TTCE   Total trichloroethylene

UV   Ultraviolet

WBDOs   Water-Borne Disease Outbreaks
WCWQ   Walkerton Centre for Water Quality
WPIPMC   Watershed Planning Implementation Project Management
                Committee

Index